ALL ■ IN ■ ONE

MCAD/MCSD Visual Basic® .NET™ Certification

EXAM GUIDE

(Exams 70-305, 70-306, 70-310)

ALL ■ IN ■ ONE

MCAD/MCSD Visual Basic® .NET™ Certification

EXAM GUIDE

(Exams 70-305, 70-306, 70-310)

Michael Linde, Anthony Sequeira,
Richard Fowler, Larry Chambers

McGraw-Hill/Osborne

New York • Chicago • San Francisco • Lisbon
London • Madrid • Mexico City • Milan • New Delhi
San Juan • Seoul • Singapore • Sydney • Toronto

The McGraw-Hill Companies

McGraw-Hill/Osborne
2600 Tenth Street
Berkeley, California 94710
U.S.A.

To arrange bulk purchase discounts for sales promotions, premiums, or fund-raisers, please contact McGraw-Hill/Osborne at the above address. For information on translations or book distributors outside the U.S.A., please see the International Contact Information page immediately following the index of this book.

MCAD/MCSD Visual Basic® .NET™ Certification All-in-One Exam Guide \ (Exams 70-305, 70-306, 70-310)

1234567890 DOC DOC 019876543

Book p/n 0-07-213129-2 and CD p/n 0-07-213128-4
parts of
ISBN 0-07-213130-6

Publisher
Brandon A. Nordin

Vice President & Associate Publisher
Scott Rogers

Acquisitions Editor
Nancy Maragioglio

Project Editor
Elizabeth Seymour

Acquisitions Coordinator
Jessica Wilson

Technical Editor
David Waddleton

Copy Editors
Cynthia Putnam, Lunaea Weatherstone

Proofreader
Pat Mannion

Indexer
Jack Lewis

Computer Designers
Tara A. Davis, John Patrus

Illustrators
Melinda Moore Lytle, Michael Mueller, Lyssa Wald

Series Design
Peter F. Hancik

Cover Design
Greg Scott

This book was composed with Corel VENTURA™ Publisher.

Special thanks to my wife, Haylee, and son, Air, who gave me more support than I needed and more support than I asked for.
Michael Linde

To my incredible wife, Joette, and our beautiful daughter, Annabella—you are the everything.
Anthony Sequeira

To my wife, Jennie, and my daughter, Kristina, for their love, patience, and support.
Richard Fowler

This book is dedicated to my two beautiful children, Courtney Ashley and Dylan Adam. "The life and love we create is the life and love we live." I live this each and every day that you are with me.
Larry Chambers

ABOUT THE AUTHORS

Michael Linde (MCSE, MCSD, MCAD, MCT) has been programming since the mid-1980s in several languages, including C, C++, Pascal, and Visual Basic. Most of his work for the past 10 years has been in building business applications from single-tier to multi-tiered enterprise applications. Michael has also been developing applications in Visual Basic .NET and C# since the early betas of the .NET Framework. He has taught MCSD and MCSE courses for many training facilities in Canada and the U.S. for the past four years. These have included .NET courses in both Visual Basic .NET and C#. He is president of LinTech Solutions Inc. (http://www.lintechsol.com), a consulting company geared toward developing application architecture and design, and building successful business solutions for organizations, no matter their size.

Anthony Sequeira has been a professional speaker and writer in the IT industry for the past eight years. He holds every major Microsoft certification including MCT, MCSE 2K, and MCSD. Anthony has written many books including titles on Internet Information and Windows 2000 Server; he has also written for several magazines and newsletters. He currently speaks about Microsoft and Cisco technologies for KnowledgeNet. When he is not speaking or writing about computer technologies, Anthony is flying his Cessna in the skies above Arizona. How did he learn to fly? Microsoft Flight Simulator, of course.

Richard Fowler provides business analysis and application development for small- and medium-sized organizations. As President of Nugget Software Incorporated for more than 20 years, he performs the roles of technical architect, project manager, software developer, and all-around get-it-done person for the organizations for which he works. Richard's areas of technical experience are Microsoft Visual Basic, SQL Server, and, of course, the .NET Framework including ASP.NET, VB.NET and C#. He lives in Centennial, Colorado (a suburb of Denver), with his wife, Jennie, and their daughter, Kristina.

Larry Chambers (B.Sc., MCSD, MCSE) is a freelance technical writer who has contributed his expertise as an editor and author to a variety of books. Larry works for a Fortune 500 financial services firm in Winnipeg, Manitoba. Before that, Larry worked with a large consulting firm that provided services for Fortune 100 companies throughout Canada. He has provided consulting, management, and technical expertise in the computer industry for the last 14 years. In his spare time, you can find him on a mountain bike somewhere in the wilderness.

CONTENTS AT A GLANCE

CONTENTS

ACKNOWLEDGMENTS

I would like to thank all who supported me though the authoring of this book, especially my wife and son. I would also like to thank friends, family, and the wonderful team at McGraw-Hill/Osborne, without whose help I would not have been able to get anything done.

Michael Linde

Foremost, I must thank my wife, Jennie, and my daughter, Kristina, for their patience during the writing of this book. So many house projects were started but not completed, so many family events were postponed. Yet their love and support was, and is, always there. My special thanks goes to the entire staff of McGraw-Hill/Osborne for taking my technical writing and making it comprehensible. Their attention to detail, consistency, and style made the book. Thank you Nancy Maragioglio, for coordinating the book and keeping us authors on track. Thank you Elizabeth Seymour and Jessica Wilson, for moving the chapters through the editing process. Thanks to the copy editors, who did a fantastic job of making everything consistent and readable. And finally, thanks to production, who took the text and turned it into a book.

Richard Fowler

I would like to thank the folks at McGraw-Hill/Osborne for giving me the opportunity to be a part of their team. I especially thank Nancy for making it so hard to "grrrr" when deadlines were tight. I would also like to thank Jessica for all the effort she put in; she doesn't say much, but I think that's because she is forever too busy. Finally, I would like to thank Elizabeth for all her effort during those final days of hard work.

Larry Chambers

INTRODUCTION

Welcome to the *MCAD/MCSD Visual Basic® .NET™ Certification All-in-One Exam Guide.* This book has been designed to help you prepare for MCSD/MCAD certifications, and also to act as an on-the job reference after your achieve your certification. We've included hands-on labs and exercises to put your knowledge to work, and we've included much of the code on the CD-ROM for your use in working through the exercises.

Due to the repetition of several objectives between the exams, this book is structured around topics rather than by exam. However, every objective from each of the three exams is covered in this book. If you would like to structure your studies by exam, Appendix B is a mapping document that will guide you to the appropriate chapter for each of the objectives, by exam.

There are several elements used within the text to help highlight information of specific interest:

- **Exam Tips** These hints contain information on the approach Microsoft has taken for a given topic. These quick elements are ideal for last-minute review before taking the test.
- **Notes** Sometimes a bit more information is provided for a topic than what is necessarily required by the exam. These elements are designed to give you further insight into a topic.
- **Hands-On Exercises** These exercises were created to allow you to put your knowledge to work in a hands-on scenario. Working through these elements will help ensure that you're familiar with the topics.
- **Questions and Answers** We've included hundreds of questions in this book to help you evaluate your comprehension of each topic and objective. There are additional questions available on the CD-ROM for further review and practice.

Why Certify?

Microsoft certification has long been recognized as an industry standard of professional qualification. With the release of the .NET initiative, and the trend toward increased integration, developers are once again experiencing increased visibility and demand. The MCAD and MCSD certifications will provide proof of qualification, particularly for those working with the .NET technologies.

MCAD vs. MCSD

According to Microsoft, candidates for the MCAD certification credential are professionals who use Microsoft technologies to develop and maintain department-level applications, components, web or desktop clients, or back-end data services, or who work in teams developing enterprise applications.

Comparatively, candidates for the MCSD certification are the lead developers who design and develop leading-edge enterprise solutions with Microsoft development tools, technologies, platforms, and the Microsoft .NET Framework.

MCSD certification encompasses the skill set of the MCAD certification, and you may wish to pursue the MCAD as a step toward MCSD certification. You may even find that MCAD matches your career interests and plans more accurately than the MCSD track. Either way, certification is a valuable asset when building your career.

MCAD Certification Requirements

Microsoft's MCAD requires three core exams and one elective, and permits the use of some exams toward either core or elective credits.

NOTE Those exams covered in this text are italicized below.

MCAD Core Exams

Web Application Development Exams (One Required)

Exam 70-305—Developing and Implementing Web Applications with Microsoft Visual Basic .NET and Microsoft Visual Studio .NET

Or

Exam 70-315—Developing and Implementing Web Applications with Microsoft Visual C# .NET and Microsoft Visual Studio .NET

Windows Application Development Exams (One Required)

Exam 70-306—Developing and Implementing Windows-Based Applications with Microsoft Visual Basic .NET and Microsoft Visual Studio .NET

Or

Exam 70-316—Developing and Implementing Windows-Based Applications with Microsoft Visual C# .NET and Microsoft Visual Studio .NET

Web Services and Server Components Exams (One Required)

Exam 70-310—Developing XML Web Services and Server Components with Microsoft Visual Basic .NET and the Microsoft .NET Framework

Or

Exam 70-320—Developing XML Web Services and Server Components with Microsoft Visual C# and the Microsoft .NET Framework

In addition to the core exams, you must pass one of the following elective exams:

- **Exam 70-229**—Designing and Implementing Databases with Microsoft SQL Server 2000, Enterprise Edition
- **Exam 70-234**—Designing and Implementing Solutions with Microsoft Commerce Server 2000

The following may be used for elective credit if they have not been used toward core exam credit.

- **Exam 70-305**
- **Exam 70-306**
- **Exam 70-310**
- **Exam 70-315**
- **Exam 70-316**
- **Exam 70-320**

MCSD Certification Requirements

Achieving the MCSD certification requires passing four core exams and one elective exam. The core exams are listed here.

NOTE Those exams covered in this text are italicized below.

MCSD Core Exams

Solution Architecture Exam (Required)

Exam 70-300—Analyzing Requirements and Defining .NET Solution Architectures

Web Application Development Exams (One Required)

Exam 70-305—Developing and Implementing Web Applications with Microsoft Visual Basic .NET and Microsoft Visual Studio .NET

Or

Exam 70-315—Developing and Implementing Web Applications with Microsoft Visual C# .NET and Microsoft Visual Studio .NET

Windows Application Development Exams (One Required)

Exam 70-306—Developing and Implementing Windows-Based Applications with Microsoft Visual Basic .NET and Microsoft Visual Studio .NET

Or

Exam 70-316—Developing and Implementing Windows-Based Applications with Microsoft Visual C# .NET and Microsoft Visual Studio .NET

Web Services and Server Components Exams (One Required)

Exam 70-310—Developing XML Web Services and Server Components with Microsoft Visual Basic .NET and the Microsoft .NET Framework

Or

Exam 70-320—Developing XML Web Services and Server Components with Microsoft Visual C# and the Microsoft .NET Framework

In addition to the core exams, you must pass one of the following elective exams:

- **Exam 70-229**—Designing and Implementing Databases with Microsoft SQL Server 2000, Enterprise Edition
- **Exam 70-230**—Designing and Implementing Solutions with Microsoft BizTalk Server 2000 Enterprise Edition
- **Exam 70-234**—Designing and Implementing Solutions with Microsoft Commerce Server 2000

EXAM TIP Visit www.microsoft.com to get the latest certification information. Exams are subject to change without notice. Check this site frequently for any changes during your exam preparation.

PART I

Fundamentals of Visual Basic .NET

CHAPTER

What Is .NET?

In this chapter, you will

- Learn what .NET is and why developers need it
- Discover the .NET Framework
- Explore the .NET Framework Class Library
- Learn about namespaces

.NET is a set of technologies designed to allow applications to work together whether they reside on the user's hard drive, the local network, a remote computer, or the Internet. Because .NET applies to almost all Microsoft products, the company divides .NET into several areas including .NET servers and the .NET Framework. The .NET servers provide services to client applications or other services. For example, Microsoft SQL Server 2000 provides relational database management system (RDBMS) services, and Microsoft Exchange Server 2000 provides messaging services. Further discussion of .NET servers is beyond the scope of this book; you can obtain more information at http://www.microsoft.com/net/products/servers.asp.

Developers of .NET applications or components primarily focus on the .NET Framework. Before we discuss the .NET Framework in detail, we will provide a brief history of Windows programming to help explain why Microsoft has developed this new set of technologies.

A History of Windows Programming

Windows was originally developed in the C programming language. The C language has existed since the introduction of the UNIX operating system in the sixties and is well established. Because Windows was developed in C, the application development functionality in the operating system was only available as C functions. As object-oriented application development, such as C++, became the favored approach, C functions became increasingly difficult to incorporate into object-oriented applications.

NOTE Object orientation allows developers to design an application according to the real-world objects they work with. For example, developers can design a car object that performs the actions that a real car does. We will discuss object orientation in detail in Chapter 6.

The functionality of the Windows operating system is exposed as a large set of functions called the Win32 API, which developers can use to implement all Windows functionality. Because these operating system functions are not object-oriented, Microsoft released a library of classes (definitions of objects) that encapsulate them. The class library released, called the Microsoft Foundation Classes (MFC), is still widely used. It includes many classes to create applications more quickly and easily.

For example, the MFC library includes a **CFrame** class that allows developers to create the window as an object. This class includes actions and attributes that allow developers to add menus, status bars, toolbars, views, and other features to the frame using a shorter string of code than when using the Win32 API directly. If the MFC library does not provide a required functionality, the MFC-based code can still call the Win32 API functions.

As MFC was being developed, Visual Basic was becoming the most widely used language for Windows business application development. One of the drawbacks of Visual Basic is that it is not easy to use the Win32 API functions, and some of the Win32 API functions cannot be used at all. In addition, Visual Basic is not an object-oriented language, although it is object driven. In other words, developers can create classes in Visual Basic, and they can create and use objects based on those classes; but they cannot perform inheritance and other object-oriented actions. Although MFC was useful to C++ developers, it was useless to Visual Basic developers.

Microsoft next released the specifications for the technology known as Component Object Model (COM). COM specifies how a component (usually distributed as a dynamic link library, or DLL), or piece of an application, must be developed and compiled so that it has binary compatibility. Binary compatibility means that once the component is compiled, it is compatible with all languages that understand the COM interfaces implemented by that component. To put it another way, the component must be language independent. There are many other advantages of COM, but in this book we will mention only the binary compatibility. For more information on COM specifications, refer to http://www.microsoft.com/com.

COM allowed C++ developers to use the Win32 API, MFC, or other libraries to create a component and pass it to developers using other languages, including Visual Basic, to use in their applications. Visual Basic developers now had the capabilities of those libraries, as long as they had a C++ developer to create the necessary components. Many languages, including Visual C++, Visual Basic, Borland C++, and Delphi, can create and use COM components.

Although COM created opportunities for sharing components among applications and languages, it also has several disadvantages. One disadvantage resulted in the coining of the term "DLL Hell". COM uses the Windows System Registry for storing the location of a component so that the location does not need to be hard-coded into the client application. When the client wants to use the component, it uses a Win32 API function to locate the component in the registry and then load it into memory. The problem comes about because the component can be registered only once on a particular computer. Let us say that we register a **ComponentA version 1** and we want to install another application that uses the same component but is registered as **version 2**. Instructions exist for allowing the new version to be installed and maintaining compatibility with **version 1**. However, the steps are difficult, and most developers do not understand them. Therefore, once **version 2** is installed, the likely incompatibilities in the **version 1** client will prevent it from working correctly.

Another disadvantage of COM is that it uses remote procedure calls (RPCs) to have a client make calls to the component. If the component exists on another machine or in another service, the RPCs used in COM are called distributed COM (DCOM). If a company wants to allow an application running on the Internet to use the services provided by a component on its server, the administrator must open specific ports on the firewall to allow access to the application. Alternatively, the administrator could use DCOM over HTTP (the Web protocol). Neither of these scenarios is viable as the security risk is too great. In addition, the client application must be able to support COM/DCOM in order to communicate with the server hosting the component. Linux machines and Java applications cannot use the component because they do not support COM. Because components today are frequently used for business logic within distributed applications, COM has substantial drawbacks related to platform independence.

The .NET Framework

To resolve the issues related to COM and other technologies, Microsoft has built a new framework that is completely different from Microsoft's previous programming models. It uses many of the concepts discussed in the preceding section.

The .NET Framework includes the runtime and compile time services required to run a .NET application. Compile time is when the developer is compiling the source. Runtime is when the compiled code is executing in memory. The compile time and runtime services include the servers (COM+, Message Queuing, Internet Information Server, Windows .NET Server, SQL Server 2000, etc.) and the Visual Studio Integrated Development Environment (IDE).

At the center of the runtime execution of .NET code is the Common Language Runtime (CLR). The CLR is a virtual machine that runs as a process on the computer on which it is installed. The virtual machine acts as a computer within the operating system and runs .NET code. If a CLR is built for a particular platform (e.g., Linux, Solaris, Windows, or Macintosh) any compliant .NET code can run on that platform. Compliant code is code that conforms to the Common Type System (CTS) specifications. For more information about the CTS, look for "Common Type System" in the MSDN Library. The compiled code to be run in the CLR is called portable executable (PE) code and is an .EXE or .DLL file.

In most development languages the compiled version of the source code is native to the machine it was compiled on, so the compiled application cannot run on any other platform. Code compiled with a .NET compiler is compiled into an intermediate byte code called Microsoft Intermediate Language (MSIL). This code is not fully compiled into native code, so the CLR must further compile the code when it is run.

The code loaded into the CLR is called an assembly, which is a collection of one or more files. All the files in an assembly are deployed as a single unit. These files may include PEs (.EXEs or .DLLs) or .BMPs. One of the PEs in the assembly will include a portion of

MSIL called the manifest. The manifest contains information about all the files in the assembly, all the classes and other data types in the assembly, and how to use the assembly. The manifest is analogous to the type library in COM programming.

When the CLR loads an assembly for use, only the manifest is compiled into memory. Methods of data types are compiled and cached in memory only when they are actually needed; this strategy is called just-in-time compiling. It allows .NET applications to load into memory quickly and minimize the use of resources. Assemblies will be discussed further in Chapter 9.

When the application needs to have memory freed up, a component of the CLR called the garbage collector (GC) performs its work. The GC tracks references to objects throughout the application's life and only destroys objects that are no longer used. Developers do not need to worry about destroying objects and implementing reference counting. This, in turn, prevents memory leaks. The garbage collector will be discussed further in Chapter 7.

The .NET Class Library

To create a .NET application, a developer must be able to use the .NET Class Library, which is a core component of the .NET Framework. The library includes support for the common type system (CTS) and provides the classes for basic and complex tasks, such as a **String** class for read-only text data and a **Form** class for creating a window. Because the library supplies hundreds of classes, Microsoft placed each class in a group that specifies what that class does. These groups are called *namespaces*.

Namespaces

A namespace is a grouping of data types that have a common purpose. For example, data types in the **System.Windows.Forms** namespace all relate to building applications that have stand-alone user interfaces (UIs). These data types include the **Form** class, the **Button** class, and the **MenuItem** class. When you create data types in a .NET application, always include them in a namespace. The convention for namespace naming is to choose the organization name and then the purpose of the namespace. For example:

```
Namespace FooCo.AccountsReceivable
```

This example declares a namespace for classes related to the accounts receivable application. This convention allows developers to distinguish their classes from other classes that have the same name. For example, there could be a **Payment** class in the **AccountsReceivable** namespace and a **Payment** class in the **Payroll** namespace.

The .NET Class Library Namespaces

Microsoft has supplied several namespaces with the .NET Framework. Developers usually use these namespaces to create applications; occasionally, they create components and their own namespaces with the Microsoft namespaces as the foundation classes. To help you understand what is provided in the .NET Class Library, this section outlines the development tasks and the namespaces to use to accomplish those tasks.

General Development

All applications must include the basic grouping of data types. These types are part of the **System** namespace. All programmers have created applications that need to store numeric or text values in memory. Depending on the size and precision of numeric values, we must try to select the most appropriate data type. In other words, selecting the data type that most closely represents the type of data being stored will optimize the application's performance. This section discusses some of the data types most commonly used.

Integer numbers (whole numbers) are referred to in different ways depending on the development language. For example, C and C++ use the **int** data type, and Visual Basic uses the **Integer** data type. Many issues have arisen due to the memory addressing structure of the computer and operating system being used. With the release of the 64-bit processor and operating systems, these data types may be represented as 32 bits of memory instead of 16 bits. This prevents developers from being able to easily port existing 32-bit applications to a 64-bit platform. To address this problem, Microsoft introduced new whole number data types in the **System** namespace: Int16, Int32, and Int64. These data types more realistically reflect the amount of memory to be used for the data, thereby maintaining precision when changing the execution platform.

The **System** namespace includes the **String** data type for storing a string of characters in memory. This set of characters is immutable; the **String** cannot be changed. The **System.Text** namespace includes data types to allow string manipulation.

NOTE Strings are, by default, Unicode in .NET. Unlike ASCII, which uses one byte for each character, Unicode uses two bytes for each character. The **System.Text** namespace includes data types for use with Unicode and ASCII strings.

Table 1-1 provides basic information about fundamental data types in the **System** namespace. There are important issues related to when each data type should be used; their discussion is beyond the scope of this book. For details, refer to the MSDN Library.

Data Type	Range of Values	Notes
Boolean	true or false	
Byte	0 through 255	Whole numbers only; 8 bits
Int16	negative 32768 through positive 32767	Whole numbers only; 16 bits; use Int16 instead of SByte
Int32	negative 2,147,483,648 through positive 2,147,483,647	Whole numbers only; 32 bits; use Int32 instead of UInt16
Int64	negative 9,223,372,036,854,775, 808 through positive 9,223,372,036,854,775,807	Whole numbers only; 64 bits; use Int64 instead of UInt32

Table 1-1 Fundamental Data Types in the System Namespace

Data Type	Range of Values	Notes
Decimal	positive 79,228,162,514,264,337,593,543,950,335 to negative 79,228,162,514,264,337,593,543,950,335	Precision of 28 decimal points; 96 bits; use Decimal instead of UInt64
Single	negative 3.402823e38 to positive 3.402823e38, as well as positive or negative zero, PositiveInfinity, NegativeInfinity, and Not a Number (NaN)	32 bits
Double	negative 1.79769313486232e308 to positive 1.79769313486232e308, as well as positive or negative zero, PositiveInfinity, NegativeInfinity, and Not a Number (NaN)	64 bits
Char	Single character	Unicode; 16 bits
String	A series of characters	Immutable (cannot be changed once created); strings will be discussed in Chapter 4
DateTime	12:00:00 midnight, January 1, 0001 C.E. (Common Era) to 11:59:59 P.M., December 31, 9999 C.E.	Unlike Visual Basic 6, you cannot assign a numeric value to a DateTime variable

Table 1-1 Fundamental Data Types in the System Namespace *(continued)*

Data Access

Microsoft has separated its data access into two areas: the in-memory data and the link to that data. The in-memory data is stored and manipulated within classes contained in the **System.Data** namespace. One of the classes in this namespace is the **DataSet** class. (Although we are listing the classes here, we will discuss them in detail in Chapter 12.) The **DataSet** can be thought of as an in-memory relational database. One advantage of the **DataSet** is that it has no link to a specific type of data source. Therefore, developers can create a **DataSet** from data contained within a SQL Server database, Oracle database, XML file, or from data created "on the fly". Developers can also create a **DataSet** from data contained in multiple data sources and then link the data through relationships in the **DataSet**.

Because the **DataSet** does not include functionality for retrieving data from a data source, the .NET Framework includes two namespaces, called providers, to connect to a data source and optionally place the data within a **DataSet** for manipulation. The two namespaces are **System.Data.SqlClient**, for accessing Microsoft SQL Server 7.0 and later databases, and **System.Data.OleDb**, for accessing data sources by using OLEDB providers (like the providers used in ADO). Microsoft also recently released the ODBC .NET Provider for accessing ODBC data sources. Data access will be discussed in further detail in Chapter 12.

Working with XML Data

Extensible Markup Language (XML) has become the de facto standard in data transmission due to its clear-text structured form. Because XML is based on open standards and almost all technologies support XML, Microsoft has developed .NET with XML as its core data and message transmission technology. Even the **DataSet** class has its data stored internally as XML. To manipulate data using the XML protocols, the .NET Framework includes the **System.Xml**, **System.Xml.Schema**, **System.Xml.Serialization**, **System .Xml.XPath**, and **System.Xml.Xsl** namespaces. XML will be discussed in further detail in Chapter 13.

Accessing the Networks and the Internet

The .NET Framework provides the **System.Net** namespace for performing most types of network access. For example, it contains the **Dns** class to perform simple domain name resolution and the **IPAddress** class to store an IP address and separate it into its node format. The second namespace used for network access is **System.Net.Sockets**. These two namespaces provide developers with classes to perform all types of TCP/IP network operations. They include classes for TCP and UDP access as well as Secure Sockets Layer (SSL) implementation.

Runtime Type Information

The .NET Framework provides a mechanism that enables developers to determine, at runtime, what data types and members of those types are available in an assembly. Because the assembly manifest is always the first item in the assembly to be compiled by the CLR when the assembly is loaded, the classes supplied allow developers to use the information in the assembly the same way the CLR does.

This technology is called reflection and is regarded as a key success of the .NET Framework. The namespaces used for reflection are **System.Reflection** and **System.Reflection .Emit.** The classes in this namespace are used in conjunction with the **System.Type** class (contained in the **System** namespace) for information about the particular data type in the assembly.

Developers not only can determine the data types and members contained within the assembly, but also, at runtime, can create new assemblies dynamically that are usable for the execution of that particular instance of the application.

Drawing and Editing Images

The Graphical Device Interface (GDI) API, called GDI+, is included as an object-oriented set of classes in the .NET Framework. This API allows developers to use the graphical features of the operating system to display and manipulate graphical images. The namespaces included with the .NET Framework are **System.Drawing**, **System.Drawing .Drawing2D**, **System.Drawing.Imaging**, and **System.Drawing.Text**.

Table 1-2 lists some of the classes in the **System.Drawing** namespace. This namespace provides basic GDI+ functionality to the .NET Framework.

Class/Structure	Description
Graphics	Encapsulates the drawing surface, which can be any GDI+ output device such as a monitor, printer, or plotter
Pen	Allows developers to draw lines and curves; often used as the outline of shapes
Brush	Used as the fill for shapes. Depending on the color and fill style that is selected, the shape is filled appropriately.
Bitmap	Provides the pixel data for a GDI+ image and its attributes
Color	Represents an ARGB color
Font	Determines the font face, style, size, and format for text
Icon	Displays a Windows icon in the form of a small bitmap. The size is determined by the operating system.
Point	An ordered pair of x- and y-coordinates; frequently used for placement of controls on a form
Rectangle	Used for representing the location and size of a logical rectangle, not for drawing rectangles; usually used to represent bounds of controls, shapes, and other visual objects
Size	Similar to the Rectangle structure; stores only the size of the logical rectangle and not the location

Table 1-2 Classes in the System.Drawing Namespace

The **System.Drawing.Imaging** namespace provides advanced GDI+ imaging functionality. The main class in this namespace is the **Metafile** class, and when used in conjunction with the **Encoder** and **Decoder** classes it can manipulate any type of image format.

The **System.Drawing.Text** namespace is quite small and is used for advanced GDI+ typographic functionality. For example, the **InstalledFontCollection** class is used to retrieve a collection of all the fonts installed on the system.

Management with the Windows Management Instrumentation (WMI)

The Windows Management Instrumentation (WMI) API is useful for accessing and manipulating most parts of the system. Members (functions or classes in an API) are used to access the operating system and hardware settings. Methods are used to shut down or restart systems locally or remotely. The **System.Management** namespace, included in the .NET Framework, includes classes that wrap the WMI API members. Further discussion of WMI is beyond the scope of this book.

Code Security

The CLR has extensive capabilities with regards to security, including the use of X509 certificates for public/private key encryption. The .NET Framework includes a number of namespaces, and therefore classes and members, to use for accessing the CLR security features within the CLR. The namespaces provided are **System.Security**, **System.Security.Cryptography**, **System.Security.Cryptography.X509 Certificates**, **System.Security.Cryptography.Xml**, **System.Security.Permissions**, **System.Security.Policy**, and **System .Secu-**

rity.Principal. Security would fit in an entire book of its own. We will touch on securing .NET assemblies in Chapter 10.

Multithreading

One feature that Visual Basic .NET developers will find extremely useful (and one that has not been available in previous versions of Visual Basic) is multithreading. Multithreading is the capability to have an application seemingly perform multiple tasks at the same time. What actually occurs is that each task (thread) is allocated a small portion of time, a time-slice, and the CLR cycles through the time-slices until each task has been completed. The namespace to use to build multithreaded applications and components is **System.Threading**. Building multithreaded applications is beyond the scope of this book.

Data Streams and Files

The **System.IO** namespace allows developers to read from and write to data streams and files. It includes members such as the **Directory** and **File** classes for working with files and folders, as well as the **Stream** class for working with generic streams (a sequence of bytes).

Interoperating with Unmanaged Code

Code that is not managed by the CLR is called unmanaged code. The CLR cannot perform type checking on the data types used in this code and the garbage collector (GC) cannot clean up unused resources in the same manner as it does with managed code. Examples of unmanaged code are Component Object Model (COM) components and function libraries (usually stored in DLLs).

The .NET Framework includes a technology for interoperating with COM components called COM Interop. COM Interop can be used by exposing a COM component to .NET components and applications or by exposing a .NET component to a COM-based component or application. COM Interop will be discussed in Chapter 25.

Summary

The .NET Framework is a paradigm shift from previous Microsoft development strategies. Points to note about .NET development are:

- Source code is compiled by a .NET compiler into byte code called Microsoft Intermediate Language (MSIL) code.
- The Common Language Runtime (CLR) is a virtual operating environment that loads and manages MSIL.
- The CLR tracks and references objects, and then destroys them once they are no longer used. This process is called garbage collection (GC).
- To allow MSIL to be 100% compatible with all .NET runtimes, no matter which platform they are run on, developers must base all their code on the .NET Framework Class Library. This library is based on the Common Type System (CTS) specification.

- The Class Library, and all libraries developed by .NET developers, is portioned into namespaces. These namespaces logically divide classes, structures, and enumerators into groups based on their functionality. Examples of these groups are ADO.NET, Web Forms, and Drawing.
- Compiled .NET files are called portable executables (PEs) and have either an .EXE or .DLL extension.
- The most basic unit of deployment is an assembly. The assembly is made up of one or more PEs and optional resource files such as .BMPs.
- Every assembly contains a section of metadata called the manifest. The manifest contains information about all the files contained in the assembly as well as all the data types and members that the assembly implements.
- When the CLR loads an assembly, only the manifest is compiled. The members are only compiled when they are needed. This strategy is called just-in-time (JIT) compilation.

Additional Resources

- http://msdn.microsoft.com/library
- http://www.microsoft.com/net
- http://msdn.microsoft.com/net

CHAPTER 2

The Visual Studio .NET IDE

In this chapter, you will

- Use the Start Page
- Customize the IDE using My Profile
- Use Document and Tool windows
- Implement the Solution Explorer, the Toolbox, and other Tool windows
- Debug your application in the IDE

Now that you understand the importance of the .NET Framework and how it fits into the overall history of Windows programming, it is time to begin studying Visual Studio.NET much more closely. Over the years, Visual Studio has evolved its integrated development environment or IDE. The IDE is a workspace for developing applications or services within Visual Studio, and it offers tools and features to simplify and enhance development processes.

A large part of mastering Visual Basic .NET development relies upon mastery of the IDE. The more you leverage the tools and features of the IDE, the more quickly and efficiently you can develop Visual Basic .NET applications. You can also customize the IDE to increase efficiency, tailoring the IDE to the way in which you work.

This chapter explores the IDE and teaches you how to exploit its valuable features. You learn to customize the interface, employ time-saving features, and debug applications using special functions of the IDE.

Using the Visual Studio .NET IDE

A key element in productivity when using Visual Basic .NET is mastering the Integrated Development Environment (IDE) presented by Visual Studio .NET. The environment is termed *integrated* because important .NET development applications rely upon this central interface for essential services and graphical user interface presentations.

EXAM TIP Although the Visual Basic exams do not test your knowledge of the IDE per se, the information in this chapter serves as a foundation for almost all other processes.

The IDE is filled with time-saving features. One of the "arts" of developing applications within the IDE is finding and exploiting these techniques. To explore the IDE, let's begin with the most logical starting point: the Start Page.

The Start Page

When you launch Visual Studio .NET for the first time, the default configuration presents the Start Page. The Start Page allows you to access important links that let you take advantage of the IDE immediately. These links are located on the left-hand side of the Start Page. When the Start Page first appears, the default selection is the My Profile pane, as seen in Figure 2-1. The options in the My Profile section of the Start Page are covered in detail later in this section.

If you decide to start each Visual Studio development session with the Start Page (you will learn how to customize this option later), the default presentation is the Projects pane of the Get Started link. The Projects pane makes it simple to open recently saved Visual Basic .NET projects. By default, this pane displays the last four saved projects. To open any of these projects, simply click the name hyperlink. The Open Project button allows

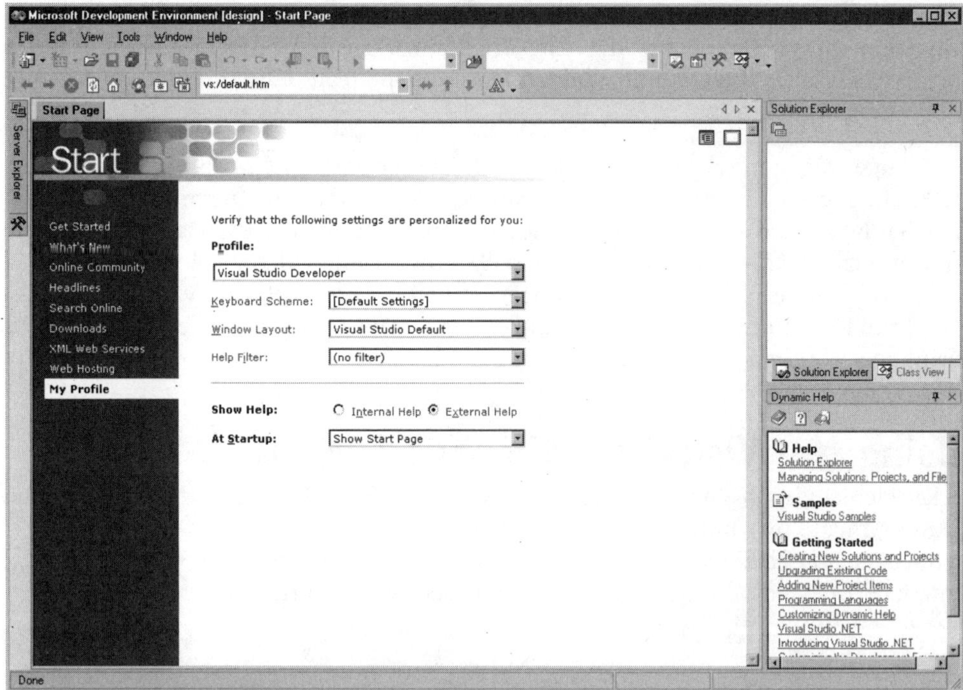

Figure 2-1 The My Profile pane of the Start Page

you to easily open another project, and the New Project button allows you to start a new project. The Projects pane of the Get Started link is depicted in Figure 2-2.

Notice that there are links other than the Get Started option. For example, the Headlines link provides featured articles relating to Visual Studio .NET, the latest news about the product, and featured Knowledge Base articles.

TIP Much of the content in the Start Page links is dynamic—the content changes frequently and is driven by the Internet. To get the most out of these features, have an active Internet connection when you browse these links.

Of particular interest to Web developers is the Web Hosting link. This link puts you in contact with Web hosting services that host ASP .NET Web applications. Some of these services offer limited free hosting, which allows students of Visual Basic .NET to quickly test and deploy their applications to the Internet without incurring the time and expense of building and deploying an Internet-based Web server.

TIP Consider configuring an internal Internet Information Server system as well as an internal SQL Server system. It is just as effective to deploy and test products within an intranet—even a lab-based intranet—as it is to deploy and test applications on the public Internet.

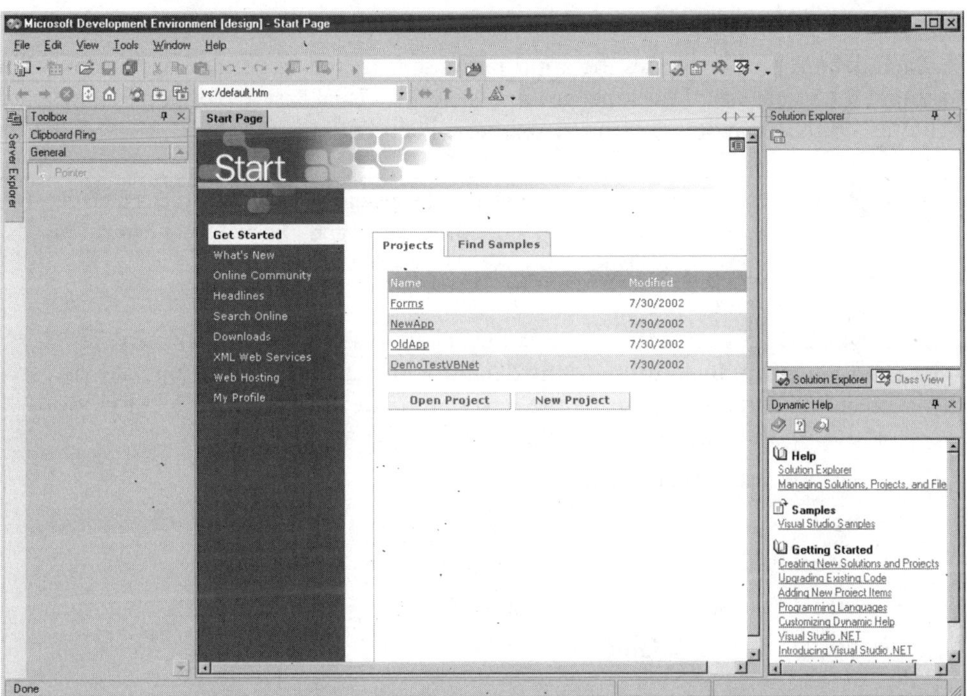

Figure 2-2 The Projects pane of the Get Started link

The My Profile link, depicted in Figure 2-1, allows you to personalize the IDE for your particular needs and work habits. The first time you launch Visual Studio .NET, the My Profile pane appears automatically. Subsequent launches of the product display the Projects pane by default.

The My Profile area includes the following options for configuration:

- **Profile** This option allows you to select a default profile that automatically sets the Keyboard Scheme, Window Layout, and Help Filter options. You can change one of the default profiles after selecting it by further modifying the Keyboard Scheme, Window Layout, or Help Filter option. A Visual Basic developer, for example, would typically want help to be filtered for Visual Basic topics, but not for other Visual Studio applications. If you do customize a default profile, the Profile displays as "Custom". The default profiles are
    - Visual Studio Developer
    - Visual Basic Developer
    - Visual C++ Developer
    - Visual InterDev Developer
    - VS Macro Developer
    - Visual C# Developer
    - Student Developer

Each default profile applies the appropriate settings for the named application. For example, the Visual Basic Developer profile assigns the Visual Basic 6.0 option for Keyboard Scheme, Window Layout, and the Visual Basic Help Filter.

NOTE The Student Developer profile specifies the Visual Studio Default Keyboard Scheme, Minimal Window Layout, and Minimal Help Filter. This profile is only available in the Academic Edition.

- **Keyboard Scheme** This option allows you to select the IDE shortcut key configuration. In addition to the default schemes in the following list, you can create custom schemes using the Keyboard pane of the Environment Options in the Options dialog box. The default schemes are:
    - Default Settings Shortcut Keys
    - Visual Studio 6.0 Default Shortcut Keys
    - Visual Basic 6.0 Default Shortcut Keys
    - Visual C++ 6.0 Default Shortcut Keys
    - Visual C++ 2.0 Default Shortcut Keys

NOTE For a list of the shortcut keys included in these schemes, check Help for the search phrase "Shortcut Keys."

Some standard shortcut key combinations work within Visual Studio .NET regardless of the preferences that have been set. They can be useful for accessing tools and navigating interfaces without the use of the mouse. Common shortcut keys are listed in Table 2-1.

Name	Shortcut Keys	Description
Activate application menu	ALT-SPACEBAR	Opens the program menu, allowing the user to manage the state of the application window, for example, by moving or resizing it
Activate document window menu	ALT-HYPHEN	Opens the document menu, allowing the user to manage the state of the active document window; available only while in MDI mode from within a document window
Activate tool window menu	ALT-HYPHEN	Opens the tool window menu, allowing the user to move the tool window within the IDE; available only when within a tool window
Close application	ALT-F4	Closes the IDE
Close document	CTRL-F6	Closes the active application document
Collapse all tree nodes	NUM – –	Collapses all nodes in the current tree view
Expand all tree nodes	NUM – *	Expands all nodes in the current tree view
Move to menu bar	ALT	Activates the main IDE menu bar
Move to next toolbar	CTRL-TAB	Moves to the next visible toolbar; available only when the main menu bar is active
Move to the previous toolbar	CTRL-SHIFT-TAB	Moves to the previous visible toolbar; available only when the main menu bar is active
Move to tool window toolbar	SHIFT-ALT	Activates the tool window toolbar; available only when in a tool window containing a toolbar
Move tree focus down	CTRL-DOWN ARROW	Moves the focus in tree view down without changing the selection
Move tree focus up	CTRL-UP ARROW	Moves the focus in tree view up without changing the selection

Table 2-1 Common Shortcut Keys of the Visual Studio .NET IDE

Name	Shortcut Keys	Description
Shortcut menu	SHIFT-F10	Displays the shortcut menu
Toggle drop-down list visibility	F4	Hides and shows a drop-down list
Toggle tree focus selection	CTRL-SPACEBAR	Toggles a selection for the current focus in tree view

Table 2-1 Common Shortcut Keys of the Visual Studio .NET IDE *(continued)*

You may realize already that the Visual Studio .NET IDE is highly customizable. In fact, even keyboard shortcuts are customizable. To customize keyboard shortcuts, access the Options dialog box of the Tools menu and choose the Keyboard option in the Environment node. If you plan to customize a keyboard shortcut scheme, consider basing the shortcuts on an existing scheme; this will save you time and effort. For example, Visual Basic developers frequently customize the Visual Basic 6.0 Default Shortcut Keys scheme.

Window Layout

The Window Layout option allows you to control the following default window configurations in the IDE:

- **Visual Studio Default** Places Server Explorer and the Toolbox window auto-hidden along the left of the IDE; Solution Explorer and Class View tab-docked on the right with Properties window and Dynamic Help window tab-docked below.
- **Visual Basic 6** Places Server Explorer auto-hidden along the left of the IDE and Toolbox docked on the left; Solution Explorer and Class View tab-docked on the right with Properties window and Dynamic Help window tab-docked below.
- **Visual C++ 6** Places Solution Explorer, Class View, and Resource View windows tab-docked on the left; Properties window and Dynamic Help window tab-docked below on the left.
- **Student Window Layout** Places Solution Explorer and Class View windows tab-docked on the left with the Dynamic Help window below; Task List and Output windows tab-docked on bottom.
- **No Tool Windows Layout** Displays the edit space only, with no tool windows open.

Help Filter

This option allows developers to select a filter for documentation when using Microsoft Developer Network (MSDN) and the Start Page links. This can be very useful, especially when considering the massive amount of information available in the MSDN documentation. If your primary development tool is Visual Basic .NET, filtering out the other development tools available in Visual Studio .NET helps ensure that you view information pertinent to Visual Basic.

NOTE For more information on the default Help Filters, see "Using Existing Filters" in Help.

Show Help

This option allows you to specify whether Help appears within a window in the IDE or within a window separate from the IDE.

TIP The Internal Help option tends to make the Help window quite small. Unless you are using a large monitor, select External Help.

At Startup

The At Startup option allows you to select which user interface appears when Visual Studio launches. The options are:

- Show Start Page
- Load Last Loaded Solution
- Show Open Project Dialog Box
- Show New Project Dialog Box
- Show Empty Environment

Windows in the IDE

Two types of windows are used in the IDE: Document windows and Tool windows. Use these windows in conjunction with each other to develop applications.

Document windows contain forms and code. Multiple document windows can be open at once; you choose between them using the tabs located under the toolbars near the top of the interface. Tool windows contain components to add to forms, or they allow access to objects or properties that help create applications.

Tool windows include Toolbox, Properties, and Solution Explorer. By default, these windows are displayed on the left and right of the Document windows. You can set Tool windows so that they are hidden and only appear as tabs within the IDE. To view the "hidden" window, hover your mouse over the tabbed representation. Hiding Tool windows helps ensure that you have adequate space within Document windows to create your Visual Basic masterpiece.

If you would like Tool windows to remain visible at all times, select the Auto Hide icon in the top right of the Tool window. This icon looks like a pushpin. If you would like to return the window to its default "auto-hide" behavior, select the icon again. Both Tool windows and Document windows are depicted in Figure 2-3.

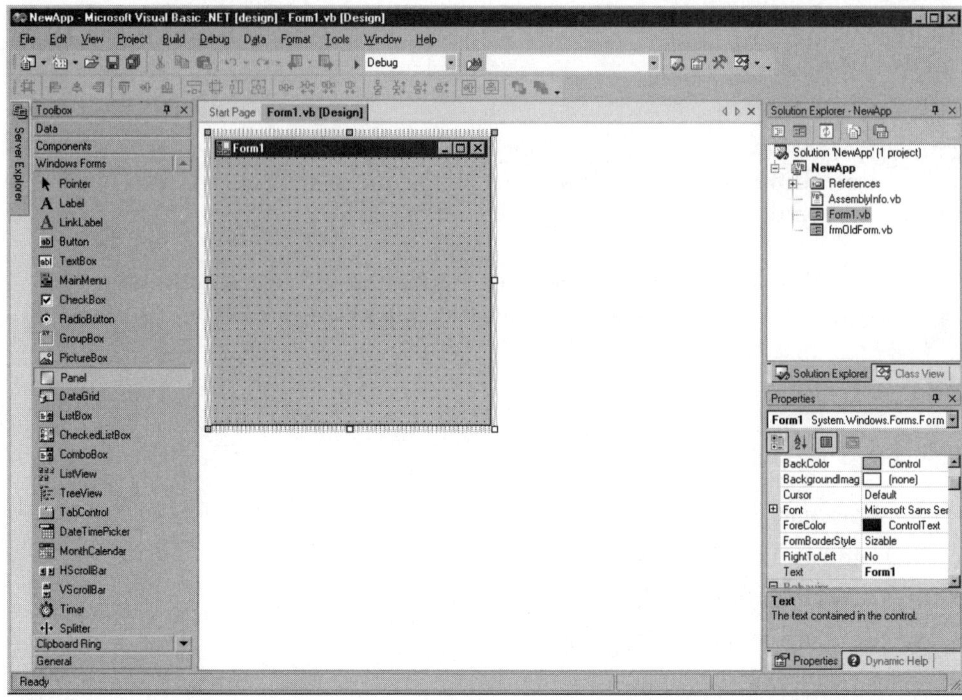

Figure 2-3 Tool windows and Document windows in the Visual Studio .NET IDE

TIP If you deliberately or unintentionally close a Tool window and then need it to return to the IDE, you can access it from the View menu of the Visual Studio .NET menu bar.

Although many Visual Basic .NET developers prefer the new tabbed page interface design of the Visual Studio .NET IDE, others will long to return to the Visual Studio interface of old. The good news for these developers is that almost every aspect of the Visual Studio IDE can be customized to resemble the old interface. For example, to return the Visual Studio .NET IDE to a Multiple Document Interface environment, use the Tools menu to access the Options dialog box. Then, click the appropriate radio button in the Environment - General section, as shown in Figure 2-4.

The Solution Explorer

Visual Studio .NET organizes applications into *projects* and *solutions*. Projects consist of files that make up a single executable, while solutions are a group of projects that make up an entire application. You view and access components of solutions and projects using the most important Tool window: Solution Explorer.

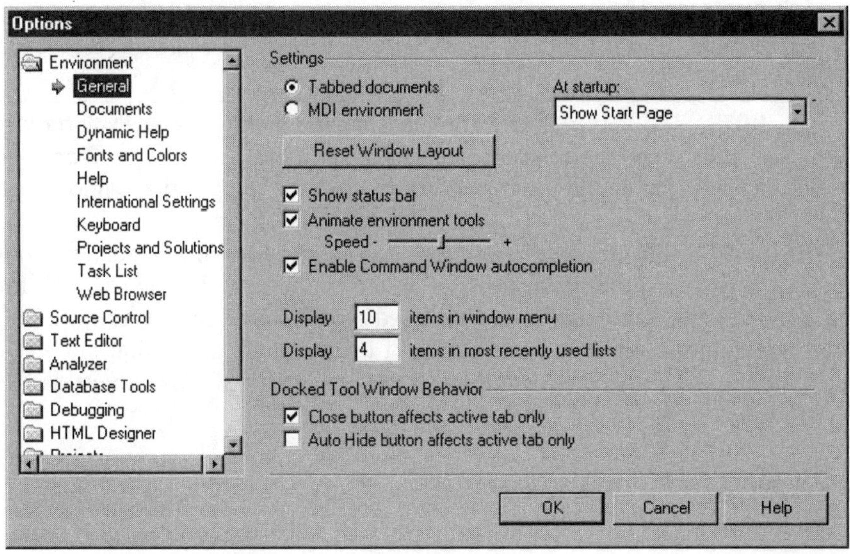

Figure 2-4 The Options dialog box

As you can see in Figure 2-5, one project in the Solution Explorer is highlighted in bold. This is the start-up project. The start-up project is the first project that executes when the solution is run. Typically, this project calls other projects in the solution during its execution.

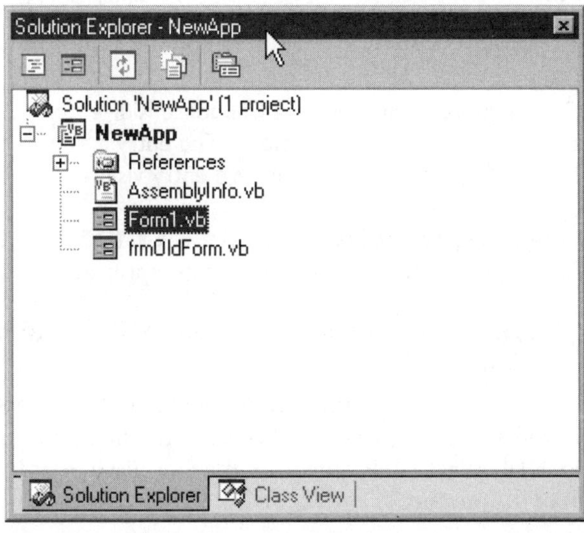

Figure 2-5 The Solution Explorer

EXAM TIP To change the start-up project within a solution, right-click the project node and choose Set As StartUp Project from the shortcut menu.

NOTE The solution information that appears in the Solution Explorer is stored in a file called the solution file. You can find this file in the My Documents folder. It has an .SLN extension and can be used to open the solution.

You use the Solution Explorer to navigate among the files that make up a solution. For example, to access a particular form in design mode, you double-click the form in the Solution Explorer. Some options are accessed by right-clicking objects in the Solution Explorer. For example, right-clicking a project brings out a menu that allows you to choose to debug the project, add objects to the project, or set the project as the new start-up project.

The Toolbox

The Toolbox is a critical Tool window in the IDE. It contains the controls and components you add to Windows or Web-based forms in order to visually create an application. The components and controls listed in the Toolbox dynamically change based on which type of object you are currently editing.

Because there is typically a large number of potential controls and components, the Toolbox contains category buttons that you select in order to view underlying controls. If the list of controls in a category is large, up and down scroll icons permit you to view all possible controls. Figure 2-6 shows a typical Toolbox.

The Clipboard Ring is a new Toolbox feature that is available during code editing. The Clipboard Ring contains the last 20 items copied to the clipboard for reuse in the current document. You can easily paste an item from the Clipboard Ring by clicking and dragging the item from the Toolbox and dropping it on the appropriate insertion point.

TIP To see more of the data in a Clipboard Ring entry, hover the mouse pointer over the entry in the Toolbox. The entry automatically expands in a tool tip, making more of the clipboard entry visible.

Exercise 2.1: Exploring the Visual Studio.NET IDE In this exercise you will explore the Visual Studio .NET IDE by creating an application.

1. Select Start | Programs | Microsoft Visual Studio .NET | Microsoft Visual Studio .NET to launch Visual Studio.
2. If this is the first time you have launched Visual Studio .NET, the Start Page appears with the My Profile pane displayed. If this is not the first time you have launched Visual Studio .NET, select My Profile from the Start Page in order to simulate the initial launch of the product.
3. Select Visual Basic Developer from the Profile drop-down list.

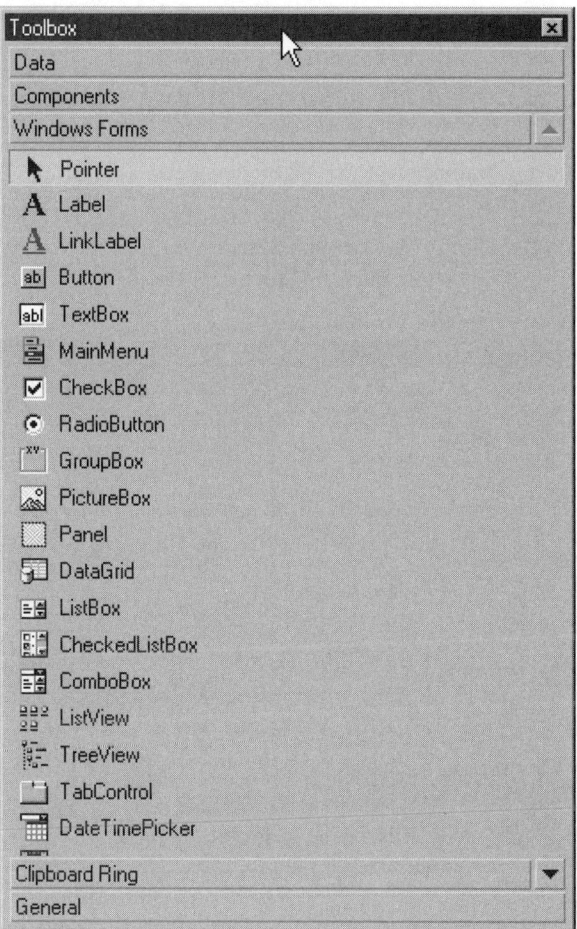

Figure 2-6 The Toolbox

4. Select External Help in the Show Help area. Select OK in the dialog box that appears warning you that changes will not take effect until Visual Studio .NET is restarted.
5. Press ALT-F4 on the keyboard to use the keyboard shortcut to close the Visual Studio .NET IDE.
6. To launch Visual Studio, select Start | Programs | Microsoft Visual Studio .NET | Microsoft Visual Studio .NET.
7. Visual Studio now launches with the Get Started pane of the Start Page selected. To get a quick glimpse of new features in Visual Basic .NET, select the What's New option in the Start Page.

8. Select the What's New in Visual Basic link. Notice the topics that are available in this category.
9. To return to the Get Started pane of the Start Page, select the Home icon in the Web toolbar.
10. In the Get Started pane, select the New Project button.
11. In the Templates area of the New Project dialog box, select ASP .NET Web Application. Name your new project **Sample** by typing over WebApplication1 in the Location field. Then, click OK to create the new project.

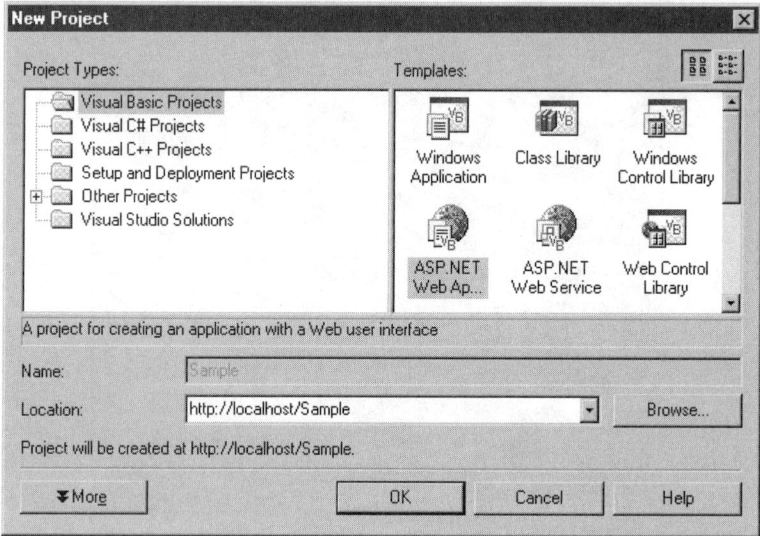

12. Notice the Toolbox window located to the left in the IDE. The Web Forms category of tools is selected because you are currently viewing a Web form in the main Document window. The Toolbox is always visible in the IDE regardless of where you click. To change this default behavior and give yourself more editing room in the IDE, click the Auto Hide icon in the top right corner of the Toolbox. When you move your mouse off the Toolbox, it automatically hides to the left in the IDE and appears as a labeled tab. To access the Toolbox, move your mouse over the tab.

13. Access the Toolbox and click and drag a TextBox onto your Web form. This is how easy it is to add controls to a form.
14. You are currently viewing your Web form in Design mode within the Document window. To view the underlying text (HTML) that makes up the form, select the HTML tab near the bottom of the IDE. When you have finished viewing the HTML code, select the Design tab to return to Design mode.

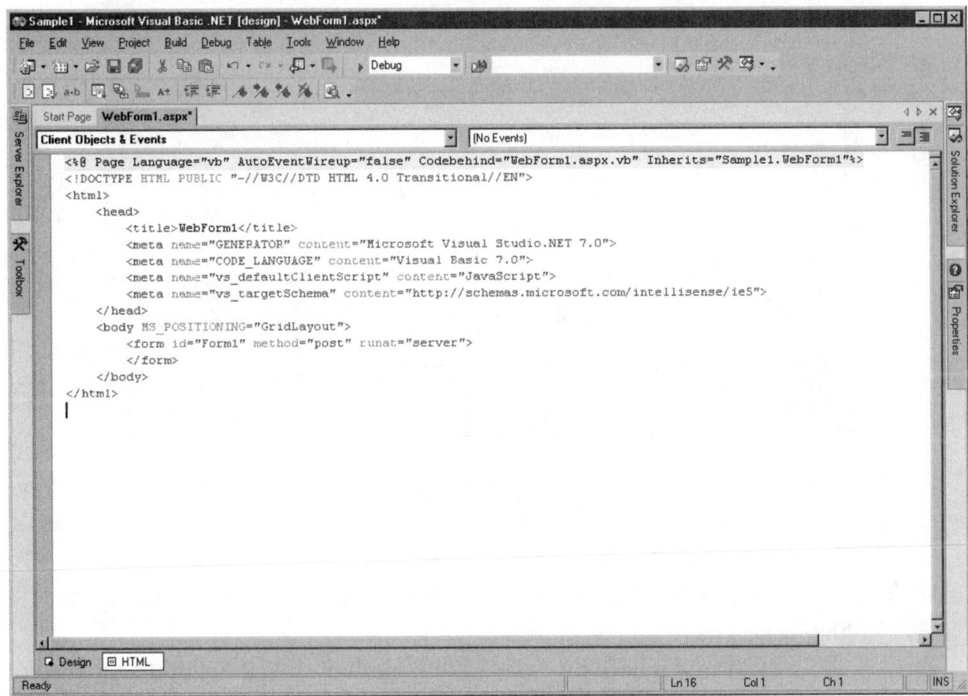

15. To add a new Web form to the project using the Solution Explorer, right-click the Sample project node in the Solution Explorer and choose Add | Add Web Form.

16. In the Add New Item - Sample dialog box, name your Web form **samplewebform.aspx** and click the Open button.

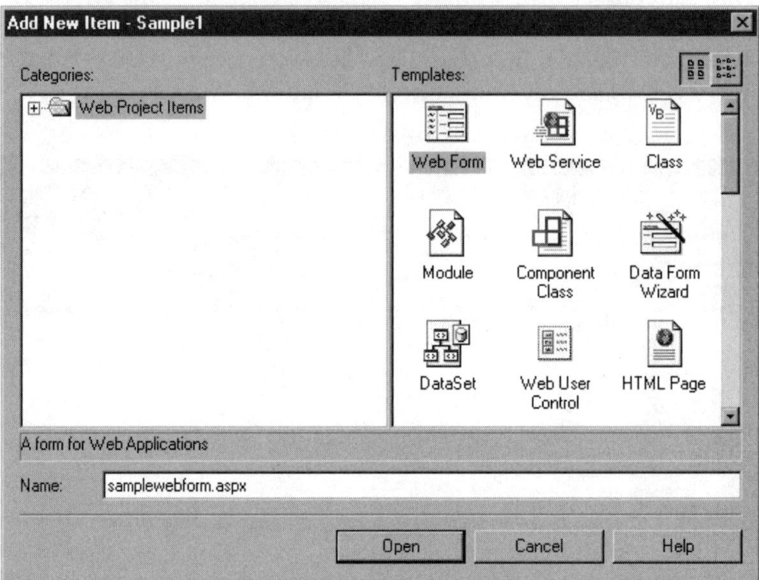

17. Your Web form is selected and is in Design mode, waiting for your modifications. To quickly access the first Web form of the project, double-click Webform1.aspx in the Solution Explorer.
18. To quickly close Visual Studio and your Web application, press ALT-F4 on the keyboard.
19. To save all the files you have modified in the solution, choose Yes in the Microsoft Development Environment dialog box that appears.

The Properties Window

The Properties window is another critical Tool window in the Visual Studio .NET IDE. It allows you to view and change the design-time properties and events of selected objects within the IDE. This powerful Tool window can also be used to view and edit file, project, and solution properties. Figure 2-7 shows a typical Properties window in the IDE.

The fields that the Properties window displays vary dynamically depending on the object selected in the IDE. For example, if a button on a form is selected, the Properties window displays Text and Location options for the button. If a form is selected, however, the Properties window displays fields that include WindowState and StartPosition.

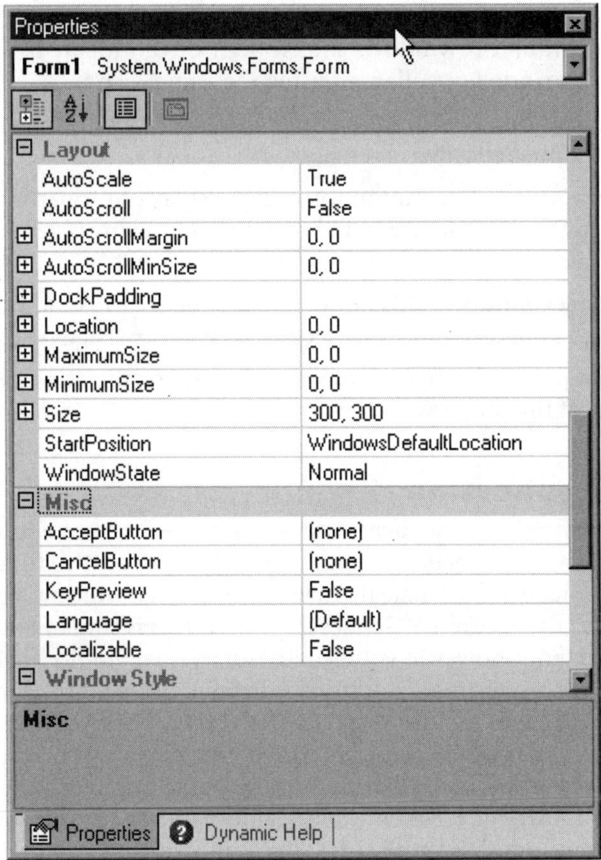

Figure 2-7 The Properties window

NOTE You may notice that some fields in the Properties window appear in gray for specific objects. These fields are read-only and cannot be changed.

The following elements in the Properties window warrant explanation so that you can make the most of this Tool window:

- **Object Name drop-down list** This field lists the currently selected object within the IDE. You can use the drop-down list to quickly move from object to object as you edit or view properties. This field appears empty if multiple objects are selected in the IDE; the only properties that appear in the window are properties common to all selected objects.

- **Categorized button** When selected, this button causes the properties to be categorized within the window. The Property categories are listed alphabetically and can be expanded or collapsed using the + and - icons.
- **Alphabetic button** This button eliminates categories and causes all properties to be listed alphabetically.
- **Properties button** This button forces the display of properties within the Tool window. This button may seem useless at first, but many objects have events that can be viewed using the Properties window.
- **Property Pages button** This button allows you to access additional properties for a selected item using the object's official Property Pages within the IDE.
- **Description pane** This area of the window displays the property type and a short description of the property.

Editing an Application

To create the user interface that clients use to interact with your application, you edit Windows or Web forms in Document windows. In the case of Web forms or HTML documents, you can visually manipulate them using the Design window, or you can edit the form using the underlying text that defines the object. This is similar to using Notepad to design these documents; however, you benefit from Visual Studio .NET IDE *IntelliSense* technology. IntelliSense technology provides dynamic assistance as you edit or write code. To access the form as text, use the HTML tab located below the object. The Design tab lets you easily switch back to the non-text representation of the form. When you edit text that comprises the form in HTML authoring mode, IntelliSense technology assists in completing the HTML code. For example, it automatically provides end tags to ensure that you do not leave out these critical HTML components.

Code exists "behind" user interfaces to give them "intelligence" and functionality. To access the Code Editor window (see Figure 2-8) in a Windows form, double-click the form. The code window is organized in blocks of code that begin with + or - signs. You can use these icons to collapse or expand code, allowing you to focus on particular class definitions or procedures that you are editing.

Several Visual Studio .NET Code Editor functions simplify programming. For example, the IntelliSense technology in Code Editor assists you in completing keywords and class members. Also, syntax errors and undeclared variables are detected as they occur. Typically these errors are underlined; hovering your mouse over the error provides a description.

The Code Editor also helps properly format code as you type, thanks to automatic indentation and code block auto-completion. Use the Options dialog box to control these features.

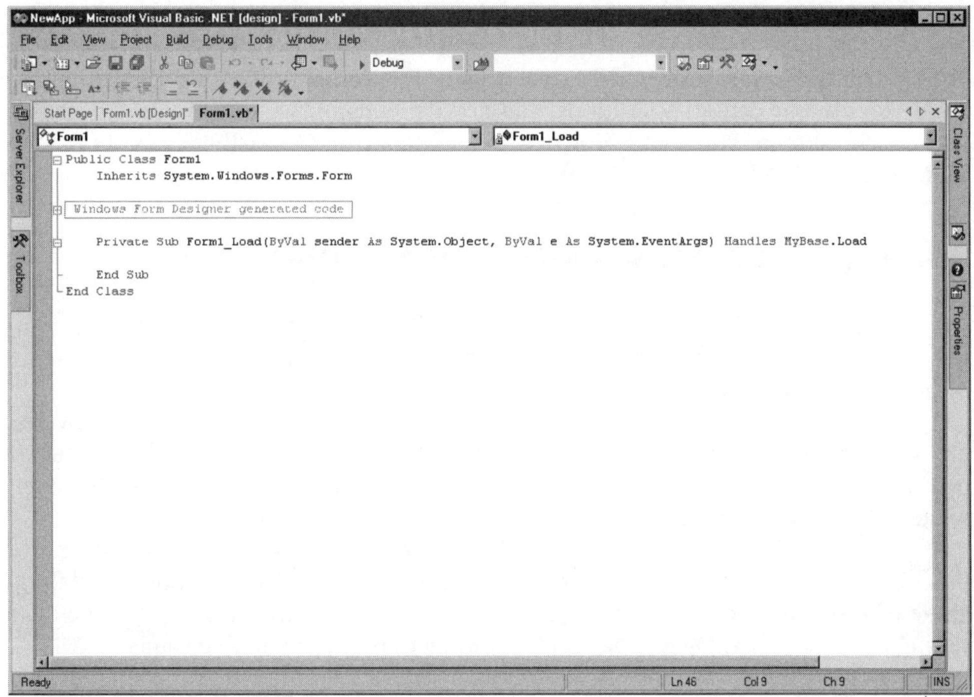

Figure 2-8 The Code Editor

Accessing Help

The Visual Studio .NET IDE provides Help in several ways. The main Help system, accessible from the Help menu in the IDE, includes Contents, Index, and Search windows. Each window acts like other Tool windows, and each offers a Filter drop-down list to narrow contents by programming language.

TIP When you are in a Help topic that includes programming language samples, a filter icon in the interface allows filtering for a particular language.

The Dynamic Help Tool window displays help topics as hyperlinks as you select objects or code in the IDE. If your IDE does not display the Dynamic Help window, use the Help menu to select Dynamic Help. You can customize Dynamic Help using the Options dialog box. The options for Dynamic Help include controlling the number of links that dynamically appear and how these links are sorted.

Debugging in the Visual Studio .NET IDE

The Visual Studio .NET Integrated Development Environment makes it very simple to build, execute, and debug applications. Additional menus and windows in the IDE enable you to set breakpoints in the execution of your application and watch the values of variables as the program executes.

Building, Running, and Debugging Applications

Once you have completed your project within the IDE, or you are at a point where you would like to test its functionality, you should build and run the project. This is accomplished by clicking the Start icon on the toolbar, choosing Start from the Debug menu, or pressing F5 on the keyboard.

When your project is built in preparation for execution, any errors that are discovered are displayed in the Task List window within the IDE. If you double-click the error description within the Task List window, the erroneous code appears within a Document window awaiting your corrections.

If no errors occur during the building of your project, the project runs after the build process completes. If errors occur during execution, you must then go about the debugging process. Typically, a major part of debugging the application at this point includes setting breakpoints and using the Watch window to monitor variable values.

Setting Breakpoints and Watching Variables

When debugging an application, it is often useful to set a breakpoint. A breakpoint allows you to stop execution at a particular line of code. When the breakpoint is reached, execution halts and the line of code appears in the Code Editor. This can be useful for determining exactly where errors are created in complex applications. One simple application of breakpoints is as a test to see if an application "survives" without error until the breakpoint is reached.

To set a breakpoint in an application, click the gray margin to the left of the line of code where you want the breakpoint. You can also select the line of code and press F9 on the keyboard. You can track breakpoints using the Breakpoints window. This Tool window is covered in detail later in this section.

Another helpful debugging technique involves evaluating the value of variables during execution. Once execution stops at a breakpoint, view the value of active variables by hovering the mouse over each variable. You can drag complex variables such as arrays or objects to the Watch window. This Tool window allows you to expand complex variables and view their subitems; it is covered in more detail later in this section.

To continue execution after an application has stopped at a breakpoint, press F5 or click Continue on the toolbar. If you would like to execute only the next statement, press F10 or F11. F10 executes each procedure call as a single statement. F11 executes procedures and stops at the first line in the called procedure.

Breakpoints and the Breakpoints Window

Breakpoints allow you to halt the execution of an application at a specific point and can be helpful when debugging an application. There are four types of breakpoints in Visual Studio .NET:

- **Function** Halts execution when a specific point in a specific function is reached
- **File** Halts execution when a specific point in a specific file is reached
- **Address** Halts execution when a specific memory address is reached
- **Data** Halts execution when a variable achieves a specific value

To make breakpoints more powerful and flexible, you can modify the Hit Count and Condition properties of breakpoints. The Hit Count property determines how many times the breakpoint must be reached before execution halts. The default Hit Count setting for a breakpoint is one. The Condition property allows you to set an expression that determines whether the breakpoint is hit or skipped.

For the most control over application breakpoints, consider using the Breakpoints window, shown in Figure 2-9. This Tool window displays all breakpoints and their properties. It allows you to add, delete, and edit these breakpoints, as well as set more advanced properties such as Hit Counts and Conditions.

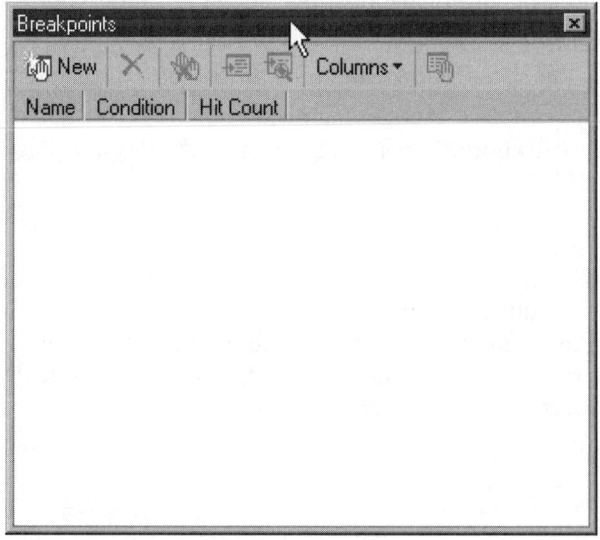

Figure 2-9 The Breakpoints window

To view the Breakpoints window, select Windows | Breakpoints from the Debug menu of the IDE. In order for the window to appear, the debugger must be running or you must be in break mode. The Breakpoint window includes the following elements:

- **New** This option opens the New Breakpoint dialog box, which provides a full set of options for creating a new breakpoint in your application.
- **Delete** This option removes the selected breakpoint. Use caution with this element because this operation cannot be undone; you will be forced to re-create the breakpoint.
- **Clear All Breakpoints** This option deletes all the breakpoints in the current project. Again, use caution with this option because it cannot be easily reversed. Reversing the action forces you to re-create all breakpoints.
- **Disable All Breakpoints** This handy option allows you to temporarily disable all the breakpoints currently set in an application. Clicking this button again enables the breakpoints.
- **Go To Source Code** This option takes you into the appropriate Code Editor and shows you the location of the currently selected breakpoint.
- **Go To Disassembly** This option displays the Disassembly window and displays the location where the breakpoint is set. The Disassembly window is an advanced debugging window that shows assembly code corresponding to the instructions created by the compiler.
- **Columns** This option allows you to set the columns displayed in the Breakpoints window.
- **Properties** This button permits you to open the Property Page for a selected breakpoint.

The Watch Window

Another excellent debugging tool is the Watch window. This Tool window allows you to examine or edit the value of a variable or variables as your application executes.

To view the Watch window, you must be running the debugger, or the application must be in break mode. Select Windows | Watch | Watch1 from the Debug menu. The Watch window offers the following columns:

- **Name** This column allows you to enter any variable name that you want to watch when debugging.
- **Value** This column displays the value of the variable that you specify in the name column. You can edit it in order to change the value of the variable or expression. You cannot, however, use this window to change the value of constants.
- **Type** This column displays the type of variable or expression that you are watching, as determined by the name column.

Exercise 2.2: Debugging an Application and Using Help In this exercise you will practice basic debugging of an application, and you will also use the sophisticated Visual Studio.NET Help system.

1. Select Start | Programs | Microsoft Visual Studio .NET | Microsoft Visual Studio .NET to launch Visual Studio.
2. Select New Project from the Get Started pane of the Start Page.
3. Select Windows Application in the Templates area and name your new project **Chapter02**. When you are finished, click the OK button.
4. Notice the default first Windows form that makes up your Windows application. The form should be selected. (If it is not selected, click inside the form to select it.) With the form selected, click the Dynamic Help tab that appears at the bottom of the Properties window. The Dynamic Help window fills with links to Windows forms; these links are categorized under Help, Sample, and Getting Started.
5. Move your mouse over the Toolbox and click and drag a Button control and place it on the form.
6. With the button selected, access the Properties window. Change the Text property of Button1 to display Close.
7. To edit the code that executes when the button is clicked, double-click the button on the form to access the Code Editor.

8. Your cursor is positioned in the private sub-routine for a click of the button. Add the following code in this sub-routine:

```
Me.Close()
```

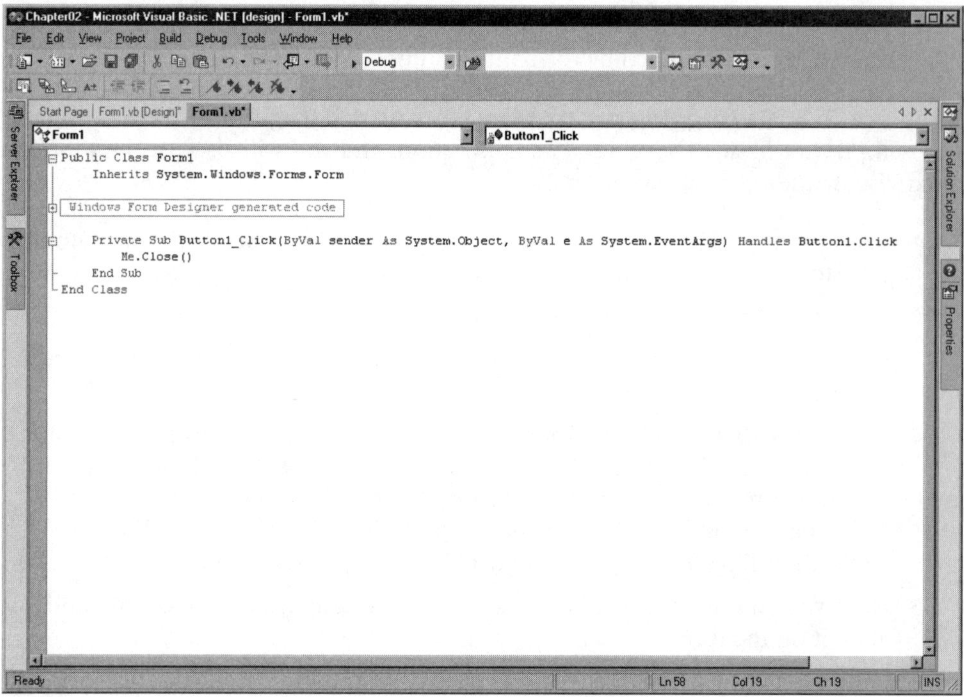

9. Notice that after typing `Me.`, IntelliSense technology suggests possible syntax for you to enter. Switch back to Design view for the form by clicking the Form1.vb [Design] tab near the top of the interface.

10. You are now going to intentionally introduce an error in your application. Switch to the Code Editor window for your form by selecting the Form1.vb tab near the top of the IDE.

11. After the line of code `Inherits System.Windows.Forms.Form` add the following line of code:

```
Din X as Integer
```

12. Press Enter on the keyboard after adding the line of code. Notice that Din is underlined in the Code Editor. The IntelliSense technology is notifying you that you have an error. Ignore the error for now.

13. Switch back to Design view for your form by clicking the Form1.vb [Design] tab near the top of the interface.

14. You are now ready to build and run your application. Click the Start icon on the Standard toolbar. The application begins the build process.
15. A dialog box appears indicating there were errors discovered during the build process. Click No to indicate that you do not want to continue.
16. The Task List window appears near the bottom of the IDE and contains an entry that represents your error. Double-click the entry in the Task List window.

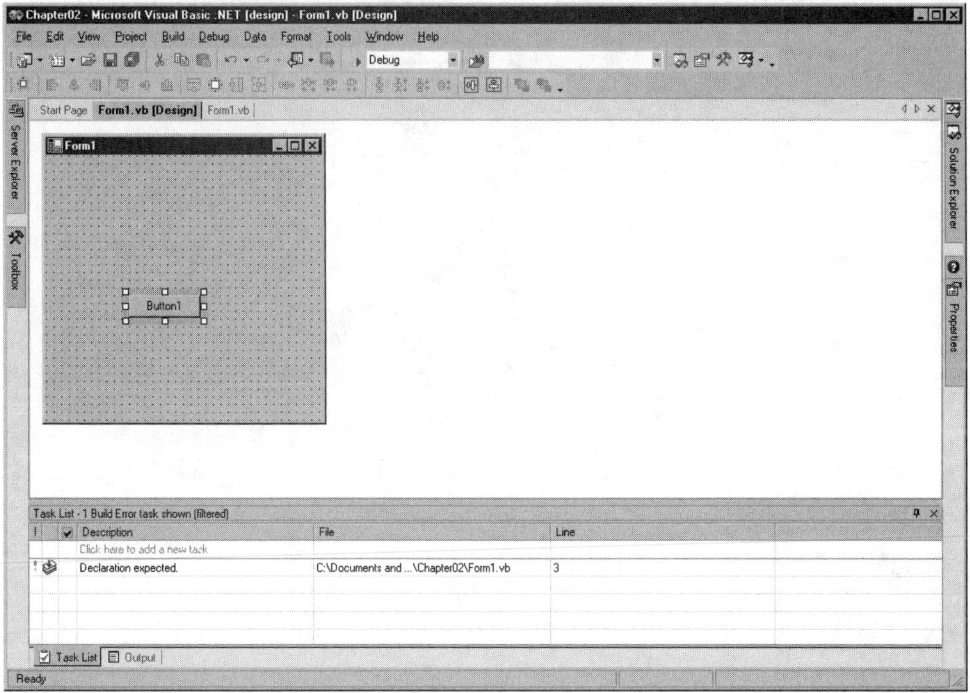

17. The Code Editor launches and the erroneous code is highlighted. Type <<Dim to correct the error, and then click the Start icon to try another build.
18. The application should execute flawlessly this time and display your form on screen. Test the functionality of the Close button by clicking it. Doing so closes the form, and because this form represents your entire application, closes the application as well. You are returned to the IDE for further development tasks.

19. To view Help information regarding packaging and deploying your application, and specifically to walk through the deployment process, select Search from the Help menu in the IDE.

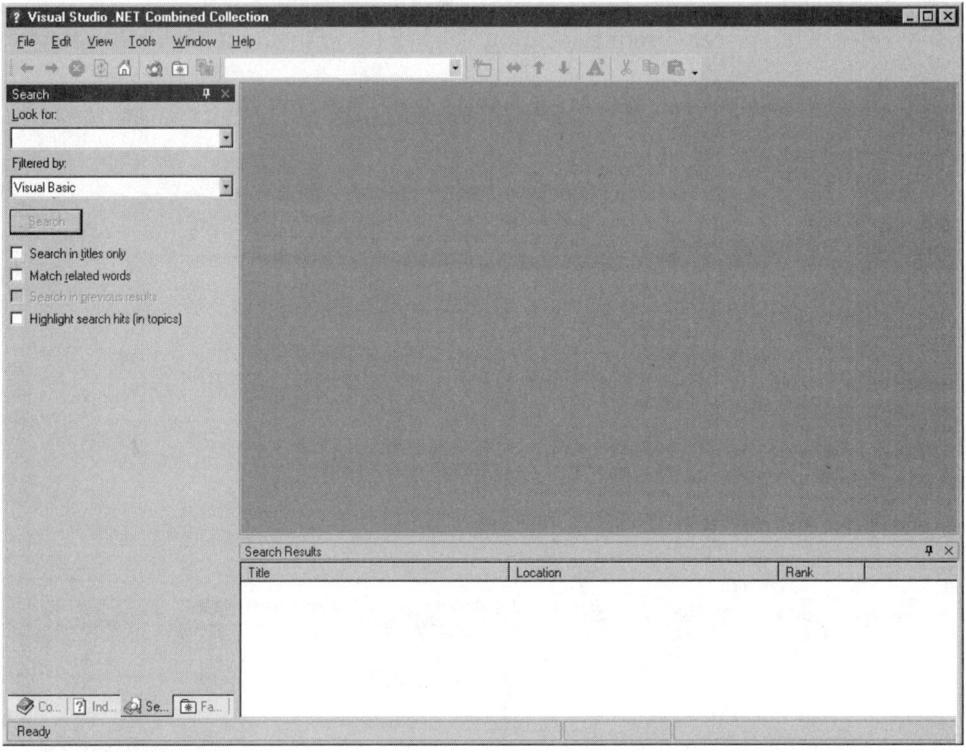

20. In the Look For: field of the Help window that appears, type `deployment walkthrough` and click the Search button.
21. In the Search Results window that appears, double-click the article entitled "Walkthrough: Deploying a Windows Application."
22. To be able to find this article quickly in the future, add it to your Favorites menu by clicking the Add to Favorites icon on the Web toolbar. Click OK in the Favorites dialog box to add the article.
23. Close the Help window using the Close icon in the top right corner.
24. Close Visual Studio by pressing ALT-F4 on the keyboard.
25. Choose Yes in the Microsoft Development Environment dialog box that appears to save all the files that you have modified in the solution.

Summary

One of the first steps to mastery of Visual Basic .NET is to master the Integrated Development Environment (IDE) used by Visual Studio .NET. Once you become familiar with the tools and options in this powerful design environment, your programming and application design skills should become sharper and more efficient than ever.

The IDE launches by default to a Start Page. This page allows you to determine the particular IDE settings that are most beneficial to you. Visual Basic .NET developers typically select the profile created for Visual Basic developers. When this profile is selected, the IDE tailors itself to the preferences and window layout that cater to Visual Basic developers. This includes filtering the vast number of Help files to narrow in on Visual Basic topics.

Once you have set your preferences using the Start Page, the Get Started pane of the Start Page serves as an excellent starting point for subsequent launches of the product. This pane allows you to quickly open previously created solutions and enables quick access to the creation of new solutions.

The IDE features two types of windows: Tool windows and Document windows. Document windows edit code and design the forms that make up an application. Tool windows provide access to controls and properties for further editing of applications. Tool windows can be "hidden" to make more room for Document windows in the design environment. Three frequently used Tool windows in the IDE are the Toolbox, the Solution Explorer, and the Properties window.

IntelliSense technology greatly enhances the editing of applications in the Code Editor and design windows. This technology examines keystrokes and searches for errors, and provides auto-completion information.

To obtain assistance developing an application, you may check the Dynamic Help window to view hyperlinks that direct you to relevant documents. To access the "full-blown" help system, use the Help menu provided in the IDE. Here you can search, view the entire contents, or access an index of help topics.

The IDE simplifies building, debugging, and executing applications. To activate these processes, you simply click the Start button on the Standard toolbar. The Breakpoint window and Watch window allow you to engage in advanced debugging techniques while in the comfort of the IDE and using familiar Tool window approaches. Visual Basic .NET even directs you to erroneous lines of code so that you can quickly and efficiently correct errors.

Test Questions

1. What is the default starting point when you first launch Visual Studio .NET?
   A. The Get Started pane of the Start Page
   B. The My Profile pane of the Start Page
   C. The What's New pane of the Start Page
   D. The last solution that was edited

2. Choosing a particular profile setting controls which of the following? Choose all that are correct.
   A. Help Filter
   B. Window Layout
   C. Language Setting
   D. Keyboard Scheme
3. Which of the following window types are found within the Visual Studio .NET IDE? Choose all that are correct.
   A. Document
   B. Event
   C. Tool
   D. Traceable
4. You must quickly and efficiently set the Startup Project in a Visual Basic .NET solution. Which tool window should you use?
   A. Toolbox
   B. Properties
   C. Watch
   D. Solution Explorer
5. You need to add several controls to a form in order to design a user interface for an application. Which tool window should you use?
   A. Toolbox
   B. Properties
   C. Watch
   D. Solution Explorer
6. You have inadvertently closed the Toolbox in the IDE. You now require the use of the Toolbox in order to properly design your application. What should you do?
   A. Open the Toolbox using the View menu in the IDE
   B. Close Visual Studio .NET and re-open the application
   C. Select the Toolbox icon in the Solution Explorer
   D. Open the Toolbox using the Debug menu in the IDE
7. What is the purpose of the Hit Count property for breakpoints?
   A. It allows you to configure an expression that triggers the breakpoint.
   B. It allows you to configure the number of times a breakpoint must be reached before it executes.

C. It allows the creation of a file breakpoint.

D. It allows you to view detailed statistics regarding the number of times a breakpoint has been reached.

8. You need to study the value that a variable receives during the execution of an application. Which Tool window should you use?

    A. Toolbox

    B. Breakpoints

    C. Watch

    D. Command

9. You are frustrated by your searches of Help in the Visual Studio .NET IDE. Your searches typically return over 200 results that match your search criteria, and many of the results have nothing to do with what you are searching for. What should you do?

    A. Use the Index feature of Help instead

    B. Use the Dynamic Help window exclusively

    C. Use the MSDN Library on the Internet

    D. Employ a Help Filter

10. You would like to return to several articles that you have located in the Visual Studio .NET Help files. What is an easy way to configure this?

    A. Save the files as text files and store them on your local hard drive

    B. Use the Bookmark feature of the Visual Studio .NET IDE

    C. Add the articles to your list of Favorites

    D. Add the articles to the Recent Documents area

Test Answers

1. B.
2. A, B, D.
3. A, C.
4. D.
5. A.
6. A.
7. B.
8. C.
9. D.
10. C.

CHAPTER 3

The Visual Basic .NET Language

In this chapter, you will

- Study the structure of a Visual Basic .NET application
- Learn how to declare variables
- Examine the scope of variables
- Learn about conditional structures and looping structures
- Study structured exception handling
- Understand how to create exception classes

Because the .NET Framework is an entirely new runtime environment, Microsoft has had to rewrite the Visual Basic language to suit the features of the .NET Framework. The Visual Basic runtime used by Visual Basic 6 and earlier was built specifically for Visual Basic, and no other language could use the features of that runtime. This meant that code created using Visual Basic could not be reused by another language and it could not execute if the runtime was not installed on the computer where the application was installed.

In this chapter, we will first take a look at the structure of a simple Visual Basic .NET application. We will then discuss .NET variables and how to use them, especially focusing on value-type variables and variable scope. We will then proceed into discussing procedures in Visual Basic .NET followed by loops and conditional structures. Finally, we will delve into the world of handling exceptions (run-time errors) within our application. The following section outlines some of the changes Visual Basic 6 developers will encounter when beginning their adventure with Visual Basic .NET.

Hello, World!

No software programming book would be complete without at least one "Hello, World!" example. The following sample code demonstrates the simplest Visual Basic

.NET application that can be developed. The file has been saved as HelloWorld.vb and the source code can be found on the CD-ROM.

```
Imports System
Class HelloWorld
      Public Shared Sub Main()
            Console.WriteLine("Hello, World!")
            Console.ReadLine()
      End Sub
End Class
```

Every application in .NET requires an entry point. The *entry point* is the first procedure that the .NET common language runtime (CLR) executes; this procedure runs the rest of the application. The sample application declares a class called **HelloWorld** that has one member procedure called Main. Main is the entry point required by the CLR to execute. We will discuss more about procedures later in this chapter.

This first line in the Main procedure uses the **Console** class in the **System** namespace. We use the Imports keyword to import the **System** namespace so that we do not need to put in the fully qualified name when we use the **Console** class. The fully qualified name of **Console** is **System.Console**. When the CLR determines that **Console** is not a class declared in our application, it will check to see whether the **Console** class belongs to the **System** namespace, which it does. We use the WriteLine method of the **Console** class to write a string to the command line. We use the ReadLine method, which takes no arguments, to wait for the user to press a key before terminating the application.

Although the sample application is not useful in the business world, it does outline the basic structural requirements of a Visual Basic .NET application:

- Every application must have at least one class.
- Every application must have at least one Main procedure.

To compile the sample application, we open the command prompt and go to the location of the source code. Save the sample code above to a file called HelloWorld.vb. Then run the following line (make sure you have the Framework SDK directory in your path or type the entire path name of the compiler to execute):

```
vbc /t:exe /r:System.dll /out:HelloWorld.exe HelloWorld.vb
```

The Visual Basic .NET compiler is run with the following parameters:

- **/t** This parameter specifies the type of portable executable (PE) to output.
- **/r** This parameter refers to components we use within our code. There can be one or more references. In this case we are using the **System** namespace, which is stored in the System.dll assembly.
- **/out** This parameter specifies the file name of the PE we want to create.
- ***name of source file*** The last parameter is the input (source) file to compile; in this case, it is HelloWorld.vb.

Describing .NET Variables

A variable is a pointer to a location in memory. It has a data type that defines what size of memory should be accessed, what operations can be performed on the data, and what type of data can be placed in that location.

The memory in an operating system can be thought of as a large set of compartments. Developers populate these compartments with data that is appropriate for the purposes of an application. Once the data is placed into memory the application manipulates and operates on the data to provide solutions and results to the user.

Internally to the operating system, the memory is accessible through addresses specified by the operating system's memory manager. Each operating system may use dissimilar addressing schemes to allocate memory, but each one will use memory addresses appropriate for the hardware platform it runs on. For example, in the x686 family of computers, the addressing is 32 bits (4 bytes) per address. The new Itanium processor from Intel, for example, uses 64 bits (8 bytes) per address. This means that on a 32-bit computer, the first address is the first 4 bytes, the second is the second 4 bytes, and so on. To complicate this more for developers, the operating system specifies the address as hexadecimal. An example of a memory address is FF05C4DA.

There are many reasons to build applications that do not use this type of address in their code. One reason is the complexity of the address. No developer wants to remember a 32-bit hexadecimal address just to access a single piece of data, never mind trying to access thousands of pieces of data during the lifetime of the application. Another reason is that the data may be loaded into a different location the next time it is saved in memory. The next time the application loads, another application may already be using that location for its own data.

Modern programming languages abstract the use of memory by allowing developers to create a pointer to a location in memory that has a human readable and understandable name. To understand this concept, imagine looking up information about volcanoes in an encyclopedia. You would not open the first volume of the encyclopedia and read from the first page to the last only to realize that volcano is not in volume one. You would open the index and find the word "volcano". Next to that word would be the volume and page where the information could be retrieved. You would then proceed directly to that volume and page, and the information would be at your disposal. Variables are located in the "index" of the application's memory and when the application needs to access or manipulate data, it looks up the variable name and finds the data's address in the "index". The application then proceeds to that location and accesses the data.

The data type specifies how much memory is used to store the data. For example, the **Int32** structure in the .NET Class Library uses 32 bits. Therefore, when we declare variable *x* to be of type **Int32**, the variable will hold the address (starting point) of the data's location in memory, and then we will access 32 bits of data from that starting point. On the other hand, if we declare variable *y* to be of type **Car**, which is a class we have created with many data members and functions, we would access enough memory from the address (starting point) in memory to hold the data for the **Car**. The size would be determined when we compile the component that contains the class and would be stored in the assembly manifest of the component.

The second purpose of the data type is to determine what type of data can be placed in the variable's location. Using a variable of type **Int16**, we can only place whole numbers ranging from -32768 to +32767 in memory. This range is based on the number of bits (16), including the sign bit for the negative or positive value. Refer to the MSDN Library for a list of numeric data types and their ranges of values.

The third purpose of the data type is to determine what actions we can perform on the variable. Using the "+" operator on two integer variables will add the two values and return an integer with the total value. Using the same operator on two string variables will return a concatenation of the two strings. Most objects do not support the "+" operator.

Value-Type Variables

Visual Basic .NET has two types of variables: value type and reference type. The two types differ in how they are copied, what they are based on, where they are created, and how they are created. The following section discusses only value-type variables. Because reference-type variables are used to point to objects, we will discuss them in Chapter 7 after we have explained object orientation.

Creating Value-Type Variables

When a value-type variable is declared, the CLR immediately allocates the location in memory that the variable is going to point to. This means that we do not use the New keyword to create the object (more about using the New keyword in the discussion on reference-type variables in Chapter 7). Examples of value-type variables are **Integer**, **Int16**, **Int32**, **Int64**, **Byte**, and **Boolean**.

```
Dim intCounter as Int32
intCounter = 58
```

The preceding code shows a simple declaration of a variable called **intCounter** that has the **Int32** data type. The CLR first creates the data location based on the **Int32** data type and initialize it to zero; zero is the initial value for all numeric value types. Then, the **intCounter** variable is created in memory and assigned the starting address of the newly allocated location. The second line of code assigns the value to the location in memory that **intCounter** points to.

EXAM TIP The location in memory is immediately allocated when a value-type variable is declared.

Two of the most important concepts to discuss when declaring variables are scope and lifetime. Scope determines where in the application we can use the variable. Lifetime determines how long the variable is available. Table 3-1 lists declaration keywords and how they impact scope and lifetime.

Keyword	Location Declared	Scope	Lifetime
Dim	In a block (e.g., If…Then…End If)	Limited to that block	From the time the block begins until the block ends
Dim	In a procedure	Limited to that procedure; local	From the time the procedure begins until the procedure ends
Static	In a procedure	Limited to that procedure; local	From the first time the procedure is executed until the class or module where the procedure resides is unloaded
Private or Dim	In a module, class, or structure; not in a procedure	Limited to all procedures in that module, class or structure; modular	From the time the module is loaded or the object is created until the module is unloaded or the object is destroyed
Protected	In a class; not in a procedure	Limited to all procedures in the class and to all procedures in any classes deriving from this class	From the time the object is created until the object is destroyed
Public	In a module, class, or structure	Available to all procedures in all modules, objects, or structures in the application	From the time the module is loaded or the object is created until the module is unloaded or the object is destroyed

Table 3-1 Scope and Lifetime of Variables

NOTE The data that a value-type variable points to in memory is deleted as soon as the variable is destroyed, that is, when the variable goes out of scope.

EXAM TIP When value-type variables go out of scope, the data in the location in memory they point to is immediately erased.

Declaring Value-Type Variables

The syntax for declaring value-type variables in Visual Basic .NET is

```
|<Scope Keyword>||<Shared>| <variable name> As <data type> _
|= <initial value>|
```

For example:

```
Dim sTemp As String = "Hello, World!"
```

NOTE The line continuation character (_) allows developers to wrap a single statement into multiple lines.

NOTE The initial value assignment when declaring the variable is new to Visual Basic .NET. In previous versions of Visual Basic, initializing a variable had to be done in a second line of code.

Using Value-Type Variables

Once a value-type variable is declared it can be used. All numeric value-type variables are assigned an initial value of zero if the value is not explicitly assigned in the statement declaration. A **Boolean** variable initializes to **False** and a **String** variable initializes to an empty string, that is, "".

Because declaring a value-type variable immediately allocates and initializes the location in memory, when we copy one value-type variable to another, the target variable's memory location will receive a copy of the value in the source variable's memory location.

In the following example there are two locations in memory and two variables. After all three lines execute, both locations will contain values of 16.

```
Dim x as Int32 = 16 'Value set to 16
Dim y as Int32 'Initial value set to 0
y = x 'Value of y now set to 16
```

Visual Basic .NET Procedures

When you want to bake a cake, you generally use a recipe. You find the title of the cake in the recipe book's table of contents, and then you turn to the page where the recipe is. You gather the necessary ingredients and follow the recipe steps. Developers use a similar concept when writing code.

A procedure is a set of statements, given a name, that can be supplied with input values and may return a value. Procedures in Visual Basic .NET that return a value are called Function procedures, and those that do not are called Sub procedures. Both Sub and Function procedures can be thought of as recipes—or sets of steps—to execute.

The syntax for declaring a Sub procedure, followed by the syntax for declaring a Function procedure, is presented here.

```
|<scope keyword>| |Shared| Sub <name of procedure>( _
||Optional| ByVal/ByRef <name of arg1> As <data type> _
|= <initial value>|, |…|)

|<scope keyword>| |Shared| Function <name of procedure>( _
||Optional| ByVal/ByRef <name of arg1> As <data type>| _
|= <initial value>|, |…|) As <data type>
```

Because the Sub procedure does not return a value, the return data type specification is the only difference between the declarations of the Sub and Function procedures. The scope keyword specifies where this procedure can be used. Use either Private, Protected, or Public depending on what level of scope is needed for the procedure. The Shared keyword will be discussed in Chapter 8. According to the Visual Basic .NET language specifications, the name of the procedure must begin with an alphabetic character.

The arguments of a procedure are specified as either ByVal or ByRef. The default is ByVal, which specifies that a copy of the input variable's value will be passed into the procedure. This creates a new variable and location in memory local to the procedure. ByRef specifies that the memory address of the location where the data is located is passed into the procedure. If the argument is ByRef and the value is changed in the procedure, the calling procedure will see the changes as the location in memory is being modified.

EXAM TIP ByVal is the default for passing arguments into procedures in Visual Basic .NET.

A procedure can have zero or more arguments. Each argument can be marked as optional, meaning that it is not required. If the argument is marked as optional, it must follow all required arguments in the list. Optional arguments must also have a default value specified in the declaration. This is because all arguments must have a value; if values are not passed in, the default can be used.

All arguments have local scope. This means that the argument's variable is not accessible to other procedures, not even procedures being called by this procedure.

The following example illustrates the difference between ByVal and ByRef.

```
Imports System
Class ByRefByVal
      Public Shared Sub Main()
            Dim x as Int32 = 6
            Dim y as Int32 = 8
            Console.WriteLine("x = " & x.ToString() & _
                 "; y = " & y.ToString())
            Sub1(x, y)
            Console.WriteLine("x = " & x.ToString() & _
                 "; y = " & y.ToString())
      End Sub
      Public Shared Sub Sub1(ByVal Sub1x As Int32, ByRef Sub1y As Int32)
            Sub1x += 1
            Sub1y += 1
            Console.WriteLine("Sub1x = " & Sub1x.ToString() & _
                  "; Sub1y = " & Sub1y.ToString())
      End Sub
End Class
```

The first WriteLine method will output 6 for the value of **x** and 8 for the value of **y**. **Sub1** is then called passing **x** in by value and **y** by reference. When the WriteLine method executes inside **Sub1**, the value of **Sub1x** is 7 and the value of **Sub1y** is 9. When the second WriteLine method is called in **Main**, the value of **x** is still 6 but the value of **y** is now 9 as it had been modified inside **Sub1**.

In distributed application development, the preference is to pass variables by value. Passing by reference causes the application to make continuous calls across the network each time the variable needs to be accessed. Passing by reference, though, is useful if you want to have a procedure that returns more than one value. Functions can only return one value, but a Sub or Function can return multiple values if the arguments are passed in by reference.

NOTE In Visual Basic .NET, procedures are always called with parentheses around the arguments. If you call a procedure that has no arguments, the procedure must be called with empty parentheses.

Conditional Structures

Applications are built around logic. The business logic in business applications refers to the set of questions asked during the flow of the application as well as the order in which the questions are asked.

Let's say we are building a class registration application for a university. For the student to be able to register for the class the student must answer several questions. Perhaps the first question is, "Is the class full?" If the answer to this question is "No" we proceed to the next question; if the answer is "Yes" we cancel the registration request or allow the user to request a different class, depending on the application logic. Figure 3-1 illustrates this logic.

We need to use a conditional statement to flow the application accordingly. The following example illustrates these statement blocks.

If...Then...End If To execute code only if the answer to a question is Yes or True, we use the If...Then...End If block. The syntax is

```
If <condition> Then <Statement>
```

or

```
If <condition> Then
      <True Clause>
End If
```

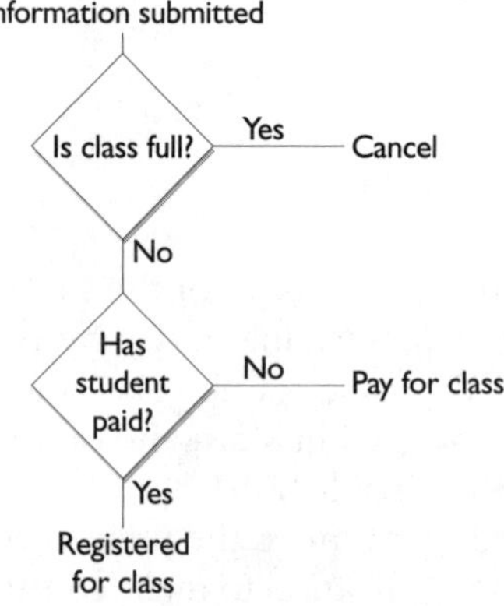

Figure 3-1 Flowchart showing the business logic in registering a student for a class

The first syntax is the single-line use of this block. It is usually used when the code to execute if the condition is True consists of only one statement. The second syntax is the most frequently used and is designed to execute multiple statements if the condition is True.

The condition to be tested will always return a True or False. It usually does this test by using the operators listed in Table 3-2. Table 3-3 lists **Boolean** operators. In these tables we assume *x* has a value of 6 and *y* has a value of 24.

The following code shows the use of the multiline syntax. We can include as many lines of code as we want within the True clause.

```
If x = 6 Then
      Console.WriteLine("x is 6")
      Console.ReadLine()
End If
```

If...Then...Else...End If In the preceding example (If...Then...End If), the code structure allows code to execute if the condition tests to be True. It does not execute code if the condition tests to be False. In the following code we have a True clause and a False clause.

```
If <condition> Then
      <True Clause>
Else
      <False Clause>
End If
```

Any code entered in the False clause section will execute if the condition tests to be False. For example:

```
If x = 6 Then
      Console.WriteLine("x is 6")
      Console.ReadLine()
Else
      Console.WriteLine("x is not 6")
      Console.ReadLine()
End If
```

Operator	Description	Test	Result
>	Greater than	x > y	False
<	Less than	(x+18) < y	False
>=	Greater than or equal to	(x+18) >= y	True
<=	Less than or equal to	(x+18) <= y	True
<>	Not equal to	(x+18) <> y	False

Table 3-2 Conditional Operators

Operator	Description	Test	Result
Or	Either operand must be true for the result to be true	x = 6 Or y < 10	True
And	Both operands must be true for the result to be true	x = 6 And y < 10	False
Not	Negation	Not ((x+18) <> y)	True
Xor	Only one of the operands can be true for the result to be true	x = 6 Xor y < 25	False

Table 3-3 Boolean Operators

If...Then...ElseIf...End If To test another condition if the first condition tests to be False, developers use the syntax of the following block.

```
If <condition1> Then
      <True Clause 1>
ElseIf <condition2> Then
      <True Clause 2>
Else
      <False Clause>
End If
```

We can include as many EndIfs inside the If block as necessary, but using too many can make code difficult to read and maintain. The following example shows a situation in which the ElseIf block can be useful.

```
If inputType <> InputType.Database Then
      'Code to open a file for reading
ElseIf dbType = "SQL Server" Then
      'Code to open connection to SQL Server database
Else
      'Code to open an Oracle database
End If
```

The first and second conditions both test for a Boolean result. In the first test we determine whether the input type is a source other than a database. If it is, we open a file for editing. If it is not, we check whether the database server we want to access is SQL Server. If it is, we open a connection to the SQL Server database. If neither of these conditions tests to be True, we open an Oracle database.

EXAM TIP If...Then structures always test for a Boolean result—True or False.

Select...Case...End Select So far the test conditions we have looked at have only resulted in True or False. The Select...Case structure allows a system to look at one expression and run code depending on one of the many possible values that the expression results in. The following example demonstrates an age categorization system.

```
Select Case iAge
      Case Is <= 1
            sTemp = "Infant"
      Case 2, 3
            sTemp = "Toddler"
      Case 4 To 12
            sTemp = "Adolescent"
      Case Else
            sTemp = "Teen"
End Select
```

In the preceding example, the expression to test is iAge. This could be a far more complex expression than simply a variable such as iAge + 10. The first test determines whether the age is less than or equal to 1. The Is keyword is used when using these operators. The second test tests for either one of the values in the list. The list could contain one or more values. The third test evaluates a range of values from the starting point to the ending point inclusive of both values. The final Case is used if none of the tests returns True; it is optional. When one of the tests is True, the set of statements between the Case keyword and the next Case keyword (or the End Select) is executed. Only the first True test result that is encountered is executed. Once it is complete, the Select block is terminated.

Looping Structures

Many tasks in an application need to be repeated several times; this is called looping. For example, we may need to validate all the students registered for a class to see that they have paid before confirming their registration. Some sets of code have a predetermined number of times they will run while other sets of code may run indefinitely. This section outlines the two main types of loops: Do...Loop and For...Next.

Do...Loop

The Do...Loop structure is used to run code an undetermined number of times. Upon entering the loop, the application does not know how many times the code inside the loop will execute. Suppose we want a logon form in our application that will validate the user, and we want to limit the number of times the user can attempt to log on. In this example, the application does not know whether the code inside the loop will execute once or five times. At any point in the loop the user may log on correctly, so the application may never reach the five logons limit.

Table 3-4 lists possible combinations of Do...Loops. The test condition will always return a Boolean result. The ellipses (...) indicate where the code statements in the loop will appear. There is no limit on how many lines can appear inside the loop, although it is better to keep code simple by calling other procedures from within the loop.

In the first two syntaxes in Table 3-4, the code may not execute at all. If, for the While test, the condition tests to be False, the code inside the loop will not execute. The same is true for the Until test if the condition tests to be False. In the second two syntaxes, the code will execute at least once as the test condition is only evaluated after the first execution.

Syntax	Minimum Number of Times Code in Loop Will Execute	Will Execute If Condition Is True or False
Do While <condition> ... Loop	Zero	True
Do Until <condition> ... Loop	Zero	False
Do ... Loop While <condition>	Once	True
Do ... Loop Until <condition>	Once	False

Table 3-4 Do ... Loops

The following example shows the logon validation limiting the user to five logon attempts.

```
Dim iCount As Byte = 1
Dim bValid As Boolean = False
Do Until iCount = 6
      ' Show the log on form
      Validate the user against a database - Set bValid to True if valid
      If bValid Then Exit Do
      iCount += 1
Loop
If (Not bValid) Then
      ' Run code to exit application gracefully
End If
```

Notice the line that uses **Exit Do**. Developers use this to exit a loop before it has finished executing. Execution will continue on the line following the loop.

NOTE While...Wend, which is used in previous versions of Visual Basic, is not used in Visual Basic .NET.

EXAM TIP Do...Loop structures are used if the application, upon entering the loop, may not know how many times the loop will execute.

For...Next

As shown in the preceding section, the Do...Loop is used when developers do not know how many times the code in a loop will execute upon entering the loop. Developers use the For...Next looping structure when they *do* know the number of times the code in the loop will execute. This section discusses the For...Next looping structure.

```
For <variable> = <start> To <end> |Step <stepping number>|
      ' Code statements to execute
Next
```

The preceding syntax above indicates that we need a starting and ending value to determine how many times the loop will execute. These values can also be expressions, such as x + 6. The variable should be declared prior to the start of the loop, but initialization is not needed.

When the loop is encountered for the first time, the variable is set to the specified starting value. The code inside the loop executes until it reaches the Next keyword. The Next keyword adds the stepping number (the number specified by the Step keyword) to the current value of the variable. Then, the code jumps back up to the first line of the loop, which determines whether the variable value is in the range specified—from the starting value through the ending value (inclusive). If it is, the loop is rerun. If it is not, execution is continued on the line following the loop. If no stepping value is included, the default stepping value is 1.

```
For iCount = 10 To 100 Step 10
      ' Code inside loop
Next
```

In the preceding example the loop will execute 10 times (10, 20 ... 100). Note that the value of **iCount** after the loop has finished executing is 110 and not 100; 110 is outside the range 10 to 100. Loops can also execute backward through a range.

```
For iCount = 100 To 10 Step -10
      ' Code inside loop
Next
```

In this situation, the variable is decreased by 10 whenever the stepping number is added to it. Therefore, the value of **iCount** after the loop is zero, and the loop has still executed 10 times.

NOTE Another For...Next looping structure is For Each...Next. This loop is used to traverse an array or collection of data. For Each...Next will be discussed in Chapter 4.

Structured Exception Handling

Visual Basic is purely a Component Object Model (COM) based language. All the objects that developers using Visual Basic work with are COM-based and all the functions we call are COM-based. The internal workings of COM are hidden from Visual Basic developers, but this section provides a little insight into why Microsoft has changed the way exceptions are handled in Visual Basic .NET.

No matter which function, method, or property developers use or manipulate in Visual Basic, a value is always returned to the application when the function (or method or property) is executed. Visual Basic developers never use this value directly. The value is a data type of **HRESULT** (not usable in .NET) and allows the calling application to determine success or failure of the execution. If the **HRESULT** is zero, the call was successful. If the **HRESULT** is non-zero, the call was unsuccessful and the **HRESULT** value is a code specifying what the error was.

In Visual Basic, exceptions are handled using the On Error statement. Every statement that is executed between the On Error statement and the procedure exit has its **HRESULT** value checked. The **HRESULT** in Visual Basic is populated into an object named **Err**. This object has several properties including the error number (**HRESULT** value) and a description of the error, but it lacks information to help developers determine how to handle the error.

Another issue with this type of exception handling is that only one On Error statement is responsible for catching all possible exceptions. If in one procedure we want to open a connection to a database, run a stored procedure on that database, open a file for logging, and email an order confirmation, only one error handler handles all the possible errors in any one of these tasks. Error handling in each of these situations would be different. The developer would have to check the **Err.Number** (**HRESULT**) property to determine what the error was and then respond accordingly.

C and C++ have included structured error handling for a long time and Microsoft has incorporated this technique into the Visual Basic .NET language. Structured exception handling uses the Try…Catch…Finally block to catch different types of exceptions and handle each one independently.

```
Try
      ' Code we want to run that could cause an error
Catch (<variable> As <Exception Type 1>)
      ' Code to handle Exception Type 1
Catch (<variable> As <Exception Type 2>)
      ' Code to handle Exception Type 2
Finally
      ' Code to execute whether the Try block works or not
End Try
```

The first section (Try) contains the code that could cause an error. This could be code to access a database or send an email or both. If code in this block fails, it "throws" an exception. Throwing an exception creates an object in memory that is based on a class of type **Exception** or its derivatives. More about the **Exception** class in a moment.

The next section is the Catch block. This block catches a specific type of **Exception** object and proceeds to handle the exception. We can have as many Catch blocks as necessary, with each one handling one type of exception.

The last section is the Finally block. Code in the Finally block always executes whether the code in the Try block succeeds or fails. The Finally block can contain code to, among other things, close connections to databases—if connections were opened in the Try block—or log the result of the procedure.

EXAM TIP The code in the Finally block always executes, whether there is an exception or not.

The Exception Class

Every exception object is based on the **Exception** class or one of its derivatives. Object orientation will be discussed in detail in Chapter 7. For now, know that a class that derives from a base class inherits functionality from the base class. This means that properties and methods of the base class can become properties and methods of the derived class.

Table 3-5 lists the properties of the **Exception** class. Most of these properties will be discussed in further detail later in the chapter.

The following example uses the Throw keyword to create an **Exception** object to be handled.

```
Imports System
Class ExceptionDemo
      Public Shared Sub Main()
            Try
                 Dim sTemp As String
                 Console.WriteLine( _
                      "Would you like to throw an exception (Y/N)?")
                 sTemp = Console.ReadLine()
                 If sTemp.ToUpper() = "Y" Then _
                       Throw New Exception("This is an exception")
                 Console.WriteLine("There was no exception")
            Catch (e As Exception)
                 Console.WriteLine(e.Message)
            Finally
                 Console.WriteLine("This is the end of Main")
            End Try
      End Sub
End Class
```

In this example, the If statement checks whether the user wants the exception to be thrown. If the answer is **y** or **Y**, then the exception is thrown by using the Throw New Exception statement. The **Exception** here is the basic **Exception** class in the **System** namespace. The Excep demo application on the CD-ROM contains the preceding code. Figures 3-2 and 3-3 show the results of this application running when an exception is thrown and when no exception is thrown, respectively.

Creating Exceptions

The **Exception** class included in the .NET Class Library is a "catch-all" class that reports the type of information that every error will produce. Most tasks have specific information that is needed if an exception occurs. For example, when accessing a SQL Server database we may want to find out in which stored procedure the error occurred. The .NET Class

Property	Description
HelpLink	A URL link to a help file and its context for the exception
InnerException	A pointer to the **Exception** object that was being handled when the exception was thrown
Message	The description of the error
Source	The name of the object or application that caused the error
StackTrace	A string representation of the call stack at the time the error was thrown
TargetSite	The method that threw the exception

Table 3-5 Properties of the Exception Class

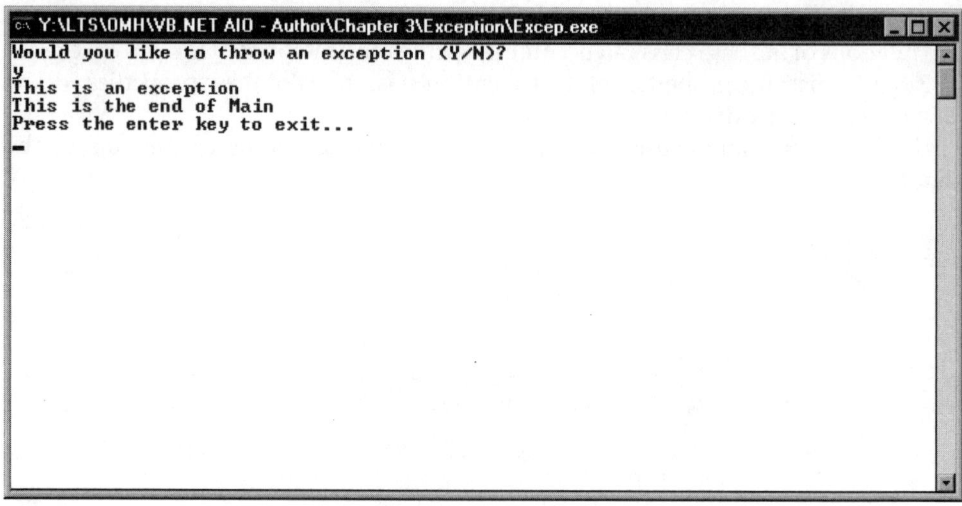

Figure 3-2 Results of exception being thrown

Library supplies an **SQLException** class, which has a Procedure property to allow developers to capture which procedure caused the error. The **SQLException** class is based on the **Exception** class and receives all its methods and properties. In the following section, we will create an exception class of our own specific to the needs of a Car application and the tasks it will perform.

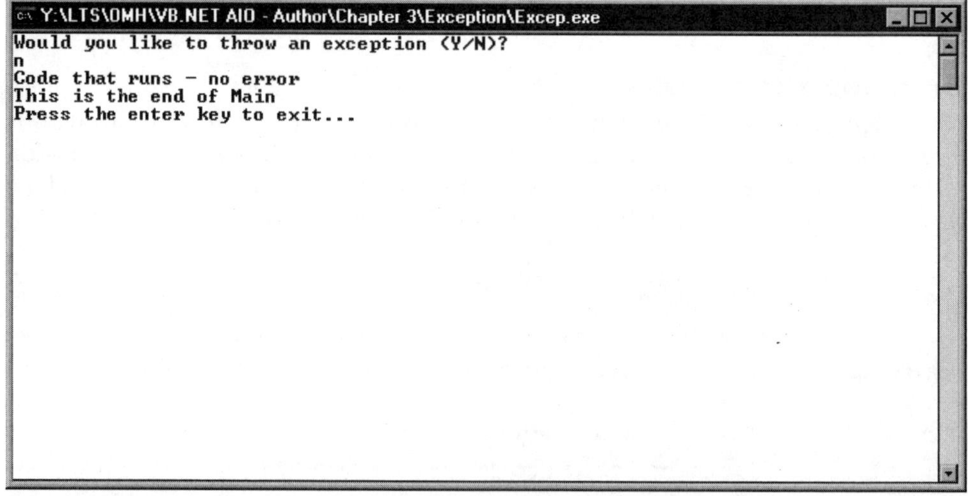

Figure 3-3 Results of no exception being thrown

Creating the Exception Class The first step in creating an exception is to declare a class that derives from an **Exception** type class; in this section we will simply derive from **Exception**. Inheritance in Visual Basic .NET is discussed in detail in Chapter 7.

In this section we will demonstrate how to create an exception for a car. In Chapter 5 you will create the car application. However, in this section we will use the car concept to demonstrate the exception that occurs when a driver would incorrectly try to refill a car. The **FuelingException** exception will be thrown when the code using the **Car** object tries to overfill or apply a negative fuel level to the car.

```
Class FuelingException
      Inherits Exception
      Private mCurrentFuelLevel As Byte
      Private mNewFuelLevel As Byte
```

The preceding code declares the exception class and shows that it derives from—or inherits—the **Exception** class. The class has all the properties and methods of the **Exception** class, including the Message property. The next code segment declares the class constructor. The constructor is the code that is executed when the exception object is first created.

```
Public Sub New(ByVal message As String, _
      ByVal currentFuelLevel As Byte, _
      ByVal newFuelLevel As Byte)
      MyBase.New(message)
      Me.mCurrentFuelLevel = currentFuelLevel
      Me.mNewFuelLevel = newFuelLevel
End Sub
```

The first line of code inside this procedure calls the New method of the base class. The MyBase keyword is used to refer to the base class of any class. When we call the base's method, we pass in the value of the **message** argument that is passed into the class constructor. Then, we set the values of the new and current fuel level variables. Then we declare any properties or methods we want the class to have. The following code declares the property used to retrieve the current fuel level.

```
Public ReadOnly Property CurrentFuelLevel() As Byte
      Get
            Return mCurrentFuelLevel
      End Get
End Property
```

Now that we have defined the exception class, we can add code to the **Car** class that will throw the exception when the incorrect value is applied to the car's FuelLevel property. The following code is declared inside the **Car** class.

```
Public Property FuelLevel() As Byte
      Get ' Read portion of the property
            Return mFuelLevel
      End Get
      Set(ByVal Value As Byte) ' Write portion of the property
            If Value < 0 Or Value > 100 Then
                  Throw New FuelLevelException( _
                        "The fuel level must be 0 to 100.", _
```

```
                                        mFuelLevel, _
                                        Value)
            End If
        End Set
End Property
```

In the **Set** section of the property procedure the **Value** argument is tested to see that it is in the range 0 through 100 (a whole number percentage). If it is not in this range we throw a new exception by creating a new **FuelingException** object and passing in the message and the current and new fuel levels. When we use the **Car** object in our client code we include a Catch block for the **FuelingException** type.

```
Try
      Dim myCar as New Car()
      myCar.FuelLevel = 110
Catch ex As FuelingException
      lblOutput.Text = ex.Message & _
           "Current Fuel Level: " & ex.CurrentFuelLevel
Catch ex As Exception
      lblOutput.Text = ex.Message
End Try
```

There are two Catch blocks in the preceding block. The rule is to catch the most specific exceptions first and then become more general. This is because only one Catch block is executed, and if we placed the Catch block for the general **Exception** class in first position it would always be executed. All exception classes are derived from the **Exception** class. Figure 3-4 shows the message box that appears when the exception is handled. The sample application, called FuelingExceptionDemo, is on the CD-ROM.

Summary

In this chapter we looked at a variety of programmatic structures within Visual Basic .NET including variables, procedures, looping, and conditional statements. This section summarized those topics.

Every application in Visual Basic must have a Main procedure entry point. To compile Visual Basic .NET source code from the command line, use the vbc.exe application included with the .NET Framework SDK.

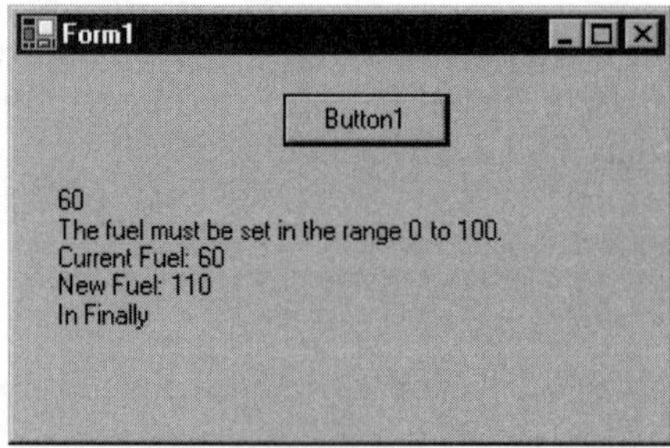

Figure 3-4 Results of handling a custom exception

The Imports keyword allows developers to use only the class name when using the class. It is not required; it just makes coding easier.

A variable is a pointer to a location in memory. There are two types of variables: reference type and value type. Reference-type variables point to objects; value-type variables point to structures and primitive data types. The location to which a value-type variable points is allocated as soon as the variable is declared. When we copy a value-type variable we copy the value that the variable points to, thereby creating another location in memory.

There are two types of procedures in Visual Basic .NET: Sub procedures do not return a value and Function procedures do return a value. Arguments are passed into procedures as ByVal or ByRef. The default in Visual Basic .NET is ByVal. When arguments are passed in ByVal, a copy of the value is passed into the procedure. If we modify the value of the argument inside the procedure, the calling procedure will not see the change. When arguments are passed in ByRef, the address of the value is passed into the procedure. If we modify the value of the argument inside the procedure, the calling procedure will see the change. Optional arguments must be placed after all required arguments and must be assigned an initial value.

The If...Then...End If block executes code if the condition tests to be True only. The If...Then...Else...End If block executes one set of code if the condition tests to be True and another set of code if the condition tests to be False. The If...Then...ElseIf...End If block tests multiple conditions and executes code in response to these tests. The Select...Case...End Select block tests one expression for multiple possible values.

The Do While...Loop tests the condition, and then executes the loop if the condition is True. The Do Until...Loop tests the condition, and then executes the loop if the condition is False. The Do...Loop While executes the loop once and the tests the condition. If then test is True, the loop will re-execute. The Do...Loop Until executes the loop once and then tests the condition. If the test is False, the loop will re-execute. The For...Next loop executes code a set amount of times based on a starting value, an ending value, and a stepping value.

Structured exception handling uses a Try...Catch...Finally...End Try block to handle several types of exceptions. Creating your own exception class requires deriving your class from an **Exception** type class. Handle exceptions in the Try...Catch...Finally...End Try block from the most specific to the most general exception.

Test Questions

1. You are creating a form that users will log on to. You want the user to type in a user name and password and then submit the information for validation. Which of the following code blocks would allow you to test the validity of the information and allow the user to resubmit the information up to four times, finally terminating the application if the information is invalid?

   A. If...Then...Else...End If

   B. Select...Case...End Select

   C. Do...Loop

   D. For...Next

2. True or False: To execute a block of code if a condition tests to be False, use the Do...Loop block with the While test.

   A. True

   B. False

3. The following code is used to square a number. The code also adds 1 to the number before squaring it. What is the value of **x** after the **SquareIt** function is called?

```
Public Sub Main()
      Dim x As Int32 = 5
      MessageBox.Show(SquareIt(x).ToString())
      MessageBox.Show(x.ToString())
End Sub
Private Function SquareIt(ByVal Num As Int32) As Int32
      Num += 1
      Return Num * Num
End Function
```

   A. 4

   B. 5

   C. 6

   D. 36

4. Which of the following properties or methods are in the **Exception** class (select all that apply)?

   A. Message

   B. Source

   C. ExceptionSource

   D. InnerException

   E. OuterException

5. You need to create an application that is going to catch all different types of exceptions. The exception classes provided with the .NET Class Library do not fit the needs of your application, so you have to create your own exception class. What is the order of steps to follow to create and use the new exception class?

   i.Throw the new exception object when necessary.

   ii.Create a new class that inherits the **Exception** class.

   iii.Create custom properties or methods for your exception class.

   iv.Call the New method of the base class to initialize the base class.

   v.Catch an exception that is based on the name of your exception class.

   A. i, ii, iii, iv, v

   B. iii, iv, ii, i, v

   C. ii, iv, iii, i, v

Test Answers

1. **C.** The validation code would be executed more than once, indicating that you need to use a looping structure. Because you do not know, when coding your application, how many times the code inside the loop will execute, the best block to use is the Do...Loop.
2. **B.** The While condition executes code only if the condition tests to be true.
3. **B.** Because we pass the **x** into the function by value we are passing in a copy of the value; **Num** points to a location in memory that is different from **x**. Therefore, when we modify the value of **Num**, we do not affect **x**.
4. **A, B, D.** The Message is the description of the exception. The Source is the location where the exception occurred. The **InnerException** gets the exception that caused the current exception.
5. **C.** The first step is to create the exception class derived from an **Exception** type of class. The next step is to call the base class constructor in the class constructor. You can then create all the properties and methods you want your exception class to contain. To cause the exception within the client, the object that throws the exception uses Throw with the New keyword and the name of your exception class. The client uses a Try...Catch...Finally...End Try block to catch and handle the specific type of exception.

CHAPTER 4

Arrays, Strings, and Collections

In this chapter, you will

- Create and use arrays
- Learn how to create multidimensional arrays
- Learn how to create and use strings
- Discover how to use the **StringBuilder** class
- Find out how to employ the **ArrayList** collection
- Understand how to use the **SortedList** collection

In Chapter 3 we discussed variables and how developers use them to point to data in memory. Until now we have only looked at creating a variable that points to one location in memory. The first section of this chapter discusses arrays, which are variables that point to a group of data in memory.

The second section of this chapter discusses strings. So far we have output strings to the console, but we have not studied how the string is stored in memory and how developers can manipulate it. The .NET Class Library provides several classes to use when working with strings.

The last section of this chapter discusses collections. Collections are similar to arrays, but they are more versatile and supply more functionality, including searching and sorting. Because they need to supply more functionality, however, they are not as efficient as arrays.

Arrays

In Chapter 3 we looked at looping structures such as Do...Loop and For...Next. When working with groups of variables, it is easier to write code that loops through all the variables instead of writing a line (or multiple lines) of code for each variable. For example, let's say we write source code that declares three variables, each holding a concert date for an artist our company is promoting. We set each variable to point to a **DateTime** object that contains July 14th, August 14th, and September 15th, respectively. We then add one and a half days to each value (for no reason other than to demonstrate this topic).

```
Dim conc0 As DateTime = New DateTime(2002, 7, 14)
Dim conc1 As DateTime = New DateTime(2002, 8, 14)
Dim conc2 As DateTime = New DateTime(2002, 9, 14)
conc1.AddDays(1.5)
Console.WriteLine(conc1.ToShortDateString())
conc2.AddDays(1.5)
Console.WriteLine(conc2.ToShortDateString())
conc3.AddDays(1.5)
Console.WriteLine(conc3.ToShortDateString())
```

To change each of the three values we need to write two lines of code, totaling six lines. This may not seem like much work, but if we had fifteen concert dates, and had to write a hundred lines of code modification for each, we would have to write 1,500 lines of code.

To the rescue comes the array. Arrays are a well-established technique in the software development world. The concept of an array is to group several locations in memory into a single name. To access each individual element (a single value's location), we follow the variable name with an index number in parentheses. For example, in the following line of code we are accessing the fourth element that the **conc** variable points to.

```
conc(3).AddDays(1.5)
```

When creating and using arrays, remember the following points:

- In Visual Basic .NET, arrays can start only at index zero. In previous versions of Visual Basic they could be set to zero or one.
- All elements of an array must be the same data type. Each data type occupies a specific amount of memory, so the index of the array states that from the first element's location we must move an amount of data equaling the size of each location multiplied by the index. For example, if we had an array of four **Int32s**, the index would range from 0 to 3. The array variable would point to the first element. To access the third element, our application would access the location calculated from the first location added to the product of 2 and 4 (the number of bytes an **Int32** occupies).
- Elements in an array are contiguous in memory; the location of each element is one after the other. This feature lets us access the elements in an array through the array index. All we have to do is move the number of elements, which is the index number, from the first element. In other words, the index number specifies how many steps over from the first element the runtime needs to move in order to access the element requested. If the items were not contiguous, we would have to know the address of each element.

Arrays in Visual Basic .NET

In most languages an array variable is a pointer to the first element in the array. In Visual Basic .NET, because everything is an object, an array is an object with the characteristics and behavior of an object. The **Array** class supplied with the .NET Class Library supports all the features of an array and provides developers with extra functionality.

Because arrays in Visual Basic .NET are objects, we will first discuss how to create an array object in memory. We will also explain how to initialize the values of the elements in the array and how to manipulate these values when using the array.

EXAM TIP Arrays are fixed-size once created. Elements cannot be added or removed.

Creating and Using an Array

Because the array is an object in Visual Basic .NET, we have to create an array object in memory before we can use it. This is done in one of two ways: implicitly by assigning the values when creating the array; or by using the CreateInstance method.

```
Dim array1() As Int16 = {5, 500, 65, 432}
Dim array2() As Int16
array2 = Array.CreateInstance(GetType(Int16), 4)
array2(0) = 5
array2(1) = 500
array2(2) = 65
array2(3) = 432
```

In the preceding code we have created two arrays. Both are four elements in length and have the same values in each element. The illustration shows how **array1** would look in memory.

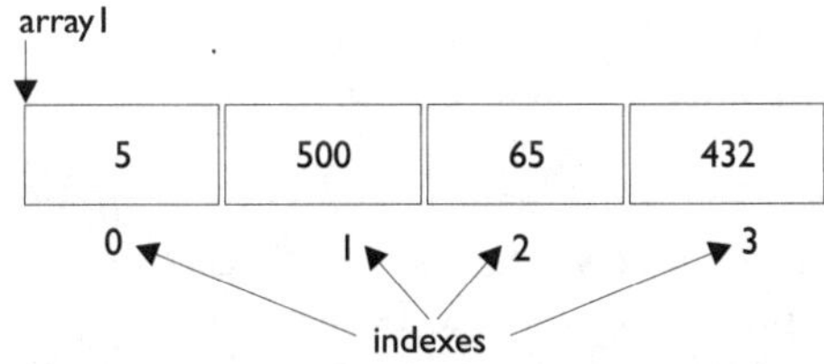

The **array1** object has been created using the single-line syntax of array creation and initialization. We declare the array the same as we declare all other variables in Visual Basic .NET, except we add parentheses after the variable name. This instructs the compiler to regard the variable name as an array and not as a single element variable. We follow the array declaration with an assignment operation. The elements of the array are immediately initialized with the values in the curly braces.

Note that we do not specify the number of elements in the array during the declaration of the array. The parentheses remain empty. The number of values placed in the initialization braces will tell the compiler the length of the array. This operation also implicitly creates the instance of the array object (creates the object in the location in memory).

The preceding example uses several lines of code to create **array2**. The first line simply declares to the compiler that we are going to create an array called **array2** that will point to **Int16**. We have not yet created the array object or used any locations for data. The next line uses the CreateInstance method of the **Array** class to create a new array. To create a one-dimensional array (if laid out in table format, this array would have only one column but a separate row for each field), this method takes the data type of each element in the array as the first argument and the number of elements in the array as the second argument. Notice that we have to use the GetType function to return a **System.Type** value—the data type of the first argument.

EXAM TIP When using the CreateInstance method you must use the GetType function to return a type in the first argument.

At this point **array2** has its elements initialized implicitly by the compiler. Because our example declares the elements of the array to be of type **Int16**, the elements are initialized to zero. For more information about the value-type variables and their initial values refer to Chapter 3.

The remaining lines of code in the example access each element in the array one by one and assign the specified values. To access the array elements we simply use the array variable name and include the index of the element in parentheses following the name. Elements in an array are read-write and can be changed at any time.

Exercise 4-1: Creating and Using an Array In this exercise you will create and initialize two arrays. You will create one array using the "declare and initialize" syntax; you will create the other using the CreateInstance method of the **Array** class.

1. Start Visual Studio .NET and create a new console application by selecting File | New | Project. Then choose Visual Basic Projects under the Project Types pane. Select Console Application from the Templates pane and type **SimpleArray** in the Name text box. Make sure the Close Solution radio button is selected and click OK.
2. Your project should have a module file called Module1 open for editing. Inside the module file you will have a declaration for the module itself (Module1) and Sub Main. You will place your code within the Sub Main procedure. To avoid having to specify the fully qualified class names in your code, place the following line at the top of this file:

```
Imports System
```

3. Create the first array by using the "declare and initialize" syntax. Type the following code within the Main procedure:

```
Dim myFirstArray() As Int16 = {5, 10, 15, 20, 25, 30}
```

4. Create the second array using the CreateInstance method of the **Array** class by entering the following:

```
Dim mySecondArray() As Int16 = Array.CreateInstance( _
      GetType(Int16), 6)
```

5. To assign values to the elements in the second array, create a loop by entering the following code. Doing so will clarify how you can use the array index to your advantage when accessing elements of an array.

```
Dim iTemp As Int16
For iTemp = 0 to 5 ' Array index are zero to n-1; n=number of elements
      mySecondArray(iTemp) = 35 + (iTemp * 5)
Next
```

6. To display the values of the preceding elements, use the **Console** class to output the values to the screen. To access the values of each array, use the For...Each loop. Your code should resemble the code that follows. Each time the loop executes, iTemp will be assigned the value of each subsequent element in the array starting from the first.

```
Console.WriteLine("These are the values in myFirstArray:")
For Each iTemp in myFirstArray
      Console.Write("{0}; ", iTemp)
Next
Console.WriteLine()
Console.WriteLine("These are the values in mySecondArray:")
For Each iTemp in mySecondArray
      Console.Write("{0}; ", iTemp)
Next
Console.ReadLine()
```

7. Run the application by selecting Debug | Start Without Debugging. The illustration shows the output of your program's execution.

```
E:\Work Files\Book\Chapter 4\SimpleArray\bin\SimpleArray.exe
These are the values in myFirstArray:
5; 10; 15; 20; 25; 30;
These are the values in mySecondArray:
35; 40; 45; 50; 55; 60; _
```

You may wonder why we would use the CreateInstance method to create an array. Why would we use a syntax that requires multiple lines when we could write a single line and initialize the array in one shot? There is method to the madness of this feature—the capability to create an array whose size is determined at run time.

Exercise 4-2: Creating an Array with a Dynamic Size In this exercise you will create a console application that accepts command line parameters when executed and creates an array of the requested size.

1. Create a new Visual Basic .NET Console application using Visual Studio .NET. Name the application **DynamicArray** and verify that the Close Solution radio button is selected.
2. Import the **System** namespace into the module by typing the following code at the top of the Module1.vb file:

```
Imports System
```

3. Change the declaration of the Main procedure to the following code. The **args** argument to our Main procedure is, in fact, an array of strings; each string follows the file name and is separated by spaces.

```
Sub Main(ByVal args() As String)
```

4. Use the following code to specify that there is only one argument passed into the application and that the application should output an error message to the user if there is more than one argument passed. Then, specify that the argument passed into the application can be converted into a number. Place this and the rest of the code inside the Main procedure.

```
If args.Length <> 1 then
      Console.WriteLine("You can pass in only 1 numeric argument")
      Console.ReadLine()
      Exit Sub
Else
      If Not IsNumeric(args(0)) Then
            Console.WriteLine("The argument must be a number")
            Console.ReadLine()
            Exit Sub
      End If
End If
```

5. If a valid argument was passed into the application from the command line, you can proceed. Convert the string argument passed into an integer value and create a variable for the converted value as follows.

```
Dim iNumElem As Int32 = Int32.Parse(args(0))
```

6. Create the array using the following code. Because the CreateInstance method takes the length of the array as an argument, you can pass the integer into this method. You use a loop to assign values to each of the elements; in this case, multiples of 5 are used.

```
Dim myArray() As Int32
Dim iTemp As Int32
myArray = Array.CreateInstance(GetType(Int32), iNumElem)
For iTemp = 0 to iNumElem - 1
      myArray(iTemp) = 5 + (iTemp * 5)
Next
```

7. Now that the array is populated with values, display those values to the command line by entering the following code.

```
Console.WriteLine("The values in the array are:")
For Each iTemp in myArray
      Console.Write("{0}; ", iTemp)
Next
Console.ReadLine()
```

8. Build the solution by selecting Build | Build Solution. To pass an argument into the application, open the command prompt and change the directory to the location of your compiled executable; this should be in the **bin** directory under the project directory. Run the application by typing **DynamicArray 10**.

Try executing the application with several different values for the number of elements to create. Also try executing the application with a string argument and with multiple arguments to test the control of the application. A word of advice: Do not type in extremely large numbers; you may have to wait a while for the application to complete. The illustration shows the output of your program's execution based on the value 10 being passed in as the size of the array.

```
E:\WINSTALL\System32\cmd.exe - dynamicarray 10

E:\Work Files\Book\Chapter 4\DynamicArray\bin>dynamicarray 10
The values in the array are:
5; 10; 15; 20; 25; 30; 35; 40; 45; 50;
```

Creating and Using a Multidimensional Array

A spreadsheet, such as a Microsoft Excel worksheet, is simply a two-dimensional array. To create a two-dimensional array we can use either of the techniques used earlier in this chapter (implicitly, by assigning the values when creating the array, or by using the CreateInstance method).

```
Dim myArray1(,) As Int16 = {{0,1},{2,3},{4,5}}
Dim myArray2(,) As Int16
myArray2 = Array.CreateInstance(GetType(Int16), 3, 2)
myArray2(0,0) = 0
myArray2(0,1) = 1
myArray2(1,0) = 2
myArray2(1,1) = 3
```

Note that to declare an array as multidimensional we have to specify within the parentheses how many dimensions the array has. Although the parentheses contain no values to indicate the number of elements in each dimension, the comma inside the parentheses indicates that these arrays have two dimensions each. In Visual Basic .NET, the number of dimensions of an array is referred to as the rank and is accessible through the Rank property of the array.

EXAM TIP To create an array whose size is determined at run time, use the CreateInstance method of the **Array** class.

Copying an Array

The **Array** class includes the Clone method. This method creates a shallow copy of the array. A shallow copy is a copy of the array elements; it produces a matching array of the original. If the elements in the array are reference types pointing to other locations in memory, however, these locations in memory are not cloned. The cloning simply copies the references from the original array into the new array, but both arrays' members point to the same locations in memory. Reference type variables will be discussed in further detail in Chapter 7.

EXAM TIP Cloning an array shallow-copies the array; it does not copy the elements.

Strings

A string, in memory, is simply an array of characters. The **String** class in Visual Basic .NET is much more, though. When we create a **String** object in .NET we are creating a read-only sequence of characters in memory and an object that points to these characters. A string is immutable in .NET; we cannot change the characters. In this section we discuss creating and building strings, combining multiple strings, and working with various types of string functionality.

EXAM TIP A string is immutable. If we change the value of the string, we are creating a new object and destroying the original.

Creating and Building Strings

The simplest way to create a string is to declare the variable and assign a value to it.

```
Dim myStr As String
myStr = "Hello, World!"
myStr = "Hello, again!"
```

We do not have to explicitly create the **String** object before we assign the value to it. The compiler will do this operation automatically. In the preceding example, the first assignment of "Hello, World!" creates a new **String** object in memory and assigns its memory address to the **myStr** variable. The next line assigns a new value to the variable; an entirely new **String** object is created and its address is assigned to the **myStr** variable. This first object has no more references to it, so the garbage collector (GC) will destroy it (more about the GC in Chapter 7).

The problem with working with a string that will have its value changed several times during the execution of an application is that a new object is created every time we change the value. This can be very costly, especially when creating distributed applications with a large number of users. The **StringBuilder** class lets us change the string value without creating a new object each time. We will look at the **StringBuilder** in more detail in the next section.

Let's look at the functionality provided with the **String** class. One of the most common tasks associated with a string is to use the Length property to determine the string's length—in other words, the number of characters it contains. Note that we are not referring to the number of bytes the string occupies. (Strings are Unicode by default; each character in a string takes two bytes. This allows for international character sets, such as Cantonese, Arabic, and Hebrew, which cannot fit into a single byte.)

```
Dim myStr As String = "Hello, World!"
Console.WriteLine(myStr.Length.ToString())
```

EXAM TIP Strings are, by default, Unicode; each character is two bytes in size.

The first line of the preceding code declares and immediately assigns the value to the string. The next line uses the Length property to retrieve the number of characters in the string. The ToString method converts this length, which is an **Integer**, into a string. The ToString method is available to every object in Visual Basic .NET as every object derives from the **Object** class. See the **Object** class in the MSDN Library for more information. The preceding example will display **13** to the command line when executed.

The Empty property of the **String** class represents the empty string "". It is useful in comparison tests for determining whether a string variable is empty.

```
Dim myStr = Console.ReadLine()
If myStr = String.Empty Then
      Console.WriteLine("Nothing was entered at the command line")
End If
```

This sample code retrieves input from the command line until the user presses ENTER. If the user presses ENTER without typing any text, the **ReadLine** method will return an empty string. We could also test this value by typing

```
If myStr = "" Then
```

But it may not be as accurate as the first test if we accidentally place a space within the quotes. The more common test is to compare the string to "".

The Chars property of the **String** class allows developers to retrieve a single character from the string based on the character's position. Remember that the argument passed into the property is the zero-based position of the character. In our "Hello, World!" string the character at position 1 is *e*.

When comparing two strings, case does not always matter. For example, in Canada the postal code is represented as *?#? #?#*, where *?* is a placeholder for a letter and # is a placeholder for a single-digit number; for example, P7F 5E2. If the user enters **p7F 5e2** when inputting the postal code, the value is still acceptable. However, we would prefer to perform comparisons of this string or extractions of individual characters in either all uppercase or all lowercase. The ToUpper and ToLower methods provide this functionality.

String Concatenation

To combine two strings in Visual Basic .NET, developers can use one of two methods. The first is to use the ampersand (&) operator or the addition (+) operator. The second is to use the Concat method of the **String** class.

```
Dim sTemp1 As String = "Hello, "
Dim sTemp2 As String = "World!"
Dim sTemp3 As String = sTemp1 & sTemp2
Dim sTemp4 As String = sTemp1 + sTemp2
Dim sTemp5 As String = String.Concat(sTemp1, sTemp2)
```

EXAM TIP Strings can be concatenated using the ampersand (&) operator, the addition (+) operator, or the Concat method of the **String** class.

In the preceding code **sTemp3**, **sTemp4**, and **sTemp5** all equal "Hello, World!". The ampersand is the most commonly used operator in Visual Basic and most experienced Visual Basic developers will use this syntax to concatenate strings in Visual Basic .NET. Keep in mind, though, that the ampersand operator calls the **Concat** method anyway. To get the quickest performance out of large-scale distributed applications, call the **Concat** method. For smaller applications, the performance increase is negligible. The choice is yours!

Searching a String

Developers frequently want to search for a particular substring or character within a string. The **String** class in the .NET Class Library includes methods that provide search capabilities. Table 4-1 lists the search functionality of the **String** class.

Developers frequently need to extract portions of the string or modify the string itself. Note that the original string is not modified using the **String** object's methods. This is to comply with the specification that the **String** object is immutable. The following example shows three methods of string manipulation.

```
Dim sTemp As String = "Hello, World!"
Console.WriteLine(sTemp.PadLeft(20))
Console.WriteLine(sTemp.PadRight(20, "."))
Console.WriteLine(sTemp.SubString(4, 3))
```

In the first line of code the string is assigned a value. The following line of code uses the PadLeft method with only one parameter. This method will fit the string into a 20-character space on the command line. Because we have used PadLeft, the string will be right-justified in this space and will be padded on the left with spaces. The space is the default padding character if none is specified in the optional second argument.

Method	Description
StartsWith	Returns a Boolean value indicating whether the string begins with the substring being passed into the method.
EndsWith	Returns a Boolean value indicating whether the string ends with the substring being passed into the method.
IndexOf	Returns the one-based index of the position in the string where the substring is found. If the substring is not found, the return value is 0. This method searches from left to right. An optional starting position can be passed into the method to start searching from a position other than the beginning of the string.
IndexOfAny	Returns the one-based index of the position of the first character it finds that matches one character in the array of characters being passed into the method. This method is useful for determining whether any of these characters is in the string. This method searches from left to right in the string.
LastIndexOf	The same as IndexOf, except it searches from right to left.
LastIndexOfAny	The same as IndexOfAny, except it searches from right to left.

Table 4-1 Search Methods of the String Class

The next line of code uses the PadRight method with two arguments. The first argument defines the space to fit the string into. PadRight will left-justify the string and, because we passed in the second argument, it will pad the remaining right characters with a period.

The last line of code shows the substring from the string starting at position 4 and retrieving 3 characters. In this case the output will be **lo,**.

The StringBuilder Class

Another useful class when working with strings is the **StringBuilder** class. It is similar to the **String** class except that it is a mutable set of characters whereas the **String** class is an immutable set of characters. The **StringBuilder** class is in the **System.Text** namespace (the **String** class is in the **System** namespace). As we've already discussed, if we assign a new value to an existing **String** variable, an entirely new **String** object is created in memory and the old one is destroyed. This can affect performance negatively if we need to use a string variable that changes frequently.

EXAM TIP The **StringBuilder** class is a mutable set of characters that is useful for strings that must be changed frequently.

The **StringBuilder** object uses more resources when created but it needs to be created only once. Even though the string value changes frequently, we use the same object. This class includes functionality to add and remove characters from the string with ease. Table 4-2 outlines some of these methods.

Method	Description
Append	Appends a new string to the end of this string (and only to the end). If an object is passed into this method, its ToString method is called to get the string representation of that object.
Insert	Inserts the new string into any location in this string as determined by the arguments passed into the method.
Remove	Removes a specified number of characters from this string. Both the point to begin removing and the number of characters to remove are passed into this method.
Replace	Replaces a substring with another substring. Both the original substring and the new substring are passed into this method.

Table 4-2 Methods of the StringBuilder Class

Collections

At the beginning of this chapter we discussed arrays. Although they are extremely useful structures within the Visual Basic .NET language, they have the following limitations:

- Array elements must be of the same data type. Developers sometimes need to group objects of different data types together to facilitate looping or to pass the group of objects into a procedure as an argument.
- We can only use an index number to access array elements. When grouping items together, developers may want to use a "user-friendly" description of each element to make element retrieval easier.
- The array is a fixed size and cannot be resized once created.

A collection is a group of related items. Unlike an array, a collection may contain items of different data types. In this section we discuss two types of collections: the **ArrayList** and the **SortedList**.

ArrayList

As just mentioned, one problem with arrays is that they cannot be resized once they are created. In other words, if we create an array with four elements it will always have four elements. The **ArrayList** provides an array that can be resized.

```
Dim myArray As ArrayList = New ArrayList() ' Empty collection
Dim sTemp As String
myArray.Add("This")
myArray.Add(" is ")
myArray.Add(" an ")
For Each sTemp in myArray
     Console.Write(sTemp)
Next
Console.WriteLine()
myArray.Add(" ArrayList")
```

```
For Each sTemp in myArray
      Console.Write(sTemp)
Next
Console.ReadLine()
```

In the first line of code we create an empty **ArrayList** object. (If this were an **Array** object, we would have to specify how many elements the array would contain, but not with the **ArrayList**.) Then, we add three string elements to the array and loop through the array to output the values of those elements to the command line. We add another string element to the array and, again, loop though the array to output the values to the command line.

This simple application would not be possible with the **Array** class because we would not be able to add a new element—nor would we be able to remove an element which is accomplished in **ArrayList** by using the Remove method.

EXAM TIP The **ArrayList** is a dynamically sizing array. Elements can be added to or removed from it.

SortedList

The **SortedList** class is a dictionary type of collection. An example of a dictionary is a table in a database that stores customer information. Each customer has a unique identifier. To access information about a specific customer, we simply enter the customer's ID.

The **SortedList** stores a unique key with each element in the collection so that we can easily retrieve the element. As long as the key is unique, it can be any type of object, including a string or number. In this way, we can store the information about a customer in a **SortedList** and use the customer ID as the unique key of each customer element.

EXAM TIP Each element in a **SortedList** object must have a unique non-null key.

The following example creates a **SortedList** object that will contain company names and their associated stock ticker.

```
Dim sList As SortedList = New SortedList()
sList.Add("MSFT", "Microsoft Corporation")
sList.Add("CSCO", "Cisco Systems, Inc.")
sList.Add("SUNW", "Sun Microsystems, Inc.")
Console.WriteLine(sList.Item("CSCO")) ' The company name will be output.
```

Two collections allow developers to retrieve elements on a first-in-first-out (FIFO) basis or a last-in-first-out (LIFO) basis. The **Queue** class provides FIFO access because the first item retrieved when looping through the collection will be the first item added to the collection. The **Stack** class provides LIFO retrieval. In this case a loop will first retrieve the last element added.

Summary

In this chapter we discussed arrays, strings, and collections. We learned that an array is a group of elements. Elements in an array must be of the same data type and are stored contiguously in memory. Arrays are fixed-size once created and therefore must be re-created if resized. Elements are retrieved from an array using their index numbers, which are zero-based. You can loop through the elements of an array or collection using the For...Each loop. To create an array whose size is determined at runtime use the CreateInstance method of the **Array** class.

After arrays, we saw that a **String** is an immutable set of characters. Changing the value of a string creates a new string object and destroys the original. There are methods to search and retrieve substrings in strings.

Even though the **String** is immutable, the **StringBuilder** class is a mutable set of characters. The **StringBuilder** provides methods to allow for the appending, inserting, removing, and replacing of substrings. A collection is a group of elements. An array is a type of collection in which the elements must be of the same type. The **ArrayList** is like the **Array** except it is resizable. The **ArrayList** provides methods that allow the addition or removal of elements in the array.

The **SortedList** is a dictionary collection, which means that each item has an index, a key, and a value. Each element added to a **SortedList** collection must be assigned a unique non-null key. You can sort the **SortedList** based on the key or the value.

Test Questions

1. You need to create an application to store information about a supplier's products. Each product's information, except for the product number, is stored as an array of strings. You must be able to retrieve each product based on its number. Which class would you use?

   A. Array

   B. ArrayList

   C. Queue

   D. SortedList

   E. Stack

2. You need to create an array that has its size entered by the user when executing the application. Which line of code allows this?

   A. `Dim myArray() = New Array(5)`

   B. `Dim myArray() As Int16 = {6, 4, 7, 3}`

   C. `Dim myArray() As Int16 = New Array(iNumOfElements)`

   D.
   ```
   Dim myArray() As Int16 = Array.CreateInstance(GetType(Int16), _
           iNumOfElements)
   ```

3. Which members of the **String** class would you use to extract a single character from the string (select all that apply)?

   A. SubString

   B. Length

   C. Chars

   D. IndexOf

4. Which line(s) of code is best to use for creating a string whose value changes often (select all that apply)?

   A. `Dim sTemp As String`

   B. `Dim sTemp() As String = New String()`

   C. `Dim sTemp As StringBuilder = "Hello, World!"`

   D. `Dim sTemp As StringBuilder = New StringBuilder("Hello, World!")`

   E. `Dim sTemp As StringBuilder = New StringBuilder()`

Test Answers

1. D. The **SortedList** is a dictionary collection requiring a unique non-null key for each element. In this case, the product number would be the unique key. Even though each product has its information stored as an array of strings, the array is considered an object; therefore it can be added as the element in the collection.
2. D. You use the CreateInstance method of the **Array** class to create the array and pass in the number of elements.
3. A, C. The Chars property is used to retrieve a single character at the position specified. The SubString method is used to retrieve a set of characters from the string. Set the length of this substring to 1 and it will retrieve a single character.
4. D, E. The code in Line D creates the object and immediately assigns it a value. The code in Line E creates the object that is zero characters in length.

CHAPTER 5

Delegates and Events

In this chapter, you will

- Develop synchronous and asynchronous communication
- Use delegates
- Learn about events and asynchronous events
- Learn about threading

Traditional programming methods in non-visual environments such as DOS, mainframe, and other command-line applications usually call functions and methods synchronously. In this chapter we will discuss the difference between synchronous and asynchronous programming, and how delegates and events accommodate the developer with asynchronous capabilities.

Synchronous Versus Asynchronous Communication

When developers call a function synchronously in an application, the calling procedure does not continue executing until the function being called completes. This is analogous to a phone call between two parties. When we speak to each other on the phone, we utter a sentence and then wait for a response before we utter the next sentence. This continues back and forth until the conversation is completed.

Asynchronous communication can be one way or two way. Again, we can analogize this to a telephone call. If the other party is not available when we call, we can usually leave a message. With one-way asynchronous communication, we don't expect a return call after the person receives the message. With two-way asynchronous communication, we do expect a return phone call. In either case, we do not sit by the phone doing nothing but waiting for the return call. We continue with our lives and if the other party returns the call, we will chat with them.

So, how does synchronous and asynchronous communication work within an application? We will demonstrate this concept by building an application that runs a car object.

Exercise 5-1: Building the Car Application In this exercise you will build a simple Windows Forms application to create and drive a car object. The car will have a private variable that will maintain the amount of fuel in the gas tank. This variable will be represented as an integer between 0 and 100 that indicates the percentage of gas left in the tank. The car will also have a Drive method to drive the car and decrease the fuel in the gas tank by 10%—not a very functional car, but it works for this example. The method will also return the amount of gas remaining in the tank after driving.

1. Create a new Windows Forms application by clicking File | New | Project. In the New Project dialog box that appears select Visual Basic Projects in the Project Types pane. Select Windows Application in the Templates pane and enter **CarApplication** in the Name text box. Set the correct location in which to save the project and click OK to create the new project. The New Project dialog box should look similar to the following illustration.

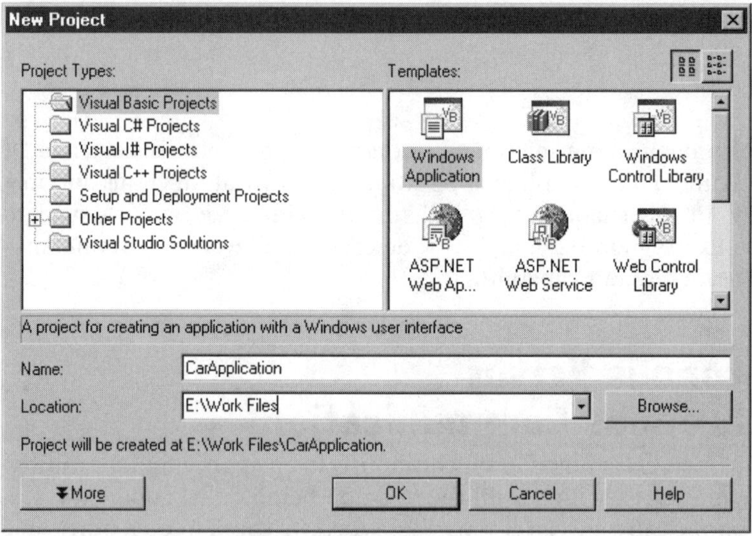

2. Once the project is created you will be presented with a default form in the Visual Studio .NET IDE called Form1. This form will be the user interface for your car application. To add the control that will drive the car, select the Button control in the Toolbox and draw it onto Form1. Once the button has been added to the form, change its Name property to **btnDrive** and its Text property to **Drive**. The form should resemble the form in the illustration.

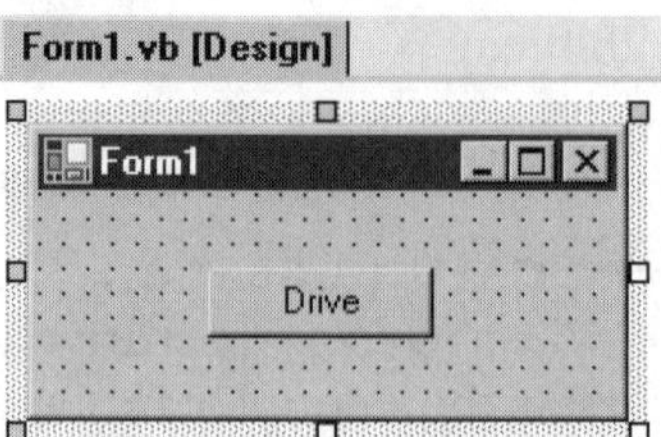

3. To create a car class that has the Drive method and the private member variable to hold the fuel level, click Add Class on the Project menu. In the Add New Item dialog box change the name of the class to **Car.vb** and click OK. The new class is created, and the Visual Studio .NET IDE opens this class for editing.

4. Add the following code between the Public Class and End Class lines:

```
Private mFuelLevel As Byte
Public Sub New()
      mFuelLevel = 100
End Sub
```

   The preceding lines of code declare the private variable that will maintain the fuel level and then initialize the value to 100 when the object is created. The New Sub procedure is called the constructor. It runs when the object is created (more about this in Chapters 6 and 7).

5. Add the following lines:

```
Public Function Drive() As Byte
      If mFuelLevel > 0 Then mFuelLevel -= 10
      Return mFuelLevel
End Function
```

   The preceding lines declare a function called Drive, which checks whether there is fuel in the tank. If so, the fuel level is decreased by 10%. Then, the amount of fuel remaining in the tank is returned to the client.

6. To create the car object, open Form1 for editing by right-clicking Form1.vb in the Solution Explorer and clicking View Code. The Code Editor window appears, displaying the contents of Form1.vb. Declare the car variable by adding the following line of code after the Inherits line:

```
Private myCar As CarApplication.Car
```

   At this point you have created the variable but not the object to which the variable is going to point. To create the car object, select the Base Class Events in the left-hand drop-down list in the Code Editor, and then select Load in the right-hand drop-down list. A new procedure, called Form1_Load, is created. This code will be executed when the form first loads. Add the following line of code as the content of this procedure:

```
myCar = New CarApplication.Car()
```

7. Now that you have a car object you can use the button on the form to drive the car. Keep in mind that you added code to the car class that set the fuel level to 100% when the car was created. Add the button's click handler to the code by selecting btnDrive from the left-hand drop-down list in the Code Editor and selecting Click from the right-hand drop-down list.

8. Add the following code for the body of the button's click event handler:

```
MessageBox.Show(myCar.Drive().ToString())
```

The MessageBox class' Show method is used to return the amount of fuel remaining in the gas tank. The ToString method is also used here to convert the Byte value returned by the Drive method to a String value, which is what the Show method displays.

9. Execute the application by clicking Debug | Start.

Delegates

There are two deficiencies in the car application: The client has no way of knowing, other than by reading the value of the fuel level after the car has been driven, whether the car is running low on fuel or whether the car has run out of fuel. All modern cars include some type of indicator to notify the driver that the car has a low fuel level. This notification is asynchronous because we continue driving the car without constantly waiting for the light to go on. Our application needs an "indicator" and code connected to the fuel level to cause the indicator to "light up."

When developers call a method, the direction of communication is from the client, in this case the form, to the object. An asynchronous call can be in either direction. In our case, we want the car to initiate the call back to the form when the car is low on fuel.

What Is a Delegate?

The word "delegate" is defined as "a person chosen to act for another." A delegate object in .NET is similar; it is delegated to run a procedure or multiple procedures. The delegate object maintains a list of the procedures it must call and when it is executed, it executes all the procedures in its list. The delegate does not have any other features. We will demonstrate this concept with an addition to the car application. Figure 5-1 shows the direction of communication of delegates and methods.

Exercise 5-2: Adding a Delegate to the Car Application A simple delegate contains only one procedure in its list. In this exercise you will create a procedure in the form to be added to the delegate's list. You will also declare a delegate and create a delegate object, which will maintain the list and execute the procedure. Use the completed code from Exercise 5-1. If you did not complete Exercise 5-1, the source code for this exercise is on the CD-ROM.

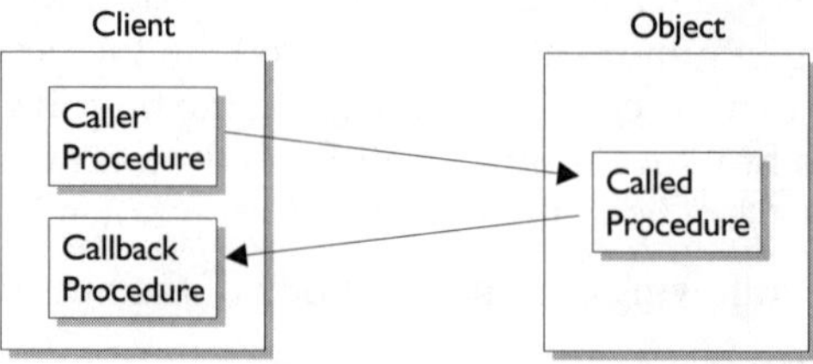

Figure 5-1 Direction of communication of delegates and methods

PART I

1. Add a button to the form and change the Name property to **btnSimpleDel**. Change the Text property to Invoke Delegate and size the button so that all the text of the button is displayed.
2. Add the following line under the line that declares the myCar variable:

```
Private Delegate Sub MyDelegate(ByVal num As Byte)
```

   This line declares a new data type, called MyDelegate, that can call any Sub procedure added to its list that matches exactly the signature (the data types and orders of parameters as well as, if a function, the return type). In other words, all the procedures to be added to the delegate's list must be Sub procedures with a single Byte argument.

NOTE The preceding declaration line using the Delegate keyword declares the delegate data type but not the delegate object. You must create the delegate object before adding procedures to the list.

3. To declare the variable that will point to the delegate object once it is created, enter the following line of code after the declaration of the delegate data type:

```
Private delList As MyDelegate
```

4. Before you can specify which procedure to add to the list you must declare the procedure in your code. Enter the following code at the bottom of the class before the End Class. This code causes a message box to pop up and show the value of the argument passed into it.

```
Private Sub ShowNumber(ByVal arg As Byte)
      MessageBox.Show("The value of the number is: " & _
            arg.ToString())
End Sub
```

5. To create the delegate object and assign a procedure to its list, enter the following code inside but at the end of the Form1_Load procedure:

```
delList = new MyDelegate(AddressOf ShowNumber)
```

   The AddressOf operator in Visual Basic retrieves the address of the procedure and, in this case, assigns that address in the list inside the delegate. The delegate will now parse through the list when it is called and know the location of functions in its list so as to call them.

EXAM TIP When using the AddressOf operator do not include parentheses or arguments after the procedure name. Only the procedure address is required for the delegate. Also note that the signature of any procedure being added to the delegate's list must match exactly the signature of the delegate itself.

6. The last step in this exercise is to add code to the button's click event in order to invoke the delegate. Add the click event handler by selecting btnSimpleDel from the left-hand drop-down list in the Code Editor and selecting Click from the right-hand drop-down list. Add the following code inside the procedure:

```
Static iCount As Int16
iCount += 1
delList.Invoke(iCount)
```

EXAM TIP You can also use delList(iCount) to invoke the delegate without calling the Invoke method explicitly.

7. Execute the application by clicking Debug | Start. Click the Invoke Delegate button several times to invoke the delegate. Even though you did not call the ShowNumber procedure, the delegate object invokes it.

Multicast Delegates

Exercise 5-2 created a simple delegate known as a single cast delegate. This delegate contains only one procedure in its list. Instead of creating a delegate in Exercise 5-2, you could have called the ShowNumber procedure directly passing in the single Byte argument. One of the handiest features of the delegate object is that you can create multicast delegates. These delegate objects contain multiple procedures in their lists and execute each of those procedures when invoked.

Exercise 5-3: Creating a Multicast Delegate In this exercise you will enhance the car application by adding a second procedure to the form, and then adding it to the delegate list. Use the completed code from Exercise 5-2, which can be found on the CD-ROM.

1. You will first create another procedure to be called by the delegate. Remember that this procedure's signature must match that of the delegate. Add the following code to the end of the class before the End Class statement:

```
Private Sub SquareTheNumber(ByVal num As Byte)
      MessageBox.Show("The square of the number is: " & _
            (num * num).ToString())
End Sub
```

2. In Exercise 5-2 you created a single delegate and set the variable delList to point to it. In this exercise you will change that line of code. To create a multicast delegate you must "combine" delegates and store the combination as a new delegate. Remove the line of code in the Form1_Load procedure that created the single cast delegate. The line should look similar to the following line:

```
delList = new MyDelegate(AddressOf ShowNumber)
```

3. In its place, you will create an array of delegate objects, and then initialize the array to the address of each procedure in the list by entering the following code:

```
Dim tDelegate() As MyDelegate = {AddressOf ShowNumber, _
      AddressOf SquareTheNumber}
```

4. You now have an array of two delegate objects. All delegate data types have a combine method to create a new delegate by combining either two delegate objects or an array of delegate objects. The resulting delegate is a multicast delegate. Enter the following line of code:

   ```
   delList = MyDelegate.Combine(tDelegate)
   ```

   In this exercise you will combine the entire array. Remember that all the delegate objects in the array must be of the same data type as the new delegate.

NOTE The order in which the procedures are added to a multicast delegate's list is the order in which they will be executed.

EXAM TIP A multicast delegate is a combination of two or more delegates.

5. Execute the application by clicking Debug | Start. Click the Invoke Delegate button several times to watch the application work. Note that even though the code in the button's click event handler only called the delegate object's Invoke method once, both procedures in its list were executed in the order you added them to the list.

Events

Events are delegates that are contained within objects and can be handled using the event handling technology of traditional Windows programming. This means that we don't have to explicitly create a delegate object; it is implicitly created when we assign the handler procedure to it. There are two steps in creating an event:

1. Declare, in the class, the event that can be handled by the client.
2. Raise the event; this is the same as invoking the delegate.

To practice this technique you will create a delegate in Exercise 5-4, and then change the delegate to an event in Exercise 5-5. This will help you differentiate between using a delegate and using an event.

Exercise 5-4: Adding a Delegate to the Car Class Your car still does not notify the driver (your form) that it is running low on or has run out of fuel. This exercise will add a delegate to the class that notifies the client that the car has run out of fuel. Use the solution code from Exercise 5-3, which can be found on the CD-ROM.

1. You must first declare the delegate data type in the class, and then declare the variable that will point to the delegate object once it is created. The object will use this variable to execute the event handler. Enter the following code after the Public Class line:

```
Public Delegate Sub OutOfFuelDelegate()
Public OutOfFuel As OutOfFuelDelegate
```

2. You must invoke the delegate at the appropriate time. To have the car application check the fuel level of the car and invoke the delegate when the tank is empty, add the following code to the Drive method before the line that uses the Return keyword.

```
If mFuelLevel = 0 Then OutOfFuel.Invoke()
```

3. To create the handler procedure in the form, add the following code to the end of the form class before the End Class line:

```
Private Sub OutOfFuelHandler()
      MessageBox.Show("The car is out of fuel.")
End Sub
```

4. To create the delegate object and assign the handler procedure to its list, add the following code to the end of the Form1_Load procedure:

```
myCar.OutOfFuel = New CarApplication.Car.OutOfFuelDelegate( _
      AddressOf OutOfFuelHandler)
```

5. Execute the application by clicking Debug | Start and clicking the Drive button until the car runs out of fuel. The illustration shows the message box that appears when the car runs out of gas.

Even though you have effectively handled an event, the code created in Exercise 5-4 was not written using the traditional event handling approach. You had to explicitly create the delegate object and expose two public members from the object: the delegate data type and the delegate variable.

Exercise 5-5 illustrates a more graceful way to implement this type of functionality by using an event to notify the form when the car runs low on fuel. Keep in mind that the event is still just a delegate object.

Exercise 5-5: Adding an Event to the Car Class This exercise will add to the source code of the completed Exercise 5-4. This code can be found on the CD-ROM.

1. The first step is to declare the event. This single line will declare the delegate data type (although not available as before) as well as declare the variable to point to the delegate object in memory. Add the following line of code at the top of the class after the Public Class line.

```
Public Event LowOnFuel(ByVal FuelLevel As Byte)
```

2. The next task is to invoke the event at the appropriate time. With events developers use a Visual Basic keyword called RaiseEvent instead of using the Invoke method. Add the following code inside the Drive method just before the Return statement.

```
If mFuelLevel < 30 And mFuelLevel > 0 Then _
      RaiseEvent LowOnFuel(mFuelLevel)
```

EXAM TIP Use the RaiseEvent keyword to invoke the event delegate object from within the object.

3. Now that you have declared the event in your class, you need to handle the event in your form. There are two ways to do this in Visual Basic. Steps 3 through 5 will use the Handles keyword to add a procedure to the delegate's list. Steps 6 and 7 introduce the second method of handling the event.

   To use the Handles keyword, you must first modify the line of code that declares the object variable so that the runtime can create the delegate object that has just had its variable declared. To do so, change the following line:

   ```
   Private myCar As CarApplication.Car
   ```

   to

   ```
   Private WithEvents myCar As CarApplication.Car
   ```

   Now create the event handler in the same way you created the event handler for the buttons' click events. Select myCar from the right-hand drop-down list in the Code Editor and select LowOnFuel from the left-hand drop-down list. This will create a new Sub procedure called myCar_LowOnFuel, but that is just the default name it creates in the Visual Studio .NET IDE. Unlike previous versions of Visual Basic, Visual Basic .NET does not bind a procedure to an event based on its name. The binding is performed based on the Handles keyword that follows the procedure declaration. In this case the code states that this procedure is to be added to the LowOnFuel delegate object's list and must be invoked when the LowOnFuel delegate is invoked. Note that the new procedure matches exactly the event signature that was declared in the class. Another important note is that the handler of an event is always a Sub procedure. If you want the handler to be a Function you must use delegates explicitly.

EXAM TIP The WithEvents keyword must be used when declaring an object variable whose events you want to handle. The variable cannot be declared inside a procedure.

4. Add the following code inside the myCar_LowOnFuel procedure:

```
MessageBox.Show("The car is low on fuel and has " & _
      FuelLevel.ToString() & "% gas left.", _
      "myCar_LowOnFuel")
```

5. Execute the application by clicking Debug | Start and "driving" the car until it runs low on gas. The following illustration shows the output when the car runs low on fuel; note the title bar caption of the message box.

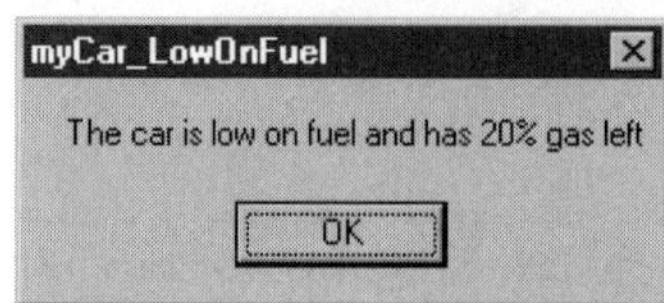

6. The second method of adding a procedure to the event delegate's list is by using the AddHandler Visual Basic .NET function. In this step you will create another procedure to be executed when the event occurs. Remember that this procedure too must match exactly the signature of the event. Add the following code at the end of the form class before the End Class statement.

```
Private Sub CustomHandler(ByVal arg As Byte)
      MessageBox.Show("The car is low on fuel and has " & _
            arg.ToString() & "% gas left", _
            "CustomHandler")
End Sub
```

7. You use AddHandler to add this procedure to the delegate list in the Form1_Load procedure. Add the following code to the end of the procedure.

```
AddHandler myCar.LowOnFuel, AddressOf CustomHandler
```

8. Execute the application again by clicking Debug | Start and "driving" the car until it runs low on gas. Notice that this time two message boxes appear showing the car is running low on fuel; however, each has a different caption in the title bar. This shows that our event is now multicast.

As Exercise 5-5 demonstrates, you can use either the Handles or the AddHandler keywords to perform event binding. You can use the Handles keyword with multiple handler procedures for the same event, or you can use the AddHandler function in the same manner. You should, however, stick to one or the other for consistency. The convention is to use the Handles keyword for single cast events and the AddHandler keyword for multicasting. The following illustration shows the output of the message box using the AddHandler function; note the caption in the title bar.

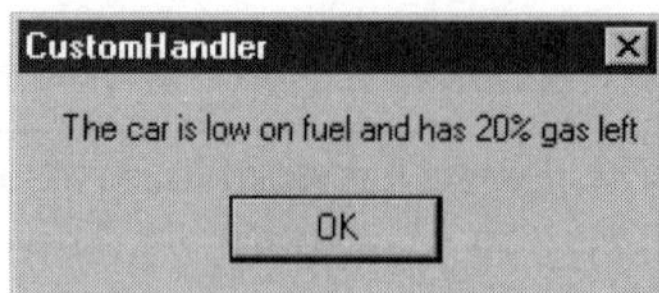

Asynchronous Delegates

One of the most important capabilities of modern programming languages is to perform multiple tasks at the same time. All modern operating systems have the capability to build multithreaded applications. This section will discuss multithreading, and where and how it is used. Specifically, it will cover multithreading in relationship to asynchronous programming and delegates.

Threads

A thread is a path of execution. The CPU in a computer has only a single thread and, therefore, can have only one process on the computer passing it data to process at a particular time.

In single-threaded operating systems such as DOS, all computer processes use the CPU thread to pass data to the CPU. Each process that needs to have a task executed must queue up in order to have the task completed.

Let's say that DOS has a task to execute. It gets the thread because it is the first in the queue, executes its task, and then releases the thread once it completes its task. If Word 2.0 (for Windows 3.x) executes a task and is next in the queue, it gets the thread, and then releases the thread to the next process in the queue once its task is complete. The problem occurs when the process executing the task does not release the thread, such as when Word runs an infinite loop. Because it does not release the thread, other processes, including the operating system, cannot acquire use of the thread. In this case the computer is left "hanging by a thread", which is where the "My computer just hung!" expression comes from.

The 32-bit operating systems such as those in the Windows NT line (Windows NT, 2000, XP, and .NET) use a different approach to solve this issue. The only process that has direct use of the CPU thread is the operating system. The operating system has a thread manager that creates multiple threads for use with each running application. One specification of a 32-bit operating system is that every process (in Windows, this would be an executing .EXE) must have at least one thread of its own.

Each process thread communicates with the operating system's thread manager and not the CPU. Instead of a queuing method, the thread manager uses a time-slicing method, called multitasking, to cycle through each thread. For example, it allocates a small amount of time to Word and then, even though Word's task may not be complete, moves to Excel, then to Explorer, and so on. It continues cycling and each task appears to be executing at the same time. If a thread is tied up in an infinite loop, the operating system will ask it a few times if it is "okay". If not, the Windows operating system will display a message to the user that the application is "Not Responding". This process prevents the hanging problem encountered in 16-bit operating systems.

The problem with a single-threaded application is that it can only perform one task at a time. If the primary thread (the first thread created by the operating system for the process) can request another thread to execute the other task, these tasks can occur at the same time. This is called multithreading. Why do we need an application to be multithreaded? Imagine building an application for anesthesiologists that monitors the vital signs of a patient in surgery and allows doctors to enter any drugs they are administering to the patient. Would we really want the vital sign monitor component of the application to stop running while the doctor types in the data? Probably not.

The .NET common language runtime (CLR) creates a thread pool for .NET applications. In this case the application requests a thread from the CLR, and not the operating system. When the CLR loads, it requests several threads from the operating system and, if need be, requests more as it runs.

How Does Multithreading Relate to Events?

Earlier in the chapter we discussed synchronous and asynchronous applications. So far you have only built synchronous applications; each task executed must complete before another task can begin. We will examine this idea by modifying the car application in two exercises. Exercise 5-6 will demonstrate the deficiency of driving the car synchronously. Exercise 5-7 will correct this deficiency by enabling asynchronous execution.

Exercise 5-6: The Synchronous Car For this exercise, use the solution code from Exercise 5-5. It can be found on the CD-ROM.

1. Modify the Drive method of the car to create a loop and change the method from a Function to a Sub. The resulting code should look as follows:

```
Public Sub Drive()
      Do Until mFuelLevel = 0
            System.Threading.Thread.CurrentThread.Sleep(1000)
            If mFuelLevel > 0 Then mFuelLevel -= 10
            If mFuelLevel = 0 Then OutOfFuel.Invoke()
            If mFuelLevel < 30 And mFuelLevel > 0 Then _
                  RaiseEvent LowOnFuel(mFuelLevel)
      Loop
End Sub
```

   Besides creating a Sub procedure, you added a loop so that the code inside the loop executes until the car is out of fuel. You also added a line that tells the current thread to sleep. The Sleep method takes an argument specifying how many milliseconds to sleep. Sleeping a thread pauses the thread for that amount of time. In this case, you sleep the thread for one second before decreasing the fuel level. The rest of the procedure is the same as before except that it doesn't return a value because it is now a Sub.

2. Add two Label controls and a Timer control to the form. Set the Name property of one of the labels to **lblStatus** and the other to **lblTime**. Erase the contents of the lblStatus label's Text property. Set the Interval property of the Timer control to 100 and the Enabled property to True. This will set the Timer's Tick event to be raised every tenth of a second. The resulting form should look similar to the illustration.

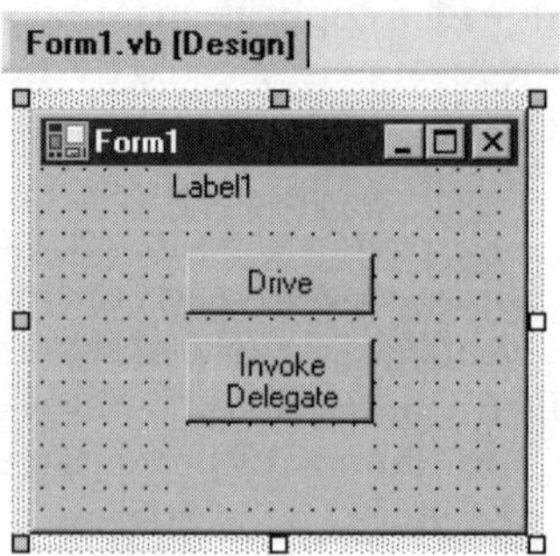

3. To show the current time in the lblTime control, you must add code to the Tick event of the Timer control. Add an event handler for the Tick event by double-clicking the Timer control. Add the following line of code inside the event handler:

```
lblTime.Text = DateTime.Now.ToLongTimeString() & " " & _
      DateTime.Now.Millisecond.ToString()
```

   This line of code will output the current time, including milliseconds, to the lblTime control to verify whether the forms code still executes when driving the car.

4. Remove all the code from inside the btnDrive_Click procedure and replace it with the following code:

```
lblStatus.Text = "Driving"
myCar.Drive()
```

5. Add the following line of code inside the OutOfFuelHandler procedure before the MessageBox.Show statement:

```
lblStatus.Text = "Stopped"
```

6. Execute the application by clicking Debug | Start. Click the Drive button and note that the time does not get updated until the first low fuel message appears. The time output returns to its consistent updating only when the Drive method of the object has completed.

In this type of application it would be preferable to have a continuously updating time and have the car notify the client when it is low on or out of fuel. This is two-way asynchronous communication; the application continues executing the code in the form (the time updates) and expects a response. Exercise 5-7 enables asynchronous communication.

Exercise 5-7: The Asynchronous Car In this exercise you will modify the car further by using the solution code from Exercise 5-6, which can be found on the CD-ROM.

1. You only need to modify the class. Start by creating a new procedure to be executed by the new thread. A thread is actually a delegate and therefore must be passed a procedure's address. A delegate, however, can only invoke Sub procedures that have no arguments. Create a new Sub procedure in the class called DriveInternal and move all the code inside the Drive procedure to the DriveInternal procedure.

2. You must now request a new thread to invoke the DriveInternal procedure asynchronously. You must also start the thread. Starting the thread is the same as starting to run the procedure using the new thread. Replace the removed code in the Drive procedure with the following code:

```
Dim driveThread As System.Threading.Thread = _
      New System.Threading.Thread(AddressOf DriveInternal)
driveThread.Start()
```

3. Execute the application by clicking Debug | Start and click the Drive button. Notice that the time does not stop updating and that the car notifies the client when it is low on and out of fuel.

Summary

In this chapter we discussed delegates, events and communication techniques. We learned that synchronous communication is when the caller procedure does not continue until the called procedure completes. One-way asynchronous communication is when the caller does not wait for the called procedure to complete its work before continuing. In addition, the caller does not expect a response from the called procedure. Two-way asynchronous communication is the same as one-way asynchronous communication, except the caller does expect a response from the called procedure.

A delegate is an object that maintains a list of procedures that it must execute when it is invoked. To add a delegate to an application, you must first declare the delegate data type. This data type has a specific signature and the procedures added to its list must match that signature exactly. To create the delegate object, you must declare a variable to be of the type of the delegate declaration, and then create the delegate object itself.

To assign a procedure to a single cast delegate, use the AddressOf keyword in the delegate objects constructor. Use the Combine method of the delegate data type to create a new delegate object that is either the combination of two delegates or the combination of an array of delegates. These delegates must all match signatures. Use the Invoke method of the delegate object to execute the procedures it is delegated to run.

An event is a delegate that can be handled using traditional Windows programming techniques. Event delegates can only execute Sub procedures. Event delegates are only created in classes and are handled in a client that creates the object. To handle the object's event in the client, the WithEvents keyword must be used to declare the variable that points to the object. Use the RaiseEvent keyword in the class to invoke the event delegate. Add the handler procedures to the event delegate's list using either the Handles keyword at the end of each handler procedure or the AddHandler function.

To execute code asynchronously, request a new thread (a path of execution) to execute the code. Every application has at least one thread called the primary thread. A Thread object is a delegate that can only execute Sub procedures with no arguments and runs on its own CLR thread.

Test Questions

1. To create and use a multicast delegate object, what is the order of steps to follow?
   - i. Create the delegate objects (usually as an array).
   - ii. Declare the delegate data type.
   - iii. Create the procedures to be called by the delegate.
   - iv. Invoke the delegate object.
   - v. Use the Combine method of the delegate data type to create a new delegate from the delegate objects.

A. i, ii, iii, iv, v

B. ii, iii, iv, i, v

C. ii, iii, i, v, iv

D. ii, i, iii, v, iv

2. You are building an application that needs to execute work on a database server in the form of a stored procedure. This stored procedure takes an extensive amount of time to complete. Instead of having the user wait for the execution on the server to complete, you want the code that executes this procedure to notify the user when it is complete. Which method should you use?

   A. Synchronous delegate

   B. Asynchronous event

   C. Synchronous event

   D. Stored procedure event

3. You have declared a delegate as follows:

```
Private Delegate Function MyFuncDel(ByVal Arg As Int32) As String
```

   Which of the following procedures can be added to a delegate object's list when the delegate object is of the data type MyFuncDel?

   A. Private Function MyProc(ByVal Num As Int32) As String

   B. Private Sub MyProc(ByVal Arg As Int32) As String

   C. Private Function MyProc(ByRef Arg As Int32) As String

   D. Private Function MyProc(ByVal Arg As Int32) As Int32

4. Which of the following is a valid procedure for a thread to execute?

   A. Private Sub MyProc(ByRef frm As Form1)

   B. Private Function MyProc() As Thread

   C. Private Sub(ByRef thrd As Thread)

   D. Private Sub MyProc()

5. Your car class has an OutOfFuel event declared. Which line(s) of code can be used to add an event handler to your form (select all that apply)?

   A. AddHandler myCar.OutOfFuel, MyHandlerProc

   B. Private Sub MyHandlerProc() Handles myCar.OutOfFuel

   C. AddHandler myCar.OutOfFuel, AddressOf MyHandlerProc

   D. Private Sub MyHandlerProc() Handles myCar

Test Answers

1. **C.** The delegate data type must be declared first. You should then create the procedures to be invoked by the delegate. Following that, you create the single cast delegates that will execute each of the procedures. You then combine those delegates to create a new multicast delegate. Call the Invoke method of the multicast delegate to execute the procedures it has in its list.
2. **B.** The code executing the stored procedure should be performed asynchronously using a new thread. Once it is complete it can notify the client that it has completed. This way the user can continue using the client to perform work.
3. **A.** This is the only procedure that matches the signature of the delegate exactly. Our delegate can only point to a Function procedure that takes one argument ByVal that is an Int32 data type and returns a String data type.
4. **D.** A thread can only execute a procedure that is a Sub and has no arguments. This is because a thread is a delegate with that type of signature.
5. **B, C.** B uses the Handles keyword at the end of the handler and is followed by the event to handle. C uses the AddHandler function to combine a delegate object to the OutOfFuel event delegate in the object.

PART II

Object Orientation in Visual Basic .NET

CHAPTER 6

Object-Oriented Analysis and Design Overview

In this chapter, you will

- Learn basic concepts of object-oriented technology
- Study object-oriented technology's terminology
- Read an overview of the unified modeling language

As software development, maintenance, and modification grow in complexity, developers are increasingly adopting object-oriented analysis, design, and programming in order to save time and money.

This chapter provides an overview of the basic concepts and terminology of object-oriented development. The goal of this chapter is to help you understand the object model as implemented in the .NET Framework and to introduce you to the object-oriented technology terminology used throughout this book.

Why Object-Oriented Development?

As computer power and software complexity increased in the 1990s, the software development methodologies of the 1980s and early 1990s became inadequate. Not only had software become more complex, but also businesses were demanding rapid modification of the software to meet the changing business environment. Software maintenance and modification became an expensive stumbling block. Businesses were spending more than fifty percent of their budget maintaining existing software.

Problems with the earlier methodologies included a high degree of *coupling* and poor *cohesion*. Coupling is the dependence of one part of the software on another part of the software or on some data. When one part of the code changes or the structure of the data changes, it is difficult and time consuming to determine the impact on the rest of the system.

Cohesion refers to how well code and its associated data form a unit. Ideally, the data required by the code should be only the data that is needed to do the task defined for the code. Also, the code should not create unexpected side effects such as modifying data that is unrelated to its task.

Businesses needed an analysis, design, and programming environment that enables the creation of maintainable and reusable code and helps ensure that software has a low degree of coupling and a high level of cohesion. Object-oriented development was designed to meet these goals through the use of *encapsulation* and *information hiding*. Encapsulation is the combining of the data and the code to process that data into a single entity, the object. Information hiding refers to the technique of only allowing access to an object's data through the use of messages and services. The only way to access data is by sending a message to an object and having one of the object's services provide that information. Information hiding also allows the object to use information that is never exposed through a service.

Defining Objects and Classes

Understanding objects and classes is key to understanding object-oriented technologies. Part of object-oriented analysis is to find all the objects in the business requirements. One approach is to look for all the nouns in the requirements documents. Depending on how the requirement documents are written, nouns can be proper or common. In the following sentence **Bill** is a proper noun.

```
Bill orders Shakespeare In Love.
```

In the following sentence, **customer** is a common noun.

```
A customer orders a movie.
```

In the preceding examples, **Bill** is an object that is an instance of the class **customer**. After identifying an object or class, you define the characteristics of the object as it relates to the class. It is important to understand the phrase "as it relates to the class". This concept helps define good cohesion. You only want to look for the characteristics of **Bill** that apply to him as a **customer**. Hair color, for example, is not important as a characteristic of a customer.

A *class* is the blueprint used for the creation of an object, an instance of a class. An *object* is an entity (real or abstract) that has attributes, services, and relations. Attributes, services, and relations are the characteristics of an object. We discuss these characteristics in the following sections.

Characteristics of an Object

The identification of objects and their characteristics is important in defining a software implementation with low coupling and good cohesion. The characteristics of an object include attributes, services, and relations.

Object Attributes

An object has descriptive attributes and naming attributes. Descriptive attributes are facts about the object. Height, weight, and eye color are descriptive attributes about a person object. Naming attributes identify the object. A person's name and social security number are naming attributes of a **person** object. Attributes are called *properties* in the Microsoft object model; we will use this term throughout this book when referring to attributes.

NOTE Microsoft VB.NET uses the term "attribute" as a class to provide additional information about code within an application. Do not confuse Microsoft's use of the term "attribute" with the *properties* of a class.

Object Services

A service is work done by the object for other objects. An object performs a service when sent a message by another object. A **person** object may have a DateOfBirth attribute (property) and an Age service. The object calculates the age of a person using the person's date of birth. Services are also called methods or behaviors. The Microsoft object model uses the word *methods;* we will use this term throughout the rest of this book when referring to services.

Object Relationships

The object model does not allow an object to use services (functions, subroutines) that are not a part of an object. For example, you cannot have a generic function that calculates age with date as an input parameter. You can only calculate the age of a person by creating an instance of the **person** object from the **person** class and requesting the age of the person using a service provided by the **person** object. Therefore, one object frequently uses the services of another object. This dependence of one object on the service of another object leads to relationships between objects. These relationships are represented as *links* between objects. A link can be represented as a phrase that describes the relationship between two objects, as shown in the following examples.

```
An employee is a person.
A verb is part of a sentence.
A person is employed by a company.
A company employs a person.
```

The bold text in the preceding sentences identifies the links.

NOTE The .NET Framework circumvents the restriction of not allowing generic functions by allowing the creation of objects that have shared methods. However, you should not use shared methods unless it is absolutely necessary. Shared methods are discussed in Chapter 8.

Three types of relationships exist in the object model: inheritance, aggregation, and association.

An inheritance relationship, also known as a generalization/specialization relationship, is a relationship in which one object inherits the attributes and services of another object and can modify them and add to them (extend them). In terms of links, inheritance is an **is a** link. That is, an employee *is a* person. An employee has all the attributes and services of a person, and an employee has additional attributes and services.

An aggregation relationship is a relationship in which one object is a part of another object. The link for aggregation is **is part of**. An order line *is part of* an order. An aggregation relationship is also referred to as a whole-parts relationship.

An association relationship is any type of relationship other than inheritance or aggregation. It is also called a catch-all relationship. An example of an association relationship is an **employee** and the employee's **supervisor**. Both objects are employees, and there is a special relationship between them. This relationship is neither inheritance nor aggregation. The link for the relationship is defined by the relationship, and the link is bi-directional. The employee *is supervised by* the supervisor. And the supervisor *supervises* the employee. Being bi-directional means that the **employee** object can request services of the **supervisor** object, and the **supervisor** object can request services of the **employee** object.

Object State and Events

The state of an object depends on the values of its attributes. When the values of an object change, its state may change. For example, if an object reads data from a database, the data may be considered to be unmodified. As soon as one of the attributes (properties) is modified, however, the object's state may change.

When an object's state changes, it may cause an event to occur. For example, an object may want to notify its users that it has changed from unmodified to modified. To do so, the object raises an event. Good examples of state changes and events in the .NET Framework are found in the ADO.NET classes.

Inheritance in More Detail

Inheritance is an important part of the object-oriented development model. Previous versions of Microsoft Visual Basic did not include inheritance so the concept may be new to you.

As described earlier in this chapter, inheritance is a relationship in which one object inherits the properties, methods, and events of another object. Inheritance is also referred to as generalization/specialization: One object is a specialization of another object. Conversely, that one object is a generalization of another object.

NOTE The definition of inheritance is actually through the class because inheritance is a technique of defining properties, methods, and events. Therefore, you will see the term "class" used when discussing inheritance as opposed to the term "object," which is an instance of a class.

In describing the inheritance relationship, developers use the terms *subclass, superclass, base class,* and *derived class.* Microsoft Visual Basic .NET specifically uses the terms *base class* and *derived class.*

We'll use the following sentence to illustrate the meaning of the preceding terms.

```
A voter is a person.
```

In the preceding relationship, a voter is a person who is 18 years old or older. Based on this criterion, the following descriptions apply:

- The voter class is a derived class from the person class.
- The person class is the base class of the voter class.
- The voter class is a specialization of the person class.
- The person class is a generalization of the voter class.
- The voter class is a subclass of the person class.
- The person class is a superclass of the voter class.

Although Microsoft has standardized on using *base class* and *derived class* in the .NET Framework, *subclass* is still used frequently because of its previous usage in Microsoft products.

Polymorphism, Overriding, and Overloading

When one object inherits methods from another object, you may want to modify the functionality of the inherited method. This is called *inheritance-based polymorphism* or *overriding.* In the preceding example using the **voter** class and the **person** class, you may have a Create method that adds a person to a database. The **voter** class inherits the Create method from the **person** class. The **voter** class may require additional work that is not handled by the **person** class. For example, the **voter** class may require that the person be at least 18 years old before allowing creation of the database entry. In this case you override the Create method of the **person** class with code for the method in the **voter** class.

It is easy to confuse the concepts of polymorphism and overloading. The premise of polymorphism is that the same method name can function differently depending upon its object. That is, **voterobject.Create** functions differently than **personobject.Create**.

Overloading is the creation of two methods with the same name. Let's say that the **person** class defines a method called Age. The Age method calculates the person's age as of the current date. The **voter** class inherits this method. If the **voter** and the **person** are different objects for the same entity, then the **voterobject.Age** and **personobject.Age** methods return the same value. Now, suppose you want to calculate the person's age as of a certain date. You create a new method within the **person** class with the same name but with a parameter called AsOfDate. You now have two methods called Age within the same class. They are two different methods because the parameters for each method are different. The combination of the method name, the data type of the return value, and the data types and sequence of the parameters form what is referred to as a *signature* for a method. If the signatures of two methods are different, they are considered different methods.

In this example of overloading, the code for both methods exists within the **person** class. And the **voter** class inherits both methods. This is different from polymorphism, where the **voter** class changes the functionality of the Create method.

Abstract Classes

A class that does not provide all the necessary implementation code is called an abstract class. The purpose of this class is to provide a common structure for a base class that can be inherited by several derived classes. You can use abstract classes when you want the derived classes to have the same external properties, methods, and events, even though the base class is not fully implemented. The derived classes provide the implementation. You cannot instantiate an object from an abstract class. All objects must be instantiated from one of the derived classes.

Multiple Inheritance

Microsoft C++ allows a class to inherit from more than one class. Visual Basic .NET allows a class to inherit from only one base class. You can work around this limitation by using interface-based inheritance. This is the same technique that has been used in previous versions of Microsoft Visual Basic to provide functionality similar to inheritance. Chapter 8 provides more details on implementation of inheritance in the .NET Framework.

The Object-Oriented Development Cycle

Object-oriented development is divided into three stages: object-oriented analysis (OOA), object-oriented design (OOD), and object-oriented programming (OOP). Sometimes the first two categories are combined into object-oriented analysis and design (OOAD). Object-oriented analysis is the application of object-oriented methodology to determine the business requirements and the definition of a set of interacting business objects. Object-oriented design is the application of object-oriented methodology in order to define the interacting software objects necessary to meet the requirements of the business objects. Object-oriented programming is the implementation of interacting objects to meet the software object requirements.

Several methodologies exist for performing analysis and design. One popular methodology is the Unified Modeling Language (UML). In the UML methodology, *use-cases* are used to help communicate requirements during the analysis stage and design the classes and the class relationships for the system. Then, the classes and the class relationships are developed using object-oriented programming.

What Is a Use-Case?

A *use-case* is a description of major processes within a system. It is developed from scenarios that describe interactions between users and the system. When creating use-cases during the analysis and design stages, you identify specific processes around which you can draw a boundary. This enables you to focus on that specific process and not be overwhelmed by the system requirements as a whole. All of the use-cases are then diagrammed and evaluated to form the basis of the system design.

Microsoft Visio 2002 supports both the diagramming of use-cases and the design of classes and class relationships. It can also generate code for the classes.

Use-Cases in the UML

The Unified Modeling Language employs use-cases during the analysis and design phases of a system. There are two sets of use-cases that can apply to a system. The first set of use-cases results from the requirements gathering phase and describes the current or desired system based on interviews with the existing or future users and experts of the system. This set of use-cases is derived from scenarios that describe the user interaction with the system, and they communicate the analyst's understanding of the user requirements. The use-cases may describe the system with respect to specific people and specific items. For example,

```
Bill orders the Shakespeare in Love DVD
```

references specific people and items. That is, these use-cases refer to objects.

The second set of use-cases describes the system, again in user terms, but it is created after the analysis and reflects the system as it is being implemented. This set of use-cases communicates to the users the reorganization of the requirements into the actual system. It also identifies the classes for the system. The use-cases in this set may describe the system in more general terms. For example,

```
A customer orders a product
```

is a more general use-case. Although care must be taken to not lose requirements when generalizations are made, generalizations help clarify the types of objects, that is, classes, within the system. In the first use-case example above, is **Bill** a person or is **Bill** a customer? The second use-case example clearly identifies the object as a customer. A customer is usually different than a person within a system.

Actors in a Use-Case

When creating a use-case, you focus on the specific process and the people, hardware, or other systems that interact with the process. In the UML methodology, the people, hardware, or other systems that interact with the process are called actors. Actors are divided into four categories:

- **Principal actors** The main users of the process; for example, an order entry clerk
- **Secondary actors** Those responsible for maintaining and administering the resources of the process; for example, the person responsible for restocking the shelves with products

- **External hardware** Hardware devices that are required to perform the processes (not including the system running the software); for example, a printer
- **Other systems** Other systems with which the process must interact; for example, a system that verifies credit cards

For the purpose of diagramming a use-case within the UML methodology, the use-case is composed of the use-case itself, which is enclosed within the system, and the actors, which are outside the system interacting with the use-case. Figure 6-1 shows a simple use-case diagram within Microsoft Visio 2002.

The Label Printing Scenario

The following scenario is used throughout this chapter to create sample use-case diagrams.

```
Jane is in charge of the mail room for the Ajax Corporation. She is
responsible for mailing announcements for the company. These announcements
include mailings to vendors, customers, or both. Jane needs to be able to
generate labels that go to the attention of the accounts payable department
for a customer, to the accounts receivable department for a vendor, or to
the company in general with no specific department identified. The labels
should be sent to the mail room printer.
```

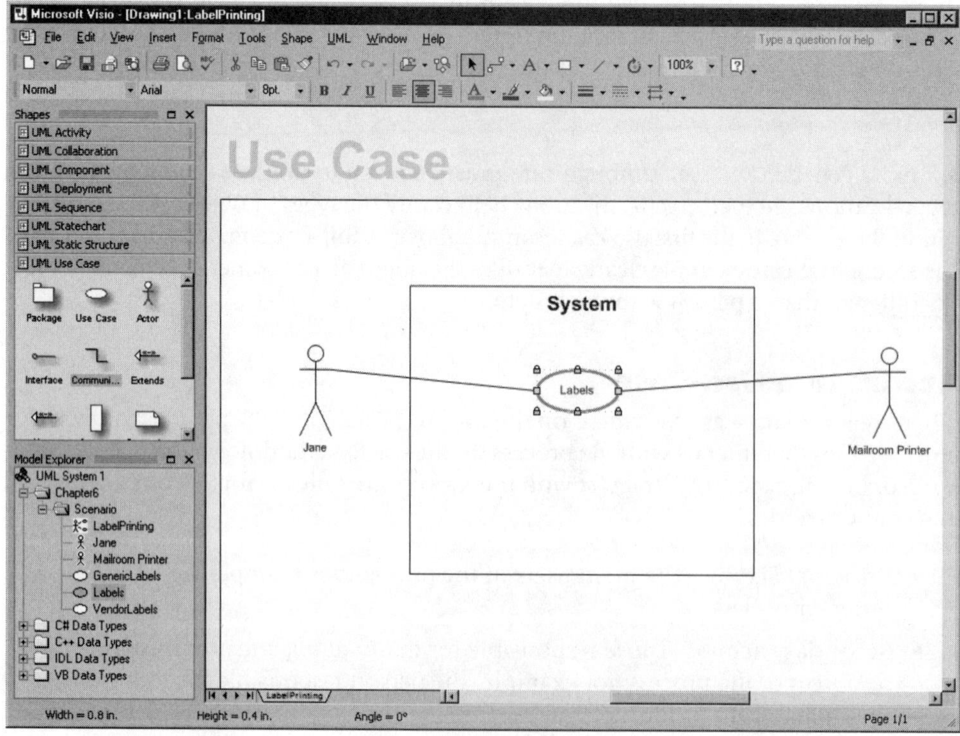

Figure 6-1 A simple use-case diagram using Microsoft Visio 2002

Use-Cases for the Scenario

As with all requirements gathering and interpretation, there is more that one way to break down the preceding scenario into use-cases. The first method is similar to Figure 6-1: There is a single use-case for printing labels. Jane and the mailroom printer are the actors and printing labels is the use-case. The details for vendor labels and customer labels become part of the textual description of the use-case.

Another interpretation of the requirements is to create three use-cases: one for printing customer labels, one for printing vendor labels, and one for printing generic labels. The actors for each of these use-cases are still Jane (or Mailroom Person) and the mailroom printer. Figure 6-2 shows this interpretation of the requirements.

The scenario and the use-cases do not focus on the details of a vendor or of a customer. In addition, they do not define the specifics of the label or the printer. At this level, the focus is on the actors and the process as a whole. The details come later. In fact, the developer must resist the temptation to insert knowledge gained from previous implementations and making assumptions about vendors and customers. All that is known at this point is that there are such objects and that labels are required for them. The focus of the design effort for this scenario is defining what makes a vendor

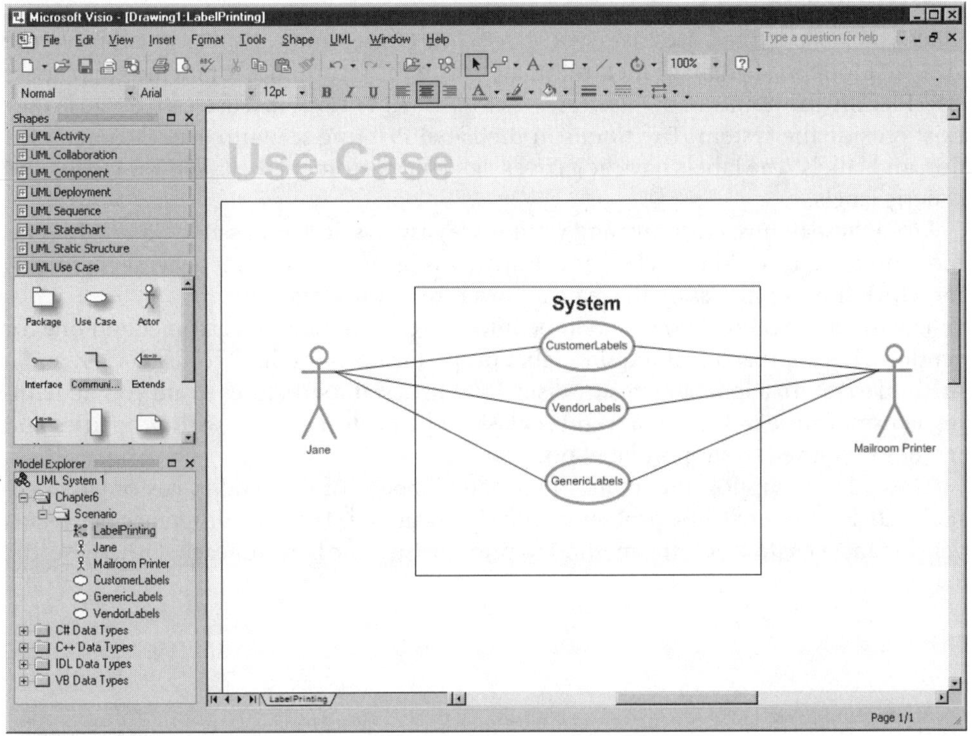

Figure 6-2 Use-case diagram for label printing scenario

different from a customer with respect to labels and what information about each is required for a label.Object-oriented development begins at the analysis stage and is propagated through the rest of the system. The following list demonstrates how to apply development concepts that were discussed earlier in this chapter during the analysis phase.

- **Low degree of coupling** The focus should be only on the label printing process, independent of the rest of the system.
- **High degree of cohesion** The information being defined should apply only to label printing, independent of the information required for the rest of the system.
- **Information hiding** Vendors and customers may have more information that is not part of the label printing and may even affect label printing, but it is not exposed.
- **Encapsulation** Everything is internal to the label printing process.
- **Isolation** Again, the focus should be only on the label printing process and the customer and vendor information required for printing labels.

Defining Classes

Once you have defined use-cases, you can define classes and class relationships. In the Unified Modeling Language methodology, one of the techniques for identifying classes is to identify the nouns in the use-cases. Actors are not nouns in a use-case because they exist outside the system. The nouns in the Label Printing scenario are customer, vendor, and labels. The labels have adjectives defining customer labels, vendor labels, and generic labels.

From these nouns, customer and vendor are easy to select as possible classes. Label is more difficult. It could be a class or a utility class (a class created for general processing for which it is not necessary to create an instance of the class).

The initial class breakdown could be into two classes: one for customer and one for vendor. This approach still requires label properties to be defined for each class and a method to return a label. Microsoft Visio 2002 uses static structures to aid you in defining classes. Figure 6-3 shows a **vendor** class and a **customer** class with properties and methods required to support label printing.

These classes support the return of formatted labels for the vendor, customer, or generic label. There are some problems with this structure. The only difference between a **vendor** and a **customer** is the method to print the specific label for each. Otherwise, the

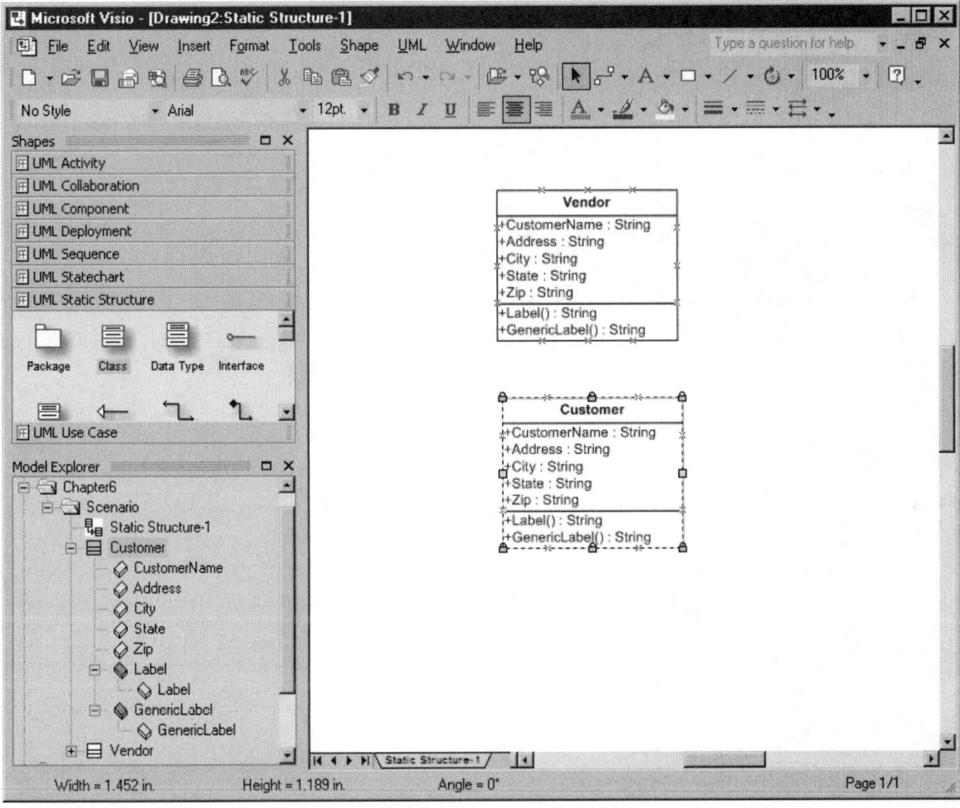

Figure 6-3 Static structures for the vendor and customer classes

structures are identical. Most of the code for each class is redundant; if a change is necessary, it must be changed in two places. Also, the code for printing the generic label is duplicated in both the **customer** class and the **vendor** class.

A possible better solution is to create another class called **company**. Figure 6-4 shows this class structure.

The **company** class contains the properties for both the **vendor** and the **customer**. In addition, it has a Label method and a GenericLabel method. The **vendor** class and the **customer** class inherit from the **company** class. The only code that needs to be implemented

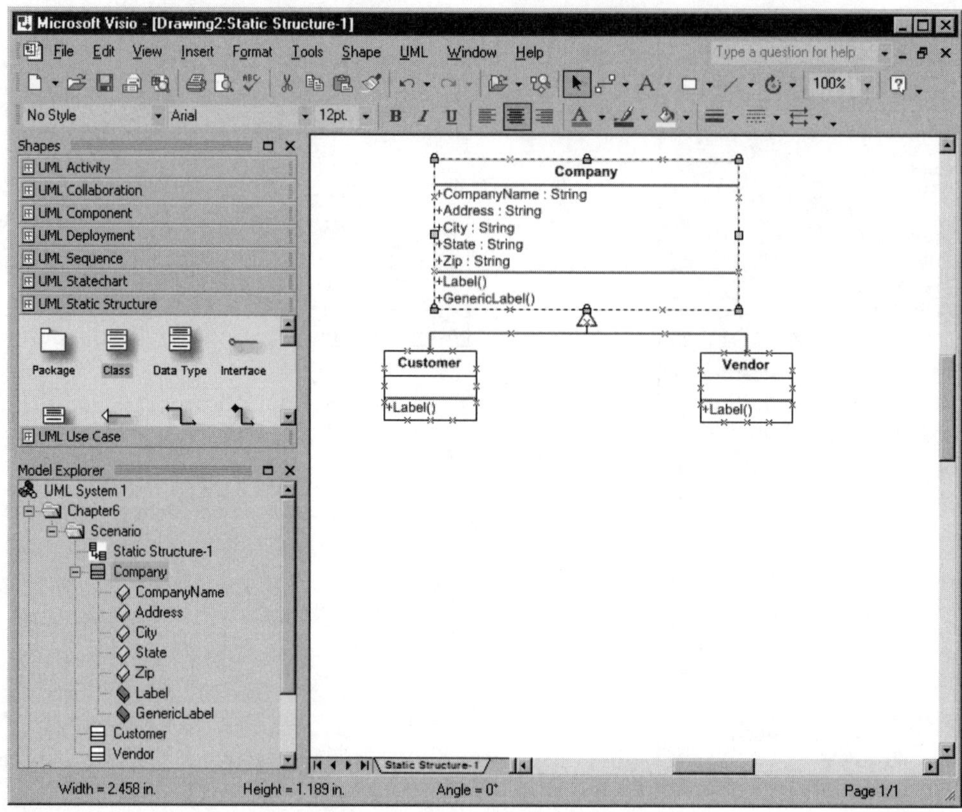

Figure 6-4 Static class structure with the vendor and customer classes inheriting properties from the company class

in the **vendor** class and the **customer** class is code that overrides the Label method for the special label requirements of these classes. More details on this implementation are presented in Exercise 8-3 in Chapter 8.

Generating Visual Basic Code from Microsoft Visio

Once you have created class diagrams within Microsoft Visio 2002, you can generate code from the definition. Figure 6-5 shows the dialog box within Microsoft Visio 2002 for generating the code. This dialog box is accessed from the UML menu item.

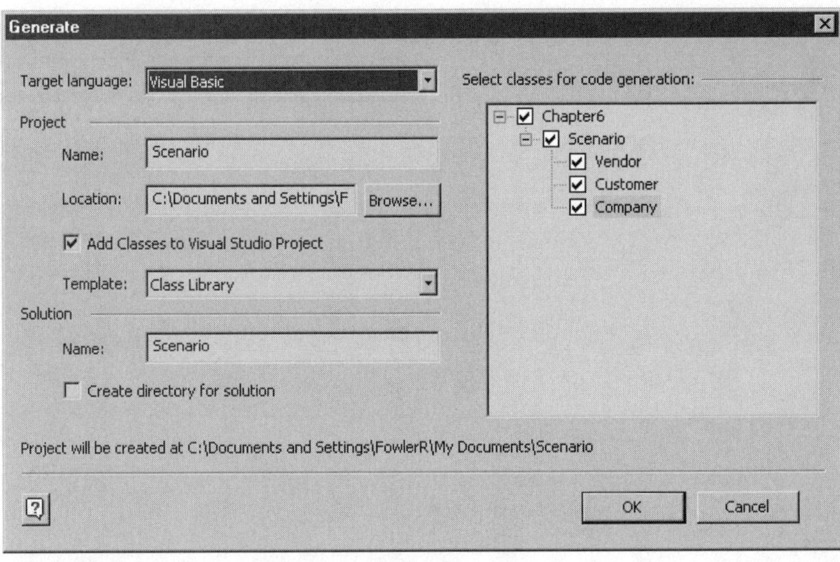

Figure 6-5 The code generation dialog box for Microsoft Visio 2002

When you are working on a specific class within Microsoft Visio 2002, you can preview the code that will be generated. Figure 6-6 shows the preview of the code.

As you can see from Figure 6-6, this code is more of a code outline that allows you to complete the code within the Visual Studio .NET integrated development environment (IDE). Other options within Microsoft Visio 2002 allow you to generate more complete code.

Generating Visio Class Structure from the Visual Studio .NET IDE

You can also generate the Microsoft Visio 2002 class structure for existing code from the Visual Studio .NET IDE. From the Visual Studio .NET IDE Project menu, select Visio UML | Reverse Engineer, as shown in Figure 6-7.

Using the Reverse Engineering option reduces the learning curve in using Microsoft Visio 2002. You can develop the structures of your classes by using the Visual Studio .NET IDE and then moving them into your class diagrams. Once the design has been solidified, you have a jump start on creating the finished classes.

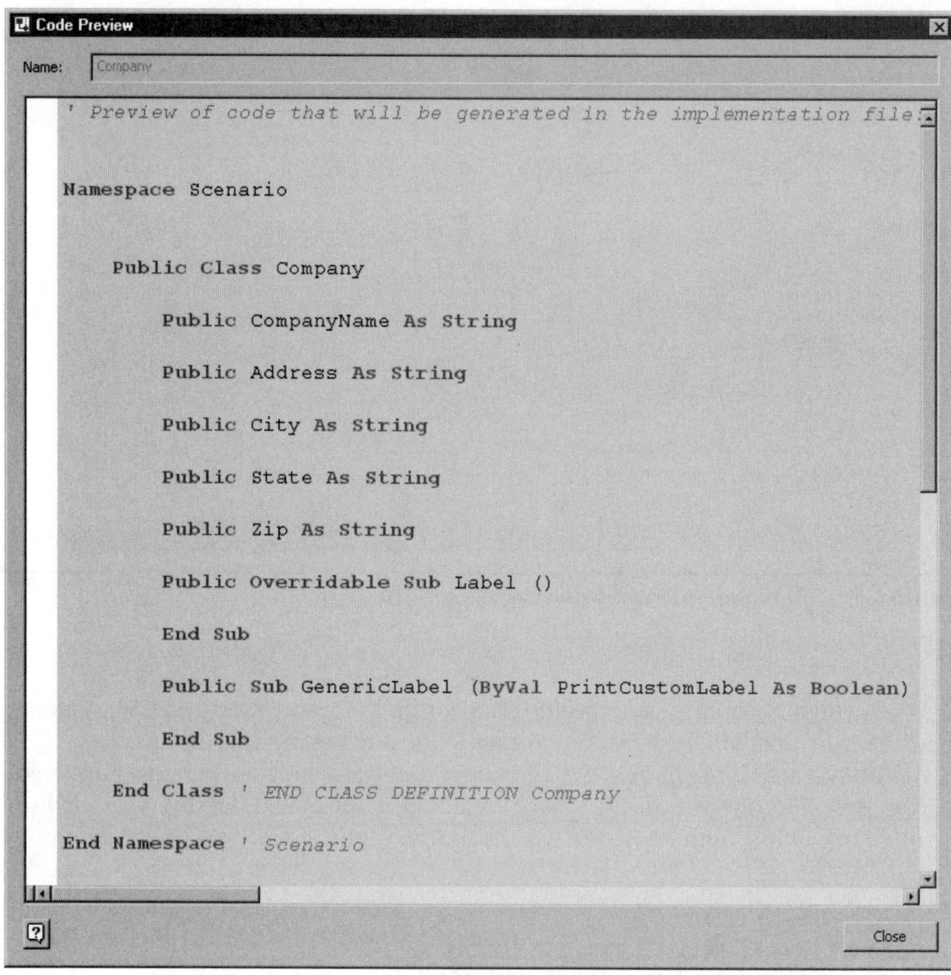
Code Preview
Name:
Company
' Preview of code that will be generated in the implementation file:
Namespace Scenario
Public Class Company
Public CompanyName As String
Public Address As String
Public City As String
Public State As String
Public Zip As String
Public Overridable Sub Label ()
End Sub
Public Sub GenericLabel (ByVal PrintCustomLabel As Boolean)
End Sub
End Class ' END CLASS DEFINITION Company
End Namespace ' Scenario
Close

Figure 6-6 Preview of code that can be generated for a class by Microsoft Visio 2002

Summary

The .NET Framework is based on the object model. Therefore, it is important that you understand the basics of object-oriented analysis, design, and programming.

One of the primary goals of object-oriented development is to reduce the cost of application maintenance and modification by minimizing coupling and optimizing cohesion. The object model accomplishes these goals using encapsulation and information hiding.

Classes are blueprints used to create objects. Objects are instances of a class. During the analysis and design of an application you isolate the classes and objects that make

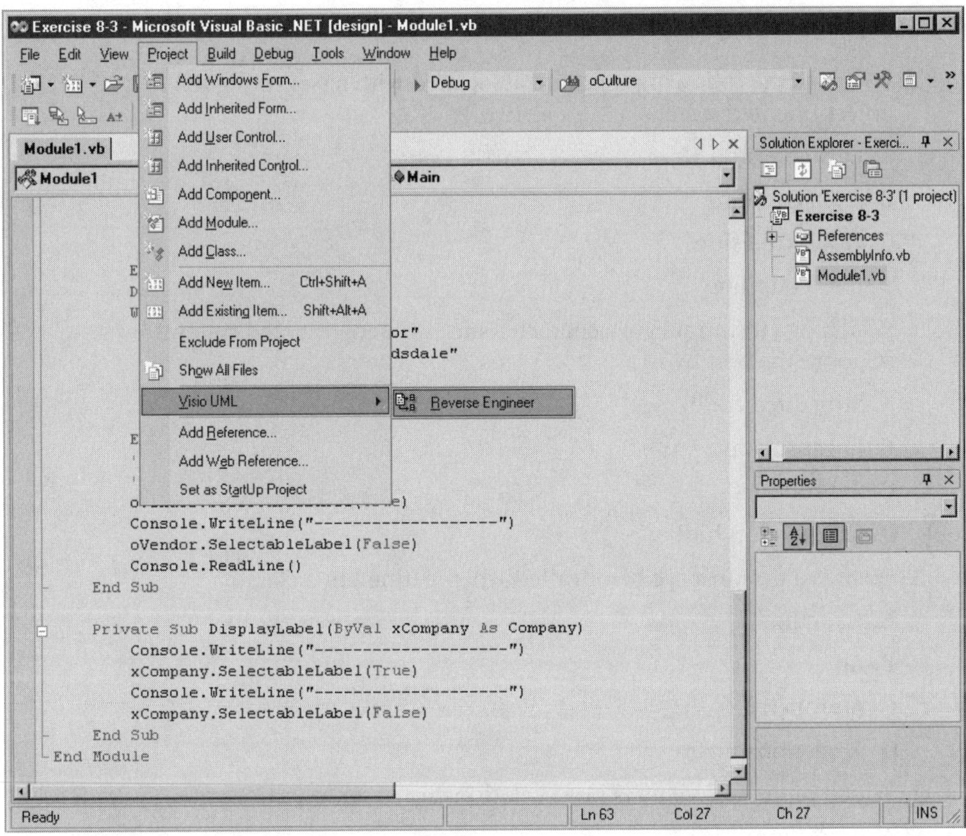

Figure 6-7 Reverse Engineering as Microsoft Visio 2002 class structure from the Visual Studio .NET IDE

up the application. Then, you define the properties, methods, events, and relationships for the classes. Object-oriented programming implements the classes.

The relationship of classes is an important part of the object model. There are three basic relationships: inheritance, aggregation, and association. These relationships can be defined using sets of words called links. Inheritance is an **is a** relationship, aggregation is an **is part of** relationship, and association is any relationship that is neither an inheritance nor aggregation relationship. The association relationship can be defined by a bi-directional link that describes the relationship. For example, an employee *is supervised by* a manager and a manager *supervises* an employee.

Microsoft Visio 2002 provides support for the Unified Modeling Language (UML) methodology for object-oriented development. The UML methodology is one of several and is commonly used. The UML methodology incorporates use-cases to diagram object-oriented systems. In addition, it supports several other diagramming techniques including class diagrams (called static structures in Microsoft Visio 2002).

Test Questions

1. Which of the following traits are associated with a well-designed object-oriented system? (Choose two.)
   A. Low cohesion
   B. High coupling
   C. Good cohesion
   D. Low coupling
2. Which two techniques are characteristic of object-oriented systems? (Choose the best two.)
   A. Structured code
   B. Encapsulation
   C. Subroutines
   D. Information hiding
3. What is a person's eye color called when defined in a class?
   A. A method
   B. An event
   C. A property
   D. A relationship
4. Which of the following is not a relationship in an object-oriented system?
   A. Association
   B. Inheritance
   C. Link
   D. Aggregation
5. Which of the following is a link for inheritance?
   A. is part of
   B. is a
   C. supervises
   D. supervised by
6. The statement

   ```
   The voter class is a specialization of the person class
   ```

   is an example of what type of relationship?
   A. Association
   B. Inheritance

C. Link

D. Aggregation

7. Which two terms are used to describe inheritance class relationships in the .NET Framework?

A. Base class

B. Subclass

C. Derived class

D. Superclass

8. What is another term for inheritance-based polymorphism?

A. Overloading

B. Overriding

C. Substitution

D. Overridable

9. What do you look for in use-case descriptions when trying to identify classes?

A. Verbs

B. Adjectives

C. Nouns

D. Adverbs

10. What technique can you use to implement multiple inheritance in Visual Basic .NET?

A. Subroutines

B. Associated classes

C. Interfaces

D. Overloading

Test Answers

1. C, D.
2. B, D.
3. C.
4. C.
5. B.
6. B.

7. A, C.
8. B.
9. C.
10. C.

CHAPTER 7

Reference-Type Variables

In this chapter, you will

- Learn about reference-type variables
- Understand class structure
- Instantiate and invoke .NET components
- Learn about memory resource management
- Learn about unmanaged resource management
- Manage garbage collection

Classes and objects are the foundation of the .NET Framework. The Visual Basic .NET and C# languages are syntaxes for implementing the .NET Framework classes and for adding your own classes to the .NET Framework. This chapter explains how to define and use classes.

When objects are created from your classes or from the .NET Framework classes, they are stored in memory. Until recently, the allocation of memory for objects and then the removal of the objects from memory when they were no longer required was a complex issue. It led to many programming errors and system crashes that were hard to resolve. The .NET Framework automates the memory management process for its objects. This chapter discusses this memory management process as well as the management of resources that are not included in the .NET Framework.

Using Reference-Type Variables

All data, variables, in Visual Basic .NET are objects that are divided into types. There are two main categories of types: value types and reference types. With the exception of the object type, all types belong to one of these categories. Value types were discussed in Chapter 3. We will cover reference types in this chapter.

Unlike value types, which are stored directly in the memory allocated for them, reference types only store a pointer to the location where the values are stored. A value type and the pointer to a reference type are stored on a stack. The *value* of a reference type is stored on the common language runtime (CLR) heap.

Because the values for value types and reference types are stored differently, value types and reference types behave differently when they are used in code. The following code assigns the value of one integer to another, and then changes the value of the second integer. An integer is a value type.

```
Dim I1 as Integer = 0
Dim I2 as Integer = I1
I2 = 15
```

In this code, the final values are I1 = 0 and I2 = 15.

The following code uses an object created from a *class*, which is a reference type. The class, **TestClass**, has a Text property.

```
Dim C1 as New TestClass()
Dim C2 as TestClass = C1
C1.Text = "Text for C1"
C2.Text = "Text for C2"
```

In this code, the final values are C1.Text = "Text for C2" and C2.Text = "Text for C2." The value for C1.Text is not "Text for C1" as you might expect. The statement

```
Dim C2 as TestClass = C1
```

only copied the pointer for C1 to the pointer for C2. That is, the assignment statement (=) applied only to the values in the stack, which are the pointers. Now, there are two *references* to the same object. Changes to either reference will change the same object.

NOTE It is important to understand that the preceding example created two references to the same object and that both references must be destroyed before the object can be removed from the common language runtime heap. This concept is fundamental to garbage collection, which we discuss later in this chapter.

Reference types can be classes, strings, standard modules, interfaces, arrays, or delegates. We already discussed strings and arrays in Chapter 4, and delegates in Chapter 5. This chapter focuses on classes and interfaces.

Defining and Using Classes

A class is the primary application building block in the .NET Framework. Almost everything in the .NET Framework is an object, and objects are instantiated from classes. In this section you learn how to build and use classes.

One of the first decisions you must make when creating a class is whether it will be local to a specific project or part of a class library that is shared with multiple projects. With a business application, most of the classes will be part of a class library. With a standalone program, such as a game, the classes may be local to the one project. When prototyping, testing coding techniques, or writing samples for books, you may frequently include the classes in a single project, and then break them out later into a class library.

In either case, you start by adding a class to a project. With the Visual Studio .NET integrated development environment (IDE) you usually create a separate file for each class, and then use the same name for both the class and the file. However, you are not restricted to this structure. You can include as many classes in the same file as you want. In fact, when you are prototyping, you may include the class within the main application project.

When declaring a class, you can provide a modifier for it. The class modifiers consist of specific modifiers and *access modifiers*, which are defined in the next section. The specific modifiers for a class are MustInherit, NotInerhitable, and Shadow. We discuss these specific modifiers in Chapter 8.

Access Modifiers

Access modifiers define the scope of a class and its classes, variables, and methods. There are five access modifiers.

- **Public** The type is accessible to everything.
- **Friend** The type is accessible within the type and within the project (assembly).
- **Private** The type is accessible only within the type where it is defined.
- **Protected** The type is accessible within the class in which it is declared and within any derived classes.
- **Protected Friend** The type is accessible within the class in which it is declared, within any derived classes, and within the assembly.

When using the access modifiers, you can only use Public and Friend when the class is not inside another type.

Creating and Instantiating a Class

To create a class, you simply declare the class with an optional modifier and the name of the class, as shown in the following code.

```
Public Class TestClass
End Class
```

The End Class statement completes the class definition, as shown here. Of course, you must add the rest of the class functionality, including properties, methods, and events, to make it complete.

Once defined, you can use the class to create an object that can be used in your program. Except for **Shared** classes, discussed in Chapter 8, you cannot use a class directly. You must create an object based on the class. Creating an object from a class is called *instantiating* an object.

Instantiating an object in Visual Basic .NET is different than doing so in Visual Basic 6.0. In both releases you can use the New keyword on the declaration line for an object. The following declaration line is from a Visual Basic 6.0 program.

```
Dim myClass as New ClassName
```

The following declaration lines are from a Visual Basic .NET program.

```
Dim oClass as New ClassName()
Dim oClass1 as ClassName = New ClassName()
```

Even though the syntax is similar in both applications, the functionality is completely different in Visual Basic .NET.

In Visual Basic 6.0 the New keyword instructs the compiler to add code to every access of the object to check whether the object has been created. If it has not been created, it will be. The object is created when used, not when declared.

In Visual Basic .NET the New keyword causes the object to be instantiated immediately. During the instantiation of the object, the .NET Framework processes the New constructor method. (Constructors are discussed in the following section.)

Exercise 7-1: Creating Simple Classes and Examining the Use of Access Modifiers In this exercise you will examine the different aspects of the access modifiers by creating a simple console project and adding classes and properties to it.

1. Open the Visual Studio .NET IDE and create a new project by clicking the New Project button on the Start Page.
2. Select Visual Basic Projects in the Project Types pane.
3. Select Console Application in the Templates pane and name the project **Exercise 7-1**. The New Project dialog box should look similar to Figure 7-1.

NOTE The Location text box in Figure 7-1 shows D:\DotNet because this setup of the Visual Studio .NET IDE has specified D:\DotNet as the default directory for new projects.

4. Modify the code in the IDE to match the following code.

```
Public Class Class1
    Public A As Integer = 1
    Friend B As Integer = 2
    Private C As Integer = 3
End Class

Module Module1
    Sub Main()
        Dim x As New Class1()
        Console.WriteLine("A=" & x.A.ToString)
        Console.WriteLine("B=" & x.B.ToString)
        Console.ReadLine()
    End Sub
End Module
```

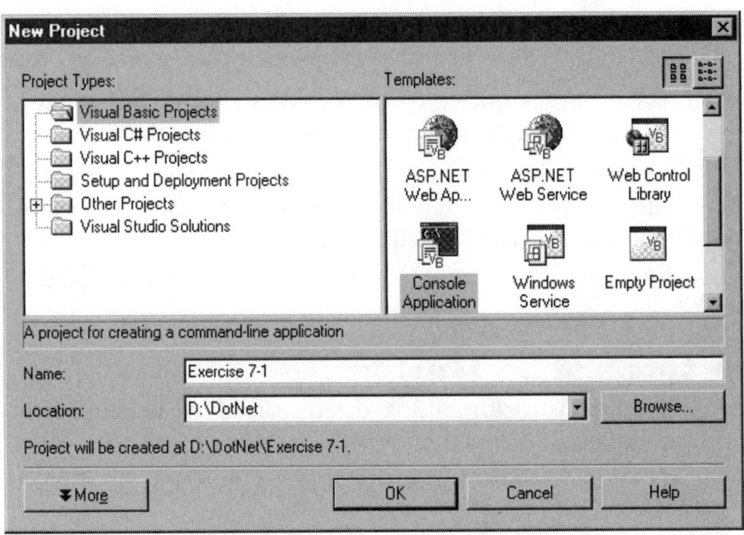

Figure 7-1 The New Project dialog box for Exercise 7-1

The preceding code defines a class, **Class1**, with the Public modifier. Therefore, it can be accessed within Module1. Class1 has two Public properties and one Private property.

The code in the Main subroutine of Module1,

```
Dim x as New Class1()
```

declares **x** as an instance of the class **Class1** and instantiates the object **x**.

```
Console.WriteLine("A=" & x.A.ToString)
Console.WriteLine("A=" & x.B.ToString)
```

These two lines build an output line for properties A and B and output the line to the console window. The syntax to access an object property or method is object.property or object.method() respectively.

```
Console.ReadLine()
```

The preceding line causes the application to wait for input from the console. Otherwise, the application ends, and the console window disappears before you can view it.

In the preceding code, **Console** is a .NET Framework object. WriteLine and ReadLine are methods of the object.

5. Press F5 to compile and run the application.
6. Press ENTER to complete the application.
7. Add the following line of code before the Console.ReadLine() line.

```
Console.WriteLine("C=" & x.C.ToString)
```

As you type in the line, notice that the C property is not available in the IntelliSense window. This is because the property is declared as Private.

8. Move the cursor off the line you just entered by clicking one of the other lines. The *x.C* is underlined with a wavy line, indicating that there is an error in the statement.
9. Place the cursor over the x.C statement but do not click it. The following message appears, as shown in Figure 7-2.

```
'Exercise_7_1.Class1.C' is not accessible in this context because it is
'Private'.
```

Constructors and Destructors

Every class needs a constructor and a destructor to create and remove objects instantiated from the class. A constructor is the New method that is called when you create a new object. It replaces the Class_Initialize event that is part of Visual Basic 6.0. The New method has the following characteristics.

- It runs before any other code in the class.
- It has no return value because it is a subroutine.

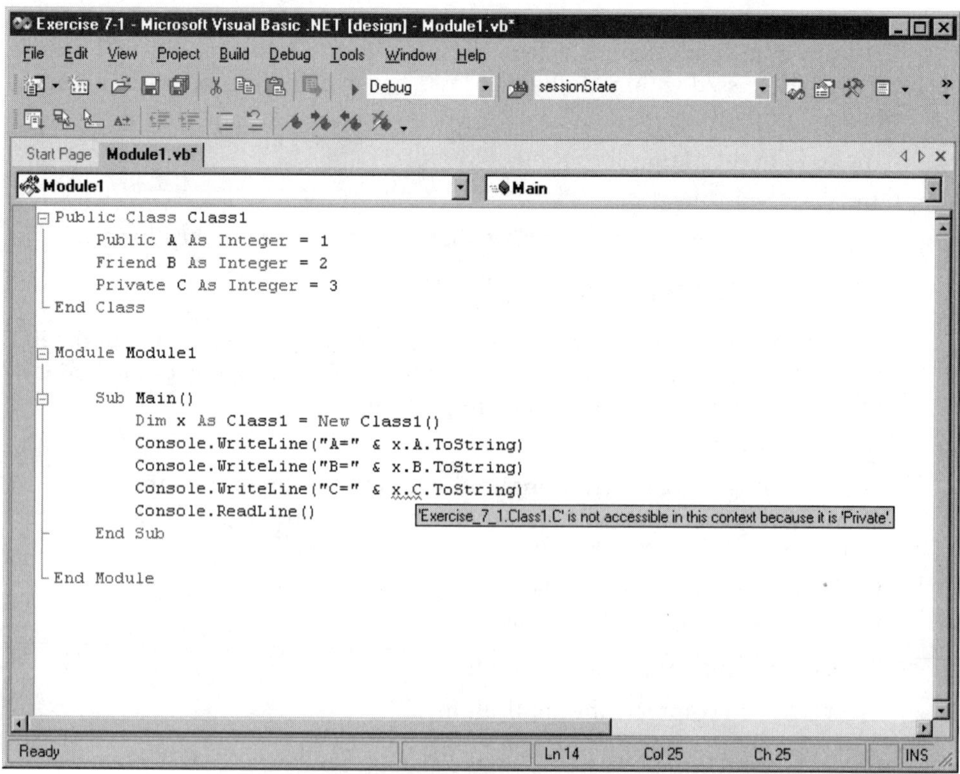

Figure 7-2 The Visual Studio .NET IDE showing the inaccessibility of a Private property in a class

- It runs only when the class is created.
- It can be overloaded. Overloading is explained later in this chapter and in Chapter 8.
- It can only be called from the first line of another constructor in its class or in a derived class.
- It can have parameters that allow the object to be initialized at the same time it is declared.

The destructor method, Finalize, is called during the removal of an object from the common language runtime heap. It replaces the Class_Terminate event that is part of Visual Basic 6.0. You use the Finalize method to clean up resources that are used by the class. This cleanup includes closing database connections and closing files. The following code shows a Finalize method.

```
Protected Overrides Sub Finalize()
    ' Close the Northwind connection
    cnNWind.close
End Sub
```

In Visual Basic 6.0, the Class_Terminate event is processed as soon as an object is removed from the application—that is, when it is set to Nothing or goes out of scope. In Visual Basic .NET, the Finalize method is not called until the object is removed from the runtime heap during garbage collection. Garbage collection and the use of the Finalize method are discussed in more detail later in this chapter.

You may have noticed that in the preceding code and in Exercise 7-1 the constructors and destructors are not defined. Also, the Protected Overrides keywords are used in the declaration of the Finalize destructor. This is because these methods are automatically derived from the base class **System.Object**. That is, the code inherits the New and Finalize methods from the **System.Object** class. The **System.Object** class declares the New method as Public, so we do not need to create our own New method. The **System.Object** class declares the Finalize method as Protected, so it must be Protected in classes that derive from it. Chapter 8 discusses these concepts in detail.

Exercise 7-2: Creating and Destroying Objects In this exercise you will create and remove objects from an application and observe some of the timing issues associated with garbage collection.

1. Open the Visual Studio .NET IDE and create a new console application project called **Exercise 7-2**. Refer to Exercise 7-1 if you have questions about creating a new console application project.
2. Modify the IDE code to match the following code.

```
Public Class Class1
    Public Sub New()
        Console.WriteLine("Class1 - New")
    End Sub
    Protected Overrides Sub Finalize()
        Console.WriteLine("Class1 - Finalize")
    End Sub
```

```
End Class

Module Module1
    Sub Main()
        Dim x As New Class1()
        x = Nothing
        Console.WriteLine("Should not see the Class1 Finalize")
        GC.Collect()
        Console.WriteLine("Wait a few seconds and press enter.")
        Console.ReadLine()
        Console.WriteLine("The Class1 - Finalize should appear above this
         line.")
        Console.ReadLine()
    End Sub
End Module
```

Class1 is a simple class that writes a line to the console when it is created and writes another line to the console when it is removed from the common language runtime heap. The program, Module1, simply creates and destroys the object to show the execution of the New and Finalize methods. The garbage collection is forced in the example, GC.Collect, in order to force the execution of the Finalize method.

3. Press F5 to compile and run the application. The illustration shows the resulting console. The console window shows execution of the New and Finalize methods of **Class1**. This exercise in repeated in Exercise 7-5, where the timing of the garbage collection is explained further.

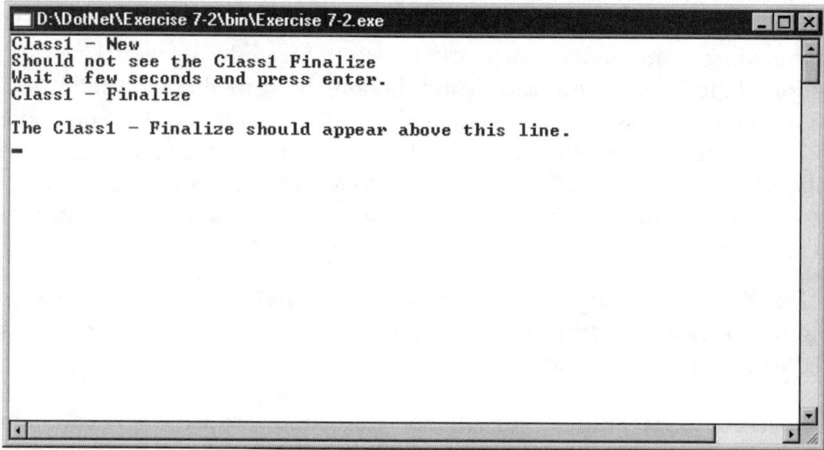
D:\DotNet\Exercise 7-2\bin\Exercise 7-2.exe
Class1 - New
Should not see the Class1 Finalize
Wait a few seconds and press enter.
Class1 - Finalize
The Class1 - Finalize should appear above this line.

Class Properties

Properties are the data of an object. When defining a class, you can create properties in two ways. The first way is to simply declare a Public variable (type). The variable becomes the property. This technique has been used so far in the exercises in this chapter. The second way is to use the Property statement. In Visual Basic 6.0 you use the Get Property, the Let

Property, and the Set Property statements to declare properties. In Visual Basic .NET you use the Property statement, which contains a Get code block and a Set code block. The Property statement supports the Default, WriteOnly, and ReadOnly keywords. In addition, it usually maintains a Private variable for specifying the value of the property.

Using the Property statement instead of creating a Public variable provides the following advantages.

- You can provide read-only or write-only properties.
- You can add error handling to enforce business rules.
- You can perform calculations to update related properties.

You use the Default keyword to specify the default property for the class. The default property has the following characteristic and restrictions.

- You must specify at least one parameter for the property. This parameter is usually a value that is used to find one of many values that are stored for the property.
- You can access the property without using the property name (classname(parameter)).
- You can use only one default property for a class.
- If you overload the property, all properties with the same name must be specified as a default property.

The WriteOnly and ReadOnly keywords have the following restrictions.

- If you do not specify either the WriteOnly or ReadOnly keyword, both the Get code block and the Set code block must exist for the property.
- You can specify only one of the two keywords.
- If you specify the WriteOnly keyword, the property can contain only the Set code block.
- If you specify the ReadOnly keyword, the property can contain only the Get code block.

The following code samples illustrate several variations in declaring and coding properties.

```
Private pValue1 as Integer
Public Property Value1() as Integer
    Get
        Return pValue1
    End Get
    Set (ByVal Value as Integer)
        pValue1 = Value
    End Set
End Property
```

```
Private pValue2 as Integer = 50
Public ReadOnly Property Value2() as Integer
    Get
        Return pValue2
    End Get
End Property

Private pValue3 as Integer
Public WriteOnly Property Value3() as Integer
    Set (ByVal Value as Integer)
        pValue3 = Value
    End Set
End Property

Private pArray(10) as Integer
Public Property Item(ByVal Index as Integer) as Integer
    Get
        Return pArray(Index)
    End Get
    Set (ByVal Value as Integer)
        pArray(Index) = Value
    End Set
End Property
```

Class Methods

Adding methods to classes is very simple. You create either a function or a subroutine to handle the method. If the method must return values, you create a function. If the method does not have to return values, you create a subroutine. The following listing illustrates the code used for adding methods.

```
Public Function Age() As Integer
    Return DateDiff(DateInterval.Year, pBirthDate, Today)
End Function

Public Sub Update()
    ... Update code
End Sub
```

Overloading Methods

Visual Basic .NET includes the capability to overload methods. Overloading allows you to define multiple methods using the same name in the same class. The methods must have different signatures. A *signature* is determined by the method name, the return value type, and the sequence and types of parameters. All the signatures within a class must be different.

Suppose that you want to create an Age method that returns the age as of today's date or as of a specific date. In Visual Basic 6.0 you can define a method with an optional parameter, and then check for the existence of the parameter. You can use optional parameters in Visual Basic .NET, too. However, you also have the option of overloading the Age method as shown in the following code.

```
Public Function Age() As Integer
    Return DateDiff(DateInterval.Year, pBirthDate, Today)
```

```
End Function
Public Function Age(ByVal AsOfDate as Date) As Integer
    Return DateDiff(DateInterval.Year, pBirthDate, AsOfDate)
End Function
```

The preceding code uses the DateDiff function in both methods, which is acceptable for simple code like this. However, you would not want to have complex code exist for each method. You could place the complex code in a Private function and call it from each method. Or you could use a technique similar to that demonstrated in the following code.

```
Public Function Age() As Integer
    Return Age(Today)
End Function
Public Function Age(ByVal AsOfDate as Date) As Integer
    Return DateDiff(DateInterval.Year, pBirthDate, AsOfDate)
End Function
```

The first Age method, the one with no parameters, calls the second Age method using Today for the AsOfDate parameter. This approach keeps the code for calculating the age in a single method.

Exercise 7-3: Creating and Using a Class with Properties and Methods In this exercise you will build a class with properties and methods, including an overloaded constructor.

1. Open the Visual Studio .NET IDE and create a new console application project called **Exercise 7-3**. Refer to Exercise 7-1 if you have questions about creating a new console application project.
2. Modify the IDE code to match the following code. Or, if you prefer, you can copy the code from the companion CD.

```
Public Class Person
    Dim pLastName As String
    Dim pFirstName As String
    Dim pBirthDate As Date
    Public Sub New()
        MyBase.New()
    End Sub
    Public Sub New(ByVal FirstName As String, ByVal LastName As String)
        pLastName = LastName
        pFirstName = FirstName
    End Sub
    Public Sub New(ByVal FirstName As String, ByVal LastName As String,
ByVal BirthDate As Date)
        Me.New(FirstName, LastName)
        pBirthDate = BirthDate
    End Sub
    Public Property LastName() As String
        Get
            Return pLastName
        End Get
        Set(ByVal Value As String)
            pLastName = Value
        End Set
```

```
        End Property
        Public Property FirstName() As String
            Get
                Return pFirstName
            End Get
            Set(ByVal Value As String)
                pFirstName = Value
            End Set
        End Property
        Public Property BirthDate() As Date
            Get
                Return pBirthDate
            End Get
            Set(ByVal Value As Date)
                pBirthDate = Value
            End Set
        End Property
        Public Function Age() As Integer
            Return Age(Today)
        End Function
        Public Function Age(ByVal AsOfDate As Date) As Integer
            Return DateDiff(DateInterval.Year, BirthDate, AsOfDate)
        End Function
        Public Function DisplayText() As String
            Return pFirstName & " " & pLastName & " Age " & Age().ToString
        End Function
    End Class

    Module Module1
        Sub Main()
            Dim oPerson1 As New Person()
            oPerson1.FirstName = "Person"
            oPerson1.LastName = "One"
            oPerson1.BirthDate = "1/1/65"
            Dim oPerson2 As New Person("Person", "Two")
            oPerson2.BirthDate = "1/1/66"
            Dim oPerson3 As New Person("Person", "Three", "1/1/67")
            Console.WriteLine(oPerson1.DisplayText())
            Console.WriteLine(oPerson2.DisplayText())
            Console.WriteLine(oPerson3.DisplayText())
            Console.ReadLine()
        End Sub
    End Module
```

Module1 creates three **Person** objects using each of the available constructors. Next, it populates the properties. Finally, it displays the **Person** information using the DisplayText method. A detailed explanation of the **Person** class code follows this exercise.

3. Press F5 to compile and run the application. The illustration on the following page shows the resulting console window.

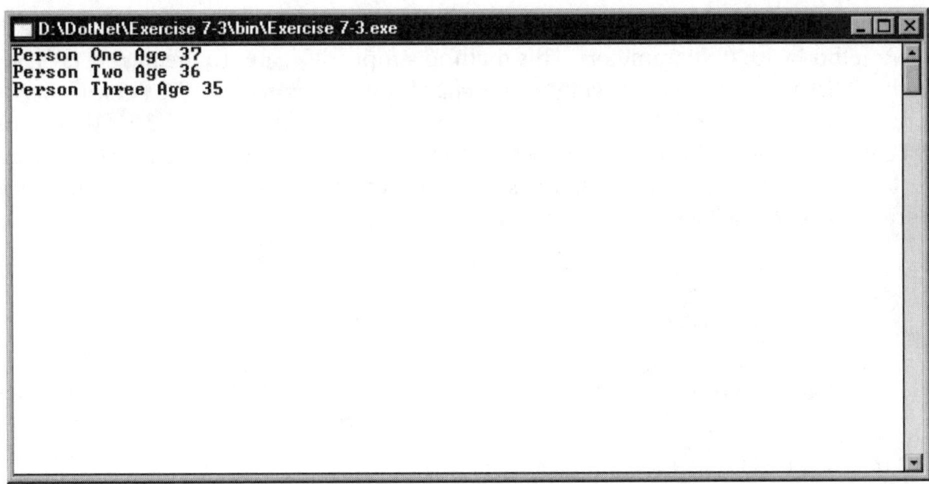

The following discussion provides a detailed explanation of each section of the Person class code from Exercise 7-3.

```
Private pLastName As String
Private pFirstName As String
Private pBirthDate As Date
```

The Private variables store the data for the class.

```
Public Sub New()
        MyBase.New()
    End Sub
    Public Sub New(ByVal FirstName As String, ByVal LastName As String)
        pLastName = LastName
        pFirstName = FirstName
    End Sub
    Public Sub New(ByVal FirstName As String, ByVal LastName As String,
ByVal BirthDate As Date)
        Me.New(FirstName, LastName)
        pBirthDate = BirthDate
    End Sub
```

The three New constructors allow for three different methods of creating the object.

- The object can be created with no parameters.
- The object can be created with first name and last name.
- The object can be created with first name, last name, and birth date.

Because overload constructors are provided for the New method, you must create the New method with no parameters. This method simply delegates to the base class's New method. Because you do not specify a base class for the **Person** class, the **Person** class inherits from the **System.Object** class. The MyBase keyword refers to a class's base class.

The third New method calls the second New method to populate the first name and the last name. The Me keyword enables a class to reference itself. The Me keyword is required here because New is also a keyword.

```
Public Property LastName() As String
    Get
        Return pLastName
    End Get
    Set(ByVal Value As String)
        pLastName = Value
    End Set
End Property
Public Property FirstName() As String
    Get
        Return pFirstName
    End Get
    Set(ByVal Value As String)
        pFirstName = Value
    End Set
End Property
Public Property BirthDate() As Date
    Get
        Return pBirthDate
    End Get
    Set(ByVal Value As Date)
        pBirthDate = Value
    End Set
End Property
```

Each property for the class is defined using the associated Private variables.

```
Public Function Age() As Integer
    Return Age(Today)
End Function
Public Function Age(ByVal AsOfDate As Date) As Integer
    Return DateDiff(DateInterval.Year, BirthDate, AsOfDate)
End Function
```

The Age method is overloaded to allow for an age based on today's date and an age based on a date provided as a parameter.

```
Public Function DisplayText() As String
    Return pFirstName & " " & pLastName & " Age " & Age().ToString
End Function
```

The DisplayText method is used to provide a common display format for the **Person** class. It calls the Age method to get the age. The Me keyword is not required for the Age method because the compiler can resolve Age() without it.

Defining and Using Interfaces

Interfaces are similar to classes in that they have properties, methods, and events. However, interfaces do not have implementation code. They simply define the signatures for the properties, methods, and events.

Interfaces are used to implement polymorphism. Visual Basic .NET implements polymorphism either through inheritance or interfaces. Although a class can be derived from only one base class (inheritance-based polymorphism), it can implement more than one interface. This capability enables multiple inheritance within Visual Basic .NET. More detail on interfaces and inheritance is provided in Chapter 8.

The implementation of the code for an interface occurs in the class that implements the interface. The following listing shows the code used to define an interface.

```
Interface iPerson
    Property LastName() As String
    Property FirstName() as String
    Property BirthDate() as Date
    Function Age() as Integer
    Function Age(ByVal AsOfDate as Date) as Integer
    Function DisplayText() as String
End Interface
```

The following code implements the interface in the **Person** class.

```
Public Class Person
    Implements iPerson
    Dim pLastName As String
    Dim pFirstName As String
    Dim pBirthDate As Date
    Public Property LastName() As String Implements iPerson.LastName
        Get
            Return pLastName
        End Get
        Set(ByVal Value As String)
            pLastName = Value
        End Set
    End Property
    Public Property FirstName() As String Implements iPerson.FirstName
        Get
            Return pFirstName
        End Get
        Set(ByVal Value As String)
            pFirstName = Value
        End Set
    End Property
    Public Property BirthDate() As Date Implements iPerson.BirthDate
        Get
            Return pBirthDate
        End Get
        Set(ByVal Value As Date)
            pBirthDate = Value
        End Set
    End Property
```

```
    Public Function Age() As Integer Implements iPerson.Age
        Return Age(Today)
    End Function
    Public Function Age(ByVal AsOfDate As Date) As Integer Implements
Person.Age
        Return DateDiff(DateInterval.Year, BirthDate, AsOfDate)
    End Function
    Public Function DisplayText() As String Implements iPerson.DisplayText
        Return pFirstName & " " & pLastName & " Age " & Age().ToString
    End Function
End Class
```

Resource Management

Resource management in the .NET Framework is divided into memory resource management and unmanaged resource management. Memory resource management is for managing the memory of value-type variables (values) and reference-type variables. Unmanaged resource management is for managing memory in all other resources, including resources that are not part of the .NET Framework. These resources include files, database connections, and unmanaged components.

Value-type memory resource management handles the allocation and de-allocation of memory on the stack. Memory is allocated for an instance of a value type when it is pushed onto the stack. Memory is de-allocated when the variable goes out of scope and is removed from the stack.

Reference-type memory resource management uses the common language runtime managed heap for storing instances of reference types. The memory is allocated when the New method for the reference type is called. The memory is made available for recovery when the instance of the reference type is explicitly set to Nothing or when it goes out of scope. Garbage collection is the process that actually frees the memory on the heap.

You can manage unmanaged resources implicitly within the garbage collection process by using the Finalize destructor of reference types. You can also manage them explicitly by adding a method to the class to release the unmanaged resources.

Memory Resource Management (Garbage Collection Without Finalize)

The garbage collector removes objects from the common language runtime heap. When an applications tries to create an object and there is insufficient memory on the heap for the object, the garbage collection process is triggered. An application can also programmatically trigger garbage collection.

The garbage collection process uses an algorithm to find all objects that are not referenced directly or indirectly by the application. The garbage collector removes the unused objects from the heap and compacts the heap to create more space. If there is insufficient space to add an object after garbage collection, the application throws an OutOfMemoryException exception.

It's important to understand that garbage collection does not occur as soon as an object is released, that is, when an object is explicitly set to Nothing or when it goes out of scope. If the object is not using unmanaged resources, this delay in removing the object from the heap is not a problem. It is best to let the .NET Framework perform the garbage collection when it needs to. Although you can use the GC.Collect method to force garbage collection, it is not advisable because you may cause unnecessary garbage collections. Garbage collection is a resource-intensive process and should be performed only when required.

Implicit Unmanaged Resource Management (Garbage Collection with Finalize)

Some objects use resources that are not included in the .NET Framework memory management process. Before completely removing an object, you may need to clean up these resources. For example, you may need to close a file or database connection, or destroy unmanaged component resources.

Suppose you have an object that creates a new file when it is instantiated and provides methods to add information to the file. You want to make sure that the file is always closed. Although you can provide a Close method, you cannot guarantee that the programmer will always call this method. If you use the Finalize method to close the file, you guarantee that the file gets closed before the object is destroyed.

Exercise 7-4: Timing the Finalize Method Open the Visual Studio .NET IDE and create a new console application project called **Exercise 7-4**. Refer to Exercise 7-1 if you have questions about creating a new console application project.

1. Modify the IDE code to match the following code. Because this is the same code used in Exercise 7-2, you may copy it into this exercise.

```
Public Class Class1
    Public Sub New()
        Console.WriteLine("Class1 - New")
    End Sub
    Protected Overrides Sub Finalize()
        Console.WriteLine("Class1 - Finalize")
    End Sub
End Class

Module Module1
    Sub Main()
        Dim x As New Class1()
        x = Nothing
        Console.WriteLine("Should not see the Class1 Finalize")
        GC.Collect()
        Console.WriteLine("Wait a few seconds and press enter.")
        Console.ReadLine()
        Console.WriteLine("The Class1 - Finalize should appear above this
line.")
        Console.ReadLine()
    End Sub
End Module
```

2. Press F5 to compile and run the application. The illustration shows the resulting console.

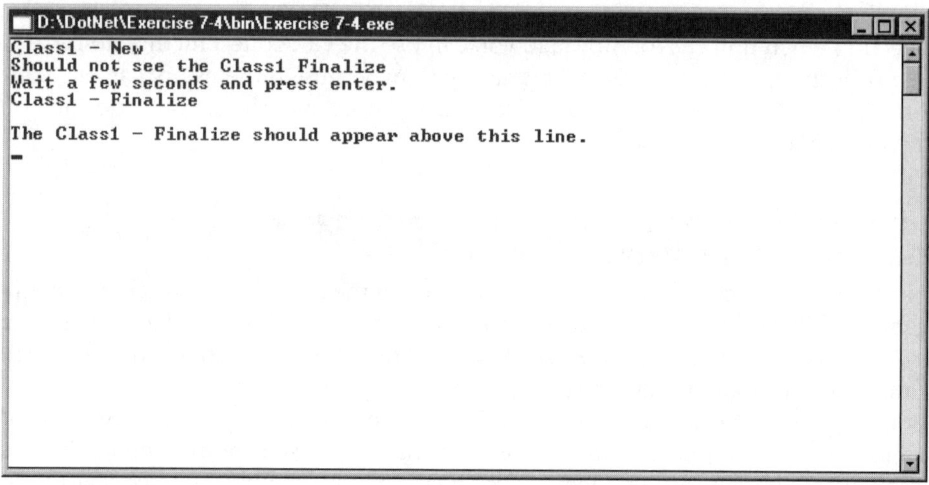
D:\DotNet\Exercise 7-4\bin\Exercise 7-4.exe
Class1 - New
Should not see the Class1 Finalize
Wait a few seconds and press enter.
Class1 - Finalize
The Class1 - Finalize should appear above this line.

The following text explains in detail the statements in the Main subroutine of Module1 in Exercise 7-4.

```
Dim x As New Class1()
```

The **x** object is instantiated from **Class1** and added to the common language runtime heap. A pointer to its location in the heap is added to the application stack. Because **Class1** has a Finalize method, a reference to the **x** object is added to a list of objects that require finalization. The New method for **Class1** is processed and the Class1 - New message is sent to the console window.

```
x = Nothing
```

The pointer to **x** in the application stack is set to Null. The application no longer has a reference to the **x** object so it can be removed by garbage collection.

```
Console.WriteLine("Should not see the Class1 Finalize")
```

The message is sent to the console window. This message appears before the message sent in the Finalize method. This verifies that the Finalize method has not been processed when the **x** object was set to **Nothing**.

```
GC.Collect()
```

Garbage collection is forced. As stated earlier, it usually is not a good idea to force garbage collection. We show it here for demonstration purposes only. During the garbage collection process, the garbage collector finds the **x** object in its list of objects that requires calling the Finalize method of the object. A pointer to the **x** object is added to the application stack indicating that the object requires finalization. Another process monitors the stack to call the Finalize methods of the objects in the stack. Until this call to the Finalize method for the **x** object is complete, the **x** object cannot be removed from the heap.

```
Console.WriteLine("Wait a few seconds and press enter.")
```

When this line appears in the console prior to the Finalize message from **Class1**, it indicates that the **Finalize** method was not executed prior to the completion of garbage collection.

```
Console.ReadLine()
```

This statement waits for a response from the user. While it waits, the Finalize method for the **x** object is processed, and the Class1 - Finalize message is sent to the console. The pointer to the **x** object in the application stack for those objects requiring finalization is removed. The **x** object can be removed from the heap when the garbage collection process runs again.

```
Console.WriteLine("The Class1 - Finalize should appear above this line.")
Console.ReadLine()
```

These two lines allow you to see the result prior to terminating the program.

Explicit Unmanaged Resource Management

The Finalize method has a major drawback in the .NET Framework. Because the garbage collection process calls the Finalize method and you do not know when the garbage collection is going to occur, you do not know when the Finalize method is going to be executed. If you provide for the clean-up of non-memory resources in the Finalize method of your classes, you do not have control of when this code is executed. You should not force a garbage collection every time you need to clean up a non-memory resource because garbage collection is a resource-intensive process.

Take the example of closing a file. If you need to access the file immediately after the object that created it has been removed from your application process, the file may not be available because the Finalize method of the object has not been called yet.

To overcome the problem of delayed execution of the Finalize method, you can explicitly provide a method to clean up non-memory resources. The user of your class must call this method to clean up the non-memory resources. Microsoft has standardized the name of this method for classes within the .NET Framework. Microsoft calls it the Dispose method. In addition, Microsoft provides the IDisposable Interface for .NET Framework classes that require the clean-up of non-memory resources. When you use these classes you should call the Dispose method when you are finished with the object. Also, any class that you derive from these classes must include the Dispose method in order to allow users of the class to clean up unmanaged resources. You can access a list of the .NET Framework classes that implement the Dispose method in the online help for the IDisposable Interface. Figure 7-3 shows the online help for the IDisposable Interface.

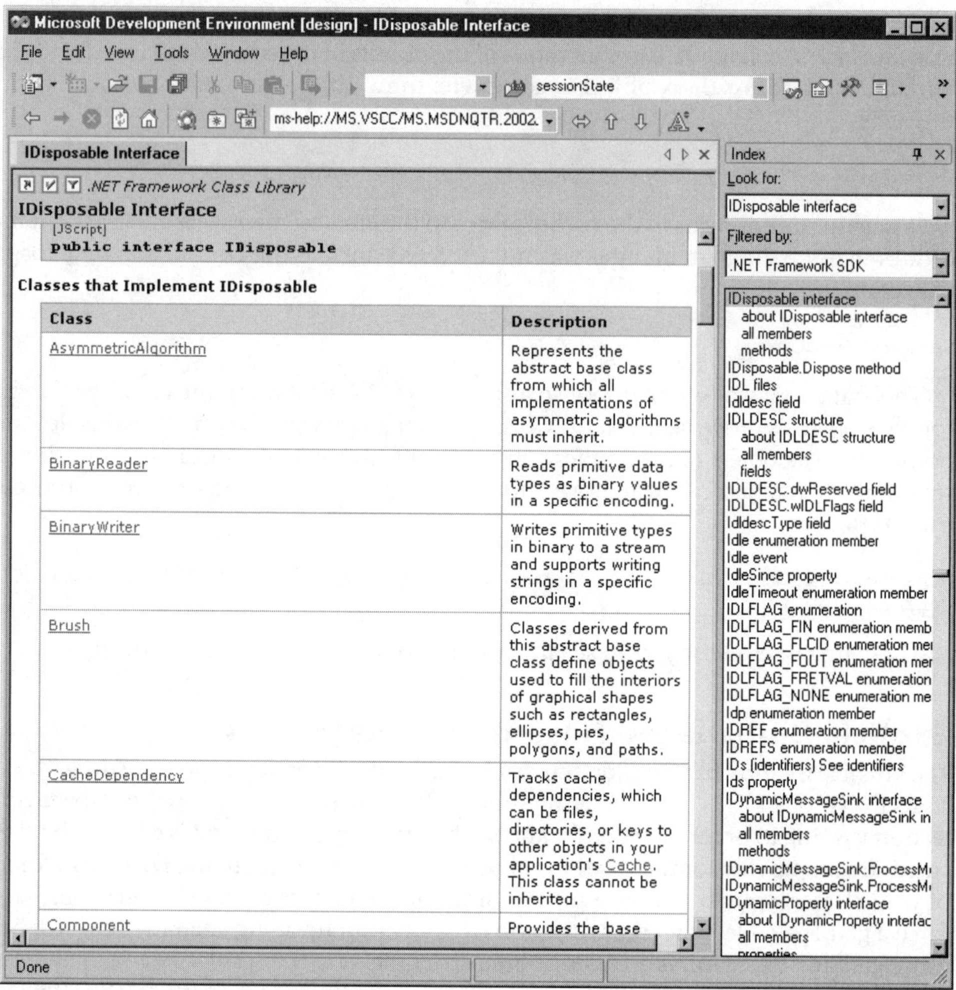

Figure 7-3 Online help for the IDisposable Interface showing a partial list of .NET Framework classes that implement the IDisposable Interface

When you explicitly implement a method to clean up unmanaged resources, you still must implement the Finalize method because you cannot guarantee that all users of the class will call the Dispose method. The Finalize method can call the Dispose method. However, the Dispose method must be able to recognize whether it has been called already. The user of your class may call it more than once, or the Finalize method may try to call it after the user of your class has called it.

NOTE Although you are not required to name the method you implement to clean up unmanaged resources *Dispose*, it is a good idea to use this common term to avoid confusion by users of your class.

Implementing the Finalize method in your class adds more overhead to the garbage collection process. When you implement your own method to clean up unmanaged resources, you want to avoid this additional processing and, because the clean-up of the unmanaged resources has already taken place, you want to avoid trying to clean them up again. The garbage collection process provides the SuppressFinalize method to remove your object from the list of objects that require finalization within the garbage collector. The use of the SuppressFinalize method is demonstrated in Exercise 7-5.

Exercise 7-5: Explicitly Managing Unmanaged Resources In this exercise you will create code to determine whether the clean-up of unmanaged resources has been performed.

1. Open the Visual Studio .NET IDE and create a new console application project called **Exercise 7-5**. Refer to Exercise 7-1 if you have questions about creating a new console application project.
2. Modify the IDE code to match the following code.

```
Public Class Class1
    Private Disposed as Boolean = False
    Private pTrackingName As String
    Public Sub New(ByVal TrackingName As String)
        pTrackingName = TrackingName
        Console.WriteLine(pTrackingName & " - New")
    End Sub
    Public Sub Dispose()
        If Not Disposed Then
            Console.WriteLine(pTrackingName & " - Dispose")
            GC.SuppressFinalize(Me)
            Disposed = True
        End If
    End Sub
    Protected Overrides Sub Finalize()
        Console.WriteLine(pTrackingName & " - Finalize")
        Dispose()
    End Sub
End Class
Module Module1
    Sub Main()
        Dim x As New Class1("Class_X")
        Dim y As New Class1("Class_Y")
        x.Dispose()
        x = Nothing
        y = Nothing
        GC.Collect()
        Console.WriteLine("Wait a few seconds and press enter.")
        Console.ReadLine()
    End Sub
End Module
```

3. Press F5 to compile and run the application. The illustration shows the resulting console.

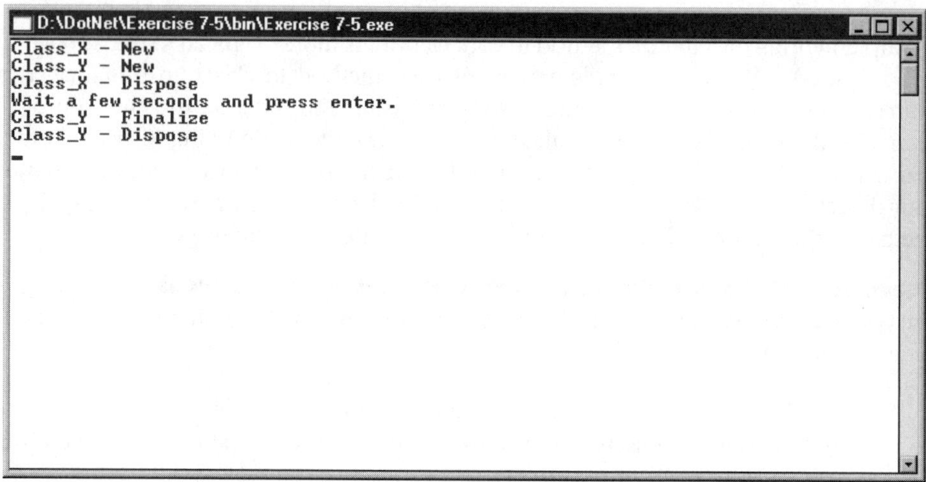

D:\DotNet\Exercise 7-5\bin\Exercise 7-5.exe
Class_X - New
Class_Y - New
Class_X - Dispose
Wait a few seconds and press enter.
Class_Y - Finalize
Class_Y - Dispose

The code in Exercise 7-5 is similar to that in Exercise 7-4. The New method has been changed to add a parameter for identifying the object after it has been created. Private properties, pTrackingName and pDisposed, have been added. The Dispose method has been added, and the Finalize method has been changed as shown here.

```
Public Sub Dispose()
    If Not Disposed Then
        Console.WriteLine(pTrackingName & " - Dispose")
        GC.SuppressFinalize(Me)
        Disposed = True
    End If
End Sub
Protected Overrides Sub Finalize()
    Console.WriteLine(pTrackingName & " - Finalize")
    Dispose()
End Sub
```

The Dispose method contains the code to clean up unmanaged resources. For this exercise, only a message is printed to the console. If the clean-up process has not been processed already, it is executed and the garbage collection finalization process is suppressed.

The Finalize method calls the Dispose method to provide the clean-up of unmanaged resources.

The console output in the preceding illustration shows the creation of the **x** and **y** objects. It then shows the call to the Dispose method for the **x** object. The Finalize method for the **x** object was never called because it was suppressed in the Dispose method. However, the Finalize method for the **y** object was called because its Dispose method was never explicitly called; the Dispose method for the **y** object is called from the Finalize method.

The processing for the **x** object is more efficient than the processing for the **y** object because the garbage collector does not have to perform finalization for **x**.

Summary

Classes and objects are the foundation of the .NET Framework. You define a class, and then create instances of objects from the class. The .NET Framework consists of several thousand classes. Understanding classes and objects and how they work is fundamental to understanding the .NET Framework.

To work with an object, you instantiate it from a class. Objects consume memory. The .NET Framework provides automatic memory management. It also enables management of resources that are not managed by the .NET Framework itself. Garbage collection is an integral part of management. It removes objects that are no longer needed and implements methods for cleaning up unmanaged resources.

Test Questions

1. Which of the following items is not a reference type?
   A. Array
   B. Structure
   C. Interface
   D. Standard module
2. Which of the following modifiers is not an access modifier?
   A. Protected
   B. Private
   C. MustInherit
   D. Friend
3. What is the value of C1.I1 after the following code is executed?

```
Dim C1 as New MyClass
Dim C2 as MyClass = C1
C1.I1 = 2
C2.I1 += 1
```

   A. 1
   B. 2
   C. 3
   D. 4
4. Which of the following lines is a valid constructor for a class?
   A. Public Function New() as Object
   B. Public Sub New(ByVal Parameter1 as String)
   C. Public Sub Initialize()
   D. Public Sub Construct()

5. Which of the following lines is a valid destructor for a class?
   A. Public Sub Finalize()
   B. Public Sub Terminate()
   C. Protected Overrides Sub Finalize()
   D. Overrides Sub Finalize()
6. Which of the following statements are true for a class constructor (choose all that apply)?
   A. It runs after the Class_Initialize event.
   B. It runs before any other code in the class.
   C. Only one constructor is allowed.
   D. The constructor can be overloaded.
   E. It can be either a subroutine or a function.
7. Based on the following code, which statement is true?

```
Private pValue1 as Integer
Public Property Value1() as Integer
    Get
        Return pValue1
    End Get
End Property
```

   A. This is a read-only property.
   B. This is a write-only property.
   C. The syntax is invalid.
   D. The value of pValue1 is returned.
8. Given the following overloaded method

```
Public Sub New()
Public Sub New(ByVal FirstName as String, ByVal LastName as String)
```

   which of the following additional overloaded methods is not valid?
   A. Public Sub New(ByVal FirstName as String, ByVal LastName as String, BirthDate as Date)
   B. Public Sub New(ByVal LastName as String, ByVal FirstName as String, BirthDate as Date)
   C. Public Sub New(ByVal FirstName as String, ByVal LastName as String, BirthDate as Date)
   D. Public Sub New(ByVal LastName as String)

9. What happens after garbage collection when there is not room on the common language runtime heap?
   A. The .NET Framework adds more memory to the heap.
   B. The least recently used object is removed.
   C. An OutOfMemoryException is thrown.
   D. The .NET Framework fails and displays "the blue screen of death."
10. Which of the follow statements are false? (Select all that apply.)
   A. You should always include the Finalize method in a class.
   B. You do not need to include a New method in a class.
   C. You should only include the Finalize method in a class when it is absolutely necessary.
   D. Including the Finalize method in a class improves performance.

Test Answers

1. B.
2. C.
3. C.
4. B.
5. D.
6. B.
7. C.
8. B.
9. C.
10. A, D.

CHAPTER 8

Inheritance in Visual Basic .NET

In this chapter, you will

- Implement polymorphism, inheritance, and interfaces
- Override properties and methods
- Implement custom namespaces
- Share class members
- Learn how to convert value types to reference types

Inheritance allows you to use one class as a basis for another. There are several methods for defining both the *base* class and the *derived* class. This chapter discusses the use of inheritance.

Once you start creating classes you are going to want to organize them into meaningful groups. You can use *namespaces* to organize classes similar to the way the .NET Framework organizes its classes. This chapter also discusses the use of *namespaces* for organizing and more efficiently referencing classes.

Most classes require that you instantiate an object from the class to have access to its members. The Shared keyword allows you access shared members of a class without instantiating an object and to share this member information with all objects instantiated from the class. This chapter helps you understand when and how to use the shared members.

Data in the .NET Framework is divided into value types and reference types. Sometimes you want to be able to handle value types as reference types. This chapter discusses why you may want to do this and how to do it using Boxing and Unboxing.

Polymorphism

Inheritance is a method of implementing polymorphism. Understanding polymorphism helps you to better understand inheritance. Within the context of object-oriented programming, polymorphism is the capability to define classes that can be used interchangeably with the same properties and methods but to behave differently. Polymorphism allows you to override functionality in a *base* class with new functionality in the *derived* class while keeping the same method name for both classes.

Visual Basic .NET provides two methods of implementing polymorphism: inheritance-based polymorphism and interface-based polymorphism.

EXAM TIP Polymorphism is the capability to have classes that can be used interchangeably using the same properties and methods but can act differently.

To understand polymorphism and inheritance, consider the following example, which will be used throughout this chapter. Suppose that we want to create a label addressing application. The basic requirements are that there are vendors and customers. When sending an invoice to a customer, the label should be addressed to its Payables Department. When sending payment to a vendor, the label should be addressed to its Receivables Department.

The first class is the **Company** class. The **Company** class in the following code defines name and address information for a company as well as the Label method used to display this information. This class will become the *base* class for the **Vendor** class and the **Customer** class.

```
Public Class Company
    Public CompanyName As String
    Public Address As String
    Public City As String
    Public State As String
    Public Zip As String
    Public Overridable Sub Label()
        Console.WriteLine(CompanyName)
        Console.WriteLine(Address)
        Console.WriteLine(City & ", " & State & " " & Zip)
    End Sub
End Class
```

The **Vendor** class listed in the following code inherits name and address information from the **Company** class but implements different code for the Label method. The **Vendor** class is the *derived* class from the **Company** *base* class.

```
Public Class Vendor
    Inherits Company
    Public Overrides Sub Label()
        Console.WriteLine(CompanyName)
        Console.WriteLine("Attn:Receivables Department")
        Console.WriteLine(Address)
        Console.WriteLine(City & ", " & State & " " & Zip)
    End Sub
End Class
```

The **Customer** class in the following code inherits from the **Company** class but implements different code for the Label method. The **Customer** class is a *derived* class from the **Company** *base* class.

```
Public Class Customer
    Inherits Company
    Public Overrides Sub Label()
        Console.WriteLine(CompanyName)
        Console.WriteLine("Attn:Payables Department")
        Console.WriteLine(Address)
        Console.WriteLine(City & ", " & State & " " & Zip)
    End Sub
End Class
```


In the preceding examples, the only difference between the **Vendor** class and the **Customer** class is the Label method. In an actual application there can be many differences. The Label methods in the **Company** class, **Vendor** class, and **Customer** class are each different. This multiple implementation of the Label method is polymorphism. Exercise 8-1 demonstrates using polymorphism and inheritance in an application.

Exercise 8-1: Implementing Polymorphism Through Inheritance

1. Open the Visual Studio .NET integrated development environment (IDE) and create a new console application project called **Exercise 8-1**. (Refer to Exercise 7-1 if you have questions about creating a new console application project.)
2. Modify the code to match the following code.

```
Public Class Company
    Public CompanyName As String
    Public Address As String
    Public City As String
    Public State As String
    Public Zip As String
    Public Overridable Sub Label()
        Console.WriteLine(CompanyName)
        Console.WriteLine(Address)
        Console.WriteLine(City & ", " & State & " " & Zip)
    End Sub
End Class
Public Class Vendor
    Inherits Company
    Public Overrides Sub Label()
        Console.WriteLine(CompanyName)
        Console.WriteLine("Attn:Receivables Department")
        Console.WriteLine(Address)
        Console.WriteLine(City & ", " & State & " " & Zip)
    End Sub
End Class
Public Class Customer
    Inherits Company
    Public Overrides Sub Label()
        Console.WriteLine(CompanyName)
        Console.WriteLine("Attn:Payables Department")
        Console.WriteLine(Address)
        Console.WriteLine(City & ", " & State & " " & Zip)
    End Sub
End Class
Module Module1
    Sub Main()
```

```
        Dim oCustomer As New Customer()
        With oCustomer
            .CompanyName = "My Customer"
            .Address = "123 S. Broadway"
            .City = "Denver"
            .State = "CO"
            .Zip = "80202"
        End With
        Dim oVendor As New Vendor()
        With oVendor
            .CompanyName = "My Vendor"
            .Address = "1200 N. Hindsdale"
            .City = "Jefferson"
            .State = "CO"
            .Zip = "80112"
        End With
        DisplayLabel(oCustomer)
        DisplayLabel(oVendor)
        Console.ReadLine()
    End Sub
    Private Sub DisplayLabel(ByVal xCompany As Company)
        Console.WriteLine("--------------------")
        xCompany.Label()
    End Sub
End Module
```

The first part of the preceding code was explained when we created the **Vendor** and **Customer** classes earlier in the chapter. We will discuss Module1 and DisplayLabel here.

Module1 creates and populates the **oVendor** and **oCustomer** objects. Even though the properties for the **Vendor** and **Customer** classes are not explicitly defined, they are inherited from the **Company** class. If a new property is added to the **Company** class, it is automatically available in the **Vendor** and **Customer** classes without requiring changes to those classes. Module1 calls the DisplayLabel subroutine using the **oCustomer** and **oVendor** objects as parameters.

The DisplayLabel subroutine has the parameter **xCompany**, which is a **Company** object. It calls the Label method of the **Company** class.

The calls to DisplayLabel from Module1 with **Vendor** and **Customer** objects are allowed even though DisplayLabel takes a **Company** parameter. This is because the **Vendor** class and the **Customer** classes both inherit from the **Company** class.

3. Press F5 to compile and run the application. The illustration shows the resulting console window.

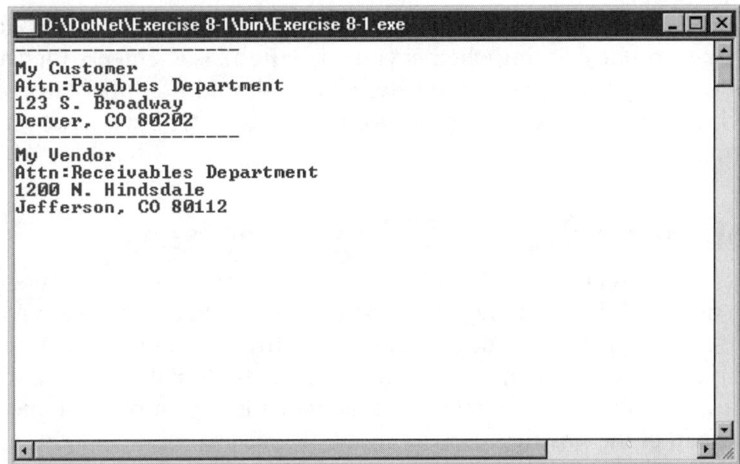

The labels displayed in the console window in the preceding illustration are the output of the code in the **Vendor** class and the **Customer** class even though the DisplayLabel calls the Label method from a **Company** object. This is polymorphism. The .NET Framework uses the type of the object as it exists at runtime to determine which method to execute. In this case, the actual objects are of type **Vendor** and type **Customer** even though the statement to call the Label method is of type **Company**.

4. Press ENTER to close the application.

Inheritance

In Exercise 8-1, all the properties of the **Company** class are available within the **Vendor** class and the **Customer** class. This functionality is gained simply by inheriting from the **Company** class. As explained in Chapter 6, inheritance is the capability to define classes that serve as the basis for other classes. The class that serves as the basis for the new class is the *base* class. The class that uses the *base* class to derive its definition is the *derived* class. The derived class inherits the properties, methods, and events of the base class. The derived class can then modify and extend the properties, methods, and events. Visual Basic .NET allows you to control which properties, method, and events can be inherited, modified, and/or extended.

EXAM TIP The class that is used as the basis for a new class is the *base* class and the new class is the *derived* class.

Inheritance is an **is a** relationship. In our example, the **Vendor** *is a* **Company** and the **Customer** *is a* **Company**. Seeing whether you can write an **is a** sentence for two classes is a good test when trying to determine whether you should use Inheritance or another method to implement a relationship between them. Chapter 6 discusses relationships in more detail.

Multiple Inheritance Using Interfaces

One limitation of Visual Basic .NET is that it allows only one *base* class. That is, you can only inherit from one class. Although you can use interfaces to implement multiple inheritance, this is not a complete solution because it requires you to duplicate code in each of the derived classes to implement the properties and methods of the interface. The primary purpose of using an interface to implement inheritance is to control which properties and methods are part of the *base* class.

In the label addressing example, primary contact information may be required for the **Customer** class and the **Vendor** class. You can create a **Contact** interface and implement it in both the **Customer** class and the **Vendor** class.

The following example lists the code for creating the **Contact** interface.

```
Public Interface Contact
    Property FirstName() As String
    Property LastName() As String
    Property Telephone() As String
    Property EmailAddress() As String
    Function DisplayContact() As String
End Interface
```

The following listing shows the code for implementing the **Contact** interface in the **Vendor** class.

```
Public Class Vendor
    Inherits Company
    Implements Contact
    Private pFirstName As String
    Private pLastName As String
    Private pTelephone As String
    Private pEmailAddress As String
    Public Property FirstName() As String _
        Implements Contact.FirstName
        Get
            Return pFirstName
        End Get
        Set(ByVal Value As String)
            pFirstName = Value
        End Set
    End Property
    Public Property LastName() As String _
        Implements Contact.LastName
        Get
            Return pLastName
        End Get
        Set(ByVal Value As String)
            pLastName = Value
        End Set
```

```
    End Property
    Public Property Telephone() As String _
        Implements Contact.Telephone
        Get
            Return pTelephone
        End Get
        Set(ByVal Value As String)
            pTelephone = Value
        End Set
    End Property
    Public Property EmailAddress() As String _
        Implements Contact.EmailAddress
        Get
            Return pEmailAddress
        End Get
        Set(ByVal Value As String)
            pEmailAddress = Value
        End Set
    End Property
    Public Function DisplayContact() As String _
        Implements Contact.DisplayContact
        Return pFirstName & " " & pLastName _
            & " " & pTelephone & " " & EmailAddress
    End Function
    Public Overrides Sub Label()
        Console.WriteLine(CompanyName)
        Console.WriteLine("Attn:Receivables Department")
        Console.WriteLine(Address)
        Console.WriteLine(City & ", " & State & " " & Zip)
    End Sub
End Class
```

Using an interface does not simplify the implementation of the contact information in the **Vendor** class. In addition, the same code must be added to the **Customer** class if the **Contact** interface is implemented in it. For these reasons, using an interface is probably not the best choice for implementing the contact information.

It can be argued that the **Vendor** and **Contact** relationship is an **is a**, or an inheritance relationship. That is, the **Vendor** *is a* **Contact**. It is more appropriate, however, to say that the **Vendor** *has a* **Contact**. The **has a** relationship is an association relationship (discussed in Chapter 6) and not an inheritance relationship. The contact information should be implemented as a **Contact** class and an association relationship established between the **Vendor** class and the **Contact** class. Implementation of association relationships is beyond the scope of this book.

Exercise 8-2: Implementing Multiple Inheritance in a Class In this exercise you will add the **Contact** interface code to your application and implement it in the **Vendor** class.

1. Open the Visual Studio .NET IDE and create a new console application project called **Exercise 8-2**. Refer to Exercise 7-1 if you have questions about creating a new console application project.
2. Copy in the code from Exercise 8-1. You can copy the code from Exercise 8-1 using the companion CD if you like.

3. Add the following **Contact** interface code.

```
Public Interface Contact
    Property FirstName() As String
    Property LastName() As String
    Property Telephone() As String
    Property EmailAddress() As String
    Function DisplayContact() As String
End Interface
```

4. Modify the **Vendor** class code to implement the **Contact** interface as follows.

```
Public Class Vendor
    Inherits Company
    Implements Contact
    Private pFirstName As String
    Private pLastName As String
    Private pTelephone As String
    Private pEmailAddress As String
    Public Property FirstName() As String _
        Implements Contact.FirstName
        Get
            Return pFirstName
        End Get
        Set(ByVal Value As String)
            pFirstName = Value
        End Set
    End Property
    Public Property LastName() As String _
        Implements Contact.LastName
        Get
            Return pLastName
        End Get
        Set(ByVal Value As String)
            pLastName = Value
        End Set
    End Property
    Public Property Telephone() As String _
        Implements Contact.Telephone
        Get
            Return pTelephone
        End Get
        Set(ByVal Value As String)
            pTelephone = Value
        End Set
    End Property
    Public Property EmailAddress() As String _
        Implements Contact.EmailAddress
        Get
            Return pEmailAddress
        End Get
        Set(ByVal Value As String)
            pEmailAddress = Value
        End Set
    End Property
    Public Function DisplayContact() As String _
        Implements Contact.DisplayContact
        Return pFirstName & " " & pLastName _
            & " " & pTelephone & " " & pEmailAddress
    End Function
    Public Overrides Sub Label()
```

```
            Console.WriteLine(CompanyName)
            Console.WriteLine("Attn:Receivables Department")
            Console.WriteLine(Address)
            Console.WriteLine(City & ", " & State & " " & Zip)
        End Sub
    End Class
```

The primary purpose of having you modify the **Vendor** code is to demonstrate how much more difficult it is to implement an interface. Using inheritance is much more efficient.

5. Add the following code to the Main subroutine in Module1 after the DisplayLabel(oVendor) statement.

```
With oVendor
     .FirstName = "Michael"
     .LastName = "Smith"
     .EmailAddress = "msmith@nowhere.com"
     .Telephone = "333 555-1212"
    Console.WriteLine(.DisplayContact)
End With
```

6. Press F5 to compile and run the application. The illustration shows the resulting console window.

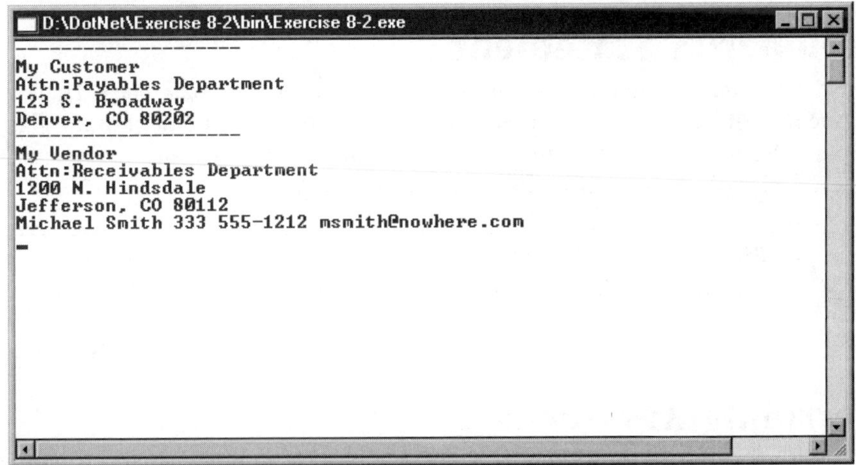

7. Press ENTER to close the application.

Special Class Modifiers

When you define a class, you can specify the access modifiers discussed in Chapter 7. These modifiers are *Public, Private, Protected, Friend,* and *Protected Friend*. There are two additional modifiers that relate specifically to inheritance. These modifiers are:

- **NotInheritable** This modifier specifies that the class cannot be inherited by a *derived* class.

- **MustInherit** This modifier specifies that an object cannot be instantiated from the class. Its properties, methods, and events must be accessed through a *derived* class.

The MustInherit modifier is useful when the class is not a complete definition of a functional object. In the label addressing example, you may not want the users of your classes to ever instantiate a **Company** object. In this case, you would use the MustInherit modifier when defining the **Company** class.

You can use the NotInheritable modifier if you do not want to worry about maintaining the contract formed when your class is used as a *base* class for another class. That is, when you create a class that can be inherited, you are guaranteeing that your class will function in a specific manner. This is referred to as the contract between your class and the classes that are derived from your class. This limits the ability for you to change the functionality of your class because changes you make may not be compatible with the classes that are derived from your class. By not allowing your class to be inherited, you can modify your class without worrying about other classes being derived from your class. Also, a **NotInheritable** class enables better performance because the compiler can make assumptions about a class that cannot be inherited and optimize the code for the class.

The Inherits Statement

You use the Inherits statement in a derived class to specify the base class. There can be only one Inherits statement in a class and it must be the first statement in the class. The **Company**, **Vendor**, and **Customer** code listings in Exercise 8-1 and Exercise 8-2 provides examples of using the Inherits statement.

NOTE If you implement an interface for multiple inheritance, the Implements statement for the interface must immediately follow the Inherits statement.

Overriding Keywords

When writing a class that can be inherited, you need to control which properties and methods can be used by the derived class. You can use the Public, Private, Protected, Friend, and Protect Friend modifiers, discussed in Chapter 7, to control which derived classes the properties and methods of the class are available. These modifiers control only if the derived class and its users have access to the properties and methods. They do not control if the derived class can change the functionality of the properties and methods.

Visual Basic .NET provides three modifiers that can be used in a base class to control how a derived class can interact with properties and methods of the base class. These three modifiers are

- **Overridable** This modifier specifies that the derived class can override the property or method.
- **NotOverridable** This modifier specifies that the derived class cannot override the property or method.
- **MustOverride** This modifier specifies that the derived class must override the property or method.

When you create a method in a derived class that has the same name as a method in the base class, you must use the Overrides keyword to override the implementation in the base class method. The code from the example for **Company** and **Vendor** is repeated in the following listing.

```
Public Class Company
    Public CompanyName As String
    Public Address As String
    Public City As String
    Public State As String
    Public Zip As String
    Public Overridable Sub Label()
        Console.WriteLine(CompanyName)
        Console.WriteLine(Address)
        Console.WriteLine(City & ", " & State & " " & Zip)
    End Sub
End Class
Public Class Vendor
    Inherits Company
    Public Overrides Sub Label()        Console.WriteLine(CompanyName)
        Console.WriteLine("Attn:Receivables Department")
        Console.WriteLine(Address)
        Console.WriteLine(City & ", " & State & " " & Zip)
    End Sub
End Class
```

In this example, the Overridable keyword modifies the Label method in the **Company** class and the Overrides keyword modifies the implementation of the Label method in the **Vendor** class.

EXAM TIP To override a property or method in a base class, you must explicitly modify it with the Overridable keyword.

Me, MyBase, and MyClass Keywords

The following keywords are useful for referencing objects in code:

- **Me** This keyword references the instance of the object in which the code is executing.
- **MyBase** This keyword references the class specified in the Inherits statement in a derived class. Instead of using the base class name, you use the MyBase keyword to reference the base class.

- **MyClass** This keyword is similar to the Me keyword except that all properties and methods in the class act as NotOverridable.

The best way to demonstrate the differences between the Me, MyBase, and MyClass keywords is by using the label addressing example. The following code shows the addition of the SelectableLabel method to the **Company** class.

```
Public Class Company
    Public CompanyName As String
    Public Address As String
    Public City As String
    Public State As String
    Public Zip As String
    Public Overridable Sub Label()
        Console.WriteLine(CompanyName)
        Console.WriteLine(Address)
        Console.WriteLine(City & ", " & State & " " & Zip)
    End Sub
    Public Sub SelectableLabel(ByVal PrintCustomLabel As Boolean)
        If PrintCustomLabel Then
            Me.Label()
        Else
            MyClass.Label()
        End If
    End Sub
End Class
```

For an instance of a **Vendor** object, the Me.Label() statement in the SelectableLabel method causes the code from the derived class (the **Vendor** class) to be executed. The MyClass.Label() statement causes the code in the **Company** class to be executed. The MyClass keyword instructs the .NET Framework to ignore any overrides, and the code in the class in which the method exists is executed.

This process changes slightly when working in the derived class. The following VendorSelectableLabel subroutine implements the same functionality in the **Vendor** class, which is derived from the **Company** class.

```
Public Class Vendor
    Inherits Company
    Public Overrides Sub Label()
        Console.WriteLine(CompanyName)
        Console.WriteLine("Attn:Receivables Department")
        Console.WriteLine(Address)
        Console.WriteLine(City & ", " & State & " " & Zip)
    End Sub
    Public Sub VendorSelectableLabel(ByVal PrintCustomLabel As Boolean)
        If PrintCustomLabel Then
            Me.Label()
        Else
            MyBase.Label()
        End If
    End Sub
End Class
```

Instead of using MyClass.Label() as in the preceding code segment, MyBase.Label() is used. The MyBase keyword refers to the base class when used in a derived class.

EXAM TIP MyClass is used to reference the properties or code in the class in which it is used. It ignores overrides in derived classes.

In Exercise 8-3, you will implement the preceding code for the SelectableLabel and VendorSelectable label methods, and then use these methods to demonstrate the use of the Me, MyBase, and MyClass keywords.

PART II

Exercise 8-3: Using the Me, MyBase, and MyClass Keywords

1. Open the Visual Studio .NET IDE and create a new console application project called **Exercise 8-3**. Refer to Exercise 7-1 if you have questions about creating a new console application project.
2. Copy in the code from Exercise 8-1. You can copy the code from Exercise 8-1 on the companion CD if you like.
3. Add the following SelectableLabel method to the **Company** class.

```
Public Sub SelectableLabel(ByVal PrintCustomLabel As Boolean)
    If PrintCustomLabel Then
        Me.Label()
     Else
        MyClass.Label()
    End If
End Sub
```

4. Change the DisplayLabel subroutine to the following code.

```
Private Sub DisplayLabel(ByVal xCompany As Company)
    Console.WriteLine("--------------------")
    xCompany.SelectableLabel(True)
    Console.WriteLine("--------------------")
    xCompany.SelectableLabel(False)
End Sub
```

5. Press F5 to compile and run the application. The illustration displays the resulting console window.

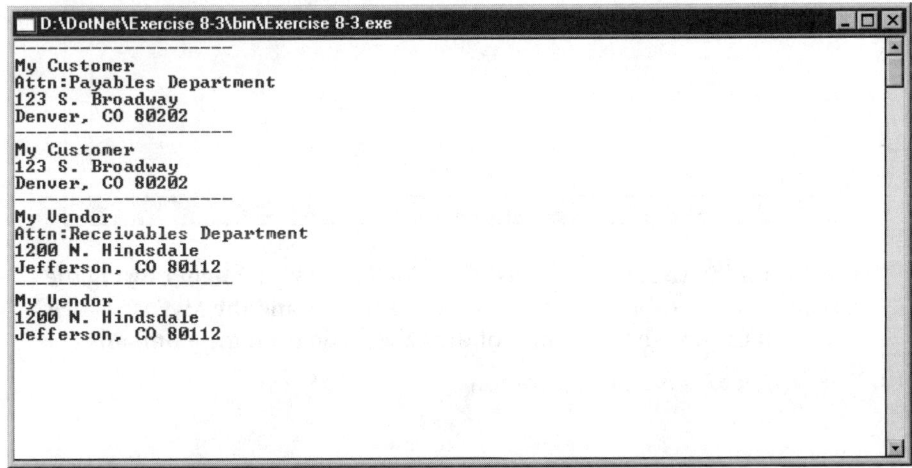

The illustration shows the results of the Me.Label() statement causing the execution of the Label code from the **Vendor** and **Customer** classes and the MyClass.Label() statement causing the execution of the Label code from the **Company** class.

6. Press ENTER to close the application.
7. Add the following VendorSelectableLabel method to the **Vendor** class.

```
Public Sub VendorSelectableLabel(ByVal PrintCustomLabel As Boolean)
    If PrintCustomLabel Then
        Me.Label()
    Else
        MyBase.Label()
    End If
End Sub
```

8. Make the following modifications to the code in the Main subroutine of Module1.

```
'DisplayLabel(oCustomer)
'DisplayLabel(oVendor)
oVendor.SelectableLabel(True)
Console.WriteLine("--------------------")
oVendor.SelectableLabel(False)
Console.ReadLine()
```

9. Press F5 to compile and run the application. The illustration shows the resulting console window.

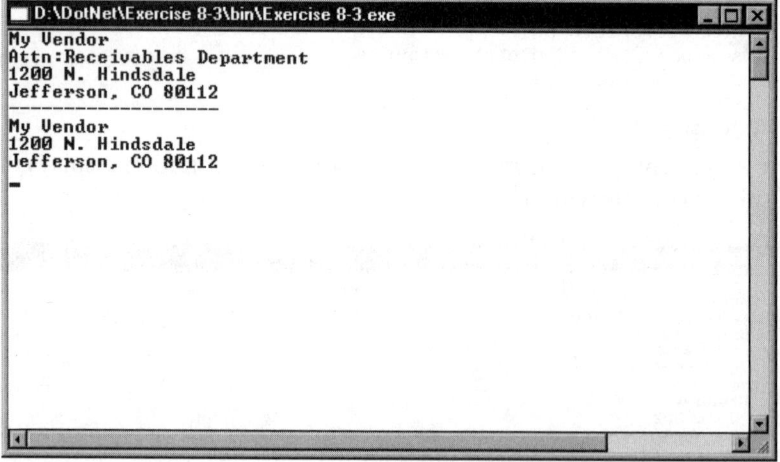

The illustration shows the results of the Me.Label() statement causing the execution of the Label code from the **Vendor** class and the MyBase.Label() statement causing the execution of the Label code from the **Company** class.

10. Press ENTER to close the application.

Special Considerations for the New() Constructor

You cannot use the Overridable keyword with the New() constructor. This is usually not a problem until you try to overload the New method. To make an overloaded New method available in the derived class, you must overload the New method in the derived class, and then call the MyBase.New overloaded method. The following code demonstrates the overloading of the New method in the **Company** class and the corresponding overloading in the **Vendor** class.


```
Public Class Company
    Public CompanyName As String
    Public Address As String
    Public City As String
    Public State As String
    Public Zip As String
    Public Sub New()
        MyBase.New()
    End Sub
    Public Sub New(ByVal xCompanyName As String, _
        ByVal xAddress As String, _
        ByVal xCity As String, _
        ByVal xState As String, _
        ByVal xZip As String)
        CompanyName = xCompanyName
        Address = xAddress
        City = xCity
        State = xState
        Zip = xZip
    End Sub
    Public Overridable Sub Label()
        Console.WriteLine(CompanyName)
        Console.WriteLine(Address)
        Console.WriteLine(City & ", " & State & " " & Zip)
    End Sub
 End Class
```

Because the New method is being overloaded, it is necessary to add the New method without any parameters. This method simply calls the New method on the base class for this class. Because this class has not inherited from any other classes, it automatically inherits from the **System.Object** class. MyBase.New() calls the **System.Object**'s New method.

The overloaded New method accepts the property information (CompanyName, Address, City, State, and Zip) for this object. This allows you to instantiate the object and populate all of its properties when you declare the object. The code for the **Vendor** class needs to be modified as shown in the following code.

```
Public Class Vendor
    Inherits Company
    Implements Contact
    Public Sub New()
        MyBase.New()
    End Sub
    Public Sub New(ByVal xCompanyName As String, _
```

```
        ByVal xAddress As String, _
        ByVal xCity As String, _
        ByVal xState As String, _
        ByVal xZip As String)
        MyBase.New(xCompanyName, xAddress, xCity, xState, xZip)
    End Sub
    Public Overrides Sub Label()
        Console.WriteLine(CompanyName)
        Console.WriteLine("Attn:Receivables Department")
        Console.WriteLine(Address)
        Console.WriteLine(City & ", " & State & " " & Zip)
    End Sub
End Class
```

You must implement both New methods in the derived class. They each call the corresponding overloaded New method for the base class using the MyBase keyword.

In Exercise 8-4 you will add the preceding overloaded New methods to the **Company**, **Vendor**, and **Customer** classes.

Exercise 8-4: Using Overloaded New Constructors in Classes

1. Open the Visual Studio .NET IDE and create a new console application project called **Exercise 8-4**. Refer to Exercise 7-1 if you have questions about creating a new console application project.
2. Copy in the code from Exercise 8-1. You can copy the code from Exercise 8-1 on the companion CD if you like.
3. Add the two following New methods to the **Company** class.

```
Public Sub New()
    MyBase.New()
End Sub
Public Sub New(ByVal xCompanyName As String, _
    ByVal xAddress As String, _
    ByVal xCity As String, _
    ByVal xState As String, _
    ByVal xZip As String)
    CompanyName = xCompanyName
    Address = xAddress
    City = xCity
    State = xState
    Zip = xZip
End Sub
```

4. Add the two following New methods to both the **Vendor** class and the **Company** class.

```
Public Sub New()
    MyBase.New()
End Sub
Public Sub New(ByVal xCompanyName As String, _
    ByVal xAddress As String, _
    ByVal xCity As String, _
    ByVal xState As String, _
    ByVal xZip As String)
    MyBase.New(xCompanyName, xAddress, xCity, xState, xZip)
End Sub
```

5. Change the Main subroutine in Module1 to the following code.

```
Sub Main()
    Dim oCustomer As New Customer("My Customer", "123 S. Broadway" _
        , "Denver", "CO", "80202")
    Dim oVendor As New Vendor("My Vendor", "1200 N. Hindsdale" _
        , "Jefferson", "CO", "80112")
    DisplayLabel(oCustomer)
    DisplayLabel(oVendor)
    Console.ReadLine()
End Sub
```

6. Press F5 to compile and run the application. The console window should be the same as in Exercise 8-1.
7. Press ENTER to close the application.

Custom Namespaces

The Visual Basic .NET Framework is divided into numerous namespaces. The purpose of the namespaces is to divide the .NET Framework into manageable pieces so that you can focus on the parts that you need to complete your tasks. For example, if you are working with Windows forms, you can focus on **System.Windows.Forms**. If you are working with data, you can focus on **System.Data**. For more details on the .NET Framework namespaces, refer to Chapter 1. The important concept here is that you can create your own custom namespaces to manage the development environment.

Creating custom namespaces is common when creating class libraries for use within applications. These class libraries are separately compiled projects that are referenced by other classes and modules within applications. A common structure for customer namespaces is *CompanyName.Application.Layer.Module*. For example, Microsoft provides namespaces for *Microsoft.Word, Microsoft.Excel,* and so on.

Figure 8-1 shows the Visual Studio .NET IDE with the Add Reference dialog box open to show some of the Microsoft namespaces.

When you create a project, the Visual Studio .NET IDE creates a namespace using the name of your project. You can change its name by selecting Project Properties | Common Properties | General | Root Namespace. Figure 8-2 shows the Project Properties window opened to this location.

In Exercise 8-5, you will add namespaces to the classes defined in Exercise 8-1.

Exercise 8-5: Creating a Class Library with Custom Namespaces

1. Open the Visual Studio .NET IDE and create a new console application project called **Exercise 8-5**. Refer to Exercise 7-1 if you have questions about creating a new console application project.
2. Copy in the code from Exercise 8-1. You can copy the code from Exercise 8-1 on the companion CD if you like.

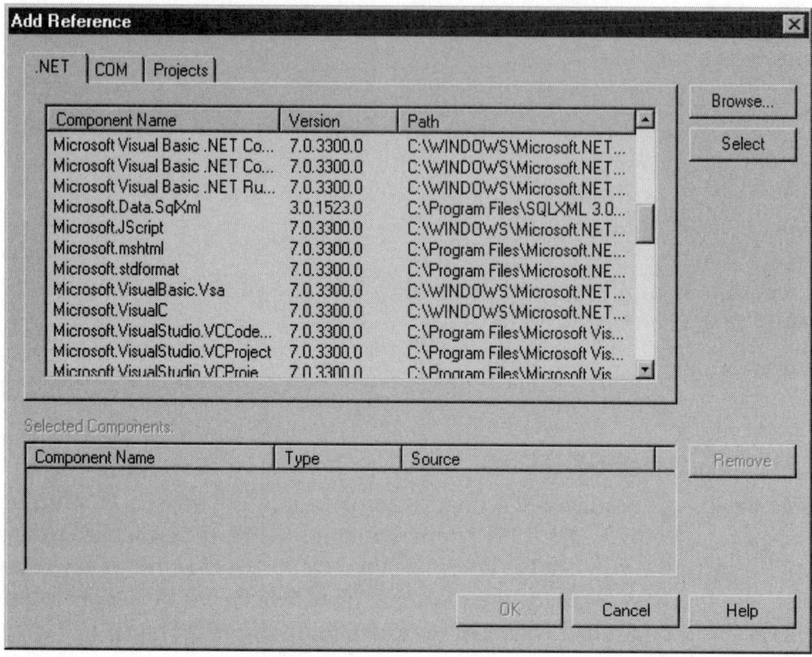

Figure 8-1 Add Reference dialog box showing Microsoft namespaces

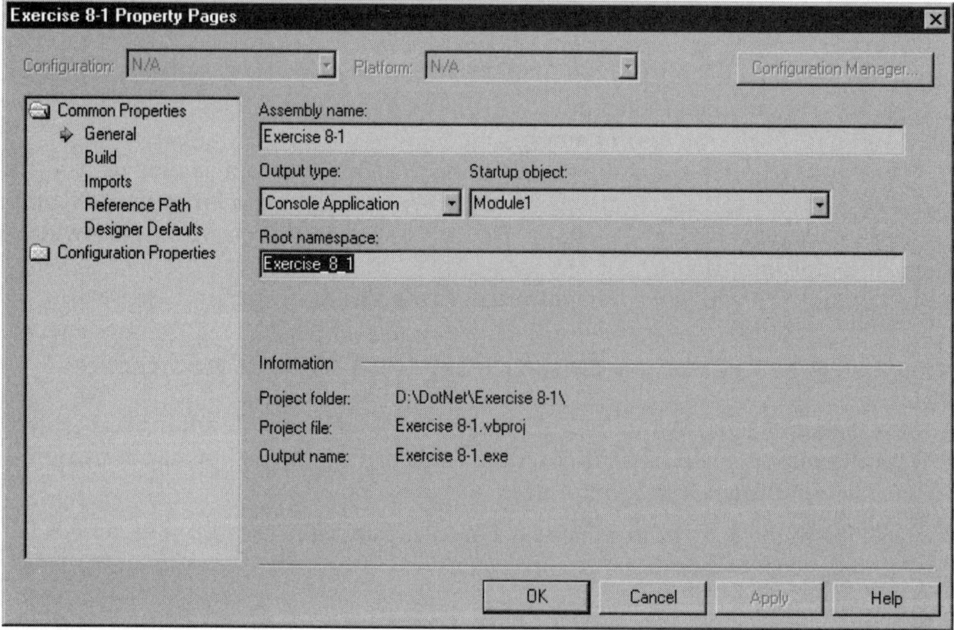

Figure 8-2 Root Namespace in the Project Properties dialog box

3. Modify the code by adding the Namespace and End Namespace statements around the classes and adding the namespaces to the declaration statements as shown in the following code.

```
Namespace MyCompany
    Namespace Business
        Public Class Company
            Public CompanyName As String
            Public Address As String
            Public City As String
            Public State As String
            Public Zip As String
            Public Overridable Sub Label()
                Console.WriteLine(CompanyName)
                Console.WriteLine(Address)
                Console.WriteLine(City & ", " & State & " " & Zip)
            End Sub
        End Class
        Namespace Payables
            Public Class Vendor
                Inherits Company
                Public Overrides Sub Label()
                    Console.WriteLine(CompanyName)
                    Console.WriteLine("Attn:Receivables Department")
                    Console.WriteLine(Address)
                    Console.WriteLine(City & ", " & State & " " & Zip)
                End Sub
            End Class
        End Namespace
        Namespace Receivables
            Public Class Customer
                Inherits Company
                Public Overrides Sub Label()
                    Console.WriteLine(CompanyName)
                    Console.WriteLine("Attn:Payables Department")
                    Console.WriteLine(Address)
                    Console.WriteLine(City & ", " & State & " " & Zip)
                End Sub
            End Class
        End Namespace
    End Namespace
End Namespace
Module Module1
    Sub Main()
        Dim oCustomer As New MyCompany.Business.Receivables.Customer()
        With oCustomer
            .CompanyName = "My Customer"
            .Address = "123 S. Broadway"
            .City = "Denver"
            .State = "CO"
            .Zip = "80202"
        End With
        Dim oVendor As New MyCompany.Business.Payables.Vendor()
        With oVendor
            .CompanyName = "My Vendor"
            .Address = "1200 N. Hindsdale"
            .City = "Jefferson"
            .State = "CO"
            .Zip = "80112"
```

```
            End With
            DisplayLabel(oCustomer)
            DisplayLabel(oVendor)
            Console.ReadLine()
        End Sub
        Private Sub DisplayLabel(ByVal xCompany As MyCompany.Business.Company)
            Console.WriteLine("--------------------")
            xCompany.Label()
        End Sub
    End Module
```

This code encloses all the classes in the **MyCompany.Business** namespace. The **Company** class is included in the namespace. The reference to the **Company** class in the DisplayLabel declaration is changed to **MyCompany.Business.Company**.

The **Vendor** class is enclosed in the **Payables** namespace within the **MyCompany .Business** namespace. All references to the **Vendor** class in the Main subroutine in Module1 are changed to **MyCompany.Business.Payables.Vendor**.

The **Customer** class is enclosed in the **Receivables** namespace within the **MyCompany.Business** namespace. All references to the **Customer** class in the Main subroutine in Module1 are changed to **MyCompany.Business .Receivables .Customer**.

4. Using the outline feature in the Visual Studio .NET IDE, close all code segments. The resulting display should look like Figure 8-3, which shows all the namespaces and the classes within the namespaces.

Shared Class Members

The .NET Framework allows you to create shared class members. These members have two useful features.

- You do not have to create an instance of an object from the class to have access to the shared members.
- All instances of the object have access to the shared members.

Because you do not need to instantiate an object to use the shared members of a class, you can use the methods as utility functions within your applications. Microsoft provides more than 25 math functions in its **Math** class. The following code is an example of using the *abs* method of the **Math** class.

```
Y = Math.abs(X)
```

It is not necessary to instantiate a **Math** object in order to access the abs method. This usage replaces the Visual Basic 6 GlobalMultiUse class interface.

Allowing all instances of a class to have access to a shared property allows you to set the values of that property once. This can provide significant performance gains if access to the file system or a database is required for the property values.

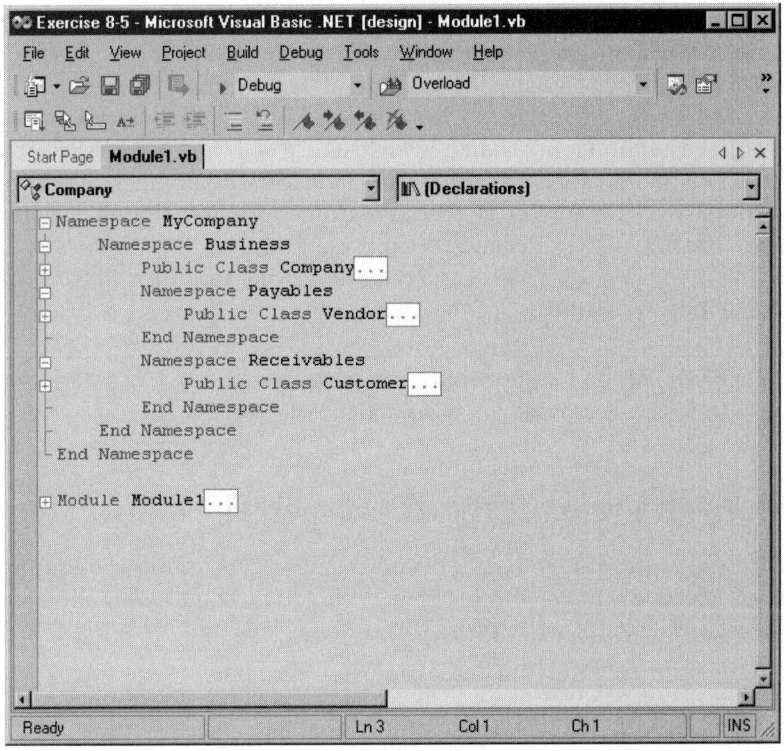

Figure 8-3 The main code window of Exercise 8-5 in the Visual Studio .NET IDE showing the namespaces for the classes

To define a shared property or method, you simply prefix the property or method with the Shared keyword as shown in the following code.

```
Public Class CustomMessages
    Public Shared Messages As New Collection()
    Shared Function DisplayMessage(ByVal MessageCode As String) As String
        PopulateMessages()
        Return Messages(MessageCode)
    End Function
    Public Function InstanceMessage(ByVal MessageCode As String)
        PopulateMessages()
        Return Messages(MessageCode)
    End Function
    Private Shared Sub PopulateMessages()
        If Messages.Count = 0 Then
            Console.WriteLine("Loading Messages")
            Messages.Add("This is Message One", "M1")
            Messages.Add("This is Message Two", "M2")
            Messages.Add("This is Message Three", "M3")
        End If
    End Sub
End Class
```

Messages is a collection that holds custom messages that can be accessed using the collection key. It is shared, which means that an instance of the object does not need to be created for it to be populated or referenced. The DisplayMessage method is also shared so an instance of the class does not need to be created to return a message. The InstanceMessage method is not shared so an instance of a **CustomMessage** object needs to be created before InstanceMessage can be accessed. The PopulateMessages method needs to be shared because it is accessed from both the shared DisplayMessage method and the non-shared InstanceMessage method. The PopulateMessages method is not available outside the class because of the Private modifier. Exercise 8-6 implements and demonstrates the use of this class.

EXAM TIP If one instance of a class changes the value of a shared property, that value is changed for all instances of the class.

Exercise 8-6: Implementing Shared Members in Classes

1. Open the Visual Studio .NET IDE and create a new console application project called **Exercise 8-6**. Refer to Exercise 7-1 if you have questions about creating a new console application project.
2. Add the following **CustomMessage** class to the code.

```
Public Class CustomMessages
    Public Shared Messages As New Collection()
    Shared Function DisplayMessage(ByVal MessageCode As String) As String
        PopulateMessages()
        Return Messages(MessageCode)
    End Function
    Public Function InstanceMessage(ByVal MessageCode As String)
        PopulateMessages()
        Return Messages(MessageCode)
    End Function
    Private Shared Sub PopulateMessages()
        If Messages.Count = 0 Then
            Console.WriteLine("Loading Messages")
            Messages.Add("This is Message One", "M1")
            Messages.Add("This is Message Two", "M2")
            Messages.Add("This is Message Three", "M3")
        End If
    End Sub
End Class
```

3. Modify the Main subroutine in Module1 to match the following code.

```
Sub Main()
    Console.WriteLine(CustomMessages.DisplayMessage("M1"))
    Console.WriteLine(CustomMessages.DisplayMessage("M2"))
    Dim oCustomMessages As New CustomMessages()
    Console.WriteLine(oCustomMessages.InstanceMessage("M3"))
    Console.ReadLine()
End Sub
```

This code calls the shared DisplayMessage method of the **CustomMessages** class without creating an instance of the object. It also creates an instance of the **CustomerMessages** class named **oCustomMessages** and calls the InstanceMessage method using the **oCustomMessages** object.

4. Press F5 to compile and run the application. The illustration shows the resulting console window.

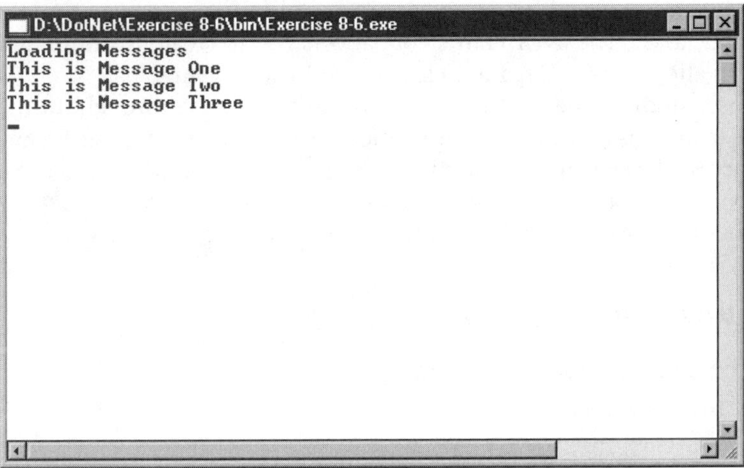

The illustration confirms that the loading of the custom messages happened only once. After the first time the messages are loaded, they are available to both the shared method and the instance method of the class.

5. Press ENTER to close the application.

Boxing and Unboxing

Boxing allows you to convert a value-type variable to a reference-type variable. Unboxing allows you to undo a conversion. Because value-type variables and reference-type variables use memory differently, you may find that it is useful for the same information to be stored as a value type sometimes and as a reference type at other times. For example, if you are using code that makes several copies of a large structure, it may be more efficient to convert the structure to an object. Now, instead of copying the entire structure, only the pointer is copied, which is much faster. Of course this all depends on your specific requirements and the performance increase you are looking for. Do not use boxing and unboxing unless there is a specific performance and/or memory usage problem. The following code shows an example of boxing and unboxing.

```
Dim I as Integer = 10
Dim O as Object = I     ' Boxing
Dim J as Integer = O    ' Unboxing
```

Summary

Inheritance is an important part of reusing code in an application. You can centralize common code in *base* classes and access this code in *derived* classes. Inheritance allows not only code reuse, but also polymorphism, which is much easier to implement than interfaces. Polymorphism allows you to override functionality in a *base* class with new functionality in the *derived* class while keeping the same method name for both classes.

When you create several classes to use in an application, you need a method of organizing these classes. The .NET Framework allows you to create custom namespaces for classes. This allows you to organize classes into logical groups.

Of course, all developers create their own utilities to use throughout their applications. This is still possible in the .NET Framework using shared properties and methods. You can access these shared properties and methods without instantiating an object. Also, when you instantiate an object from a class with a shared property or method, these properties and classes are available to all instances of the class.

Test Questions

1. In the following code, what is the *base* class?

```
Public Class Customer
  Inherits Company
  Public oContact as Contact
End Class
```

   A. Customer

   B. Company

   C. Contact

   D. None of the above

2. In the code for Question 1, what is the derived class?

   A. Customer

   B. Company

   C. Contact

   D. None of the above

3. What keyword is used to allow derived classes to modify a property or method?

   A. AllowChanges

   B. Overridable

   C. Overloadable

   D. Shadows

4. Which of the following is not a class modifier?

   A. NotInheritable

   B. Inheritable

C. MustInherit

D. Public

5. If a class does not specify a base class, which of the following statements is true?

A. The class cannot use the MyBase keyword.

B. The class inherits from **System.Object**.

C. The class cannot use the MyClass keyword.

D. The class cannot use the Me keyword.

6. If you want to be sure that the code for a method in a class is executed when that method is called, what keyword do you use?

A. Me

B. MyBase

C. MyClass

D. None of the above

7. If you want to be sure that the code in the base class is executed, what keyword do you use?

A. Me

B. MyBase

C. Child

D. MyClass

8. Which of the following declarations is invalid in a *derived* class if **MyMethod** is an overridable method in the *base* class?

A. Public Sub MyMethod()

B. Public Overrides Sub MyMethod()

C. Public NotOverridable Overrides Sub MyMethod()

D. Public Overloads Sub MyMethod()

9. Which of the following statements is not true of classes that contain shared members?

A. You must create an instance of the class to access members that are not shared.

B. You can access the shared members without creating an instance of the class.

C. Values for shared properties are unique for each instance of the class.

D. Members that are not shared can access the values of shared properties.

10. Which of the following statements are true for the terms boxing and unboxing? (Choose two.)

A. Boxing and unboxing are used for handling strings that contain special characters.

B. Boxing and unboxing describe methods of converting value-type variables to reference-type variables and back again.

C. When you box a variable, it is moved to the stack.

D. When you box a variable, it is moved to the common runtime heap.

E. When you box a variable, it is copied to the common runtime heap.

11. Which of the following statements best describes polymorphism?

A. It is the ability to derive one class from another.

B. It is the ability to define different classes with methods and properties of the same name that can be used interchangeably in code.

C. It is the parent-child relationship between classes.

D. It is the ability to create classes with the same name in different namespaces.

12. If you have overloaded the New method in a *base* class, what must you do in the *derived* class?

A. Override all New methods of the base class in the derived class.

B. Implement a New method in the derived class for each New method of the base class that you want available in the derived class.

C. Nothing; all New methods are automatically inherited by the derived class.

D. None of the above.

13. How can you implement multiple inheritance in Visual Basic .NET?

A. Include multiple Inherits statements in the derived class.

B. Include one Inherits statements in the derived class and implement interfaces for the additional inheritance required.

C. Multiple inheritance is not available in Visual Basic .NET, even if using interfaces.

D. Nest inheritance by using multiple classes in a hierarchy.

14. If you are defining a method in a class and do not want to allow it to be modified by a class that uses your class as a base class, what keyword do you use?

A. NotInheritable

B. NotOverloadable

C. NotOverridable

D. Private

15. What is the root namespace for the .NET Framework classes?

A. Microsoft.NET

B. Microsoft.System

C. Windows

D. System

Test Answers

1. B.
2. A.
3. B.
4. B.
5. B.
6. C.
7. B.
8. A.
9. C.
10. B.
11. B.
12. B.
13. B.
14. C.
15. D.

PART III

Components and Assembly Deployment

CHAPTER

Creating and Using Assemblies

In this chapter, you will

- Use the Visual Basic Compiler to create assemblies
- Learn how to use ildasm.exe to view the contents of an assembly
- Use the Assembly Linker (al.exe) to create multifile assemblies
- Create and use satellite assemblies

In the Visual Basic .NET Framework, the final result of development and implementation is one or more assemblies. An assembly is a file that gets distributed as an application. It contains the code that is executed by the common language runtime. It also contains support information for types, references to other assemblies, and versioning. An assembly is the primary unit for deployment and security in the .NET Framework.

This chapter describes the assembly, how to create and modify assemblies, and how to create and implement satellite assemblies.

An Overview of Assemblies

When developers use the Visual Studio .NET integrated development environment (IDE) to build a Windows application, the Visual Studio .NET IDE builds an assembly. The assembly contains the code necessary to run the application, information about the types that are created and used in the application, and references to other assemblies and resources needed by the application. By default, this assembly is placed in the bin directory of the project. The assembly file for a Windows application has the .exe extension. By looking at the file name alone, you might easily mistake it for a standard Windows executable file. If the project is for a class library or a Web application, the file extension is .dll. This file can be mistaken for a standard Windows dynamic link library. However, these files are quite different from the standard Windows executable files or the dynamic link files.

Assemblies are the building blocks for applications. They provide the basic unit for application activation, deployment, versioning, and security.

Assembly Features

Assemblies allow the Visual Basic .NET Framework to manage an application, including other dependent assemblies, versioning, and security. Assemblies include the following attributes:

- Assemblies contain the Microsoft Intermediate Language (MSIL) code that is compiled by the just-in-time compiler for executing an application.
- Assemblies are a versioning unit. An assembly version is the smallest unit to which versioning in the .NET Framework is applied.
- Assemblies are a deployment unit.
- Assemblies are a security boundary; permissions are granted to individual assemblies.
- Assemblies are a type boundary. The identifiers for all types that are defined in an assembly are prefixed by the assembly name, making the identifiers unique to that assembly.
- Assemblies support side-by-side execution, which allows different versions of an assembly to execute at the same time.

The combination of versioning and side-by-side execution helps resolve DLL conflicts which occur when different programs running at the same time require different versions of the same DLL. DLL conflicts have been a major problem for both developers and users for a long time. Chapter 10 covers versioning and side-by-side execution in detail.

Assembly Structure

An assembly consists of four parts:

- The assembly manifest or assembly metadata
- The type metadata
- The Microsoft Intermediate Language (MSIL) code
- Resources

These parts are discussed in the following sections.

The Assembly Manifest

The assembly manifest, also called the assembly metadata, describes the assembly, its contents, and the location of other files that are part of the assembly. An assembly is self-describing. It does not depend on information stored in locations that are not part of its metadata, such as the Windows registry. The manifest includes the following elements:

- **Assembly name** Although the manifest includes an assembly name, the assembly's actual identity is composed of its name, version number, culture, and strong name information.
- **Version number** This four-part number identifies the assembly version. Versioning is described in detail in Chapter 10.
- **Culture** This element identifies the culture and language of the assembly. It applies only to satellite assemblies, which are described later in this chapter and in Chapter 11.
- **Strong-name information** If the assembly has been strongly named, this element contains the strong-name information. Strong naming is discussed later in this chapter.
- **List of files that make up the assembly** An assembly can consist of one or more files. This list identifies the files. Multifile assemblies are discussed later in this chapter.
- **Type reference information** All types implemented by the application do not need to be declared and implemented in the same file as the assembly manifest. Type reference information identifies in which files the types are declared and implemented.
- **Referenced assembly information** The assembly may depend on other assemblies. Referenced assembly information identifies these assemblies and provides information about them.

The Type Metadata

The type metadata contains the declaration information for the types defined in the MSIL code that is included in the assembly file. If the assembly consists of more that one file that contains type implementations, the type metadata is included in the file that contains the MSIL code for the type.

MSIL Code

The assembly file contains Microsoft Intermediate Language (MSIL) code for the implementation of types in the file. All code in the Visual Basic .NET Framework is included in a type. These types include, but are not limited to, modules, classes, and applications.

Resources

Many programs have resources that are required but are not part of the executable code. Resources, as applied to assemblies, are any nonexecutable data that is part of the application. Strings and images are commonly used resources. These resources need to be available to the application. Creating resource-only assemblies and implementing localization using resource assemblies are covered in more detail in Chapter 11.

EXAM TIP An assembly is made up of the assembly manifest, type metadata, MSIL code, and resources.

Multifile Assemblies

An assembly can consist of one or more files in the Windows file system. Many applications consist of a single assembly file. There can be performance gains by using multiple files for assemblies. Files that make up assemblies are not loaded until they are required; developers can move seldom-used types and resources into separate files that are loaded only when required. This is especially helpful if the assemblies require downloading across a local area network or a wide area network.

Strong-Named Assemblies

Most assemblies that are created for an application are application-private assemblies. These assemblies live within the directory structure of the application, and other applications cannot use these assemblies. Some assemblies are shared across several applications. These shared assemblies need a method of guaranteeing their name, culture, and version. A public key is used to help identify these shared assemblies. This public key is used in conjunction with the assembly name, the culture, and the version to create a strong-named assembly. Creating and using strong-named assemblies are discussed in Chapter 10.

Creating and Modifying Assemblies

The simplest method of creating and managing assemblies is to let the Visual Studio .NET IDE do it for you. However, it is useful in learning about assemblies to create and manage them the hard way—using the command-line tools.

Many programs do not require versioning, security, or many of the other features provided by the .NET Framework. A good example of a program that does not require these features is the HelloWorld program shown in the following code.

```
Imports System
Public Module HelloWorld
    Sub Main
        Console.WriteLine("Hello World")
    End Sub
End Module
```

If the name of the file that contains the preceding code is HelloWorld.vb, you can compile this program using the Visual Basic .NET Compiler (vbc.exe) provided with the .NET Framework SDK. Using the Visual Studio .NET Command Prompt window you can compile the program as shown in the following code.

```
vbc HelloWorld.vb
```

The Visual Basic .NET Compiler creates the HelloWorld.exe file in the same directory as the HelloWorld.vb file.

NOTE To access the Visual Studio .NET Command Prompt, select Programs | Microsoft Visual Studio .NET | Visual Studio .NET Tools. Use this command window for running .NET command-line utilities. It automatically configures the correct Path information to allow easy access to the utilities.

You can run the program by entering

```
HelloWorld
```

in the Command Prompt window.

You can view the details of the HelloWorld.exe assembly using the Intermediate Language Disassembler (ildasm.exe) utility provided with the .NET Framework SDK. Use the following command-line prompt to start this utility.

```
ildasm HelloWorld.exe
```

In Exercise 9-1 you will create the HelloWorld program, and then view the resulting assembly.

Exercise 9-1: Creating an Assembly and Viewing the Assembly Structure

1. Create a directory for the files in this exercise. The directory in this example is D:/DotNet/Exercise 9-1. If you use a different name for your directory, replace any reference to D:/DotNet/Exercise 9-1 with your directory name.
2. Using Notepad, create a file called **HelloWorld.vb** in the D:/DotNet/Exercise 9-1 directory.
3. Add the following code to the file.

```
Imports System
Public Module HelloWorld
    Sub Main
        Console.WriteLine("Hello World")
    End Sub
End Module
```

4. Save the file. Be sure to save the file without the .txt extension.
5. To open the Visual Studio .NET Command Prompt window, select Start | All Programs | Microsoft Visual Studio .NET | Visual Studio .NET Tools | Visual

PART III

Studio .NET Command Prompt. The Command Prompt option is usually the last item listed on the menu. The illustration shows this path using Windows XP.

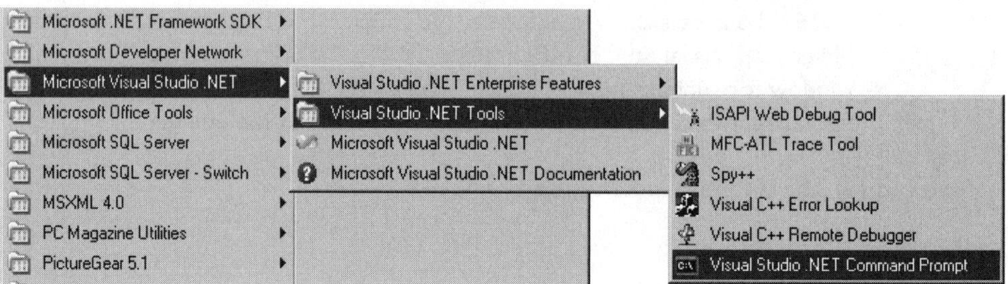

6. Navigate to the D:/DotNet/Exercise 9-1 directory in the Command Prompt window and enter the following text at the command-line prompt.

```
vbc HelloWorld.vb
```

7. Press ENTER to compile HelloWorld.vb and create the HelloWorld.exe assembly.
8. Enter the following text at the command-line prompt and press ENTER.

```
HelloWorld
```

The Hello World message should appear as shown here.

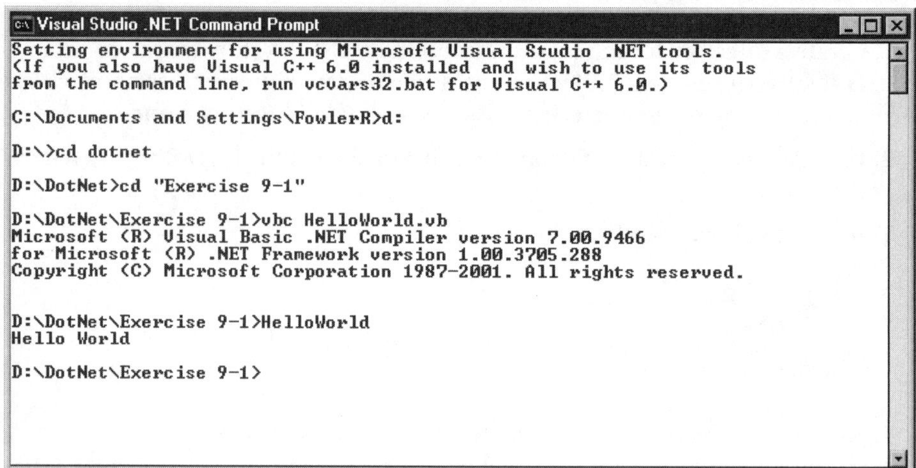

9. Enter the following text at the command-line prompt and press ENTER.

```
dir
```

You should see two files: HelloWorld.vb and HelloWorld.exe.

10. Enter the following text at the command-line prompt and press ENTER.

```
ildasm HelloWorld.exe
```

The Intermediate Language Disassembler (IL DASM) window appears as shown on the following page.

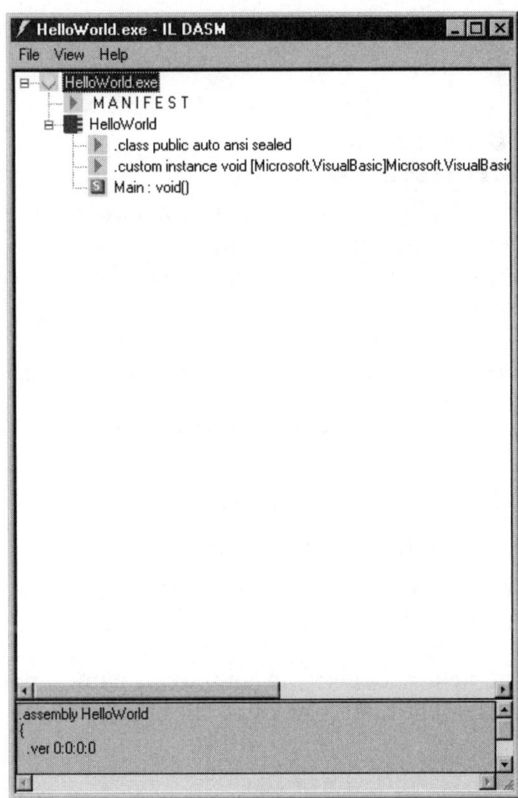

11. Double-click the MANIFEST node. The MANIFEST window opens as shown here.

```
MANIFEST
.assembly extern mscorlib
{
  .publickeytoken = (B7 7A 5C 56 19 34 E0 89 )                    // .z\
  .ver 1:0:3300:0
}
.assembly extern Microsoft.VisualBasic
{
  .publickeytoken = (B0 3F 5F 7F 11 D5 0A 3A )                    // .?_
  .ver 7:0:3300:0
}
.assembly HelloWorld
{
  .hash algorithm 0x00008004
  .ver 0:0:0:0
}
.module HelloWorld.exe
// MVID: {AF0BD7C0-DE26-423D-ADDA-9E002C50EFD6}
.imagebase 0x00400000
.subsystem 0x00000003
.file alignment 512
.corflags 0x00000001
// Image base: 0x02d90000
```

12. Close the MANIFEST window. Then, close the IL DASM window. Finally, close the Visual Studio .NET Command Prompt window.

Visual Basic Compiler Options for Dealing with Assemblies

The Visual Basic .NET Compiler (vbc.exe) provides a number of options when creating assemblies. This section discusses the options that can be used for various types of code. Chapter 10 covers the options for strong-named assemblies, and Chapter 11 covers the options for resources and localization.

You can create four types of assemblies for code (as differentiated from resources). You use the target option to specify the type of assembly you are creating. The target options are:

- **/target:exe (/t:exe)** Creates a console application (.exe). This is the default option
- **/target:winexe (/t:winexe)** Creates a Windows application (.exe)
- **/target:library (/t:library)** Creates a library (.dll)
- **/target:module(/t:module)** Creates a module that can be added to an assembly (.netmodule)

You can use the /out: option to specify the output file name. The following command lines are examples of using the target and out options.

```
vbc /out:Hello.exe /target:exe HelloWorld.vb
vbc /out:Hello.exe /t:exe HelloWorld.vb
```

In Exercise 9-2 you will create two separate code files, and then combine them into a single file assembly.

Exercise 9-2: Creating a Single File Assembly from Multiple Code Files

1. Create a directory for the files in this exercise. The directory in this example is D:/DotNet/Exercise 9-2. If you use a different name for your directory, replace any reference to D:/DotNet/Exercise 9-2 with your directory name.
2. Using Notepad, create a file called **HelloWorld.vb** in the D:/DotNet/Exercise 9-2 directory.
3. Add the following text to the file. This text *is not* the same as in Exercise 9-1.

```
Imports System
Imports HelloWorldClass
Public Module HelloWorld
    Sub Main
        Dim oHelloWorld as New HelloWorldClass()
        Console.WriteLine(oHelloWorld.HelloWorld)
    End Sub
End Module
```

The program imports the **HelloWorldClass**, creates an instance of the **HelloWorldClass** object, and uses that object to get the message to display.

4. Save the file.
5. Using Notepad, create a file called **HelloWorldClass.vb** in the D:/DotNet/Exercise 9-2 directory.
6. Add the following text to the file.

```
Imports System
Public Class HelloWorldClass
    Public Function HelloWorld() as String
      Return "Hello World"
    End Function
End Class
```

This code defines a simple class that returns the Hello World message.

7. Save the file.
8. Open the Visual Studio .NET Command Prompt window (see Step 5 of Exercise 9-1 for directions on opening this window) and navigate to the D:/DotNet/Exercise 9-2 directory in the command window.
9. Enter the following text at the command-line prompt and press ENTER to compile both the class and the program into a single file assembly.

```
vbc HelloWorld.vb HelloWorldClass.vb
```

10. Enter the following text at the command-line prompt and press ENTER to run the program displaying the Hello World message.

```
HelloWorld
```

11. Enter the following text at the command-line prompt and press ENTER to open the IL DASM window.

```
Ildasm HelloWorld.exe
```

You can see both the class and the main program as shown in Figure 9-1.

12. Close the IL DASM window. Then, close the Visual Studio .NET Command Prompt window.

When you create assemblies from multiple code files, you can have only one starting point. For example, you cannot have two modules with a Main subroutine. You can also simplify the compiling of several visual basic files into a single application by using wildcards for the file name. For example, you can use the following command.

```
vbc *.vb
```

EXAM TIP Only one entry point (starting point for the program) can exist in an assembly.

PART III

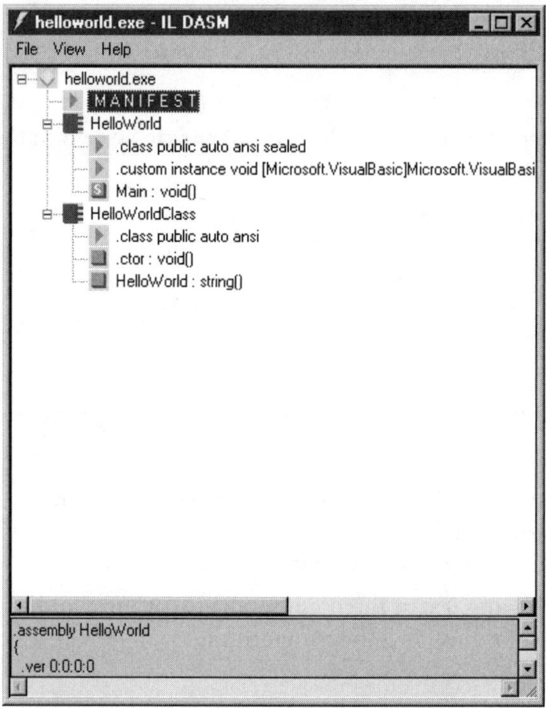

Figure 9-1 The Intermediate Language Disassembler window for the HelloWorld program and **HelloWorldClass** class

Including Resources in Assemblies

As explained earlier in this chapter, within the scope of assemblies, the term *resource* is defined as any nonexecutable data that is part of an application. In Chapter 11, which covers globalization and localization in detail, it becomes very important to be able to separate code from resources. This section explains how to add a resource file to a single file assembly. Creating satellite assemblies for resource files is discussed later in this chapter. Chapter 11 covers creating and implementing resource-only assemblies for localization.

The Visual Basic .NET Compiler (vbc.exe) uses the /resource: (/res:) option to specify a resource file to add to an assembly. The following command lines are examples of using the resource option.

```
vbc /resource:strings.resources HelloWorld.vb
vbc /res:strings.resources HelloWorld.vb
```

The resource file that is added to an assembly must be a common language runtime (CLR) binary resource file. The Resource File Generator (resgen.exe) tool creates this resource file from a text file (.txt) or from an XML-based resource file (.resx). Exercise 9-3 demonstrates the use of this tool with a simple text file.

EXAM TIP A resource file that is added to an assembly must be in the CLR binary resource file format. It cannot be a text file or the XML-based resource file you use to define the resources. To create the resource file, use the resgen.exe utility.

Exercise 9-3: Adding a Resource File to a Single File Assembly

1. Create a directory for the files in this exercise. The directory in this example is D:/DotNet/Exercise 9-3. If you use a different name for your directory, replace any reference to D:/DotNet/Exercise 9-3 with your directory name.
2. Using Notepad, create a file called **HelloWorld.vb** in the D:/DotNet/Exercise 9-3 directory.
3. Add the following text to the file.

```
Imports System
Imports System.Resources
Public Module HelloWorld
    Sub Main
    Dim rm As ResourceManager = NewResourceManager("HelloWorldStrings", _
        System.Reflection.Assembly.GetExecutingAssembly())
        Console.WriteLine(rm.GetString("HelloWorld"))
    End Sub
End Module
```

   This code creates an **rm** object that is a ResourceManager for a resource called HelloWorldStrings. The code uses **rm** to get the value for a string named HelloWorld. You define the resource in Steps 5 through 9.

4. Save the file.
5. Using Notepad, create a file called **HelloWorldStrings.txt** in the D:/DotNet/ Exercise 9-3 directory.
6. Add the following text to the file.

```
HelloWorld = Hello World From Resources
```

7. Save the file.
8. Open the Visual Studio .NET Command Prompt window (see Step 5 of Exercise 9-1 for directions on opening this window) and navigate to the D:/DotNet/Exercise 9-3 directory in the command window.
9. Enter the following text at the command-line prompt and press ENTER.

```
resgen HelloWorldStrings.txt
```

10. Enter the following text at the command-line prompt and press ENTER.

```
dir
```

PART III

The HelloWorldStrings.resources file should appear in the directory listing as shown in the illustration.

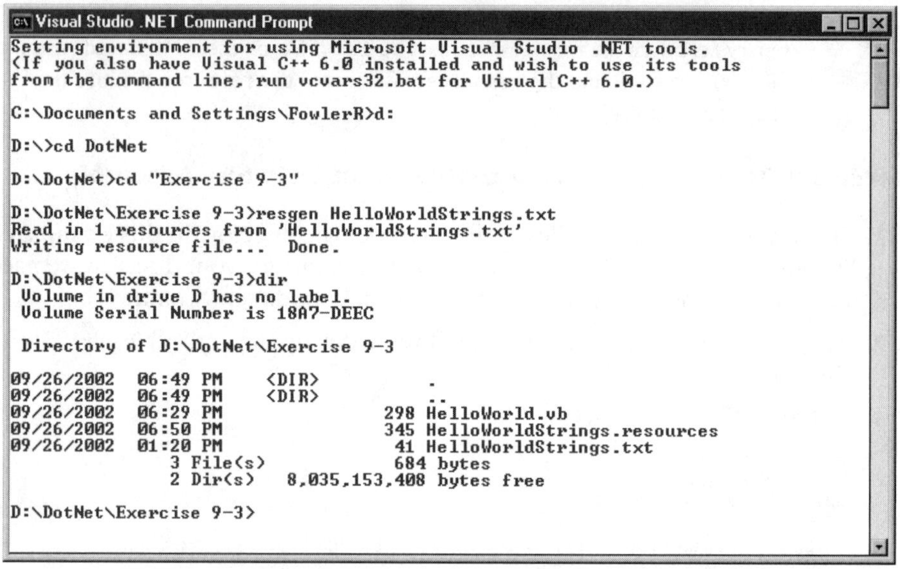

```
Visual Studio .NET Command Prompt
Setting environment for using Microsoft Visual Studio .NET tools.
(If you also have Visual C++ 6.0 installed and wish to use its tools
from the command line, run vcvars32.bat for Visual C++ 6.0.)

C:\Documents and Settings\FowlerR>d:

D:\>cd DotNet

D:\DotNet>cd "Exercise 9-3"

D:\DotNet\Exercise 9-3>resgen HelloWorldStrings.txt
Read in 1 resources from 'HelloWorldStrings.txt'
Writing resource file...  Done.

D:\DotNet\Exercise 9-3>dir
 Volume in drive D has no label.
 Volume Serial Number is 18A7-DEEC

 Directory of D:\DotNet\Exercise 9-3

09/26/2002  06:49 PM    <DIR>          .
09/26/2002  06:49 PM    <DIR>          ..
09/26/2002  06:29 PM               298 HelloWorld.vb
09/26/2002  06:50 PM               345 HelloWorldStrings.resources
09/26/2002  01:20 PM                41 HelloWorldStrings.txt
               3 File(s)            684 bytes
               2 Dir(s)   8,035,153,408 bytes free

D:\DotNet\Exercise 9-3>
```

11. Enter the following text at the command-line prompt and press ENTER.

    ```
    vbc /res:HelloWorldStrings.resources HelloWorld.vb
    ```

    The /res: option specifies to include the HelloWorldStrings.resources resource file in the assembly.

12. Enter the following text at the command-line prompt and press ENTER.

    ```
    HelloWorld
    ```

    The Hello World From Resources message appears.

13. Close the Visual Studio .NET Command Prompt window.

Creating Multifile Assemblies

In complex applications, it is not always appropriate to include all the information for an application in a single assembly file. For example, you might improve performance by only loading seldom-used classes when they are needed. A multifile assembly is different from an application that references multiple assemblies. A multifile assembly has one primary file that contains, at minimum, the assembly manifest and other files to make up a single assembly.

To create a multifile assembly, developers perform the following steps:

1. Compile all the files that contain types that are referenced by other modules.

2. Compile all modules that reference other modules; reference the modules created in Step 1 where needed.
3. Use the Assembly Linker (al.exe) to create the assembly manifest. The Assembly Linker is a command-line program that creates a file with an assembly manifest from one or more files.

Exercise 9-4 walks you through the creation of a multifile assembly.

Exercise 9-4: Creating Multifile Assemblies

1. Create a directory for the files in this exercise. The directory in this example is D:/DotNet/Exercise 9-4. If you use a different name for your directory replace any reference to D:/DotNet/Exercise 9-4 with your directory name.
2. Using Notepad, create a file called **HelloWorld.vb** in the D:/DotNet/Exercise 9-4 directory.
3. Add the following text to the file. This text is the same as in Exercise 9-2.

```
Imports System
Imports HelloWorldClass
Public Module HelloWorld
    Sub Main
      Dim oHelloWorld as New HelloWorldClass()
        Console.WriteLine(oHelloWorld.HelloWorld)
    End Sub
End Module
```

4. Save the file.
5. Using Notepad, create a file called **HelloWorldClass.vb** in the D:/DotNet/Exercise 9-4 directory.
6. Add the following text to the file. This text is the same as in Exercise 9-2.

```
Imports System
Public Class HelloWorldClass
    Public Function HelloWorld() as String
      Return "Hello World"
    End Function
End Class
```

7. Save the file.
8. Open the Visual Studio .NET Command Prompt window (see Step 5 of Exercise 9-1 for directions on opening this window) and navigate to the D:/DotNet/Exercise 9-4 directory in the command window.
9. Enter the following text at the command-line prompt.

```
vbc /target:module HelloWorldClass.vb
```

   This is the first use of the /target: option. In the preceding exercises, the target was a console application, the default target.

10. Press ENTER to create HelloWorldClass.netmodule. It will be used in creating both the .netmodule file for the HelloWorld.vb and for creating the final assembly that contains the assembly manifest.
11. Enter the following text at the command-line prompt and press ENTER to create HelloWorld.netmodule.

    ```
    vbc /addmodule:HelloWorldClass.netmodule /target:module HelloWorld.vb
    ```

    Because HelloWorld.vb references the **HelloWorldClass** class, the /addmodule: option is required.
12. Enter the following text at the command-line prompt and press ENTER.

    ```
    dir
    ```

    The HelloWorldClass.netmodule file and the HelloWorld.netmodule file should appear in the directory listing, as shown in Figure 9-2.
13. Enter the following text at the command-line prompt.

    ```
    al HelloWorldClass.netmodule HelloWorld.netmodule /main:HelloWorld.Main
    /out:HelloWorld.exe /t:exe
    ```

    The /main: option specifies the location of the application startup code. In this case, it is the Main subroutine in the HelloWorld.vb module.

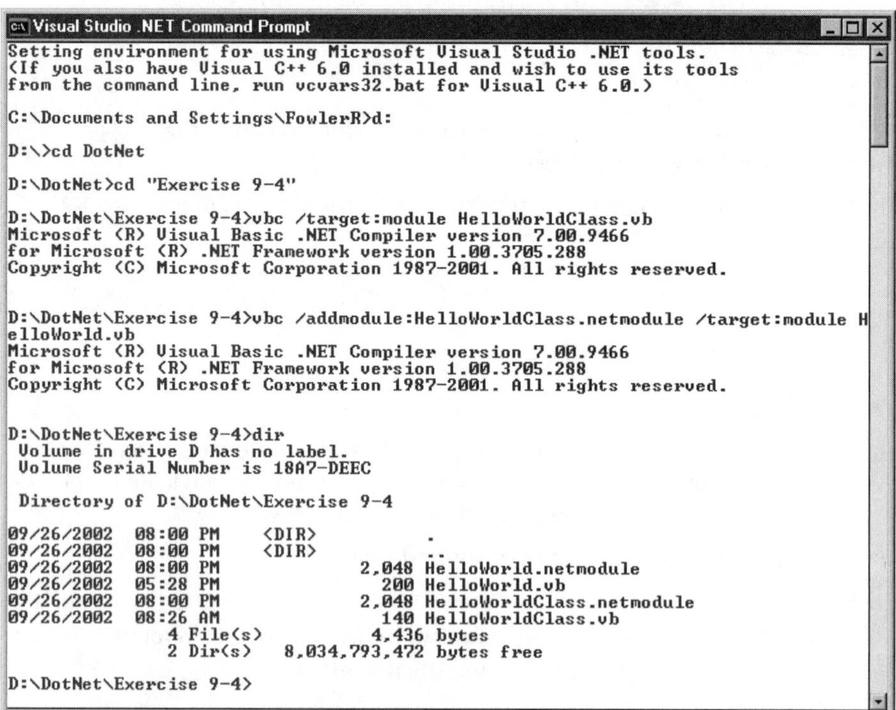

Figure 9-2 The Visual Studio .NET Command Prompt window showing the HelloWorldClass .netmodule file and the HelloWorld.netmodule file

14. Press ENTER to create HelloWorld.exe. To examine HelloWorld.exe, HelloWorld .netmodule, and HelloWorldClass.netmodule, use ildasm.exe. These three files make up the application. Instead of a single file for the assembly, there are now three files. The HelloWorld.exe file contains the assembly manifest but no MSIL code.
15. Close the Visual Studio .NET Command Prompt window.

Creating Satellite Assemblies

Satellite assemblies contain only resources; these resources are not included in the assembly manifest. Satellite assemblies are used primarily for localization. Localization and resource-only (satellite) assemblies are covered in more detail in Chapter 11. Besides localization, there are other reasons to use satellite assemblies. Among other things, they allow easy modification of textual data after an application has been completed. For example, you may need to complete an application, even though the departments within your organization have not agreed on terminology. By separating the textual data from the application code, you can easily modify a user interface without modifying the application code.

Exercise 9-5 makes a simple change to the HelloWorld application to allow changes to the message without changing the application code.

Exercise 9-5: Creating and Using Satellite Assemblies

1. Create a directory for the files in this exercise. The directory in this example is D:/DotNet/Exercise 9-5. If you use a different name for your directory, replace any reference to D:/DotNet/Exercise 9-5 with your directory name.
2. Using Notepad, create a file called **HelloWorld.vb** in the D:/DotNet/Exercise 9-5 directory.
3. Add the following text to the file.

```
Imports System
Imports System.Resources
Public Module HelloWorld
    Sub Main
        Dim rm As ResourceManager
        rm = ResourceManager.CreateFileBasedResourceManager( _
            "HelloWorldStrings", ".", Nothing)
        Console.WriteLine(rm.GetString("HelloWorld"))
    End Sub
End Module
```

   This code differs from the code in Exercise 9-2. The ResourceManager CreateFileBasedResourceManager method is used to create **rm**.
4. Save the file.
5. Using Notepad, create a file called **HelloWorldStrings.txt** in the D:/DotNet/Exercise 9-5 directory.

6. Add the following text to the file.

```
HelloWorld = Hello World From Resources
```

7. Save the file.
8. Open the Visual Studio .NET Command Prompt window (see Step 5 of Exercise 9-1 for directions on opening this window) and navigate to the D:/DotNet/Exercise 9-5 directory in the command window.
9. Enter the following text at the command-line prompt and press ENTER.

```
resgen HelloWorldStrings.txt
```

10. Enter the following text at the command-line prompt and press ENTER.

```
al /out:HelloWorldStrings.resources.dll
/linkresource:HelloWorldStrings.resources
```

This command creates the HelloWorldStrings.resources.dll as a resource-only assembly.

11. Enter the following text at the command-line prompt and press ENTER.

```
dir
```

The HelloWorldStrings.resources.dll file should appear in the directory listing as shown in Figure 9-3.

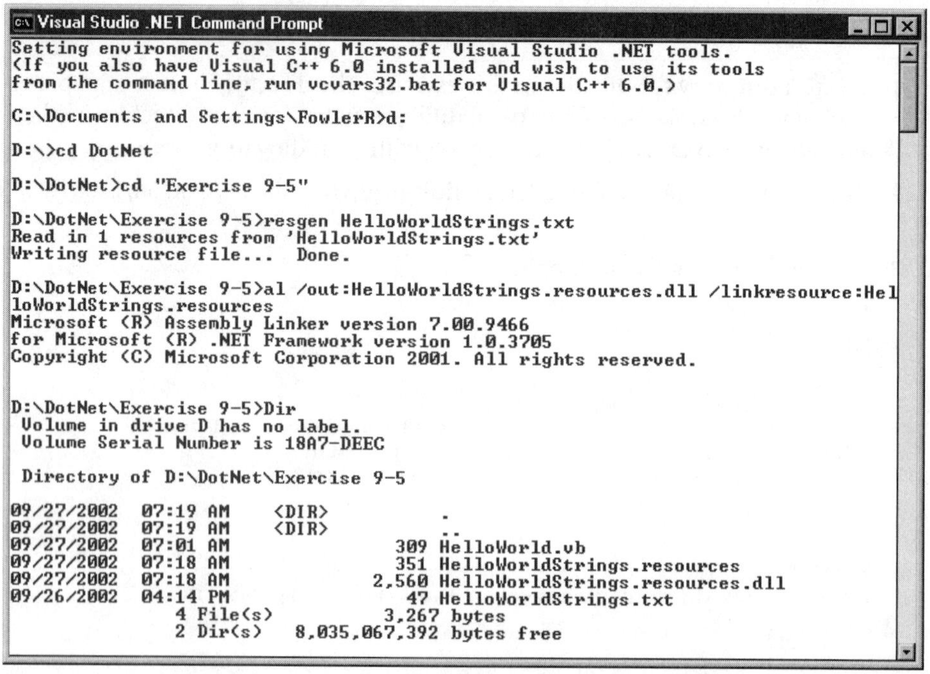

```
Visual Studio .NET Command Prompt
Setting environment for using Microsoft Visual Studio .NET tools.
(If you also have Visual C++ 6.0 installed and wish to use its tools
from the command line, run vcvars32.bat for Visual C++ 6.0.)

C:\Documents and Settings\FowlerR>d:

D:\>cd DotNet

D:\DotNet>cd "Exercise 9-5"

D:\DotNet\Exercise 9-5>resgen HelloWorldStrings.txt
Read in 1 resources from 'HelloWorldStrings.txt'
Writing resource file...  Done.

D:\DotNet\Exercise 9-5>al /out:HelloWorldStrings.resources.dll /linkresource:Hel
loWorldStrings.resources
Microsoft (R) Assembly Linker version 7.00.9466
for Microsoft (R) .NET Framework version 1.0.3705
Copyright (C) Microsoft Corporation 2001. All rights reserved.


D:\DotNet\Exercise 9-5>Dir
 Volume in drive D has no label.
 Volume Serial Number is 18A7-DEEC

 Directory of D:\DotNet\Exercise 9-5

09/27/2002  07:19 AM    <DIR>          .
09/27/2002  07:19 AM    <DIR>          ..
09/27/2002  07:01 AM               309 HelloWorld.vb
09/27/2002  07:18 AM               351 HelloWorldStrings.resources
09/27/2002  07:18 AM             2,560 HelloWorldStrings.resources.dll
09/26/2002  04:14 PM                47 HelloWorldStrings.txt
               4 File(s)          3,267 bytes
               2 Dir(s)   8,035,067,392 bytes free
```

Figure 9-3 The Visual Studio .NET Command Prompt window showing the HelloWorldStrings .resources.dll file

12. Enter the following text at the command-line prompt and press ENTER.

    ```
    vbc /linkresource:HelloWorldStrings.resources.dll HelloWorld.vb
    ```

    The /linkresources: option specifies that a reference to the HelloWorldStrings .resources.dll resource-only assembly should be included in the assembly.

13. Enter the following text at the command-line prompt and press ENTER

    ```
    HelloWorld
    ```

    The Hello World From Resources message appears.

14. Using Notepad, change the HelloWorldStrings.txt file to the following message.

    ```
    Hello World From Resources - New
    ```

15. Save the file.

16. Enter the following text at the command-line prompt and press ENTER.

    ```
    resgen HelloWorldStrings.txt
    ```

17. Enter the following text at the command-line prompt and press ENTER.

    ```
    al /out:HelloWorldStrings.resources.dll
    /linkresource:HelloWorldStrings.resources
    ```

18. Enter the following text at the command-line prompt and press ENTER.

    ```
    HelloWorld
    ```

    The Hello World From Resources - New message appears. You changed the message without changing or recompiling HelloWorld.vb.

19. Close the Visual Studio .NET Command Prompt window.

PART III

Summary

Assemblies are the primary building blocks for Visual Basic .NET applications. They contain the Microsoft Intermediate Language (MSIL) code, metadata about the assembly and types in the application, and references to other files, assemblies, and resources required by the application.

The contents of assemblies make the applications self-describing. That is, they do not depend on other means, such as the Windows registry, for finding their resources. Assemblies also provide an easy method for separating application code from nonexecutable data (resources). This not only simplifies the implementation of localization, but also allows more flexibility in applications.

Test Questions

1. Which of the following is not a feature of assemblies?

   A. They allow side-by-side execution.

   B. They allow execution on UNIX systems.

C. They are a unit of deployment.

D. They provide security boundaries.

2. What makes up the identity of an assembly?

A. The assembly name and version.

B. The assembly name, version, and culture.

C. The assembly name, version, culture, and strong-name public key.

D. The assembly name, version, culture, and strong-name private key.

3. What is the name of the file that results from the following command?

```
vbc /t:module HelloWorld.vb
```

A. HelloWorld.exe

B. HelloWorld.dll

C. HelloWorld.netmodule

D. HelloWorld.resources

4. If you have a resource file called Strings.txt that you want to include in a single file assembly with the MyApp.vb programs, what two steps are required? (Choose two.)

A. make MyApp.vb /resource:Strings.txt

B. resgen Strings.txt

C. vbc /res:Strings.resources MyApp.vb

D. vbc /res:Strings.txt MyApp.vb

5. What utility can you use to view the contents of an assembly?

A. resgen

B. vbc

C. al

D. ildasm

6. What is the extension of the file created by the resgen.exe utility?

A. dll

B. resx

C. resources

D. netmodule

7. You have a source code file that contains classes called **MyClasses.vb**. You do not want to include **MyClasses.vb** in the main assembly file for your application, MyApp.vb. What command do you use to compile the source code?

A. vbc /target:library MyClasses.vb

B. vbc MyApp.vb MyClasses.vb

C. vbc /t:module MyClasses.vb

D. vbc /target:winexe MyClasses.vb

8. If you have the files MyClasses.netmodule, MyApp.netmodule, and MyApp.exe, which file contains the assembly manifest?

A. MyClasses.netmodule

B. MyApp.netmodule

C. MyApp.exe

D. All of the above

9. If you have the files MyClasses.netmodule and MyApp.netmodule, what is the command to create MyApp.exe?

A. al MyClasses.netmodule MyApp.netmodule

B. al MyClasses.netmodule MyApp.netmodule /out:MyApp.exe /t:exe

C. vbc MyClasses.netmodule MyApp.netmodule

D. al MyClasses.netmodule MyApp.netmodule /main:MyApp.Main /out:MyApp.exe /t:exe

10. If you have a resource file called Strings.resources and you want to create a resource-only assembly, what command do you use to create the assembly?

A. vbc /res:Strings.resources /t:library

B. al /out:HelloWorldStrings.resources.dll /linkresource:HelloWorldStrings.resources

C. al /out:HelloWorldStrings.resources.dll /res:HelloWorldStrings.resources

D. al /link:HelloWorldStrings.resources

Test Answers

1. B.
2. C.
3. C.
4. B.
5. D.
6. C.
7. B.
8. C.
9. D.
10. B.

CHAPTER

Assembly Deployment

In this chapter, you will

- Add assemblies to the global assembly cache
- Learn about registering components and assemblies
- Learn how to verify security policies for a deployed application
- Find out how to launch a remote application
- Learn about registering the component in the global assembly cache
- Implement versioning
- Plan, configure, and deploy side-by-side deployments and applications

Assemblies are either private assemblies for a single application or shared assemblies available to multiple applications. Applications that do not share assemblies usually do not require versioning. Versioning helps prevent problems that occur when, for example, a COM class or a Win32 DLL is updated to a new version that does not include features that were available in the older version and are required by an application.

Applications that share assemblies require versioning and other complex capabilities:

- Different versions of the same assembly must be able to run at the same time (side-by-side execution).
- Applications must be able to find and load the version of an assembly required for a specific application.
- When third-party assemblies are upgraded, there must be a guarantee that the provided assembly is from the third party.
- Developers and administrators must be able to override the default version of an assembly.

This chapter focuses on shared assemblies and discusses the .NET Framework features that enable the reliable and appropriate sharing of assemblies: strong-named assemblies, versioning, the global assembly cache, and configuration files.

Strong-Named Assemblies

The reason for strongly naming an assembly is to ensure that the assembly is what it says it is, especially when the assembly is being used by several applications. In order for an assembly to be added to the global assembly cache, it must be strong-named. Also, versioning applies only to assemblies that are strong-named.

A strong name consists of the assembly name, version, culture, public key, and digital signature. The public key and digital signature guarantee that the assembly name, version, and culture have not been tampered with. (The culture applies only to resource-only assemblies. Resource-only assemblies are covered in detail in Chapter 11.)

Strong names provide the following assurances:

- Guarantee the uniqueness of the assembly name
- Confirm that the assembly version is correct
- Verify that the contents of the assembly have not changed

Strong-named assemblies apply to both code assemblies and resource-only assemblies. The procedure for creating a strong-named assembly is the same for either type of assembly. An assembly cannot have a strong name added after it is created. Developers perform the following steps to create a strong-named assembly:

1. Generate or acquire a public/private key pair.
2. Build the .netmodule or .resources file from the source file.
3. Create the assembly using the Assembly Linker (al.exe) with the /keyfile: option.

Creating the Public/Private Key Pair

A public/private key pair is required to generate a strong-named assembly. You can create this pair using the Strong Name tool (sn.exe), or you can acquire the pair from a control source within your organization. The public/private key pair must be in a file that is accessible to the Assembly Linker (al.exe) when the assembly is created.

The following command creates the StrongNamedKey.snk public/private key pair file.

```
sn -k StrongNamedKey.snk
```

EXAM TIP Use the sn.exe utility to create a public/private key pair.

Building the .netmodule or .resources File

You must use Assembly Linker (al.exe) to create a strong-named assembly; you cannot use the Visual Basic .NET Compiler (vbc.exe) to do so. If you are creating a code-based assembly (a .NET library), use the Visual Basic .NET Compiler to create a .netmodule. If you are creating a resource-only assembly, use the Resource Generator (resgen.exe) to create the .resources file.

The following command creates a .netmodule file from Visual Basic .NET source code.

```
vbc /target:module HelloWorldClass.vb
```

The following command creates a .resources file from a text resource file.

```
resgen HelloWorldStrings.txt
```

Generating the Strong-Named Assembly

To create a strong-named assembly, the Assembly Linker (al.exe) requires the private/public key pair file. This file must be located in either the source directory or the output directory. Before creating the strong-named assembly, you must copy the private/public key pair file to the appropriate directory.

The following command creates a strong-named assembly.

```
al /out:HelloWorldClass.dll HelloWorldClass.netmodule
/keyfile:StrongNamedKey.snk
```

The /keyfile: option specifies the private/public key pair filename.

Creating strong-named resource-only assemblies is covered in Chapter 11.

Using Strong-Named Assemblies

Once you have created a strong-named assembly, you can use it when creating application assemblies. Use the /reference: option of the Visual Basic .NET Compiler to use the strong-named assembly.

The following command creates a console application using a strong-named assembly.

```
vbc HelloWorld.vb /reference:HelloWorldClass.dll
```

In Exercise 10-1 you create the HelloWorldClass.dll strong-named assembly, and then use it in the HelloWorld.vb application.

Exercise 10-1: Building and Using a Strong-Named Assembly

1. Create a directory for the files in this exercise. The directory in this example is D:/DotNet/Exercise 10-1. If you use a different name for your directory, replace any reference to D:/DotNet/Exercise 10-1 with your directory name.
2. Using Notepad, create a file called **HelloWorld.vb** in the D:/DotNet/ Exercise 10-1 directory.
3. Add the following text to the file. This text is the same as in Exercise 9-2.

```
Imports System
Imports HelloWorldClass
Public Module HelloWorld
    Sub Main
      Dim oHelloWorld as New HelloWorldClass()
        Console.WriteLine(oHelloWorld.HelloWorld)
    End Sub
End Module
```

This program imports the **HelloWorldClass**, creates an instance of the **HelloWorldClass** object, and uses the object to return the message to display.

4. Save the file.
5. Using Notepad, create a file called **HelloWorldClass.vb** in the D:/DotNet/Exercise 10-1 directory.
6. Add the following text to the file. This text is the same as in Exercise 9-2.

```
Imports System
Public Class HelloWorldClass
    Public Function HelloWorld() as String
      Return "Hello World"
    End Function
End Class
```

   This code defines a simple class that returns the Hello World message.
7. Save the file.
8. Open the Visual Studio .NET Command Prompt window (see Step 5 of Exercise 9-1 for directions on opening this window) and navigate to the D:/DotNet/Exercise 10-1 directory in the command window.
9. Run (enter the command-line prompt and press ENTER) the following text at the command-line prompt to create the HelloWorldClass.netmodule file.

```
vbc /t:module HelloWorldClass.vb
```

10. Run the following text at the command-line prompt to generate a private/public key pair in the StrongNamedKey.snk file.

```
sn -k StrongNamedKey.snk
```

11. Run the following text at the command-line prompt to create the strong-named assembly HelloWorldClass.dll file.

```
al /out:HelloWorldClass.dll HelloWorldClass.netmodule
/keyfile:StrongNamedKey.snk
```

12. Run the following text at the command-line prompt to create the HelloWorld.exe assembly using the strong-named HelloWorldClass.dll assembly.

```
vbc HelloWorld.vb /reference:HelloWorldClass.dll
```

13. Run the following text at the command-line prompt to run the program displaying the Hello World message.

```
HelloWorld
```

14. Run the following text at the command-line prompt.

```
ildasm HelloWorldClass.dll
```

15. Double-click MANIFEST to open the MANIFEST window. You can see the public key as shown in Figure 10-1.
16. Close the MANIFEST window, and then close the IL DASM window.

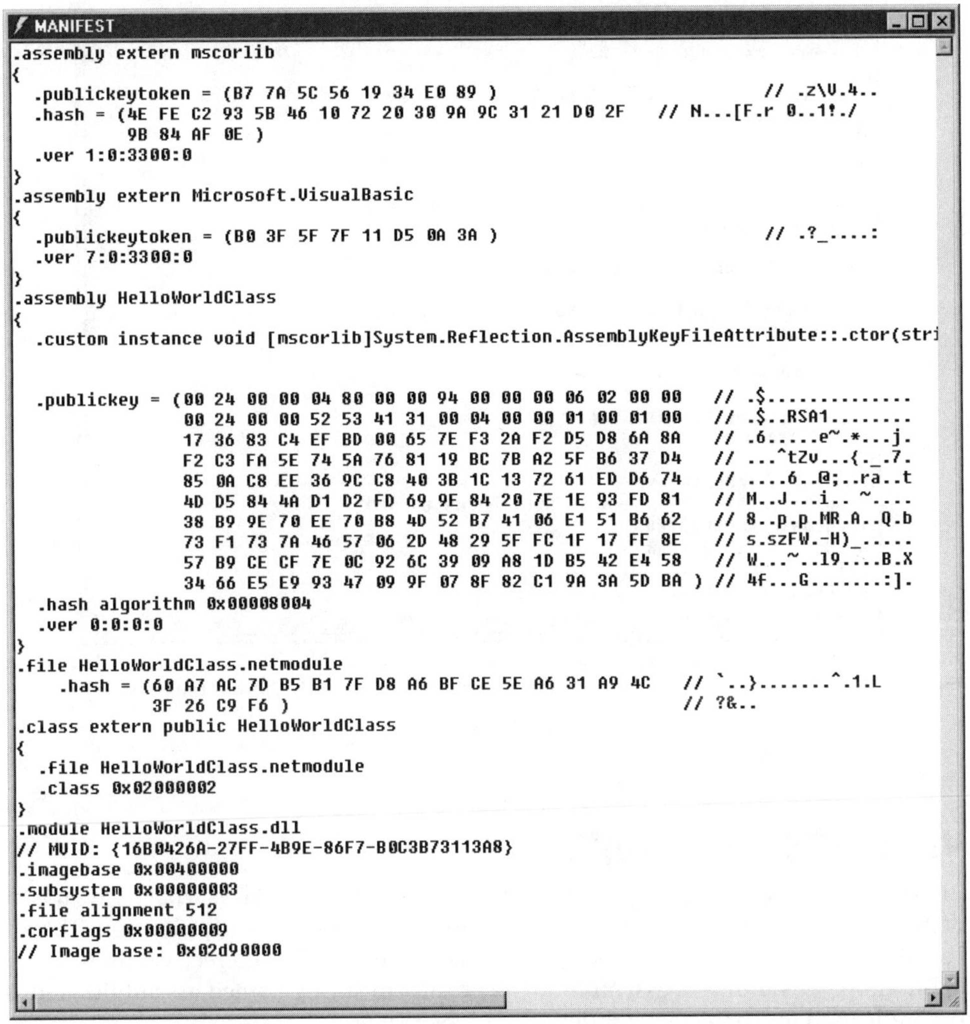

```
MANIFEST
.assembly extern mscorlib
{
  .publickeytoken = (B7 7A 5C 56 19 34 E0 89 )                         // .z\V.4..
  .hash = (4E FE C2 93 5B 46 10 72 20 30 9A 9C 31 21 D0 2F   // N...[F.r 0..1!./
           9B 84 AF 0E )
  .ver 1:0:3300:0
}
.assembly extern Microsoft.VisualBasic
{
  .publickeytoken = (B0 3F 5F 7F 11 D5 0A 3A )                         // .?_....:
  .ver 7:0:3300:0
}
.assembly HelloWorldClass
{
  .custom instance void [mscorlib]System.Reflection.AssemblyKeyFileAttribute::.ctor(stri


  .publickey = (00 24 00 00 04 80 00 00 94 00 00 00 06 02 00 00   // .$..............
                00 24 00 00 52 53 41 31 00 04 00 00 01 00 01 00   // .$..RSA1........
                17 36 83 C4 EF BD 00 65 7E F3 2A F2 D5 D8 6A 8A   // .6.....e~.*...j.
                F2 C3 FA 5E 74 5A 76 81 19 BC 7B A2 5F B6 37 D4   // ...^tZv...{._.7.
                85 0A C8 EE 36 9C C8 40 3B 1C 13 72 61 ED D6 74   // ....6..@;..ra..t
                4D D5 84 4A D1 D2 FD 69 9E 84 20 7E 1E 93 FD 81   // M..J...i.. ~....
                38 B9 9E 70 EE 70 B8 4D 52 B7 41 06 E1 51 B6 62   // 8..p.p.MR.A..Q.b
                73 F1 73 7A 46 57 06 2D 48 29 5F FC 1F 17 FF 8E   // s.szFW.-H)_.....
                57 B9 CE CF 7E 0C 92 6C 39 09 A8 1D B5 42 E4 58   // W...~..19....B.X
                34 66 E5 E9 93 47 09 9F 07 8F 82 C1 9A 3A 5D BA ) // 4f...G.......:].
  .hash algorithm 0x00008004
  .ver 0:0:0:0
}
.file HelloWorldClass.netmodule
    .hash = (60 A7 AC 7D B5 B1 7F D8 A6 BF CE 5E A6 31 A9 4C   // `..}.......^.1.L
             3F 26 C9 F6 )                                      // ?&..
.class extern public HelloWorldClass
{
  .file HelloWorldClass.netmodule
  .class 0x02000002
}
.module HelloWorldClass.dll
// MVID: {16B0426A-27FF-4B9E-86F7-B0C3B73113A8}
.imagebase 0x00400000
.subsystem 0x00000003
.file alignment 512
.corflags 0x00000009
// Image base: 0x02d90000
```

Figure 10-1 The MANIFEST window for the HelloWorldClass.dll assembly showing the public key

17. Run the following text at the command-line prompt.

    ```
    ildasm HelloWorld.exe
    ```

18. Double-click MANIFEST to open the MANIFEST window. You can see the public key token as shown in Figure 10-2.
19. Close the MANIFEST window and the IL DASM window. Then, close the Visual Studio .NET Command Prompt window.

PART III

```
MANIFEST
.assembly extern mscorlib
{
  .publickeytoken = (B7 7A 5C 56 19 34 E0 89 )
  .ver 1:0:3300:0
}
.assembly extern Microsoft.VisualBasic
{
  .publickeytoken = (B0 3F 5F 7F 11 D5 0A 3A )
  .ver 7:0:3300:0
}
.assembly extern HelloWorldClass
{
  .publickeytoken = (37 AF 85 2F 4C 56 3C 68 )
  .ver 0:0:0:0
}
.assembly HelloWorld
{
  .hash algorithm 0x00008004
  .ver 0:0:0:0
}
.module HelloWorld.exe
// MVID: {22A77B9C-CB53-4F9E-8DF7-A27A358AEB4B}
.imagebase 0x00400000
.subsystem 0x00000003
.file alignment 512
.corflags 0x00000001
```

Figure 10-2 The MANIFEST window for the HelloWorld.exe assembly showing the public key token

Versioning Assemblies

Although the assembly's strong name guarantees that the assembly is what it says it is, it does not guarantee that an assembly is the correct assembly for an application. The assembly version is used to determine whether an assembly is the correct assembly for an application. Versioning of assemblies applies only to strong-named assemblies and is primarily used for shared assemblies.

EXAM TIP Versioning applies only to strong-named assemblies.

The version number for an assembly is divided into four parts. These parts are the major version, the minor version, the build, and the revision. Although these parts have specific names, you can use a version number to mean anything that you want. The part names simply imply a usage, as identified in the following list.

- **Major version** A major release that may not be compatible with previous versions, or added or significantly modified features.

- **Minor version** Minor changes to the assembly that may not be compatible with the previous version.
- **Build** Changes that happen over a short time period and may be compatible with the previous version.
- **Revision** Release to a build that fixes a single bug or is a minor modification that is compatible with the previous version.

When any of the version parts change, the assembly is considered to be a new version. The .NET Framework looks at the whole version number (all four parts) to determine whether the assembly version has changed.

EXAM TIP All four parts of the version number are used to uniquely identify an assembly.

You use the Assembly Linker (al.exe) to assign a version number when you create a strong-named assembly. The following command applies a version number to an assembly.

```
al /out:HelloWorldClass.dll HelloWorldClass.netmodule /version:1.0.0.0
/keyfile:StrongNamedKey.snk
```

The /version: (/v:) option specifies the version for the assembly.

In Exercise 10-2 you create a strong-named assembly with a version number, and then use the assembly in an application.

Exercise 10-2: Applying Versioning to a Strong-Named Assembly

1. Create a directory for the files in this exercise. The directory in this example is D:/DotNet/Exercise 10-2. If you use another name for your directory, replace any reference to D:/DotNet/Exercise 10-2 with your directory name.
2. Copy the following files from the D:/DotNet/Exercise 10-1 directory to the D:/DotNet/Exercise 10-2 directory. If you have not completed Exercise 10-1, you can copy the files from the companion CD.
   - HelloWorldClass.vb
   - HelloWorldClass.netmodule
   - HelloWorld.vb
   - StrongNamedKey.snk
3. Open the Visual Studio .NET Command Prompt window (see Step 5 of Exercise 9-1 for directions on opening this window) and navigate to the D:/DotNet/Exercise 10-2 directory in the command window.

4. Run the following text at the command-line prompt to create the strong-named assembly HelloWorldClass.dll file.

```
al /out:HelloWorldClass.dll HelloWorldClass.netmodule /version:1.0.0.0
/keyfile:StrongNamedKey.snk
```

5. Run the following text at the command-line prompt.

```
vbc HelloWorld.vb /reference:HelloWorldClass.dll
```

6. Run the following text at the command line-prompt to run the program displaying the Hello World message.

```
HelloWorld
```

7. Run the following text at the command-line prompt.

```
ildasm HelloWorldClass.exe
```

8. Double-click MANIFEST to open the MANIFEST window. You can see the version as shown in the illustration.

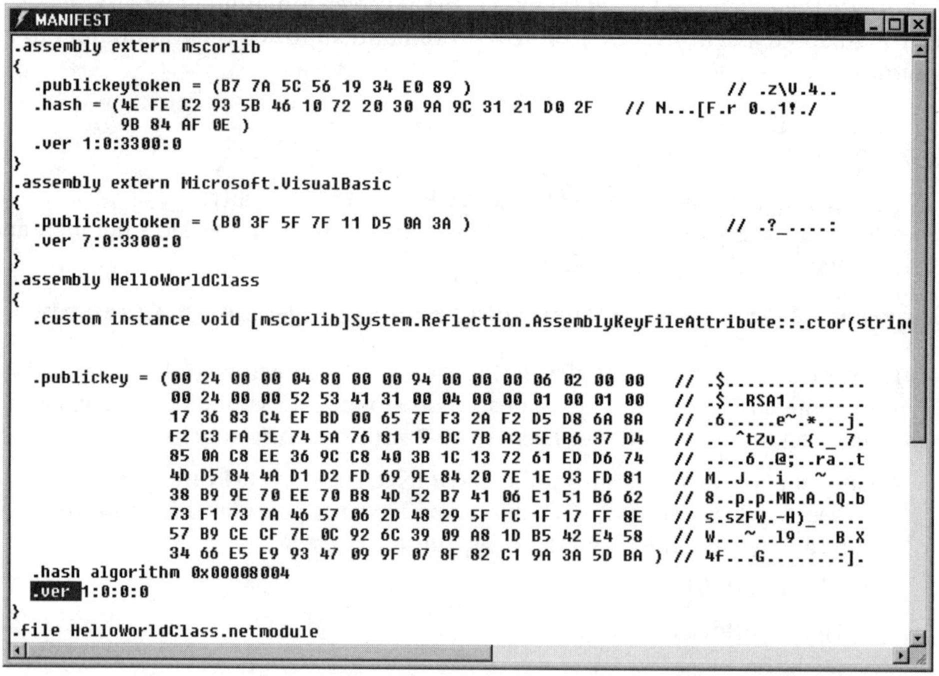

```
MANIFEST
.assembly extern mscorlib
{
  .publickeytoken = (B7 7A 5C 56 19 34 E0 89 )                         // .z\V.4..
  .hash = (4E FE C2 93 5B 46 10 72 20 30 9A 9C 31 21 D0 2F   // N...[F.r 0..1!./
           9B 84 AF 0E )
  .ver 1:0:3300:0
}
.assembly extern Microsoft.VisualBasic
{
  .publickeytoken = (B0 3F 5F 7F 11 D5 0A 3A )                         // .?_....:
  .ver 7:0:3300:0
}
.assembly HelloWorldClass
{
  .custom instance void [mscorlib]System.Reflection.AssemblyKeyFileAttribute::.ctor(strin


  .publickey = (00 24 00 00 04 80 00 00 94 00 00 00 06 02 00 00   // .$..............
                00 24 00 00 52 53 41 31 00 04 00 00 01 00 01 00   // .$..RSA1........
                17 36 83 C4 EF BD 00 65 7E F3 2A F2 D5 D8 6A 8A   // .6.....e~.*...j.
                F2 C3 FA 5E 74 5A 76 81 19 BC 7B A2 5F B6 37 D4   // ...^tZv...{._.7.
                85 0A C8 EE 36 9C C8 40 3B 1C 13 72 61 ED D6 74   // ....6..@;..ra..t
                4D D5 84 4A D1 D2 FD 69 9E 84 20 7E 1E 93 FD 81   // M..J...i.. ~....
                38 B9 9E 70 EE 70 B8 4D 52 B7 41 06 E1 51 B6 62   // 8..p.p.MR.A..Q.b
                73 F1 73 7A 46 57 06 2D 48 29 5F FC 1F 17 FF 8E   // s.szFW.-H)_.....
                57 B9 CE CF 7E 0C 92 6C 39 09 A8 1D B5 42 E4 58   // W...~..19....B.X
                34 66 E5 E9 93 47 09 9F 07 8F 82 C1 9A 3A 5D BA ) // 4f...G.......:].
  .hash algorithm 0x00008004
  .ver 1:0:0:0
}
.file HelloWorldClass.netmodule
```

9. Close the MANIFEST window and the IL DASM window.
10. Run the following text at the command-line prompt.

```
ildasm HelloWorld.exe
```

11. Double-click MANIFEST to open the MANIFEST window. You can see the public key token in the section for the HelloWorldClass as shown here.

```
MANIFEST
.assembly extern mscorlib
{
  .publickeytoken = (B7 7A 5C 56 19 34 E0 89 )                    // .z\
  .ver 1:0:3300:0
}
.assembly extern Microsoft.VisualBasic
{
  .publickeytoken = (B0 3F 5F 7F 11 D5 0A 3A )                    // .?_
  .ver 7:0:3300:0
}
.assembly extern HelloWorldClass
{
  .publickeytoken = (37 AF 85 2F 4C 56 3C 68 )                    // 7..
  .ver 1:0:0:0
}
.assembly HelloWorld
{
  .hash algorithm 0x00008004
  .ver 0:0:0:0
}
.module HelloWorld.exe
// MVID: {710FEC5F-D7DD-4F43-9B51-C8BAA13A321E}
.imagebase 0x00400000
```

12. Close the MANIFEST window and the IL DASM window. Then, close the Visual Studio .NET Command Prompt window.

Adding Assemblies to the Global Assembly Cache

When you use strong-named and versioned assemblies, you usually add them to the global assembly cache (GAC). The GAC is a machine-wide code cache for the common language runtime (CLR) used for storing shared assemblies. Only strong-named assemblies can be stored in the global assembly cache.

EXAM TIP Only strong-named assemblies can be stored in the global assembly cache.

During application development you can use the global assembly cache tool (gacutil.exe) to add the shared assembly to the GAC, or you can use Windows Explorer to drag and drop the shared assembly into the GAC. The GAC is located in the operating system directory (WinNT or Windows) and the *assembly* subdirectory.

The global assembly cache tool and Windows Explorer do not provide the full functionality needed on a production system. Use Windows Installer 2.0 or another appropriate installation tool instead. This allows for the appropriate tracking (reference counting) of the assemblies that exist in the assembly cache.

The following command adds an assembly to the global assembly cache.

```
gacutil /i HelloWorldGClass.dll
```

The GAC directory is unique in that multiple versions of the same file can exist in the directory. For example, version 1.0.0.0 and version 1.1.0.0 of HelloWorldClass.dll can exist in the directory at the same time. This allows the CLR to load different versions of an assembly with the same filename at the same time. This is discussed in more detail later in this chapter.

Side-by-Side Execution

Allowing multiple versions of the same assembly file to exist in the global assembly cache enables side-by-side execution of different versions of the same assembly. In Exercise 10-3 you create multiple versions of the HelloWorldClass.dll file in the GAC, and then create an application to run each of them.

Exercise 10-3: Adding Assemblies to the Global Assembly Cache and Enabling Side-by-Side Execution

1. Create a directory for the files in this exercise. The directory in this example is D:/DotNet/Exercise 10-3. If you use a different name for your directory, replace any reference to D:/DotNet/Exercise 10-3 with your directory name.
2. Copy the following files from the D:/DotNet/Exercise 10-2 directory to the D:/DotNet/Exercise 10-3 directory. If you have not completed Exercise 10-2, you can copy the files from the companion CD.
   - HelloWorldClass.vb
   - HelloWorldClass.dll
   - HelloWorldClass.netmodule
   - HelloWorld.vb
   - HelloWorld.exe
   - StrongNamedKey.snk
3. Open the Visual Studio .NET Command Prompt window (see Step 5 of Exercise 9-1 for directions on opening this window) and navigate to the D:/DotNet/Exercise 10-3 directory in the command window.
4. Run the following text at the command-line prompt to add the HelloWorld Class.dll to the global assembly cache (GAC).
   ```
   gacutil -i HelloWorldClass.dll
   ```
5. Delete the following two files from the D:/DotNet/Exercise 10-3 directory.
   - HelloWorldClass.dll
   - HelloWorldClass.netmodule

6. Run the following text at the command-line prompt to run the program displaying the Hello World message.

```
HelloWorld
```

   Because the HelloWorldClass.dll and HelloWorldClass.netmodule files have been deleted from the application directory, you know that the versions in the GAC are being used.

7. Open My Computer and navigate to the Windows/assembly directory (Windows may be WinNT or another directory where the operating system is installed). You should see the HelloWorldClass entry as shown in Figure 10-3.

8. Using Notepad, create a file called **HelloWorldV11.vb** in the D:/DotNet/Exercise 10-3 directory.

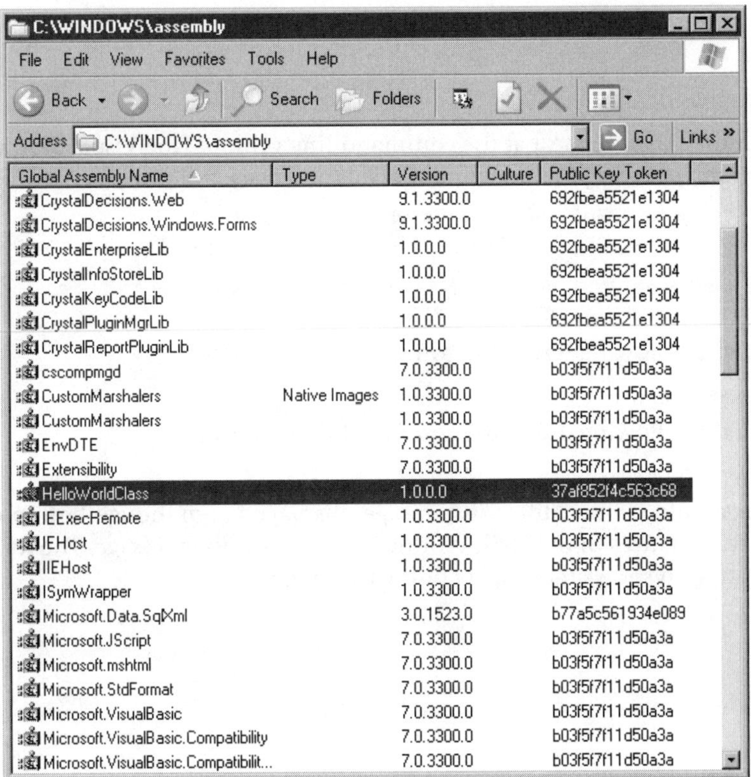

Figure 10-3 The Windows/assembly directory showing HelloWorld in the global assembly cache

9. Add the following text to the file.

```
Imports System
Imports HelloWorldClass
Public Module HelloWorld
    Sub Main
        Dim oHelloWorld as New HelloWorldClass()
        Console.WriteLine(oHelloWorld.HelloWorld)
    Console.ReadLine()
    End Sub
End Module
```

The only difference between HelloWorldV11.vb and HelloWorld.vb is the addition of the Console.ReadLine statement.

10. Save the file.
11. Modify the following line of code in the HelloWorldClass.vb file

```
Return "Hello World"
```

to

```
Return "Hello World - Version 1.1.0.0"
```

12. Save the file.
13. Run the following text at the command-line prompt (the Visual Studio .NET Command Prompt window should still be open) and press ENTER.

```
vbc /t:module HelloWorldClass.vb
al /out:HelloWorldClass.dll HelloWorldClass.netmodule /version:1.1.0.0
/keyfile:StrongNamedKey.snk
vbc HelloWorldV11.vb /reference:HelloWorldClass.dll
gacutil -i HelloWorldClass.dll
```

14. Run the following text at the command-line prompt.

```
HelloWorld
```

15. Run the following text at the command-line prompt.

```
HelloWorldV11
```

You should see two different messages displayed even though both programs create instances of the HelloWorldClass to access the message. The following illustration shows the display of the two messages.

Visual Studio .NET Command Prompt

```
D:\DotNet\Exercise 10-3>vbc HelloWorldV11.vb /reference:HelloWorldClass.dll
Microsoft (R) Visual Basic .NET Compiler version 7.00.9466
for Microsoft (R) .NET Framework version 1.00.3705.288
Copyright (C) Microsoft Corporation 1987-2001. All rights reserved.


D:\DotNet\Exercise 10-3>gacutil -i HelloWorldClass.dll

Microsoft (R) .NET Global Assembly Cache Utility.  Version 1.0.3705.0
Copyright (C) Microsoft Corporation 1998-2001. All rights reserved.

Assembly successfully added to the cache

D:\DotNet\Exercise 10-3>Del HelloWorldClass.dll

D:\DotNet\Exercise 10-3>Del HelloWorldClass.netmodule
D:\DotNet\Exercise 10-3>HelloWorld
Hello World

D:\DotNet\Exercise 10-3>HelloWorldV11
Hello World - Version 1.1.0.0

D:\DotNet\Exercise 10-3>
```

16. Open My Computer and navigate to the Windows/assembly directory (Windows may be WinNT or another directory where the operating system is installed). You should see two HelloWorldClass entries as shown in Figure 10-4.
17. Close the Visual Studio .NET Command Prompt window.

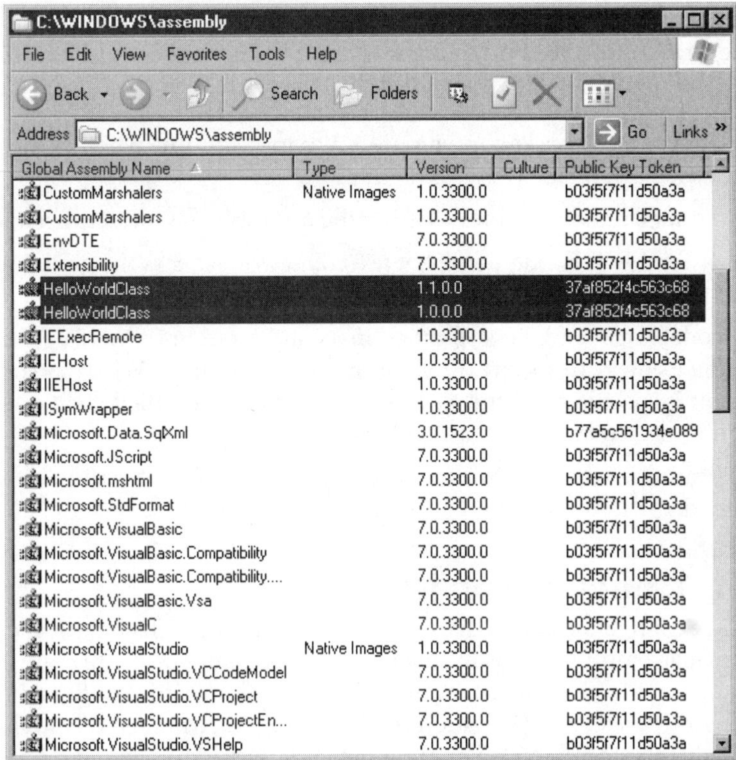

Global Assembly Name	Type	Version	Culture	Public Key Token
CustomMarshalers	Native Images	1.0.3300.0		b03f5f7f11d50a3a
CustomMarshalers		1.0.3300.0		b03f5f7f11d50a3a
EnvDTE		7.0.3300.0		b03f5f7f11d50a3a
Extensibility		7.0.3300.0		b03f5f7f11d50a3a
HelloWorldClass		1.1.0.0		37af852f4c563c68
HelloWorldClass		1.0.0.0		37af852f4c563c68
IEExecRemote		1.0.3300.0		b03f5f7f11d50a3a
IEHost		1.0.3300.0		b03f5f7f11d50a3a
IIEHost		1.0.3300.0		b03f5f7f11d50a3a
ISymWrapper		1.0.3300.0		b03f5f7f11d50a3a
Microsoft.Data.SqlXml		3.0.1523.0		b77a5c561934e089
Microsoft.JScript		7.0.3300.0		b03f5f7f11d50a3a
Microsoft.mshtml		7.0.3300.0		b03f5f7f11d50a3a
Microsoft.StdFormat		7.0.3300.0		b03f5f7f11d50a3a
Microsoft.VisualBasic		7.0.3300.0		b03f5f7f11d50a3a
Microsoft.VisualBasic.Compatibility		7.0.3300.0		b03f5f7f11d50a3a
Microsoft.VisualBasic.Compatibility....		7.0.3300.0		b03f5f7f11d50a3a
Microsoft.VisualBasic.Vsa		7.0.3300.0		b03f5f7f11d50a3a
Microsoft.VisualC		7.0.3300.0		b03f5f7f11d50a3a
Microsoft.VisualStudio	Native Images	1.0.3300.0		b03f5f7f11d50a3a
Microsoft.VisualStudio.VCCodeModel		7.0.3300.0		b03f5f7f11d50a3a
Microsoft.VisualStudio.VCProject		7.0.3300.0		b03f5f7f11d50a3a
Microsoft.VisualStudio.VCProjectEn...		7.0.3300.0		b03f5f7f11d50a3a
Microsoft.VisualStudio.VSHelp		7.0.3300.0		b03f5f7f11d50a3a

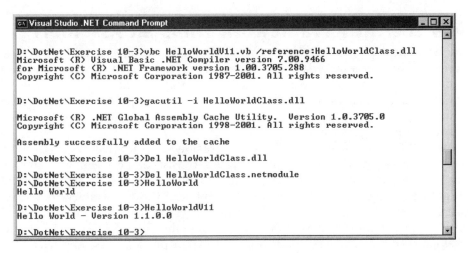

Figure 10-4 The Windows/assembly directory showing two entries for the HelloWorldClass assembly

How the .NET Framework Finds an Assembly

One key to deploying a .NET Framework application is to understand how the .NET Framework finds the appropriate assembly when it is required. You must be sure that all the dependent assemblies for your application are located in the appropriate folder. By default, the .NET Framework uses the exact version of the assembly requested by an application. However, configuration file settings can be made to override the default behavior for finding assemblies.

The .NET Framework usually uses the full assembly reference (identity) to try to find the correct assembly. The full assembly reference consists of the assembly's name, version, culture, and public key token. (The culture applies only to resources, and the public key token applies only to strong-named assemblies.) The .NET Framework also uses partial references to search for assemblies. Partial assembly references are not covered in this book. Search for Partial Assembly References in the Visual Studio .NET integrated development environment (IDE) for more information on partial assembly references.

References to assemblies can be either static or dynamic. Static references are references that the Compiler or Assembly Linker creates and places in the assembly manifest. Dynamic references are created during runtime as a result of methods that load assemblies. The System.Reflection.Assembly.Load method and AppDomain.Load method are examples of Load methods. Once a reference request is established, the steps to locate the assembly are the same regardless of whether the reference is static or dynamic.

To locate an assembly, the.NET Framework performs the following basic steps. Details for each step are provided after this outline.

1. .NET Framework checks configuration files to determine whether the reference is modified by entries in the configuration files.
2. .NET Framework determines whether the assembly has already been loaded.
3. If the assembly is strong-named, .NET Framework checks the global assembly cache for the assembly and loads it if found.
4. If a <codeBase> element is specified in a configuration file, .NET Framework uses the element to specify the location of the assembly. When a <codeBase> element is specified and the assembly is not in the specified location, the assembly search stops with a TypeLoadException.
5. .NET Framework probes for the assembly. If the correct assembly is found, it is loaded; otherwise a TypeLoadException is thrown.

Checking Configuration Files

There are three configuration files that can modify a requested reference or alter where the common language runtime looks for the requested assembly. These files are the application configuration file, the publisher policy file, and the machine configuration file. The .NET Framework checks the application configuration file first, then the publisher policy file, and finally the machine configuration file. Any overrides made in one step may be overridden by the next step. That is, the machine configuration file has the final say.

All three configuration files have the same structure for assembly binding information. The following XML code shows the structure.

```
<assemblyBinding>
  <probing/>
  <publisherPolicy/>
  <dependentAssembly>
    <assemblyIdentity/>
    <bindingRedirect/>
    <codeBase/>
    <publisherPolicy>
  </dependentAssembly>
</assemblyBinding>
```

The <assemblyIdentity> and <bindingRedirect> elements are used in Step 1 to identify any changes in the assembly reference. The <probing> and <codeBase> elements are used during Steps 4 and 5.

A <dependentAssembly> section is created for each node that requires redirection.

The <assemblyIdentity> element identifies the node providing name, culture, and publicKeyToken attributes. The name attribute is required; the culture and publicKeyToken attributes are optional.

The <bindingRedirect> element identifies version redirection. The redirection is specified using the *oldVersion* attribute and the *newVersion* attribute. The oldVersion attribute can be a single version number (major.minor.build.revision) or a range of versions (major.minor.build.revision-major.minor.build.revision). The newVersion attribute is a single version number that becomes the new version for the referenced assembly. The following configuration redirects version 1.0.0.0 of the MyHelloClass.dll assembly to version 1.1.0.0.

```
<configuration>
  <runtime>
    <assemblyBinding xmlns="urn:schemas-microsoft-com:asm.vl">
      <dependentAssembly>
        <assemblyIdentity
          name="HelloWorldClass"
          publicKeyToken="37af852f4c563c68"
        />
        <bindingRedirect oldVersion="1.0.0.0" newVersion="1.1.0.0"/>
      </dependentAssembly>
    </assemblyBinding>
  </runtime>
</configuration>
```

The **xmlns="urn:schemas-microsoft-com:asm.vl"** namespace specification for the <assemblyBinding> section is required.

The *publisher policy file* usually applies to assemblies provided by a third party. When an update is made to a third party's assembly, the publisher can provide a policy file that redirects old versions of the assemblies to new versions. When using these assemblies, you may find it necessary to ignore these policies. The <publisherPolicy> element in the application configuration file allows you to disable the processing of the publisher policy file. Using the <publisherPolicy> element to turn off processing of the publisher policy file is called *using safe mode*. You can use safe mode for individual assemblies by including the <publisherPolicy> element within the <dependentAssembly> section. Or you can use safe mode for all publisher policy files by specifying it in the <assemblyBinding> section. The following configuration uses safe mode for all publisher policy files.

```
<configuration>
  <runtime>
    <assemblyBinding xmlns="urn:schemas-microsoft-com:asm.vl">
      <publisherPolicy apply="no"/>
    </assemblyBinding>
  </runtime>
</configuration>
```

The *apply* attribute of the <publisherPolicy> element sets the policy. It can be either "yes" or "no". Publisher policy files are applied unless explicitly turned off.

The <publisherPolicy> element is available only in the application configuration file.

EXAM TIP The <publisherPolicy apply="no"/> element is used to disable checking of the publisher policy file. It applies only to the application configuration file.

In Exercise 10-4 you use the application configuration file to change the version number of a referenced assembly.

Exercise 10-4: Using the Application Configuration File to Change a Referenced Assembly's Version Number This exercise assumes that you have completed Exercise 10-3, which adds two versions of the HelloWorldClass.dll assembly to the global assembly cache (GAC).

1. Create a directory for the files in this exercise. The directory in this example is D:/DotNet/Exercise 10-4. If you use a different name for your directory, replace any reference to D:/DotNet/Exercise 10-4 with your directory name.
2. Copy the HelloWorld.exe file from the D:/DotNet/Exercise 10-3 directory to the D:/DotNet/Exercise 10-4 directory.
3. Open My Computer and navigate to the Windows/assembly directory (Windows may be WinNT or another directory where the operating system is installed).
4. Find one of the two HelloWorldClass entries. Write down the Public Key Token number for the entry. The Public Key Token number should be the same for both entries.
5. Using Notepad, create a file called **HelloWorld.exe.config** in the D:/DotNet/Exercise 10-4 directory.
6. Add the following text to the file.

```
<configuration>
    <runtime>
        <assemblyBinding xmlns="urn:schemas-microsoft-com:asm.v1">
            <dependentAssembly>
                <assemblyIdentity
```

```
                    name="HelloWorldClass"
                    publicKeyToken="37af852f4c563c68"
                 />
                 <bindingRedirect oldVersion="1.0.0.0" newVersion="1.1.0.0"/>
             </dependentAssembly>
         </assemblyBinding>
     </runtime>
 </configuration>
```

7. Replace the publicKeyToken value with the value you wrote down in Step 4, and then save the file.
8. Open the Visual Studio .NET Command Prompt window (see Step 5 of Exercise 9-1 for directions on opening this window) and navigate to the D:/DotNet/Exercise 10-4 directory in the command window.
9. Run the following command-line prompt.

   ```
   HelloWorld
   ```

   The Hello World Version 1.1.0.0 message should appear.
10. Close the Visual Studio .NET Command Prompt window.

Verifying Whether an Assembly Has Loaded

After any changes have been made to the assembly reference (identity), the common language runtime checks to see if the assembly has already been loaded. If it has already been loaded, it uses the loaded assembly.

NOTE There is a slight possibility of conflict if an application tries to load an assembly that does not have a strong name. If two assemblies exist, MyApp.exe and MyApp.dll, and the MyApp.exe tries to load MyApp.dll, it will not be loaded.

Checking the Global Cache

If the assembly is strong-named and it has not already been loaded, the global cache assembly is checked for it. The global assembly cache contains assemblies that are shared among several applications.

EXAM TIP The global assembly cache is checked only for strong-named assemblies. It is checked before the application's base (root) directory is checked.

Locating the Assembly Using the <codeBase> Element

The location of an assembly can be specified by the <codeBase> element in a configuration file. The <codeBase> element can exist in the application configuration file, the publisher policy file, and the machine configuration files. As with the version, the .NET Framework checks the application file first, then the publisher policy file, and finally the machine configuration file. Any <codeBase> element made in one step for a specific assembly may be overridden by the next step. That is, the machine configuration file has the final say. If a <codeBase> element is specified in the publisher policy file or the machine configuration file, the assembly must be strong-named. Also, if the assembly is strong-named, the <codeBase> element can exist anywhere on the intranet or the Internet.

EXAM TIP Only strong-named assemblies are resolved using the <codeBase> element in the machine configuration file or the publisher policy file.

If a <codeBase> element is specified for an assembly and the assembly is not found at the specified location, the search for the assembly stops with a TypeLoadException exception.

The <codeBase> element has a *version* attribute and an *href* attribute. The version attribute specifies to which version the href attribute applies. The href attribute contains the location of the assembly. The following configuration specifies the location of an assembly.

```
<configuration>
  <runtime>
    <assemblyBinding xmlns="urn:schemas-microsoft-com:asm.vl">
      <dependentAssembly>
        <assemblyIdentity
          name="HelloWorldClass"
          publicKeyToken="37af852f4c563c68"
        />
        <codeBase
          Version="1.0.0.0"
          href="bin/HelloWorldClass.dll"/>
        <codeBase Version="1.1.0.0"
          href="http://www.MyWebServer/HelloWorldClass.dll"/>
      </dependentAssembly>
    </assemblyBinding>
  </runtime>
</configuration>
```

In Exercise 10-5 you change the location of an assembly using the <codeBase> element.

Exercise 10-5: Changing the Location of an Assembly Using the <codeBase> Element

1. Open My Computer and navigate to the Windows/assembly directory (Windows may be WinNT or another directory where the operating system is installed).
2. Delete the two HelloWorldClass entries.
3. Create a directory for the files in this exercise. The directory in this example is D:/DotNet/Exercise 10-5. If you use a different name for your directory, replace any reference to D:/DotNet/Exercise 10-5 with your directory name.
4. Copy the HelloWorld.exe file from the D:/DotNet/Exercise 10-2 directory to the D:/DotNet/Exercise 10-5 directory.
5. Create a bin subdirectory of the D:/DotNet/Exercise 10-5 directory.

6. Copy the following files from the D:/DotNet/Exercise 10-2 directory to the D:/DotNet/Exercise 10-5/bin directory.
   - HelloWorldClass.dll
   - HelloWorldClass.netmodule
7. Using Notepad, create a file called **HelloWorld.exe.config** in the D:/DotNet/Exercise 10-5 directory.
8. Add the following text to the file.

```
<configuration>
    <runtime>
        <assemblyBinding xmlns="urn:schemas-microsoft-com:asm.v1">
            <dependentAssembly>
                <assemblyIdentity
                   name="HelloWorldClass"
                   publicKeyToken="37af852f4c563c68"
                />
                <codeBase version="1.0.0.0" href="bin/HelloWorldClass.dll"/>
            </dependentAssembly>
        </assemblyBinding>
    </runtime>
</configuration>
```

9. Replace the publicKeyToken value with the value you wrote down in Step 4 of Exercise 10-4.
10. Save the file.
11. Open the Visual Studio .NET Command Prompt window (see Step 5 of Exercise 9-1 for directions on opening this window) and navigate to the D:/DotNet/Exercise 10-5 directory in the command window.
12. Run the following command-line prompt.

```
HelloWorld
```

    The Hello World message should appear.
13. Close the Visual Studio .NET Command Prompt window.

PART III

Probing for the Assembly

If the assembly's location has not yet been resolved and no <codeBase> element exists for the assembly, the common language runtime searches the application's root directory using several criteria and techniques. This search is called *probing*.

Probing uses the following data:

- **Application base** The root directory for the application
- **Culture** If specified; resource-only assemblies
- **Assembly name** The textual name for the assembly
- **binpath** The privatePath attribute of the <probing> element in the application configuration file, or the value set by the AppDomain.AppendPrivatePath method

If a culture is specified, probing looks for the following files.

[*application base*]/[*culture*]/[*assembly name*].dll
[*application base*]/[*culture*]/ [*assembly name*]/[*assembly name*].dll
[*application base*]/[*binpath*]/[*culture*]/[*assembly name*].dll
[*application base*]/ /[*binpath*]/[*culture*]/ [*assembly name*]/[*assembly name*].dll

If a culture is not specified, probing looks for the following files.

[*application base*]/[*culture*]/[*assembly name*].dll
[*application base*]/[*culture*]/ [*assembly name*]/[*assembly name*].dll
[*application base*]/[*binpath*]/[*culture*]/[*assembly name*].dll
[*application base*]/ /[*binpath*]/[*culture*]/ [*assembly name*]/[*assembly name*].dll

In Exercise 10-6, you structure the application directory to force the common language runtime to use probing to find the required assembly.

EXAM TIP If the <codeBase> element has been used for specifying the location of an assembly and the assembly is not found at that location, the common language runtime does not do probing.

Exercise 10-6: Using Probing to Find a Requested Assembly

1. Create a directory for the files in this exercise. The directory in this example is D:/DotNet/Exercise 10-6. If you use a different name for your directory, replace any reference to D:/DotNet/Exercise 10-6 with your directory name.
2. Copy the HelloWorld.exe file from the D:/DotNet/Exercise 10-2 directory to the D:/DotNet/Exercise 10-6 directory.
3. Create a bin subdirectory of the D:/DotNet/Exercise 10-6 directory.
4. Copy the following files from the D:/DotNet/Exercise 10-2 directory to the D:/DotNet/Exercise 10-6/bin directory.
    - HelloWorldClass.dll
    - HelloWorldClass.netmodule
5. Using Notepad, create a file called **HelloWorld.exe.config** in the D:/DotNet/ Exercise 10-6 directory.
6. Add the following text to the file.

```
<configuration>
    <runtime>
        <assemblyBinding xmlns="urn:schemas-microsoft-com:asm.v1">
            <dependentAssembly>
                <assemblyIdentity
                   name="HelloWorldClass"
                   publicKeyToken="37af852f4c563c68"
                />
                <codeBase version="1.0.0.0" href="bin/HelloWorldClass.dll"/>
            </dependentAssembly>
        </assemblyBinding>
```

```
    </runtime>
</configuration>
```

7. Replace the publicKeyToken with the value you wrote down in Step 4 of Exercise 10-4.
8. Save the file.
9. Open the Visual Studio .NET Command Prompt window (see Step 5 of Exercise 9-1 for directions on opening this window) and navigate to the D:/DotNet/Exercise 10-6 directory in the command window.
10. Run the following command-line prompt.

    ```
    HelloWorld
    ```

    The Hello World message should appear. It is using the HelloWorldClass.dll assembly in the D:/DotNet/Exercise 10-6/bin directory.
11. Delete the HelloWorld.exe.config file.
12. Rename the bin directory to **HelloWorldClass**.
13. Run the following command-line prompt.

    ```
    HelloWorld
    ```

    The Hello World message should appear. It is using the HelloWorldClass.dll assembly in the D:/DotNet/Exercise 10-6/HelloWorldClass using the automatic probing feature of the common language runtime.
14. Close the Visual Studio .NET Command Prompt window.

Accessing Remote Assemblies

There are two primary methods for accessing a remote application. You can store the application on a remote server, and then download and execute it on your system; or you can actually run the application on a remote server (remoting). Remoting is covered in Chapter 26.

You can access applications directly over the local area network on a remote server, or you can access them using a URL. Your application can use the <codeBase> element in a configuration file to specify a remote location for an assembly. (We discussed the <codeBase> element earlier in this chapter.) You can run the following command line to access an application on another machine.

```
"\\computername\DotNet\Exercise 10-6\HelloWorld"
```

Or, from a browser, you can start an application using a URL, as shown in the following line.

```
http://www.myinternet.com/HelloWorld.exe
```

When an application is loaded from a remote server, that server's location becomes the application base (root) and is used in the probing for dependent assemblies.

Checking the Security Policy

During the development cycle of an application, security is not usually an issue. Developers usually work in a closely connected environment and have more access privileges than the normal user. As an application is deployed, however, security becomes more of a concern. The .NET Framework Configuration tool (mscorcfg.msc) allows developers to review and maintain the security policy that has been established for an application. This section discusses the .NET Framework Configuration tool.

The Runtime Security Policy for the .NET Framework is divided into three major sections: Enterprise, Machine, and User. Each of these sections contains three sections: Code Groups, Permission Sets, and Policy Assemblies. Figure 10-5 shows the .NET Framework Configuration tool with the outline structure of the Runtime Security Policy.

Code groups are used to determine whether an assembly meets a predefined set of membership conditions. If the assembly meets the conditions, the permissions that are defined for the code group are applied to the assembly.

Permission sets include preset permissions that can be applied to code groups. You can define custom permissions if required.

Policy assemblies are used during policy evaluation. You can create custom policy assemblies.

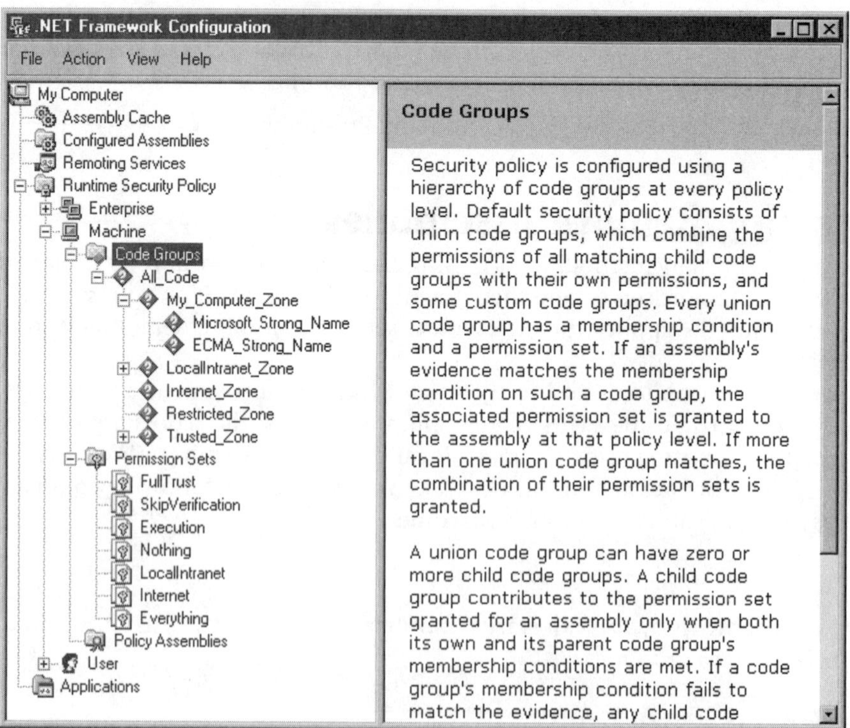

Figure 10-5 The .NET Framework Configuration tool with the expanded Runtime Security Policy node

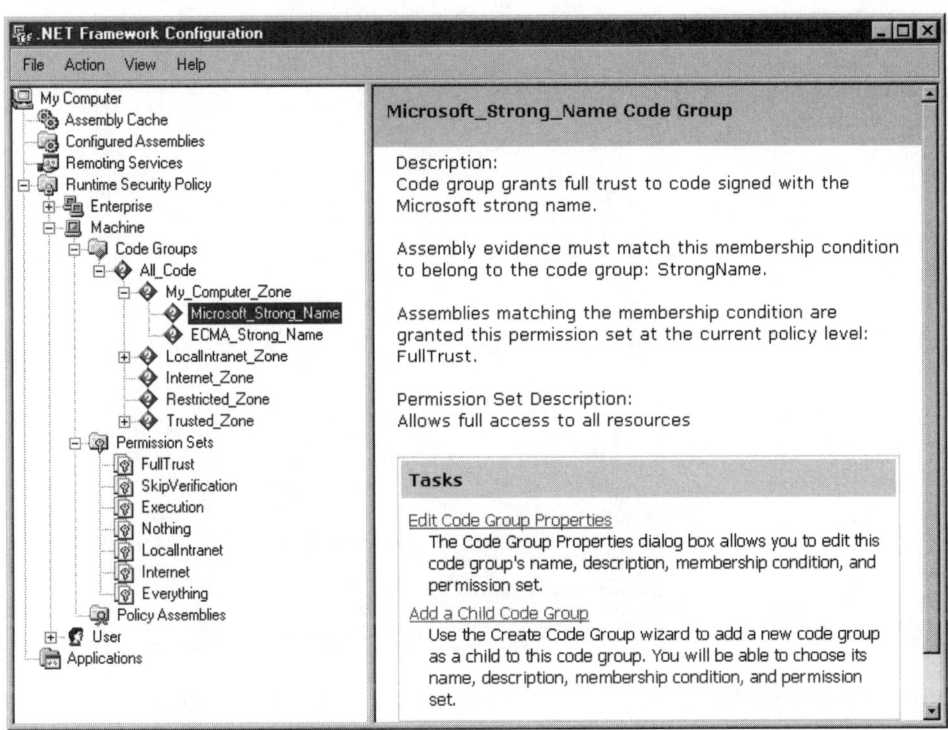

Figure 10-6 Editing and viewing properties of a Runtime Security Policy code group

You can view and edit the properties of a code group by selecting the code group, and then selecting Edit Code Group Properties in the right window as shown in Figure 10-6.

The Code Group Properties dialog box provides a General tab, a Membership Condition tab, and a Permission Set tab as shown in Figure 10-7.

The General tab allows you to enter a name and description, and set two options as shown in Figure 10-7.

The Membership Condition tab allows you to view and set the membership condition for a specific code group. Each membership condition requires different properties. Figure 10-8 shows the Strong Name membership condition and its properties.

There are several predefined membership conditions. These are All Code, Application Directory, Hash, Publisher, Site, Strong Name, URL, and Zone.

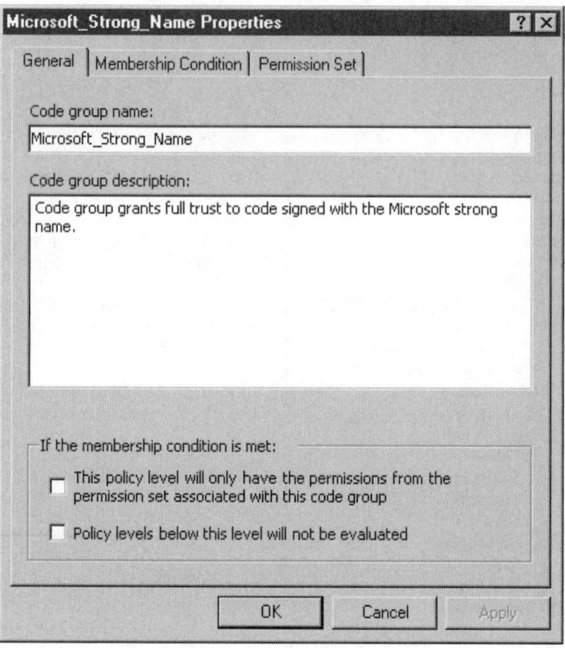

Figure 10-7 The General tab in the Code Group Properties dialog box

The Permission Set tab allows you to select a set of predefined permissions. If the membership condition is met, the assembly receives these permissions. Figure 10-9 shows the LocalIntranet permission set.

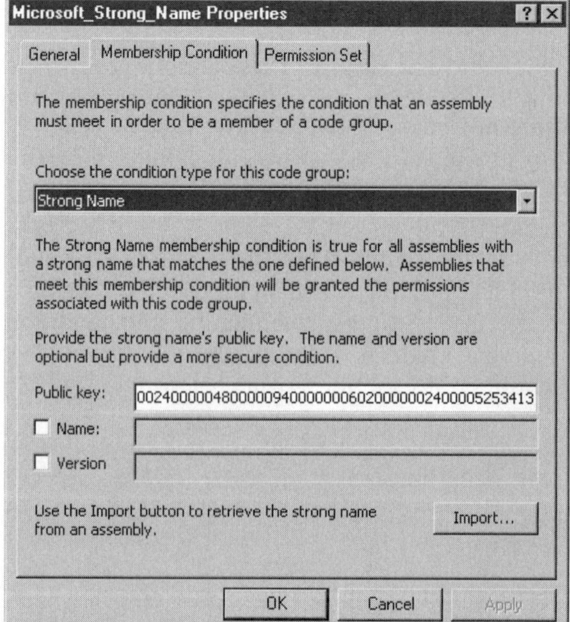

Figure 10-8 Membership conditions for a Runtime Security Policy code group

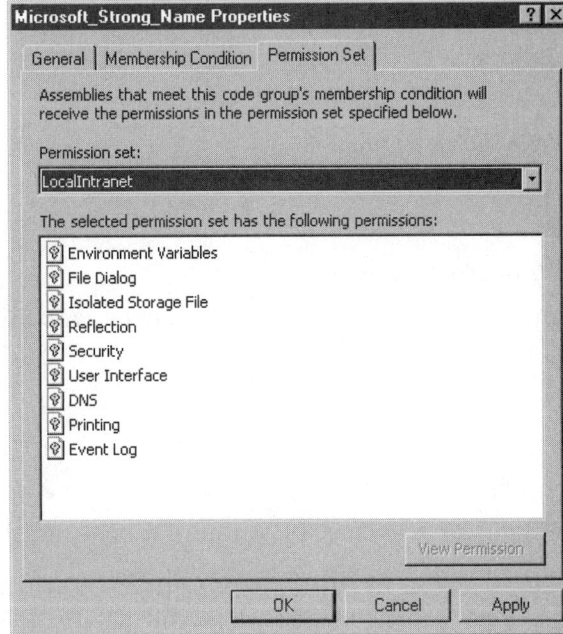

Figure 10-9 Permission set for a Runtime Security Policy code group

Summary

In the .NET Framework you can develop multiple versions of assemblies and allow them to run on the same machine at the same time. Strong-named assemblies are used to distinguish different versions of the same assembly and to guarantee that an assembly has not been modified.

Most assemblies are located in the directory or a subdirectory of the application that references them. This isolates the application from other assemblies on the machine, and makes it more self-contained.

When assemblies need to be shared across multiple applications, the assemblies can be stored in the global assembly cache. Even though the file names of different versions of an assembly are the same, different versions of the files can be stored in the global assembly cache.

You can customize the location of assemblies using the machine configuration file, the publisher policy file, and the application configuration file. These configuration files give you flexibility in choosing the versions of an assembly that run on your system. You can also specify where an assembly can be accessed or downloaded, if the assembly does not exist on your system—that is, if the assembly is on a remote system.

Test Questions

1. Which of the following elements is not part of a strong-named assembly's identity?

   A. Assembly name

   B. Private key

C. Version number
D. Public key

2. Where are shared assemblies stored?
   A. %WinDir%/system32
   B. Program Files/common
   C. %WinDir%/shared
   D. %WinDir%/assembly
3. What utility is used to create a private/public key pair?
   A. vbc
   B. al
   C. sn
   D. ipconfig
4. What is the correct syntax for creating a strong-named assembly?
   A. vbc /t:module MyClass.vb key:KeyFile.snk
   B. al /out:MyClass.dll MyClass.vb /keyfile:KeyFile.snk
   C. al /out:MyClass.dll MyClass.netmodule /keyfile:KeyFile.snk
   D. vbc /t:library MyClass.dll /keyfile:KeyFile.snk
5. Which of the following is not true about versioning?
   A. Multiple versions of the same assembly can execute at the same time.
   B. Multiple versions of the same assembly can be stored in the global assembly cache.
   C. Multiple versions of the same assembly can be stored in the application's root directory.
   D. The version in the application's assembly manifest can be overridden by a configuration file.
6. Which of the following elements is not part of the version number?
   A. Major version
   B. Sub version
   C. Minor version
   D. Build
7. Which part of the version number is used only for informational purposes and not to determine uniqueness?
   A. Major version
   B. Revision

C. Build

D. None

8. What utility can be used to display assembly information?

A. al

B. vbc

C. sn

D. ildasm

9. What does the term side-by-side execution refer to when applied to assemblies?

A. The capability to run two copies of the same application at the same time.

B. The capability to reference the same assembly from two different applications.

C. The capability to run different versions of the same assembly at the same time.

D. None of the above.

10. Which of the following is not a configuration file that the common language runtime checks when resolving the correct assembly to load?

A. The machine configuration file

B. The .NET configuration file

C. The application configuration file

D. The publisher policy file

11. Which configuration file has the higher precedence in determining the location of an assembly?

A. The machine configuration file

B. The .NET configuration file

C. The application configuration file

D. The publisher policy file

12. Which of the following configuration entries inhibits the checking of the publisher policy file?

A. <probing PublisherPolicy="no"/>

B. <publisherPolicy="no"/>

C. <publisherPolicy apply="no"/>

D. <assemblyIdentity publisherPolicy="no" />

13. If a <codeBase> element is specified for an assembly in the application configuration file and the assembly is not found at that location, what happens?

A. The common language runtime looks for a newer version.

B. The common language runtime stops searching and throws an error.

C. The common language runtime continues with probing.

D. The common language runtime looks in the global assembly cache.

14. Choose the location that is checked first for a strong-named assembly?

    A. The application's root directory

    B. The %WinDir%/system directory

    C. The global assembly cache

    D. None of the above

15. Which of the following is not one of the three main levels of the Runtime Security Policy?

    A. System

    B. Machine

    C. User

    D. Enterprise

Test Answers

1. B.
2. D.
3. C.
4. C.
5. C.
6. B.
7. D.
8. D.
9. C.
10. B.
11. A.
12. C.
13. B.
14. C.
15. A.

CHAPTER 11

Resources and Localization

In this chapter, you will

- Implement localizability for the user interface
- Convert existing encodings
- Learn about right-to-left and left-to-right mirroring
- Prepare culture-specific formatting
- Create resource-only assemblies
- Provide multicultural test data to components, pages, and applications

The .NET Framework has several features to aid in developing applications for multiple languages and cultures. If there is a chance that an application is going to provide international support, consider building it to meet this requirement. It is much more difficult to incorporate international support after an application has been implemented.

Globalization and localization are two terms commonly used in discussing international applications. *Globalization* enables an application to handle multiple cultures and languages. *Localization* implements the application for a specific culture, location, or region.

EXAM TIP Globalization is the capability of an application to operate with multiple cultures. Localization is the implementation of the application for a specific culture.

This chapter covers the techniques used in developing your application to allow it to be localized for multiple cultures. The chapter then describes the steps necessary to localize your application for a specific culture.

Globalization

Globalization starts during the design process of an international application. You must identify the cultures and locations that the application is going to support, design the support for these cultures and locations, and then implement code that functions properly independent of which culture or location is implemented. The Microsoft operating systems and the .NET Framework use a concept called cultures/locales (culture). Cultures define sets of rules that are specific to a language and geographic area. These rules include:

- The character set to represent the language
- The direction in which the language is displayed (e.g., right-to-left, left-to-right, or top-to-bottom)
- The formatting of dates, times, and numbers
- How words and lines are wrapped from one line to the next line

In addition to the rules that apply to a culture, you must provide for the translation of the text and images displayed to the user. The .NET Framework enables the system to separate application code from data that is displayed to the user. You use resource assemblies to globalize an application. Then, you create specific culture resource assemblies to localize it. Chapter 9 described—and provided a simple exercise for—using resource assemblies to localize an application.

Culture Property and UICulture Property in the .NET Framework

The names of the cultures in the Windows operating systems and the .NET Framework conform to the Internet RFC 1766 standard *Tags for the Identification of Languages* format. This format is *<languagecode>-<country/regioncode>*. The <languagecode> codes are specified in the ISO 369 standard, *Code for the representation of names of languages,* and the <country/regioncode> codes are specified in the ISO 3166 standard, *Codes for the representation of names of countries*. The <languagecode> codes use two lowercase characters and the <country/regioncode> codes usually use two uppercase characters. Table 11-1 is a sample list of culture names. For a full list of culture names see the CultureInfo Class section in the .NET Framework documentation.

The .NET Framework includes the **System.Globalization** namespace, which contains classes that define culture-related information about language, calendars, formats, currency, numbers, and sorting order. The .NET Framework uses two different specifications: the culture and the UICulture. The *culture* specifies the language characteristics, environment, and conventions. The *UICulture* is used solely for determining which resources are used. For example, the culture setting is used when determining the format of a date or number. The UICulture setting is used when loading specific text to be displayed from a resource-only assembly.

EXAM TIP The *UICulture* is used for accessing resource assemblies.

Table 11-1 Sample of Internet RFC 1766 Culture Names

Culture Name	Language-Country/Region
ar-DZ	Arabic - Algeria
ar-EG	Arabic - Egypt
bg-BG	Bulgarian - Bulgaria
da-DT	Danish - Denmark
en-CA	English - Canada
en-US	English - United States
fr-FR	French - France
fr-CA	French - Canada
de-DE	German - Germany
de-AT	German - Austria
zh-CN	Chinese - China

Specific Culture, Neutral Culture, and Invariant Culture Definitions

The terms *specific culture, neutral culture,* and *invariant culture* are used throughout the .NET Framework documentation. Their definitions follow.

- **Specific culture** A fully qualified culture containing both the <languagecode> code and the <country/regioncode> code. *fr-FR* and *fr-CA* are examples of a specific culture.
- **Neutral culture** A culture that contains only the <languagecode> code. *fr* and *en* are examples of neutral cultures.
- **Invariant culture** A culture that can be used to work with data that is not culture dependent. It is based on the English language and has no region or country specification. It is distinguished from the *en* neutral culture because it can be used for culture information when a neutral culture cannot be used. For example, you may need to store information such as dates in an invariant culture so that you can access the information knowing that it is in a specific format and then display it in the user's culture.

Working with the CultureInfo Class

The **CultureInfo** class in the **System.Globalization** namespace is used for working with culture information. You can create instances of culture information that can be used with other classes or for changing the current culture information. Culture information is thread specific, so when changing the current culture information, you change it on the current thread. The following code changes the current culture to the German language in Germany (de-DE).

```
Thread.CurrentThread.CurrentCulture = new CultureInfo("de-DE").
```

CurrentCulture must be a specific culture. It cannot be a neutral or invariant culture.

EXAM TIP When you set CurrentCulture for a thread, CurrentCulture must be culture specific.

In Exercise 11-1 you change the current culture to display different dates.

Exercise 11-1: Changing the Culture Setting

1. Create a directory for the files in this exercise. The directory in this example is D:/DotNet/Exercise 11-1. If you use a different name for your directory, replace any reference to D:/DotNet/Exercise 11-1 with your directory name.
2. Using Notepad, create a file called **ChangeCulture.vb** in the D:/DotNet/Exercise 11-1 directory.
3. Add the following text to the file.

```
Imports System
Imports System.Globalization
Imports System.Threading
Module Module1
    Sub Main()
        Dim DateString As String = "03/07/03"
        Dim TestDate As DateTime = DateString
        Console.WriteLine(TestDate.ToLongDateString)
        Thread.CurrentThread.CurrentCulture = New CultureInfo("en-GB")
        TestDate = DateString
        Console.WriteLine(TestDate.ToLongDateString)
    End Sub
End Module
```

   This code sets the appropriate imports for **System.Globalization** and **System.Threading.** The **CultureInfo** class is in the **System.Globalization** namespace. The **Thread** class for setting the CurrentCulture of the CurrentThread is also in the **System.Globalization** namespace.

   The code initializes the DateString variable to **03/07/03**. The DateString variable is used for setting the TestDate variable before and after the culture has been changed, thereby simulating user input. The code assumes that the default culture is en-US. The long format for the date is written to the console for both the default culture and the en-GB culture.

4. Save the file. Be sure to save the file without the .txt extension.
5. Open the Visual Studio .NET Command Prompt window (see Step 5 of Exercise 9-1 for directions on opening this window) and navigate to the D:/DotNet/Exercise 11-1 directory in the command window.
6. Run the following text at the command-line prompt.

```
vbc ChangeCulture.vb
```

7. Run the following text at the command-line prompt.

```
ChangeCulture
```

   The two dates should appear as shown in the following illustration. There are two significant differences in the dates. First, the date formats are different.

Second, the dates themselves are different. The month and day values have been changed. This difference is discussed in more detail later in the chapter.

```
Visual Studio .NET Command Prompt
Setting environment for using Microsoft Visual Studio .NET tools.
(If you also have Visual C++ 6.0 installed and wish to use its tools
from the command line, run vcvars32.bat for Visual C++ 6.0.)

C:\Documents and Settings\FowlerR>d:

D:\>cd DotNet

D:\DotNet>cd "Exercise 11-1

D:\DotNet\Exercise 11-1>vbc ChangeCulture.vb
Microsoft (R) Visual Basic .NET Compiler version 7.00.9466
for Microsoft (R) .NET Framework version 1.00.3705.288
Copyright (C) Microsoft Corporation 1987-2001. All rights reserved.


D:\DotNet\Exercise 11-1>ChangeCulture
Friday, March 07, 2003
03 July 2003

D:\DotNet\Exercise 11-1>
D:\DotNet\Exercise 11-1>
```

8. Close the Visual Studio .NET Command Prompt window.

Unicode and Code Pages for Languages in the .NET Framework

Each character of a specific language is processed internally as a number. When applications were limited to a single language, this did not present a problem. In fact, different operating systems used different encodings (numbering) for the same character set. With the expansion of information technology, a more standardized method of language encoding has evolved.

Code pages were developed for use with a specific language or set of languages that use the same characters. The Windows operating systems use code pages that contain 256 code points (characters, punctuation, symbols, and special characters). Most of these code pages have a common set of points for the code points 0 through 127. The code points 128 through 255 are significantly different for each code page. Because 256 characters are not sufficient for some languages, double-byte character sets (DBCS) were developed for languages such as Chinese and Japanese. Numbers are used to identify code pages. Table 11-2 lists sample code pages and their numeric identifiers.

One problem with code pages is that they do not allow the mixing of multiple code pages within the same data stream; therefore, it is difficult to display multiple languages on the same page. The .NET Framework uses the Unicode standard as its default character scheme. Unicode is designed to support multilingual character sets. Every character (regardless of language), operating system, or program is represented by a unique code point. Unicode is an industry standard supported by the Unicode Consortium; the consortium's Web site is located at www.unicode.org.

Table 11-2 Sample Code Pages and Their Numeric Identifiers

Code Page	Description
437	MS-DOS U.S. English
850	Multilingual (MS-DOS Latin1)
950	Chinese (Traditional)
1250	Central European
1252	Latin1 (ANSI)
1253	Greek
1254	Turkish
1255	Hebrew
1256	Arabic
1257	Baltic
1258	Vietnamese

EXAM TIP The .NET Framework is Unicode by default.

The .NET Framework provides classes in the **System.Text** namespace that allow you to convert between code pages and Unicode. The following list summarizes these classes.

- **ASCIIEncoding** Encodes between Unicode characters and 7-bit ASCII characters
- **UnicodeEncoding** Encodes between Unicode characters and consecutive bytes
- **UTF7Encoding** Encodes between Unicode characters and UTF-7 characters
- **UTF8Encoding** Encodes between Unicode characters and UTF-8 characters

The GetBytes method for each of these classes converts arrays of Unicode characters to arrays of bytes. The GetChars method for each of these classes converts arrays of bytes to arrays of Unicode characters.

Bi-directional Text and Mirroring

Some languages read right-to-left. Sometimes, Windows forms and Web forms must be able to display some text left-to-right and other text, in a different language on the same page, from right-to-left. The term *bi-directional* is used to describe applications that provide this capability. Windows forms in the .NET Framework allow you to specify the form and/or individual controls to display text right-to-left by setting the RightToLeft property for the form or controls.

ASP.NET uses the *dir* attribute to set the text direction. You can use this attribute with the <HTML> tag, the <BODY> tag, the <TABLE> tag, and many other HTML tags. You can also set the dir property for the HTML server controls. The attribute values are *rtl* and *ltr* for right-to-left and left-to-right respectively. The following HTML code provides an example of using the dir attribute.

```
<HTML dir="rtl">
```

Windows 2000 and later support mirroring to handle right-to-left language conversion for the localized culture. Mirroring is also supported in Windows 98 for the localized versions of Arabic and Hebrew. Mirroring depends upon Windows and is not directly supported in the .NET Framework. In addition, it does not address the issue of displaying multiple languages on the same Windows form.

Using Fonts

Fonts are used to format the language characters for output to devices. Developers have become accustomed to changing default fonts to custom fonts that enhance their applications. This luxury should be avoided when developing international applications. Fonts do not contain all the characters necessary to support all Unicode characters. Using the default font allows the system to adjust to the language that has been established for the user's machine.

Working with Strings

Textual data and images for international applications should be stored in resource-only assemblies. More details on using resource-only assemblies to store the textual data and images is covered later in this chapter. When you use strings in international applications, you must be careful to take into account concatenation, string length, and sorting and comparison.

String Concatenation

When expressions are concatenated in the English language they may make sense to the user. However, the same concatenation in other languages may not make sense. Strings that make perfect sense as individual strings may not make sense as concatenated strings because of gender, word order, or translation. It is best to work with strings as a whole and not form new strings by concatenating multiple strings. This increases the size of resource files but it avoids difficulties (bugs) when localizing an application.

String Length

Most languages require more space for textual information than the English language. The .NET Framework documentation provides guidelines for allowing for string size increases in international applications, as shown in Table 11-3.

Sorting and Comparison

The sorting and comparison of string data is a complex issue in an international application. Even within the English language sorting and comparing data has not been straightforward. For example, case-sensitive and case-insensitive sorting and comparisons are often an issue. The .NET Framework allows you to specify the culture when performing sorting and comparison functions. The **Array** class allows you to sort based on the current culture, and the **CompareInfo** class in the **System.Globalization** namespace allows you to specify various compare options for comparing strings and characters.

Table 11-3 String Size Increase for Language Translation, As Described in the .NET Framework Documentation

English Size	Added Size
1 to 4 characters	100%
5 to 10 characters	80%
11 to 20 characters	60%
21 to 30 characters	40%
31 to 50 characters	20%
Over 50 characters	10%

Working with Dates

Date formatting is a good example of why the culture is divided into two sections, the language and the location. Depending on whether you are in the United States or in Europe, the short date format is different. In the United States the format is mm/dd/yy. In Europe, the format is dd/mm/yy. If a user enters **03/07/03**, what date does the entry refer to? It depends on the location of the user or more precisely, the culture in effect for processing the entered date. Exercise 11-1 provided a simple example of how date information can vary depending on culture. The code for the Main() subroutine in the exercise is repeated here.

```
Dim DateString As String = "03/07/03"
Dim TestDate As DateTime = DateString
Console.WriteLine(TestDate.ToLongDateString)
Thread.CurrentThread.CurrentCulture = New CultureInfo("en-GB")
TestDate = DateString
Console.WriteLine(TestDate.ToLongDateString)
```

Assuming the default culture is en-US, the DateString value represents March 7, 2003. However, when the culture is changed to en-GB, the DateString value represents July 3, 2003.

In addition, the ToLongDateString method is different for each culture. The en-US culture format is Friday, March 7, 2003. The en-GB culture format is 03 July 2003.

It is not always appropriate to change the current culture in order to format information. An application may not reside on the machine that is requesting the information. An application may be responding to Web requests, acting as a Web service, or running remotely. In this case you may need to format the data with respect to the requestor's culture. Once you have determined the requestor's culture, you can use the ToString method of the date object to format the information.

The ToString method allows you to specify a format string and a format provider, as shown in the following code segment.

```
TestDate.ToString("D", oUserCulture.DateTimeFormat)
```

The format string *"D"* specifies the long date format; oUserCulture is an instance of the **CultureInfo** class for the user's culture; and DateTimeFormat specifies the format information for that class. The **CultureInfo** class implements the IFormatProvider interface, which is discussed later in this chapter. Some of the format strings for dates are listed in Table 11-4. A complete list can be found in the DateTimeFormatInfo Class section of the .NET Framework documentation.

Table 11-4 Sample Format Characters for Dates and Times (Format Sample for en-US)

Format Character	Description
d	Short date (7/3/2003)
D	Long date (Friday, July 3, 2003)
f	Full date and short time (Friday, July 3, 2003 10:12 PM)
F	Full date and time (Friday, July 03, 2003 10:12:53 PM)

The ToString method also allows you to specify format patterns. However, for international applications, this is not a good technique because it does not allow the format to change for different cultures.

In Exercise 11-2 you change the culture for date formats using a **CultureInfo** class.

Exercise 11-2: Formatting Dates Using the ToString Method and a CultureInfo Object

1. Create a directory for the files in this exercise. The directory in this example is D:/DotNet/Exercise 11-2. If you use a different name for your directory, replace any reference to D:/DotNet/Exercise 11-2 with your directory name.
2. Using Notepad, create a file called **DateFormats.vb** in the D:/DotNet/Exercise 11-2 directory.
3. Add the following text to the file.

```
Imports System
Imports System.Globalization
Imports System.Threading
Module Module1
    Sub Main()
        Dim TestDate As DateTime = "03/07/03 10:12:53 PM"
        Dim oUserCulture As New CultureInfo("en-US")
        Console.WriteLine(TestDate.ToString("d", UserCulture.DateTimeFormat))
        Console.WriteLine(TestDate.ToString("D", UserCulture.DateTimeFormat))
        Console.WriteLine(TestDate.ToString("f", UserCulture.DateTimeFormat))
Console.WriteLine(TestDate.ToString("F", UserCulture.DateTimeFormat))
    End Sub
End Module
```

4. Save the file.
5. Open the Visual Studio .NET Command Prompt window (see Step 5 of Exercise 9-1 for directions on opening this window) and navigate to the D:/DotNet/Exercise 11-2 directory in the command window.
6. Run the following text at the command-line prompt.

```
vbc DateFormats.vb
```

7. Run the following text at the command-line prompt.

```
DateFormats
```

8. Change the following line

```
Dim oUserCulture As New CultureInfo("en-US")
```

to

```
Dim oUserCulture As New CultureInfo("en-GB")
```

PART III

9. Save the file.
10. Run the following text at the command-line prompt.

    ```
    vbc DateFormats.vb
    ```

11. Run the following text at the command-line prompt.

    ```
    DateFormats
    ```

    The two sets of formats should be displayed in the Visual Studio .NET Command Prompt window as shown in the illustration.

```
Visual Studio .NET Command Prompt
D:\DotNet\Exercise 11-2>vbc DateFormats.vb
Microsoft (R) Visual Basic .NET Compiler version 7.00.9466
for Microsoft (R) .NET Framework version 1.00.3705.288
Copyright (C) Microsoft Corporation 1987-2001. All rights reserved.


D:\DotNet\Exercise 11-2>DateFormats
3/7/2003
Friday, March 07, 2003
Friday, March 07, 2003 10:12 PM
Friday, March 07, 2003 10:12:53 PM

D:\DotNet\Exercise 11-2>vbc DateFormats.vb
Microsoft (R) Visual Basic .NET Compiler version 7.00.9466
for Microsoft (R) .NET Framework version 1.00.3705.288
Copyright (C) Microsoft Corporation 1987-2001. All rights reserved.


D:\DotNet\Exercise 11-2>DateFormats
07/03/2003
07 March 2003
07 March 2003 22:12
07 March 2003 22:12:53

D:\DotNet\Exercise 11-2>
```

12. Close the Visual Studio .NET Command Prompt window.

When extracting month, day, year, hour, minute, and second information you use properties provided with the **DateTime** class. As demonstrated in Exercise 11-2, you cannot depend on the value's position in the string representation of the date. The DateTime properties for the date parts are *day, month, year, hour, minute,* and *second.* The following code gets the month from a DateTime variable.

```
Dim TestMonth as Integer = TestDate.Month
```

Working with Numbers and Currency

Number formatting in international applications is similar to date formatting. Number and currency formats are different for different languages and for different countries and regions within a language. You use the number variable's ToString method and the **CultureInfo** class. The **CultureInfo** class method for number formats is NumberFormat as shown in the following code segment.

```
TestNumber.ToString("c", oUserCulture.NumberFormat)
```

Table 11-5 lists the format strings for numbers. More details can be found in the NumberFormatInfo Class section of the .NET Framework documentation.

Table 11-5 Format Characters for Numbers (Format Sample for en-US)

Format Character	Description
c, C	Currency format
d, D	Decimal format
e, E	Scientific (exponential) format
f, F	Fixed-point format
g, G	General format
n, N	Number format
r, R	Roundtrip format
x, X	Hexadecimal format

In Exercise 11-3 you change the culture for number formats using a **CultureInfo** object.

Exercise 11-3: Formatting Numbers Using the ToString Method and a CultureInfo Object

1. Create a directory for the files in this exercise. The directory in this example is D:/DotNet/Exercise 11-3. If you use a different name for your directory, replace any reference to D:/DotNet/Exercise 11-3 with your directory name.
2. Using Notepad, create a file called **NumberFormats.vb** in the D:/DotNet/Exercise 11-3 directory.
3. Add the following text to the file.

```
Imports System
Imports System.Globalization
Imports System.Threading
Module Module1
    Sub Main()
       Dim TestDouble As Double = "1234.666"
       Dim TestInteger As Integer = 1234
       Dim oUserCulture As New CultureInfo("en-US")

Console.WriteLine(TestDouble.ToString("c",oUserCulture.NumberFormat))
       Console.WriteLine(TestInteger.ToString("d", UserCulture.NumberFormat))
Console.WriteLine(TestDouble.ToString("e",UserCulture.NumberFormat))

Console.WriteLine(TestDouble.ToString("f",oUserCulture.NumberFormat))

Console.WriteLine(TestDouble.ToString("g",oUserCulture.NumberFormat))

Console.WriteLine(TestDouble.ToString("n",oUserCulture.NumberFormat))

Console.WriteLine(TestDouble.ToString("r",oUserCulture.NumberFormat))

Console.WriteLine(TestInteger.ToString("x",oUserCulture.NumberFormat))
    End Sub
End Module
```

PART III

When entering the preceding text, be sure to distinguish between TestDouble variable and TestInteger variable. The *d* and *r* format characters do not accept variables of the double type.

4. Save the file.
5. Open the Visual Studio .NET Command Prompt window (see Step 5 of Exercise 9-1 for directions on opening this window) and navigate to the D:/DotNet/Exercise 11-3 directory in the command window.
6. Run the following text at the command-line prompt.

```
vbc NumberFormats.vb
```

7. Run the following text at the command-line prompt.

```
DateFormats
```

8. Change the following line

```
Dim oUserCulture As New CultureInfo("en-US")
```

to

```
Dim oUserCulture As New CultureInfo("fr-FR")
```

9. Save the file.
10. Run the following text at the command-line prompt.

```
vbc NumberFormats.vb
```

11. Run the following text at the command-line prompt.

```
NumberFormats
```

The two sets of formats should be displayed in the Visual Studio .NET Command Prompt window as shown in the illustration.

```
D:\DotNet\Exercise 11-3>vbc NumberFormats.vb
Microsoft (R) Visual Basic .NET Compiler version 7.00.9466
for Microsoft (R) .NET Framework version 1.00.3705.288
Copyright (C) Microsoft Corporation 1987-2001. All rights reserved.


D:\DotNet\Exercise 11-3>NumberFormats
$1,234.67
1234
1.234666e+003
1234.67
1234.666
1,234.67
1234.666
4d2

D:\DotNet\Exercise 11-3>vbc NumberFormats.vb
Microsoft (R) Visual Basic .NET Compiler version 7.00.9466
for Microsoft (R) .NET Framework version 1.00.3705.288
Copyright (C) Microsoft Corporation 1987-2001. All rights reserved.


D:\DotNet\Exercise 11-3>NumberFormats
1 234,67 ?
1234
1,234666e+003
1234,67
1234,666
1 234,67
1234,666
4d2

D:\DotNet\Exercise 11-3>
```

12. Close the Visual Studio .NET Command Prompt window.

Classes That Implement the IFormatProvider Interface

The IFormatProvider interface provides the format interface for the **CultureInfo** class. The **CultureInfo** class uses the **DateTimeFormatInfo** class and the **NumberFormatInfo** class to provide culture-specific formatting information. When a method has a parameter of type **IFormatProvider**, you can use the DateTimeFormat and the NumberFormat objects to provide the necessary formatting details. The ToString method is an example of a method that has a parameter of type **IFormatProvider**. Exercise 11-2 and Exercise 11-3 demonstrated the use of the ToString method for variables of the DateTime, Double, and Integer type. The following code segments demonstrate the IFormatProvider interface as used in these exercises.

```
TestDate.ToString("d", oUserCulture.DateTimeFormat))
TestDouble.ToString("c",oUserCulture.NumberFormat))
TestInteger.ToString("d", oUserCulture.NumberFormat))
```

Working with Resource-Only Assemblies for Cultural Resources

One of the major tasks in implementing an international application is working with the different languages. Writing the application code to handle the different cultures does not address the actual textual information that is presented to the user. The .NET Framework uses resource-only assemblies (satellite assemblies) to provide for the variations in textual information and images for different languages and cultures. The UICulture setting within a .NET application automatically identifies the correct resource assemblies to use. The UICulture setting can be specified as a configuration setting or it can be set in code. The value of this setting is the CultureInfo.CurrentUICulture property. It is a different setting than the Culture setting, which is the value of the CultureInfo.CurrentCulture property that has been used in previous examples in this chapter.

You can create different resource assemblies for each culture in an application. It is common to develop an application using the en-US culture. The resources for this culture are incorporated into the main assembly for the application. You use them to test the successful implementation of a globalization of the application. This is the normal unit testing and system testing for any application.

NOTE Even if you are not creating international applications, it is a good practice to use resource files for the main application. Doing so allows you to create the application while others are still deciding on the actual wording of the textual information presented to the user. You do not want to have to modify the application code every time a manager or potential user decides that the wording for a prompt should be changed.

Creating Resource Assemblies

You create resource files that can be included into assemblies or used to create resource-only assemblies. The .NET Framework supports only one type of resource file. It is a special binary file and has the .resources extension. You define the resources in another file, and then use the Resource File Generator (resgen.exe) to create the .resource file. In Exercise 9-3 in Chapter 9, you created and used a resource assembly that is included in the main assembly for the HelloWorld.exe application.

The Resource File Generator (resgen.exe) works with text files (.txt) and with XML-based resource files (.resx). XML-based resource files are fairly complex to edit using a text editor. You can edit XML-based resource files using the Visual Studio .NET integrated development environment (IDE) or the Windows Forms Resource Editor (WinRes.exe). During application development, the Visual Studio .NET IDE provides the best functionality for creating resource files and synchronizing multiple resource files for different cultures. Groups that localize the application to individual cultures can use the Windows Forms Resource Editor. You may not want to provide these groups with the entire application.

In Exercise 11-4 you use the Visual Studio .NET IDE to create resource files for a simple HelloWorld application. This exercise assumes that you are familiar with the basics of creating Windows form applications using the Visual Studio .NET IDE. If you need help in creating the application and using the IDE, please review Chapter 15.

Exercise 11-4: Creating and Using Resource Files with the Visual Script .NET IDE

1. Open the Visual Studio .NET IDE and select the **New Project** object from the Start Page.
2. Under Project Types, select Visual Basic Projects.
3. Under Templates, select Windows Application.
4. Change the Name text box to read **MyResources**. Select OK. The resulting application should look similar to Figure 11-4. Be sure that the Solution Explorer is open as shown in the illustration.

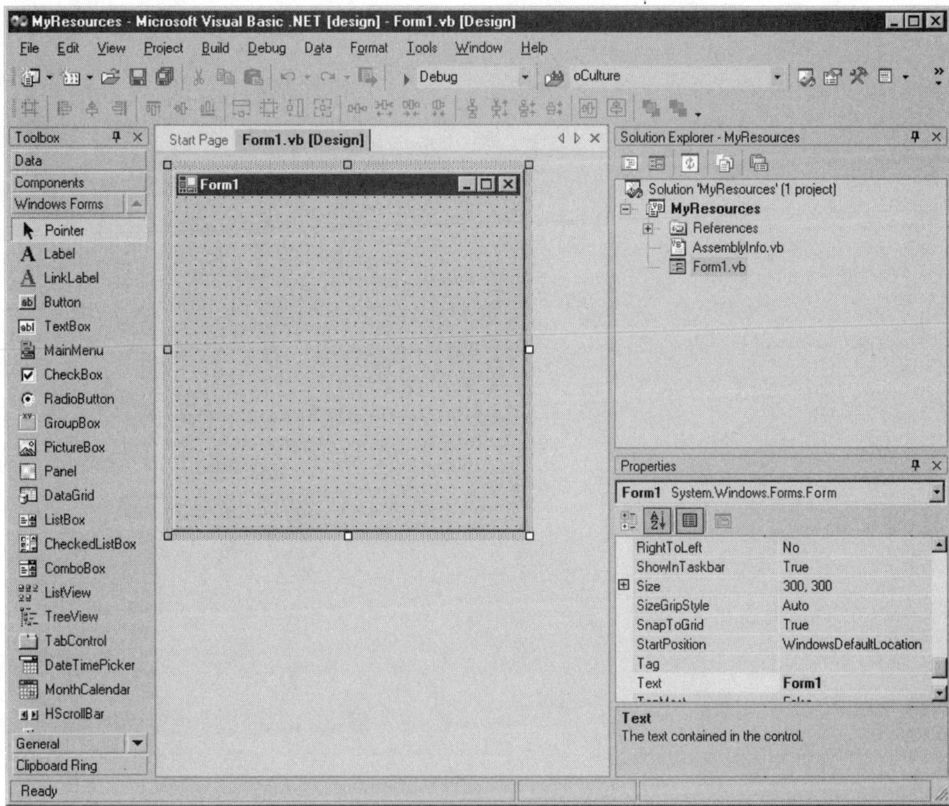

5. To delete Form1, right-click Form1.vb in the Solution Explorer and select Delete. Then, click OK.

6. To add a new form to the project, right-click MyResources in the Solution Explorer. Select Add | Add Windows Form and name the form **ResourcesForm.vb**.
7. To set the Start Object to the ResourcesForm, right-click MyResources in the Solution Explorer, select Properties, and then set the Start Object in the MyResources Property Page.
8. To set the ResourcesForm form Localizable property to True, be sure that the Properties window is visible in the Visual Studio .NET IDE. Then, click ResourcesForm in the main edit window to display the form's properties. In the Properties window, find the Localizable property and set it to True. The following illustration shows the Visual Studio .NET IDE with the Solution Explorer, Properties, Toolbox, and main window displayed.

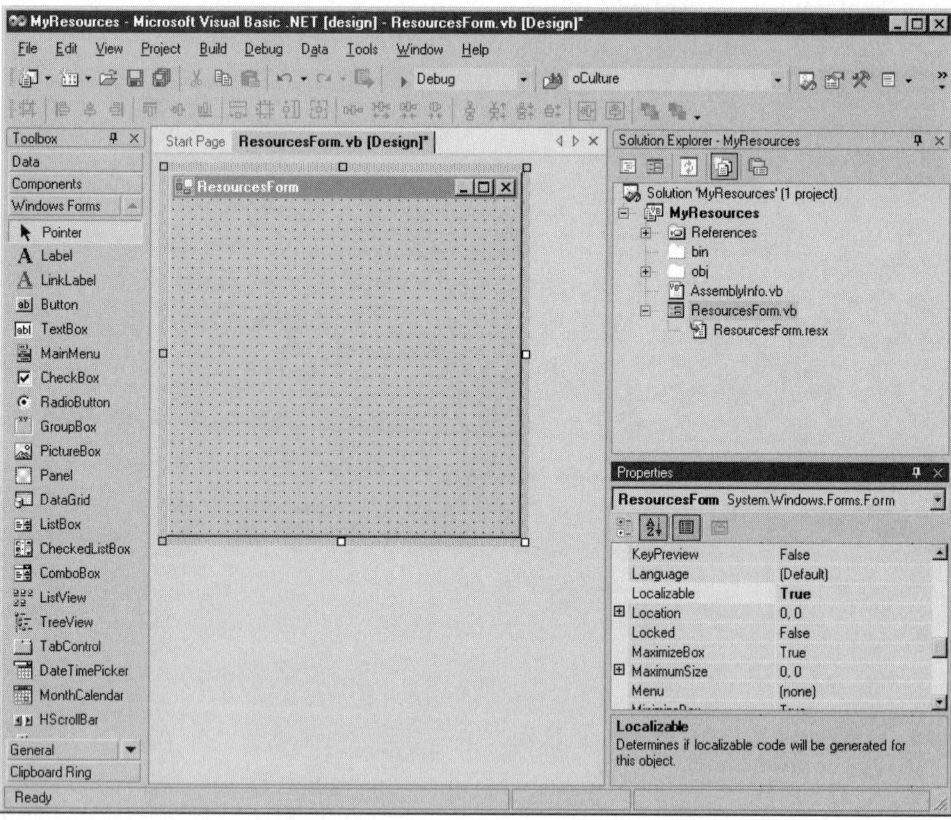

9. Add a Label control to the ResourcesForm.
10. Set the Text property of the label to **Hello World**.
11. If the Explorer Window is not showing all files, select the Show All Files icon in the Solution Explorer. Expand the ResourcesForm.vb node in the Solution Explorer. The Solution Explorer window should look like this.

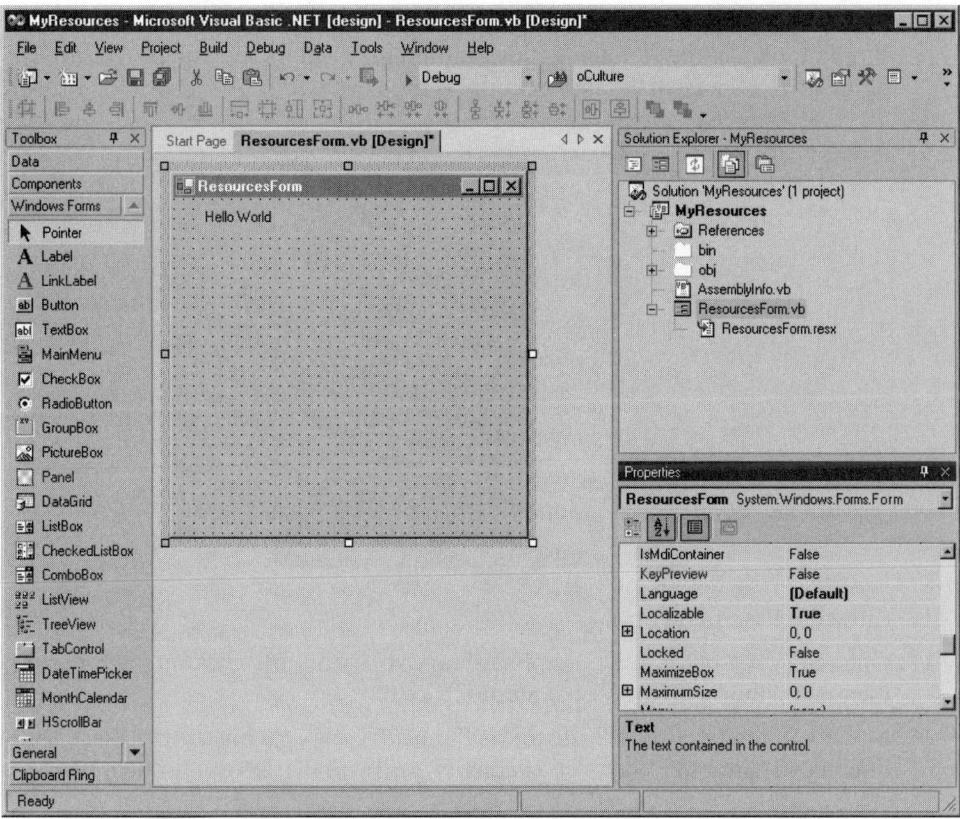

The preceding illustration shows the ResourcesForm.resx file that is automatically created by the Visual Studio .NET IDE. This resource file is used for creating the resource information in the MyResources.exe assembly.

12. Set the ResourcesForm Language property to German. (See Step 9 for instructions on accessing the properties for ResourcesForm.) The Language property is directly above the Localizable property. The ResourcesForm.de.resx file is now added to the Solution Explorer.
13. Set the Text property for the Label1 control to **Hallo Welt**.
14. Move the Label1 control to a different location on the form.
15. Press F5 to compile and run the application. The resulting Windows form should look like the following illustration. This displays the English version of the form because the default culture is used.

16. Close the ResourcesForm.
17. Open the code-behind file, ResourcesForm.vb, by double-clicking the form in the main window of the Visual Studio .NET IDE.
18. Add the following line of code to the Public Sub New() constructor. Place the line of code after the line of code containing the MyBase.New() statement.

```
System.Threading.Thread.CurrentThread.CurrentUICulture _
    = New System.Globalization.CultureInfo("de-DE")
```

The resulting code should look like that in the illustration on the next page. This line of code simulates running the application in the German language.

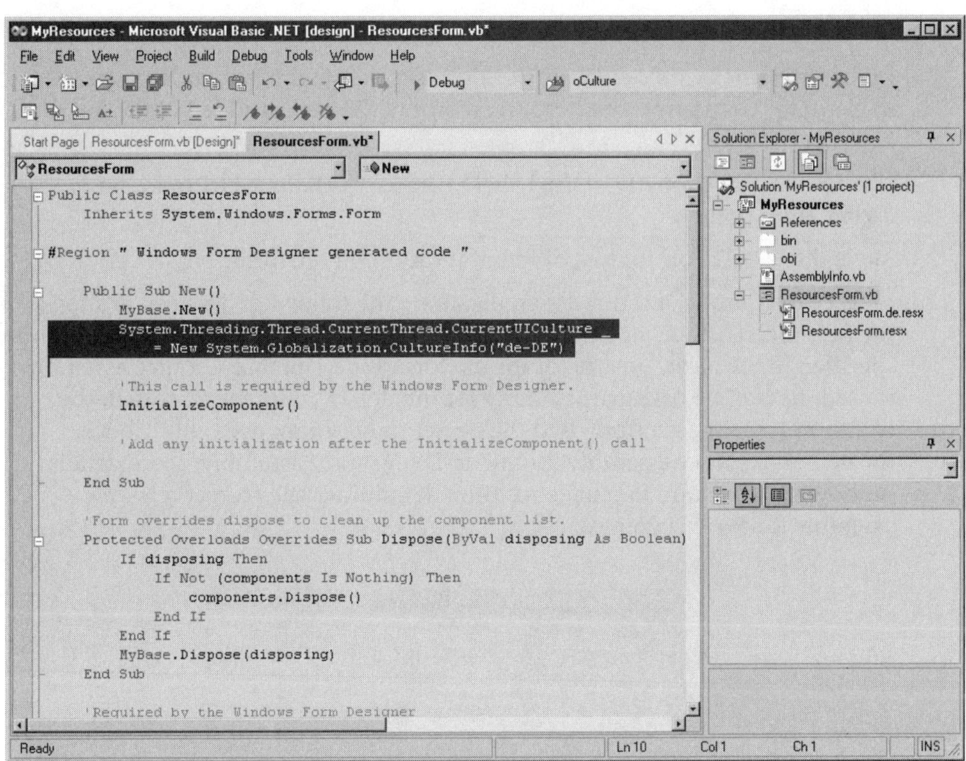

19. Press F5 to compile and run the application. The following illustration shows the ResourcesForm using the German language.

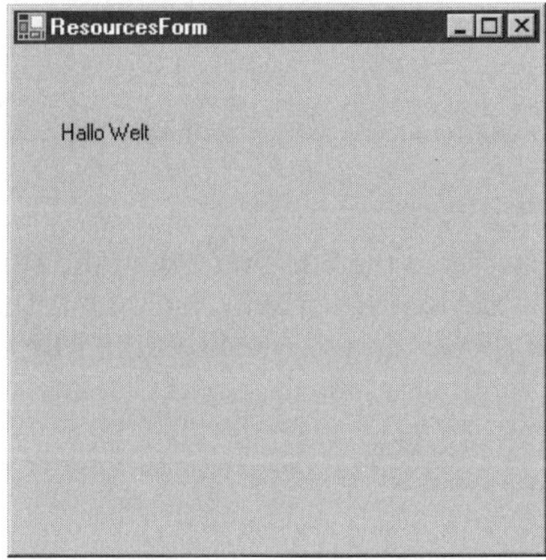

20. Close the ResourcesForm.
21. In the Properties window for the ResourcesForm, set the Language property to German (Germany). The ResourcesForm.de-DE.resx is added to the Solution Explorer.
22. Change the Text property of the Label1 control to **Hallo Welt!** (add the exclamation point).
23. Move the Label1 control to a different location on the form.
24. Press F5 to compile and run the application. The following illustration shows the ResourcesForm using the German language of Germany. Because the culture specified in the New constructor for the form is de-DE, that resource assembly is used. Before the resource assembly for the de-DE culture was created, the common language runtime used the de neutral resource assembly. This is the default resource assembly for the de-DE resource assembly. More details on how the common language runtime determines the correct resource assembly follow this exercise.

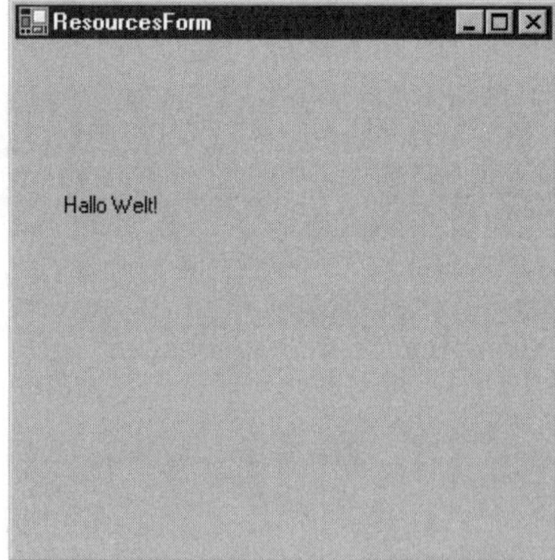

25. Close the ResourcesForm assembly.
26. Expand all the directories in the bin directory in the Solution Explorer. The directory structure should look like that in Figure 11-1. The structure and files in this directory are discussed in the next section, which describes how the common language runtime selects the correct assembly.

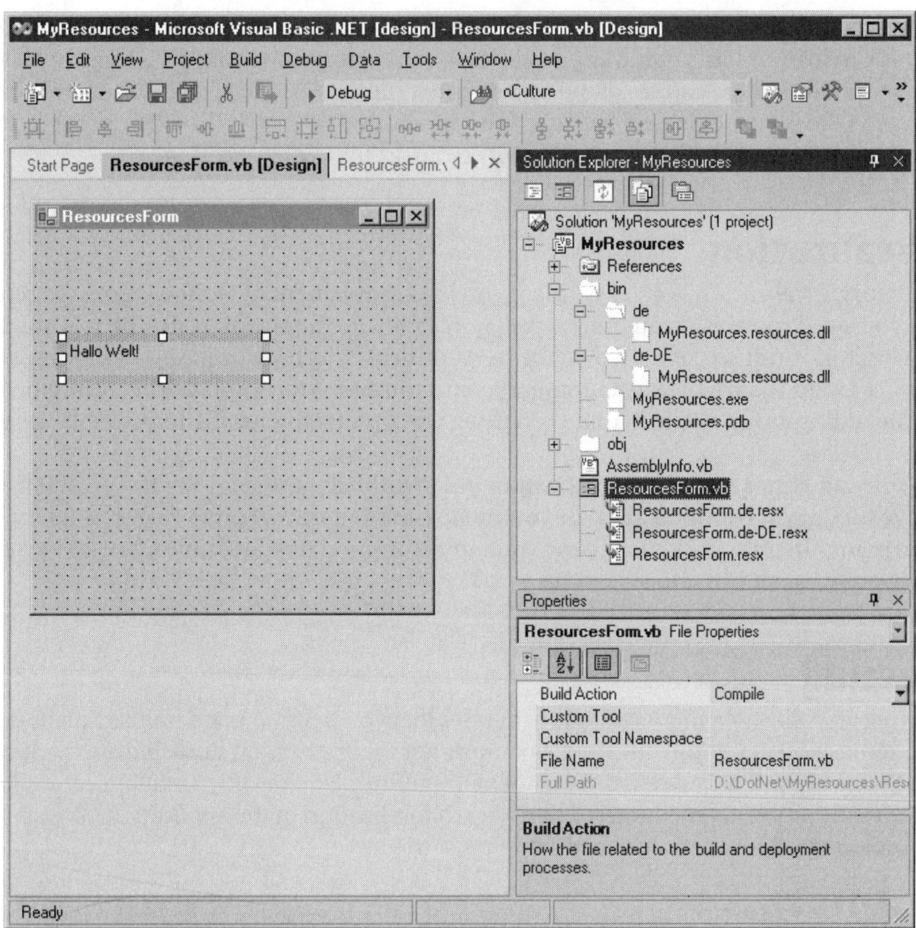

Figure 11-1 The VS.NET IDE showing the resource directories and assemblies for Exercise 11-4

Resource Assembly Selection by the Common Language Runtime

Figure 11-1 shows the bin directory for the MyResources project. The main assembly for the project is MyResources.exe. This main assembly contains the resources from the ResourcesForm.xres file, the default culture for the application. The Visual Studio .NET IDE created two directories for satellite resource assemblies: the de directory and the de-DE directory. Each of these directories contains a satellite resource assembly, MyResources.resources.dll. These assemblies contain the resources for the culture of the directory they are located in.

PART III

The common language runtime (CLR) uses the culture to determine the correct assembly to load. It starts in the application's root directory and looks for a directory with the same name as the culture. If the CLR does not find the assembly in the root directory, it checks the parent culture. The parent culture for de-DE is *de*. If the CLR does not find the resource assembly, it uses the default resources for the application.

Localization

In theory, localization is an easy task if you have implemented globalization correctly. All you need to do is create new resource files for the application. In the real world, however, it is not so easy. Two of the most difficult localization tasks are finding the correct group to do the translation and communicating the application requirements to the testing group to verify that everything works correctly for the localized language and cultures.

You can either allow the localization group to use the Visual Studio .NET IDE to make the resource modification or you can use the Windows Forms Resource Editor. It is very important to not change the code to accommodate localization unless you are ready to retest all other localizations.

Testing

Testing globalization and localization requires that you develop good unit test plans during application development. Then, you must test the application's capability to be localized. This capability is referred to as the application's *localizability*. Testing localizability reduces the problems encountered during each localization of the application. As each localization of an application is made, you must test it.

EXAM TIP Localizability is the application's capability to be localized. It is not the actual localization of the application.

As you develop each unit, test the globalization using the default culture and another culture in order to confirm that the application code is properly separated from the data. An exact translation of the second culture is not required. It should be sufficiently different from the default culture to identify where the data is not properly separated from the code. Specifically, you should test dates, numbers, and currency to identify the problems of fixed formats and patterns. Also, if special code is required for string manipulation, arithmetic operation, or date conversion, test the appropriate cultures to exercise this code.

You should use the Windows 2000 or later operating system to do the initial testing. Afterward, you can test your application against other operating systems. In addition, there may be components in your application that do not support Unicode. To test non-Unicode components, perform tests using a double-byte character set such as Japanese as the system default culture. If your application is going to support a culture that has right-to-left formatting, test these cultures. The key to this testing is to verify that your application can be localized, not necessarily to implement the actual localization.

As an application is localized, retest it. In addition to date, currency, and number testing, verify that the appropriate telephone and address structures are implemented. Besides the application itself, you must verify the online help, error messages, and printed document for consistency and accuracy. You also need to make sure that the presentation order is consistent with the language constructs.

Summary

There are two parts to creating an international application. The first part, globalization, is developing the application to allow it to be localized to a specific culture. The second part, localization, is the actual implementation of the application for a specific culture. Confirming the localizability of the application verifies that the globalization of the application is complete and the application can be localized.

The globalization of an application requires that you account for cultural differences in the display and input of information. The .NET Framework provides the **CultureInfo** class for working with different formatting characteristics of different cultures. You can use the culture information to control the formatting of dates, currency, and numbers.

The .NET Framework is based on the Unicode character representation. This allows the processing of multiple languages at the same time. Conversion utilities allow the conversion of code pages to and from the Unicode characters.

The testing of an international application includes not only the usual application testing, but also the testing of the localizability of the application. The application must be tested for every localization.

Test Questions

1. Which of the following is a valid neutral culture name in the .NET Framework?

   A. German-Germany

   B. en

   C. English

   D. de-DE

2. Which of the following statements sets the current culture information for accessing resource assemblies?

   A. CurrentCulture = CultureInfo("de")

   B. Thread.CurrentThread.CurrentCulture = CultureInfo("de")

   C. Thread.CurrentThread.UICurrentCulture = CultureInfo("de-DE")

   D. CurrentCulture = CultureInfo("de-DE")

3. Which of the following statements sets the current culture information for controlling the date format?
   A. Thread.CurrentThread.CurrentCulture=CultureInfo("de")
   B. Thread.CurrentThread.UICurrentCulture=CultureInfo("de-DE")
   C. UICurrentCulture = CurrentInfo("de-DE")
   D. Thread.CurrentThread.CurrentCulture = CultureInfo("de-DE")
4. What namespace is the **CultureInfo** class part of?
   A. System.Cultures
   B. System.Languages
   C. System.Globalization
   D. System.Localization
5. Given the en-GB culture and the date 03/07/03, what is the correct long date format?
   A. March 07, 2003
   B. Friday, March 07, 2003
   C. July 07, 2003
   D. 03 July 2003
6. Given the en-US culture and the date 03/07/02, what is the correct long date format?
   A. March 07, 2003
   B. Friday, March 07, 2003
   C. July 07, 2003
   D. 03 July 2003
7. If **oUserCulture** is an instance of the **CultureInfo** class and TestDate is a DateTime variable, which of the following statements is correct for accessing the long date for the culture of the **oUserCulture** object?
   A. TestDate.ToLongDateString
   B. TestDate.ToLongDateString(oUserCulture.DateTimeFormat)
   C. TestDate.String("D")
   D. TestDate.String("D", oUserCulture.DateTimeFormat)
8. What interface is used for accessing culture-specific formats?
   A. ICultureInfo
   B. ICultureFormats

C. IFormatProvider

D. IFormats

9. What is the extension of the XML resource file created by the Visual Studio .NET IDE?

A. .dll

B. .exe

C. .xres

D. .txt

10. You are developing a Windows application project in the Visual Studio .NET IDE. It is named MyApp and contains the MyForm form. Where does the common language runtime get the default resources for MyForm?

A. MyForm.xres

B. MyApp.xres

C. MyApp.exe

D. MyApp.resources.dll

11. Where does the common language runtime find the resources for the de-DE culture for the MyApp.exe running from the C:/MyApp directory (assuming the resources for the de-DE culture exist)?

A. C:/MyApp/MyApp.resources.dll

B. C:/MyApp/de/de-DE/MyApp.resources.dll

C. C:/MyApp/de-DE/MyApp.resources.dll

D. C:/MyApp/MyApp.de-DE.resources.dll

12. Using the Visual Studio .NET IDE, what property is set to create resources for the de-DE culture when adding a label to the MyForm form in the MyApp project?

A. MyForm.Language

B. MyForm.Localizable

C. MyApp.Language

D. MyApp.Localizable

13. What program can a localization group use to localize an application if it cannot have access to the application source code?

A. resgen.exe

B. al.exe

C. vb.exe

D. winres.exe

14. What is globalization of an application?
    A. The modification of application data for a specific culture
    B. The development of an application to support multiple cultures
    C. The modification of existing application code to a different language
    D. The rewriting of an application for a different language
15. What is localization of an application?
    A. The modification of application data for a specific culture
    B. The development of an application to support multiple cultures
    C. The modification of an existing application code to a different language
    D. The rewriting of an application for a different language

Test Answers

1. B
2. C.
3. D.
4. C.
5. D.
6. B.
7. D.
8. C.
9. C.
10. C.
11. C.
12. A.
13. D.
14. B.
15. A.

PART IV

Data Access

CHAPTER 12

ADO.NET and the DataSet Class

In this chapter, you will

- Work with connected data access
- Use the **DataReader**
- Work with the disconnected data model
- Understand the **DataSet**, **DataTable**, and **DataAdapter** classes
- Use the **DataTable** without the **DataSet**
- Create a **Typed DataSet**
- Update the data source with the changes made to the **DataSet**

This chapter discusses ADO.NET classes and their uses. It focuses in detail on the **DataReader** class and also covers the **DataSet** class and its related classes.

Why a New Data Model?

Microsoft developed three data access APIs prior to developing ADO.NET. The first was Data Access Objects (DAO), which was used to access Microsoft Jet data sources such as Microsoft Access. Because open database connectivity (ODBC) was rapidly becoming the *de facto* standard in database connections, Microsoft released Remote Data Objects (RDO) to enable communication using the ODBC technology. The RDO API allowed developers to communicate with any data source for which there was an ODBC manager.

However, to develop an application that communicated with a variety of data sources, including Jet and ODBC, developers had to use multiple object models. This was cumbersome; to upgrade from Microsoft Access to Microsoft SQL Server, code had to be rewritten to use an entirely different object model, namely RDO.

To address this issue and enable data access with Windows applications, Microsoft developed OLEDB technology. OLEDB works similarly to ODBC in that the client communicates with the data source through a wrapper driver. In ODBC the wrapper driver is called an ODBC manager, and in OLEDB it is called an OLEDB provider. In either case, this wrapper communicates with the data source using the data source's appropriate communication technology. When communicating with SQL Server 7.0 (or later) the wrapper uses tabular data services (TDS). When working with Oracle the wrapper uses

SQLNET. The client, in either case, uses OLEDB to communicate with the OLEDB provider. This technology allows developers to change the type of wrapper to what is appropriate for the data source being accessed without having to change the client code.

Because the provider wrapper technology is well established, it works well for code portability. OLEDB is easier to use than ODBC because developers (in C++) can write their own OLEDB provider with fair ease. Almost every data source has an OLEDB provider, bringing about the acronym UDA, which stands for universal data access.

ActiveX Data Objects (ADO) was developed as the ActiveX-compliant object model. It uses OLEDB to communicate with the OLEDB provider. Developers use the ADO library with languages such as Visual Basic and Visual Basic Scripting Edition (VBScript) to use the OLEDB technology.

ADO has nine objects; three of them are top-level objects: **Connection**, **Command**, and **Recordset**. The **Connection** object is the pipeline to, or communication with, the data source. We open a Connection object before we interact with the data source. The **Command** object is a statement we execute on the data source. With most data sources the statement is an SQL query or stored procedure call.

The **Recordset** object is the container that holds the data returned from the statement execution. For example, executing an SQL SELECT query returns a result set that ADO places inside the **Recordset** object. The **Recordset** object provides methods and properties to manipulate the data, such as MoveNext and MovePrevious for navigation, and EOF and BOF to indicate the end or beginning of the result set.

One problem with ADO is that it was originally created as a connected data access object model. This means that developers primarily use a **Recordset** object while connected to the data source. Microsoft modified the **Recordset** to allow disconnected access (using the **Recordset** while not connected to the data source), but this solution did not work as well as if it had been designed as a disconnected data access model from the beginning. For one thing, the **Recordset** object can contain only one result set. This means we cannot relate result sets using a primary/foreign key type of relationship and we cannot relate result sets from different data sources.

With .NET, Microsoft developed an entirely new data model that uses the provider wrapper technology but eliminates the old-style **Recordset** object. That new data model is ADO.NET. ADO.NET still uses **Connection** and **Command** types, but it replaces the Recordset with two data types: **DataReader** and **DataSet** objects. The **DataReader** object provides connected data access. The **DataSet**, the core object of ADO.NET, is an in-memory cache of disconnected data.

The ADO.NET Classes

The ADO.NET classes are segmented into .NET namespaces according to their uses. This section discusses the use of each namespace in developing applications.

The System.Data Namespace

The primary namespace of ADO.NET, the **System.Data** namespace, contains classes used in all types of data access and manipulation, no matter which data source we access or whether we access a data source at all. At the core of this namespace is the **DataSet** class. Table 12-1 lists many of the **System.Data** classes and briefly explains their purpose.

Table 12-1 Selection of System.Data Classes

Class	Description
DataSet	This is an in-memory cache of data that can hold several **DataTable** objects of data, and the relationships among those tables. It is used for disconnected data access.
DataTable	Each table in the **DataSet** object is stored in a **DataTable** object. This object can be independent of the **DataSet** object if we want to create a single disconnected result set. The **DataTable** contains collections of **DataRows**, **DataColumns**, and **Constraint** objects, which make up the structure and data of the table.
DataRow	This object represents a row of the result set in a **DataTable**. It is used to access and manipulate the data in a **DataTable**.
DataColumn	This object represents a column in a result set and maintains the schema (structural) information about the column, such as the data type and default value.
DataRelation	This object sets up the primary/foreign key relationships in a **DataSet** object.
DataView	This object is a virtual **DataTable**. Without modifying the data in the **DataTable** we can filter the rows and columns we are viewing within the table at a particular time.

The Provider Namespaces

As with ADO, ADO.NET uses wrapper functionality to connect to various data sources using the same client model. None of the classes in the **System.Data** namespace has binding to a specific type of data source. No matter which data source you access, you will always use the same **DataSet**, **DataTable**, or **DataRow** class. You can even use these classes without connecting to a data source.

To allow generic functionality, Microsoft puts the data source-specific classes in their own namespace. Each namespace is based on the data source the class will access. Table 12-2 outlines the provider namespaces available at the time this book was written. Many more will be available in the future as vendors develop the .NET providers themselves.

Several classes are common among namespaces. To establish a connection to a data source before executing statements on it, developers use an object similar to the ADO **Connection** object. The classes are named based on the data source each object will access.

Table 12-2 ADO.NET Data Provider Namespaces

Namespace	Used To Access
System.Data.SqlClient	Microsoft SQL Server 7.0 or later using tabular data services communication
Microsoft.Data.Odbc	All ODBC drivers using ODBC communication; available for download from Microsoft
System.Data.OracleClient	Oracle 8i Release 3 (8.1.7) Client or later; available for download from Microsoft
System.Data.OleDb	OLEDB providers using OLEDB communication

Table 12-3 Common Provider Classes

Class	Description
Connection	Establishes a connection to the data source.
Command	Provides a statement to execute on the data source that the data source can understand.
DataReader	Provides a forward-only, read-only data set similar to the default ADO **Recordset**.
DataAdapter	Populates a **DataSet** object and reconciles changes made to the data.

For example, to connect to a SQL Server 2000 data source, we use the **System.Data.SqlClient.SqlConnection** class. Similarly, to connect to an OLEDB data source we use the **System.Data.OleDb.OleDbConnection** class. Notice that the names of the connection classes are really just the data source prefixed to the class name. Table 12-3 lists some of the common classes in the provider namespaces; prefix each class with the provider prefix. This chapter explains each of these classes in detail.

This chapter uses the **OleDb** namespace for all data access to a Microsoft Access database.

Connected Data Access

Connected data access means that we are connected to the data source while we use the data. To work with data in this manner, we must first use the **Connection** object to establish a connection to the data source.

Some properties and methods are specific to each provider's **Connection** object, but the general ones are shown in Table 12-4.

Some of the exercises in this chapter use the Northwind sample database that is distributed with Microsoft SQL Server 7.0 and later. This database is also distributed as an Access file (mdb) with many of Microsoft's products including Microsoft Office and Visual Studio.

Member Name	Property/Method	Description
ConnectionString	Property	Establishes the connection to the data source by providing a file name or server name, or the database to access on the server. This property is provider specific.
ConnectionTimeout	Property	Specifies the length of time (in seconds) to attempt to connect before timing-out with an error.
State	Property	Gets the state of the connection—whether it is connected, connecting, not connected, and so on.

Table 12-4 Common Properties and Methods of the Connection Object

Member Name	Property/Method	Description
Provider	Property	Used by the **OleDbConnection** object to specify which OLEDB provider will be used to communicate with the data source.
Open	Method	Attempts to open the **Connection** object based on the ConnectionString.
Close	Method	Closes the connection to the data source. The connection must be open; otherwise this method will result in an exception.
BeginTransaction	Method	Begins a database transaction. Database transactions are discussed later in this chapter.

Table 12-4 Common Properties and Methods of the Connection Object *(continued)*

Exercise 12-1: Creating a Connected Data Access Application In this exercise you will create an application that retrieves data from a Microsoft SQL Server 2000 database.

1. Create a new Windows Forms application by clicking File | New | Project. In the New Project dialog box select Visual Basic Projects in the Project Types pane and select Windows Application in the Templates pane. Type **DataReaderApp** in the Name text box and type the appropriate location in the Location text box. Click OK to create the new project.
2. The Visual Studio .NET IDE should now display the default form in design view. Place the controls shown in Table 12-5 on the form.

Type	Name	Properties
The form itself	frmDataReader	Text = Customers Size = 408,224
Button	btnOpenConnection	Location = 8,8 Text = Open Connection Size = 112,23 Enabled = True
Button	btnRetrieveData	Location = 8,40 Text = Retrieve Data Size = 112,23 Enabled = False
Button	btnCloseConnection	Location = 8,72 Text = Close Connection Size = 112, 23 Enabled = False

Table 12-5 Controls for DataReader Application

PART IV

Type	Name	Properties
ListBox	lstCustomers	Location = 128,8 Size = 264,173
Label	lblStatus	Location = 8,168 Size = 112,16 Text = Not Connected

Table 12-5 Controls for DataReader Application *(continued)*

The resulting form should look similar to the illustration.

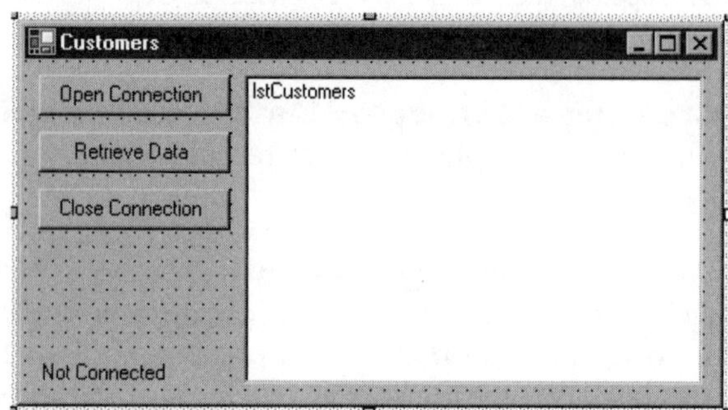

3. Because you have changed the name of the form, you must modify the project settings to specify that frmDataReader is the startup form. Right-click the DataReaderApp project in the Solution Explorer and click Properties. In the Startup object combo box, select frmDataReader. To allow easier coding using the **System.Data.SqlClient** namespace, import it before declaring the **frmDataReader** class, by entering the following code.

```
Imports System.Data.SqlClient
```

4. To declare the variables that will point to the **Connection** and **DataReader** objects in memory, enter the following lines of code immediately after the Inherits statement in the **frmDataReader** class.

```
Protected WithEvents cnNWind As SqlConnection
Protected drCustomers As SqlDataReader
```

5. Now you must create the **SqlConnection** object and open it when the button is clicked. Select btnOpenConnection from the left-hand drop down list in the code editor and select Click from the right-hand drop down list to create the handler for the event. Then, add the following code to the event handler to create and open the connection.

```
cnNWind = New SqlConnection()
cnNWind.ConnectionString = _
      "Data Source=(local);Initial Catalog=Northwind;" & _
      "Integrated Security=SSPI"
cnNWind.Open()
```

EXAM TIP The **Connection** object must be open the entire time you use the **DataReader**.

You could also have instantiated the **SqlConnection** and initialized the ConnectionString in one line using the overloaded constructor, as shown in the following code.

```
cnNWind = New SqlConnection("Data Source=(local);" & _
      "Initial Catalog=Northwind;Integrated Security=SSPI")
```

NOTE The ConnectionString is specific to each provider you use. Refer to the provider's documentation for the string syntax.

6. To allow the user to see the state of the connection, you must include a Label control on the form. To handle this event in your form, select cnNWind from the left-hand drop-down list in the Code Editor and select StateChange from the right-hand drop-down list. Add the following code to the event handler.

```
lblStatus.Text = e.CurrentState.ToString()
```

7. To make the application more user friendly (and less error prone), you must enable or disable the appropriate buttons depending on the state of the application. Add the following code to the StateChange event handler created in the preceding step.

```
If e.CurrentState = ConnectionState.Open Then
      Me.btnCloseConnection.Enabled = True
      Me.btnOpenConnection.Enabled = False
      Me.btnRetrieveData.Enabled = True
End If
```

8. Add the Click event handler for the btnRetrieveData button to the form and add the following code to the procedure to retrieve the data into the **DataReader**.

```
lstCustomers.Items.Clear()
If cnNWind.State = ConnectionState.Open Then
      Dim cmCustomers As New SqlCommand("SELECT * FROM Customers", _
            cnNWind)
      drCustomers = cmCustomers.ExecuteReader()
      Do While drCustomers.Read()
      lstCustomers.Items.Add(drCustomers.Item("CompanyName").ToString())
      Loop

      Me.btnRetrieveData.Enabled = False
      drCustomers.Close()
Else
      MessageBox.Show("The connection must be opened first.")
End If
```

EXAM TIP Use the State property of the **Connection** object to determine whether the connection is open.

The first line of code in this procedure clears the contents of the ListBox control. The next line executes the True clause of the If statement if the **Connection** object is open. If not, a message box informs the user that the connection must first be opened. The first statement in the True clause creates a **Command** object that is used to retrieve all the records from the Customers table. Every field is retrieved for each record. The first argument in the constructor of the **Command** object is the statement to execute on the data source, and the second argument passes a pointer to the **Connection** object that the **Command** object must use.

The next statement runs the ExecuteReader method of the **Command** object, which returns a pointer to the newly created **DataReader** object. The Read method of the **DataReader** object allows you to move to the next record. When you use this method, it returns a Boolean result, indicating whether the **DataReader** has moved to a valid record. In other words, when Read returns False, you have no more records to access and are at the end of the **DataReader**'s data.

EXAM TIP Use the ExecuteReader method of the **Command** object to return a **DataReader** pointer. Use the ExecuteScalar method with queries that return a single value and not a row set, such as the COUNT SQL function.

NOTE You must call the Read method of the **DataReader** at least once to move to the first record. If you try to access data in the **DataReader** without calling Read, an exception will be thrown.

In Step 8 of this exercise you created a loop that calls the Read method and executes the loop if the method returns True. In that case the code inside the loop adds the value of the CompanyName column to the list box's Items collection. Once the loop is completed, you close the **DataReader** object.

Remember this statement: *Acquire resources late and release them early.* This means that as soon as you have finished using a resource, you should close it to allow other applications, or portions of your application, to use the resource. This is one of the key advantages of the **DataSet** object.

NOTE When the **DataReader** is open, the active **Connection** object it is using is not usable by any other objects. Therefore, close it as soon as possible.

9. To close the **Connection** object, add the event handler for the btnCloseConnection's Click event by selecting btnCloseConnection from the left-hand drop-down list box in the code editor and selecting the Click event in the right-hand drop-down list; then add the following code.

```
cnNWind.Close()
Me.btnCloseConnection.Enabled = False
Me.btnOpenConnection.Enabled = True
Me.btnRetrieveData.Enabled = False
```

This code closes the connection to the data source, releasing resources on the data source and, most importantly in many cases, freeing up one database license. The code also modifies the Enabled property of the buttons to make them more user friendly.

10. Execute the application by clicking Debug | Start. Make sure the data source you will be using is accessible to the client application.

    The result of the execution will look similar to the illustration.

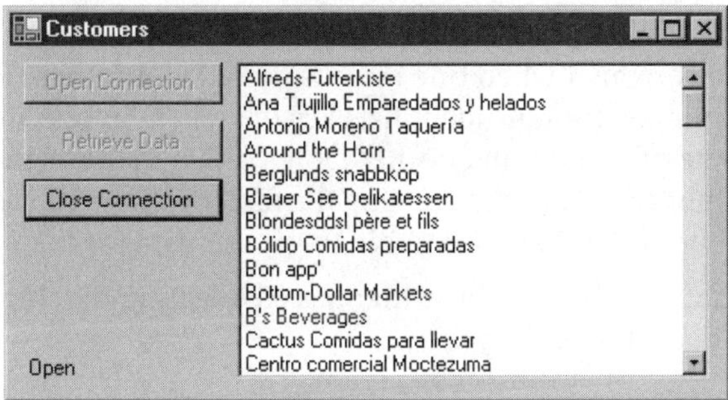

Disconnected Data Access

Although connected data access using the **DataReader** is fairly simple, the **DataReader** lacks functionality. Once we reach the end of the data in the **DataReader** we can no longer use the **DataReader**. In addition, the **DataReader** is read-only. Finally, it requires an open connection to the data source the entire time we use it and, as we saw previously, the **Connection** object cannot be used by any other object while the **DataReader** is using it.

The applications that developers build today are different from the applications that developers built when ADO was first released. Developers at that time mainly built one- and two-tier applications in which it was accepted practice to have an open connection to the data source while using the data. Developers usually had only employees accessing the data at a particular time; therefore, database licensing was not the largest concern within application development.

The whole idea of connected data access changed with the explosion of Web-based and intranet-based applications. Hundreds, if not thousands of users, can access data simultaneously. The cost of database licenses would be astronomical and resource usage on database servers would be dramatic if another data access strategy were not utilized. Disconnected data access solves these issues.

Disconnected data access is similar to connected data access in that the application opens a connection to the data source and retrieves the data into a container that will hold the data. The difference is that once the data is placed into this container, we close the connection to the data source. The data is cached where the **Container** object is created.

The **DataSet** object, mentioned earlier, is a **Container** object that is generic to all types of disconnected data access. Developers can use this container even if they are not retrieving data from a data source. The container, unlike the ADO **Recordset** object, holds multiple tables of data and cannot communicate with the data source.

Microsoft defines a DataSet as "an in-memory cache of data." What does this mean? Before answering that question, let's look at what a relational database is.

- A *database* is a collection of information organized into tables.
- A *table* is a collection of rows and columns in which each row represents one item within the table, and each column represents one attribute of each item. Therefore, all items in a table will have the same attributes.
- A *relationship* is created when one table is linked to another table through a set of keys. The primary (unique identifier) key of an item in one table can be specified as the attribute of an item in another table (called the foreign key). Instead of having to duplicate data when creating the table with the foreign key, developers can link over to the primary key table to get the data for the matching item.
- A *relational database* is a database that has a collection of tables that are related by using primary/foreign keys.

We won't go into database design details such as normalization, but the preceding concepts are important to understand when discussing the **DataSet** object.

A **DataSet** contains a collection of tables that can be related using primary/foreign key relationships. And, it is an in-memory object; the data is cached in-memory. Therefore, the **DataSet** object is an in-memory relational database.

Because the **DataSet** object has no understanding of specific data sources, it can be populated with data from multiple data sources and related through its own relationships. Suppose we are using Microsoft SQL Server as the data source for a sales application and Oracle as the data source for an accounts application. Because these data sources are different, we cannot create a relationship between them using the ADO **Recordset**. With the **DataSet**, however, we can create one table from the SQL Server and another from the Oracle server, and then relate them with a **DataRelation** object.

Some of the objects that work in conjunction with the **DataSet** are the **DataTable**, the **DataRelation**, and the **DataAdapter**.

The DataTable

The **DataTable** object holds the data. Because it is a table, and has rows and columns, it has a Rows collection of **DataRow** objects and a Columns collection of **DataColumn** objects. Table 12-6 lists the properties and methods of the **DataTable** class.

Each row in the **DataTable** is represented as a **DataRow** object. The **DataRow** is used for reading and manipulating the data. Table 12-7 lists some members of the **DataRow** class.

Member	Type	Description
CaseSensitive	Property	A Boolean value; specifies whether string comparisons within the table are case sensitive. The default is False. If the table is created in a **DataSet**, this value will be inherited from the **DataSet**.
ChildRelations	Property	If other tables use this table as their primary key table, this collection contains a pointer to each of those **DataRelation** objects.
Columns	Property	Specifies the collection of **DataColumn** objects in the table.
Constraints	Property	Defines the restrictions, such as unique fields, that are placed upon the table.
DataSet	Property	If the **DataTable** belongs to a **DataSet**, this property acts as a pointer to the DataSet; otherwise it is Nothing.
DefaultView	Property	Acts as the default **DataView** object for this table. DataViews are discussed later in this chapter.
ParentRelations	Property	Like ChildRelations, this property serves as a collection of all the **DataRelation** objects that specify relationships to parent tables.
PrimaryKey	Property	Specifies the array of columns used for the table's primary key.
Rows	Property	Specifies the collection of **DataRow** objects in the table.
TableName	Property	Specifies the name of the table–Read/Write property.
AcceptChanges and RejectChanges	Methods	Accepts/rejects changes to the data for the entire table.
Clear	Method	Clears the table of data; does not clear the structure.
Select	Method	Gets an array of **DataRow** objects. Good for retrieving an array of rows that match specific criteria.

Table 12-6 Properties and Methods of the DataTable Class

Member	Type	Description
Item	Property	Retrieves or sets data in an individual cell in the table.
ItemArray	Property	Retrieves or sets data in an array of cells in the row.
Table	Property	Retrieves a pointer to the **DataTable** that the row belongs to.
BeginEdit, CancelEdit, EndEdit, AcceptChanges, and RejectChanges	Methods	Modify and accept/reject the changes made to the cells.

Table 12-7 Properties and Methods of the DataRow Class

Exercise 12-2: Using the DataTable Object In this exercise you will populate a **DataTable** object with data. This **DataTable** is not contained within the **DataSet**.

1. Create a Visual Basic .NET Windows Application in Visual Studio .NET. Name the application **DataTableApp**.
2. Add the controls and property settings listed in Table 12-8. The resulting form should look similar to the following illustration.

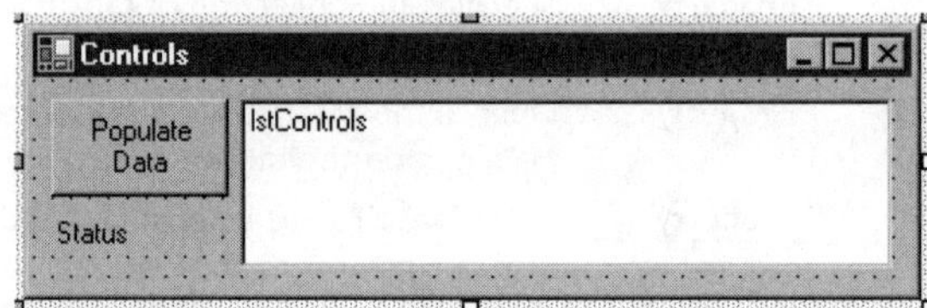

3. To modify the project settings so that they specify the new form name as the startup form, right-click the project in the Solution Explorer and click Properties. Set the **Startup** Object to frmControls.
4. To add code to the button's event handler, click btnPopulate in the left-hand drop-down list of the Code Editor and select Click in the right-hand drop-down list.
5. In the btnPopulate_Click event handler, create a new **DataTable** object to hold the data by adding the following line of code.

```
Dim dtControls As New DataTable("Controls")
```

The data to be held is simply the name and data type of each control on the form. The constructor you use creates and names the table. Although not useful here, naming the table is extremely important when working with **DataSets**, which can contain multiple **DataTable** objects.

Table 12-8 Controls on the DataTableApp Form

Type	Name	Properties
The form itself	frmControls	Size = 376,120 Text = Controls
Button	btnPopulate	Location = 8,8 Size = 75,40 Text = Populate Data
Label	lblStatus	Location = 8,56 Size = 72,16 Text = Status
ListBox	lstControls	Location = 88,8 Size = 272,69

6. So far your table is empty; it contains no rows or columns. Before you can add rows to the table, you must structure the table according to the data's structure—that is, according to the table's schema. In this exercise, each row in the table has a Name attribute and a Type attribute. The Name is the control's name and the Type is the control's .NET data type. Therefore, to create the columns in the table you enter the following code.

   ```
   dtControls.Columns.AddRange(New DataColumn() _
         {New DataColumn("Name"), New DataColumn("Type")})
   ```

   The preceding line of code uses the Columns collection's AddRange method to add an array of **DataColumn** objects to the **DataTable**. You could also use the collection's Add method, but this approach requires one statement for each column you add. AddRange uses a single Visual Basic .NET statement.

7. You will now add the rows of data to the table. To have the application loop through the Controls collection of the form and add a row for each control in the collection, enter the following code.

   ```
   Dim ctl As Control
   For Each ctl In Me.Controls
         dtControls.Rows.Add(New Object() {ctl.Name.ToString(), _
               ctl.GetType().ToString()})
   Next
   ```

   The first line of code declares the variable that points to each control as the loop executes. The second line of code uses For...Each to loop through the Controls collection of the form.

   The third line of code uses the **Rows** collection's Add method to add a new row to the table. In this case, the Add method takes an array of **Objects** as its argument. The array specifies the values used in each column in the row. These values must be specified in the array initialization in the same order the columns are specified in the Columns collection of the **DataTable**.

8. To use the data in the table, loop through each row and add items to the list box by entering the following code.

   ```
   Dim drControl As DataRow
   For Each drControl in dtControls.Rows
         lstControls.Items.Add(drControl.Item("Name").ToString() & _
               " - " & drControls.Items("Type").ToString())
   Next
   ```

9. To let the user know the procedure is complete, change the Text property of the Status label to "Complete" by entering the following code.

   ```
   lblStatus.Text = "Complete"
   ```

10. Execute the application by clicking Debug | Start.

The result of executing the application should look similar to the illustration.

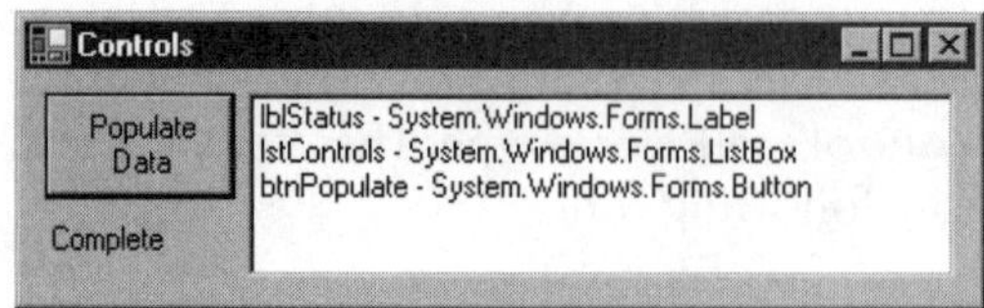

The DataSet

As stated earlier in this chapter, the **DataSet** is an in-memory relational database. Therefore, it will contain zero or more tables (usually one or more) and possibly include relationships between the tables.

Exercise 12-3: Creating a Basic DataSet Application In this exercise you will create a **DataSet** object and add two **DataTables** to it. Then, you will add a **DataRelation** object to the **DataSet** to establish a relationship between the two tables. Finally, you will display the data on the form and utilize the relationship between the tables.

1. Create a new Visual Basic .NET Windows Application using the Visual Studio .NET IDE. Name the application **BasicDataSet**.
2. Add the controls and property settings listed in Table 12-9. The resulting form should look similar to the illustration.

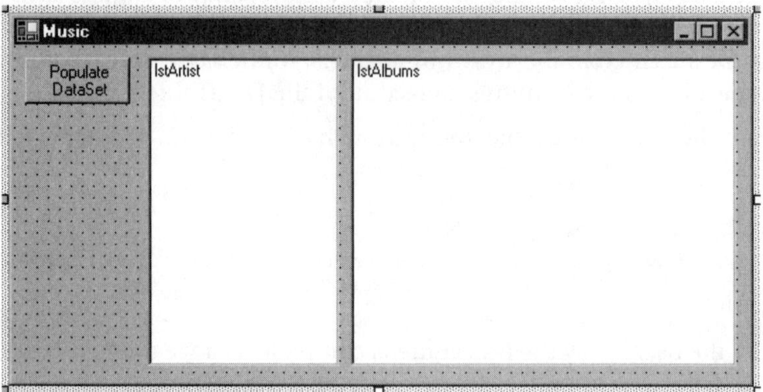

3. To declare the variable that will point to the **DataSet** object, place the following statement after the Inherits statement at the top of the Class declaration.

```
Protected dsMusic As DataSet
```

This variable is modular so that you can use it between multiple procedures.

Although you have not specified an Imports statement at the top of this file, the **System.Data** namespace is, by default, imported into every file in the project. The default specification is an option in the project settings.

Table 12-9 Controls on the BasicDataSet Form

Type	Name	Properties
The form itself	frmMusic	Size = 528,264 Text = Music
Button	btnPopulate	Location = 8,8 Size = 75,32 Text = Populate DataSet
ListBox	lstArtist	Location = 96,8 Size = 136,212
ListBox	lstAlbums	Location = 240,8 Size = 272,212

4. Add the btnPopulate's Click event handler to the form.
5. To create the **DataSet** object inside the event handler, use the following statement.

```
dsMusic = New DataSet("Music")
```

This statement also gives the **DataSet** a name that, although not required, makes it easier to identify when using multiple **DataSets**.

EXAM TIP The **DataSet** object must be instantiated before it can be used. When instantiated, it contains zero **DataTable** or **DataRelation** objects.

6. To create the **DataTable** object that will hold information about each music artist, add the following code.

```
Dim dt As DataTable
dt = dsMusic.Tables.Add("Artists")
dt.Columns.AddRange(New DataColumn() _
     {New DataColumn("Name"), New DataColumn("Type")})
dt.PrimaryKey = New DataColumn() {dt.Columns.Item("Name")}
dt.Rows.Add(New Object() {"Dire Straits", "Group"})
dt.Rows.Add(New Object() {"Bob Marley & the Wailers", "Group"})
dt.Rows.Add(New Object() {"Billy Joel", "Solo"})
```

The first line of code declares the variable you use to point to each of the **DataTable** objects you add to the **DataSet**. The second line uses the **DataSet**'s Add method to create and add a **DataTable** called "Artists". The third line adds **DataColumns** to the Artists **DataTable** using the AddRange method of the **Columns** collection. It adds one column for the artist's name and another for the type of artist (Solo or Group).

The fourth line of code gives the Artists **DataTable** a primary key. The PrimaryKey property of a **DataTable** is an array of **DataColumn** objects. In this case it is a single element array containing only a pointer to the Name column.

The last three lines in this code segment use the Add method of the **Rows** collection to add each artist's data to the table.

PART IV

7. You will now create the child table in this relationship. Each artist will have one or more albums. The table will hold the name and release year of each album. Each row in the table will also contain the primary key of the Artists table that relates to each album. To create the child table, enter the following code.

```
dt = dsMusic.Tables.Add("Albums")
dt.Columns.AddRange(New DataColumn() _
      {New DataColumn("Name"), New DataColumn("Year"), _
      New DataColumn("Artist")})
dt.Rows.Add(New Object() {"Alchemy Part One", "1984", _
      "Dire Straits"})
dt.Rows.Add(New Object() {"Alchemy Part Two", "1984", _
      "Dire Straits"})
dt.Rows.Add(New Object() {"Storm Front", "1989", _
      "Billy Joel"})
dt.Rows.Add(New Object() {"Communique", "1979", _
      "Dire Straits"})
dt.Rows.Add(New Object() {"Confrontation", "1983", _
      "Bob Marley & the Wailers"})
dt.Rows.Add(New Object() {"Natty Dread", "1974", _
      "Bob Marley & the Wailers"})
```

In the preceding code, you first add the Albums **DataTable** to the **DataSet** and then add the Name, Year, and Artist **DataColumns** to it. The Artist **DataColumn** is the foreign key in the relationship. You do not need to give this table a primary key as it will not be the parent table in any relationship.

Next, you add each of the albums to the **DataTable**'s **Rows** collection using the Add method. Feel free to replace the artists and albums used in the sample code with those that fit your tastes. Remember, though, that the primary and foreign keys must match exactly.

8. The **DataRelation** objects in a **DataSet** are contained within the **Relations** collection. To create the relationship between the Artists and Albums tables, enter the following code.

```
dsMusic.Relations.Add("ArtistAlbum", _
      dsMusic.Tables("Artists").PrimaryKey, _

      New DataColumn() _
      {dsMusic.Tables("Albums").Columns.Item("Artist")})
```

The first argument in the Add method specifies the name that the **DataRelation** object has within the **DataSet**. The second argument specifies an array of **DataColumns** representing the primary key of the parent table. Because you created the primary key by assigning the PrimaryKey property of the Artists **DataTable**, you can use the PrimaryKey property as the value. The third argument specifies an array of **DataColumn** objects representing the foreign key of the child table. You create the new table and assign the **Artist** column as the single element in the array.

9. To populate the lstArtist ListBox control with the names of all the artists, enter the following code.

```
Dim dr As DataRow
For Each dr In dsMusic.Tables("Artists").Rows
      lstArtist.Items.Add(dr.Item("Name").ToString())
Next
```

10. The application populates the **DataSet** and adds the items to the lstArtist ListBox control. There is, however, no code that executes when the artist's name is selected in the list box. Create the event handler for the lstArtist control's SelectedIndexChanged event.

11. The items displayed in the lstAlbums control must only be albums that were recorded by the selected artist. To clear the list box of any items currently there, add the following code to the event handler.

```
lstAlbums.Items.Clear()
```

12. To retrieve the albums for the selected artist, you must retrieve a pointer to the row in the Artists **DataTable** whose Name value matches the selected artist's name. To do so, enter the following code.

```
Dim parentRow As DataRow = dsMusic.Tables("Artists").Select( _
      "Name = '" & lstArtist.SelectedItem.ToString() & "'")(0)
```

In this statement, the Select method of the **DataTable** object returns a **DataRow** array in which the Name value matches the string representation of the selected artist. Note that you use the zero in parentheses at the end of the statement to return only the first element in the array. Because the Name column of the Artists table is a unique primary key, there will always be only one element in the array. However, you still need to retrieve the **DataRow** by using the array index.

13. To add items to the lstAlbums ListBox control, you must retrieve them from an array of **DataRows** whose Artist value matches the parent **Row**'s Name value. To retrieve the items, enter the following code, which uses the GetChildRows method of the parent row to return an array of **DataRow** objects.

```
Dim childRows() As DataRow = parentRow.GetChildRows( _
      dsMusic.Relations("ArtistAlbum"))
```

The argument to pass into the GetChildRows method is the **DataRelation** object that specifies the relationship between these two tables. Because you have already created the object, you use the ArtistAlbum relationship.

14. Now that you have the rows containing the data for the ListBox, loop through the array and display the details by entering the following code.

```
Dim dr As DataRow
For Each dr In childRows
      lstAlbums.Items.Add(dr.Item("Name").ToString() & " - " & _
            dr.Item("Year").ToString())
Next
```

15. Execute the application by clicking Debug | Start. Select different artists and notice that the album list changes. The following two illustrations show what the application looks like when you execute it and select different artists.

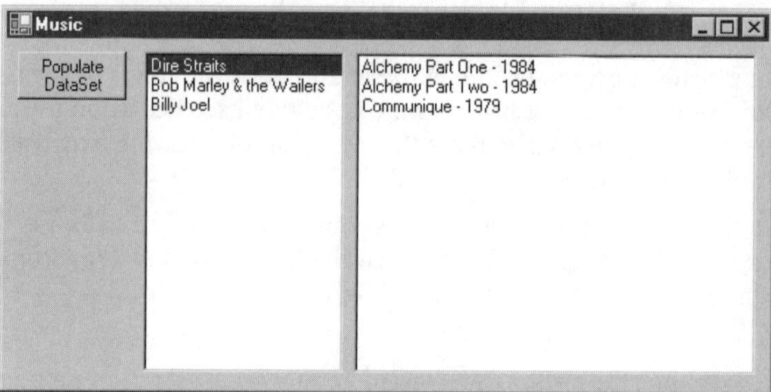

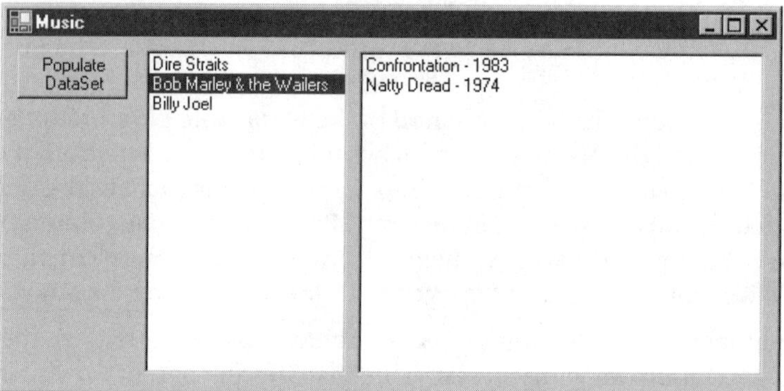

Retrieving Data from a Data Source

Exercises 12-2 and 12-3 demonstrated how to work with disconnected data. They did not, however, demonstrate how to retrieve data from a data source and work with that data when disconnected from the data source. At the beginning of this chapter we discussed the creation of applications that work with the data while staying connected to the data source. In this section, we restate the importance of using the disconnected approach.

As applications become larger they use more resources on the server. Web applications require rapid server response. Because thousands of users may hit a server at once, a server may become increasingly slow as more clients are added to an application. Distributing applications among multiple systems is the most common approach to solving this issue.

Because server resources are scarce, the idea is to free them as soon as possible. The "acquire resources late and release them early" concept is satisfied by a data access technology that retrieves the data, places it in memory, and releases the connection resources that the client occupies while retrieving that data. Once the connection is closed, the server can handle other clients' requests while each client works with its data locally.

The **DataSet**, as stated earlier, has no ability to communicate with a particular data source. It does not retrieve data; it simply stores it. Therefore, developers must use a combination of the **DataSet** and a data provider to work with the disconnected data.

The following steps outline how to work with a DataSet and data from a data source.

1. Retrieve the data from the data source and place it in a **DataSet**.
2. Disconnect from the data source.
3. Work with the in-memory data. Any changes will be flagged within the **DataSet**.
4. Reconnect to the data source.
5. Reconcile the changes in the **DataSet** back to the data source.
6. Disconnect from the data source.

Not all of these steps must be executed when working with disconnected data. If we do not need to update the data source with the changes made to the **DataSet**, we do not execute Steps 4 through 6.

Exercise 12-4: Retrieving Data from a Data Source In Exercise 12-4 you will retrieve data from the Microsoft SQL Server Northwind sample database. You will use the SQL Server .NET data provider, which is contained in the **System.Data.SqlClient** namespace. If you wish to retrieve data from a different data source, modify the code according to the connection information and data structure of the provider and data source.

1. Create a Visual Basic .NET Windows Application using the Visual Studio .NET IDE named CustomersApp.
2. Add the controls and property settings listed in Table 12-10. The resulting form should look similar to the illustration.

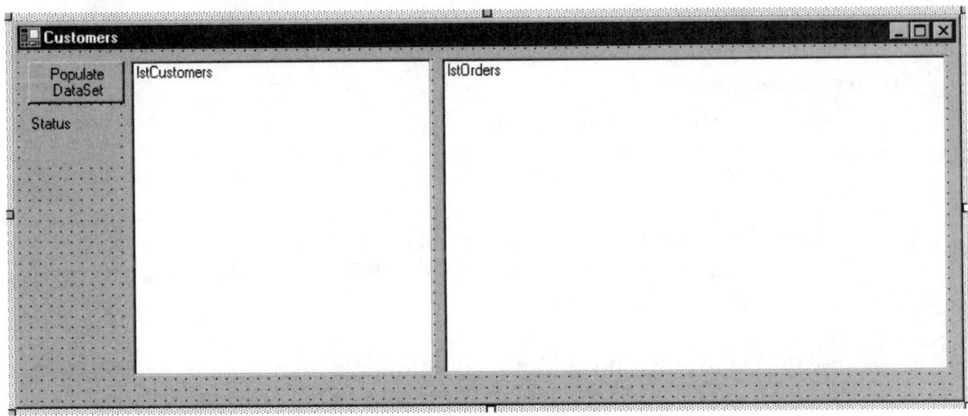

Table 12-10 Controls on the CustomersApp Form

Type	Name	Properties
The form itself	frmCustomers	Size = 736,300 Text = Customers
Button	btnPopulate	Location = 8,8 Size = 75,32 Text = Populate DataSet
ListBox	lstCustomers	Location = 88,8 Size = 232,238
ListBox	lstOrders	Location = 328,8 Size = 392,238
Label	lblStatus	Location = 8,48 Size = 72,40 Text = Status

3. In the project settings, set the Startup Object to frmCustomers.
4. To declare the **DataSet** variable to be modular, add the following statement immediately after the Inherits statement at the top of the Class declaration.

```
Protected dsCustomers As DataSet
```

5. Create the btnPopulate control's Click event handler. Because the **DataSet** may take several seconds to populate, you must let the user know the operation is underway. You must also clear the two list boxes of any values. Add the following code to the event handler.

```
lblStatus.Text = "Please wait …"
lstCustomers.Items.Clear()
lstOrders.Items.Clear()
```

6. You must now create a **Connection** object to connect to the data source. This object is provider specific. Because you will be connecting to a Microsoft SQL Server 2000 database, you will use the **SqlConnection** data type for the **Connection** object. Again, if you wish to use another data source, use the appropriate .NET data provider. The connection string used when creating the **Connection** object will most likely be different for each provider. Enter the following code.

```
Dim cnNWind As New SqlConnection( _
      "Integrated Security=SSPI;Initial Catalog=Northwind;" _
      "Data Source=(local)")
```

EXAM TIP Because the **DataSet** has no ability to communicate directly with any type of data source, you must use a .NET data provider to access the data on behalf of the **DataSet**.

7. Because the **DataSet** has no ability to communicate directly with the data source, the **DataSet** object can be used whether it is connected to a data source or independent of a data source. To establish the connection between the data source

and the **DataSet**, the provider namespace will include an object; this object is the **DataAdapter** class. The **DataAdapter** object contains a SelectCommand property that points to a **Command** object used to retrieve a row set from the data source. For each row set (**DataTable** created by the **DataAdapter**) to be added to the **DataSet**, there must be one **DataAdapter** object. To create three **DataAdapter** objects that populate three **DataTables** in the single **DataSet**, enter the following code.

```
Dim daCustomers As New SqlDataAdapter( _
      "SELECT CustomerID, CompanyName FROM Customers", _
      cnNWind)
Dim daOrders As New SqlDataAdapter( _
      "SELECT OrderID, OrderDate, CustomerID, EmployeeID FROM Orders", _
      cnNWind)
Dim daEmployees As New SqlDataAdapter( _
      "SELECT EmployeeID, LastName, FirstName FROM Employees", _
      cnNWind)
```

For each **DataAdapter** object, the constructor used is passed the SELECT query for each row set. The second argument passed into the constructor is a pointer to the **Connection** object to use when executing the query. This constructor creates the **Command** object and assigns it to the SelectCommand property of the **DataAdapter** object.

8. To create the **DataSet** object, enter the following line.

```
dsCustomers = New DataSet("Customers")
```

9. So far you have created a **Connection** object that is closed (the connection has not yet been established); three **DataAdapters** whose queries have not yet been executed on the data source; and an empty **DataSet** object. Enter the following code to populate the **DataSet** with the result of each of the queries.

```
daCustomers.Fill(dsCustomers, "Customers")
Dim dtCustomers As DataTable = dsCustomers.Tables("Customers")
daOrders.Fill(dsCustomers, "Orders")
Dim dtOrders As DataTable = dsCustomers.Tables("Orders")
daEmployees.Fill(dsCustomers, "Employees")
```

The Fill method of the **DataAdapter** object opens the connection to the data source if necessary (if the **Connection** object is currently open the **DataAdapter** simply uses it and leaves the object open when complete). It then executes the statement on the data source. The result is a new **DataTable** in the **DataSet** filled with the row set returned from the data source. The first argument of the Fill method specifies the **DataSet** in which to place the **DataTable**, which is named with the second argument of the method.

EXAM TIP Use the Fill method of the **DataAdapter** object to populate the **DataTable** in the **DataSet**.

For each of the Customers and Orders **DataTables**, you have created a variable and assigned it a pointer to each of the tables. This variable is for simplicity when using the tables later in this procedure.

PART IV

10. To create the **DataRelation** object, enter the following code.

```
dsCustomers.Relations.Add("CustomerOrders", _
      New DataColumn() {dtCustomers.Columns("CustomerID")}, _
      New DataColumn() {dtOrders.Columns("CustomerID")})
```

11. To populate the lstCustomers ListBox control with a list of the customers and their IDs, add the following code.

```
Dim dr As DataRow
For Each dr In dtCustomers.Rows
      lstCustomers.Items.Add(dr.Item("CustomerID").ToString() & _
           " --- " & dr.Item("CompanyName").ToString())
Next
```

12. To tell the user that the population is complete, add the following code.

```
lblStatus.Text = "Data Retrieved"
```

13. To execute code when the user selects a customer from the ListBox, enter the following code, which is similar to the code in Exercise 12-3.

```
lstOrders.Items.Clear()
Dim parentRow As DataRow = dsCustomers.Tables("Customers").Select( _
"CustomerID = '" & lstCustomers.SelectedItem.ToString().Substring(0, 5) & _
      "'")(0)

Dim childRows() As DataRow = parentRow.GetChildRows( _
      dsCustomers.Relations("CustomerOrders"))
Dim dr As DataRow
For Each dr In childRows
      Dim drEmp As DataRow = dsCustomers.Tables("Employees").Select( _
           "EmployeeID = '" & dr.Item("EmployeeID").ToString() & "'")(0)
      lstOrders.Items.Add(dr.Item("OrderID").ToString() & " - " & _
           dr.Item("OrderDate").ToLongDateString() & " - " & _
           drEmp.Item("FirstName").ToString() & " " & _
           drEmp.Item("LastName").ToString())
Next
```

14. Execute the application by clicking Debug | Start. The resulting execution will look similar to the sample shown in the illustration.

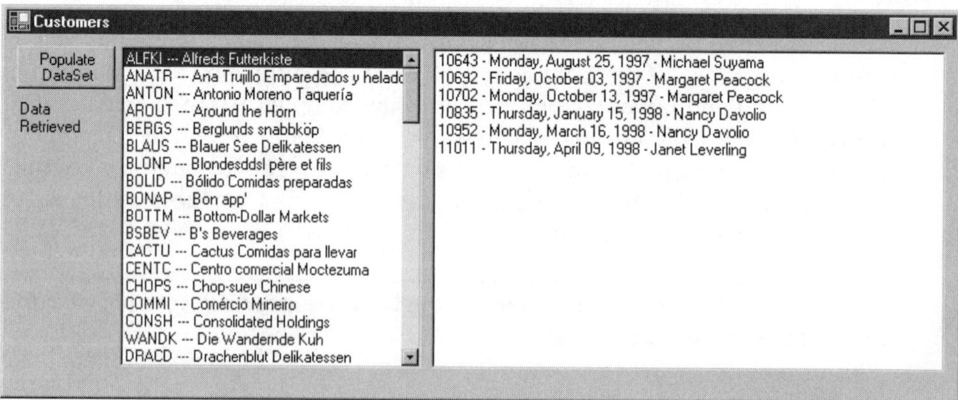

The Typed DataSet

So far in this chapter, accessing items within the **DataSet** object has required the use of the item's name in quotes: for example, using *dsCustomers.Tables("Customers")* to access a table and using *dRow.Items("CompanyName")* to access a particular value. In each of these examples, the application works perfectly well as long as the developer does not make a typo.

Even if the developer typed the name of the table or field incorrectly, the error would only be detected at runtime. To the compiler, the code would look correct. When executed, however, the table or field would not be found, causing an exception.

Microsoft has provided a feature with the Visual Studio .NET IDE to go along with its IntelliSense technology. The feature, called **Typed DataSets**, creates a file that describes the structure of the **DataSet**. This XML schema file does not contain the data; it contains only the structure of the data. XML and XML schemas are discussed in detail in Chapter 13.

With **Typed DataSets**, developers can use *dsCustomers.Customers* instead of dsCustomers .Tables("Customers") to access the Customers **DataTable**. This provides a type-safe manner of using the **DataSet** because the compiler compares the code to the XML schema file representing the **DataSet** to determine whether the name of the table or field has been entered correctly.

Exercise 12-5: Creating a Typed DataSet In this exercise you will create an application similar to the application created in Exercise 12-4. This application, however, will have a **Typed DataSet** and will utilize features in the Visual Studio .NET IDE that are related to the **Typed DataSet**.

1. Create a new Visual Basic .NET Windows Application using the Visual Studio .NET IDE named TypedCustomers.
2. Add the controls and property settings listed in Table 12-11. The resulting form should look similar to the illustration.

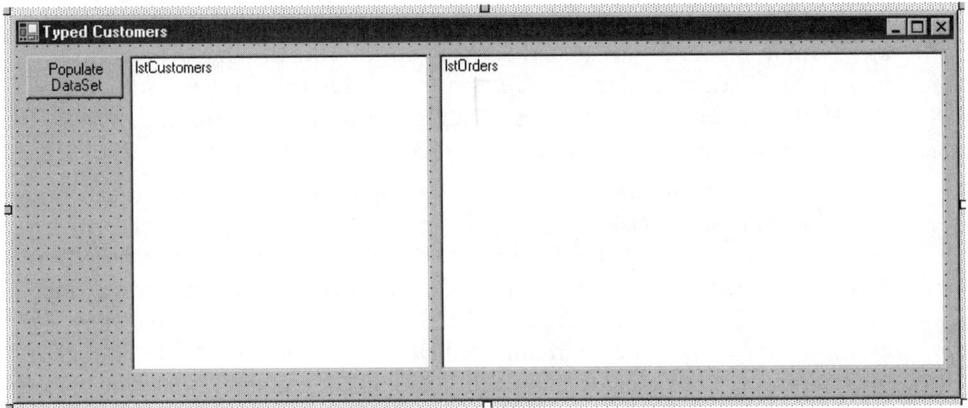

PART IV

Table 12-11 Controls on the TypedCustomers Application Form

Type	Name	Properties
The form itself	frmTypedCustomers	Size = 736,300 Text = Typed Customers
Button	btnPopulate	Location = 8,8 Size = 75,32 Text = Populate DataSet
ListBox	lstCustomers	Location = 88,8 Size = 232,238
ListBox	lstOrders	Location = 328,8 Size = 392,238

3. Modify the project settings to specify the frmTypedCustomers form as the Startup Object.

   In the previous exercises you created the **Connection**, **Command**, and other data access objects by manually coding them. In this exercise you will use the Visual Studio .NET designer to create them. This is not a replacement for manually coding the objects, just an alternative.

4. Because this application will be accessing a SQL Server 2000 database, you will use the **SqlConnection** object to create the Connection object in the integrated development environment (IDE). While viewing the form in Design Mode, select the Data tab on the Toolbox. Double-click the SqlConnection icon to add a new **Connection** object to the form. An object called **SqlConnection1** will be added to the objects pane below the form. Select this object and rename it to **cnNWind**.
5. To create a Connection string, select the ConnectionString property in the Properties window and click the drop-down arrow. Select the New Connection option. The Data Link Properties dialog box, which is shown in Figure 12-1, appears. Type the name of the server; to access the local machine use "(local)" as the value. Select the Integrated Security option (the difference between the two options is described in the *SQL Server Books Online*). Select Northwind as the database to access and click the Test Connection button to verify that the connection string is correct. Click OK to return to the Visual Studio .NET IDE.
6. You must now create the **DataAdapter** to retrieve the Customers row set from the data source. Using the Data tab on the Toolbox, double-click the SqlDataAdapter icon to add the object to the object pane and invoke the Data Adapter Configuration Wizard. Click Next and choose the connection created in Step 5. For SQL Server, this will be the fully qualified connection format—for example, NDWHQ1.Northwind.dbo. Click Next and select SQL statements as the query type. Click Next to enter the SQL SELECT statement that you will use to retrieve the data. You can manually type the SQL statement in the box provided or click the Query Builder button to invoke the graphical tool for generating the query.

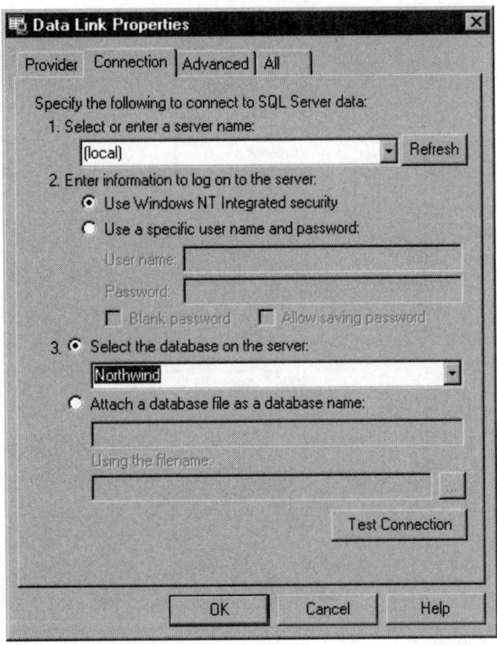

Figure 12-1 Data Link Properties dialog box

For this exercise, invoke the Query Builder and add the Customers table to the query. There are four panes in the Query Builder, which can be seen in Figure 12-2. The top pane displays the tables in a graphical view and allows you to select which columns of the tables you want in the query. The second pane gives you an alternate method for adding fields to the query. It also allows you to specify criteria and sorting attributes. The third pane displays the SQL representation of the query, which you can also modify. The last pane is the output pane, which is useful for verifying the correct output from the query. To invoke the Run, simply right-click anywhere in the Query Builder and click Run.

So far you have no fields in the query. In the top pane click the check box next to the CustomerID and CompanyName columns. Click OK to accept the query and return to the Wizard. Click Advanced Options. The top check box specifies that the Wizard will generate the INSERT, DELETE, and UPDATE queries based on the SELECT query you have created. The Advanced Options can be seen in Figure 12-3. This is a very useful feature of the Wizard; without it you would have to create the queries manually. To allow the **DataAdapter** to provide data source update support (used if you modify any data in the **DataSet**), you must assign queries to the **Commands**. Each of the **Command** objects is contained within the **DataAdapter** as properties called SelectCommand, DeleteCommand, UpdateCommand, and InsertCommand.

Click OK to close the Advanced Options, and then click Finish to generate the **DataAdapter**. Rename the **DataAdapter** in the Properties window to **daCustomers**. Expand each **Command** in the **DataAdapter** and notice the SQL statement that has been generated. Even though the SELECT statement is quite simple, the UPDATE statement is complex.

Figure 12-2 Query Builder

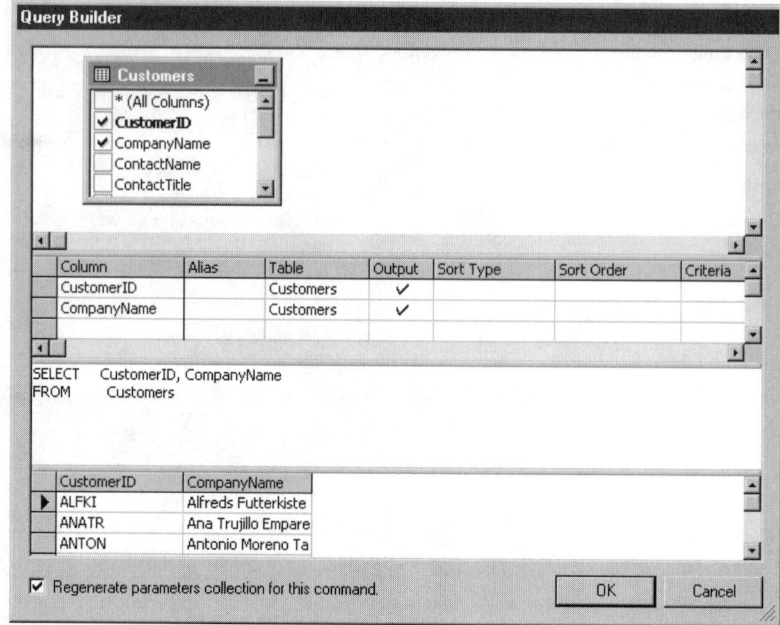

7. To create daOrders and daEmployees, follow the instructions in Step 6. Table 12-12 shows the SELECT statements for each.

Figure 12-3 Advanced options of the Data Adapter Configuration Wizard

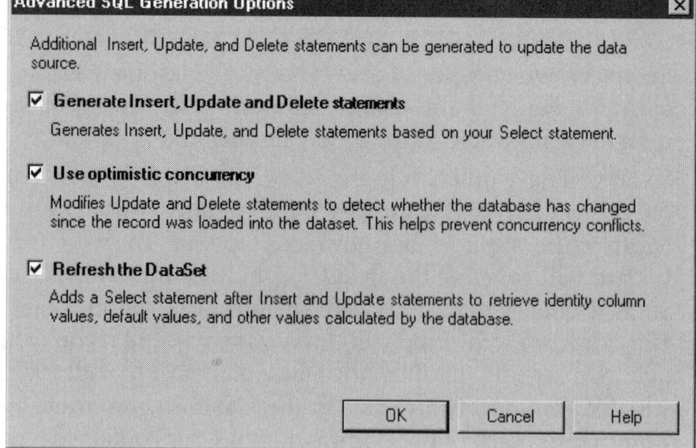

Table 12-12 daOrders and daEmployees SELECT Statements

DataAdapter Name	SELECT Statement
daOrders	SELECT OrderID, OrderDate, CustomerID, EmployeeID FROM Orders
daEmployees	SELECT EmployeeID, FirstName, LastName FROM Employees

8. To generate the **Typed DataSet** using the IDE, select the form in Design Mode and click Data | Generate DataSet. The Generate Dataset dialog box, which can be seen in Figure 12-4, appears. Create a new **DataSet** called **CustomersTypedDS**. Note that this action does not generate the **DataSet** object but rather the XML schema representing the structure of the **DataSet**. Leave all the DataAdapters checked so that all three tables will be part of the **DataSet**. Click OK to generate the XML schema definition (XSD) file. This action also creates a **DataSet** object and adds it to the object pane below the form. Rename this **DataSet** to **dsCustomers**.
9. Now that you have created the user interface and the data access objects, you must write the code within the event handlers. Add the btnPopulate control's Click event handler to the form. Clear the list boxes of any content by entering the following code.

```
lstCustomers.Items.Clear()
lstOrders.Items.Clear()
```


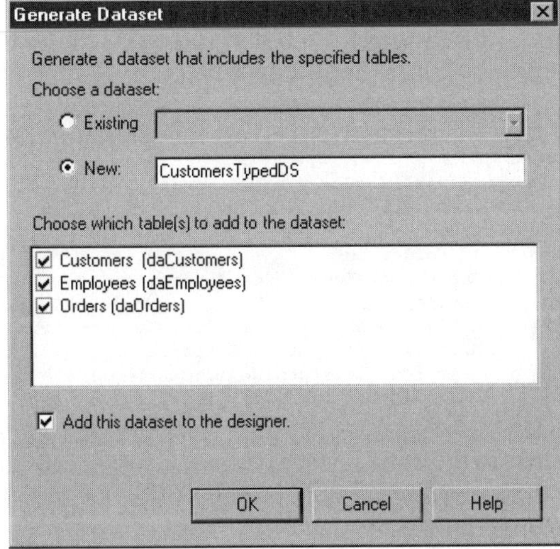

Figure 12-4 Generate Dataset dialog box

10. Even though you have specified which tables will be part of the **DataSet**, you have not yet retrieved the data. As with the previous exercise, enter the following code to use the Fill method of the **DataAdapters** to add the table to the **DataSet**.

```
daCustomers.Fill(dsCustomers, "Customers")
daOrders.Fill(dsCustomers, "Orders")
daEmployees.Fill(dsCustomers, "Employees")
```

11. To create the **DataRelation** object establishing the relationship between the Customers and Orders tables, enter the following code.

```
dsCustomers.Relations.Add("CustomerOrders", _
      New DataColumn() {dsCustomers.Customers.CustomerIDColumn}, _
      New DataColumn() {dsCustomers.Orders.CustomerIDColumn})
```

In this statement, you have used the table and column names as properties of the **DataSet** instead of using the Tables and Items collections.

12. To add the customers to the lstCustomers ListBox, enter the following code.

```
Dim dr As DataRow
For Each dr In dsCustomers.Customers.Rows
      lstCustomers.Items.Add(dr.Item("CustomerID").ToString() & _
            " --- " & dr.Item("CompanyName").ToString())
Next
```

13. To add the SelectedIndexChanged event handler for the lstCustomers ListBox control, first clear the lstOrders ListBox control of any values by entering the following code.

```
lstOrders.Items.Clear()
```

14. The following code is almost exactly the same as the code used in the previous exercise. The only difference is that you use table and column names as properties instead of the Tables and Items collections. Enter the code.

```
Dim parentRow As DataRow = dsCustomers.Customers.Select( _
      "CustomerID = '" & lstCustomers.SelectedItem.ToString().Substring( _
      0, 5) & "'")(0)
Dim childRows() As DataRow = parentRow.GetChildRows( _
      dsCustomers.Relations("CustomerOrders"))
Dim dr As DataRow
For Each dr In childRows
      Dim drEmp As DataRow = dsCustomers.Employees.Select( _
            "EmployeeID = '" & dr.Item("EmployeeID").ToString() & "'")(0)
      lstOrders.Items.Add(dr.Item("OrderID").ToString() & " - " & _
            dr.Item("OrderDate").ToLongDateString() & " - " & _
            drEmp.Item("FirstName").ToString() & " " & _
            drEmp.Item("LastName").ToString())
Next
```

As shown in the code above, you must still specify the column names when using the **DataRow** variable because only the **DataSet** is typed. There is no such thing as a Typed DataRow.

15. Execute the application by clicking Debug | Start. The following illustration shows the executed application.

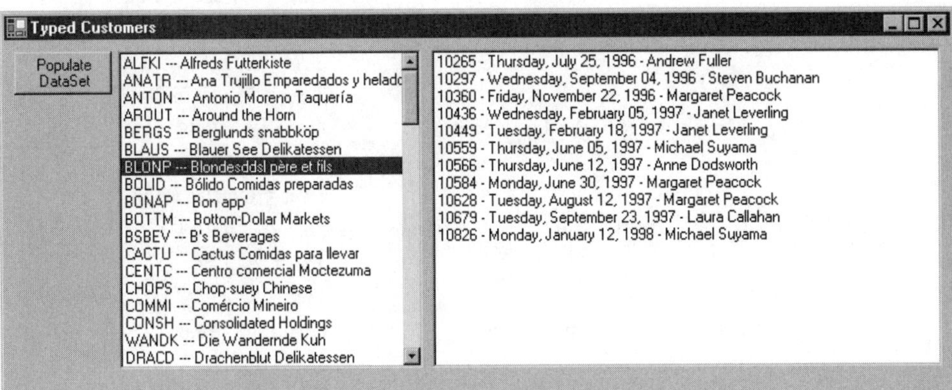

Updating the Data Source

Developers can manipulate the **DataSet** while it is in memory, and then use the **DataAdapter** object to reconcile the changes back to the data source. In Exercise 12-5, you created the **DataAdapter** using the Data Adapter Configuration Wizard, which generated the INSERT, UPDATE, and DELETE statements based on the SELECT statement you entered.

EXAM TIP To have the **DataAdapter** reconcile changes back to the data source, the **DataAdapter** UpdateCommand, DeleteCommand, and InsertCommand properties must be set with the appropriate statements.

Exercise 12-6: Updating the Data Source In this exercise you will create an application that retrieves the unit price of each of the products in the Products table and increases the price by 10%. You will see that even though the data in the **DataSet** changes, the data in the data source stays the same as when you retrieved it. Then, you will update the data source and see how the values change to match the DataSet.

1. Create a new Visual Basic .NET Windows Application using the Visual Studio .NET IDE named UpdatingData.
2. Add the controls and property settings listed in Table 12-13. The resulting form should look similar to Figure 12-5.
3. Modify the project settings to specify frmUpdatingData as the Startup Object.

Table 12-13 Controls on UpdatingData Form

Type	Name	Properties
The form itself	frmUpdatingData	Size = 328,368 Text = Updating Data
Button	btnPopulate	Location = 8,8 Size = 75,32 Text = Populate DataSet
Button	btnUpdatePrice	Location = 8,48 Size = 75,32 Text = Update Price
Button	btnUpdateDataSource	Location = 8,88 Size = 75,32 Text = Update Data Source
Label	lblDataSet	Location = 96,8 Size = 104,16 Text = Data Set
Label	lblDataSource	Location = 208,8 Size = 104,16 Text = Data Source
ListBox	lstDataSetValues	Location = 96,32 Size = 104,277
ListBox	lstDataSourceValues	Location = 208,32 Size = 104,277

4. Add a **SqlConnection** object to the form by double-clicking the SqlConnection icon on the Data tab of the Toolbox. Set the ConnectionString to establish a connection to the local server and the Northwind database. Name the **Connection** object **cnNWind**.

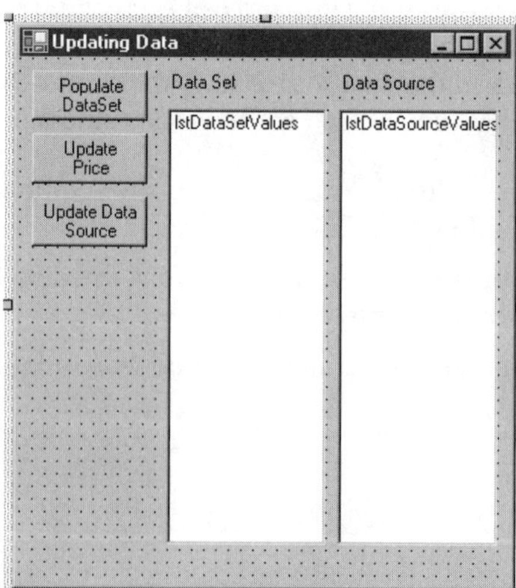

Figure 12-5 UpdatingData form

5. Add a **SqlDataAdapter** object to the form by double-clicking the SqlDataAdapter icon on the Data tab of the Toolbox. Set the SELECT query of the **DataAdapter** to **SELECT ProductID, UnitPrice FROM Products**. Make sure that the Generate check box in the Advanced Options dialog box is selected to generate the INSERT, UPDATE, and DELETE statements. Name the **DataAdapter** object **daProducts**.
6. Generate a **Typed DataSet** by clicking Data | Generate Dataset. Select the daProducts **DataAdapter** as the only table in the **Typed DataSet** and name the **DataSet** object **ProductsTypedDS**. Rename the new **DataSet** object in the object pane below the form to **dsProducts**.
7. Add the following Imports statement to the form.

```
Imports System.Data.SqlClient
```

8. Create a new Sub procedure that has no arguments. Name it **ShowDataValues**.
9. Inside the ShowDataValues procedure, clear the ListBox controls of their values by entering the following code.

```
lstDataSourceValues.Items.Clear()
lstDataSetValues.Items.Clear()
```

10. To create a loop that will add each of the prices in the **DataSet** to the lstDataSetValues ListBox control, enter the following code.

```
Dim dr As DataRow
For Each dr In dsProducts.Products.Rows
      lstDataSetValues.Items.Add(dr.Item("UnitPrice").ToString())
Next
```

11. To retrieve a **DataReader** from the data source and add the unit price values to the lstDataSourceValues ListBox control, add the following code to the procedure.

```
cnNWind.Open()
Dim drProducts As SqlDataReader = daProducts.SelectCommand.ExecuteReader()
Do While drProducts.Read()
      lstDataSourceValues.Items.Add(drProducts.Item("UnitPrice"))
Loop
drProducts.Close()
cnNWind.Close()
```

12. To add the event handler for the btnPopulate control's Click event, use the Fill method of the **DataAdapter** to populate the **DataTable** in the **DataSet** and call the ShowDataValues procedure by entering the following code.

```
daProducts.Fill(dsProducts, "Products")
ShowDataValues()
```

13. To add the event handler for the btnUpdatePrice control's Click event, loop through the **Rows** collection and multiply the value by 110% by entering the code below. Note that using the CType function to convert the String value to a Double ensures that you perform the correct mathematical calculation.

```
Dim dr As DataRow
For Each dr In dsProducts.Products.Rows
      dr.Item("UnitPrice") = CType( _
            dr.Item("UnitPrice").ToString(), Double) * 1.1
Next
ShowDataValues()
```

14. Add the event handler for the btnUpdateDataSource control's Click event by entering the code below. Because the daProducts **DataAdapter** has the appropriate UPDATE statement for the **DataSet**, you can use its Update method to reconcile the changes to the data source. Only the rows in the **DataSet** that have been changed are flagged to be updated to the data source. In this exercise, every row has been updated. In another application only certain rows may be changed. The **DataAdapter**, once it opens the **Connection** object, creates an appropriate INSERT, UPDATE, or DELETE statement for each row that is flagged—all by executing a single method!

```
daProducts.Update(dsProducts)
ShowDataValues()
```

15. Execute the application by clicking Debug | Start. Figures 12-6, 12-7, and 12-8 show the progressive execution of the application. In Figure 12-6 the **DataSet** contains the same values as the data source. In Figure 12-16 the **DataSet**'s values have increased while the data source has not been affected. In Figure 12-8 the data source has been updated, and the DataSet and data source values are now the same.

NOTE Many issues related to disconnected data access are beyond the scope of this book. The most important issue relates to what happens when the data is updated by another user while we are updating the data. In this situation, which change is saved to the data source? The decision is usually based on each application's business rules.

Figure 12-6 Original values retrieved

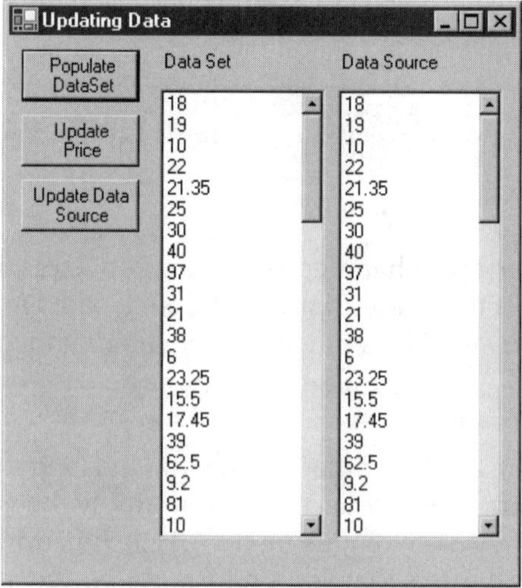

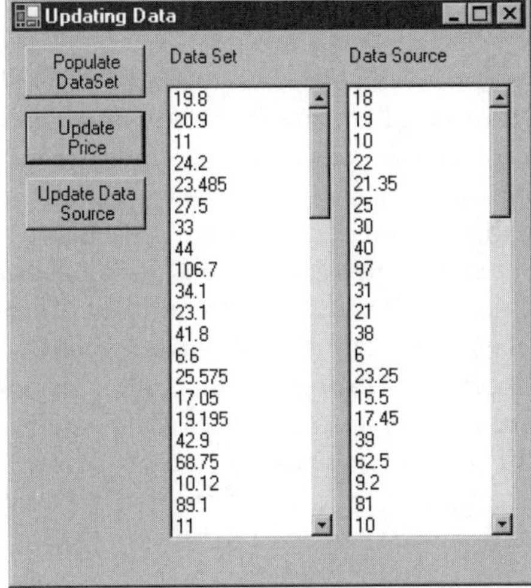

Figure 12-7 DataSet and data source values are different

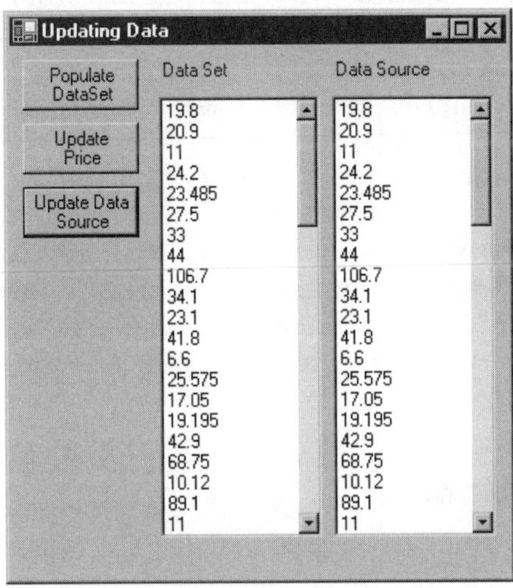

Figure 12-8 Data source reflects the changes made to the DataSet

Summary

In this chapter, we discussed data access using the ADO.NET classes. We focused mainly on the DataReader class and the DataSet class with its associated classes. The **DataSet** is an in-memory cache of data, as well as an in-memory relational database. The **DataSet** has no ability to communicate directly with any particular data source. This quality allows developers to use it with any type of data source as well as with no data source at all.

The **DataSet** contains **DataTable** and **DataRelation** objects. Each **DataTable** is a table of data represented as **DataColumns** and **DataRows**. Developers use these three objects to manipulate data. The **DataRelation** object represents a primary/foreign key relationship between **DataTables** in a **DataSet**. This relationship allows multiple tables to be retrieved from multiple data sources and related as if they were from the same data source. A **Typed DataSet** is a **DataSet** in which **DataTables** and the **DataColumns** of those tables are available as properties of the **DataSet**. The definition of a **Typed DataSet** is stored as an XML schema definition (XSD) file.

The **DataAdapter** is used to retrieve and update the data between a data source and a **DataSet**. The **DataAdapter** has a **Command** object property for each of the SELECT, INSERT, UPDATE, and DELETE statements that will be executed by the **DataAdapter**. The **DataSet** flags the **DataRows** that have been changed while working in disconnected mode. The **DataAdapter** creates an individual statement for each row that is to be reconciled to the data source when the Update method of the **DataAdapter** is called. Developers can use the DataAdapter Configuration Wizard in the Visual Studio .NET IDE to generate a **DataAdapter** object and its **Commands**. Developers can use the Query Builder to generate SQL statements for the **DataAdapter**.

The **DataReader** is a provider-specific read-only, forward-only data set. It is meant for use in a connected data access scenario. The **Connection** object must be open while the **DataReader** is open. Remember to acquire resources late and release them early, which means that you must remember to close the **DataReader** as soon as you are finished using it.

Test Questions

1. You need to develop a Web-based application that retrieves your company's catalog from a SQL Server 2000 database. The catalog information is changed once a day by the marketing department through a Windows Forms application. Which object would use the fewest resources to send the catalog information to a Web browser?

   A. SqlDataAdapter

   B. DataSet

   C. SqlDataReader

   D. DataTable

2. Which of the following lines of code will correctly create a **DataTable** called "Products" in a **DataSet** called dsProductInfo?

   A. daProducts.Fill(dsProductInfo, "Products")

   B. daProducts.Fill(dsProductInfo)

   C. daProducts.FillDataSet("Products")

   D. daProducts.CreateTable("Products", dsProductInfo)

3. You are developing an application for a client that is used by the inventory department to reconcile stock quantities. There are two tables on the data source to be accessed; one table stores the product information for each inventory item, and the other table stores the inventory categories for the products that the client sells. The Categories table has a primary key and the Products table has a foreign key corresponding to the primary key. Which strategy is best for developing the application?

   A. Create an **OracleDataReader** object and set the object to allow editing. Retrieve a row set from the database using a JOIN query.

   B. Create an **OracleDataAdapter** object and populate a **DataSet** with the Fill method of the **DataAdapter** object. The query on the database will be performed with an INNER JOIN statement.

   C. Create an **OracleDataAdapter** object and populate a **DataSet** with the Fill method of the **DataAdapter** object. The query on the database will retrieve only the Categories table. Create an event handler to be executed when the user selects a particular category. Have the procedure create an **OracleDataReader** object that retrieves only products that are part of the selected category.

   D. Create two **OracleDataAdapter** objects. Have one **DataAdapter** retrieve the Categories table and the other retrieve the Products table. Execute the Fill method on each of the **DataAdapters** to fill the **DataSet**. Create a **DataRelation** object in the **DataSet** that relates the two tables.

4. Which of the following steps are used to update a data source from a **DataSet**? Select the most appropriate order for the steps you choose.

   i. Create the **DataSet**.

   ii. Open the **Connection**.

   iii. Modify the data in the **DataSet**.

   iv. Execute the Fill method of the **DataAdapter**.

   v. Execute the Update method of the **DataAdapter**.

   vi. Set the SELECT query of the **DataAdapter**.

   vii. Create the **DataAdapter** using the Data Adapter Configuration Wizard.

A. ii, i, vii, vi, v, iii, iv

B. i., vii, vi, iv, iii, v

C. ii, i, vii, vi, iv, iii, v

D. vii, vi, iv, iii, v

5. What is wrong with the following code?

```
Dim drProducts As SqlDataReader = _
      cmProducts.ExecuteReader()
MessageBox.Show(drProducts.Item("ProductName"))
```

A. The ToString method has not been called in the MessageBox.Show method.

B. The code did not explicitly create the **DataReader** instance.

C. The Execute method should have been called and not the ExecuteReader method.

D. The Read method of the **DataReader** should have been called.

Test Answers

1. **C.** In this case the code on the server is simply going to open a connection to the server and send the output to the Web browser line-by-line. This way you can open the **DataReader** and loop until the end of the data set. At that point you only need to close the **DataReader** and **SqlConnection** objects.

2. **A.** The Fill method populates a **DataTable** in a **DataSet**. The first argument of the method is a pointer to the **DataSet** you wish to add the data to, and the second argument is the name of the **DataTable** you wish to add the data to.

3. **D.** Even though you could retrieve the data using a JOIN query and populate the table of the **DataSet** with the results of this query, it is more useful (especially if you wish to use one of the tables in another query) to retrieve each table and create a relationship in the **DataSet**.

4. **B.** You must create the **DataSet** before you can place data within it. You must also create the **DataAdapter**, using the Wizard if you wish. During the Wizard's execution you must enter the SELECT statement so that the Wizard can generate the appropriate **Commands**. You then call the Fill method to populate the **DataSet**. After data has been modified you call the Update method of the **DataAdapter**. At no point do you explicitly have to open the connection to the data source. This is done implicitly when you execute the Fill or Update methods.

5. **D.** You must call the Read method to move to the first row in the row set. Because it may be an empty row set, it is common to place the code that uses the data in a Do While drProducts.Read() loop so that the code is called only if there is at least one row.

CHAPTER 13

Introduction to XML

In this chapter, you will

- Study XML and how it is used
- Create an XML document
- Learn how to define the syntax of XML documents
- Find out how to format XML documents by applying Extensible Stylesheet Language (XSL) templates to the XML document
- Understand how to use Extensible Stylesheet Language Transformations (XSLT)
- Explore the use of cascading style sheets

Extensible Markup Language (XML) has become the lingua franca of the development world. XML is a language defined by the World Wide Web Consortium (W3C) to describe the way in which content within a document should be interpreted. In practice, XML has primarily been used to:

- Exchange information among applications, databases, and other devices
- Enable formatting and presentation of information for different types of devices, such as palmtops, laptops, desktops, and cellular phones
- Act as a storage format for document-centric information, such as manuals and enterprise data

Although XML may be new to you, markup languages in general probably are not. You use a markup language whenever you open Internet Explorer. HTML, which is used to create Web pages, is an example of a markup language. It specifies to the Web browser how Web content should be displayed to end users. However, HTML does not provide information about what the data being displayed means. This type of information is known as metadata. Unlike HTML, XML focuses on providing information about the data itself and how it relates to other data. To do this, XML not only lets you specify the data, but the structure of the data and how various elements are integrated into other elements. This chapter explores these concepts and how they are used to define XML documents.

Because you can create your own tags within XML, it's up to you to set their syntax. XML documents whose syntax has been checked successfully are called valid documents. To be valid, an XML document must be associated with an XML schema and comply with the syntax specified by the XML schema. This chapter explores XML schemas and how they can be used to validate XML documents.

Although XML is used to describe the data within a document, it does not describe how the data is to be formatted or rendered for the end user. Formatting is the job of Cascading Style Sheets (CSS). Cascading Style Sheets provide a centralized and modular way to format HTML output. We will take the opportunity in this chapter to explore how to create CSS Stylesheets and how they can be applied to our XML documents.

Basic XML

In HTML, approximately 100 tags, or elements, are defined. When a Web browser receives a Web page from a server, it renders the page to the end user based on the tags defined within the page. Although this technology has transformed the computer industry, it is inflexible and doesn't provide enough functionality for anything beyond creating standard Web pages. XML on the other hand gives developers the flexibility—and responsibility—of defining tags and how they should be used.

XML has a stringent set of rules that are much less forgiving than HTML. These rules and specifications allow a computer to process information in a reproducible way. We will begin this section with a simple exercise and a discussion of the syntax, semantics, and rules of XML.

Exercise 13-1: Creating a Simple XML Document In this exercise you will create a simple XML document in order to gain a basic understanding of what an XML document looks like and how it works.

1. To open a copy of Notepad on your computer, select Start | Run. Type **notepad** in the Run dialog box that appears, as shown in the illustration.

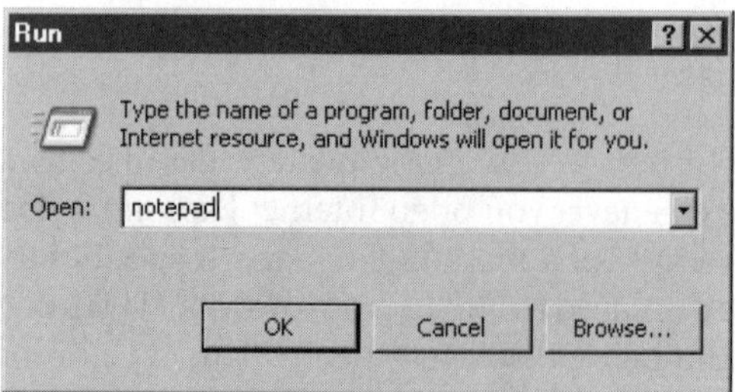

2. Copy the following code into Notepad.

```
<?xml version="1.0" encoding="UTF-8"?>
<DOCUMENT>
      <GREETING>
            Hello World
      </GREETING>
      <MESSAGE>
            Welcome to the wonderful world of XML
      </MESSAGE>
</DOCUMENT>
```

When copying the preceding code, be careful to enter the double quotes as shown; otherwise Internet Explorer may not process the XML document correctly. If you do not enter the quotes correctly, you may receive an error message when you save the document. An example of an error message is shown in the illustration.

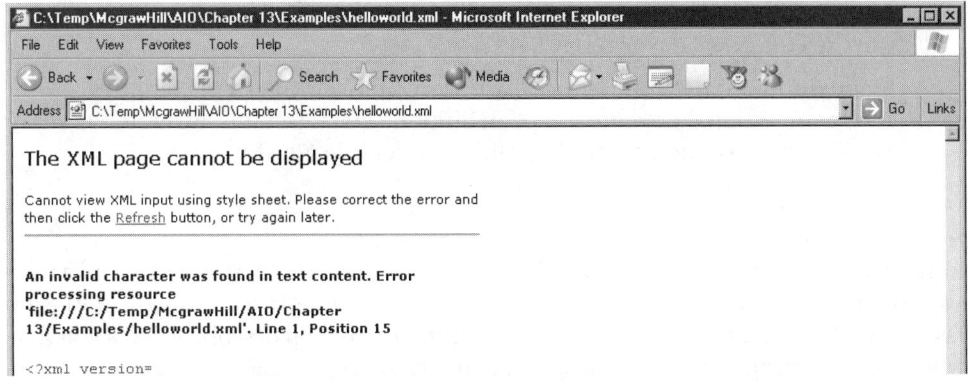

3. Save the file as **helloworld.xml**.
4. To view this XML document, open an instance of Internet Explorer and type the full path to helloworld.xml in the Address text box, as shown in the illustration.

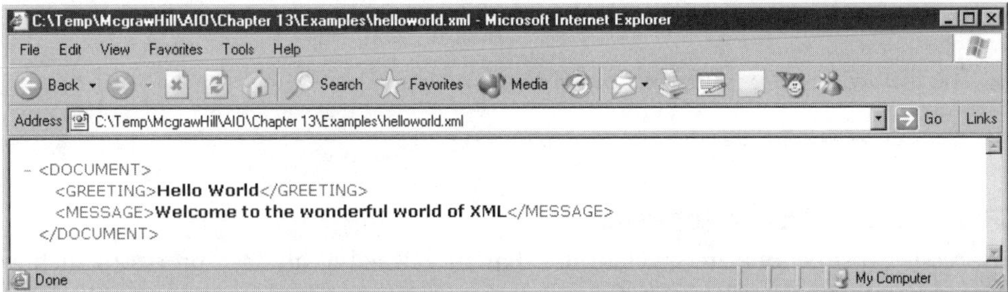

The code in Exercise 13-1 begins with a prolog. Prologs come at the beginning of XML documents. They contain XML declarations, comments, processing instructions, white space, and document-type declarations. In this exercise, you only used an XML declaration. We will discuss the other prolog elements later in the chapter, but for now, let's look at the XML declaration.

The XML Declaration

The XML declaration indicates to an XML processor that the document is written in XML. Although it is not required, it is good practice. If you use an XML declaration, it should be the first line in the document. Nothing should precede it.

PART IV

The <?xml?> tag has three attributes:

- **Version** Specifies the version of XML that is used within the document.
- **Encoding** Specifies the language encoding and character set used within the document. A character set specifies the characters that can be used. Different character sets define and accommodate different symbols and support different languages. The default encoding is UTF-8; however, you can use Unicode, UCS-2, or UCS-4.
- **Standalone** Indicates whether the document refers to external entities such as an external document type definition (DTD); set this attribute to Yes if it refers to external entities; otherwise set it to No.

Comments

Although XML for the most part is self-describing (Exercise 13-1 had a greeting and a message to convey), it is a language of its own. Because the meaning of a document may be difficult to understand at times, developers use comments to help describe what is going on within the document. Comments are in a commonly understood language, usually English. A comment within an XML document begins with <! - - and ends with - - !>.

The following rules apply to comments:

- Comments cannot precede an XML declaration.
- Comments cannot be put inside tags.
- Comments cannot include - -.

The following code is an example of a comment.

```
<!-- Welcome to our HelloWorld example --!>
```

Processing Instructions

Processing instructions are special rules that are relayed to an XML processor such as Internet Explorer to instruct it how to process or interpret the content of an XML document. Processing instructions begin with <? and end with ?>. Processing instructions are platform dependent; not all XML processors support the same processing instructions and XML processors may define their own unique processing instructions.

The main processing instruction that is implemented by virtually all XML processors/Web browsers is the XML Stylesheet processing instruction. This instruction associates a style sheet with the XML document. The instruction must appear in the prolog, before the document or root element.

The syntax for a Stylesheet processing instruction is

```
<?xml-stylesheet type="type" href="uri" ?>
```

where *type* is text/css or text/xsl. The text/css type is a cascading style sheet; the xsl type is a link to an XSLT file. Each type is used to assist in the rendering of the XML document to the browser. Href="uri" specifies the uniform resource identifier (URI) of the style sheet. The following code is an example of an XML Stylesheet processing instruction utilizing a cascading style sheet.

```
<?xml-stylesheet href="/cssstyle.css" type="text/css" ?>
```

Tags and Elements

An XML document consists of a series of elements that allow developers to create structures that can be manipulated with programs or style sheets. Each element usually consists of a start tag and an end tag. The exception is an element that is defined as empty; an empty element consists of only one tag. Start tags, or opening tags, begin with < and end with >. End tags, or closing tags, begin with </ and end with >. You can use start and end tags to create elements within a document.

The tag name can begin with a letter, an underscore, or a colon. However, you should avoid beginning a tag name with a colon because a colon is used to specify namespaces in XML. Because XML processors are case-sensitive, the <DOCUMENT> tag is different from the <document> tag. In Exercise 13-1, you defined three elements: the <DOCUMENT> element, the <GREETING> element, and the <MESSAGE> element.

As mentioned, empty elements have only one tag. In XML you use /> to close an empty element. You can also indicate an empty element by using start and end tags that have no white space or content in between the start and end tags. For example, you can represent an acknowledgement of a message as <ACKNOWLEDGEMENT></ ACKNOWLEDGEMENT>, or you can use an empty tag, <ACKNOWLEDGEMENT/>. The two forms produce identical results in an XML parser.

One element is more significant than the other elements: the root element. The root element contains all the other elements that make up a document. Although the root element must contain all the content considered to be part of the document itself, the root element can be preceded and followed by other markups, such as declarations, processing instructions, and comments. In Exercise 13-1, the root element for the XML document is the <DOCUMENT> element.

Attributes

Attributes are used within XML to specify additional data in start and empty tags. They are often used to define element properties that are not considered to be the content of the element. In some cases, however, the attribute determines the content of the element. For example, in the HTML img tag, the content is specified within the attribute value. An attribute is represented within an element as a name value pair. Names without values are not permitted and an element cannot have two attributes with the same name. An equal sign (=) is used to assign a value to an attribute.

In the following example we assign a Status attribute to customer elements to indicate the status of the customers' credit ratings.

```
<?xml version="1.0" standalone="yes"?>
<DOCUMENT>
      <CUSTOMER STATUS="Bad Credit">
            <NAME>
                  <LASTNAME>Blow</LASTNAME>
                  <FIRSTNAME>Joe</LASTNAME>
            </NAME>
      </CUSTOMER>
</DOCUMENT>
```

You can use attributes to assign additional information to a tag. In the preceding example, we created an attribute called STATUS to add information to the customer tag. Attribute names can start with a letter, an underscore, or a colon, which is followed by digits, underscores, letters, periods, hyphens, and colons. You cannot use white space.

The value assigned to the attribute is text. Because markup is always text, attribute values also are considered text. Even if you assign a number, you must treat the number as a text string and enclose it with quotes. If you do not use quotes around attribute values, the XML parser will reject the document and report an error. The XML specification allows you to use either single or double quotes to indicate attributes, though the type of quote used must be the same on both sides of the attribute value.

Although using attributes to specify additional information for an element is useful, using too many attributes makes a document difficult to read. If you find your markup becoming unwieldy and hard to read, consider breaking some of the attributes into separate elements.

XML Namespaces

XML provides great flexibility in defining your own tags. However, the more XML applications you develop, the more you run the risk of defining tags that have been used already. This causes a tag name conflict. For example, you might have two properties named *Date* that are used for two different types of information. The first Date element might be used for storing information about when a resource or record was created, as outlined in the following example.

```
<RECORD>
      <DATE>101002</DATE>
      <EVENTID>1033</EVENTID>
      <DESCRIPTION>Event Description</DESCRIPTION>
</RECORD>
```

The second Date property might be used for storing information about a person's birth date.

```
<PERSON>
      <DATE>040664</DATE>
      <NAME>Joe, Blow</NAME>
</PERSON>
```

If you use both XML documents within your application and make a reference to the DATE element, the application will not know which DATE element to use. The solution is to use namespaces. Namespaces let you prepend a name, followed by a colon, to tag and attribute names, uniquely identifying them so that one set of tags does not conflict with another.

To illustrate how namespaces are created, we will use an XML application that is designed to catalog books, as shown in the following code.

```
<LIBRARY>
       <BOOK>
             <TITLE>Dinosaurs Are Us</TITLE>
       </BOOK>
</LIBRARY>
```

Because books are usually held within a library, the root element is <LIBRARY>. Within the library we have books, each having its own title. To add a comment to each book, we start by explicitly defining a prefix that we can then substitute for the full name of the namespace. In this example we confine the catalog XML application to its own namespace. To define a new namespace, we use the XMLNS:prefix attribute, where *prefix* is the prefix that we want to use for the namespace; in this case, we will use the prefix *book:*. The following code shows the catalog XML with the new namespace prefix defined.

```
<LIBRARY
      xmlns:book="http://www.booksrus.com/spec">
      <BOOK>
            <TITLE>Dinosaurs Are Us</TITLE>
      </BOOK>
</LIBRARY>
```

To define this namespace, we assign the XMLNS:prefix attribute to a unique identifier, which in XML is usually a uniform resource identifier (URI). This URI can help direct the XML processor to a document-type definition for the namespace although it is not a requirement for the URI. The namespace represented by the URI ensures global uniqueness when merging XML sources, while the associated prefix substitutes for the namespace URI and is only required to be unique within the tightly scoped context of the document. After defining the book namespace, we can preface every tag and attribute name in the namespace with *book:*, as shown in the following code.

```
<book:LIBRARY
      xmlns:book="http://www.amazingbooks.com/spec">
      <book:BOOK>
            <book:TITLE>Dinosaurs Are Us</book:TITLE>
      </book:BOOK>
</book:LIBRARY>
```

In the preceding code, all the tag and attribute names have become part of the **book:** namespace, freeing us to use tags that would cause a conflict otherwise.

PART IV

Now that we have defined the namespace, we can add comments to the book. To do so, we add a namespace that uniquely identifies the tags and attributes used within the same XML as library tags, as shown in the following code.

```
<book:LIBRARY
      xmlns:book="http://www.amazingbooks.com/spec"
      xmlns:comment=http://www.comment.com/comment">
      <book:BOOK>
            <book:TITLE>Dinosaurs Are Us</book:TITLE>
      </book:BOOK>
      <comment:review comment:ID="12345">
            The best book I have ever read.
      </comment:review>
</book:LIBRARY>
```

In the preceding code, we used the XMLNS attribute in the root element of the XML document to explicitly define prefixes for the tags. We could have also used the XMLNS attribute by itself (without defining a prefix) to define a default namespace for the document. In this case, all the enclosed elements would be assumed to belong to that namespace if not explicitly prepended with a prefix for another namespace. The following code specifies a default namespace for the catalog element and all its descendants.

```
<book:LIBRARY
      xmlns:book="http://www.amazingbooks.com/spec"
      xmlns:comment=http://www.comment.com/comment">
      <book:BOOK>
            <book:TITLE>Dinosaurs Are Us</book:TITLE>
      </book:BOOK>
      <comment:review comment:ID="12345">
            The best book I have ever read.
      </comment:review>
      <catalog xmlns=http://www.amazingbooks.com/catalog>
            <bookid>
                  bk101
            </bookid>
      </catalog>
</book:LIBRARY>
```

Namespace declarations are scoped using the element container. All namespace prefixes are valid only within the element in which they are defined. Unqualified elements that are not defined with an explicit namespace use the default namespace.

CDATA Sections

XML is very sensitive to the types of characters that are used within a document. XML processors such as the one included with Microsoft's Internet Explorer are unforgiving if you use characters such as < or & in the wrong context. You can avoid using them by using < and &, instead, but using a lot of these characters makes a document difficult to read.

CDATA sections indicate to the XML processor that there is no markup contained within a particular section of code. Without this construct all the text in an XML document is parsed and searched for characters such as < and &. With this construct, the data remains unparsed until the end of the CDATA section. CDATA sections are commonly used for scripting language content and sample XML or HTML content.

A CDATA section starts with the markup <![CDATA and ends with]]>. Note that although CDATA sections are not parsed for markup, they are parsed for the text *]]>*. For this reason, you should not include]]> within the CDATA section. The following code provides an example of a CDATA section within an XML document.

```
<?xml version="1.0" standalone="yes"?>
<DOCUMENT>
      <MARKUP>
            <![CDATA
                  <RECORD>
                        <DATE>101002</DATE>
                        <EVENTID>1033</EVENTID>
                        <DESCRIPTION>Event Description</DESCRIPTION>
                  </RECORD>
            ]]>
      </MARKUP>
</DOCUMENT>
```

In this example, the markup between the CDATA tags will not be processed by the XML processor; it will be passed through and handled "as is."

Well-Formed XML Documents

XML documents are long chains of bytes that contain data and information that can be processed by an application. The application processes the information based on the data passed to it. The XML processor acts as a bridge between the XML document and the application. Its job is to ensure that the XML document has the correct syntax and meets any constraints outlined within the document's schema. (We will discuss schemas later in the chapter; for now consider them as templates to which a particular XML document must conform.)

To be well formed, an XML document must have a prolog and a root element; it may also have an optional miscellaneous part. The prolog should include an XML declaration and may contain an optional miscellaneous part that includes comments and processing instructions. Each well-formed XML document must have one root element, and all other elements in the document must be enclosed in the root element. (This rule does not apply to the parts of the prolog, because items such as processing instructions and comments are not considered elements.) The miscellaneous part can be made up of XML comments, processing instructions, and white space.

As with any language, knowing its syntax does not necessarily allow you to be conversant in it. To give a language meaning, you must be able to use the syntax in a way that will convey meaning. This is no different for XML.

To create a well-formed XML document, you must apply the following rules:

- Begin the XML document with an XML declaration.
- Include one or more elements. At a minimum, a well-formed XML document must include the root element. If other elements are included, they must be nested within the root element.

- Nest elements correctly; overlapping elements are not allowed.
- Include both start and end tags for elements that aren't empty. In HTML you do not have to include an end tag. A Web browser generally handles this gracefully and still processes the data properly. In XML, this is not the case. To ensure that every document is well formed, every element that is not empty must have both a start and an end tag.
- Close empty elements with /> as shown in the following code. Because empty elements do not include content it is not necessary to include an end tag.

```
<GREETING TEXT="Hello World"/>
```

- Use unique attribute names. Ensure that no attribute name appears more than once in the same start or empty element. Although this is fairly intuitive, it is possible to violate this rule when including a large number of attributes in a tag.
- Use only the five pre-existing entity references: &, <, >, ', and ".
- Surround attribute values with quotes.
- Use < and & only to start tags and entities.

Using these rules and the proper syntax ensures that documents are well formed. If a document is not well formed, the XML processor will not process it. Web browsers are more forgiving. However, being forgiving introduces incompatibilities between different Web browsers because each can handle the rendering in its own way. XML processors require strict compliance to well-formed rules and syntax to ensure that they do not introduce the same incompatibilities as HTML browsers.

XML Schemas

XML provides flexibility by allowing developers to define custom tags, which can be used to mark up data with metadata and turn the raw data into meaningful information. However, with flexibility comes interpretation. One application's interpretation may be different from another application's interpretation. For example, in one application a <BOOK> element may contain plain text, while in another application it may contain other elements such as <CHAPTER> and <PARAGRAPH>.

When you develop an XML document containing custom tags, you must define the syntax with which those tags can be used within the document. You must be specific about how the document is constructed for applications that deal with the document through code. Applications are very unforgiving when it comes to interpretation.

To ensure that an XML document is constructed properly using custom tags, the document must comply with an XML schema. An XML schema specifies the structure and syntax of XML documents, but not their content. The content specification is left to the XML document itself. XML schemas specify not only the structure and syntax, but also the actual data types to be used. Documents that comply with an associated schema are said to be valid XML documents.

Creating an XML Schema

An XML schema defines the elements, attributes, and data types that make up an XML document. The XML schema definition (XSD) language enables developers to define the structure and data types that can be used within an XML document.

```
The following XML document illustrates the development of a schema.<?xml
version="1.0" encoding="UTF-8"?>
<book isbn="1234567">
      <title>Books Are Us</title>
      <author>Book R. Worm</author>
</book>
```

To create an XML schema for the document, we begin by specifying the top-level schema element within the schema file. We call this file *book.xsd.*

```
<?xml version="1.0" encoding="UTF-8"?>
<xsd:schema xmlns:xsd=http://www.w3.org/2001/XMLSchema
       targetNamespace=http://tempura.org/po.xsd">
...
</xsd:schema>
```

Within the top-level element of the preceding code, we specify the namespace that the schema is associated with and define a prefix, *xsd,* for the namespace. We also specify an attribute for the schema tag called targetNamespace. One advantage of schemas is that they allow XML processors to validate documents that use namespaces. The targetNamespace attribute specifies the namespace to which the schema is targeted. An XML processor can determine which schema to use when it is validating a document based on the namespace that is used within the document. When the XML processor finds the schema and verifies that its target namespace is the same as the document's, it can validate the document.

To declare the elements and attributes for our XML document we use the <xsd:element> and <xsd:attribute> elements. With this declaration we also specify the type of the elements and attributes. To create types, we use the <xsd:simpletype> and <xsd:complextype> elements. Elements that enclose subelements or have attributes are complex types; elements that enclose simple data such as dates, strings, and numbers are simple types. Simple types are easy to create as many simple types are already declared in the XML schema specification. Complex types are defined by the developer. The following code shows the XML schema for our XML document.

```
<?xml version="1.0" encoding="UTF-8"?>
<xsd:schema xmlns:xsd=http://www.w3.org/2001/XMLSchema
      targetNamespace=http://tempura.org/po.xsd">

      <xsd:element name="book">
            <xsd:complexType>
                  <xsd:element name="title" type="xsd:string"/>
                  <xsd:element name="author" type="xsd:string"/>
                  <xsd:attribute name="isbn" type="xsd:integer"/>
            </xsd:complexType>
      </xsd:element>
</xsd:schema>
```

PART IV

In the preceding code we define an element named *book* as a complex type. It is a complex type because it has attributes and non-text children. The book element is defined with an attribute and a list of children elements that are defined with simple types. Table 13-1 lists some of the simple types that are included in the XML specification. For a more comprehensive list refer to the XML specification.

You are not limited to pre-defined simple types. You can create your own simple types. For further information on creating custom simple types, refer to the XML schema specification.

Not only elements and attributes can be defined with simple types. In fact, attributes can be defined *only* with simple types because their internal content cannot be made up of other elements or attributes. Elements can be defined with complex types that have been defined elsewhere. For example, to create a "publishers address" element, we can define it using a complex type called *address* that can be used as the definition not only for the publisher's address, but also for other types of addresses, as shown in the following code.

```
<?xml version="1.0" encoding="UTF-8"?>
<xsd:schema xmlns:xsd=http://www.w3.org/2001/XMLSchema
      targetNamespace=http://tempura.org/po.xsd">

      <xsd:complexType name="address">
            <xsd:element name="street" type="xsd:string"/>
            <xsd:element name="city" type="xsd:string"/>
            <xsd:element name="province" type="xsd:string"/>
            <xsd:element name="postal code" type="xsd:string"/>
      <xsd:element name="street" type="xsd:string"/>

      <xsd:element name="book">
            <xsd:complexType>
                  <xsd:element name="title" type="xsd:string"/>
                  <xsd:element name="author" type="xsd:string"/>
                  <xsd:element name="publishers address" type="address"/>
                  <xsd:attribute name="isbn" type="xsd:integer"/>
            </xsd:complexType>
      </xsd:element>
</xsd:schema>
```

Table 13-1 Schema Simple Types

Type	Description
Binary	Holds binary values, such as 00110011
Boolean	Holds values such as True, False, 0, and 1
Byte	Represents a byte value, such as 64; the maximum is 255
Date	Holds a date value in YYYY-MM-DD format
Decimal	Holds a decimal value such as 7.4, 1, or -120.6
Integer	Holds an integer value
Long	Holds a long integer value
String	Holds a string value

Specifying Constraints and Default Values

Simple types are deterministic. That is, a specific set of values can be specified for the type. Complex types, however, are just that: complex. With complex types developers can define not only syntax (how the type is specified), but also semantics (how the type is used). For example, to specify the minimum number of times that an element can occur, you can specify the minOccurs attribute within an element tag. You don't have to include the minOccurs attribute; if you don't the attribute defaults to 1, indicating that the element should appear at least once within the complex type. The maxOccurs attribute specifies the maximum number of times that an element can occur within the complex type. To be able to specify the element as many times as desired, we set the maxOccurs attribute to unbounded, as shown in the following example.

```
<xsd:element name="author" type="xsd:string" maxOccurs="unbounded"/>
<xsd:element name="publishers address" type="address" minOccurs="10"/>
```

In the preceding code we specify that the author element can occur an unlimited number of times. Although we may never have more than a handful of authors, setting the maxOccurs attribute to unbounded provides the freedom to specify as many authors as desired. Because the minOccurs attribute defaults to 1 if not specified, there will be at least one author.

In the publisher's address element we specify that the minimum number of elements is 0. This means that the publisher's address may or may not appear within the book. If we don't specify a value for maxOccurs, the maxOccurs attribute takes on the value of the minOccurs attribute.

Two other useful attributes are the Fixed and Default attributes. The Fixed attribute specifies that an element must have a specific value. The Default attribute specifies that the element has a default value that can be changed if you specify a value within the document. Suppose we are developing an XML schema that will be used to define XML documents for clinical trials of new medications. Due to testing regulations there is a requirement to specify a fixed number of trials before the drug can be approved. Within the XML schema we must define an element that is fixed at the fixed number of trials. Let's assume that 50 trials must be conducted. To do this within XML we use the Fixed attribute as shown in the following code.

```
<xsd:element name="clinical trials" type="xsd:integer" fixed="50"/>
```

This method is fairly rigid. We have no choice but to modify the schema if the required number of clinical trials changes. To address this issue, we can set the value as 50 by default while providing the capability to specify a different value if desired. To do this, we use the Default attribute as shown in the following code.

```
<xsd:element name="clinical trials" type="xsd:integer" default="50"/>
```

Unlike elements, schema attributes do not specify the minOccurs or maxOccurs properties. This is because attributes can appear only once. To specify the semantics of an attribute—for example, whether an attribute is required or optional, or whether it has a fixed or default value—developers use the Use and Value attributes within the <xsd:attribute> tags of the XML schema. By combining the Use and Value attributes in various ways you can constrain attributes similar to the way in which you constrain elements. Table 13-2 describes the possible values of the Use attribute.

We can rework the clinical trials example to specify the number of clinical trials as an attribute. We do so by using the following code within the XML schema.

```
<xsd:attribute name="clinical trials" type="xsd:integer"
                 use="fixed" value="50"/>
```

To use a default value instead of a fixed value we can use the following code.

```
<xsd:attribute name="clinical trials" type="xsd:integer"
                 use="default" value="50"/>
```

Sequences

Developers sometimes want to ensure that elements appear in a certain sequence within the XML document. The <xsd:sequence> element ensures that the elements within the complex type appear in the specified sequence within the containing element. Here is an example.

```
<xsd:element name="personalinfo">
      <xsd:complexType>
            <xsd:sequence>
                  <xsd:element name="firstname" type="xsd:string"/>
                  <xsd:element name="lastname" type="xsd:string"/>
                  <xsd:element name="address" type="xsd:string"/>
                  <xsd:element name="city" type="xsd:string"/>
                  <xsd:element name="country" type="xsd:string"/>
            </xsd:sequence>
      </xsd:complexType>
</xsd:element>
```

In this example we specify an element named *personalinfo* and define it as a complex type. Within this complex type we specify that the requested information be provided

Table 13-2 Use Attribute Values

Value	Description
Required	The attribute value is required and may have any value.
Optional	The attribute is optional and may have any value.
Fixed	The attribute is fixed and the value is specified within the value attribute of the <xsd:attribute> tag.
Default	If the attribute does not appear within a defined element, the attribute takes on the default value specified by the Value attribute of the <xsd:attribute> tag. If the attribute does appear within a defined element, it takes on the value specified within the XML document.
Prohibited	The attribute must not appear.

in a specific order. This specification does not require that all information be provided, but the information that is provided must be provided in the order specified via the <xsd:sequence> tag.

Making Choices

Choices allow developers to specify a number of elements, of which only one can be chosen or used at a time. To implement choices within the XML schema, developers use the `<xsd:choice>` element, as shown in the following code.

```
<xsd:element name="person">
      <xsd:complexType>
            <xsd:choice>
                  <xsd:element name="employee" type="employee"/>
                  <xsd:element name="member" type="member"/>
            </xsd:choice>
      </xsd:complexType>
</xsd:element>
```

Here we have specified a complex type for the element named *person*. The </xsd:choice> element allows one of two subelements to be used—either the employee element or the member element—but not both.

Empty Elements

The img tag in HTML allows developers to specify an image that is then rendered to the browser. The tag or element itself contains no data; to specify the image you want to use, you set the appropriate attribute of the tag. To illustrate how an image is defined within an XML schema, we will define our own image tag. This tag will take three attributes: SRC, Width, and Height. The SRC attribute specifies the path to the image; the Width and Height attributes are self-explanatory. The following code shows an example of the tag.

```
<image src="/images/graphic.jpg" width="10" height="15"/>
```

To specify an element with no content, we define a complex type that allows only elements in its content, but we do not declare any elements. The following code provides an example of the XML schema that is used to describe our fictitious image tag.

```
<xsd:element name="image">
      <xsd:complexType>
            <xsd:complexContent>
                  <xsd:attribute name="src" type="xsd:string"/>
                  <xsd:attribute name="width" type="xsd:integer"/>
                  <xsd:attribute name="height" type="xsd:integer"/>
            </xsd:complexContent>
      </xsd:complexType>
</xsd:element>
```

In this example, we create an element named *image* and define it as a complex type. However, we specify that the complex type should be made up of complex content, indicating that it should be made up of elements. Because we are creating an empty element, we do not specify any elements as part of the complex content; we specify only the attributes. Once we have done this, the image element is ready to use.

Mixed Content Elements

In HTML, developers can specify text and tags within the same Web page. The text is formatted based on the tags that are specified. In some cases the text is not formatted at all and appears "as is" within the Web page. XML provides the same capability. However because XML requires you to define content very specifically, you must be able to specify through the XML schema definition how the XML content will be defined within the document. To specify that the elements support mixed content, you use the Mixed attribute within the complex type tag.

To illustrate this we will specify a schema that uses the Mixed attribute in the complex type tag to describe the following XML document.

```
<letter>
Dear Mr.<name>John Doe</name>
You have been selected for the <prize>1,000,000</prize> dollar sweepstakes
You may collect your prize on <prizedate>2002-10-12</prizedate>
</letter>
```

This document combines both elements and character data within the letter element itself. To define the associated schema for this we use the complex type and specify the Mixed attribute, as shown in the following schema definition.

```
<xsd:element name="letter">
      <xsd:complexType mixed="true">
            <xsd:sequence>
                  <xsd:element name="name" type="xsd:string"/>
                  <xsd:element name="prize" type="xsd:positiveInteger"/>
                  <xsd:element name="prizedate" type="xsd:date"/>
            </xsd:sequence>
      </xsd:complexType>
</xsd:element>
```

By specifying the Mixed attribute of the complex type we have indicated that the character data will appear within the document. The element definitions have been defined as a sequence, indicating that they must appear in the document in the order defined within the schema.

Annotating Schemas

As mentioned earlier, XML is much like any other language in that sometimes the meaning is lost within the code. To resolve this issue, developers add comments to XML schemas to explain what the schema code is doing. To add user comments to schemas, developers use two elements: the <xsd:annotation> element and the <xsd:documentation> element. The <xsd:annotation> element is the container for the <xsd:documentation> element. The following code provides an example of how to add a comment to the preceding schema definition example.

```
<?xml version="1.0" encoding="UTF-8"?>
<xsd:schema xmlns:xsd=http://www.w3.org/2001/XMLSchema
      targetNamespace=http://tempura.org/po.xsd">
      <xsd:annotation>
            <xsd:documentation>
                  This is our book example documentation.
            </xsd:documentation>
      </xsd:annotation>

       <xsd:element name="book">
            <xsd:complexType>
                  <xsd:element name="title" type="xsd:string"/>
                  <xsd:element name="author" type="xsd:string"/>
                  <xsd:attribute name="isbn" type="xsd:integer"/>
            </xsd:complexType>
       </xsd:element>
</xsd:schema>
```

Transforming Documents Using XSL

The Extensible Stylesheet Language (XSL) can be broken down into two functions. The first function describes the transformation language (known as XSL Transformations or XSLT for short), which allows developers to transform documents into various formats. Using XSLT developers can perform very powerful operations such as transforming data from one application so that it can be used in another application. This frees developers from being locked into proprietary data formats that are difficult to integrate with other applications. Using an XML schema to separate the data from the semantics enables developers to take advantage of the information that is contained within the schema to transform the data into various formats.

The second function of XSLT is to provide a formatting language that allows developers to format and style documents according to the display device or output media that is to be targeted. Because there is limited support for formatting objects in Microsoft XML, we will not discuss the formatting language further. We will focus on the transformation language instead.

To illustrate the concepts we discuss throughout this section, we will use an example in which we transform an XML document into HTML using XSLT. The XML document we will use for these examples is shown here.

```
<?xml version="1.0"?>
<?xml-stylesheet type="text/xsl" href="booksxslt.xsl"?>
<BOOKS>
      <BOOK>
            <TITLE>Horton Hears a Who</TITLE>
            <AUTHOR>Cindy Lou Who</AUTHOR>
            <ISBN>123456</ISBN>
            <PUBLISHER>Books R Us</PUBLISHER>
            <NUMBEROFCHAPTERS>2</NUMBEROFCHAPTERS>
            <PAGECOUNT>10</PAGECOUNT>
      </BOOK>
      <BOOK>
            <TITLE>Yertle the Turtle</TITLE>
            <AUTHOR>Billy Bob Who</AUTHOR>
```

```
            <ISBN>654321</ISBN>
            <PUBLISHER>Seuss Classics</PUBLISHER>
            <NUMBEROFCHAPTERS>4</NUMBEROFCHAPTERS>
            <PAGECOUNT>20</PAGECOUNT>
      </BOOK>
      <BOOK>
            <TITLE>Hunches in Bunches</TITLE>
            <AUTHOR>Joe Author</AUTHOR>
            <ISBN>456123</ISBN>
            <PUBLISHER>Classics Inc</PUBLISHER>
            <NUMBEROFCHAPTERS>7</NUMBEROFCHAPTERS>
            <PAGECOUNT>90</PAGECOUNT>
      </BOOK>
</BOOKS>
```

At the top of the example we specify a processing instruction using the Type attribute to indicate the style sheet we will associate the document with. In this example we connect to an XSLT style sheet. The HREF attribute specifies the uniform resource identifier (URI) of the style sheet. The path to the style sheet is relative to the XML document location.

Building XSLT Style Sheets

To transform the XML document in our example, we use the XLST style sheet. The following code provides an example style sheet.

```
<?xml version="1.0"?>
<xsl:stylesheet version="1.0" xmlns:xsl="http://www.w3.org/1999/XSL/Transform">
      <xsl:template match="/BOOKS">
            <HTML>
                  <xsl:apply-templates/>
            </HTML>
      </xsl:template>
      <xsl:template match="BOOK">
            <P>
                  <xsl:value-of select="TITLE"/>
            </P>
      </xsl:template>
</xsl:stylesheet>
```

As with XML documents, XSLT style sheets must be well formed. Therefore, we begin the style sheet with an XML declaration, followed by a <stylesheet> element. The style sheet element is made up of an attribute and a namespace definition. The namespace definition refers to the w3 namespace for XSLT style sheets and associates the xsl prefix with the namespace definition. The Version attribute specifies the current version being used, which is 1.0.

We follow the <stylesheet> element with <template> elements that refer to nodes within the XML document. XSLT views XML documents as trees built of nodes. XSLT recognizes seven types of node. Table 13-3 provides an overview of each node and how XSLT processes it.

Node	Description
Document root	The top-level node; represents the document itself.
Attribute	Represents an attribute of an XML element. For example, the <book title= "Left foot, right foot"/> element has a corresponding attribute node with *title* as the node name and "The Encyclopedia of Cows" as the node value.
Comment	Represents a comment in the XML document. For example, **<!--** this is a comment **-->** is represented by a comment node.
Element	Represents an XML element. For example, a <book title="Horton Hatches the Egg"/> element is represented by a book node.
Namespace	Represents a namespace prefix that is in scope for an element. A namespace is declared with an XMLNS: attribute of an element. For example, for <xsl:stylesheet version="1.0" xmlns:xsl="http://www.w3.org/1999/XSL/Transform">, the namespace node refers to the "xmlns:xsl="http://www.w3.org/1999/XSLT/Transform" part of the element.
Processing instruction	Represents a processing instruction within an XML document, such as <?xml-stylesheet type="text/xsl" href="myXSLT.xsl"?>. However, <?xml version="1.0"?> does not correspond to a processing node because it is an XML declaration.
Text	Represents a sequence of consecutive characters that forms non-markup character data of an XML element. For example, for the <book>The Many Adventures of Gerald McBoing Boing</book> element in the XML document, there is a corresponding text node for the text of " The Many Adventures of Gerald McBoing Boing ". However, for <book>The Many Adventures of<who>Gerald McBoing Boing</who></book>, there will be two text nodes: one for the text of " The Many Adventures of " and the other for "C Gerald McBoing Boing."

Table 13-3 Document Tree Nodes

To work with specific nodes in a document developers apply XSLT templates. When a particular node is specified, the XSLT processor transforms the node according to the instructions specified within the template. In our example style sheet we have specified two templates. One template applies to the <BOOKS> element node, and the other applies to the <BOOK> element node. The following code provides the XSLT markup for the <BOOKS> element node.

```
<xsl:template match="/BOOKS">
      <HTML>
            <xsl:apply-templates/>
      </HTML>
</xsl:template>
```

Here we indicate that when the XSLT processor matches the <BOOKS> element of the XML document, it should replace the Node with two tags: an <HTML> tag and an

</HTML> tag in the transformed output. The template also specifies an <xsl:apply-templates> element. This element is an instruction to the XSLT processor and informs the processor that it should process all child nodes of the current node and match with an appropriate <xsl:template> if one applies. If the XSLT processor were to continue based on our example XSLT style sheet, we would end up with the following output.

```
<HTML>
      <P>Horton Hears a Who</P>
      <P>Yertle the Turtle</P>
      <P>Hunches in Bunches</P>
</HTML>
```

The title of each book is included in the output using the <xsl:value-of> element. When the XSLT processor encounters the <xsl:value-of> element it extracts the value of the <TITLE> element in the XML document and substitutes it in the output XML document. Notice that we use the Select attribute within the <xsl:value-of> element. This attribute is also available with the <xsl:apply-template>, <xsl:for-each>, and <xsl:sort> elements. The Select attribute allows us to be specific about which node within our XML document tree to use.

The Select attribute allows us to only select the first node that matches the selection criteria, even if there are multiple nodes that could match. For instance, assume that a book is known by multiple titles, as shown in the following XML document.

```
<BOOKS>
       <BOOK>
             <TITLE>Horton Hears a Who</TITLE>
             <TITLE>A Who Is Heard by Horton</TITLE>
             <AUTHOR>Cindy Lou Who</AUTHOR>
             <ISBN>123456</ISBN>
             <PUBLISHER>Books R Us</PUBLISHER>
             <NUMBEROFCHAPTERS>2</NUMBEROFCHAPTERS>
             <PAGECOUNT>10</PAGECOUNT>
      </BOOK>
</BOOKS>
```

If we were to use only the Select attribute of the <xsl:value-of> element, then only the first <TITLE> element would be processed. The second <TITLE> element would be bypassed. To resolve this we use the <xsl:for-each> element. Using this element modifies our template as shown in the following code.

```
<xsl:template match="BOOK">
      <xsl:for-each select="TITLE">
            <P>
                  <xsl:value-of select="TITLE"/>
            </P>
      </xsl:for-each>
</xsl:template>
```

Using this element we can now catch all titles of a book. The modified XML document generates the following output document.

```
<HTML>
      <P>Horton Hears a Who</P>
      <P>A Who Is Heard by Horton</P>

      <P>Yertle the Turtle</P>
      <P>Hunches in Bunches</P>
</HTML>
```

Pattern Matching

Up to this point we have been specific in the matching we have done within <xsl:template> elements. To match the root node we use / in the Select attribute. To match on a particular element we specify the element in the Select attribute. XSLT also supports more complex matching rules.

Suppose we want to specify a match that applies only to the <TITLE> element of our book. To do so, we simply specify that we want to match on BOOK/TITLE as shown in the following XSLT template.

```
<xsl:template match="BOOK/TITLE">
       <H1><xsl:value-of select="."/></H1>
</xsl:template>
```

Using this template we match on the BOOK/TITLE element. Then, we select the value of the current node and surround it with <H1> tags. Using the "." within an XSLT element Select attribute indicates that we want to work with the current node.

To indicate that we want to work with any node that is a descendant of the <BOOK> element, we use the * wildcard, as shown in the following example.

```
<xsl:template match="BOOK/*">
      <H1><xsl:value-of select="."/></H1>
</xsl:template>
```

Using the XSLT template we match on any element and surround the resulting element value with <H1> tags.

To match on attributes, developers prefix the Select match term with an @ character. For example, let's say our <BOOK> element contained ISBN as an attribute, as shown in the following code.

```
<BOOK ISBN="123435">
```

To specify that we want to work with the ISBN attribute in our template, we use the following XSLT code.

```
<xsl:template match="BOOK">
      <H1><xsl:value-of select="."/></H1>
      <xsl:value-of select="@ISBN"/>
</xsl:template>
```

Besides working with individual elements of the same type, developers must be able to work with more than one element of the same type. To do this, developers use the "or" operator, which is specified by the vertical bar (|). To apply the same template to both the <AUTHOR> and the <TITLE> elements in our book example and set them both to bold when encountered, we use the following code.

```
<xsl:template match="TITLE | AUTHOR">
      <B><xsl:value-of select="."/></B>
</xsl:template>
```

The [ ] operator is an important tool when using the Select attribute for matching. It enables developers to test whether certain conditions are true. For example, you can test the value of an attribute in a given string; the value of an element; whether an element encloses a particular child, attribute, or other element; or the position of a node in a node tree. Table 13-4 provides examples of how the [ ] operator can be used.

Specifying Comments

As mentioned earlier, comments help explain what is happening in a document. XSLT enables developers to automate the generation of comments using the <xsl:comment> element. Suppose that we would like to specify the number of pages by using a comment in the HTML output when we list each title. To do so, we modify the template that matches on the <BOOK> element as shown in the following code.

```
<xsl:template match="BOOK">
      <xsl:for-each select="TITLE">
            <P>
                  <xsl:value-of select="TITLE"/>
                  <xsl:comment>
                  This title has
                        <xsl:value-of select="PAGECOUNT"/>
                        pages.
                  </xsl:comment>
            </P>
      </xsl:for-each>
</xsl:template>
```

Table 13-4 [ ] Operator Examples

Example	Description
<xsl:template match="BOOK[TITLE]">	This example matches <BOOK> elements that have child <TITLE> elements.
<xsl:template match="*[TITLE]">	This example matches any element that has a <TITLE> child element.
<xsl:template match="BOOK[TITLE | AUTHOR]">	This example represents a comment in the XML document. For example, <!-- this is a comment --> is represented by a comment node.

Using the <xsl:comment> element will result in the following HTML document as output.

```
<HTML>
      <P>Horton Hears a Who</P>
      <!--This title has 10 pages-->
      <P>A Who Is Heard by Horton</P>
      <!--This title has 10 pages-->
      <P>Yertle the Turtle</P>
      <!--This title has 20 pages-->
      <P>Hunches in Bunches</P>
      <!--This title has 90 pages-->
</HTML>
```

Copying Nodes

To copy nodes from an input XML document to an output XML document, developers use the <xsl:copy> element. The <xsl:copy> element creates a node in the output with the same name, namespace, and type as the current node. Attributes and children are not copied automatically. In the following example we strip all comments, XML declarations, processing instructions, and attributes out of our books.xml document. In effect we copy only text and elements.

```
<?xml version="1.0"?>
<xsl:stylesheet version="1.0" xmlns:xsl="http://www.w3.org/1999/XSL/Transform">
      <xsl:template match="* | text()">
            <xsl:copy>
                  <xsl:apply-templates select="* | text()"/>
            </xsl:copy>
      </xsl:template>
</xsl:stylesheet>
```

Note that we use text() in the <xsl:apply-template> element. This pattern matches any text node within the XML document. Therefore, the template specifies that we copy any element and text nodes from the source XML document to the output document.

Sorting Elements

XSLT provides the capability to sort information within a document. Developers use the <xsl:sort> element to sort the nodes within an XML document before they are delivered to the output. The Select attribute within the `<xsl:sort>` element specifies the sort criteria for node lists selected by <xsl:for-each> or <xsl:apply-templates>. In the following example we create a table of the books contained within the books.xml file. These books will be sorted based on the <AUTHOR> element.

```
<?xml version="1.0"?>
<xsl:stylesheet version="1.0" xmlns:xsl="http://www.w3.org/1999/XSL/Transform">
   <xsl:template match="BOOKS">
```

```
        <BODY>
           <H1>Books sorted by Author</H1>
           <TABLE>
              <TD>Title</TD>
              <TD>Author</TD>
              <TD>Chapters</TD>
              <TD>Page Count</TD>
              <xsl:apply-templates>
                 <xsl:sort select="AUTHOR"/>
              </xsl:apply-templates>
           </TABLE>
        </BODY>
     </xsl:template>
     <xsl:template match="BOOK">
        <TR>
           <TD><xsl:apply-templates select="TITLE"/></TD>
           <TD><xsl:apply-templates select="AUTHOR"/></TD>
           <TD><xsl:apply-templates select="NUMBEROFCHAPTERS"/></TD>
           <TD><xsl:apply-templates select="PAGECOUNT"/></TD>
        </TR>
     </xsl:template>
  </xsl:stylesheet>
```

By default <xsl:sort> performs an alphabetic sort, which means that 10 will come before 2. To perform a numeric sort, set the DataType attribute to "number". You can also create descending sorts by setting the <xsl:sort> element's Order attribute to "descending". By default it is set to "ascending."

Making Choices

To make choices within a document, you use the <xsl:if> element. To use this element, you set its test attribute to an expression that evaluates to a Boolean value. In the following example, the document will output the text "Found ISBN" if the ISBN element matches 123456.

```
<xsl:template match="BOOK">
      <xsl:apply-templates/>
      <xsl:if test="ISBN=123456">FOUND ISBN</xsl:if>
</xsl:template>
```

XPath

The XPATH language enables developers to use matching expressions that are more powerful than expressions used with the Match attribute and Select attribute. The XPATH language enables developers to address and filter elements and text within XML documents. XPATH expressions provide the capability to address parts of an XML document; manipulate strings, numbers and Booleans within the document; and match sets of nodes based on some matching criteria. XPATH is much more of a true language than the expressions used within the Match attribute. With XPATH, you can return not only lists of nodes, but also Boolean, string, and numeric values.

XPATH works by modeling an XML document as a tree made up of different types of nodes. To specify a node or set of nodes in XPATH, you use a location path, which consists of one or more locations steps, separated by / or //. If the location path begins with /, the path is called an absolute location path because you specify the path explicitly from the root node. If the location path does not begin with /, the path is relative starting at the current node, which is known within XPATH as the context node.

As mentioned, an XPATH location path consists of location steps. A location step is made up of an axis, a node test, and zero or more predicates. The axis specifies how the nodes selected by the location step are related to the context node. The node test specifies the node type and expanded name of the nodes selected by the location step. Finally, the predicate is a filter that further refines the selection of nodes in the location step. The following code is an example of a location step.

```
child::BOOK[position()=5]
```

In this example, child is the name of the axis, BOOK is the node test, and [position()=5] is a predicate. Location paths can have more than one location step. For example, to select all <TITLE> elements that are children of the <BOOK> element, we use the following XPATH expression.

```
/descendant::BOOK/child::TITLE
```

In the preceding example we refer to the <TITLE> element, which is a descendant of the <BOOK> element. The descendant is the axis. A number of axes can be used within expressions. Table 13-5 describes these axes.

Axis	Description
ancestor::	The ancestors of the context node. The ancestors of the context node consist of the parent of the context node, the parent's parent, and so on through to the root node. ancestor::BOOK returns all <BOOK> ancestors of the context node.
ancestor-or-self::	The context node and its ancestors. attribute-or-self::BOOK returns the <BOOK> ancestors of the context node. If the context node is a <BOOK> element, then it returns the <BOOK> element as well.
attribute::	The attributes of the context node. attribute::ISBN returns the ISBN attribute of the context node.
child::	The children of the context node. A child is any node immediately below the context node in the tree. child::BOOK returns the <BOOK> element children of the context node.
descendant::	The descendants of the context node. A descendant is a child, a child of a child, and so on. /descendant::BOOK returns all the <BOOK> elements in the document.
descendant-or-self::	The context node and its descendants. descendant-or-self::BOOK returns the <BOOK> element descendants of the context node. If the context node is <BOOK>, it returns the context node as well.

Table 13-5 Axes

Axis	Description
following::	All nodes that follow the context node in the tree, excluding any descendants other than the immediate descendant, attribute nodes, and namespace nodes.
following-sibling::	All the following siblings of the context node. A sibling is a node on the same level as the context node.
namespace::	The namespace nodes of the context node. There is a namespace node for every namespace that is in scope for the context node.
parent::	The parent of the context node, if there is one.
preceding::	All nodes that immediately precede the context node in the tree, excluding any ancestors, attribute nodes, and namespace nodes.
preceding-sibling::	All the preceding siblings of the context node. A sibling is a node on the same level as the context node.
self::	The context node itself. self::BOOK returns the context node if it is a <BOOK> element.

Table 13-5 Axes *(continued)*

To specify a node test, developers use either the wild card character * to select element nodes or the node tests outlined in Table 13-6.

The predicate provides the bulk of the power within an XPATH expression. The following types of expressions can be derived using predicates:

- **Node set** Involves manipulation of a set of nodes
- **Boolean** Assists in evaluating expressions to a True or False value
- **Number** Involves manipulation of numeric data
- **String** Involves manipulation of textual strings made up of Unicode characters
- **Result tree fragment** Returns parts of an XML document that are not complete nodes

Node Test	Description
comment()	Selects comment nodes. following::comment() returns all comment nodes that appear after the context node.
node()	Selects any type of node. preceding::node() returns all nodes that appear before the context node.
processing-instruction()	Selects a processing instruction node. You can specify the name of the processing instruction to select in the parentheses. self::processing instruction() returns all processing instruction nodes within the context node.
text()	Selects a text node. child::text() returns the text nodes that are children of the context node.

Table 13-6 Node Tests

Table 13-7 Node Set Functions

Node Test	Description
last()	Returns the number of nodes in a node set
position()	Returns the index number of the context node in the context node set
count(node-set)	Returns the number of nodes in the node-set argument
id(string ID)	Selects elements by their unique ID
local-name(node-set)	Returns the local part of the expanded name of the node in the node-set argument
namespace-uri(node-set)	Returns the namespace uniform resource identifier (URI) of the first node in the node set
name(node-set)	Returns the fully qualified name of the first node in the node set

As mentioned, an XPATH expression involving a node set returns a set of nodes based on the expression being evaluated. To select a node or nodes from a node set, you can use various functions that work on node sets in predicates. Table 13-7 lists these functions.

Using Boolean values in XPATH expressions allows you to evaluate expressions used in filter patterns to determine the flow of action. You can use XPATH logical operators to produce Boolean True/False results. The standard set of operators includes !=, <, <=, =, >, and >=. Be careful about using these operators, however, as they contribute to the markup within XML documents and it is easy to misuse them. Use entity references such as **<** and **>** instead. In addition to the logical operators, you can use the And and Or keywords to connect Boolean clauses. Finally, the XSLT language provides a number of functions that can be used in evaluating Boolean expressions. Table 13-8 lists these functions.

XPATH also supports numerical expressions. Several operators allow developers to work with numerical expressions, including +, -, *, div, and mod. These operators work as they do in other languages. For example, the element <xsl:value-of select="100 + 400"/> inserts the string *500* into the output document. In addition to these operators, XPATH provides numerical functions as outlined in Table 13-9.

The last XPATH expressions we will discuss are string expressions. Expressions involving strings use functions. Table 13-10 describes these functions.

This discussion has only covered XPATH expressions. To learn more about XPATH, refer to the XPATH documentation located on the MSDN Web site at http://msdn.microsoft.com/.

Table 13-8 Boolean Functions

Node Test	Description
boolean()	Converts the argument to a Boolean
false()	Returns False
lang()	Returns True if the XML:lang attribute of the context node is the same as the argument string
true()	Returns True
not()	Returns True if the argument is False, otherwise, False

Table 13-9 Numerical Functions

Function	Description
ceiling()	Returns the smallest integer that is larger than the number that is passed
floor()	Returns the largest integer that is smaller than the number that is passed
round()	Rounds the number that is passed to the nearest integer
sum()	Returns the sum of the numbers that are passed.

Controlling Output

Part of the process of using XSLT to transform an XML document is to produce the output document. XSLT enables developers to control the output using the <xsl:output> element. Three types of output can be generated:

- **XML** The default document; starts with <**?xml?**>
- **HTML** Standard HTML document without an XML declaration
- **Text** Plain text document

Using the Method attribute of the <xsl:output> element, developers can explicitly define the output as XML, HTML, or TEXT. Besides explicitly defining the output you can use additional attributes to create or modify XML declarations. Table 13-11 provides a list of these attributes.

Table 13-10 String Functions

Function	Description
starts-with()	Returns True if the first argument string starts with the second argument string; otherwise returns False
contains()	Returns True if the first argument string contains the second argument string; otherwise returns False
substring()	Returns the substring of the first argument, starting at the position specified in the second argument and the length specified in the third argument
substring-before()	Returns the substring of the first argument string that precedes the first occurrence of the second argument string in the first argument string
substring-after()	Returns the substring of the first argument string that follows the first occurrence of the second argument string in the first argument string
string-length()	Returns the number of characters in the string
normalize-space()	Returns the argument string with the white space stripped
translate()	Returns the first argument string with occurrences of characters in the second argument string replaced by the character at the corresponding position in the third argument string
concat()	Returns the concatenation of the arguments

Table 13-11 <xsl:output> Attributes

Attribute	Description
Version	Specifies the value for the XML declaration's Version attribute
Encoding	Specifies the value for the XML declaration's Encoding attribute
Omit-xml-declaration	Specifies whether the XML declaration should be omitted
Standalone	Specifies the value for the XML declaration's Standalone attribute
Media-type	Specifies the MIME type of the output document. For example, <xsl:output media-type="text/xml"/>

Cascading Style Sheets

As we discussed in the preceding section, XSLT has two functions: to transform data, which we covered, and to format objects. However, Microsoft views XSLT strictly as a method for manipulating and transforming XML data in a source document, not for formatting data. As such, Microsoft leaves the formatting of data to other technologies, specifically cascading style sheets (CSS). Cascading style sheets provide a centralized and modular way to format HTML output. Although a CSS can be linked directly to an XML source document, it is more effective to use a CSS as a complement to XSLT. This section provides a brief overview of cascading style sheets and how they can be used with XSLT to transform and format documents for display.

Creating Style Sheets

In the preceding section we used style sheets to specify XSLT code to manipulate XML documents. Of course, style sheets were not originally intended for specifying XSL transformation code. Originally they contained a list of style rules that specified how elements were to be displayed within a document.

Cascading style sheets meet the original definition of style sheets. They are used to specify style rules and how the rules are to be used to process elements within an XML document. Within a CSS is a set of rules. An individual rule consists of a selector, which specifies to which element or elements you want to apply the rule, and the rule specification, which is enclosed in curly braces. For example, the following CSS can be used to format the <TITLE> and <AUTHOR> elements of our XML document. To create this style sheet, we use Notepad to enter the following code, and then save it as style.css to the same location as our books.xml document.

```
TITLE {display: block; font-size: 24pt; font-weight:bold; text-align: center;
      text-decoration: underline}
AUTHOR {display: block; font-size: 24pt; font-weight:bold; text-align: center;
      text-decoration: underline}
```

Once a CSS has been defined and saved, you attach it to a XML document using the <?xml-stylesheet?> processing instruction. To attach the <?xml-stylesheet?> instruction to the CSS, use the Type attribute to specify "text/css" and then specify the URI of the stylesheet using the HREF attribute, as shown in the following example.

```
<?xml version="1.0"?>
<?xml-stylesheet type="text/css" href="style.css"?>
<BOOKS>
      <BOOK>
            <TITLE>Horton Hears a Who</TITLE>
            <AUTHOR>Cindy Lou Who</AUTHOR>
            <ISBN>123456</ISBN>
            <PUBLISHER>Books R Us</PUBLISHER>
            <NUMBEROFCHAPTERS>2</NUMBEROFCHAPTERS>
            <PAGECOUNT>10</PAGECOUNT>
      </BOOK>
      <BOOK>
            <TITLE>Yertle the Turtle</TITLE>
            <AUTHOR>Billy Bob Who</AUTHOR>
            <ISBN>654321</ISBN>
            <PUBLISHER>Seuss Classics</PUBLISHER>
            <NUMBEROFCHAPTERS>4</NUMBEROFCHAPTERS>
            <PAGECOUNT>20</PAGECOUNT>
      </BOOK>
      <BOOK>
            <TITLE>Hunches in Bunches</TITLE>
            <AUTHOR>Joe Author</AUTHOR>
            <ISBN>456123</ISBN>
            <PUBLISHER>Classics Inc</PUBLISHER>
            <NUMBEROFCHAPTERS>7</NUMBEROFCHAPTERS>
            <PAGECOUNT>90</PAGECOUNT>
      </BOOK>
</BOOKS>
```

Once you have saved the XML document and style sheet to disk in the same location, use Internet Explorer to open the XML document. You will be presented with the output, as shown in Figure 13-1.

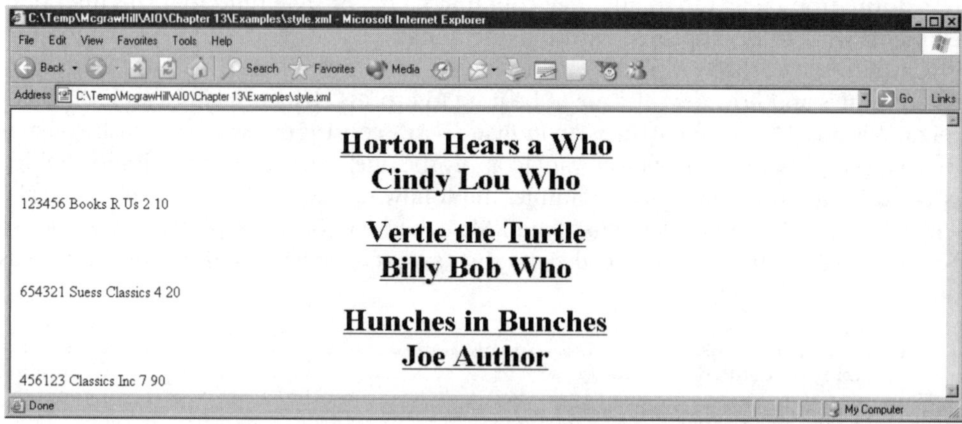

Figure 13-1 Books document displayed using a cascading style sheet

The Mechanics of Style Sheets

As mentioned, a CSS rule is composed of a selector, which identifies the element or set of elements you want to work with and the rule specification, which is enclosed in curly braces. In the preceding CSS example, we specified the <TITLE> and <AUTHOR> elements as the selector, and we used the rule specification to outline the style to apply to the selector. We can take the example a step further and minimize the CSS code within the file. To do this we group elements together. Instead of specifying two rules (one for each element), we group the <TITLE> and <AUTHOR> elements together by inserting a comma between them. This applies the same style to both elements. An example is shown in the following code.

```
TITLE, AUTHOR {display: block; font-size: 24pt; font-weight:bold;
               text-align: center; text-decoration: underline}
```

Besides using elements as selectors, developers can use classes to create selectors. A class defines a template that can be re-used. This is similar to the way in which a class can be re-used in Visual Basic .NET. To do this, make modifications to the style.css style sheet as shown here.

```
TITLE, AUTHOR {display: block; font-size: 24pt; font-weight:bold;
               text-align: center; text-decoration: underline}
.GREEN {color:white; background-color:green}
```

In the preceding code, we add a class called **.GREEN** in which elements to which it is applied will have a foreground color of white and a background color of green. To create this class we prefix a dot to its name. Once we have created the class we can apply the class to individual elements within the XML document. For this example, we use the <TITLE> element and add the class attribute to the element specifying that we want to use the **.GREEN** class we have defined in our cascading style sheet. We modify our book.xml document, as illustrated in the following code.

```
<?xml version="1.0"?>
<?xml-stylesheet type="text/css" href="style.css"?>
<BOOKS>
      <BOOK>
            <TITLE CLASS="GREEN">Horton Hears a Who</TITLE>
            <AUTHOR>Cindy Lou Who</AUTHOR>
            <ISBN>123456</ISBN>
            <PUBLISHER>Books R Us</PUBLISHER>
            <NUMBEROFCHAPTERS>2</NUMBEROFCHAPTERS>
            <PAGECOUNT>10</PAGECOUNT>
      </BOOK>
</BOOKS>
```

Besides applying classes to elements in general, you can apply classes to specific elements. For example, you can create a style for the first paragraph in a document that will add space before the paragraph. We will do this in our example by adding a class named

PART IV

TOP that applies only to <P> elements. This is specified using P.TOP. This is different than classes such as **.GREEN**, used above, which apply to all elements. Classes that apply to all elements are prefixed by a dot; classes that apply to specific elements are prefixed by the element name. Let's look at the cascading style sheet.

```
TITLE, AUTHOR {display: block; font-size: 24pt; font-weight:bold;
              text-align: center; text-decoration: underline}
.GREEN {color:white; background-color:green}
P {display:block; margin-top:30}
P.TOP {display: block; margin-top:30}
```

This class can be applied specifically to the P element within our document. Because the XML document is being rendered to our browser, we can use this for any paragraph element. However, we apply it only to the first paragraph within our XML document, as shown in the following example.

```
<?xml version="1.0"?>
<?xml-stylesheet type="text/css" href="style.css"?>
<BOOKS>
      <BOOK>
            <TITLE CLASS="GREEN">Horton Hears a Who</TITLE>
            <AUTHOR>Cindy Lou Who</AUTHOR>
      </BOOK>
      <P CLASS="TOP">
           This is the first paragraph within our document.
        </P>
</BOOKS>
```

To specify the style of elements that appear within other elements, developers use contextual selectors. For example, you may want an element to appear one way when it is by itself, but another way when it is enclosed in another element. In the following example we specify that the <UL> element must underline its enclosed text when used within a <P> element.

```
TITLE, AUTHOR {display: block; font-size: 24pt; font-weight:bold;
              text-align: center; text-decoration: underline}
.GREEN {color:white; background-color:green}
P {display:block; margin-top:10}
P UL {text-decoration:underline}
```

Now we modify our XML document as shown here.

```
This is the first <UL>paragraph</UL> within our document.
```

Note that although we specify that the text surrounded by the <UL> element be underlined, the text appears in the same font as the surrounding text. This occurs because style elements inherit the styles of their parent elements. In this particular example, the <UL> element inherited the parent element's <P> style.

Creating Style Rules

In the preceding section we focused on selectors in our rules. This section briefly examines rule specifications and how they are created. As outlined previously, a style rule is composed of a selector and a rule specification. The rule specification is composed of a list of property value pairs enclosed in curly braces and separated by semicolons. In the following style rule we specify the display, font-size, font-weight, text-align, and text-decoration properties.

```
TITLE, AUTHOR {display: block; font-size: 24pt; font-weight:bold;
              text-align: center; text-decoration: underline}
```

A number of the properties specified within this rule specification are related to setting text styles. Table 13-12 describes some of the properties that can be set.

Many more properties can be defined for cascading style sheets. For more information, go to the MSDN site at http://msdn.microsoft.com/.

Table 13-12 Styling Text Properties

Attribute	Description
Float	Indicates how text should flow around an element. Set this to Left to move the element to the left of the display area and have text flow around it to the right. Set it to Right to do the opposite.
Font-family	Sets the font face
Font-size	Sets the size of the text font
Font-stretch	Indicates the desired amount of condensing or expansion in the letters used to draw the text
Font-style	Specifies whether the text is to be rendered using a normal, italic, or oblique face
Font-variant	Indicates whether the text is to be rendered using the normal letters or small cap letters for lowercase characters
Font-weight	Refers to the boldness or lightness of the text
Line-height	Indicates the height given to each line
Text-align	Sets the alignment of text. This can be set to Left, Right, Center, or Justify.
Text-decoration	Specifies whether the text should be underlined, overlined, lined-through, or blinking
Text-indent	Sets the indentation of the first line of block level elements
Text-transform	Indicates whether you want to display text in all uppercase, all lowercase, or with initial letters capitalized. Set this to Capitalize, Uppercase, Lowercase, or None.
Vertical-align	Sets the vertical alignment of text. Can be set to Baseline, Sub, Super, Top, Text-top, Middle, Bottom, or Text-bottom.

Summary

In this chapter we introduced a wealth of information on XML. We began with an introduction to XML, describing how an XML document is structured. We outlined the various sections of an XML document, including the prolog and processing instructions. We then moved into a discussion about elements and attributes and how they are constructed and used within a document. We introduced namespaces and discussed how they play an important part in the definition of an XML document. We rounded out our discussion on XML documents by explaining well-formed documents and their qualities.

We then moved on to discuss XML schemas and how they are used to specify how the elements and attributes within a document are put together, in effect specifying the semantics of the document. We looked at how to specify the type information for elements within documents. We examined how to use the built-in simple types, and then we delved into complex types and how they are used to define the types of elements. We also discussed how various XML schema elements are used to specify how elements are constructed within a document. We looked at defining sequences, making choices, and how to add constraints.

We discussed the Extensible Stylesheet Language and more specifically the transformation part of the language, or XSLT. We looked at how to specify style sheets that contain XSLT transformation elements and how to use these elements to transform data. We looked at various transformation elements, including elements for sorting and making choices, expressions that can be used to select elements, and construction of these expressions. We finished the section on XSLT by looking at XPATH and how it is used to evaluate various types of expressions.

We concluded the chapter with an overview of cascading style sheets (CSS) and how they are used in conjunction with XSLT to transform data into the appropriate format prior to rendering it to the display. We looked at how to create a cascading style sheet and specify the rules within. We examined how to create and use the selector part of a rule. We ended by providing an overview of the rule specifications and some of the properties that can be used within these specifications.

Test Questions

1. What is wrong with the following XML document?

```
<!--BOOK XML document--!>
<?xml version="1.0"?>
<?xml-stylesheet type="text/css" href="style.css"?>
<BOOKS>
      <BOOK>
            <TITLE CLASS="GREEN">Horton Hears a Who</TITLE>
            <AUTHOR>Cindy Lou Who</AUTHOR>
      </BOOK>
</BOOKS>
```

A. There is no declaration for the **.GREEN** class.

B. The XML declaration is not complete.

C. The HREF tag does not completely specify the path to the style.css style sheet.

D. There is a comment before the XML declaration.

2. What is wrong with the following code fragment?

```
<?xml version="1.0" standalone="yes"?>
<DOCUMENT>
        <MARKUP>
                <![CDATA
                        <RECORD>
                                <DATE>101002</DATE>
                                <EVENTID>1033</EVENTID>
                                <DESCRIPTION>[[Event Description]]</DESCRIPTION>
                        </RECORD>
                ]]>
        </MARKUP>
</DOCUMENT>
```

A. The CDATA element is not specified correctly. There should be no ! in the specification.

B. You cannot include a CDATA section within a <MARKUP> element.

C. The XML declaration is specified incorrectly.

D. The CDATA section contains]] characters.

3. Which of the following conditions is not required to ensure that an XML document is well formed?

A. The root element must contain all other elements.

B. Elements that are not empty must include both start and end tags.

C. The XML document must begin with an XML declaration.

D. Attribute values must be enclosed in quotes.

Test Answers

1. **D.** Comments cannot precede XML declarations. The XML declaration, if specified, must be the first line within the XML document.

2. **D.** CDATA sections cannot contain]] characters. When the XML processor encounters a CDATA section, it scans it for]] characters to determine the end of the CDATA section; therefore these characters cannot be included in the content of the section.

3. **C.** An XML declaration is not required for an XML document to be well formed, although it is good practice to include it.

CHAPTER 14

Using XML with the ADO.NET Classes

In this chapter, you will

- Access an XML file by using the document object model (DOM) and an **XmlReader**
- See how to transform **DataSet** data into XML data
- Write an SQL statement that retrieves XML data from a SQL Server database
- Find out how to update an SQL Server database by using XML
- Learn how to validate an XML document

XML and the Document Object Model were developed to provide a dynamic, platform-agnostic approach to Web content creation and presentation. In this chapter we explore the use of XML data stored on servers, the retrieval of XML data using ADO.NET, and the manipulation of XML data through the document object model (DOM).

Even though XML is text-based and readable by humans, you still must be able to programmatically read, inspect, and change it. Microsoft provides two mechanisms for this: a tree-based XML processor and an event-based XML processor. Tree-based processors read the XML file or stream in its entirety to construct a tree of XML nodes. However, if the XML stream is very large, the tree may become too large and consume a lot of memory.

An event-based processor reads the XML stream as it is fed into the processor. As the stream is read the processor raises events, notifying the application of the tag or text the parser just read. Unlike the tree-based processor, it does not attempt to create the complete tree of all XML nodes. Therefore, the consumption of resources is not as noticeable as when a tree-based processor is used.

The Document Object Model (DOM)

A document object model (DOM) is a hierarchical structure in which all the tags of an XML document are stored. Before the introduction of the DOM, different XML parsers and processors had different ways of interacting with XML documents. The DOM provides a uniform approach for manipulating XML documents. It is useful for reading XML data into memory to change its structure, add or remove nodes, or modify the data held by a node (such as the text contained by an element).

You can think of an XML document as an in-memory tree of nodes. Every discrete data item is a node, and child elements or enclosed text are subnodes of this node. Everything in a document becomes a node within the DOM architecture, and each node is represented by an **XMLNode** object. The **XMLNode** object is the basic object used throughout a document. The **XMLDocument** class, which is derived from the **XMLNode** class, provides methods for performing operations on the document as a whole, including loading it into memory or saving the XML to a file. There are a number of possible nodes within an XML document. Table 14-1 provides an overview of node types. Each node type corresponds to the type of XML element within the XML document.

As an XML document is read into memory, nodes are created. However, not all nodes are the same type. An element in XML has different rules and syntax than a processing

Node Type	Contains Child Elements	Description
Element	Yes	Represents an element node
Entity	No	Represents the <!ENTITY...> declarations in an XML document, either from an internal document type definition (DTD) subset or from external DTDs and parameter entities
Attribute	Yes	Represents the attribute of an element
Text	No	Represents the text belonging to an element or attribute
CDATA Section	No	Represents a CDATA section
Entity Reference	Yes	Represents an entity reference, such as **&**, **<**, and **>**
Processing Instruction	No	Represents a processing instruction
Comment	No	Represents a comment
Document	Yes	Indicates the container of all the nodes in the tree; also known as the document root, which is not always the same as the root element
Document Type	No	Represents the <!DOCTYPE...> node
Document Fragment	Yes	Represents a temporary collection containing one or more nodes without any tree structure
Notation	No	Represents a notation declared in a DTD

Table 14-1 DOM Node Types

instruction. So as various data is read, a node type is assigned to each node. This node type determines the characteristics and functionality of the node. Let's look at an example.

```
<?xml version="1.0" encoding="UTF-8"?>
<DOCUMENT>
   <GREETING>
      Hello World!
   </GREETING>
   <MESSAGE>
      Welcome to the DOM
   </MESSAGE>
</DOCUMENT>
```

In the preceding example, the document begins with a processing instruction node and then is followed with a root element node of the Document type that corresponds to the <DOCUMENT> element. Under the <DOCUMENT> root node are two children of the lElement type. The first child is <GREETING> and the second is <MESSAGE>. If either of these elements contained attributes, an additional **XmlNode** of the Attribute type would have been created.

EXAM TIP Be sure that you have a solid understanding of the different parts of an XML document.

DOM Objects

There are a number of DOM classes, and each includes methods and properties. Table 14-2 outlines the DOM classes that are defined within MSXML 4.0, the version of DOM supported by Microsoft.

XML Classes	Description
XMLNode	Represents a single node in the XML document
XMLDocument	Represents an XML document
XMLDataDocument	Allows structured data to be stored, retrieved, and manipulated through a relational **DataSet** using ADO.NET
XMLDocumentFragment	Represents an object that is useful for tree insert operations
XMLEntity	Represents an entity declaration: <!ENTITY...>
XMLNotation	Represents a notation declaration: <!NOTATION...>
XMLAttribute	Represents an attribute. Valid and default values for the attribute are defined in a DTD or schema
XMLLinkedNode	Gets the node immediately preceding or following this node
XMLCharacterData	Provides text manipulation methods that are used by several classes
XMLComment	Represents the content of an XML comment
XMLText	Represents the text content of an element or attribute

Table 14-2 MSXML DOM Classes

XML Classes	Description
XMLCDATASection	Represents a CDATA section
XMLWhiteSpace	Represents white space in element content
XMLSignificantWhitespace	Represents white space between markup in a mixed content mode or white space within an xml:space= 'preserve' scope. This is also referred to as *significant white space*
XMLElement	Represents an element
XMLDeclaration	Represents the XML declaration node <?xml version='1.0'...?>
XMLDocumentType	Represents the document type declaration
XMLEntityReference	Represents an entity reference node
XMLProcessingInstruction	Represents a processing instruction, which XML defines to keep processor-specific information in the text of the document
XMLImplementation	Defines the context for a set of **XmlDocument** objects
XMLNodeList	Represents an ordered collection of nodes
XMLNamedNodeMap	Represents a collection of nodes that can be accessed by name or index
XMLAttributeCollection	Represents a collection of attributes that can be accessed by name or index
XMLNodeChangedEventArgs	Provides data for the NodeChanged, NodeChanging, NodeInserted, NodeInserting, NodeRemoved, and NodeRemoving events

Table 14-2 MSXML DOM Classes *(continued)*

As mentioned previously, when an XML document is processed by a tree-based processor each node within the document is represented by an **XmlNode** object. Almost every other object within the XML DOM derives from **XmlNode**. Instead of working with each of the individual node types, developers can work with **XmlNode** objects and XML documents using methods such as AppendChild(), PrependChild(), InsertBefore(), InsertAfter(), and Clone(). The **XmlNode** class also supports a set of properties that assist in navigation within an XML document tree. These properties include FirstChild, NextSibling, PreviousSibling, LastChild, ChildNodes, and ParentNode. For example, you can use the ChildNodes property to navigate down from the root of the XML document tree. Or, to traverse backwards up the tree, you can use the ParentNode property.

An **XmlNode** object represents a single node. The **XmlNodeList** class allows developers to work with a collection of nodes independent of the nodes' individual types. In our example XML document we could traverse the document tree using the **XmlNode** ChildNodes property of the <DOCUMENT> root element. This property is actually an XmlNodeList and would return a collection consisting of the <GREETING> and <MESSAGE> elements. Because this is a collection, we can iterate over the collection, retrieving **XmlNode** objects and working with the individual elements.

Just as **XmlNodeList** provides a collection of elements, the **XmlNamedNodeMap** class provides a collection of **XmlAttribute** objects that allow developers to iterate over attributes of an element. In our example, there are no attributes attached to elements so we cannot use this object.

The **XmlDocument** object is derived from an **XmlNode** object, just as all objects are. **XmlDocument** extends **XmlNode** and adds a number of helper functions. These helper functions are used to create other types of **XmlNodes** such as XmlAttribute, XmlComment, XmlElement, and XmlText.

Loading XML Documents

The **XmlDocument** object also supports methods for loading XML data into XML document trees. The LoadXml method takes a string XML format as input and builds an XML document tree.

Exercise 14-1: Loading an XML Document In this exercise you will build an XML document tree.

1. In Visual Studio .NET, create a new Console application by selecting File | New | Project. The New Project dialog box will appear, as shown in Figure 14-1.
2. Select Visual Basic Projects in the Project Types pane and choose Console Application from the Templates pane. Specify the path for your project and name the application **XMLApp1**.
3. Within the Module1 code window, make the following modifications.

```
Imports System
Imports System.IO
Imports System.Xml

Module Module1
   Public Sub Main()
      Dim doc As New XmlDocument()

      doc.LoadXml(("<DOCUMENT>" & _
                   "<GREETING>Hello World!</GREETING>" & _
                   "<MESSAGE>Welcome to the DOM</MESSAGE>" & _
                   "</DOCUMENT>"))
      doc.Save("data.xml")
   End Sub
End Module
```

4. Once you have modified the code, build the solution. Then run the solution from a command window. After you execute the application, a file called data.xml is created containing the XML data that you loaded via the LoadXml method.

As demonstrated, the LoadXml method is useful for loading strings of XML that are specified within an application. Another method that is available with the **XMLDocument** class is the Load method. This method provides more flexibility than the LoadXml method when loading XML documents into an XML document tree. The Load method is an overloaded method, which means it can take as input a number of

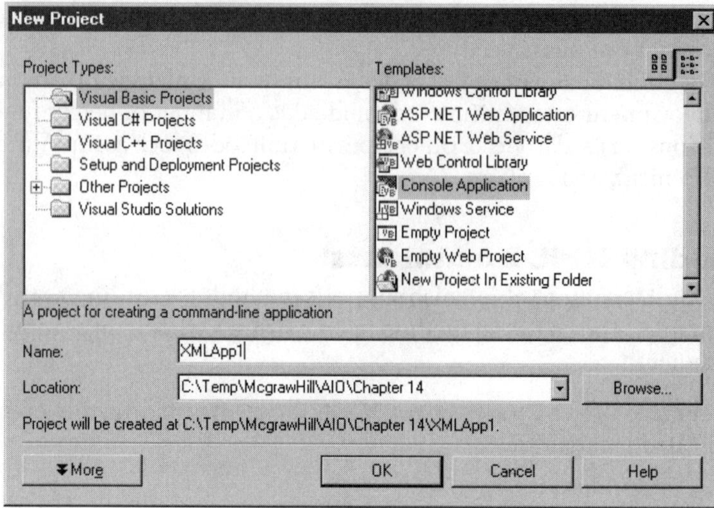

Figure 14-1 New Project dialog box

parameters that specify the location of the XML data to be loaded. The Load method can take the following parameters:

- **URL** Specifies the URL from which the XML data will be loaded
- **Stream** Specifies the stream from which the XML data will be loaded
- **TextReader** Specifies a reader that can read a sequential series of characters from a file
- **XmlReader** Specifies a reader that provides rapid, non-cached, forward-only access to XML data

Loading XML documents from a URL or file is straightforward. You simply specify the URL or file name of the XML document.

The **XmlReader** class provides rapid access to streamed XML data that checks to ensure that the XML is well-formed. **XmlReader** is an abstract class that is implemented in the following derivatives:

- **XmlTextReader** The fastest implementation of **XmlReader**; checks for well-formed XML, but does not provide validation
- **XmlValidatingReader** Provides a reader that can validate data using XML schemas or document type definitions (DTDs)
- **XmlNodeReader** Reads a stream of nodes from an **XMLDocument** object. The stream can start at the beginning of the XML file to enable reading of the whole **XMLDocument**, or it can start at a specific node of the **XMLDocument** to enable partial reading

The **XmlTextReader** supports reading from a text-based stream, whereas the **XmlNodeReader** is designed for working with in-memory DOM trees or DOM subtrees. When deciding which reader to use, consider the following guidelines.

Use the **XmlTextReader** in the following circumstances:

- You are concerned about memory and processing resources, particularly for large documents.
- You are looking for specific pieces of information in the document.
- You do not need to modify the document structure.
- You want to only partially parse the document before handing it off to another application.

Use an **XmlNodeReader** in the following circumstances:

- You need random access to all of a document's contents.
- You need to modify the document structure.

EXAM TIP Be sure that you know the different types of **XmlReaders**, and how they are used.

Exercise 14-2: Using the XmlNodeReader In this exercise you will use the **XmlTextReader** to read the XML document. Then, you will use the **XmlNodeReader** to process the nodes within the XML document tree.

1. Within the sample Visual Studio .NET application, XMLApp1, make the following modifications.

```
Imports System
Imports System.IO
Imports System.Xml

Module Module1

    Private Const FILE_NAME As String = "MyFile.xml"

    Public Sub Main()
        Dim objXMLdoc As XmlDocument
        Dim objFileSystemIn As FileStream
        Dim objStreamReader As StreamReader
        Dim objTxtRdr As XmlTextReader
        Dim objNodeReader As XmlNodeReader

        If Not File.Exists(FILE_NAME) Then
            Console.WriteLine("{0} does not exist!", FILE_NAME)
            Return
        End If
```

```
            objFileSystemIn = New FileStream(FILE_NAME, FileMode.Open, _
                                             FileAccess.Read, FileShare.Read)
            objStreamReader = New StreamReader(objFileSystemIn)

            objTxtRdr = New XmlTextReader(objStreamReader)
            Do While (objTxtRdr.Read())
                If (objTxtRdr.NodeType = XmlNodeType.Element _
                    And objTxtRdr.Name = GREETING") Then
                    Console.WriteLine("We have just processed the _
                    Greeting element using an XmlTextReader")
                End If
            Loop

            objXMLdoc = New XmlDocument()
            objXMLdoc.Load(FILE_NAME)
            objNodeReader = New XmlNodeReader(objXMLdoc)
            Do While (objNodeReader.Read())
                If (objNodeReader.NodeType = XmlNodeType.Element _
                    And objNodeReader.Name = "MESSAGE") Then
                    Console.WriteLine("We have just processed the _
                    Message element using  XmlNodeReader")
                End If
            Loop

        End Sub
    End Module
```

In the preceding example, you start by opening a file and assigning it to a stream. The stream is passed to an **XmlTextReader**, which is used to process the XML one node at a time. Within the body of the While loop, each XML node is checked to determine whether it is an element and has the name GREETING. If so, a message is written to the console. Next, the application creates an **XmlDocument** that is loaded with the XML contained in the specified file name. The **XmlDocument** is used to create an **XmlNodeReader** object that is used within the body of the loop to process nodes one at a time until it encounters a node of type Element with the name MESSAGE, at which time a message is written to the console.

The preceding exercise includes some of the methods that are available with the **XmlTextReader** and **XmlNodeReader** objects. Tables 14-3 and 14-4 describe the methods and properties that are available with the **XmlReader** object, on which the **XmlTextReader** and **XmlNodeReader** objects are based.

Writing XML Documents

Just as Microsoft .NET defines classes that provide a fast, noncached way of reading streamed XML data, it also provides a fast noncached way of writing streamed XML data. This is done through the **XmlWriter** class. The **XmlWriter** class includes the **XmlTextWriter** class, which can be used to write XML data.

XmlWriter supports namespaces by providing a number of overloaded functions that take a namespace to associate with the element. If the namespace is already defined and there is an existing prefix, **XmlWriter** automatically writes the element name with the defined prefix.

Table 14-3 Commonly Used XmlTextReader and XmlNodeReader Properties

Property	Description
AttributeCount	Returns the number of attributes of the current node
Depth	Returns the depth (nesting level) of the current node
EOF	Returns True if the XML reader is at the end of the file
HasAttributes	Returns True if the current node has attributes
HasValue	Returns True if the current node can have a value
IsEmptyElement	Returns True if the current node is an empty element (for example, <ElementName/>)
Item	Returns the value of an attribute
LocalName	Returns the name of the current node without a namespace prefix
Name	Returns the name of the current node with a namespace prefix
NodeType	Returns the type of the current node
Value	Returns the value of the current node

We will use the following XML document to demonstrate some of the methods and properties of the **XmlTextWriter** class.

```
<?xml version="1.0" encoding="us-ascii" ?>
<!--This is a comment-->
<world>
    <country name="China" pop="1,300" cont="Asia">
        <headofstate>President Jiang Zemin</headofstate>
    </country>
    <country name="India" pop="1,100" cont="Asia">
        <headofstate>President Kocheril Raman Narayanan</headofstate>
    </country>
    <country name="United States" pop="281" cont="North America">
        <headofstate>President George W. Bush</headofstate>
    </country>
</world>
```

Table 14-4 Commonly Used XmlTextReader and XmlNodeReader Methods

Method	Description
Close	Closes the XML file and reinitializes the reader
GetAttribute	Gets the value of an attribute
IsStartElement	Returns True if the current node is a start element or an empty element
MoveToAttribute	Moves to a specific attribute
MoveToElement	Moves to the element that contains the current attribute
MoveToFirstAttribute	Moves to the first attribute
MoveToNextAttribute	Moves to the next attribute
Read	Reads the next node from the XML file. Returns True on success or False if there are no more nodes to read

To create the XML documentin the preceding listing, we modify the code within the console application. We create an **XmlTextWriter** object, and then use various methods to write the XML document to a local file, as shown in the following code. The code is indented to make it more readable.

```
Imports System
Imports System.IO
Imports System.Xml

Module Module1
    Private Const FILE_NAME As String = "MyFile.xml"

    Public Sub Main()
        Dim objXmlTXTWriter As XmlTextWriter

        objXmlTXTWriter = New XmlTextWriter("writerexample.xml", _
                          New System.Text.ASCIIEncoding())
        objXmlTXTWriter.Formatting = Formatting.Indented
        objXmlTXTWriter.Indentation = 4
        objXmlTXTWriter.WriteStartDocument()
        objXmlTXTWriter.WriteComment("This is a comment")

        objXmlTXTWriter.WriteStartElement("World")
           objXmlTXTWriter.WriteStartElement("Country")
              objXmlTXTWriter.WriteAttributeString("name", "China")
              objXmlTXTWriter.WriteAttributeString("pop", "1,300")
              objXmlTXTWriter.WriteAttributeString("cont", "Asia")
              objXmlTXTWriter.WriteElementString("Headofstate", _
                              "President Jiang Zemin ")
           objXmlTXTWriter.WriteEndElement()

           objXmlTXTWriter.WriteStartElement("Country")
              objXmlTXTWriter.WriteAttributeString("name", "United States")
              objXmlTXTWriter.WriteAttributeString("pop", "281")
              objXmlTXTWriter.WriteAttributeString("cont", "North America")
              objXmlTXTWriter.WriteElementString("Headofstate", _
                              "President George W. Bush")
           objXmlTXTWriter.WriteEndElement()

        objXmlTXTWriter.WriteEndDocument()
        objXmlTXTWriter.Flush()
        objXmlTXTWriter.Close()
    End Sub
End Module
```

In this code we create an **XmlTextWriter** object and then specify formatting information to indicate how the XML data is to be laid out in the output file. Next, we generate the XML document. We use the WriteStartDocument method to write the XML declaration with the version 1.0, and we write an XML comment for the document. Then, we write elements and attributes, and associated text values for each. We complete the application with a WriteEndDocument method, which closes any open elements or attributes, puts the

Table 14-5 Commonly Used XmlTextWriter Properties

Property	Description
AttributeCount	Returns the number of attributes of the current node
Depth	Returns the depth (nesting level) of the current node
EOF	Returns True if the XML reader is at the end of the file
HasAttributes	Returns True if the current node has attributes
HasValue	Returns True if the current node can have a value
IsEmptyElement	Returns True if the current node is an empty element (for example, <ElementName/>)
Item	Returns the value of an attribute
LocalName	Returns the name of the current node without a namespace prefix
Name	Returns the name of the current node with a namespace prefix
NodeType	Returns the type of the current node
Value	Returns the value of the current node

XmlTextWriter back into the Start state, flushes whatever is left in the buffer to the stream, and closes down the stream.

Tables 14-5 and 14-6 describe the properties and methods that can be used with the **XmlTextWriter** object.

Table 14-6 Commonly Used XmlTextWriter Methods

Method	Description
Close	Closes the XML file and reinitializes the reader
GetAttribute	Gets the value of an attribute
IsStartElement	Returns True if the current node is a start element or an empty element
MoveToAttribute	Moves to a specific attribute
MoveToElement	Moves to the element that contains the current attribute
MoveToFirstAttribute	Moves to the first attribute
MoveToNextAttribute	Moves to the next attribute
Read	Reads the next node from the XML file. Returns True on success or False if there are no more nodes to read

Validating XML Documents

Although the **XmlTextReader** ensures that an XML document is well-formed, it cannot validate the document against a schema to ensure that the XML within the document is properly structured and complies with XML schema rules for using elements and attributes.

- To check the validity of an XML document, developers use the **XmlValidatingReader** class. This class is used to validate an XML document against a document type definition (DTD) or XML schema. As a derivative of the **XmlReader** class, the **XmlValidatingReader** class provides the same access to document contents as the **XmlTextReader** class. The methods and properties of this class are virtually identical to the methods and properties of the **XmlTextReader** and **XmlNodeReader** classes, except the **XmlValidatingReader** class has the following four additional properties:
- **ValidationType** Determines the type of validation performed by the XmlValidatingReader. You must set this property before calling the Read method and use the XmlResolver property if external DTDs or schemas are required for validation. Table 14-7 describes the values that can be assigned to the ValidationType property.
- **ValidationEventHandler** Sets an event handler for receiving information about document type definition (DTD) or schema validation errors.
- **Schemas** Gives the reader access to schemas within the built-in XmlSchemaCollection. Because these schemas are cached, the reader can validate a schema without having to reload it each time, thereby improving performance significantly.
- **XmlResolver** Resolves external entities such as a DTD or schema location through the use of an **XmlResolver** or **XmlUrlResolver** class. An **XmlResolver** is an abstract class that resolves external XML resources that have been named by a URI. It is used to load external DTDs, entities, schemas, and XmlSchema/XslTransform include/import elements. An **XmlUrlResolver** is used to resolve references to XML resources from file systems using *file://* and Web servers using *http://*. The **XmlUrlResolver** is the default resolver used by all XML classes within Visual Basic .NET.

The following example demonstrates how to use the **XmlValidationReader** to validate the XML within an XML document using an associated schema. In the example, the names of XML programmers are held in a document whose root is *<PROGRAMMING_TEAM>*.

```
<?xml version="1.0"?>
<PROGRAMMING_TEAM xmlns="schema.xsd">
   <PROGRAMMER>Jill Samson</PROGRAMMER>
   <DESCRIPTION>Program Manager</DESCRIPTION>
   <PROGRAMMER>Fred Langdon</PROGRAMMER>
   <DESCRIPTION>Head Programmer</DESCRIPTION>
   <PROGRAMMER>Sam Pollock</PROGRAMMER>
   <DESCRIPTION>Programmer</DESCRIPTION>
</PROGRAMMING_TEAM>
```

Table 14-7 ValidationType Constants

Constant	Description
ValidationType.Auto	Validates using information in the XML document (a DTD defined in a DOCTYPE element, a "schema location" attribute, or an inline schema). If no validation information is found, it acts as a nonvalidating parser.
ValidationType.DTD	Validates against a DTD
ValidationType.None	Does not validate
ValidationType.Schema	Validates against an XML schema definition (XSD) schema
ValidationType.XDR	Validates against an XML-data reduced (XDR) schema

Associated with this XML document is the following schema, which creates a complex type comprised of two elements: <PROGRAMMER> and <DESCRIPTION>. The complex type is then associated with the <PROGRAMMING_TEAM> element.

```
<xsd:schema xmlns:xsd=http://www.w3.org/2001/XMLSchema
    xmlns="schema.xsd"
    elementFormDefault="qualified"
    targetNamespace="schema.xsd">

  <xsd:element name="PROGRAMMING_TEAM" type="pttype"/>

  <xsd:complexType name="pttype">
     <xsd:sequence maxOccurs="unbounded">
        <xsd:element name="PROGRAMMER" type="xsd:string"/>
        <xsd:element name="DESCRIPTION" type="xsd:string"/>
     </xsd:sequence>
  </xsd:complexType>
</xsd:schema>
```

To validate this document against the associated schema we use the following code.

```
Imports System
Imports System.IO
Imports System.Xml
Imports System.Xml.Schema

Module Module1

    Private Const XMLdoc As String = "ProgrammingTeam.xml"
    Private Const XSDdoc As String = "schema.xsd"
    Private Success As Boolean = True

    Sub Main()
        Dim myXmlValidatingReader As XmlValidatingReader
        Dim myXmlTextReader As XmlTextReader
        Dim myXmlSchemaCollection As XmlSchemaCollection
        Dim strResult As String

        Try
            myXmlSchemaCollection = New XmlSchemaCollection()
            myXmlSchemaCollection.Add("schema.xsd", New XmlTextReader(XSDdoc))
```

```
                Success = True
                Console.WriteLine("Validating XML file " &_
                   "ProgrammingTeam.xml with schema File schema.xsd ...")
                myXmlTextReader = New XmlTextReader(XMLdoc)
                myXmlValidatingReader = New XmlValidatingReader(myXmlTextReader)
                AddHandler myXmlValidatingReader.ValidationEventHandler, _
                           AddressOf ValidationEvent
                myXmlValidatingReader.Schemas.Add(myXmlSchemaCollection)
                myXmlValidatingReader.ValidationType = ValidationType.Schema

                While myXmlValidatingReader.Read()
                End While

                If (Success = True) Then
                    strResult = "successful"
                Else
                    strResult = "failed"
                End If
                Console.WriteLine("Validation finished. Validation " & strResult)

                If Not myXmlValidatingReader Is Nothing Then
                    myXmlValidatingReader.Close()
                End If

            Catch e As XmlSchemaException
                Console.WriteLine("LineNumber = {0}", e.LineNumber)
                Console.WriteLine("LinePosition = {0}", e.LinePosition)
                Console.WriteLine("Message = {0}", e.Message)
                Console.WriteLine("Source = {0}", e.Source)

            Catch e As Exception
                Console.WriteLine(e)
            End Try
        End Sub

        Public Sub ValidationEvent(ByVal errorid As Object, _
                                   ByVal args As ValidationEventArgs)

            Success = False
            Console.WriteLine(Strings.Chr(9) & "Validation error: " & args.Message)

            If (args.Severity = XmlSeverityType.Warning) Then
                Console.WriteLine("No schema found to enforce validation.")
            ElseIf (args.Severity = XmlSeverityType.Error) Then
                Console.WriteLine("validation error occurred " & _
                                 "when validating the XML Document.")
            End If

            If Not (args.Exception Is Nothing) Then
                Console.WriteLine(args.Exception.SourceUri & "," & _
                                 args.Exception.LinePosition & "," & _
                                 args.Exception.LineNumber)
            End If
        End Sub
    End Module
```

In the preceding code, we begin by adding the schema to the schema collection object. This object contains a cache of XML schema definition (XSD) language or XML-data reduced (XDR) schemas that can be used to validate documents programmatically. Next, we begin the XML document validation by reading the XML document into an **XmlTextReader**. At this point we create an **XmlValidatingReader** object and associate various information with it. We begin by associating the XML document through the **XmlTextReader** object. Next, we associate an event handler with the object and the schema that was loaded into the XmlSchemaCollection. The event handler is used to indicate how and where a validation has gone wrong within the XML document if an invalid XmlDocument is passed to it. Finally we set the ValidationType to Schema to explicitly tell the **XmlValidatingReader** that we want to validate based on a schema. The application begins to validate the document through the Read method, and then generates a message to the console based on the results of the validation.

Although we set the ValidationType property for the **XmlValidatingReader** to Schema, we could have also set it to Auto to allow the **XmlValidatingReader** to determine how to validate the document. Depending on the situation, the **XmlValidatingReader** uses one of the following approaches to validate the data:

- If there is no document type definition (DTD) or schema, the reader parses the XML without validation.
- If a DTD is defined in a <!DOCTYPE ...> declaration, the reader loads the DTD and processes the DTD declarations so that default attributes and general entities are made available. General entities are loaded and parsed only if they are used (expanded).
- If there is no <!DOCTYPE ...> declaration but there is an XSD "schemaLocation" attribute, the reader loads and processes the XSD schemas and returns any default attributes that are defined in the schemas.
- If there is no <!DOCTYPE ...> declaration and no XSD or XDR schema information, the parser is a nonvalidating parser and will only check for well formed documents (i.e., ValidationType=ValidationType.None).
- If there is no <!DOCTYPE ...> declaration and no XSD schemaLocation attribute but some namespaces are using the MSXML "x-schema:" Universal Resource Name (URN) prefix, the reader loads and processes the schemas and returns any default attributes defined in them.
- If there is no <!DOCTYPE ...> declaration but there is a schema declaration <schema>, the reader validates the data using the inline schema.

PART IV

Using the DOM to Traverse XML Documents

Although the reader objects provide very fast forward-only/read-only processing capabilities to an application, they do not allow you to traverse a document in different directions or write information into the XML document. For example, when working with XML documents in an application, you may need to randomly access nodes to insert, update, or delete a particular node. The XML DOM provides these capabilities via the **XmlNode** class hierarchy.

To help explain the DOM and its capabilities, we will use the following GREETING XML document.

```
<?xml version="1.0" encoding="UTF-8"?>
<DOCUMENT>
   <GREETING>Hello World!</GREETING>
   <MESSAGE>Welcome to the DOM</MESSAGE>
</DOCUMENT>
```

To traverse the XML document once it is loaded in memory, we retrieve an object that corresponds to the document's root element <DOCUMENT>, as shown in the following code.

```
Imports System
Imports System.IO
Imports System.Xml

Module Module1

    Private Const FILE_NAME As String = "MyFile.xml"

    Public Sub Main()
        Dim objXMLdoc As XmlDocument
        Dim objFileSystemIn As FileStream
        Dim objDocRootNode As XmlNode

        If Not File.Exists(FILE_NAME) Then
            Console.WriteLine("{0} does not exist!", FILE_NAME)
            Return
        End If

        objFileSystemIn = New FileStream(FILE_NAME, FileMode.Open, _
                                         FileAccess.Read, FileShare.Read)

        objXMLdoc = New XmlDocument()
        objXMLdoc.Load(FILE_NAME)

        objDocRootNode = objXMLdoc.DocumentElement
        Console.WriteLine("The Documents Root Element is, " & _
                          objDocRootNode.Name)
    End Sub
End Module
```

In the preceding example we load the XML document into an **XmlDocument** object and then retrieve the document's root element by using the ocumentElement property. Now we can move around the document using the properties that are available with the DOM.

Table 14-8 describes DOM properties for traversing the XML document.

Table 14-8 DOM Properties for Traversing Documents

Property	Description
DocumentElement	Gets the document's root XML element
FirstChild	Gets the first child of the node
LastChild	Gets the last child of the node
HasChildNodes	Gets a value indicating whether this node has any child nodes
ParentNode	Gets the parent of this node (for nodes that can have parents)
NextSibling	Gets the node immediately following this node
PreviousSibling	Gets the node immediately preceding this node

These DOM properties allow you to traverse the XML document tree within memory to process nodes, retrieve information, and base decisions within the application. For example, the <GREETING> element in our preceding example is the first child of the document root element <DOCUMENT>. To retrieve the <GREETING> element using the DOM, we can use the irstChild property. To do this, we modify the code within the XML application, as shown in the following lines.

```
Dim objDocRootNode As XmlNode
Dim objXMLNode As XmlNode

objXMLdoc = New XmlDocument()
objXMLdoc.Load(FILE_NAME)

objDocRootNode = objXMLdoc.DocumentElement
Console.WriteLine("The Document's Root Element is, " & objDocRootNode.Name)
objXMLNode = objDocRootNode.irstChild
Console.WriteLine("The FirstChild is, " & objXMLNode.Name)
```

To get the next node that follows the child node at the same level in the XML document tree, we can use the extSibling property, as shown in the following code. This code will retrieve the <MESSAGE> element.

```
Dim objDocRootNode As XmlNode
Dim objXMlNode As XmlNode

objXMLdoc = New XmlDocument()
objXMLdoc.Load(FILE_NAME)

objDocRootNode = objXMLdoc.DocumentElement
Console.WriteLine("The Documents Root Element is, " & objDocRootNode.Name)
objXmlNode = objDocRootNode.firstChild
Console.WriteLine("The FirstChild is, " & objXMLNode.Name)
objXmlNode = objXmlNode.nextSibling
Console.WriteLine("The nextSibling is, " & objXMLNode.Name)
```

To illustrate how to use the information within the XML document tree, let's assume that we would like to use the text within the <GREETING> element to display a message to the end user. To do this, we must traverse to the actual text, which represents the text in the <GREETING> element and is represented by a text node. To display the actual text, therefore, we must navigate to the text node for this element. To display the text of the text node, we add the following code.

```
Dim objDocRootNode As XmlNode
Dim objXMlNode As XmlNode

objXMLdoc = New XmlDocument()
objXMLdoc.Load(FILE_NAME)

objDocRootNode = objXMLdoc.DocumentElement
Console.WriteLine("The Documents Root Element is, " & objDocRootNode.Name)
objXmlNode = objDocRootNode.firstChild
Console.WriteLine("The FirstChild is, " & objXMLNode.Name)
objXmlNode = objXmlNode.firstChild
Console.WriteLine("The text node is is, " & objXMLNode.Value)
```

Note that in this code we use the Value property of the text node object. In previous nodes we used the Name property to indicate the name of the element we were working with. In this case, however, we want the value of the text node and not its name.

Retrieving Elements by Name

Traversing an XML document tree one node at a time can be time-consuming. Instead of traversing the entire XML document tree looking for the element we want to use, we can use the document object's getElementsByTagName method to return a node list object containing all elements of a given name. In the following code, we modify our example XML document to illustrate the use of this method and retrieve the <MESSAGE> element from the document.

```
Dim objXMLdoc As XmlDocument
Dim listNodesMeeting As XmlNodeList
Dim intCounter As Integer

objXMLdoc = New XmlDocument()
objXMLdoc.Load(FILE_NAME)

objDocRootNode = objXMLdoc.DocumentElement
listNodesMeeting = objXMLdoc.GetElementsByTagName("MESSAGE")
intCounter = 0
While intCounter < listNodesMeeting.Count
   Console.WriteLine("The Value of listNodesMeeting is, " & _
                     listNodesMeeting(intCounter).Name)
   intCounter = intCounter + 1
End While
```

Retrieving Attribute Values from Elements

Besides enabling developers to work with individual elements and the document tree in general, the XML DOM provides methods to work with attributes as well. To explore these techniques we will modify our example XML document, as shown in the following code.

```
<?xml version="1.0" encoding="UTF-8"?>
<DOCUMENT>
   <GREETING type="verbal">Hello</GREETING>
   <GREETING type="verbal">Bonjour</GREETING>
   <GREETING type="verbal">Aloha</GREETING>
   <GREETING type="direct">HandShake</GREETING>
   <GREETING type="gesture">Wave</GREETING>
   <MESSAGE>Welcome to the DOM</MESSAGE>
</DOCUMENT>
```

To read attributes in elements, we get a named node map object of the attributes of the current element using the element's attributer property. In this example we read the *type* attribute of the element containing the text string *HandShake,* as shown in the following code.

```
Public Sub Main()
   Dim objXMLdoc As XmlDocument
   Dim objXMLAttributes As XmlAttributeCollection
   Dim objXMLAttrNode As XmlAttribute
   Dim objFileSystemIn As FileStream
   Dim listNodesMeeting As XmlNodeList
   Dim intCounter As Integer

   If Not File.Exists(FILE_NAME) Then
       Console.WriteLine("{0} does not exist!", FILE_NAME)
       Return
   End If

   objFileSystemIn = New FileStream(FILE_NAME, FileMode.Open, _
                                    FileAccess.Read, FileShare.Read)
   objXMLdoc = New XmlDocument()
   objXMLdoc.Load(FILE_NAME)
   listNodesMeeting = objXMLdoc.GetElementsByTagName("GREETING")
   intCounter = 0
   While intCounter < listNodesMeeting.Count
      If listNodesMeeting(intCounter).FirstChild.Value = _
         "HandShake" Then
         objXMLAttributes = listNodesMeeting(intCounter).Attributes
         objXMLAttrNode = objXMLAttributes.GetNamedItem("type")
         Exit While
      End If
      intCounter = intCounter + 1
   End While
   Console.WriteLine("The Value of the handshake " & _
                     "attribute is, " & objXMLAttrNode.Value)
End Sub
```

In this example we retrieve all <GREETING> elements and then search through each one for the text *HandShake.* Once the text is found, we retrieve the attributes associated with that element and look for the specific attribute named *type.* Once the attribute is found, we break out of the loop and write the value of the attribute to the console. Note, attribute nodes do not have internal text nodes. For this reason, we use the Value property to retrieve the value of the attribute.

Editing XML Documents

The XML DOM enables developers not only to traverse and read existing documents, but also to edit them. The XmlDocument includes a number of properties to facilitate editing. Table 14-9 describes some of these properties.

To illustrate how to edit XML documents, we will modify our example code to insert a new element called <TOKEN_GIFT> into the XML document, as shown in the following lines.

```
<?xml version="1.0" encoding="UTF-8"?>
<DOCUMENT>
   <GREETING type="verbal">Hello</GREETING>
   <GREETING type="verbal">Bonjour</GREETING>
   <GREETING type="verbal">Aloha</GREETING>
   <GREETING type="direct">HandShake</GREETING>
   <GREETING type="gesture">Wave</GREETING>
   <TOKEN_GIFT>Key to the city</TOKEN_GIFT>
   <MESSAGE>Welcome to the DOM</MESSAGE>
</DOCUMENT>
```

The following code outlines how we arrive at the preceding document.

```
Public Sub Main()
    Dim objXMLdoc As XmlDocument
    Dim objNewNode As XmlNode
    Dim objDocRootNode As XmlNode
    Dim objFileSystemIn As FileStream
    Dim listNodesMeeting As XmlNodeList
    Dim intCounter As Integer

    If Not File.Exists(FILE_NAME) Then
        Console.WriteLine("{0} does not exist!", FILE_NAME)
        Return
    End If

    objFileSystemIn = New FileStream(FILE_NAME, FileMode.Open, _
                                     FileAccess.Read, FileShare.Read)

    objXMLdoc = New XmlDocument()
    objXMLdoc.Load(FILE_NAME)
    objDocRootNode = objXMLdoc.DocumentElement

    listNodesMeeting = objXMLdoc.GetElementsByTagName("MESSAGE")
    If listNodesMeeting.Count = 1 Then
        objNewNode = objXMLdoc.CreateElement("TOKEN_GIFT")
        objNewNode = objDocRootNode.InsertBefore(objNewNode, _
                                    listNodesMeeting(0))
        objNewNode.AppendChild(objXMLdoc.CreateTextNode("Key to the city"))
    End If
    objFileSystemIn.Close()
    objXMLdoc.Save(FILE_NAME)
End Sub
```

Table 14-9 Editing Properties of the XmlDocument Class

Property	**Description**
CreateElement	Creates an XML element
CreateTextNode	Creates an XmlText node with the specified text
AppendChild	Adds the specified node to the end of the list of children of this node
CreateAttribute	Creates an XML attribute with the specified name
CreateCDATASection	Creates an XML CDATA section containing the specified data
CreateComment	Gets the node immediately preceding this node
CreateEntityReference	Creates an XML entity reference with the specified name
CreateProcessingInstruction	Creates an XML processing instruction with the specified name and data
CreateXmlDeclaration	Creates an XML declaration node with the specified values
InsertAfter	Inserts the specified node immediately after the specified reference node
InsertBefore	Inserts the specified node immediately before the specified reference node
RemoveChild	Removes the specified child node

To add the element, we create a new node corresponding to the <TOKEN_GIFT> element and use the InsertBefore property to insert it before the <MESSAGE> element. Next, we use the CreateTextNode property to create the text for the element. Once we have modified the document in memory we save it, overwriting the input XML document.

Using ADO.NET to Work with XML

One of the most important design goals of ADO.NET is to ensure support for XML. Microsoft designed ADO.NET hand-in-hand with the .NET Framework; each is a component of a single architecture. To facilitate this integration, Microsoft introduced the **DataSet** object into ADO.NET. This object is an amalgamation of the ADO **Recordset** with XML. If you are an ADO developer, you might think of a **DataSet** as a disconnected **Recordset** that contains one or more tables of data. As an XML developer, you're more likely to see the **DataSet** and its related objects as a highly specialized DOM, tuned to represent tables of data that contain sets of elements with a regular, strongly typed structure.

Over the years, the ADO **Recordset** has evolved from something that was generally used only to process the results of database queries into a much more powerful and general-purpose data structure. The ADO.NET **DataSet** uses this process, introducing a formal separation between data and its source. As a result, the **DataSet** has no knowledge of data sources, and separate objects are used to populate the **DataSet** and write changes back to the data source. For example, the **DataSet** has methods that can both read and write XML. To use these methods, you pass an XML parser to the method. For reading, you use an **XmlReader** object. For writing you use an **XmlWriter** object.

To populate a **DataSet** using XML is a two-stage process. First, the schema is created, and then the data is loaded. If the XML document comes with a schema, the schema is used to create the relational structure of the **DataSet**. If the schema is not available, then the **DataSet** infers the schema from the XML itself. It does this by determining which elements will be inferred as tables, and then inferring the columns for those tables. The following list outlines the rules of the inference process.

- Elements that have attributes are referenced as tables
- Elements that have child elements are referenced as tables
- Elements that repeat are referenced as a single table
- Attributes are referenced as columns
- Elements that have neither attributes nor child elements and do not repeat are referenced as columns
- If the document, or root, element has neither attributes nor child elements that would be inferred as columns, it is referenced as a **DataSet**. Otherwise, the document element is inferred as a table.
- For elements that are referenced as tables that are nested within other elements that are also inferred as tables, a relationship between the two tables is created through a DataRelation which is an association between two tables. A new, primary key column named *TableName_Id* is added to both tables and used by the DataRelation. A ForeignKeyConstraint is then created between the two tables using the *TableName_Id* column. This explicitly makes the association.
- For elements that are inferred as tables and contain text but have no child elements, a new column named *TableName_Text* is created for the text of each element. If an element is inferred as a table and has text, but also has child elements, the text is ignored.

The process of inferring schema is useful when constructing an application that has to consume XML that comes with no schema. For production applications, it is highly desirable to modify the inferred schema as appropriate, and then load it before the actual data is loaded. This will significantly improve performance as ADO.NET will not have to use the inference process to determine schema.

Reading an XML Document into a DataSet

To load an XML document into a **DataSet**, you can load the XML document directly into a **DataSet**, or you can build an **XmlDataDocument** object from an existing **DataSet**. In this section we examine how to load an XML document directly into a **DataSet**; we explore how to create an XmlDocument from a **DataSet** later in this chapter.

To read an XML document directly from a file into an ADO.NET **DataSet,** you use the ReadXml method of the **DataSet** class. Doing so converts an XML DOM object or document into a **DataSet**. Once the XML document is loaded into a **DataSet**, it can be synchronized automatically. Therefore, if you add a new "row" to the **DataSet**, it will automatically appear as a new "element" in the DOM and vice versa.

Exercise 14-3: Loading a DataSet with an XML Document In this exercise you will load the following XML document into a **DataSet**. Then, you will bind the **DataSet** to a DataGrid control that allows you to display the data within the DataSet.

```
<?xml version="1.0" encoding="UTF-8"?>
<MENU>
   <MENUITEM>
      <FOOD>French Toast</FOOD>
      <PRICE>5.40</PRICE>
   </MENUITEM>
   <MENUITEM>
      <FOOD>Scrambled Eggs</FOOD>
      <PRICE>3.89</PRICE>
   </MENUITEM>
</MENU>
```

1. Create a new Windows Application Console application by selecting File | New | Project. The New Project dialog box appears.
2. Select Visual Basic Projects in the Project Types pane and choose Windows Application from the Templates pane. Specify the path for your project and name the application **ADOXMLApp1**.
3. Within the designer window for the form, select a DataGrid control from the Toolbox and drag it onto the form.
4. Rename the DataGrid control to **dgrdMenu** by selecting Properties and changing the Name property.
5. Within the code window for the form, modify the existing code to match the following code.

```
Imports System.Data
Public Class Form1
    Inherits System.Windows.Forms.Form

    Private Sub Form1_Load(ByVal sender As System.Object, _
                ByVal e As System.EventArgs) Handles MyBase.Load
        Dim dstMenu As New DataSet()
```

PART IV

```
            dstMenu.ReadXml("menu.xml")
            dgrdMenu.DataSource = dstMenu
        End Sub
    End Class
```

6. Once finished, select Build Solution from the Build menu to run the application. Expand the DataGrid control and then click MenuItem to display the items on the menu, as shown in the illustration.

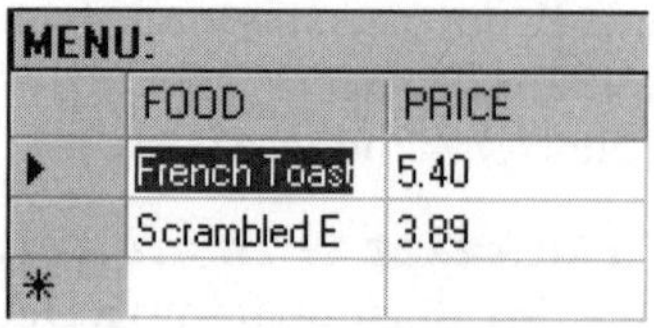

MENU:		
	FOOD	PRICE
▶	French Toast	5.40
	Scrambled E	3.89
*		

In the preceding exercise, you create a **DataSet** and then read the XML data into the **DataSet** using the ReadXml method. Instead of specifying a file name you could have specified a stream or an **XmlReader**. The ReadXml method takes as an optional argument an XmlReadMode parameter. The XmlReadMode parameter indicates to ReadXml whether a relational schema already exists or whether one needs to be created. Table 14-10 describes the values that can be specified for this parameter.

Because each table within a **DataSet** has a regular two-dimensional structure of data held in memory, **DataSets** provide a more convenient syntax for data manipulation than is possible using the XML DOM, which supports a more generic navigational model.

Table 14-10 XmlReadMode Parameters

Parameter	Description
Auto	This is the default parameter value and specifies how the ReadXml method should examine the XML; it chooses the most appropriate option in the following order: • If the XML is a DiffGram, DiffGram is used. • If the **DataSet** contains a schema or the XML contains an inline schema, ReadSchema is used. • If the **DataSet** does not contain a schema and the XML does not contain an inline schema, InferSchema is used.
ReadSchema	Reads any inline schema and loads the data and schema. If the **DataSet** already contains a schema, new tables are added from the inline schema to the existing schema in the **DataSet**. If the **DataSet** does not contain a schema, and there is no inline schema, no data is read.
IgnoreSchema	Ignores any inline schema and loads the data into the existing **DataSet** schema. Any data that does not match the existing schema is discarded. If no schema exists in the **DataSet**, no data is loaded.
InferSchema	Ignores any inline schema and infers the schema per the structure of the XML data; then, loads the data. If the **DataSet** already contains a schema, the current schema is extended by adding tables where there is no existing table, or by adding columns to existing tables.

Table 14-10 XmlReadMode Parameters *(continued)*

Parameter	Description
DiffGram	Reads a DiffGram and adds the data to the current schema. A DiffGram is an XML format that is used to identify current and original versions of data elements; it is primarily used in the transport of **DataSets** between Web services.
Fragment	Continues reading multiple XML fragments until the end of the stream is reached. Fragments that match the **DataSet** schema are appended to the appropriate tables. Fragments that do not match the **DataSet** schema are discarded.

Using a Schema with the ReadXML Method

In the Table 14-10 we described the XmlReadMode default parameter, Auto. When an XmlReadMode parameter is not specified, the **DataSet** determines the structure of the XML document by systematically evaluating data to make "an educated guess."

When an XML file is read into the **DataSet**, the **DataSet** infers the structure of the file. For example, it checks whether the elements directly under the root node can be interpreted as tables. If they can be, the root node is interpreted as a **DataSet**; otherwise, the root node represents a table. Allowing the **DataSet** to infer the structure of an XML document has disadvantages. One problem is that the **DataSet** must interpret all the elements as strings; it is not possible to specify other types for the data contained within the XML document. So, even if the <PRICE> element in Exercise 14-3 is a decimal value, the **DataSet** will interpret it as a string in the absence of an associated schema to define its proper type.

To specify a schema when loading XML documents, you can include the schema inline with the XML document itself, or you can read the schema separately by using the ReadXmlSchema method of the **DataSet** object. The following code specifies the associated schema for the document in Exercise 14-3.

```
<xsd:schema id="menu" xmlns:xsd=http://www.w3.org/2001/XMLSchema
                      xmlns:msdata="urn:schemas-microsoft-com:xml-msdata">
   <xsd:element name="MENUITEM">
      <xsd:complexType>
         <xsd:all>
            <xsd:element name="FOOD" minOccurs="0" type="xsd:string"/>
            <xsd:element name="PRICE" minOccurs="0" type="xsd:decimal"/>
         </xsd:all>
       </xsd:complexType>
   </xsd:element>
      <xsd:element name="MENU" msdata:IsDataSet="true">
      <xsd:complexType>
         <xsd:choice maxOccurs="unbounded">
            <xsd:element ref="MENUITEM"/>
         </xsd:choice>
       </xsd:complexType>
   </xsd:element>
</xsd:schema>
```

This schema definition specifies the data types for both the <FOOD> and <PRICE> elements. The <FOOD> element contains string values, while the <PRICE> element contains decimal data.

Note that the schema definition uses the msdata:IsDataSet="true" attribute for the <MENU> element. In most cases, schema elements, whether created to validate XML documents or to define associated **DataSet** classes, are defined in accordance with the W3C schema specification. In situations where schema syntax is not sufficient to describe features that are specific to ADO.NET **DataSets**, custom attributes are used. These custom attributes are identified with the msdata: qualifier as illustrated in the preceding code. The W3C specification permits custom attributes, which are to be ignored by applications that do not understand them. To use this schema within the example application, the application code must be modified, as shown in the following example.

```
Imports System.Data
Public Class Form1
    Inherits System.Windows.Forms.Form

    Private Sub Form1_Load(ByVal sender As System.Object, _
            ByVal e As System.EventArgs) Handles MyBase.Load
        Dim dstMenu As New DataSet()

        dstMenu.ReadXmlSchema("menu.xsd")
        dstMenu.ReadXml("menu.xml")
        dgrdMenu.DataSource = dstMenu
    End Sub
End Class
```

Although this application does not add anything significant to the visual display of the information, it adds a lot in the background by allowing you to specify the types of data that are loaded into the **DataSet**.

EXAM TIP To firmly grasp how ADO.NET works in conjunction with XML, be sure that you understand how schemas are used to specify the structure of **DataSets**.

Writing an XML Document from a DataSet

The **DataSet** class includes several methods for retrieving an XML representation of the data contained in a **DataSet**. You can use these methods regardless of whether you originally loaded the **DataSet** with data from an XML file or from a database table.

To retrieve a string representation of XML data, you use the GetXML method.

Exercise 14-4: Using the GetXML Method In this exercise you will use the GetXml method to retrieve a string that contains an XML representation of the **DataSet**.

1. In Visual Studio .NET, create a new console application by selecting File | New | Project. The New Project dialog box appears. Select Visual Basic Projects in the Project Types pane and choose Console Application from the Templates pane. Specify the path for your project and name the application **XMLApp2**.
2. Within the Module1 code window make the following modifications to the code.

```
Imports System.Data
Imports System.Data.OleDb
Imports System.IO
Imports System.Xml
Imports System.Xml.Schema

Module Module1
    Private Const FILE_NAME As String = "MyADOFile.xml"
    Sub Main()
        Dim NWConn As OleDbConnection
        Dim dadCustomers As OleDbDataAdapter
        Dim dstCustomers As DataSet
        Dim objStreamWriter As StreamWriter
        Dim strXmlData As String

        objStreamWriter = File.CreateText(FILE_NAME)
        NWConn = New OleDbConnection("Provider=Microsoft.Jet.OLEDB.4.0;" & _
                                     "Data Source=c:\Temp\McgrawHill\" & _
                                     "Data\nwind.mdb;")
        dadCustomers = New OleDbDataAdapter("SELECT * FROM Customers", NWConn)
        dstCustomers = New DataSet()
        dadCustomers.Fill(dstCustomers, "Customers")

        strXmlData = dstCustomers.GetXml()
        objStreamWriter.Write(strXmlData)
        objStreamWriter.Close()
    End Sub
End Module
```

3. Build the solution and then run the application from a command window. After you execute the application, a file called data.xml is created with the XML data that you loaded using the LoadXml method.

In Exercise 14-4, you retrieve the XML data using the GetXml method; this method also retrieves the underlying schema. To explicitly retrieve the XML schema, you can use the GetXmlSchema method.

In the preceding example, you explicitly convert the retrieved XML data to a string and then write the string directly to a text file. This is unnecessary, however, as the **DataSet** class contains the WriteXml and WriteXmlSchema methods for writing XML data to a file. To see how these methods are used, modify the code in the console application, as shown in the following lines.

```
Sub Main()
    Dim NWConn As OleDbConnection
    Dim dadCustomers As OleDbDataAdapter
    Dim dstCustomers As DataSet
    Dim strXmlData As String

    NWConn = New OleDbConnection("Provider=Microsoft.Jet.OLEDB.4.0;" & _
                                 "Data Source=c:\Temp\McgrawHill\" & _
                                 "Data\nwind.mdb;")
    dadCustomers = New OleDbDataAdapter("SELECT * FROM Customers", NWConn)
    dstCustomers = New DataSet()
    dadCustomers.Fill(dstCustomers, "Customers")
    dstCustomers.WriteXml(FILE_NAME)
End Sub
```

Using XMLDataDocuments with DataSets

A **DataSet** provides a relational view of XML data. All the information within the XML document is represented with tables, rows, and columns. In some situations, it is more convenient to work with a nonrelational view of the data in a **DataSet**. In other words, sometimes it makes more sense to represent data as nodes within a DOM document tree instead of representing it as tables, rows, or columns.

Consider the following XML documents.

```
<?xml version="1.0" standalone="yes"?>
<NewDataSet>
  <Customers>
    <CustomerID>ALFKI</CustomerID>
    <CompanyName>Alfreds Futterkiste</CompanyName>
    <ContactName>Maria Anders</ContactName>
    <ContactTitle>Sales Representative</ContactTitle>
    <Address>Obere Str. 57</Address>
    <City>Berlin</City>
    <PostalCode>12209</PostalCode>
    <Country>Germany</Country>
    <Phone>030-0074321</Phone>
    <Fax>030-0076545</Fax>
</NewDataSet>

<?xml version="1.0" standalone="yes"?>
<NewDataSet>
  <Customers>
    <ProductID>1</ProductID>
    <ProductName>Chai</ProductName>
    <SupplierID>1</SupplierID>
    <CategoryID>1</CategoryID>
    <QuantityPerUnit>10 boxes x 20 bags</QuantityPerUnit>
    <UnitPrice>18</UnitPrice>
    <UnitsInStock>39</UnitsInStock>
    <UnitsOnOrder>0</UnitsOnOrder>
    <ReorderLevel>10</ReorderLevel>
    <Discontinued>false</Discontinued>
  </Customers>
</NewDataSet>

<?xml version="1.0" standalone="yes"?>
<NewDataSet>
  <Customers>
    <OrderID>10330</OrderID>
    <CustomerID>LILAS</CustomerID>
    <EmployeeID>3</EmployeeID>
    <OrderDate>1994-11-16T00:00:00.0000000-06:00</OrderDate>
    <RequiredDate>1994-12-14T00:00:00.0000000-06:00</RequiredDate>
    <ShippedDate>1994-11-28T00:00:00.0000000-06:00</ShippedDate>
    <ShipVia>1</ShipVia>
    <Freight>12.75</Freight>
    <ShipName>LILA-Supermercado</ShipName>
    <ShipAddress>Carrera 52 con Ave. Bolívar #65-98 Llano Largo</ShipAddress>
    <ShipCity>Barquisimeto</ShipCity>
    <ShipRegion>Lara</ShipRegion>
    <ShipPostalCode>3508</ShipPostalCode>
    <ShipCountry>Venezuela</ShipCountry>
  </Customers>
</NewDataSet>
```

This XML is composed of three different XML documents. It has a customer, a product, and an order document. In a relational environment, these documents would be represented as three different tables, with the orders table defining a relationship between the product being sold and the customer purchasing the product. However, in a nonrelational environment, maintaining these relationships can be difficult.

For example, the preceding XML documents are the partial results of extracting information from the underlying tables directly. This process produces the data from the tables; however, the relationships are only implied in the data. To maintain the relationships between the data in the tables you would have to define a custom translation layer when attempting to read a **DataSet** into an XML document, or, alternatively, attempting to save an XML document into a relational **DataSet**.

The Microsoft .NET Framework addresses this issue by integrating the relational view with the node-based hierarchical view provided by the DOM. The intermediary class used to facilitate this is the **XmlDataDocument** class. This class represents data as nodes on a tree. It allows you to translate the contents of the relational data into an XML document and explicitly maintain the relationships between the data. Similarly, you can translate the XML documents into a relational **DataSet**, defining the relationships from the XML document itself.

EXAM TIP Have a good understanding of how the **XmlDataDocument** class works and how it is used to provide an XML view of the underlying **DataSet**.

At a basic level, the **XmlDataDocument** provides an XML view of a **DataSet** in a separate object so that it can be manipulated using the DOM. Manipulating the contents of the **XmlDataDocument** automatically synchronizes the two views as they are changed. Instead of viewing the contents of the relational **DataSet** as a set of tables, you can view the contents of the XML document nonrelationally. The following example demonstrates this concept by converting a **DataSet** to an XML document and then writing the contents of the XML document to a file using the **XmlDataDocument** class.

```
Module Module1
    Private Const FILE_NAME As String = "MyADOXMLDataDocument.xml"

    Sub Main()
        Dim NWConn As OleDbConnection
        Dim dadCustomers As OleDbDataAdapter
        Dim dstCustomers As DataSet
        Dim xddDataDocument As XmlDataDocument

        NWConn = New OleDbConnection("Provider=Microsoft.Jet.OLEDB.4.0;" & _
                                     "Data Source=c:\Temp\McgrawHill\" & _
                                     "Data\nwind.mdb;")
        dadCustomers = New OleDbDataAdapter("SELECT * FROM Orders", NWConn)
        dstCustomers = New DataSet()
        dadCustomers.Fill(dstCustomers, "Customers")
        xddDataDocument = New XmlDataDocument(dstCustomers)
        xddDataDocument.Save(FILE_NAME)

    End Sub
End Module
```

Using SQL Statements to Retrieve XML Data

Up to this point we have used basic SQL queries to retrieve data into a DataSet directly and then made use of the methods available with the DataSet class to retrieve the associated XML documents. Instead, we can execute SQL queries directly that will return data into an XML document instead of into standard rowsets. In addition to retrieving data into an XML document, SQL queries can be used to directly update or insert data into a table from an XML document. Let's begin with a discussion of how to retrieve data into an XML document using SQL.

To retrieve data from an SQL Server using SQL, we make use of the following FOR XML clauses within our SELECT statements:

- FOR XML AUTO
- FOR XML RAW
- FOR XML EXPLICIT

The FOR XML AUTO clause returns XML elements that are nested, based on which tables are listed in the "from" part of the query, and which fields are listed in the "select" part. As an example, consider the following query that can be executed against our NorthWind database:

```
SELECT Customers.CustomerID, Orders.OrderID, Customers.ContactName
FROM Customers, Orders
WHERE Customers.CustomerID = Orders.CustomerID
FOR XML AUTO
```

This results in an XML document that contains the data specified by the query. The partial results of this query are as follows:

```
<Customers CustomerID="ALFKI" ContactName="Maria Anders">
<Orders OrderID="10643"/>
   <Orders OrderID="10692"/>
   <Orders OrderID="10702"/>
   <Orders OrderID="10835"/>
   <Orders OrderID="10952"/>
   <Orders OrderID="11011"/>
</Customers>
```

As can be seen from the partial results, each CustomerID, OrderID, and ContactName were returned based on the selection criteria. As can be seen in the results, an element is created for each table referenced in the FROM CLAUSE. Each of the column values requested from the table is specified as an attribute in the corresponding table element. In the example results, the CustomerID whose value is "ALKFI" and the ContactName whose value is "Maria Anders" are represented in the Customer element. For each of the orders placed by that customer ID, an Orders element representing the table that the information is retrieved from is nested under the corresponding Customers element.

The FOR XML RAW clause returns XML elements with "row" prefixed (eg. "`<row tProduct ...>`"). Each column in a table is represented as an attribute and null column values are not included. As an example, let's modify our preceding example query as follows:

```
SELECT Customers.CustomerID, Orders.OrderID, Customers.ContactName
FROM Customers, Orders
WHERE Customers.CustomerID = Orders.CustomerID
FOR XML AUTO
```

In this particular example, the partial results for this query would be as follows:

```
<row CustomerID="ALFKI" OrderID="10643" OrderDate="1997-08-25T00:00:00"/>
<row CustomerID="ANATR" OrderID="10308" OrderDate="1996-09-18T00:00:00"/>
<row CustomerID="ANATR" OrderID="10625" OrderDate="1997-08-08T00:00:00"/>
<row CustomerID="AROUT" OrderID="10355" OrderDate="1996-11-15T00:00:00"/>
```

Here we see that a row element is returned for each result of our query. This differs from the FOR XML AUTO query in that the elements are not nested. As can be seen from the partial results, the column names and values returned by the query are specified as attributes within the XML element.

Finally, the FOR XML EXPLICIT clause is used to allow users to query a data source in such a way that the names and values of the returned XML are specified before the query batch is executed. The query must be written in a specific way so that the additional information about the expected nesting is explicitly specified as part of the query. Let's rewrite our example query to make use of the FOR XML EXPLICIT clause:

```
SELECT 1                      as Tag,
       NULL                   as Parent,
       Customers.CustomerID as [Customer!1!CustomerID],
       NULL                   as [Order!2!OrderID]
FROM Customers

UNION ALL
SELECT 2, 1, Customers.CustomerID, Orders.OrderID
FROM Customers, Orders
WHERE Customers.CustomerID = Orders.CustomerID
ORDER BY [Customer!1!CustomerID], [Order!2!OrderID]
FOR XML EXPLICIT
```

In this example, we have actually specifed two queries. In the first query all the customer elements and their associated customer ID and order ID attribute values are returned. Finally, in the second query all the order elements and their attribute values are returned. The results of these queries are then combined using the UNION ALL statement. Before explaining the specifics of the query, let's look at the partial results that are returned by this query. The results are shown in Table 14-11.

For the data to be transformed into an XML document, the results of the query are returned in what is known as a Universal table format. This in turn requires the query to be written in a particular way to produce the results in the proper format so that they can be transformed into an XML document. First the EXPLICIT mode requires the query to produce two metadata columns:

- The first column specified in the SELECT clause must be a named tag column that contains the tag number of the current element.
- The second column specifies the parent tag which contains the tag number of the parent element.

Table 14-11 Results of FOR XML EXPLICIT Querynb

Tag	Parent	Customer!1!CustomerID	Order!2!OrderID
1	NULL	ALFKI	NULL
2	1	ALFKI	10643
2	1	ALFKI	10692
2	1	ALFKI	10702
2	1	ALFKI	11011
2	1	ALFKI	...
1	NULL	ANATR	NULL
2	1	ANATR	10308
2	1	ANATR	10625
2	1	ANATR	...

These columns specify the parent-child hierarchy in the XML tree. This information is then used to produce the desired XML tree. If the parent tag value stored in the Parent column is 0 or NULL, then the row is placed at the top level of the XML hierarchy.

To specify the column names within the universal table, the column names in the universal table are encoded within the SELECT statement using XML generic identifiers and attribute names. The encoding of the element name, the attribute names, and other transformation information in the column name in the universal table are specified as

```
ElementName!TagNumber!AttributeName!Directive
```

The arguments for the encoding are outlined in Table 14-12.

Table 14-12 Arguments for Column Name Specifications

Argument	Description
ElementName	Is the resulting generic identifier of the element (for example, if Customers is specified as ElementName, then <Customers> is the element tag).
TagNumber	Is the tag number of the element. TagNumber, with the help of the two metadata columns (Tag and Parent) in the universal table, is used to express the nesting of XML elements in the XML tree. Every TagNumber correspond to exactly one ElementName.
AttributeName	Is either the name of the XML attribute (if Directive is not specified) or the name of the contained element (if Directive is either xml, cdata, or element). If Directive is specified, AttributeName can be empty. In this case, the value contained in the column is directly contained by the element with the specified ElementName.
Directive	This option is used to encode ID, IDREF, and IDREFS by using the keywords ID, IDREF, and IDREFS. It is also used to indicate how to map the string data to XML using the keywords hide, element, xml, xmltext, and cdata. Combining directives between these two groups is allowed in most of the cases, but not combining among themselves.

Using SQL Statements to Write XML Data

Not only can we retrieve data into an XML Document using an SQL Query, but we also have the ability to construct a rectangular rowset from an XML Document using an SQL Query. To do this we make use of the OPENXML function within our SELECT and SELECT INTO statements. The OpenXML function decomposes XML hierarchies into relational structures. To write queries against an XML document using OPENXML, you must first call sp_xml_preparedocument, which parses the XML document, builds a tree representation of the document in memory and returns a handle to the parsed document. This handle is then passed to the OPENXML function along with an XPATH expression that will identify the nodes to be processed as rows, and a mapping between the rowset columns and XML nodes. Table 14-13 outlines the types of mappings that can be done.

The OPENXML function will then return a rowset view of the data for our SELECT and SELECT INTO query statements. Once the in memory version of the XML document is finished being used, it should be removed using the sp_xml_removedocument stored procedure. Let's look at an example of how this works. In the following query we will use OPENXML to add a row to a database table from an XML document.

```
DECLARE @h int
DECLARE @xmldoc varchar(1000)

set @xmldoc =
'<root>
<customer customerID="ALFKJ"
      companyName="Who Inc."
      contactName="Dr. Seuess"
      contactTitle="author"
      address="123 Any St."
      city="WhoVille"
      region="North East"
      state="MB"
      PostalCode="R3J2Y2"
      country="Canada"
      phone="(204) 888-6543"
      fax="(204) 989-3456 />
</root>'

EXEC sp_xml_preparedocument @h OUTPUT, @xmldoc
INSERT INTO customers
SELECT *
FROM OpenXML(@h,'/root/customer')
WITH customers
EXEC sp_xml_removedocument @h
```

In this example, because of the one-to-one relationship between attributes of the authors elements and the columns in the underlying SQL Server table, the WITH schema clause doesn't contain the column names, types, or XPath expressions that identify document locations. If we only wanted to retrieve certain columns then we would need to

Table 14-13 Mapping Flags

Flag	Description
0	Defaults to attribute centric mapping
1	Use the attribute centric mapping. Can be combined with XML_ELEMENTS in which case, attribute centric mapping is applied first, and then element centric mapping is applied for all columns not yet dealt with.
2	Use the element centric mapping. Can be combined with XML_ATTRIBUTES in which case, attribute centric mapping is applied first, and then element centric mapping is applied for all columns not yet dealt with.
8	Can be combined with XML_ATTRIBUTES or XML_ELEMENTS. In context of retrieval, this flag indicates that the consumed data should not be copied.

specify the schemaDeclaration within our WITH clause. The following selects only the customerID and companyName from the XML Document provided:

```
DECLARE @h int
DECLARE @xmldoc varchar(1000)

set @xmldoc =
'<root>
<customer customerID="ALFKJ"
      companyName="Who Inc."
      contactName="Dr. Seuess"
      contactTitle="author"
      address="123 Any St."
      city="WhoVille"
      region="North East"
      state="MB"
      PostalCode="R3J2Y2"
      country="Canada"
      phone="(204) 888-6543"
      fax="(204) 989-3456/>
</root>'

EXEC sp_xml_preparedocument @h OUTPUT, @xmldoc
SELECT *
FROM OpenXML(@h,'/root/customer',1)
WITH (CustomerID  varchar(10),
      ContactName varchar(20))
EXEC sp_xml_removedocument @h
```

Here we have indicated that we wish to use an attribute centric mapping between our XML Document and the rowset. We have also specified the schemaDeclaration indicating our column names and the valuetypes they specify.

We have provided only a brief introduction into how to make use of the OPENXML function and how it can be used to retrieve information from XML Documents. It is recommended that you refer to the documentation on the MSDN library at http://msdn.microsoft.com/ or the documentation within Visual Studio .NET for an in-depth discussion on how the OPENXML function can be used within an SQL SELECT or SELECT INTO query.

Typed DataSets

Typically, when you work with a **DataSet**, you must work with several collections. To retrieve the value of a specific column in a specific row, you must work with the **DataSet's** Tables and Rows collections. For example, to display the value of the CustomerID for all the rows of the Customers table, you would use the following code.

```
Dim rwDataRow As DataRow
For each rwDataRow in dstDataSet.Tables("Customers").Rows
   Console.Writeline(rwDataRow("CustomerID"))
Next
```

Instead of accessing data in a **DataSet** by working with collections, you can access the data by using strongly typed methods and properties specified by an XML schema. Using a strongly typed **DataSet**, you can create more readable code, and you can refer to tables and columns by name. In addition, you can, for example, display the value of the CustomerID column for all the rows in the Customers table, as shown in the following code.

```
Dim rwCustomerIDRow As CustomerIDRow
For each rwCustomerIDRow in objCustomersDS.Customers
   Console.Writeline(rwDataRow(rwCustomerIDRow.CustomerID))
Next
```

When you create a typed **DataSet**, you create a new class that represents the **DataSet**. In the preceding example, you create a new class named **objCustomersDS** that represents the **DataSet**. Once you create this class, you can retrieve a reference to the Customers DataTable by using the Customers property. Furthermore, you can refer to the value of the CustomerID column by using the CustomerID property. A strongly typed **DataSet** simply provides a more intuitive means of referring to the members of a **DataSet**.

To create a strongly typed **DataSet**, complete the following steps:

1. Create an XML schema that specifies the structure of the **DataSet**.
2. Use the XML schema with the XSD.EXE command line tool to generate the source code for a class that represents the **DataSet**.
3. Compile the source code for the class and copy the compiled class into your application's /bin directory.

Exercise 14-5: Creating a Strongly Typed DataSet In this exercise you will create a strongly typed DataSet that contains the Customers table from the NWind .MDB database.

1. To automatically generate an XML schema that specifies the structure of the **DataSet** and Customers table, use the GetXmlSchema method, as shown in the following code.

PART IV

```
    Private Const FILE_NAME As String = "CustomersDS.xsd"
    Sub Main()
        Dim NWConn As OleDbConnection
        Dim dadCustomers As OleDbDataAdapter
        Dim dstCustomers As DataSet
        Dim xddDataDocument As XmlDataDocument

        NWConn = New OleDbConnection("Provider=Microsoft.Jet.OLEDB.4.0;" & _
                 "Data Source=c:\Temp\McgrawHill\" & _
                 "Data\nwind.mdb;")
        dadCustomers = New OleDbDataAdapter("SELECT * FROM Orders", NWConn)
        dstCustomers = New DataSet()
        dadCustomers.Fill(dstCustomers, "Customers")
        dstCustomers.WriteXmlSchema(FILE_NAME)
    End Sub
```

In the preceding code you write the schema for the Customers table by using the WriteXmlSchema method of the **DataSet**. This produces the following schema for the table.

```
<?xml version="1.0" standalone="yes"?>
<xs:schema id="NewDataSet" _
              xmlns="" xmlns:xs="http://www.w3.org/2001/XMLSchema"
              xmlns:msdata="urn:schemas-microsoft-com:xml-msdata">
  <xs:element name="NewDataSet" msdata:IsDataSet="true">
    <xs:complexType>
      <xs:choice maxOccurs="unbounded">
        <xs:element name="Customers">
          <xs:complexType>
            <xs:sequence>
              <xs:element name="CustomerID" type="xs:string" minOccurs="0" />
              <xs:element name="CompanyName" type="xs:string" minOccurs="0" />
              <xs:element name="ContactName" type="xs:string" minOccurs="0" />
              <xs:element name="ContactTitle" type="xs:string" minOccurs="0" />
              <xs:element name="Address" type="xs:string" minOccurs="0" />
              <xs:element name="City" type="xs:string" minOccurs="0" />
              <xs:element name="Region" type="xs:string" minOccurs="0" />
              <xs:element name="PostalCode" type="xs:string" minOccurs="0" />
              <xs:element name="Country" type="xs:string" minOccurs="0" />
              <xs:element name="Phone" type="xs:string" minOccurs="0" />
              <xs:element name="Fax" type="xs:string" minOccurs="0" />
            </xs:sequence>
          </xs:complexType>
        </xs:element>
      </xs:choice>
    </xs:complexType>
  </xs:element>
</xs:schema>
```

Notice that the schema's ID in the preceding code is the name of the **DataSet** (CustomersDS), and the schema includes a Customers element that represents the Customers database table.

2. To generate the source code for the class, use the schema definition tool (XSD.EXE) from the command line. Open a DOS prompt and change to the directory that contains the schema file. In this exercise the schema file is named CustomersDS.xsd. Next, execute the following statement.

```
Xsd /d l:vb CustomersDS.XSD
```

This statement generates the source for a new Visual Basic class file named CustomersDS.vb. The /d directive indicates that a **DataSet** should be generated, and the /l directive specifies the language to use for the class file. Once you have the source for the class file, you must compile it.

3. To compile the source, execute the following statement from the command line.

```
Vbc /t:library /r:system.dll,system.data.dll,system.xml.dll CustomersDS.vb
```

A new file named CustomersDS.dll is created.

4. To use the component within your application, add a reference to the component, and then modify the example console application, as shown in the following code.

```
Sub Main()
    Dim NWConn As OleDbConnection
    Dim dadCustomers As OleDbDataAdapter
    Dim objCustomersDS As CustomersDS
    Dim objCustomerIDRow As CustomersDS.CustomerID

    NWConn = New OleDbConnection("Provider=Microsoft.Jet.OLEDB.4.0;" & _
                                 "Data Source=c:\Temp\McgrawHill\" & _
                                 "Data\nwind.mdb;")
    dadCustomers = New OleDbDataAdapter("SELECT * FROM Customers", NWConn)
    objCustomersDS = New CustomersDS()
    dadCustomers.Fill(objCustomersDS, "Customers")

    For Each objCustomerIDRow In objCustomersDS.Customers
        Console.WriteLine(objCustomersIDRow.CustomerID)
    Next
End Sub
```

In this exercise you use the **DataSet** Fill method to fill the typed **DataSet** with all the rows from the Customers table. After the rows are added, a For Each loop is used to display the values of the CustomerID for each row.

Notice that the Customers table is returned as a property of the **DataSet**. Also, notice that each column name is returned as a property of the **CustomerRow** object.

```
public void RaisePostBackEvent(String eventArgument){
      OnClick(EventArgs.Empty);
}
```

EXAM TIP Be sure that you understand how typed **DataSets** work and when best to use them within an application.

PART IV

Summary

The use and manipulation of XML data is a complex subject. Microsoft offers a number of XML classes for reading data. Useful readers include the **XmlTextReader**, the **XmlNodeReader**, and the **XmlValidatingReader**. Of particular significance is the **XmlValidatingReader**, which allows developers to validate XML documents to ensure that they conform to schema specifications and goals.

The readers are efficient at reading XML data in a forward-only, read-only manner. However, they do not allow you to traverse XML documents in other directions or edit documents. The XML document object model (DOM) provides this functionality. This class enables you to read an XML document into memory as an XML document tree and traverse the document in different directions based on the logic and requirements of the application. The DOM also provides facilities for manipulating, augmenting, or removing nodes from the document tree.

Microsoft has taken great strides to ensure support for XML within ADO.NET and has designed ADO.NET hand in hand with the .NET XML Framework to provide a single architecture. To facilitate this integration, Microsoft introduced a new object called a **DataSet** that provides the foundation for integration with XML. Using various methods of the **DataSet** class, you can load XML documents into a relational data structure and generate XML documents from relational data stored in the **DataSet**.

The **XmlDataDocument** class facilitates the translation of a **DataSet** to an XML document. This is useful for applications that must manipulate data in a hierarchical tree fashion using the DOM instead of manipulating data in a relational structure using a **DataSet**.

Typically, when you work with a **DataSet** you must work with several collections to process the information contained within the **DataSet**. Typed **DataSets** provide an alternative way of working with the information contained in a DataSet. Instead of accessing data in a **DataSet** by working with a collection, you can access the data by creating and using strongly typed methods and properties specified by an XML schema.

Test Questions

1. You have an XML document that you want to validate before using it within your application. Which of the following classes would you use? Choose all that apply.

   A. XmlDataDocument

   B. XmlTextReader

   C. XmlValidatingReader

   D. XmlNodeReader

2. When would you use an **XmlNodeReader** instead of an **XmlTextReader**?
   A. You need read-only access to your document.
   B. You need to modify the structure of your document.
   C. Your application does not require random access to your document.
   D. Your application requires random access to your document's contents.
3. Which tool can be used to generate a class that can then be used to provide a typed **DataSet** to your application?
   A. VBC.EXE
   B. XSDL.EXE
   C. XSD.EXE
   D. ASMGEN.EXE

Test Answers

1. C. The XmlValidatingReader is used to validate XML documents.
2. B, D. You would use the XmlNodeReader document when you need to modify the structure of your document or randomly access the nodes within it.
3. C. The XSD.EXE tool is used to generate the necessary class code from an XML schema that can then be compiled and used within your application.

PART V

Windows Forms Applications

CHAPTER 15

Creating Form Classes

In this chapter, you will

- See how to create a Windows Form using the Windows Form Designer
- Discover how to set properties of Windows Forms
- Learn how to create Windows Forms using Visual Inheritance
- Understand how to create Windows Forms without using the Windows Form Designer
- Find out how to create custom graphics on Forms using the **System.Drawing** namespaces
- Understand how to implement error handling in Windows user interfaces
- Learn how to incorporate existing code into applications

A key element of the Visual Basic .NET framework is Windows Forms. This object-oriented, extensible class set allows developers to develop rich Windows applications with ease, facilitating the creation of rich user interfaces in applications.

Forms define the screen "real estate" in an application, including the overall application interface, Property pages, dialog boxes, and any other objects that display data or accept input from users.

It is easy to design "perfect" forms for an application using Visual Basic .NET. Forms are designed in the Windows Form Designer of the integrated development environment (IDE), or they can be created completely in code. You place controls on the form and adjust their properties as well as the properties of the form in order to tailor the form to your exact needs. You also can manipulate the methods of the form to cause forms to interact with end users according to the application's requirements.

This chapter covers everything you need to know about Windows Forms for the certification exam. This includes the creation of forms both programmatically and visually. It also explores how you can validate user information entered into your Windows forms.

Creating Windows Forms

The most common method of creating Windows Forms is to use the Windows Form Designer, shown in Figure 15-1. This IDE interface allows you to create the form's visual content by placing controls on its surface and modifying the properties of the controls

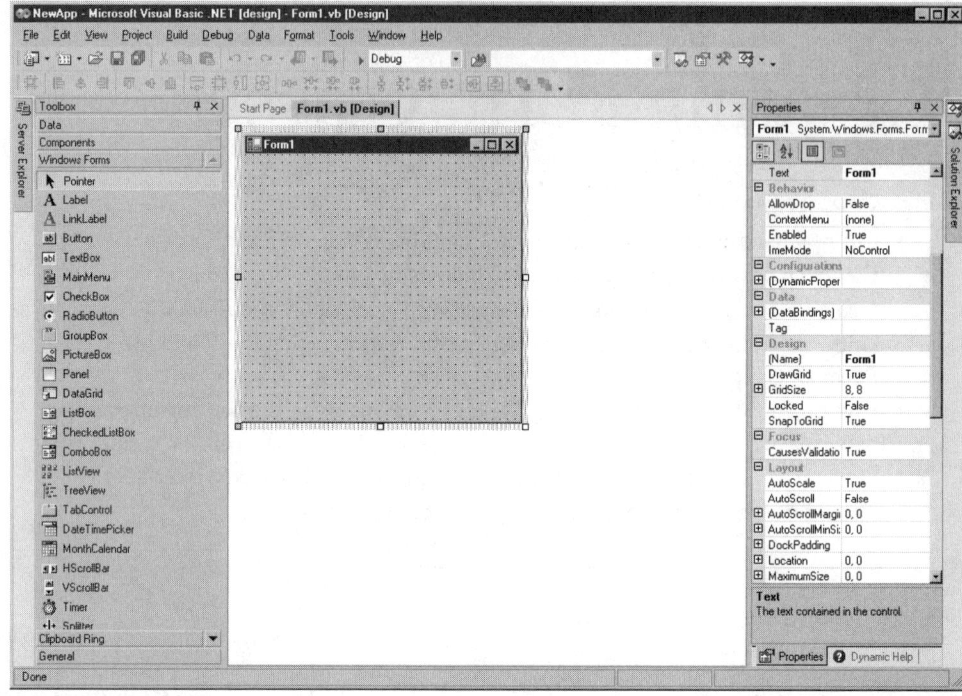

Figure 15-1 The Windows Form Designer

and the form appropriately. Although controls are covered later in this book, this chapter focuses on the underlying forms and the properties and methods of these important objects. In this section you create Windows Forms in the Windows Form Designer and in code, and you take advantage of advanced techniques including Visual Inheritance and the **System.Drawing** namespace.

Creating Forms

A major step in application development is creating the forms that present the various user interfaces to end users. This section explores various ways to do this, including leveraging the IDE and exploiting Visual Basic .NET code.

Creating Forms in the IDE

As applications grow and incorporate more functions for end users, developers typically have to add more forms. Although forms can be added using code (covered later in this section), it is often easiest and sometimes even necessary to create these additional forms in the IDE. There are many ways to add forms in the IDE. The most common method is as follows.

1. Select the Project menu in the IDE.
2. Click Add Windows Form. The Add New Item dialog box appears.
3. Ensure that Windows Form is selected, as shown here.

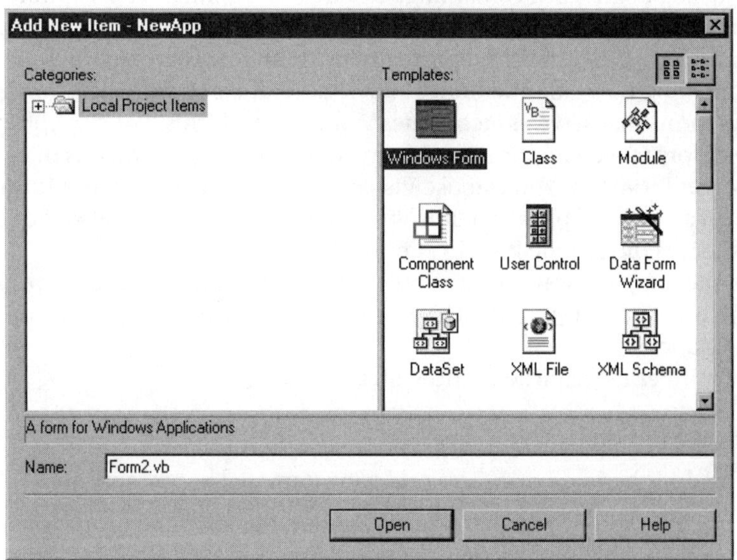

4. Click Open.

TIP Alternatively, you can use the Solution Explorer to quickly add a new form to a project. To do so, right-click the current project and choose Add | Add Windows Form from the shortcut menu.

Creating Forms in Code

Developers do not have to use the IDE to add forms to applications. Forms can also be created using code. As for other objects, to create a form in code you simply declare a variable that represents the form and then create an instance of the form. Once the form has been created, it can be displayed during the execution of the application. Although you cannot access the form during design, creating forms programmatically is an excellent method for displaying new forms that have been designed previously.

The following example shows the code used to create a new form. The example assumes that a form named frmDialogTemplate exists already.

```
Dim frmMyNewForm As frmDialogTemplate
frmMyNewForm = New frmDialogTemplate()
```

Creating Forms Using Visual Inheritance

Some applications include a large number of forms. Just think of the number of forms utilized in a product like Microsoft Outlook. This application not only presents many different user interfaces for reading email and scheduling appointments, but also features a vast number of dialog boxes, each containing several tabs of configuration options.

The Visual Inheritance capabilities of Visual Basic .NET are ideal for applications that require many forms, especially when many of these forms are going to be similar in function and design. Visual Inheritance allows developers to create new forms based on pre-existing forms that serve as "templates" for the new forms. For example, you might create a basic form for an application that includes controls and menus that will appear in several other locations. You can use Visual Inheritance to create new forms for these additional areas of the application quickly and efficiently. You can also modify the new forms for the specific unique functions of the new location.

Perhaps the simplest way to carry out Visual Inheritance is to use the Inheritance Picker, which is a clever graphical user interface for controlling and implementing Visual Inheritance.

To use the Inheritance Picker, follow these steps:

1. Select the Projects menu in the IDE.
2. Click Add Inherited Form. The Add New Item dialog box appears.
3. Choose a location in the left pane that hosts the template form. For example, choose Local Project Items, as shown in the following illustration.

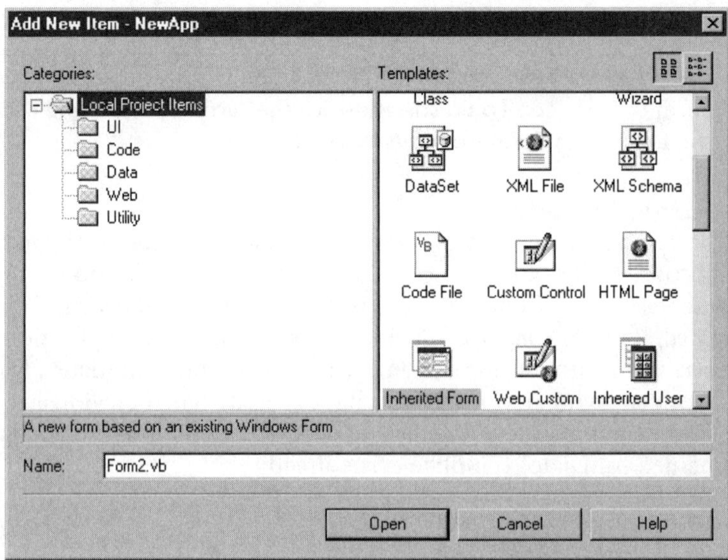

4. In the right pane, ensure that Inherited Form is selected.
5. Provide a name for the new form in the Name field and click Open.
6. The Inheritance Picker displays the forms from the location you specified. Choose the form to inherit from and click OK.

TIP You can use the Browse button to inherit a form from outside a project. To do so, the form must be in a project or it must be compiled in an .EXE or .DLL file.

You can also use the Inherits keyword to create an inherited form in your code. For example, the following code creates an inherited form from a form named frmMainForm.

```
Public Class frmMyForm
      Inherits frmMainForm
End Class
```

Form Lifetime Events

During the lifetime of a form, regardless of how it was created in the application, various events are raised. Visual Basic .NET includes the following events:

- Load
- Activated
- VisibleChanged
- Deactivated
- Closing
- Closed

You can place code in these various events to add additional and necessary functionality in an application. For example, you could use the Closed event to provide clean-up code for the form.

EXAM TIP You can place code in the Closing event of a form to prevent the form from closing if a given condition is not met.

Setting Properties of Windows Forms

A major part of tailoring Windows Forms for an application involves setting the properties of these forms. This section explores these properties and explains how to control everything from which form loads initially in an application to where forms display in the application when they launch.

You can set almost all properties using the Properties window in the IDE, or you can use code. Setting a property value in the Properties window involves simply clicking in the appropriate field and setting the desired value, as shown in Figure 15-2. Setting a property value in code for a Windows Form is accomplished as shown in the following example.

```
Dim frmAccountDialog as New Form()
Set frmAccountDialog.DesktopLocation = new Point (100,100)
```

Setting the Startup Form

Most of your Windows applications will consist of many forms. It is up to you to designate the startup form. This form loads upon execution of the application. You designate the startup form by setting the **Startup** object for the application.

To set the **Startup** object, follow these steps:

1. Click the name of the project in the Solutions Explorer.
2. Select the Project menu and choose Properties.

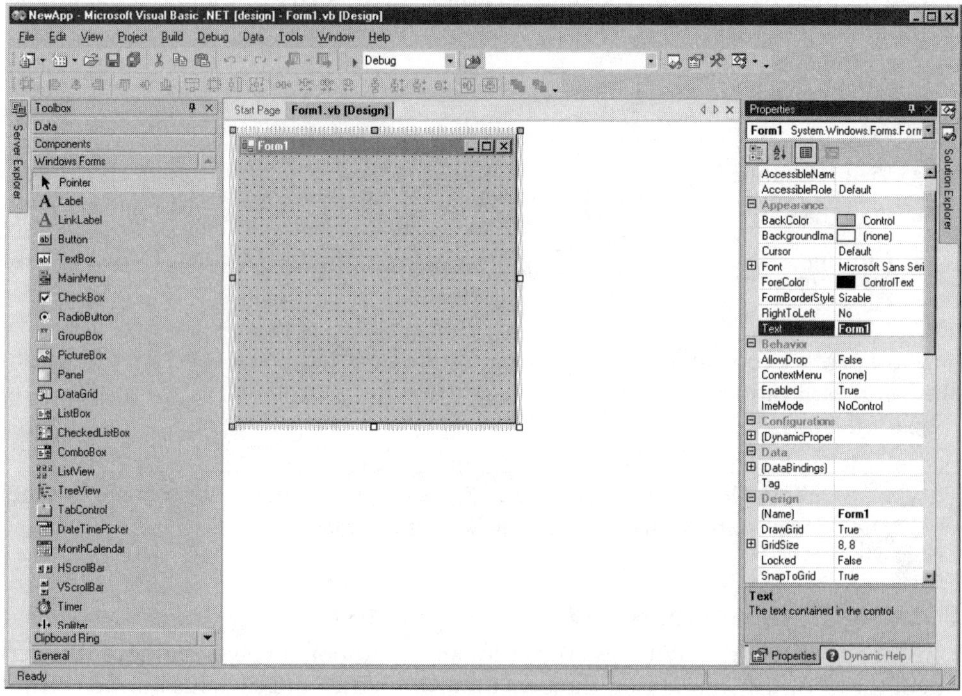

Figure 15-2 Setting properties using the Properties window

3. Choose the appropriate form in the Startup Object drop-down list.

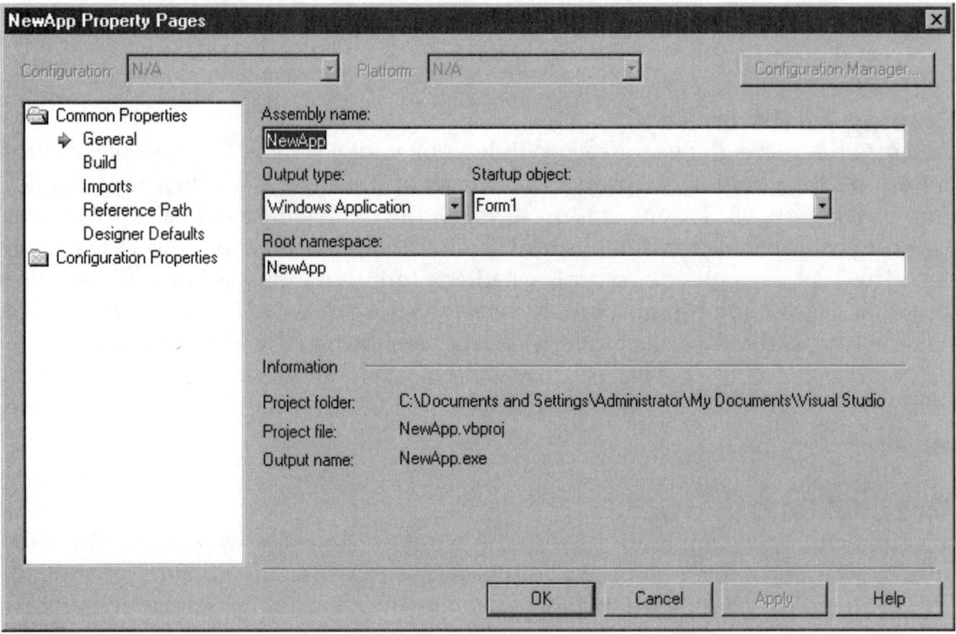

Controlling the Visibility of Forms

You typically control a form's visibility using the Visible property. Unfortunately, if you want the main form of a Windows application to be invisible at the application's startup, setting the Visible property to False is not effective (the form shows itself anyway). However, there is a solution to this problem in Visual Basic .NET.

First, understand that typically the lifetime of the startup form determines the lifetime of the application. However, it is possible to abstract the application's startup logic into a module to separate the lifetime of the application from the lifetime of the form. Once this is done, you may freely make forms visible (and invisible), because the application ends when you "close" the module.

To separate the lifetime of the application from the lifetime of the form, follow these steps:

1. Add a module to the Windows application by right-clicking the project in the Solution Explorer and choosing Add Module.
2. Add the following code in the Main subroutine of the new module.

```
Sub Main()
   Dim frmSample as New Form1()
   System.Windows.Forms.MessageBox.Show( _
```

```
        "The application is running now, but no forms have been shown.")
    frmSample.Text = "Running Form"
    frmSample.ShowDialog()
End Sub
```

3. Set the **Startup** object as the Sub Main.

Keeping Forms on Top

Onscreen form level differs for each Windows operating system. For example, in Windows 2000, a topmost form always stays in front of all windows within a given application. In Windows 98, a topmost form stays in front of all windows in all applications. Suppose you want to keep a floating tool window in front of an application's main window. The TopMost property controls whether a form is a topmost form. The topmost form floats above non-topmost forms even when it is not active. To ensure that a form stays on top, set the TopMost property to True, as shown in the following code.

```
Public sub MakeOnTop()
   myTopForm.TopMost = True
End Sub
```

Accessibility Properties

It is simple to design applications with the Windows Accessibility features. These features make it possible for end users with hearing and visual impairments to easily use applications. Visual Basic .NET includes the following Accessibility properties for forms:

- **AccessibleDescription** This property describes the form. You can use a text string for the description; typically you want to be descriptive enough so that the visually impaired understand the purpose of the form.
- **AccessibleName** This property allows the name of the form to be exposed to accessibility aids. You can use a text string for the name and again you should concentrate on making the form understandable to those with impairments.
- **AccessibleRole** This property describes the user interface role of the form. The default for this property setting is Default and the role is indicated as a form. The options in this property more accurately describe the form to the accessibility functions, for example, Window, Application, Document, Pane, Dialog, and Property Page.

Appearance Properties

Numerous Appearance properties allow developers to control everything from form colors to fonts used on the form. Visual Basic .NET includes the following Appearance properties for forms:

- **BackColor** This property controls the background color of the Windows Form. The default is controlled by another property called DefaultBackColor, which in turn is controlled by SystemColors.Control. To change the BackColor property via the Properties window, simply click in the field. A drop-down menu allows you to choose from three color palettes: Custom, Web, and System.

- **BackgroundImage** This property sets an image as the background on the Windows Form. When you click in this field in the Properties window, a dialog box appears that allows you to navigate to the image file you want to use as the background.

NOTE Images with translucent or transparent colors are not supported as background images.

- **Cursor** This property controls the cursor image that appears when the mouse is positioned over the form. Clicking in the field reveals a drop-down menu that allows you to choose from a list of possible cursor images.
- **Font** This property controls the font that displays on the form. The default is controlled by the DefaultFont property. This property has additional properties that you can control including Name, Size, Unit, Bold, GdiCharSet, GdiVerticalFont, Italic, Strikeout, and Underline.
- **ForeColor** This property controls the fore color of the Windows Form. The default is the value of the DefaultForeColor property. To change the ForeColor property via the Properties window, simply click in the field. A drop-down menu allows you to choose from three color palettes: Custom, Web, and System.
- **FormBorderStyle** This property controls the border style of the form, which determines how the outer edge of the form appears. Besides changing the border display for a form, certain border styles prevent the form from being sized. For example, the FormBorderStyle.FixedDialog border style changes the border of the form to that of a dialog box and prevents the form from being resized. The border style can also affect the size or availability of the caption bar section of a form. The default value is Sizeable. Other options for this property are None, FixedSingle, Fixed3D, FixedDialog, FixedToolWindow, and SizableToolWindow.
- **RightToLeft** This property indicates whether a form's elements are aligned to support locales using right-to-left fonts such as Hebrew and Arabic. The default value is No. When this property is set to Yes, control elements that include text are displayed from right to left.
- **Text** This property allows developers to provide a name for the form. This string appears in the title bar that appears along the top of the form. Typically, this is used for the application or document name.

Behavior Properties

The behavior-related properties of forms allow developers to control various properties such as the shortcut menu that appears when the form is right-clicked and also to control whether the form is enabled. Visual Basic .NET includes the following behavior properties for forms:

- **AllowDrop** This property determines whether the form can accept data that the user drags and drops on the form. The default setting for this property is False.
- **ContextMenu** This property determines the shortcut menu associated with the form. The shortcut menu appears if a user right-clicks the form.

EXAM TIP Another common term for shortcut menu is *context menu*. These terms tend to be used interchangeably in Microsoft Visual Basic exams.

- **Enabled** This property controls whether the form can respond to user interaction. It allows forms and controls to be enabled or disabled at runtime. For example, you can disable forms that do not apply to the current state of the application. When the Enabled property of a form is set to False, all the controls on the form are disabled as well. The default for this property is True.
- **ImeMode** This property controls the Input Method Editor (IME) mode of the form. An IME is a program that allows users to enter complex characters and symbols, such as Japanese kanji characters, using a standard keyboard. By default, this property is set to NoControl for a form.

Configurations Properties

The Configurations category of form properties allows developers to create dynamic properties. Dynamic properties allow you to configure an application so that some or all of its property values are stored in an external configuration file rather than in the application's compiled code. By making it easier to update property values that may need to change over time, these properties help reduce the cost of maintaining the application after deployment. For example, if you are creating an application that is database driven, and you are using a Test database during development, using dynamic properties for the database values allows you to easily switch the database used after deployment without recompiling the source codes.

Data Properties

The Data properties of a form allow developers to bind data values to the form object. Typically, this category consists of the following two properties:

- **DataBindings** This property configures the data bindings for the form and is used to access the ControlBindingsCollection. By adding Binding objects to the collection, you can bind any property of a control to the property of an object.
- **Tag** This property sets the object that contains data about the form. When using the Windows Form Designer to set this property, only text may be assigned. A common use for the Tag property is to store data that is closely associated with the form or control. For example, if you have a form that

displays information about a customer, you can store a DataSet that contains the customer's order history in the form's Tag property so the data can be accessed quickly.

Design Properties

The Design properties of a Windows Form provide options for controlling how the Windows Form Designer functions. Visual Basic .NET includes the following Design properties:

- **Name** This property allows developers to name the Windows Form. This name can be used at runtime to evaluate the object by name rather than type and programmatic name. Because the Name property returns a String type, it can be evaluated in case-style logic statements such as Select statements in Visual Basic.
- **DrawGrid** This property toggles the display of the grid on Windows Forms during design in the Windows Form Designer. The default value is True and causes a grid pattern to appear across the form. This grid pattern is designed to assist developers when laying out controls on the form. It does not appear during runtime.
- **GridSize** This property controls the spacing used in the grid during design time (if the grid is visible). You specify a height and width value (in pixels) in order to control the spacing.
- **Locked** This property controls the size of the form and locks this size in the Windows Form Designer. The default value is False. When set to true, the Windows Form cannot be resized in the Designer.
- **SnapToGrid** This property causes controls placed on the form in the Designer to "snap to" the grid coordinates specified in properties for the form. The default value is True. It is typically recommended that developers use the SnapToGrid property to assist in aligning controls on a form.

Layout Properties

The Layout properties are very important and control how developers form displays on screen. Visual Basic .NET includes the following Layout properties for forms:

- **AutoScale** This property controls whether the form resizes itself automatically based upon the size font used on the form and its controls. The default value is True. Developers use this property to allow the form and its controls to automatically adjust based on changes in the font. This can be useful in applications where the font might increase or decrease based on the language specified for use by Windows.
- **AutoScroll** This property defaults to True and permits the form to exhibit automatic scrolling behavior. If this property is kept at the default value, scroll bars display on the form if any controls are located outside the form's client

region. In addition, when AutoScroll is kept at True, the client area of the form automatically scrolls to make the control with input focus visible. This property is very useful for preventing users from losing the capability to view controls when their video resolution settings are set at a low resolution.

- **StartPosition** This property controls the starting position of the form when it is displayed at runtime. The form can be displayed manually or in the default location specified by Windows. You can also position the form to display in the center of the screen or in the center of its parent form. Centering against the parent form is particularly useful for multiple document interface (MDI) child forms.
- **WindowState** This property determines whether the form is displayed normally, minimized, or maximized. The default for this property is normal.

EXAM TIP Another often used property for setting the size and location of the form on the Windows desktop is the DesktopBounds property. This property uses a **Rectangle** to represent the bounds of the form on the Windows desktop using desktop coordinates. We discuss the **Rectangle** object later in this chapter.

Miscellaneous Properties

Although the following form properties do not fall under a convenient category, they are still very useful when designing applications in Visual Basic .NET.

- **AcceptButton** This property allows developers to designate a default action to occur when the user presses ENTER in the application. It allows users to quickly complete a form by pressing ENTER when they are finished instead of clicking Accept with their mouse.
- **CancelButton** This property allows developers to designate a default action to occur when the user presses ESC in the application. It allows users to quickly complete a form by pressing ESC to close a window without committing changes instead of clicking Cancel with their mouse.

Window Style Properties

The Window Style properties allow developers to control the "look and feel" of Windows forms as well as the functions that the form presents to the user. For example, one important property controls whether a Help button is displayed to the end user. Visual Basic .NET includes the following Window Style properties:

- **ControlBox** This property determines whether or not a control box appears in the caption bar of the Windows Form. When the control box is pressed, it reveals the system menu. This object exists in most parent windows and often takes on an icon representing the application. The system menu it reveals allows you to close the application, minimize it, or move it. The default for this property is True.

EXAM TIP If a form does not display a control box, it cannot be closed using ALT-F4.

- **HelpButton** When this property is set to True, a small button with a question mark appears in the caption bar to the left of the Close button. The user clicks the Help button to display Help for the application. You create an event handler for the HelpRequested event of the Control class to display Help information to the user when the Help button is clicked. The default for this property is False.

NOTE Even if this value is set to True, the Help button does not appear if the maximize or minimize boxes are shown.

- **Opacity** This property enables developers to specify a level of transparency for the form and its controls. When this property is set to a value less than 100% (1.00), the entire form, including borders, becomes more transparent. Setting this property to a value of 0% (0.00) makes the form completely invisible. You can use this property to provide different levels of transparency or to provide effects such as phasing a form in or out of view. For example, you can phase a form into view by setting the Opacity property to a value of 0% (0.00) and gradually increasing the value until it reaches 100% (1.00).
- **TransparencyKey** This property controls the color used by transparent areas of the form. When the TransparencyKey property is assigned aColor, the areas of the form that have the same BackColor will be displayed transparently. Any mouse actions, such as a click, that are performed on the transparent areas of the form are transferred to the windows below the transparent area. For example, if the client region of a form is made transparent, clicking the mouse on that area sends the event notification of the click to any window that is below it. If the color assigned to the TransparencyKey property is the same as any controls on the form, the controls also will be displayed transparently. For example, if a Button control on a form has its TransparencyKey property set to SystemColors.Control, the control will be displayed transparently unless the BackColor property of the Button control is changed to a different color.

Exercise 15-1: Building Windows Forms In this exercise you will build a Windows Form and manipulate several key properties.

1. Select Start | Programs | Microsoft Visual Studio .NET | Microsoft Visual Studio .NET to launch Visual Studio.
2. Click New Project on the Start Page.
3. In the New Project dialog box, ensure that Windows Application is selected and name your project **Forms**. Then, click OK.

4. To change the name of your initial form from the default, click Form1 in the Windows Form Designer. Click the Name property in the Properties toolbox. Change the name to **frmSampleForm.**
5. Use the Text property of the form to change the text in the title bar to "This is a sample form!"
6. Right-click Form1.vb in the Solution Explorer and choose Rename from the shortcut menu that appears. Rename the file **frmSampleForm.vb**.
7. To add a new form to your project, select File | Add New Item.
8. In the Add New Item dialog box, ensure that Windows Form is selected and name the form **frmNewStartup.vb**. Then, click Open.
9. To set the added form as the new startup form, ensure that the project name is highlighted in the Solution Explorer. Then, select the Projects menu from the IDE and choose Properties.
10. Select frmNewStartup in the Startup Object drop-down list, and then click OK.
11. You are ready to build and test your new application. Choose the Start button on the toolbar of the IDE to launch your Forms application. The new startup form that you created and set as the new startup form for the project appears.

The System.Drawing Namespaces

Windows applications consist of a graphical user interface that consists primarily of Windows Forms. The .NET framework includes many controls and methods for creating diverse interface designs; however, developers must also have the freedom to create custom graphical content.

Visual Basic .NET includes the Graphics Device Interface (GDI) and the managed implementation called GDI+ to allow you to customize graphical content. The **System.Drawing** namespaces allow you to exploit the power of GDI+ in Visual Basic .NET.

EXAM TIP Because the range of **System.Drawing** namespaces is so vast, Microsoft tends to test on the popular aspects, which are the topics covered in this chapter.

Visual Basic .NET includes the following **System.Drawing** namespaces:

- **System.Drawing** This namespace is typically used to render custom graphics. It contains most of the classes you need, and is the primary namespace for graphics programming.
- **System.Drawing.Design** This namespace contains classes that extend design-time user interface (UI) logic and drawing. You can further extend this design-time functionality to create custom Toolbox items, type-specific value editors that can edit and graphically represent values of their supported types, and type converters that can convert values between certain types.

- **System.Drawing.2D** This namespace contains classes that are designed to render advanced visual effects in applications.
- **System.Drawing.Imaging** This namespace provides classes that allow advanced manipulation of images. Remember that almost all basic image manipulation techniques are possible using the **System.Drawing** namespace classes.
- **System.Drawing.Printing** This namespace provides print-related services. Typically, you create a new instance of the PrintDocument class, set the properties that describe what to print, and then call the Print method to print the document.
- **System.Drawing.Text** This namespace provides advanced GDI+ typography functionality. The classes in this namespace allow you to create and use collections of fonts.

The Graphics Object

When it comes to creating custom graphics within GDI+, the **Graphics** object is the principal object used for rendering graphics. Not surprisingly, it is located in the **System.Drawing** namespace. Developers use the **Graphics** object to create a drawing surface on a visual element such as a Windows Form.

Forms and other visual elements expose a CreateGraphics method that you use to access a **Graphics** object associated with the form. The following code demonstrates how to access the **Graphics** object for a Windows Form entitled frmMainForm.

```
Dim mySampleGraphics As System.Drawing.Graphics
mySampleGraphics = frm.MainForm.CreateGraphics()
```

Once we have created the **Graphics** object using the preceding code, we use it to render graphics on the form.

Graphics are rendered on the form using coordinates. These coordinates are X and Y values that measure distance on the form or control. By default, measurement begins from the top left corner, and the unit of measurement is in pixels. Table 15-1 defines the structures used to describe regions of a form.

Table 15-1 Structures for Describing Regions of a Form

Structure	Description
Point	A single point with Integer values of X and Y
PointF	A single point with Single values of X and Y
Size	A rectangular size consisting of paired Height and Width values as Integers
SizeF	A rectangular size consisting of a pair of Single values for Height and Width
Rectangle	A rectangular region specified with Top, Bottom, Left, and Right Integer values
RectangleF	A rectangular region specified with Top, Bottom, Left, and Right Single values

TIP Notice that the coordinate structures can accept Integer or floating-point values. These values can be converted in code when necessary.

The Size structure indicates the size of a rectangle, but does not specify position. The Rectangle structure, however, indicates the actual position of the rectangle on the form or control. You typically create a Rectangle by applying a Size and Point, which function as the upper left corner of the Rectangle. This procedure is demonstrated in the following code.

```
Dim myStartingPoint As New Point(5,5)
Dim myRectangleSize As New Size(30,30)
Dim myRectangle As New Rectangle(myStartingPoint,myRectangleSize)
```

This code creates a rectangle that is 30 by 30 in size and has an upper left corner at the point 5,5.

To enable the rendering of shapes on the screen, the **Graphics** object includes methods that incorporate simple and complex shapes. Some methods begin with Draw and create line structures; other methods begin with Fill and render solid shapes. Tables 15-2 and 15-3 list these methods.

NOTE Each method accepts parameters for the specification of coordinates, and each method requires an object to perform the rendering. Use a **Pen** object for line structures; use a **Brush** object for fill structures.

Table 15-2 Methods for the Creation of Line Drawings

Method	Description
DrawArc	Creates an arc representing a portion of an ellipse
DrawBezier	Creates a Bezier spline
DrawBeziers	Creates a series of Bezier splines
DrawClosedCurve	Creates a closed curve through a series of points
DrawCurve	Creates an open curve through a series of points
DrawEllipse	Creates an ellipse defined by a bounding rectangle
DrawLine	Creates a line connecting two points
DrawLines	Creates a series of lines connecting an array of points
DrawPath	Creates a specified **GraphicsPath** object representing a complex shape
DrawPie	Creates a pie shape representing a slice of an ellipse
DrawPolygon	Creates a polygon drawn from a specified series of points
DrawRectangle	Creates a rectangle
DrawRectangles	Creates a series of rectangles

Table 15-3 Methods for the Creation of Filled Shapes

Method	Description
FillClosedCurve	Creates a filled, closed curve specified by an array of points
FillEllipse	Creates a filled ellipse
FillPath	Creates a filled **GraphicsPath** object representing a complex shape
FillPie	Creates a filled pie shape
FillPolygon	Creates a filled polygon specified by an array of points
FillRectangle	Creates a filled rectangle
FillRectangles	Creates a series of filled rectangles
FillRegion	Creates a filled **Region** object that usually corresponds to a complex shape

Colors, Brushes, and Pens

The **Color**, **Brush**, and **Pen** objects control the way in which graphics are rendered. The **Color** object specifies the display color. As we just explained, the **Brush** object renders filled shapes and the **Pen** object renders lines.

The **Color** object represents a single color for the rendering. The color consists of four values:

- Alpha (the transparency of the color)
- Red
- Green
- Blue

To specify a color using these values, you provide a number for each ranging from 0 to 255 and use the Color.FromArgb method, as shown in the following code.

```
Dim myColor As Color
myColor = Color.FromArgb(100,12,255,30)
```

TIP To create an opaque color, omit the Alpha parameter from the syntax.

A less flexible alternative to specifying a color exactly using the Color.FromArgb method is to use the named colors of the .NET Framework in your code, as shown in the following example.

```
Dim myColor As Color
myColor = Color.LightBlue
```

There are several Brush types for rendering filled objects in different styles. Table 15-4 describes these Brush types.

PART V

Table 15-4 Brush Types in Visual Basic .NET

Name	Description
SolidBrush	Uses a single, solid color
TextureBrush	Fills closed objects with an image
HatchBrush	Paints using a hatched pattern
LinearGradientBrush	Blends two colors along a gradient
PathGradientBrush	Renders complex gradient effects

Each Brush type requires different parameters. Some are as simple as specifying a color, while others are more complex. The following example creates a simple SolidBrush of the color Lime.

```
Dim myBrush As New SolidBrush(Color.Lime)
```

You use the **Pen** object to draw lines and arcs. Here is a simple example that creates a Pen of width 6 and color of LightBlue.

```
Dim myPen As New Pen(Color.LightBlue,6)
```

NOTE To create graphics that utilize the system colors in use at runtime, use the **SystemColors**, **SystemPens**, and **SystemBrushes** classes.

Rendering Graphics

Rendering custom graphics is a complex, multistep process. Here is a summary of the steps:

1. Create a **Graphics** object representing the drawing surface.
2. Create the objects required for rendering the desired graphic. This might include specifying coordinates using Points and Rectangles and then using the appropriate **Pen** and **Brush** objects.
3. Reference the appropriate methods of the **Graphics** objects.
4. Dispose of the rendering objects, and then dispose of the **Graphics** object.

Disposing of **Graphics** objects is important because they can consume a lot of resources. The following example demonstrates the preceding steps.

```
Dim myBrush As New SolidBrush(Color.LightBlue)
Dim myGraphic As Graphics = Me.CreateGraphics()
Dim myRectangle As New Rectangle(0,0,40,40)
myGraphics.FillEllipse(myBrush,myRectangle)
myGraphics.Dispose()
myBrush.Dispose()
```

Notice that this code renders a filled ellipse inside a rectangular area as defined by myRectangle. The code also disposes of the **Brush** and **Graphic** objects when they are no longer needed.

Enabling Form Validation and Feedback

Developers must be able to validate information entered in forms and provide feedback to users if they enter information erroneously. Suppose you have a customer tracking application that includes a field for customer numbers. The customer numbers consist of two alphabetic characters followed by a hyphen and four numbers. You should code the application to validate these customer numbers as they are entered to ensure that the underlying database is not filled with bad data. If an incorrect entry occurs, you should also provide feedback to the user, educating the user about the correct value format for the field.

To validate information entered in Windows Forms, developers typically use either field-level or form-level validation. Field-level validation examines the data input as it is entered in each field. For example, as each character is entered in a Zip Code field, field-level validation ensures that each entered character is numeric.

Form-level validation, on the other hand, validates the entered data once the form is submitted for processing.

Field-Level Validation

One of the simplest ways to perform field-level validation is to use the following properties of a TextBox control on your form.

- **MaxLength** This property limits the number of characters that can be entered into a text box on a form. When this limit is reached, the next character is not accepted and the system automatically beeps to indicate the error condition.
- **PasswordChar** This property allows developers to display asterisks (or whatever character is desired) as users enter data into the field. This feature is often used for fields where the user must enter a password or other confidential information.
- **ReadOnly** This property causes the text displayed in a text box to be locked down so that it cannot be edited.
- **MultiLine** This property allows multiple lines of text to be entered in a text box. Each line of text is separated by a carriage return and the text is stored in an array of strings.

To validate user input as it is entered, developers use the keyboard events KeyDown, KeyPress, and KeyUp. The KeyDown and KeyUp events are raised when a key is pressed and released. Each event packages the key or the combination of keys in a class called **KeyEventArgs**, which is used to determine whether the ALT, CONTROL, or SHIFT key was pressed. **KeyEventArgs** can also examine the actual key value that triggered the event.

The KeyPress event is raised only when a user presses a key that corresponds to an ASCII value.

NOTE Because they do not have ASCII values, CONTROL, ALT, and the function keys do not raise the KeyPress event.

PART V

When the KeyPress event is raised, the KeyPressEventArgs.KeyChar property contains the ASCII value that triggered the event. To evaluate the captured character, developers use the following Shared methods of Char data types:

- Char.IsDigit
- Char.IsLetter
- Char.IsLetterOrDigit
- Char.IsPunctuation
- Char.IsLower
- Char.IsUpper

The following example uses the Char.IsLower function to validate that the pressed key is lowercase.

```
Private Sub txtMyTextBox_KeyPress (ByVal sender as Object, ByVal e As _
      System.Windows.Forms.KeyPressEventArgs) Handles txtMyTextBox.KeyPress
      If Char.IsLower(e.KeyChar) = True Then
            MessageBox.Show("You pressed a lowercase character")
      End If
End Sub
```

Developers can also use the Focus events of controls on the form to assist in field-level data validation. When a control is active on a form it has focus. The Focus events that occur, and the order in which they occur, are listed here.

- Enter
- GotFocus
- Leave
- Validating
- Validated
- LostFocus

As you might guess, the Validating event is used most frequently for data validation. This event occurs before a control loses focus. The Validated event occurs immediately after a control has been successfully validated.

EXAM TIP The previous version of Visual Basic relied more heavily upon LostFocus for data validation. If you are converting these applications to the .NET platform, consider using Leave instead.

To use the Validating event for field-level validation, the CausesValidation property of the control must be set to True.

TIP The CausesValidation property of the *next* control on the form must also be set to True.

The following example demonstrates the use if the Validating event.

```
Private Sub myTextBox_Validating (ByVal sender As Object, ByVal e As _
      System.ComponentModel.CancelEventArgs) Handles myTextBox.Validating
      If myTextBox.Text = "" Then
           e.Cancel = True
      End If
End Sub
```

Notice that the preceding example uses the Validating event to check the Text value of myTextBox. If there is no data in the control, the focus remains on that control.

Form-Level Validation

As its name implies, form-level validation involves validating the data for all the controls on a form at once. Typically this occurs through the use of a procedure called in code.

The following sample code cycles through all the text boxes on the form checking for input. If a text box is empty, focus is returned to that control. This process occurs when the btnSampleFormValidate button is pressed.

```
Private Sub btnSampleFormValidate_Click (ByVal sender As _
      System.Object, ByVal e As System.EventArgs) Handles _
      btnSampleFormValidate.Click
      Dim aControl As System.Windows.Forms.Control
      For Each aControl In Me.Controls
            If TypeOf aControl Is TextBox AndAlso aControl.Text = "" Then
                  aControl.Focus()
                  Exit Sub
            End If
      Next
End Sub
```


Providing Feedback

One key to designing a successful application is to ensure that the application provides adequate feedback to its users. This is particularly important in the area of errors and data validation. Giving users feedback when they enter erroneous data in an application not only reduces their frustration, but also helps to prevent bad data from being entered in the future. Visual Basic .NET provides a number of ways in which to supply feedback to end users.

Perhaps the simplest method of indicating an error is to provide an audio cue using the Beep method. The following example demonstrates how simple this feedback option is to produce in code.

```
Beep()
```

Another method of providing feedback is to display a simple visual clue, such as a red highlight, using the BackColor or ForeColor properties of a control.

To provide more information, developers often use a message box, as shown in the following illustration. The MessageBox.Show method allows you to present a small dialog box that cannot be ignored by the end user. The message window displays text that you have entered to describe the problem and/or educate the end user. The following example demonstrates how simple this is to do in code.

```
MessageBox.Show("Sorry - you have input an invalid Customer Number.")
```

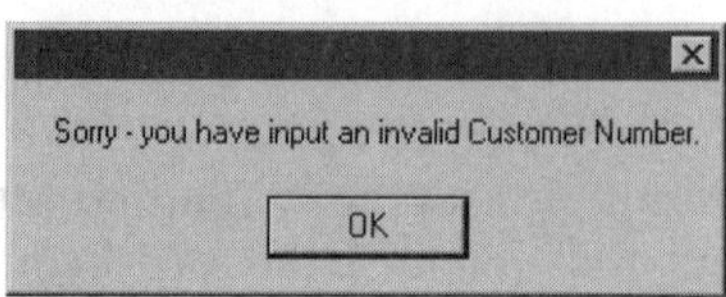

The ErrorProvider component is another excellent method for providing feedback to end users. The ErrorProvider component displays an error icon next to the control when a user enters invalid data, as shown in Figure 15-3. If the user lets the mouse hover over the icon, any message text configured using the SetError method appears in a Tool Tip.

To use the ErrorProvider component, follow these steps:

1. Create two text boxes on your Windows Form.
2. Add an ErrorProvider component to the form. The ErrorProvider component is found in the Windows Forms category of the Toolbox.
3. Select the first control and add the following code to its Validating event handler.

```
Private Sub TextBox1_Validating(ByVal Sender As Object, ByVal _
      e As CancelEventArgs) Handles TextBox1.Validating
   If Not IsNumeric(TextBox1.Text) Then
      ErrorProvider1.SetError (TextBox1, "Not a numeric value.")
   Else
      ErrorProvider1.SetError (TextBox1, "")
   End If
End Sub
```

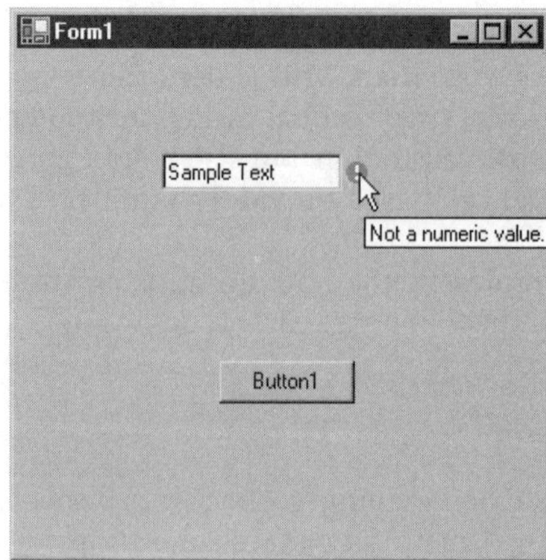

Figure 15-3 Using the ErrorProvider component

Incorporating Existing Code

Visual Studio.NET makes it very simple to incorporate existing objects and code into Windows-based applications. This allows developers to leverage objects that have been created in other projects, accelerating the development of new applications dramatically.

To utilize existing forms in a current project, follow these steps:

1. Choose File from the Visual Studio .NET menu bar in the IDE.
2. Select Add Existing Item.
3. Use the Look In field to find the solution folder that stores the form you want to utilize. Select the form and click Open.
4. The existing form is now part of the current project and can be easily incorporated in your new application.

You can also import entire projects into a current solution. For example, if an existing project includes many of the forms that the new application needs, you can simply import the existing project into the new solution.

To import the project, follow these steps:

1. Choose File from the Visual Studio .NET menu bar in the IDE.
2. Select Add Project | Existing Project.
3. Select the appropriate folder and click Open. The project (and all of its code and objects) is now part of your new project. Remember, you can use the Solutions Explorer to quickly navigate between the various components.

Summary

Windows Forms are one of the most critical components of an application. Forms comprise almost the entire user interface, designing the screen "real estate" that application end users view and interact with. Forms hold the controls that make up the application. These controls include text boxes, drop-down menus, check boxes, and other objects that allow users to control the application and provide data.

There are several techniques for adding forms to an application. You can add forms to an application using the IDE, and then visually create them using the Windows Form Designer of the IDE. Forms can also be created in the IDE using Visual Inheritance. Visual Inheritance allows you to create additional forms based on a form that acts as a template for the new forms. This saves development time, and allows you to leverage existing forms. Finally, you can use code to add forms to applications, including forms created using Visual Inheritance. Using code permits you to create forms dynamically during runtime as opposed to creating them in the Windows Form Designer during design time.

Once forms are created in design time or in runtime, you can control their appearance and behavior using the many properties available with forms. For example, the Opacity property controls the level of transparency of the form. This property allows end users to see a form or other object behind the active form in an application. Property values are set in the Windows Form Designer during design time using the Properties tool window. These properties are also set with code during runtime.

To create custom graphics in an application, you can use the **System.Drawing** namespaces. These namespaces allow you to create simple or complex **Graphic** objects. These objects are enhanced using **Pen**, **Color**, and **Brush** objects that provide vibrant colors and textures.

It is important to be able to communicate with the end users of your forms, especially if they input errors when working with them. You should plan on performing either field-level or form-level validation when designing an application. Field-level validation checks input as the user moves from field to field in the form; form-level validation checks all the input at once during a particular event, such as a button press.

If errors are detected during the validation process, beeps, color changes, or dialog boxes can provide feedback to the end user. This critical process ensures that the end user is educated in how the application functions. It also helps ensure that the end user is not frustrated by the application and will continue to use it.

If you have used the information in this chapter to build forms, you certainly want to easily include these forms in your applications. And that might include an application you are currently working in. The Add feature in the File menu of the IDE makes this possible. Using the Add Existing Item menu option, it is easy to re-use forms from applications that you have composed previously. In fact, you can add earlier projects to an existing solution and re-use every component of these projects.

Test Questions

1. Which of the following code samples creates a form dynamically within an application?
   - A. Create New Form
   - B. Dim frmMyNewForm As frmDialogTemplate
   - C. Dim frmMyNewForm As frmDialogTemplate
     frmMyNewForm = New frmDialogTemplate()
   - D. Dim frmMyNewForm As frmDialogTemplate
     Create New frmMyNewForm
2. You would like to quickly design a form using a form that you created earlier as a template for the new form. Which feature of Visual Basic .NET are you going to take advantage of?
   - A. Visual Inheritance
   - B. Modularity
   - C. Code re-use
   - D. Code share

3. You need to control the way in which a form appears when it launches in your application. Specifically, you want the form to appear centered against the form that called the child form. What property should you use?

   A. Start

   B. StartPlace

   C. WindowState

   D. StartPosition

4. You need to quickly change the title that appears in the title bar of your Windows Form. What property do you use to control this value?

   A. Caption

   B. Text

   C. Title

   D. Heading

5. Which namespace contains classes that are designed to render advanced visual effects in your applications?

   A. System.Drawing

   B. System.Drawing.Design

   C. System.Drawing.2D

   D. System.Drawing.Imaging

6. Which of the following objects do you use to draw a simple line in your application?

   A. Brush

   B. Color

   C. Line

   D. Pen

7. If you are using the MaxLength property of your text boxes in order to validate user input, which type of validation are you most likely using?

   A. Form-level

   B. Field-level

   C. Text-level

   D. User-driven

8. You would like to incorporate data validation within your application to ensure that users are entering data correctly within certain fields. Specifically, you want

to check data prior to a particular control losing focus. Which event should you use for this purpose?

A. Validated

B. Validating

C. LostFocus

D. LosingFocus

9. Your application contains a sophisticated form that users complete in order to provide data for a customer tracking application. You validate the information they have entered in all fields using the OK button when it is clicked. What type of validation are you engaging in with the application?

A. Form-level

B. Field-level

C. Control-level

D. Text-level

10. You need to provide feedback to users of your application if they enter text inappropriately within the application. Which object should you use to provide this feedback?

A. Beep

B. BackColor

C. MessageBox

D. DialogBox

Test Answers

1. C.
2. A.
3. D.
4. B.
5. C.
6. D.
7. B.
8. B.
9. A.
10. C.

CHAPTER 16

Creating and Using Controls

In this chapter, you will

- Learn how to add controls and ActiveX controls to Windows Forms
- Understand how to set properties of controls
- See how to handle control events
- Explore how to create menus and menu items
- Find out how to configure tab order
- Discover how to create custom Windows controls
- Learn how to configure licensing for controls

Windows Forms would fail miserably without controls and components. Controls, such as TextBoxes and Buttons, allow end users to input data into an application. Other controls, such as Labels or PictureBoxes, permit developers to display data.

Although components are as important to an application as controls, components are not visible in the application. Components, like controls, are pre-constructed units of code that facilitate functionality within an application. Without controls and components an application would lack almost any functionality. Users would be unable to enter and view data, and many features of Visual Basic .NET would be unavailable.

This chapter explores controls and their usage in Windows Forms applications. The events and properties of controls are examined, and the creation of custom controls is explored.

Adding Controls to Windows Forms

Controls and components exist in the Toolbox, as shown in Figure 16-1. They can be dragged from the Toolbox and dropped onto forms. Or, for slightly quicker placement of controls, you can double-click the control icon in the Toolbox. The control is automatically placed on the active form following the double-click. Once controls are on the form, repositioning them is a simple matter of clicking within the control and dragging it into a new position. Handles appear around most controls, allowing you to resize the controls to meet end user interface needs.

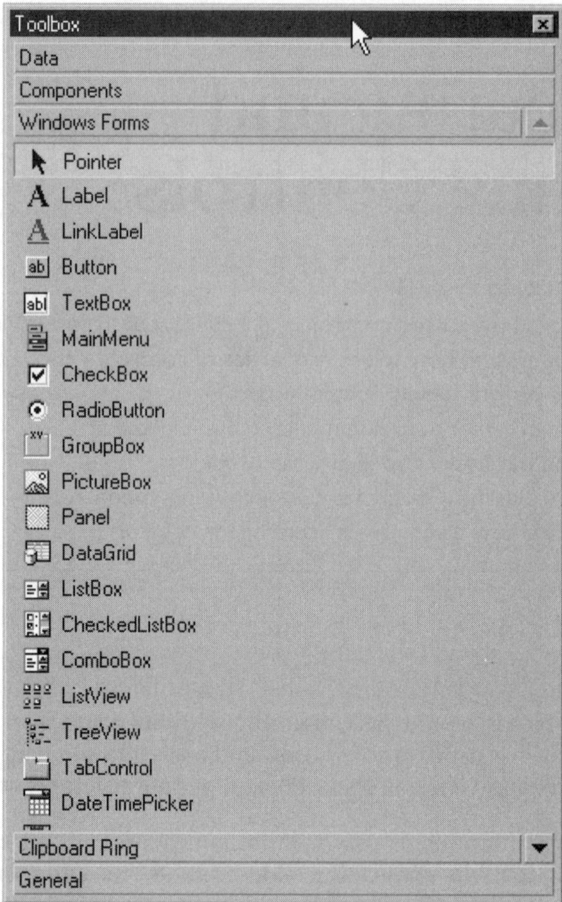

Figure 16-1 Windows Forms controls in the Toolbox

Table 16-1 describes the default Windows Forms controls and components that are available in Visual Basic .NET.

Control/Component	Description
Label	Used to provide descriptive text for other controls
LinkLabel	Used to display hyperlinks within labels
Button	Used to trigger an event, such as submitting data to an underlying database
TextBox	Used to allow users to enter text in an application

Table 16-1 Controls and Components of Visual Basic .NET

Control/Component	Description
MainMenu	Used to represent the container for the menu structure of a form
CheckBox	Used to give end users an option, such as True/False or Yes/No
RadioButton	Used to display mutually exclusive options to the end user
GroupBox	Used to logically group controls on a form
PictureBox	Used to display graphics from a bitmap, metafile, icon, .JPEG, .GIF, or .PNG file
Panel	Used to group collections of controls
DataGrid	Used to provide a user interface to ADO.NET data sets; displays tabular data and allows for updates to the data source
ListBox	Used to display a list of items from which the user can select one or more
CheckedListBox	Used to display a list of items, like the ListBox control, and also display a check mark next to items in the list
ComboBox	Used to display data in a drop-down combo box
ListView	Used to display a list of items with icons; can create a user interface that resembles the right pane of Windows Explorer
TreeView	Used to display a hierarchy of nodes that resembles the way files and folders are displayed in the left pane of Windows Explorer
TabControl	Used to display multiple tabs that resemble dividers in a notebook or labels in a set of folders in a filing cabinet
DateTimePicker	Used to select a single item from a list of dates or times
MonthCalendar	Used to present an intuitive graphical interface for users to view and set date information
HscrollBar	Used to provide easy navigation through a long list of items or a large amount of information by scrolling horizontally within an application or control
VscrollBar	Used to provide easy navigation through a long list of items or a large amount of information by scrolling vertically within an application or control
Timer	A component that is used to raise an event at regular intervals
Splitter	Used to resize docked controls at runtime
DomainUpDown	Used to display and set a text string from a list of choices
NumericUpDown	Used to display and set a single numeric value from a list of choices
TrackBar	Used for navigating through a large amount of information or for visually adjusting a numeric setting; often called a "slider" control
ProgressBar	Used to indicate the progress of an action by displaying an appropriate number of rectangles arranged in a horizontal bar
RichTextBox	Used for displaying, entering, and manipulating text with formatting
ImageList	Used to display images on controls such as the ListView, TreeView, ToolBar, Button, and TabControl controls

Table 16-1 Controls and Components of Visual Basic .NET *(continued)*

Control/Component	Description
HelpProvider	Used to associate an HTML Help 1.x Help file with a Windows application
ToolTip	Used to display text when the user points at controls
ContextMenu	Used to provide users with an easily accessed menu of frequently used commands that are associated with the selected object
ToolBar	Used on forms as a control bar that displays a row of drop-down menus and bitmapped buttons that activate commands
StatusBar	Used on forms as an area, usually displayed at the bottom of a window, in which an application can display various kinds of status information
NotifyIcon	Used to display icons for processes that run in the background and would not otherwise have user interfaces
OpenFileDialog	A component that is the same as the Open File dialog box exposed by the Windows operating system
SaveFileDialog	A component that is the same as the standard Save File dialog box used by Windows
FontDialog	A component that is the same as the Font dialog box exposed by the Windows operating system
ColorDialog	A component used to select a color from a palette and to add custom colors to the palette
PrintDialog	A component used to select a printer, choose the pages to print, and determine other print-related settings in Windows applications
PrintPreviewDialog	A component used to display how a document will appear when printed; it is the same as the dialog box exposed by the Windows operating system
PrintPreviewControl	Used to display a document as it will appear when printed
ErrorProvider	A component used to show the user in a non-intrusive way that an error has been committed
PrintDocument	A component used not only to set the properties that describe what to print, but also to print the document within Windows applications
PageSetupDialog	A component used to set page details for printing in Windows applications
CrystalReportViewer	Used to allow a Crystal Report to be viewed in an application

Table 16-1 Controls and Components of Visual Basic .NET *(continued)*

Adding ActiveX Controls to Windows Forms

Although ActiveX controls are not intended for Windows Forms, they can be used if necessary. Bear in mind that using ActiveX controls may affect performance in a Windows application. Use these controls only if you do not have a Windows form control that provides the same functionality.

ActiveX controls use component object model (COM) technology to provide interoperability with other types of COM objects. Specifically, ActiveX control technology was designed to facilitate the distribution of controls over low-bandwidth, high-latency environments like the Internet. ActiveX control technology was also designed to enable controls in Web browser interfaces.

Because ActiveX is a COM implementation, references can be added to an ActiveX control type library in virtually the same manner that they are added to a COM library. Once you have added the reference, you simply add the ActiveX control to the Toolbox for use on the Windows Forms.

To add an ActiveX control to a Windows application, follow these steps:

1. To add a reference to the type library that contains the ActiveX control, right-click the References node under your project in the Solution Explorer. Choose Add Reference from the shortcut menu that appears.
2. Select the reference that contains the ActiveX control from the Add Reference dialog box, shown in the illustration. COM type libraries are listed on the COM tab, .NET assemblies are listed on the .NET tab, and projects that you have created are listed on the Projects tab.

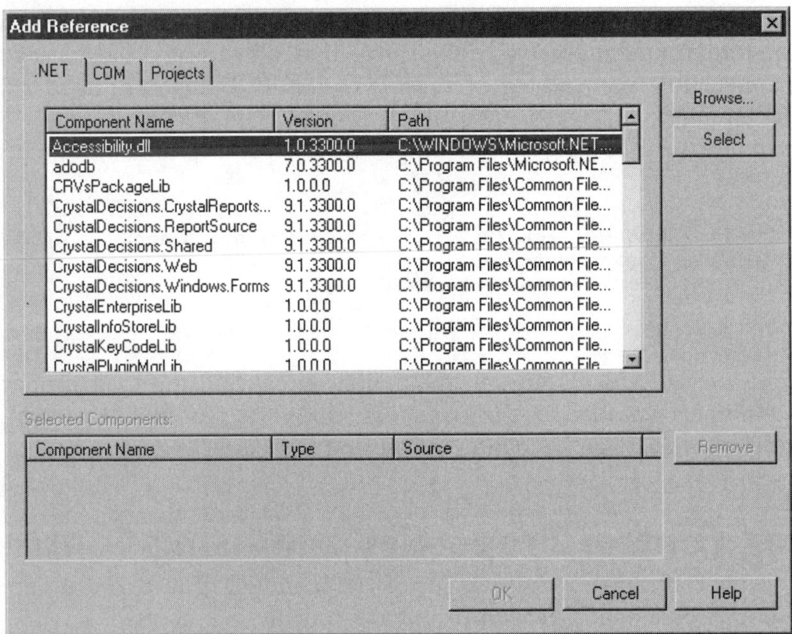

3. Add the ActiveX control to the Toolbox. Right-click the Toolbox and choose Customize Toolbox from the shortcut menu. Use the Customize Toolbox dialog box to navigate to and open the ActiveX control.
4. Use the Toolbox to place the ActiveX control on your Windows form during design time, *or* instantiate the ActiveX control in the form using code.

Keep in mind that security is a consideration when using ActiveX controls on Windows Forms. Thanks to enhancements in the common language runtime (CLR) environment of Visual Basic .NET, Windows Forms run in fully trusted or semi-trusted environments. However, ActiveX controls on Windows Forms do not share these security enhancements. As a result, you might encounter problems with your application's execution. To resolve this, ensure that you have unmanaged code permissions by searching Help for SecurityPermissionAttribute.

Besides affecting performance and raising security issues, ActiveX controls in a Windows application can also increase file sizes in deployments. This is because ActiveX controls must be deployed in their entirety.

Finally, ActiveX controls within Windows Forms require that your application writes to the Windows registry. This is not typically required with Windows Forms applications. Some users might have concerns about registry modifications required to run your application.

Adding Controls Dynamically

Instead of using the Windows Form Designer to add controls, developers can also add controls to forms or other objects dynamically—that is, by using code. Adding controls in this manner allows controls to be created dynamically during runtime as opposed to during design time.

For example, the following code creates a new label control on a form when a user clicks a button.

```
Private Sub btnAddLabel_Click (ByVal sender As System.Object, _
      ByVal e As System.EventArgs) Handles
            Dim lblMyLabel As New Label()
            lblMyLabel.Location = New Point (50,50)
            Me.Controls.Add (lblMyLabel)
```

The next section explains how to manipulate controls using their properties. Although developers typically use the Properties window to manipulate controls during design, property values can be manipulated using code as well.

Setting Control Properties and Using Controls

Simply placing controls on Windows Forms is not enough. These controls are useless unless you manipulate their properties and add code to their events.

The Properties window, shown in the Figure 16-2, allows developers to set control properties during design time. When the control is selected, the window displays the properties available for the control.

Figure 16-2 Setting properties for controls during design time

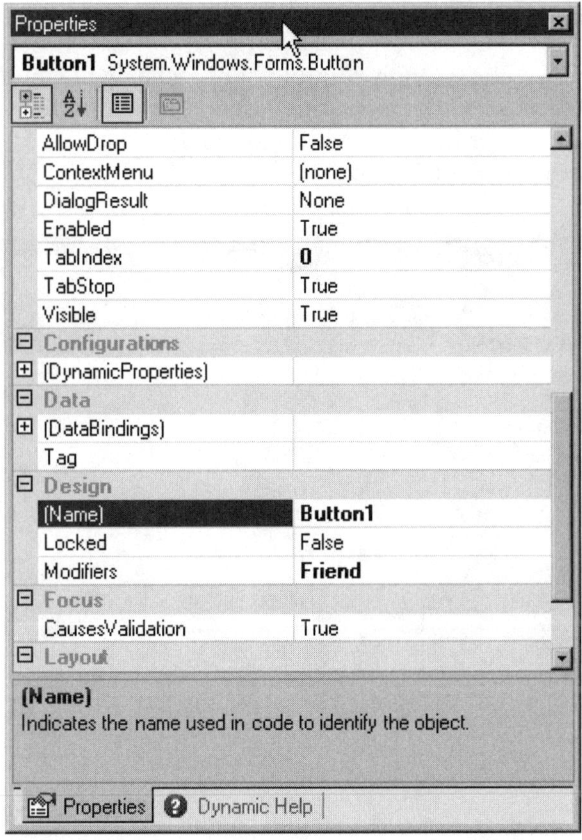

TIP The Properties window contains a drop-down list that allows you to select a particular control. This eliminates the need for you to find and select the control in the Windows Form Designer. Keep in mind that property values for controls can also be manipulated in code, ensuring that values you set in design time are flexible during runtime.

To set a property value for a control during design time, follow these steps:

1. Select the control in the Windows Form Designer.
2. Edit the particular property value using the Properties window. If the Properties window is not visible, choose Properties from the View menu.

At times, you may have a group of controls for which you need to modify properties. If you need to set all these properties to a consistent value across the controls, you are in luck.

To edit properties for multiple controls at design time, follow these steps:

1. To select the multiple controls, click and drag the mouse around the controls that you want to manipulate. Notice that the Properties window displays only those properties that are common to the multiple controls that are selected, as shown in the illustration.

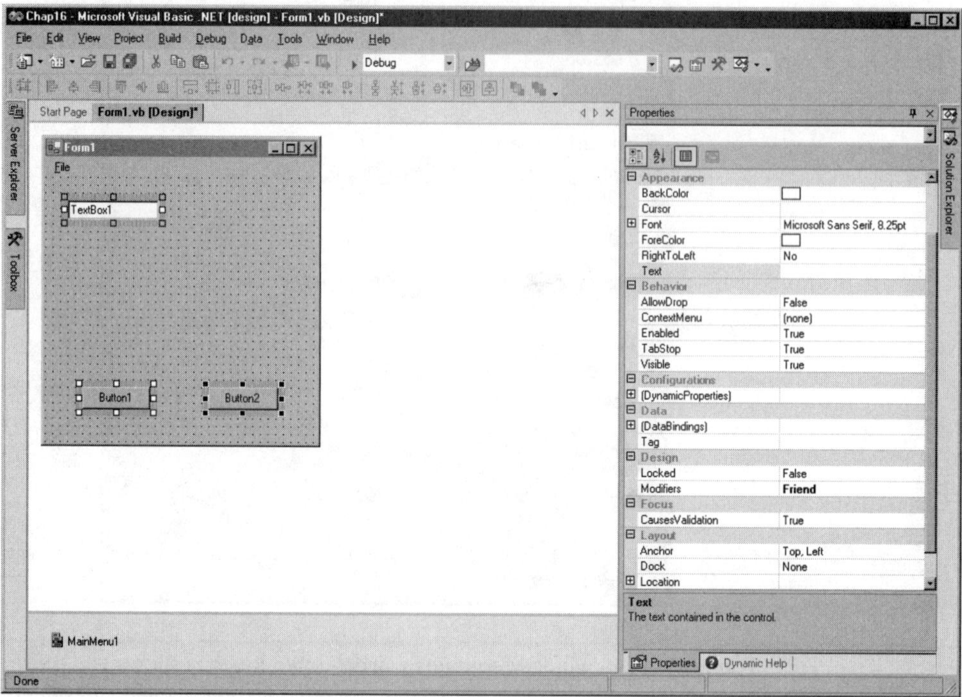

TIP You can also hold down CONTROL to select each control you want to include in the group.

2. Edit the property value in the Properties window just as you would manipulate a single control.

The Toolbox also has components for use in applications. Because components are not visible within the user interface, you handle these a bit differently at design time.

When you add a component from the Toolbox to an application, it appears in the *component tray* of the Windows Form Designer. The component tray is a rectangular region near the bottom of the IDE below the form, as shown in Figure 16-3. Because components also contain properties that must be set, you use the Properties window in design time just as you would for controls.

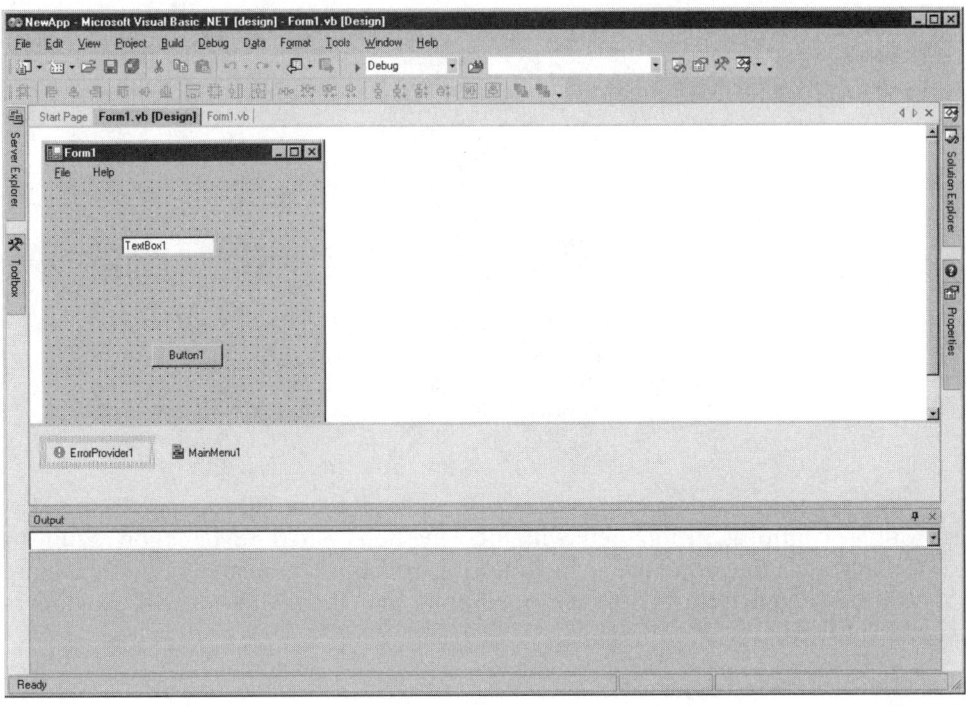

Figure 16-3 Components in the component tray of the Windows Form Designer

Using Extender Providers

Some components provide additional properties to the controls on a form. These components are known as extender providers. An example of an extender provider component is the ToolTipProvider. When you use this extender provider component on a form, the controls on the form receive a new property. This property is called ToolTip on n, where *n* is the name of the ToolTipProvider. When you complete this property with a string value, the text appears in a small yellow box during runtime; the box appears when an end user hovers the mouse over the control, as shown in Figure 16-4. Tool Tips are very useful for describing controls in the application that do not possess labels or that require additional explanation.

Although developers can access and change the properties that the extender provider supplies in code, the process differs a bit from modifying properties of other objects because the properties supplied by extender providers do not actually reside in the affected controls. The properties reside in the extender provider itself. As such, the extender provider implements methods that permit access to the properties in code. These methods are always called Getn and Setn where *n* is the name of the property provided. To use the earlier example of the ToolTipProvider, there are methods called GetToolTip and SetToolTip, which you can reference in code. You must reference the

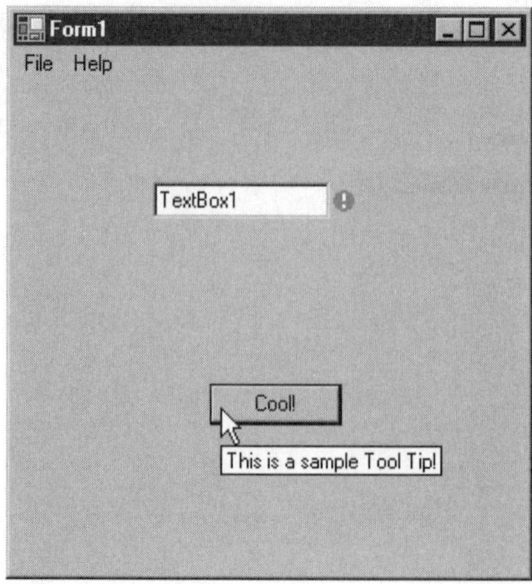

Figure 16-4 ToolTips in use in an application

appropriate control as an argument with these methods, and the Set method requires a value that you set the property to. The following example demonstrates how to acquire the value of a ToolTip for a button named btnSubmitData. The extender provider is named ToolTip1.

```
Dim myToolTip As String
myToolTip = ToolTip1.GetToolTip(btnSubmitData)
```

You use the Set method of the extender provider to set the property provided in code. In the following example, the ToolTip is set for a button named btnVerify:

```
ToolTip1.SetToolTip(btnVerify, "Click when finished")
```

Using Container Controls

Container controls hold other controls on a form. Common examples of these controls include Panel, GroupBox, and TabControl. Developers typically use these controls to logically group other controls on a form, as shown in Figure 16-5. This is usually done for two reasons: for easier manipulation of controls programmatically and to organize the form more logically for the end users of the application.

The properties of container controls affect the controls within the container. For example, changing the value of the Font property of a container automatically changes the Font property for the controls within the container.

NOTE You can still change the individual property of a control within the container to make the control unique. However, there is an exception. If the Enabled property of the container control is set to False, there is no way to enable individual controls within the container.

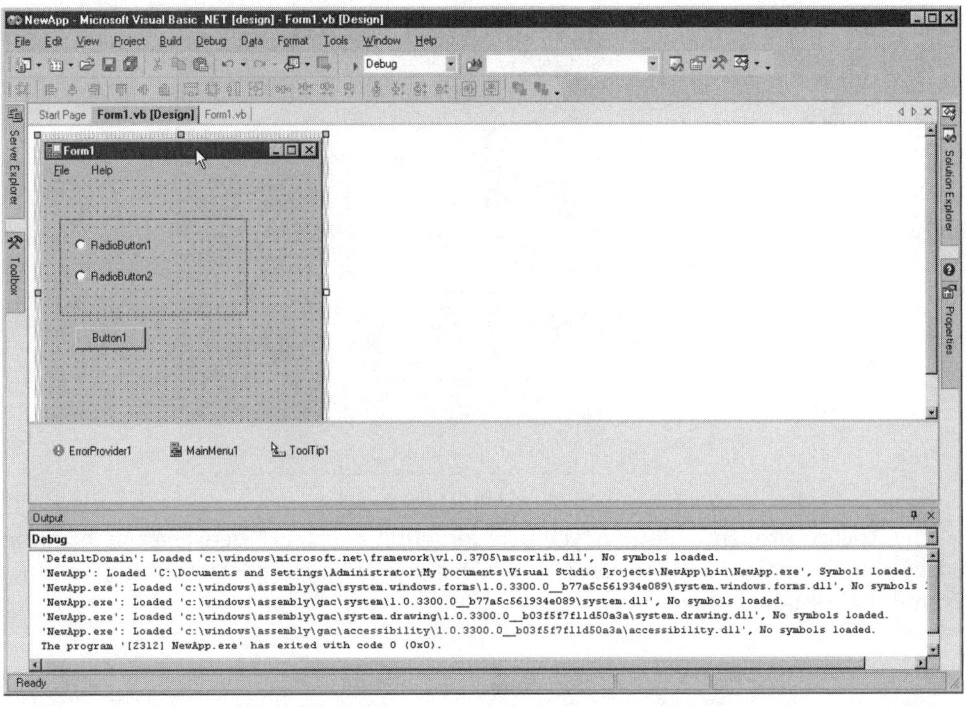

Figure 16-5 Using container controls in Windows Forms

The most popular container controls are GroupBoxes, Panels, and TabControls. GroupBoxes and Panels are similar; you use both of them to logically group controls in the form. You can control the properties of the controls within the container by manipulating the properties of the container. You can also move all the controls at once by moving the container control. GroupBoxes provide a caption for labeling the groups of controls, as shown in Figure 16-6; this is accomplished using the Text property. The Panel control lacks a caption but is scrollable if the AutoScroll property is set to True.

The TabControl allows developers to organize controls in a window that contains tabbed pages, as shown in Figure 16-7. This type of interface is often used for property pages in an application. The TabControl includes TabPage controls. Each TabPage consists of its own set of properties. You add TabPages to the TabControl using the TabPages property.

Anchoring and Docking Controls

The Anchor and Dock properties help ensure that a control is positioned correctly inside its container, whether the control is contained by a form or by a container control.

Figure 16-6 A typical use of a GroupBox container control

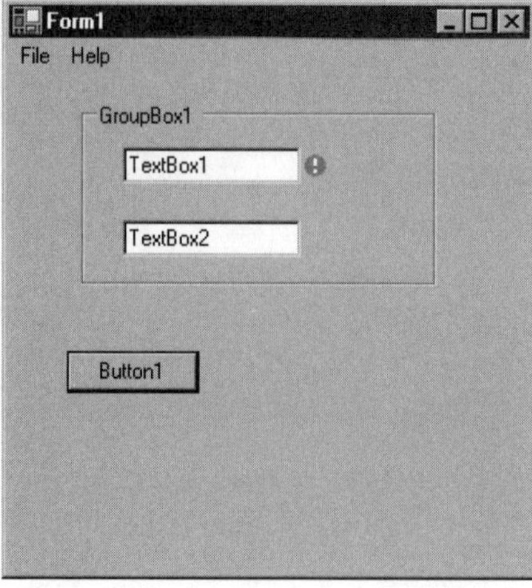

The Anchor property allows developers to define a distance between one or more edges of the container and the control. This distance remains constant during runtime, even if the container object is resized.

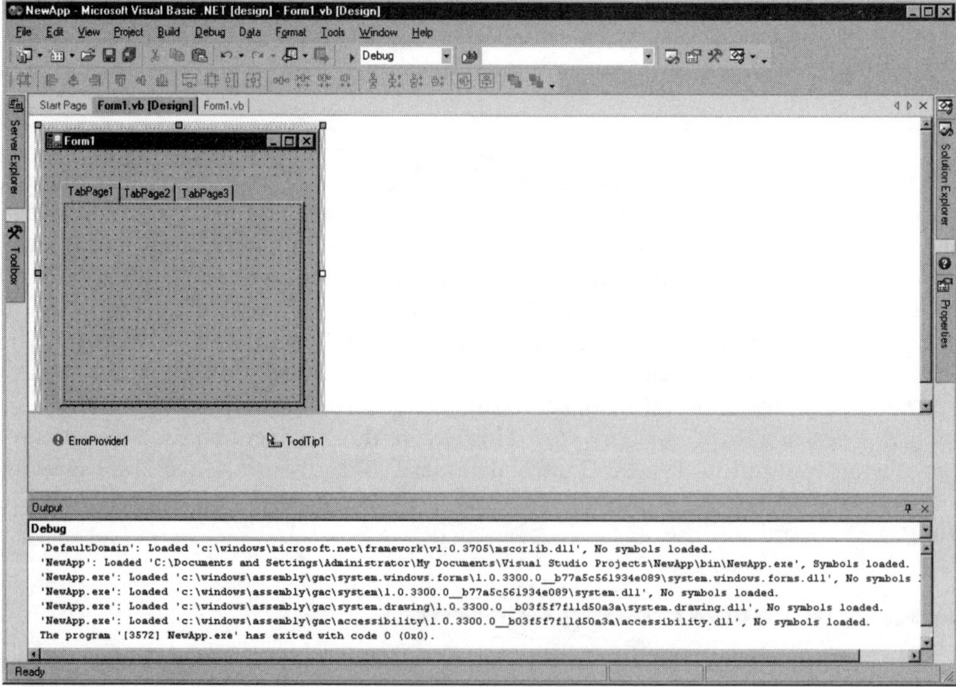

Figure 16-7 Using a TabControl

To set the Anchor property during design time, select the control in the Windows Form Designer and locate the Anchor property in the Properties window. When you select the Anchor property drop-down menu, an interface appears that allows you to select the edges that you want to anchor to. Notice the default setting is Top, Left. This is an excellent default choice because most forms are resized from the bottom right corner. Setting controls with this default ensures that controls maintain their position during a form resize.

Exercise 16-1: Anchoring Controls In this exercise you will experiment with the Anchor property of Windows Forms controls.

1. Create a new Windows Application named **Anchor**.
2. Double-click the Button control in the Toolbox to add a button to Form1.
3. Click the button to ensure that it is selected.
4. Select the Anchor property in the Properties window, as shown in the illustration. Notice the default Top, Left setting.

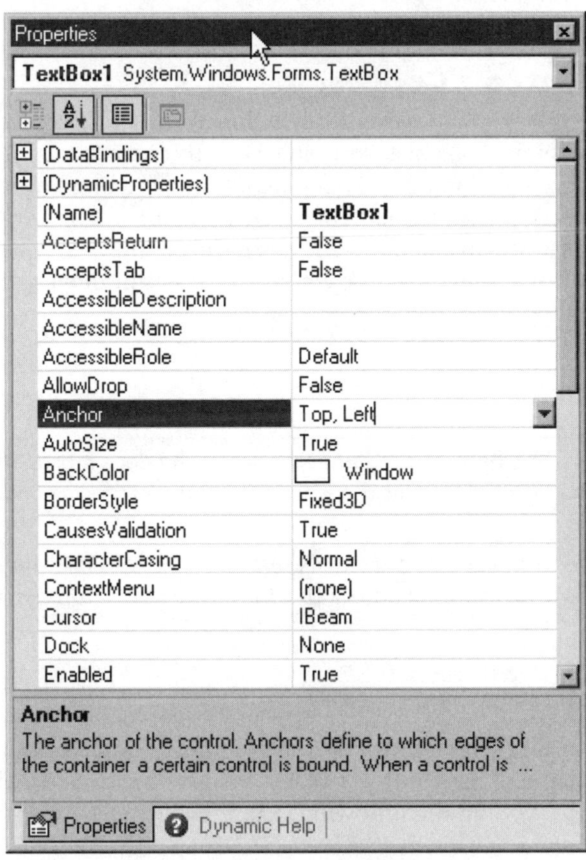

5. Resize the form in the Windows Form Designer by clicking and dragging the bottom-right corner of the form. Notice that the control maintains its distance from the Top and Left edges of the form.
6. Access the Anchor property again and click the bar indicating the Left side of the container to deselect it. Now the control is only anchored to the Top edge.
7. Resize the form again using the bottom-right corner and observe the behavior of the control.

When you dock a control, you attach the control to an edge of the container object. Menu bars are typically docked along the top edge of the form.

To set the Dock property of a control during design time, select the control and then select the Dock property drop-down menu in the Properties window. Like the Anchor property, a window appears allowing you to graphically select the area of the container where the control should be docked.

EXAM TIP Clicking the center square in the Dock property window causes the control to fill the form that it lives in.

Using the Controls Collection

All container objects in Visual Basic .NET, including forms, include a collection of all the controls that they contain. This collection, which is aptly named the controls collection, includes its own methods and properties. For example, a Count property returns the number of items in the collection, while the Item property returns a specific item. The exposed methods allow developers to add and remove controls in the collection.

To specify a control of the collection, you use the Index number of the item, as shown in the following example.

```
Dim myControl As Control
myControl = frmMyControl.Controls.Item(3)
```

EXAM TIP Because the Item property is the default property of the controls collection, you can omit the word *Item* in the preceding code.

To dynamically add or remove controls in the collection, use the Add and Remove methods. The following example adds a button to the collection dynamically.

```
Dim btnNewButton As New Button()
btnNewButton.Text = "New Button"
frmMyForm.Controls.Add(btnNewButton)
```

You use the Remove or RemoveAt method to remove controls dynamically from collections. Use the name of the control with the Remove method; use the index number with RemoveAt, as shown in the following example.

```
frmMyForm.Controls.RemoveAt(3)
```

Similar syntax is used to add or remove controls from the controls collection of a Panel, GroupBox, or TabControl. For example, the following code dynamically adds a control to a TabPage of a TabControl.

```
Dim txtTextBox As New TextBox()
myTabControl.TabPages(2).Controls.Add(txtTextBox)
```

Configuring the Tab Order

A common convenience added to end user interfaces is the use of the TAB key. Almost all Windows applications should permit the end user to press TAB to advance from control to control within the graphical user interface. As each control is reached using TAB, the control receives focus. Remember, having focus means the control is ready for manipulation by the end user. This can dramatically speed the process of data entry in a large form designed for data input.

To set the Tab order for the controls on the form, developers use the TabIndex property of each control. The control set with the lowest TabIndex value receives focus first, the control with the next lowest value receives focus second, and so on.

TIP If two or more controls have the same TabIndex setting (a design error on your part) the focus goes first to the control nearest the "front" of the form. You control this order by right-clicking the control and choosing Bring to Front or Send to Back.

Visual Studio .NET includes a dialog box that helps you easily set the Tab order. Simply choose Tab Order from the View menu. The controls on the selected container appear in the dialog box. To set the Tab order, simply click the controls in the order you would like used when the end user tabs through the interface.

EXAM TIP You use the TabStop property to ensure that a control cannot be "tabbed to" by an end user. Just set the TabStop property to False.

Control Event Handlers

Event handlers are procedures in code that are called when a corresponding event occurs. Because Visual Basic programming uses event handlers, it is event-driven. That is, code does not simply execute in a linear fashion; it executes as certain events occur within the application.

A very common event that occurs in an application and involves controls is the clicking of a button. A button click raises the Button.Click event. If a method is configured to handle this event, it is known as an event handler. As shown in this section, it is very simple to create event handlers in Visual Basic .NET.

Each control in an application contains a default event. This default event is the most common event for that type of control. For example, the most common event for a Button control is Click, so Click is the default event for the Button control.

To create event handlers for the default events of controls, follow these steps:

1. In the Windows Form Designer, double-click the control for which you want to create a default event handler. The code window appears with the cursor placed in an empty event handler for the default event of the control.

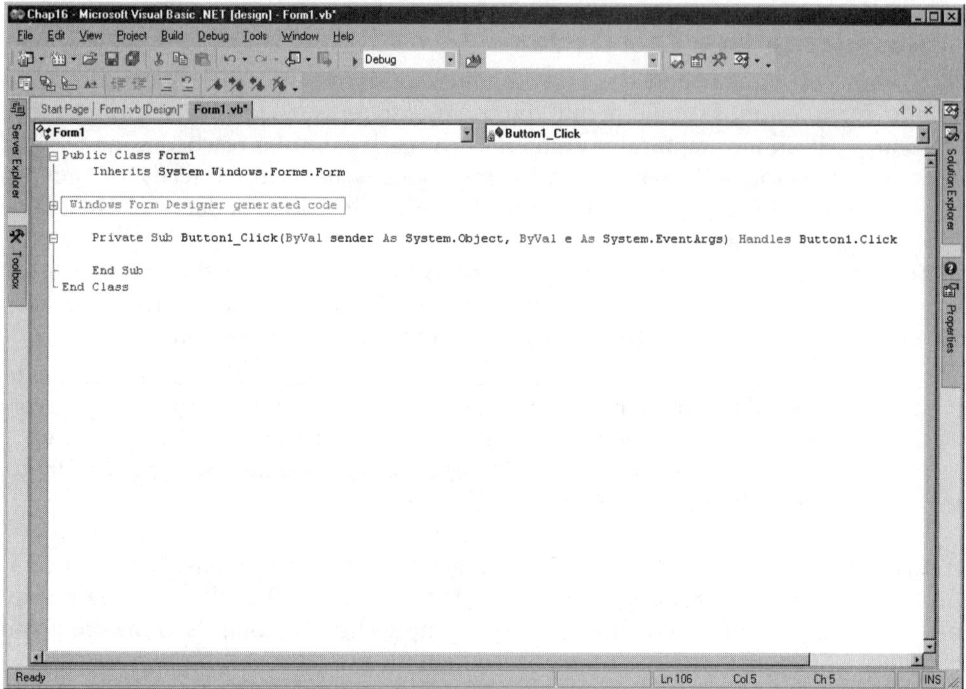

2. Place your code in the event handler.

Besides the default event for a control, you can use many other events with controls. For example, the MouseHover event allows you to add code in response to the mouse pausing over a control.

To create the event handler for one of these events, follow these steps:

1. Enter the code window for the form using the appropriate tab in the Windows Form Designer.
2. Select the control from the Class Name drop-down menu at the top of the code window.
3. In the Method Name drop-down menu, select the event you want to code, as shown in the illustration. Notice that the cursor is placed within the event handler; you may now code the event.

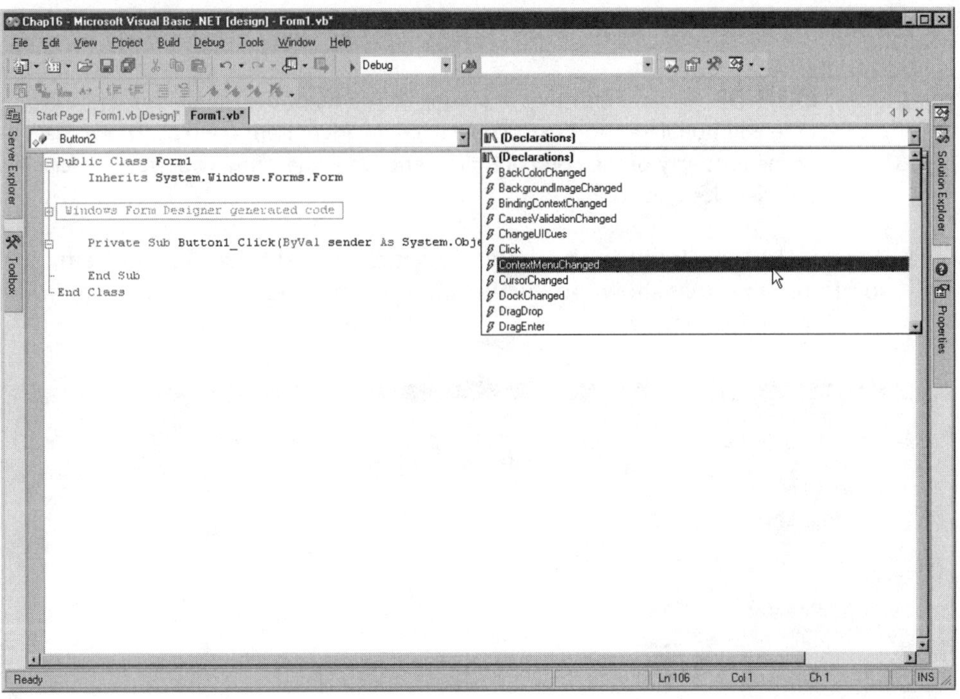

Creating Menus and Menu Items

The menu system is another critical component of most applications. This system allows users to access key functions and dialog boxes within the software in an easy-to-understand interface. You should always design the menu system prior to coding in Visual Basic .NET to ensure adherence to typical Windows conventions, and to group similar items logically.

Creating Menus at Design Time

Creating the menu system during design time is very easy in Visual Basic .NET thanks to the MainMenu component. This critical component manages a collection of MenuItem controls, which work together to form the menu interface within an application.

The MainMenu Component and MenuItem Controls

To use the MainMenu component to create MenuItems, follow these steps:

1. Double-click the MainMenu component in the Toolbox to add a Main Menu component to the component tray within the Windows Form Designer. The menu system appears in the form, with Type Here highlighting the area you can use to add the first MenuItem.

2. Enter text for the first menu item—this is typically File.

EXAM TIP Remember that in setting the name of the menu item at design time you populate the Text property of the MenuItem control. The actual Name property of the control is different and is the name you use to reference the MenuItem in code.

3. As you add MenuItems in the designer, notice that additional MenuItem locations appear, as shown in the illustration. You can build the entire menu structure in this manner.

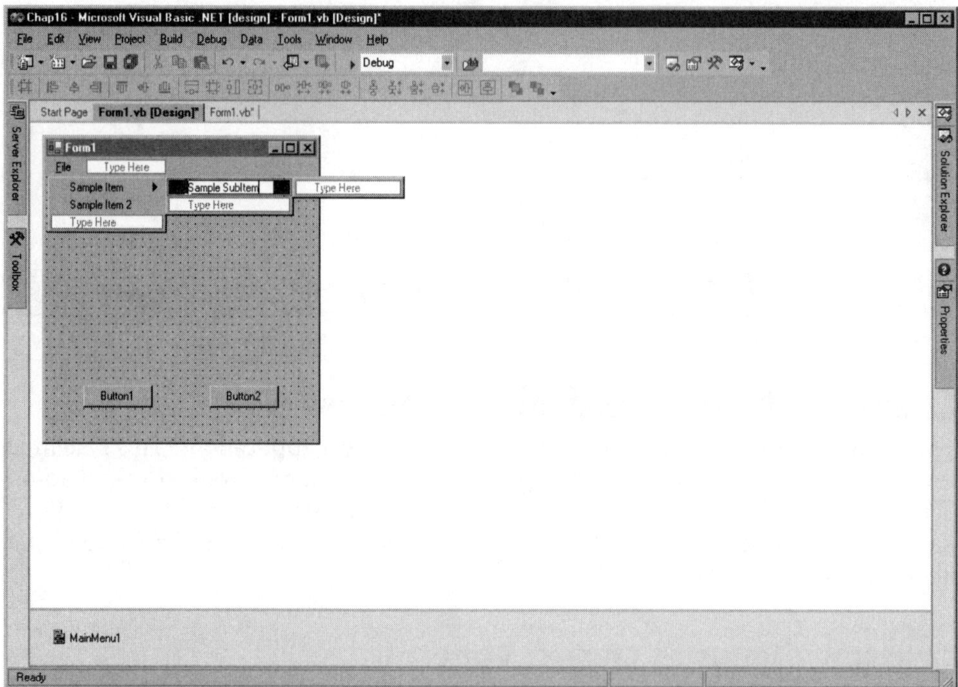

4. Use the Properties window to set the individual properties of the MenuItems you have created.

TIP If you create multiple menus for a form, ensure that the Menu property of the form is set to the menu you actually want displayed at runtime.

Separator Menu Items

To make a menu system easier to use and understand, developers often use separator items. Separator items allow you to include a horizontal line in a menu, as shown in Figure 16-8. This line helps to visually group controls on a drop-down menu and is

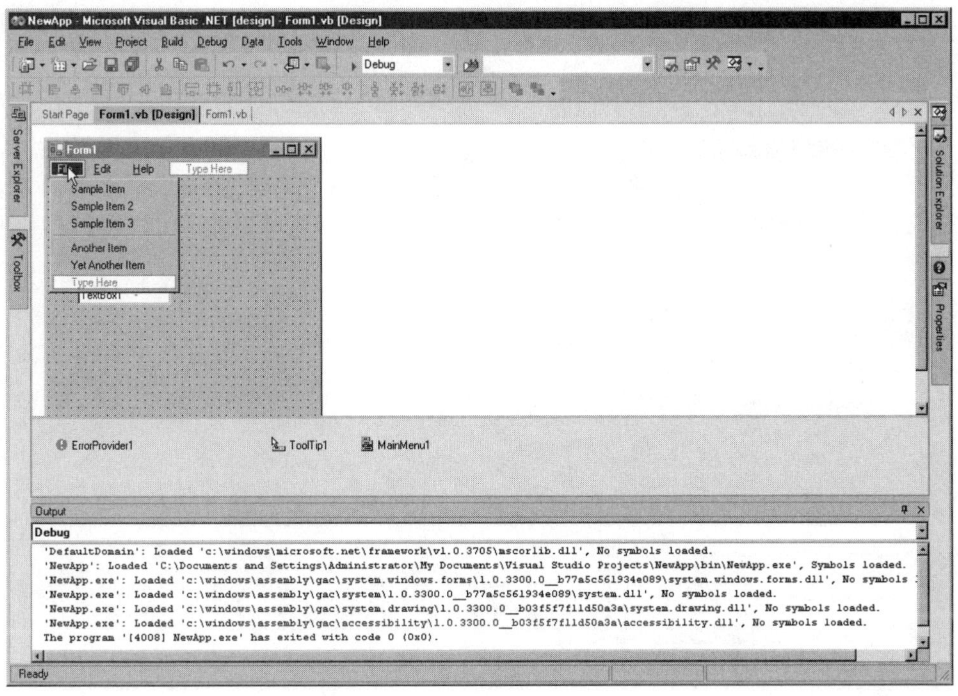

Figure 16-8 Using separator items

especially useful when creating large menus that contain many items. To add a separator in a menu system, simply enter a hyphen as the text of the menu item.

Access Keys and Shortcut Keys

Access and shortcut keys also make a menu system easier to use. Access keys make the menu system more accessible by allowing users to open a menu from the menu bar using only the keyboard. This is accomplished by pressing ALT in conjunction with a letter of your choosing. For example, in most Windows programs, pressing ALT-F opens the File menu. Once the menu is opened using this shortcut, the user presses DOWN or UP to select a particular item. Once the menu item is highlighted, selecting it is as simple as pressing ENTER. Or, for even easier access to a menu item, the user can press ALT-*LETTER*, where *letter* refers to the letter that is underlined in the menu item.

The letter of the main menu item that functions with the ALT key is also underlined, as shown in Figure 16-9. When choosing the underlined letters for a menu system, it is best to adhere to Windows conventions whenever possible. For example, the Help menu is typically accessed using ALT-H; therefore the *H* is underlined in Help.

Choose access keystrokes carefully. Suppose you use the ALT-F combination to allow users to easily access the File menu in an application. Inside the File menu you have the items Open and Organize. Because you have selected O as the access key for both items, pressing O on the keyboard when the File menu is displayed will not launch an action.

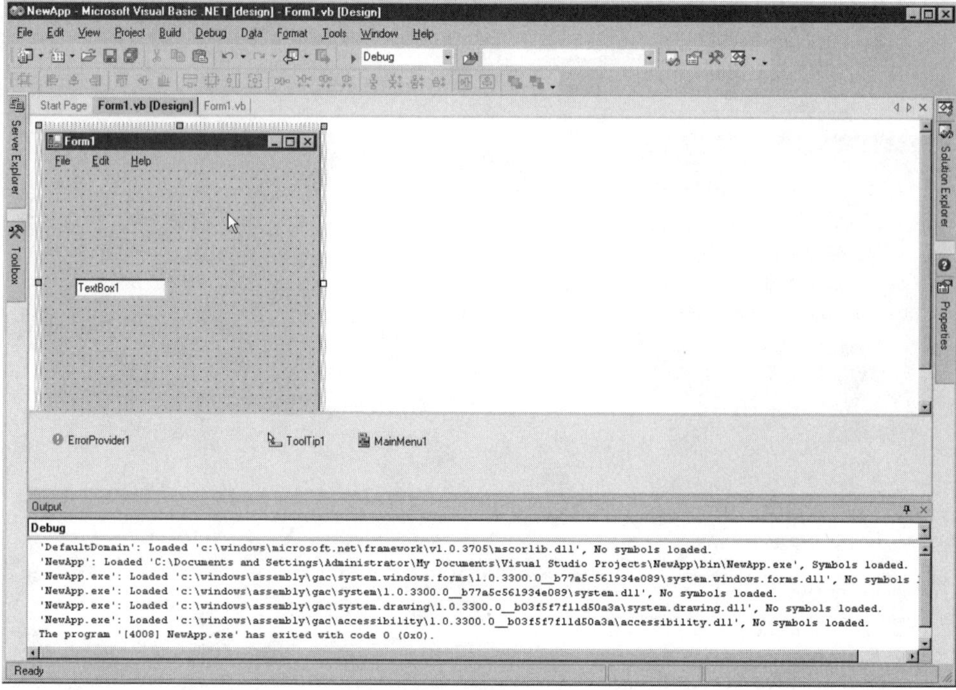

Figure 16-9 Using Access keys

NOTE In this case, pressing O highlights Open but does not select it. Pressing O again moves the highlight to Organize. The user can continue to press O to toggle between the commands. Pressing ENTER with the menu item highlighted actually selects the item.

To create an access key for a menu item, follow these steps:

1. In the Windows Form Designer, select the menu item to which you would like to assign an access key.
2. Type an ampersand (&) in front of the letter that is to be underlined and is to function as the access key.

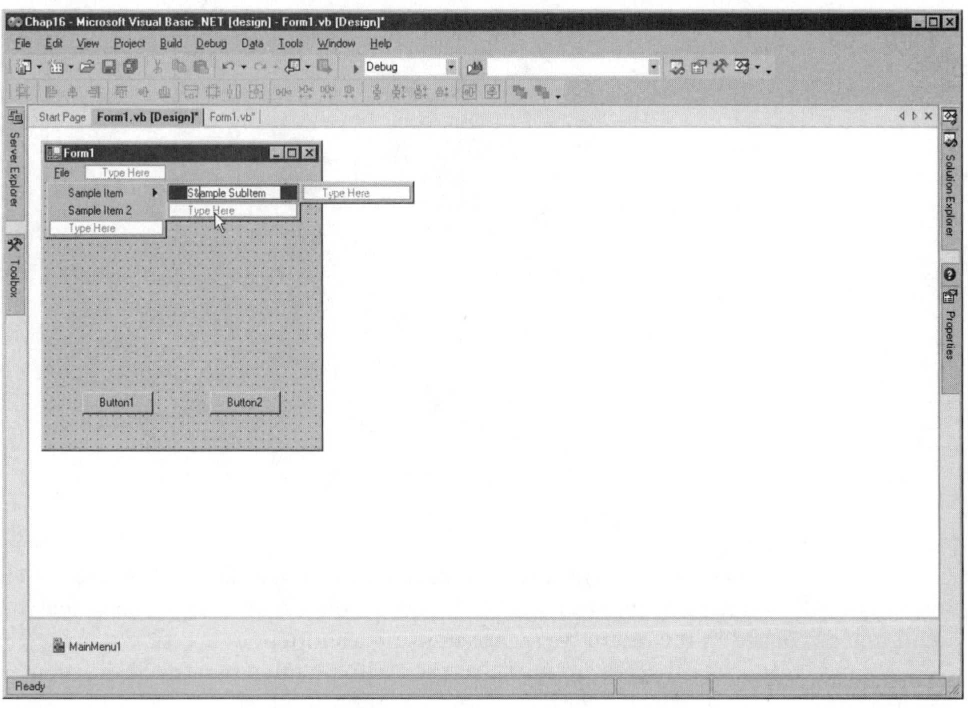

Developers use shortcut keys to provide instant access to menu items. A good example is CONTROL-C. This Windows convention copies the current selection to the user's Windows clipboard, eliminating the task of opening even a single menu. When a shortcut key is designated for a menu item, the key or key combination appears to the right of the menu text in the menu item, as shown in Figure 16-10. This serves to educate users as to the shortcut keys available in the application.

EXAM TIP To suppress the display of the shortcut key in the menu, set the ShowShortcut property of the menu item to False.

To assign a shortcut key in a menu system, follow these steps:

1. From within the Windows Form Designer, select the menu item for which you want to enable a shortcut key.
2. Access the Properties window and select the Shortcut property.
3. Select the appropriate shortcut key combination from the drop-down menu that appears.

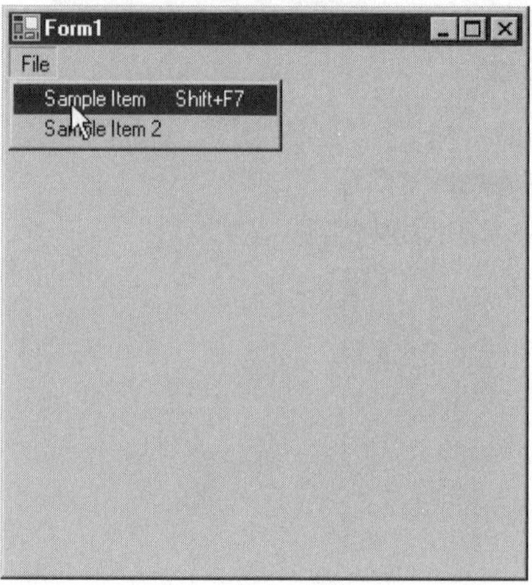

Figure 16-10 Using shortcut keys

MenuItem Events

Like other Windows Forms controls, menu items have event handlers. In fact, as with a Button control, the default event is the Click event. This event is triggered when the menu item is clicked in the interface or chosen using a shortcut or access key.

Select and Popup are other common events used with menu items. The Select event is raised when the menu item is highlighted and is often used to provide help for the menu item. The Popup event is raised just before the list of menu items is displayed. It is often used to enable or disable particular items prior to the menu being displayed. It could be used, for example, to disable a MenuItem due to the status of a particular control.

TIP You create event handlers for MenuItems just like you create them for other controls, as demonstrated earlier in this chapter.

Creating Context Menus

Context menus (or shortcut menus as they are often called) allow users to right-click a form or other control and receive a menu system that appears at the point of the right-click, as shown in Figure 16-11. You create these menus using the ContextMenu component. This process is almost identical to the MainMenu component process described earlier in this chapter.

NOTE You can use shortcut keys for context menu items, but you cannot use access keys.

To associate a context menu with a control or form, you set the ContextMenu property of that form or control.

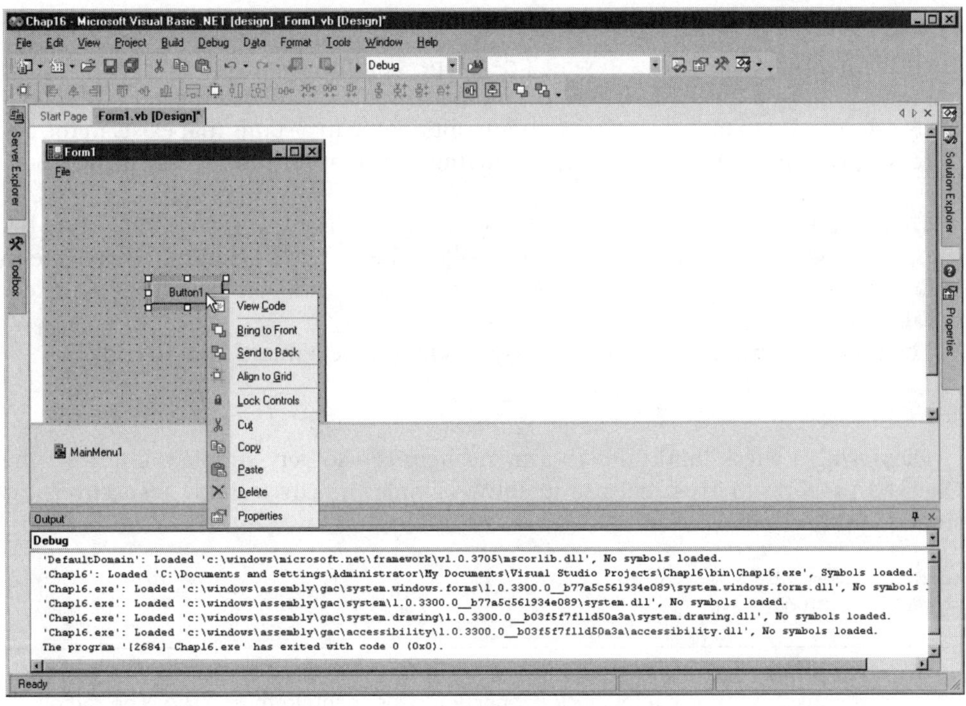

Figure 16-11 Using context menus

To create a context menu in an application, follow these steps:

1. Double-click the ContextMenu component in the Toolbox. The ContextMenu component appears in the component tray.
2. Build the context menu by typing the text of the menu items directly into the Windows Form Designer.
3. Use the Properties window to set properties for any of the menu items that you create.
4. Select the form or control that you want to associate the context menu with and edit the ContextMenu property of the control using the Properties window.

NOTE You can associate a single context menu with many different controls, but each control can be associated with only one context menu.

Modifying Menus at Runtime

There are many circumstances in which developers modify menus during runtime. For example, to show a check mark next to a menu item to indicate that the item was previously selected. Or to hide a particular menu option due to a status that exists in the application. Whatever the case may be, modifying menus at runtime is easy using Visual Basic .NET code.

There are also situations in which developers must disable a menu item, often because the state of the application should not allow the item to be chosen. When a menu item is disabled, it appears dimmed in the menu system, and access and shortcut keys are also disabled for the item.

The following example shows how easy it is to disable a menu item in code.

```
mnuMyMenuItem.Enable = False
```

Displaying a check mark next to a menu item is also very simple. Simply set the Checked property to True or False to show or hide the check mark, respectively, as shown in the following code.

```
mnuMyMenuItem.Checked = True
mnuMyMenuItem.Checked = False
```

NOTE To display a radio button next to the menu item rather than a check mark, set the RadioCheck property for the menu item to True. The radio button appears whenever the Checked property of the menu item is True.

Controlling the visibility of menu items is also quite simple. Use the Visible property of the item and set it to False as shown in the following code.

```
mnuMyMenuItem.Visible = False
```

NOTE Hiding the menu in this manner also hides any sub-menu items.

Cloning and Merging Menus

Developers sometimes make copies of menus during runtime and use them in other places within an application. This is done, for example, to clone the Help menu and make it available as a context menu when certain controls are right-clicked. To copy a menu, you use the CloneMenu method, which creates an exact duplicate of the menu, including all members, property settings, event handlers, and so on. You can then assign the cloned menu to the new control or form.

Cloning is illustrated in the following example.

```
Dim mnuMyContextMenu As New ContextMenu()
mnuMyContextMenu.MenuItems.Add(MyMenuItem.CloneMenu())
btnMyButton.ContextMenu = mnuMyContextMenu
```

Developers sometimes need to merge menus at runtime, for example, to create a context menu that is the combination of two other menu systems. You can merge multiple main or context menus easily in code and display these new menus in your application dynamically. Simply use the MergeMenu method of the menu to be displayed and call upon the incorporated menu as the argument, as shown in the following example.

```
mnuMainMenu.MergeMenu(MyContextMenu)
```

Adding Menu Items

It is also possible to add menu items dynamically during runtime. To do this, you specify a method to handle the Click event of these new menu items by specifying the method name as an argument to the constructor of the new menu item.

To add new menu items dynamically, follow these steps:

1. Declare and instantiate the new menu item; typically you specify a method to handle the click event at this time, as shown in the following code.

```
Dim mnuMyNewMenuItem As MenuItem
mnuMyNewMenuItem = New MenuItem("Sample New Item", _
New EventHandler(AddressOf MyMethodClick))
```

2. Add the new method to the MenuItems collection of the menu you want to modify as shown in the following code.

```
mnuMyMainMenu.MenuItems.Add(mnuMyNewMenuItem)
```

Creating Custom Windows Controls

As if the wealth of capabilities provided by the default Windows Forms controls was not enough, you also can author your own controls in Visual Basic .NET. Although this capability existed in previous versions of Visual Basic, you are no longer limited to designing user controls that act as a collection of pre-existing controls. Now, thanks primarily to inheritance, you can inherit functionality from pre-existing user controls or pre-existing Windows Forms controls.

Visual Basic .NET also provides increased flexibility in how you employ controls. You can author them as part of a Windows desktop application project, and then use them only on forms in the project. Or you can author them in a Windows Control Library project, compile the project into an assembly, and use the controls in other projects. You can even inherit from them, and use Visual Inheritance to customize them quickly for special purposes.

EXAM TIP For the certification exam, you should be familiar with the basic steps of authoring your own controls for Windows applications.

To author a custom user control in Visual Basic .NET, follow these basic steps:

1. Open a new Windows Application project in Visual Studio .NET.

2. From the Project menu, choose Add User Control.

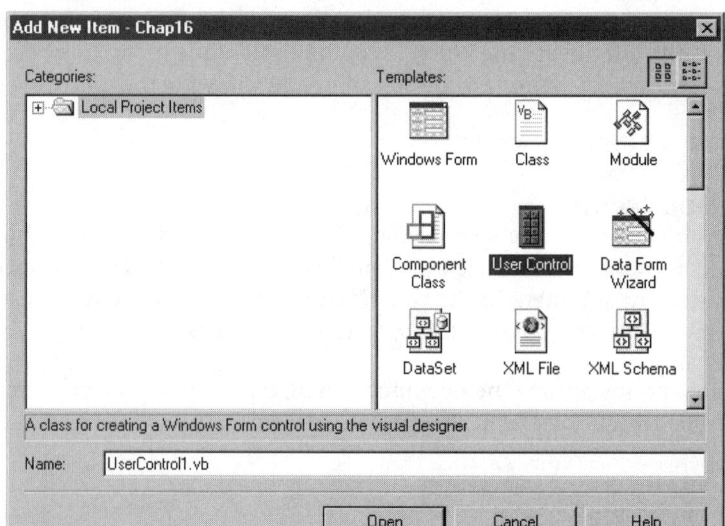

3. Add existing controls from the Toolbox to the Windows application's forms as required. Customize the properties and event handlers for these controls as necessary.
4. Close the form or forms that make up the user control and save all files.

TIP Give the class file (.vb or .cs file) the name you want the user control to have.

5. Choose Build from the Build menu.
6. Once the custom user control is built, you may add it to the Toolbox for use in Windows applications.

Configuring Control Licensing

Developers protect custom Windows controls by licensing them. This is fairly straightforward in Visual Basic .NET because the .NET Framework provides a licensing model that is identical for all components (including Windows Forms controls and ASP.NET server controls) and is fully compatible with licensing for ActiveX controls.

Licensing protects intellectual property by verifying that a user (that is, another developer) is authorized to use the control. If the user is not authorized to use the control, the control cannot be implemented in the developer's application. Of course, this check is more important at design time, when the control is incorporated into an application, than at runtime. When a licensed control is used legitimately at design time, the application receives a runtime license that can be distributed freely.

Licensing and validation logic is performed by a license provider, which is a class that derives from **System.ComponentModel.LicenseProvider**.

To enable licensing of custom controls, follow these steps:

1. Apply a LicenseProviderAttribute to your class.
2. Call LicenseManager.Validate or LicenseManager.IsValid in the constructor.
3. Call Dispose on any granted license prior to the completion of the **Finalizer** class code.

   The following code provides a simple example of control licensing.

```
Imports System
Imports System.ComponentModel
Imports System.Web.UI
<LicenseProvider(GetType(LicFileLicenseProvider))> _
       Public Class MyCustomControl
Inherits Control
Private license As License
Public Sub New()
      license = LicenseManager.Validate _
            (GetType(MyCustomControl), Me)
End Sub
Public Overloads Overrides Sub Dispose()
      If Not (license Is Nothing) Then
            license.Dispose()
            license = Nothing
      End If
End Sub
End Class
```

Summary

Windows Forms would not be very useful if not for the controls that you place on them. These controls add functionality to applications and allow users to input data and view output from your application. You can add controls to Windows Forms using the Windows Form Designer during design time, or you can add controls to forms dynamically during runtime using code. Whichever method you choose, you can always modify the properties of these controls to tailor their behavior to your exact specifications. Properties can be controlled both in design time and runtime.

To make controls really useful, it is important that you properly code the event handlers of the controls and components. These code areas respond to particular events that happen to your controls during the application's execution. Each control includes a default event handler. This event handler contains the code response to the most common event in the control's life—for example, the default event handler for a Button control is Click.

An important feature of a user interface is the menu system, including convenient "shortcut" menus that allow quick access using a simple right-click of the mouse. Menus can include shortcut keys or access keys for easy access; they can even include visual elements such as check boxes and radio buttons. You create the menu system during design time, but can easily manipulate it during runtime as well.

Finally, you are not limited to the controls and components that ship with Visual Basic .NET. You can create your own controls if the default controls do not meet your particular needs. You can start from scratch, or you can use the existing controls of Visual Basic as a starting point. You can even inherit control functionality from other applications. Of course, you will want to protect your custom controls by licensing them. The control licensing features of the .NET Framework make it easy for you to accomplish this.

Test Questions

1. Which of the following controls is used to display mutually exclusive options to the end user?
   A. TextBox
   B. CheckBox
   C. RadioButton
   D. GroupBox
2. Which of the following controls is used to group collections of controls?
   A. Panel
   B. TrackBar
   C. ComboBox
   D. MainMenu
3. Which of the following considerations should you be aware of when using ActiveX controls in Windows Forms? Choose all that apply.
   A. Security
   B. Performance
   C. File sizes
   D. Registry modifications
4. Which of the following partial code samples demonstrates the proper dynamic addition of a control during runtime?
   A. Me.Add (lblMyLabel)
   B. Add (lblMyLabel)
   C. Controls.Add (lblMyLabel)
   D. Me.Controls.Add (lblMyLabel)
5. Which of the following is an example of an extender provider?
   A. ToolTipProvider
   B. Panel

C. GroupBox

D. MainMenu

6. There is a control on your form that you do not want to include in the tab order for data entry. Which property should you use to control this?

   A. Tab

   B. TabStop

   C. TabOrder

   D. TabIndex

7. Which of the following objects is used to create menus in a Windows application?

   A. MainMenu

   B. Menu

   C. CreateMenu

   D. CreateMenuItem

8. You want to define a distance between one or more edges of a container and a control. You need the distance to remain constant during runtime, even if the container object is resized. Which property should you use?

   A. Dock

   B. Anchor

   C. TabIndex

   D. Fill

9. Which component should you use in your application to create a menu that appears when a particular control is right-clicked?

   A. ShortcutMenu

   B. PopUpMenu

   C. PopUp

   D. ContextMenu

10. Licensing and validation logic is performed by a license provider class. From which of the following classes is the license provider class derived?

    A. System.ComponentModel.LicenseProvider

    B. LicenseProvider

    C. System.LicenseProvider

    D. License

Test Answers

1. C.
2. A.
3. A, B, C, D.
4. D.
5. A.
6. B.
7. A.
8. B.
9. D.
10. A.

CHAPTER 17

Windows Forms Applications Options

In this chapter, you will

- Learn how to implement online user assistance
- Discover how to enable print capabilities
- Find out how to provide accessibility features
- Configure a Windows-based application
- Explore methods for configuring security
- Understand how to configure authorization

Typically, end users must print from an application, as well as access Help to learn about an application's features. Users with physical handicaps sometimes need special assistance in an application. This chapter helps you provide assistance and add other functionality to Windows-based applications. It also outlines how you can provide security in an application.

Implementing Online User Assistance

Even if a Windows application is carefully designed and has an intuitive interface, it should incorporate end user help. Providing users with online help ensures that they fully leverage the application's features, maximize productivity, and have a satisfying experience.

Developers typically implement help in an application using either HTML files that link to particular help topics or compressed HTML (CHM) files that are created using the Microsoft HTML Help Workshop.

Using the Help Class

The **Help** class enables developers to display help to users via HTML or CHM files. This class encapsulates the HTML Help 1.0 engine and allows you to easily display help files. Two static methods of the **Help** class enable you to implement help in an application. These static methods are ShowHelp and ShowHelpIndex.

EXAM TIP The ShowHelp method is a Shared (static) method. Therefore, you do not need to create an instance of the **Help** class to use it.

The ShowHelp method is used to display a help file for a particular control in an application. The syntax for this method is simple. You specify the control that the help file relates to, the file itself, and its location. When specifying the location, you can use a Uniform Resource Location (c:\help_files\samplehelp.htm) or an HTTP URL (http://samplehelp.htm). The following example sets the help file for a form to a help file located on the C: drive.

```
Help.ShowHelp(frmMyForm, "c:\help_files\frmMyFormHelp.htm")
```

The ShowHelp method also allows you to specify a HelpNavigator parameter, which allows you to display a specific location within the help file. You can use a pre-built HelpNavigator value, or you can specify a string value to search for as a keyword. Table 17-1 describes the possible HelpNavigator values.

The following code enables the application to display help for a form and navigate to the Format keyword.

```
Help.ShowHelp(frmMyForm, _
      "c:\help_files\frmMyFormHelp.htm", "Format")
```

To enables users to navigate directly to the Index of a help file, developers use the ShowHelpIndex method. This method, shown in the following example, accepts the control name and the URL of the help file just as the ShowHelp method did.

```
Help.ShowHelpIndex(frmMyForm, _
      "c:\help_files\frmMyFormHelp.htm"
```

You typically call the preceding methods of the **Help** class to respond to a variety of end user actions in an application interface. For example, you might implement a Help main menu item that displays help files in the application. Another common practice is to implement a context menu for controls that includes a Help option. When this option is selected, the appropriate help file is called by the ShowHelp method.

Table 17-1 HelpNavigator Values for the ShowHelp Method

Name	Description
AssociateIndex	Specifies that the index for the desired topic appears in the URL parameter
Find	Specifies that the search page of the URL is displayed
Index	Specifies that the index of the URL is displayed
KeywordIndex	Specifies a keyword to search for and the action to take in the URL
TableOfContents	Specifies that the table of contents of the URL is displayed
Topic	Specifies that the topic referenced by the URL is displayed

Using the HelpProvider Component

The HelpProvider component, shown in Figure 17-1, is another valuable way to provide help to users while they are in an application. In fact, it is a superb method for providing help for controls that are in use in the application. The HelpProvider component is used to associate HTML help files with the application. It allows developers to provide help in the following ways:

- Provide context-sensitive help for controls on Windows Forms
- Provide context-sensitive help for a particular dialog box or specific controls on a dialog box
- Open a help file to a specific area, such as the Table of Contents or Index

The HelpNameSpace property of the HelpProvider component allows developers to associate the help file with the component. Once again, you may use a CHM or HTML file and the file may be specified using a URL or HTTP URL.

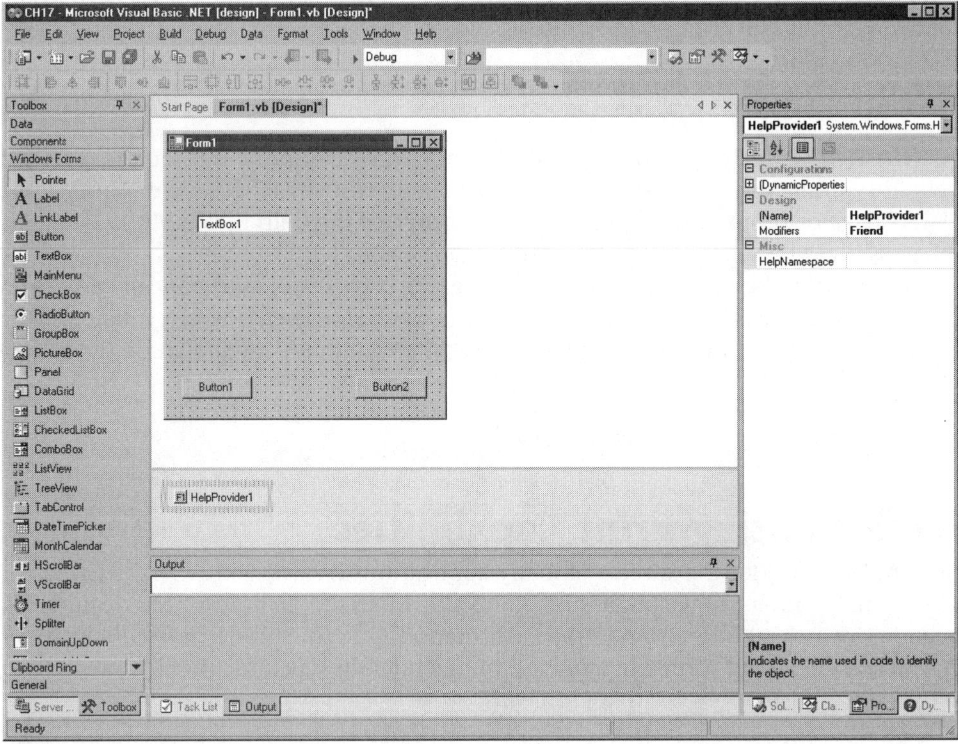

Figure 17-1 The HelpProvider component

The HelpProvider is an extender provider that adds the following properties to each control on the form where the HelpProvider component is used:

- HelpString
- HelpKeyWord
- HelpNavigator

Developers use the HelpString property to assign a string value to the control. This string value is displayed in a pop-up window when the user presses F1 while the specified control has focus.

TIP This behavior occurs only if the HelpNameSpace property of the HelpProvider component is not set. If the property is set, the appropriate help file appears when the user presses F1.

You can easily set these properties in design time using the Properties window or code. To set the properties using code, use the SetHelpString method, as shown in the following example.

```
myHelpProvider.SetHelpString(btnMyButton, _
"Use this button to complete the data input")
```

If the HelpNameSpace property of the HelpProvider component is set, the specified help file appears when the user presses F1. Developers use the HelpKeyWord and/or the HelpNavigator properties to display a specific area of the help file. Table 17-1 details the possible values for the HelpNavigator property.

As you know, the contents of the HelpString property are not automatically displayed for a control if the HelpNameSpace property is used. However, you can still access the value in your application by using the GetHelpString method, as shown in the following example.

```
myHelpProvider.GetHelpString(btnMyButton)
```

Implementing Print Capabilities

Printing is critical for the success of many applications created with Visual Basic .NET. The **PrintDocument** object makes it easy to allow users to print text files, documents, and graphics. In addition to the **PrintDocument** object, the .NET Framework includes classes to support and configure printer settings. End users rely upon these printer-setting classes to control print jobs in applications.

Using the PrintDocument Component

The properties, methods, and events of the **PrintDocument** class provide all the logic necessary to print pages within an application. Table 17-2 details the properties, methods, and events of this frequently used object.

Creating a PrintDocument component in an application is simple. In design time, simply drag a PrintDocument component from the Toolbox into the Windows Form Designer. The **PrintDocument** object appears in the component tray, ready for modifications.

You can also use code to add a PrintDocument component to an application. To do so, use the syntax in the following example.

```
Dim myPrintDocument As New PrintDocument()
```

TIP When the PrintDocument component is added in either manner, it is ready to work with the system's default printer object.

You allow print jobs to be initiated in the application using the PrintDocument.Print method. This method activates one or more PrintPage events depending upon the number of pages to be printed. The PrintPage event is the main event used in printing documents. It is up to you to provide the appropriate code to handle this event in the respective event handler. The good news is that all the objects and information you need are contained in the **PrintPageEventArgs** object that is received by the event handler. This object includes the properties listed in Table 17-3.

Name	Type	Description
DefaultPageSettings	Property	Gets or sets page settings used as defaults for all pages to be printed
DocumentName	Property	Gets or sets the document name to display while printing the document, for example, in a print status dialog box
PrintController	Property	Gets or sets the print controller that guides the printing process
PrinterSettings	Property	Gets or sets the printer that prints the document
Print	Method	Starts the document printing process
BeginPrint	Event	Occurs when the Print method is called and before the first page prints
EndPrint	Event	Occurs when the last page of the document has printed
PrintPage	Event	Occurs when the output to print for the current page is needed
QueryPageSettings	Event	Occurs immediately before each PrintPage event

Table 17-2 Properties, Methods, and Events of the PrintDocument Component

Name	Description
Cancel	Gets or sets a value indicating whether the print job should be canceled
Graphics	Retrieves the **Graphics** object used to render content on the printed page
HasMorePages	Gets or sets a value indicating whether an additional page should be printed
MarginBounds	Retrieves the rectangular area that represents the portion of the page inside the margins
PageBounds	Retrieves the rectangular area that represents the total area of the page
PageSettings	Retrieves the page settings for the current page

Table 17-3 Properties of the PrintPageEventArgs Object

As shown in Table 17-3, content is rendered to the printed page using the **Graphics** object. You use the same methods you use to render content on a form or other object. The following code demonstrates the use of the Graphics property to print a Bitmap image.

```
Private Sub PrintPage(sender As Object, _
      ev As PrintPageEventArgs)
ev.Graphics.DrawImage(Image.FromFile _
      ("C:\Pictures\MyBitmapFile.bmp"), _
      ev.Graphics.VisibleClipBounds)
ev.HasMorePages = False
End Sub
```

Notice from the properties of the **PrintPageEventArgs** object that the MarginBounds and PageBounds properties represent areas of the page's printing surface. Use the MarginBounds property to specify the location of printing within the page margins, and use the PageBounds property to specify printing outside the margin bounds. An example of printing outside the margins of the page is headers and footers.

NOTE The default unit of measurement when printing is pixels.

Use the HasMorePages property to specify that the print job has multiple pages to print. By default, this property is set to False. Typically, program logic is coded to detect multiple pages. If they are detected, you set the HasMorePages property to True. After the last page has printed, be sure program logic sets the property back to False.

To allow end users to cancel a print job in an application, simply set the Cancel property of PrintPageEventArgs to True. Obviously, this property maintains a default value of False.

The following example demonstrates the use of several **PrintPageEventArgs** properties to print a file. Notice that the code dynamically calculates the number of pages to print and controls printing through the use of the HasMorePages property.

```
Private Sub pd_PrintPage(sender As Object, _
      ev As PrintPageEventArgs)
Dim linesPerPage As Single = 0
Dim yPos As Single = 0
Dim count As Integer = 0
Dim leftMargin As Single = ev.MarginBounds.Left
Dim topMargin As Single = ev.MarginBounds.Top
Dim line As String = Nothing
linesPerPage = ev.MarginBounds.Height _
       / printFont.GetHeight(ev.Graphics)
       While count < linesPerPage
            line = streamToPrint.ReadLine()
                  If line Is Nothing Then
                        Exit While
                  End If
            yPos = topMargin + count * _
                  printFont.GetHeight(ev.Graphics)
            ev.Graphics.DrawString(line, _
                  printFont, Brushes.Black, _
                  leftMargin, yPos, New StringFormat())
           count += 1
      End While
      If Not (line Is Nothing) Then
            ev.HasMorePages = True
      Else
            ev.HasMorePages = False
      End If
End Sub
```

The PrinterSettings.SupportsColor property determines whether the current printer supports printing in color. If the printer does print in color, the DefaultPageSettings.Color property is set to True. By default, the printer then prints in color.

TIP To force black-and-white printing when a color printer is the current printer, set the DefaultPageSettings.Color property to False.

The following steps summarize the process used to enable printing in an application:

1. Add the PrintDocument component to the application. Use the Toolbox and the Windows Form Designer if this is to be accomplished in design time, or use code for runtime.
2. Create a method that handles the PrintDocument.PrintPage event.
3. Ensure that application logic exists in the PrintPage event handler to render content to the printer. Use the **PrintPageEventArgs.Graphics** object to render content.
4. If multiple pages are possible, include logic that controls the printing of multiple pages.

Using the PrintPreviewControl

It is a good idea to enable end users to preview their documents before they print. The preview displays the document exactly as it will appear once printed. To add this control to an application in design time, drag the PrintPreviewControl from the Toolbox to the Windows Form Designer, as shown in Figure 17-2.

To make the PrintPreviewControl function, you must associate it with a PrintDocument component of the application. To make this association in design time, select the PrintPreviewControl in the Windows Form Designer and access the Properties window. Then, set the Document property of the control to the PrintDocument component of the application. To associate the PrintPreviewControl with the PrintDocument using code, use the syntax shown in the following line.

```
myPrintPreview.Document = myPrintDocument
```

As soon as the association is made, the PrintPreviewControl displays the preview of the printed document. As changes are made to the document in the application or other conditions arise, the print preview that displays might become stale. To ensure that this does not happen, you can use the InvalidatePreview method of the PrintPreviewControl. This

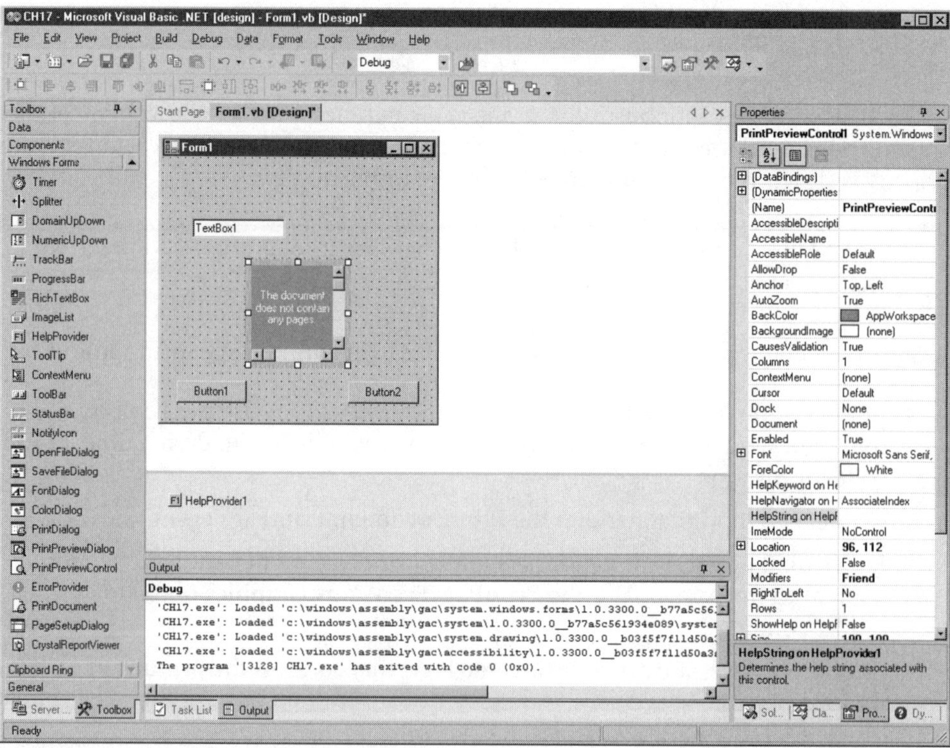

Figure 17-2 The PrintPreviewControl

method causes a refresh of the PrintPreviewControl and an associated refresh of the print preview. The following line provides an example of forcing a refresh in code.

```
myPrintPreview.InvalidatePreview()
```

The Zoom property is another important feature of the PrintPreviewControl. As its name implies, developers use this property to control the level of magnification of the print preview. Setting this value to 1 causes the print preview to be full-sized. Assigning a value less than 1 causes the preview to decrease in size, while a value greater than 1 causes the image to enlarge.

Using the PrintPreviewDialog

The PrintPreviewControl provides great flexibility when allowing users to preview their printed documents. However, if you do not need to provide a great deal of flexibility, the PrintPreviewDialog control, shown in Figure 17-3, provides a simpler way to enable the most common print preview functions. In fact, in many cases, you will find that this control outdoes your own attempts at manually building print preview functionality into an application.

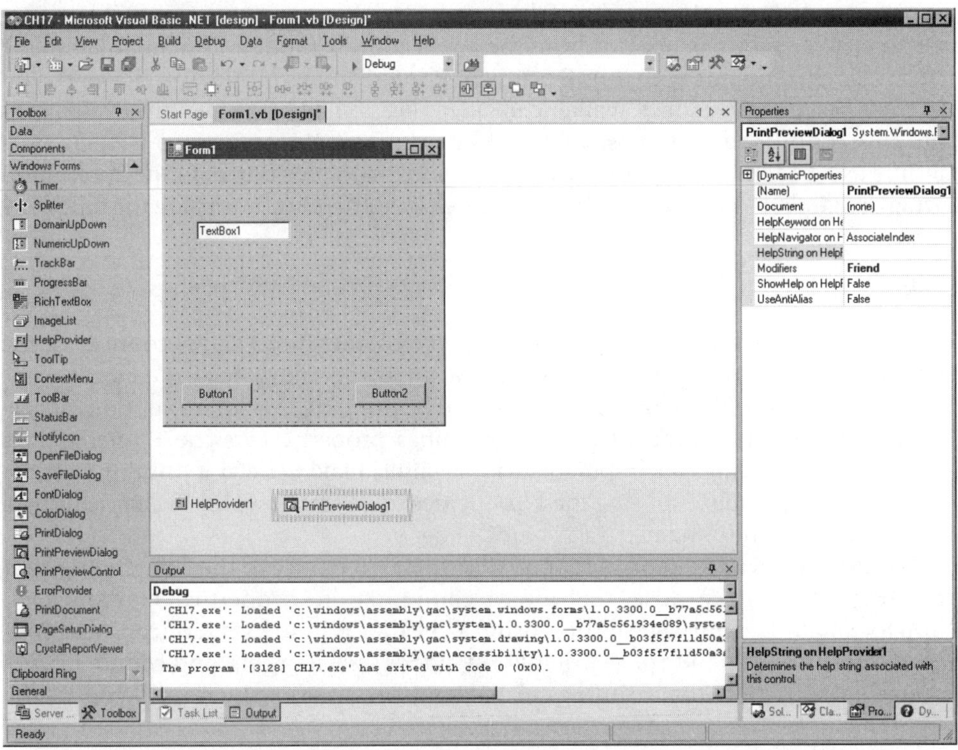

Figure 17-3 The PrintPreviewDialog control

To add the PrintPreviewDialog control to an application, drag it from the Toolbox to the Windows Form Designer. It appears in the component tray. To make the control functional, set the Document property of the PrintPreviewDialog to the PrintDocument of the application. (Notice how similar this process is to the steps for implementing PrintPreviewControl.) Display the PrintPreviewDialog box in the application just as you would display any other form, by calling the Show or ShowDialog method, as shown in the following example.

```
Private Sub btnPrintPreview_Click(ByVal sender _
      As Object, ByVal e As _
      System.Drawing.Printing.PrintPageEventArgs) _
      Handles btnPrintPreview.Click
myPrintPreviewDialog.ShowDialog()
End Sub
```

Configuring Printing

There are many possible printer configuration options in an application. The PrintDocument.PrinterSettings property contains configuration settings for all the available printers on a system. There are many possible settings for this object, but when you create a **PrintDocument** object in an application, these settings are automatically populated with the default settings of the end user's default printer. It is possible, therefore, to enable end users to print from the application without ever manipulating the many settings associated with PrintDocument.PrinterSettings properties. However, you can easily make these settings available in an application by using the PrintDialog control. This control exposes most of the PrintDocument.PrinterSettings properties at runtime using a familiar Windows interface. Simply add the control to the application during design time, and then display the dialog box during runtime using the following syntax.

```
myPrintDialog.ShowDialog()
```

Just be sure to set the Document property of the PrintDialog control to the PrintObject you are using, as you have done with other printing-related controls.

What about the settings for the page that is to be printed? These many options are exposed by the PrintDocument.DefaultPageSettings property. Like the PrinterSettings properties, these options are populated with defaults, making default printing possible without further coding. Exposing these properties to a user, however, is simple using a printing-related control named PageSetupDialog.

The PageSetupDialog control is almost identical in nature to the PrintDialog control. It is used to expose the many configuration properties contained in PrintDocument.DefaultPageSettings using a familiar Windows interface. These configuration options include page orientation, paper size, margins, and certain printer settings. Just like the other printing-related controls, to use this control, you set the

Document property of the PageSetupDialog to the correct PrintDocument from the application. When you are ready to display the object in the runtime environment, use the Show syntax, as demonstrated in the following code.

```
myPageSetupDialog.ShowDialog()
```

Finally, to enable end users to print a certain page of a print job with page settings that are different from the rest of the job, change the page settings using the PrintPageEventArgs.PageSettings property. This setting only affects the current page being printed and does not affect other pages in the job. For example, the following sample code changes the layout of a particular page in a print job to a landscape layout. This line of code would exist in the PrintPage event handler and the value *e* in the code represents the PrintPageEventArgs.

```
e.PageSettings.Landscape = True
```

Implementing Accessibility Features

A superior Windows Forms application interface design includes features to make the application useful to all potential users. This includes individuals that possess visual or hearing impairments that would make a typical Windows interface impossible to utilize.

While an increasing number of Microsoft operating systems are adding features to assist in the accessibility of all Windows applications, Visual Basic .NET includes a full range of accessibility features that developers can build into an application to ensure the richest possible experience for all users.

Accessibility begins with a well-planned design. In fact, an accessible design is a requirement of the Certified for Windows logo; the logo handbook about this program lists the following requirements to make applications more accessible:

- **Support standard system size, color, font, and input settings** Ensuring support for the Windows standards provides a consistent user interface across all applications on the user's system. This has tremendous implications even for users without special needs.
- **Ensure compatibility with the High Contrast option** Application users who desire a high degree of legibility can select the High Contrast option of Display settings. When this option is selected several restrictions are imposed upon the application. For example, only system colors selectable through Control Panel or colors set by the user may be used by the application.
- **Provide documented keyboard access to all features** Providing this support in an application allows users to interact with the application without using a pointing device, such as a mouse. Again, this support also benefits users without special needs.

- **Provide notification of the keyboard focus location** End users should always be able to identify the part of the application that has focus. Meeting this requirement also enables use of the Magnifier and Narrator accessibility aids.
- **Convey no information by sound alone** Any application that conveys information by sound must also provide other options to express this information.
- **Strive to make applications accessible** An application should offer built-in options and make the user interface familiar and consistent.

Microsoft outlines five basic principles underlying accessible design:

- **Flexibility** Provide users with a flexible, customizable user interface that accommodates a variety of needs and preferences.
- **Choice of input methods** Provide users with keyboard access to all features and simple mouse-click access for common tasks.
- **Choice of output methods** Enable users to choose discrete and redundant output combinations of sound, visuals, text, and graphics.
- **Consistency** Be sure that applications interact with other applications and system standards in a consistent, predictable manner.
- **Compatibility with accessibility aids** Whenever possible, build applications using standard and common user interface elements that are compatible with accessibility aids.

Supporting Accessibility Aids

As more Windows operating systems support enhanced accessibility aids such as the Magnifier, Narrator, and On Screen Keyboard, you must ensure that applications support these features to the fullest possible extent. To do this, you must populate the properties listed in Table 17-4. These properties are available for each visual control.

Although most Accessibility Properties are self-explanatory, one exception is the AccessibleRole property. This property contains an enum value that helps determine how an accessibility aid treats a control. Typically, you leave this value set to Default so that each control behaves in its usual manner. You should modify this property value, however, if you want to modify the control's behavior or if you are using a custom control.

Configuring an Application

What if you need to make configuration changes to your application following its deployment? The .NET Framework provides tools to help ensure that an application is properly configured and optimized following deployment.

Table 17-4 Accessibility Properties of Windows Forms Controls

Name	Description
AccessibleDescription	Describes the control to the accessibility aid
AccessibleName	Provides the name of the control to the accessibility aid
AccessibleRole	Provides the role of the control to the accessibility aid
AccessibilityObject	Provides an instance of AccessibleObject, which provides information about the control to accessibility aids; this property is read-only and is set by the designer
AccessibleDefaultActionDescription	Describes the default action of a control; this property cannot be set at design time and must be set in code

Developers use a configuration file to allow application properties to be adjusted without recompiling and redistributing the application, to enable certain properties of an application to change dynamically during runtime, and to ensure that an application is optimized for the particular operating system environment in which the deployment occurs.

Using a Configuration File

To use a configuration file, you create an XML document of a specific name that consists of specific tags. The configuration file name requires the following format.

```
<name>.<extension>.config
```

In this format, *<name>* is the name of the application and *<extension>* is the extension used on the application, typically .EXE. For example, the configuration file for an application named DataModeler.exe would be named DataModeler.exe.config. This file must be located in the same folder as the application assembly it configures.

The Visual Basic .NET documentation outlines the specific structure that the configuration file must follow. This structure is known as the .config file schema.

To create the basic structure of the file, follow these steps:

1. Select File from the main menu.
2. Select Add New Item.
3. In the Add New Item window choose Application Configuration File in the Templates area.

4. Click Open. The .config file appears in the document window of the IDE ready for you to customize it. When you build the application, this file is appropriately named.

The file must follow the following basic structure.

```
<?xml version="1.0" encoding="utf-8" ?>
<configuration>
</configuration>
```

Notice the <configuration> element; it is the root element in every configuration file used by the common language runtime and .NET Framework applications. This element can contain the following child elements:

- Startup Settings Schema
- Runtime Settings Schema
- Remoting Settings Schema
- Network Settings Schema
- Cryptography Settings Schema
- Configuration Sections Schema
- Trace and Debug Settings Schema
- ASP.NET Settings Schema

Table 17-5 describes some common elements that are based upon these schemas.

Using Dynamic Properties

The configuration file can help you dynamically set property values for objects in an application. You accomplish this by mapping selected properties to entries in the configuration file. During runtime, you retrieve values from the file for the properties. Using this approach greatly increases the flexibility of an application and reduces the need for recompilation.

You use the Properties window during design time to set a property value as configurable. You accomplish this using the DynamicProperties node. This node is populated automatically by control properties likely to be linked to external resources. You add other control properties by clicking the ellipses button next to the (Advanced) entry.

EXAM TIP Not all properties can be added as Dynamic Properties. The property value must be of the string type, or it must be explicitly converted from a string in order to be used.

Element	Description
<startup>	Used to provide the <requiredRuntime> element, which specifies the version of the common language runtime that should run the application
<runtime>	Used to provide information about assembly binding and the behavior of garbage collection
<system.runtime.remoting>	Used to provide information about remote objects and channels
<defaultProxy>	Used to specify the proxy server used for HTTP requests to the Internet
<system.net>	Used to specify the settings for Internet applications
<mscorlib>	Used to provide the <cryptographySettings> element, which provides the cryptography settings
<add>	Used to add custom application settings
<appSettings>	Used to provide custom application settings
<configSections>	Used to provide configuration section and namespace declarations
<system.diagnostics>	Used to specify trace listeners that collect, store, and route messages and the level where a trace switch is set
<trace>	Used to specify listeners that collect, store, and route tracing messages

Table 17-5 Sample .config Schema Elements

The property value links to and reads from the .config file using a key that is written to the .config file. This key corresponds to the property value. The Visual Basic .NET integrated development environment (IDE) guides you through the creation of the key and makes the modification to the .config file for you. After you complete the Dynamic Properties window, the configuration file is modified. For example, if you make the Visible property of a button (Button1) in an application dynamic, the following element is added for you to the configuration file.

```
<add key="Button1.Visible" value="True" />
```

Once the appropriate tag exists in the .config file and you deploy the application, you can change the startup value of the property simply by changing the value in the .config file. To modify the .config file, use Notepad or any other text editor. Find the particular property value you want to change and enter the new value.

Exercise 17-1: Using Dynamic Properties In this exercise you will experiment with the use of dynamic properties in Visual Basic. NET.

1. Start Microsoft Visual Studio .NET and choose New Project from the Get Started pane of the Start Page.

2. Create a new Windows Application named **Chapter17**.
3. Select File | Add New Item.
4. Select Application Configuration File in the Templates area and click Open.

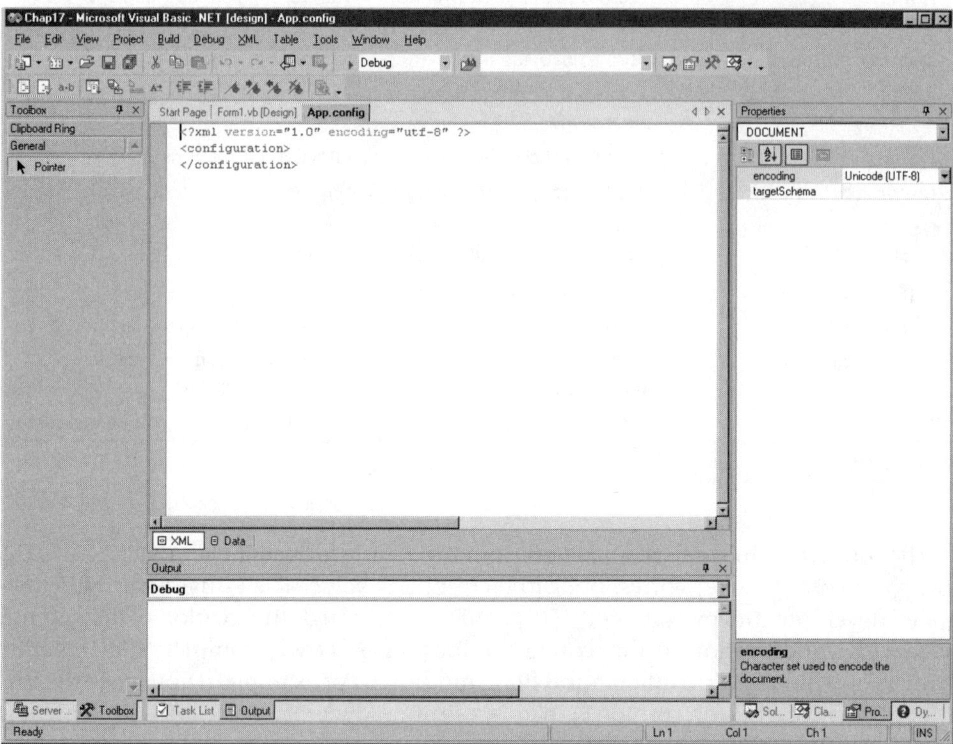

5. Select the Form1.vb tab to return to the Windows Form in design mode.
6. Double-click the button control in the Toolbox to add a button to the initial Windows Form of your application.
7. Position the button in the center of the form.
8. Ensure that the button is still selected and access the Properties window.
9. Ensure that the button properties are in the Categorized view, and then expand the (DynamicProperties) node under the Configurations area.
10. Select the file next to (Advanced) and click the ellipses button.
11. In the Dynamic Properties for Button1 window, click the Text check box in the Properties area. Notice the default key mapping name of Button1.Text. Then, click OK.

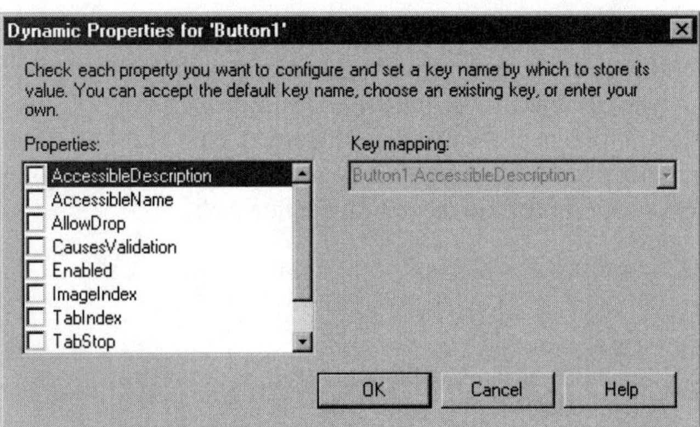

12. Select the App.config tab to view the automatic alteration to your configuration file.
13. Select Build | Build Solution.
14. Select File | Close Solution.
15. Open the Windows Explorer and navigate to your solution's directory. This is most likely in My Documents\Visual Studio Projects\Chapter17.
16. Open the Chapter17 folder, and then open the Bin folder within it.
17. Right-click the file named Chapter17.exe.config and choose Open With.
18. Select Notepad in the Open With window.
19. Change the value for the button text from Button1 to NewText.
20. Choose File | Save and close the file.
21. Double-click the Chapter17.exe file in the Bin directory to run the application. Notice the change in the button text that has been driven by the property change in the configuration file.

Visual Basic .NET also enables you to dynamically change properties that do not appear in the user interface. Perhaps you are instantiating a class in runtime and the class must have different property settings at different times. At runtime, you can easily provide default properties in the configuration file for these dynamically created objects. You retrieve these settings from the .config file using the **AppSettingsReader** class. As you might expect, the **AppSettingsReader** class uses a key to retrieve a value from the .config file.

NOTE The **AppSettingsReader** class is part of the **System.Configuration** namespace.

PART V

You use the GetValue method of the **AppSettingsReader** class to specify the value to retrieve. This method requires you to provide the String value for the key and a Type value that indicates the type of object to be retrieved. Even though you must specify a type, the value is returned as an object and must be converted to the appropriate data type.

The following example demonstrates the use of the **AppSettingsReader** class for retrieving the Text property for a dynamically created object.

```
Dim myAppSettingsReader As New _

      System.Configuration.AppSettingsReader()
Dim mySampleObject As New SampleObject()
mySampleObject.Text = CType(myAppSettingsReader.GetValue _
      ("DynamicSampleObject.Text", GetType(System.String)), _
      String)
```

Optimizing an Application

Another step in ensuring the success of an application is to implement optimization techniques during design. Microsoft recommends taking the following steps during design time to help ensure that an application is optimized:

- **Use the As Object syntax sparingly when declaring object variables** Declaring an object variable with the As Object clause creates a variable that can contain a reference to any type of object. However, access to the object through that variable is "late bound;" that is, the binding occurs when the program is run. There are a lot of reasons to avoid late binding, including slower application performance. To create an object variable that results in early binding (that is, binding when the program is compiled), add a reference to the type library for the object using the COM tab of the Add Reference dialog box on the Project menu. Then, declare the object variable of the specific type of the object.
- **Use global variables sparingly** Use local variables and constants whenever possible. Only use global variables when you truly need global scope.
- **Design loops in an application carefully** Improperly constructed loops could cause poor application performance or even failure of the application.

Understanding Visual Basic .NET Resource Management Capabilities

It is important to understand how Visual Basic .NET handles resources, especially compared to previous versions of the language. The common language runtime (CLR) in Visual Basic .NET uses a process called garbage collection to manage allocated resources. The system garbage collector releases an object's resources when the object can no longer be reached by any running code in the application.

Visual Basic .NET uses the Nothing keyword to indicate that an object variable does not contain a reference to an object. Previous versions of Microsoft Visual Basic encouraged developers to assign unused objects to Nothing to disassociate the object variable from the object and release resources. You can still assign unused objects to Nothing, but because of the way Visual Basic .NET manages resources this process does not guarantee that objects will be released immediately. Generally speaking, you should only assign long-lived objects, such as shared members or global variables, to Nothing.

Some objects support the Dispose method, whose purpose is to release system resources more expeditiously. Classes that support the Dispose method should implement the IDisposable interface. The Dispose method needs to be explicitly called when you want to release object resources, as shown in the following example.

```
MyObject.Dispose
```

Finalize is another method supported by some classes. The Finalize method runs automatically when an object is released and can be used to perform other cleanup tasks. It is similar to the Class_Terminate() method used in previous versions of Microsoft Visual Basic. Unlike the Dispose method, the Finalize method is called automatically by the CLR after an object is no longer needed.

The Optimization Process

Optimizing code should be an ongoing process in which you continually attempt to identify bottlenecks, and then tune code in an attempt to remove the bottlenecks. A bottleneck is caused by poor resource utilization or some other design problem and impedes performance. The following steps outline the process of optimizing code:

1. Obtain performance data through careful measurements.
2. Identify performance bottlenecks.
3. Tune your code.
4. Repeat the process.

Performance Monitoring Windows Tools

Fortunately, Windows operating systems provide plenty of tools to assist you as the developer in monitoring an application. Building and executing an application while using many of these tools is a critical component in the optimization process.

Event Viewer Console The Event Viewer, shown in Figure 17-4, is an ideal tool for monitoring events that occur on a Windows system as an application executes. It reports events related to applications, the system, security, or the underlying directory service. The Event Viewer is critical for obtaining information "post-mortem". For example, if an application fails, the Event Viewer may provide valuable clues as to why. You frequently check Event Viewer messages against Microsoft's support Web site to troubleshoot applications.

The Event Viewer contains logs that are specific to various areas of performance management. Table 17-6 describes these logs.

You may find that additional services that you install in Windows cause additional logs to be created. For example, installing the Domain Name System (DNS) on a Windows system causes a DNS log to be installed in Event Viewer.

To use the Event Viewer, go to the Start Menu, choose Programs, and then select Administrative Tools. In the Administrative Tools area, select Event Viewer.

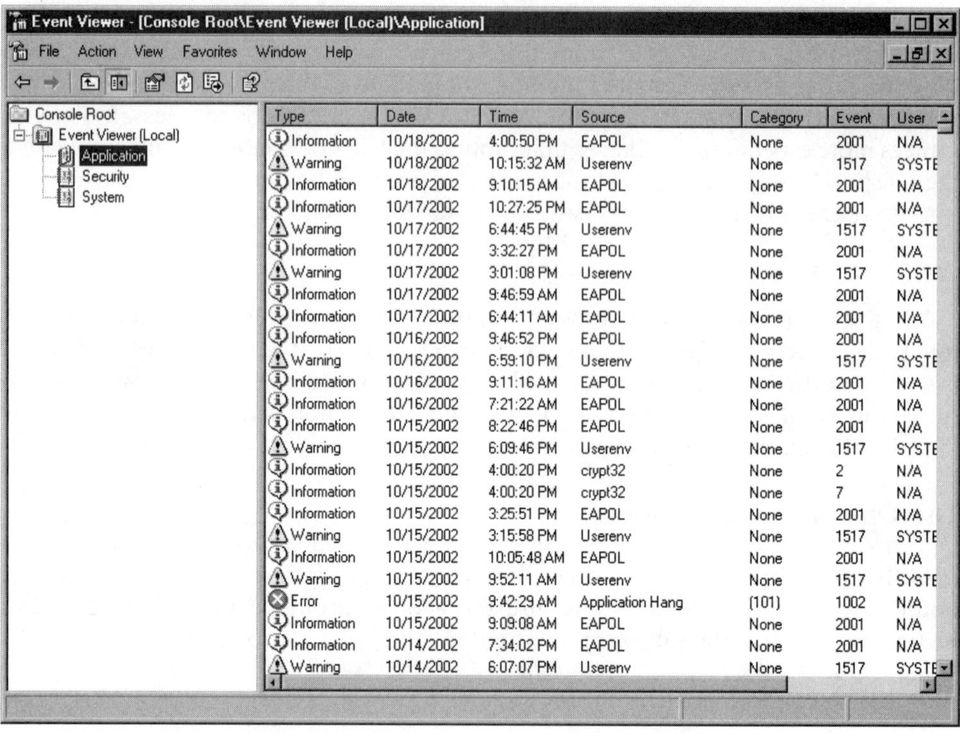

Figure 17-4 The Event Viewer

Performance Console The ultimate performance-monitoring tool in Windows is the Performance Console, as shown in Figure 17-5. This tool allows you to monitor local and remote systems in a Windows 2000 network. This console is made up of two components: the System Monitor and Performance Logs and Alerts. The combination of

Table 17-6 Event Viewer Logs

Log	Description
Application	Contains errors, warnings, or information generated by applications
Directory Service	Contains errors, warnings, or information generated by Active Directory services
Security	Contains information about the success or failure of audited events
File Replication Service	Contains errors, warnings, and information that the File Replication Service generates
System	Contains errors, warnings, and information generated by Windows 2000

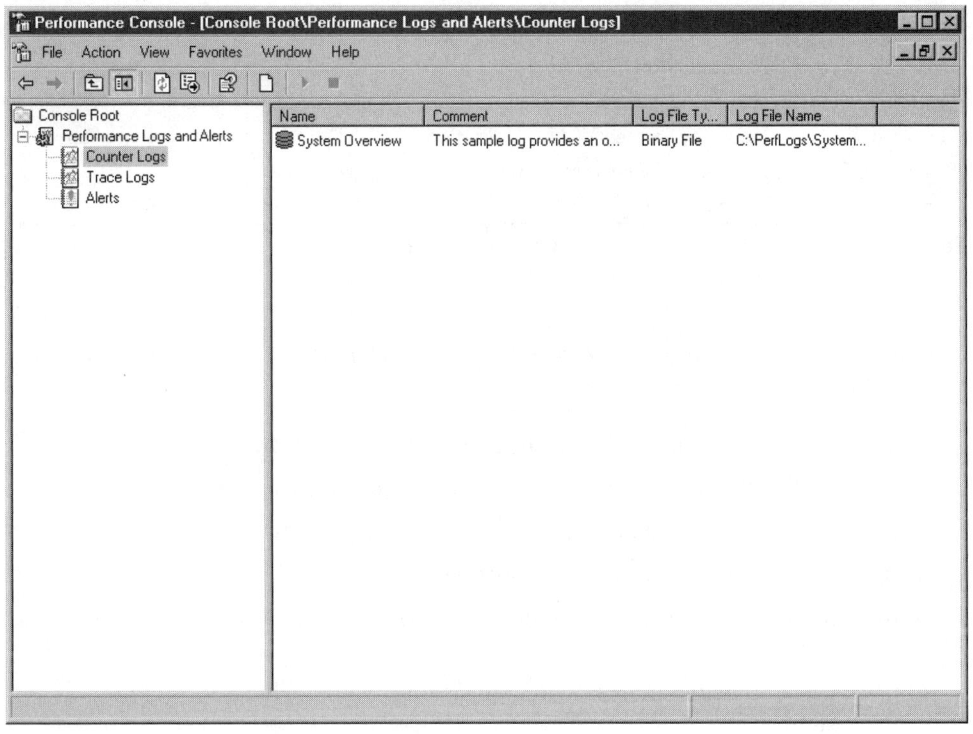

Figure 17-5 The Performance Console

these tools allows you to create baselines, diagnose historical performance issues, and send alerts regarding resource issues.

System Monitor The System Monitor tool allows you to measure the performance of a Windows system and specific services and applications. This flexible tool allows you to define the type and source of data to monitor, as well as the sampling parameters for data collection. For example, you can have System Monitor capture a specific memory statistic at fixed intervals such as every five minutes for a period of several hours. You also have a lot of flexibility in how the data is displayed. Possible displays include charts, histograms, and report views with full control over all formatting options including font, colors, and other characteristics.

To use System Monitor to monitor the health of the system and the application, you must specify the performance objects and performance counters to be monitored. A performance object provides counters for measuring the performance of a certain system component. The many performance objects in Windows 2000, and the number of counters associated with each of these objects, enable an incredible number of statistics to be monitored. Some of these, along with guidelines for their usage, are listed in Table 17-7.

Resource	Object/Counter	Suggested Threshold
Disk	PhysicalDisk\% Disk Time	90%
Memory	Memory\Available Bytes	Less than 4MB
Network	Network Segment\% Net Utilization	Depends on network medium
Processor	Processor\% Processor Time	85%
Server	Server\Pool Paged Peak	Amount of physical RAM

Table 17-7 Possible System Monitor Statistics and Positive Values

To use the System Monitor to collect statistical information about the performance of a server, follow these steps:

1. Select Start | Programs | Administrative Tools | Performance.
2. Right-click System Monitor in the right pane and choose Add Counters.
3. In the Add Counters dialog box, select Use Local Computer Counters.
4. In the Performance Object list, choose Memory.
5. In the Select Counters From List area, choose Available Bytes and click Add to add this counter.
6. Click Close to begin analyzing data regarding available bytes of memory on the system.

Choose what you would like to monitor carefully; monitoring an excessive number of counters at once can hinder system performance.

Performance Logs and Alerts The Performance Logs and Alerts component permits you to create counter logs, trace logs, and system alerts. Counter logs collect performance data in a log file format. Later, you can import this data into a database or spreadsheet application for analysis, or you can use the built-in System Monitor application to view the data.

You use trace logs to record data when certain activities such as disk I/O operations or page faults occur. Trace logs are much different than counter logs, which do not wait for an event to occur, but simply sample data at a prescribed interval.

For both counter and trace logs you define the start and stop times, file names, file types, file sizes, and other parameters. Typically, administrator permissions are required to configure these options and create a counter or trace log.

Alerts are another powerful option. With an alert, you use the performance objects and counters to monitor information regarding system performance. Using this data, you create an alert for a counter. If the selected counter's value exceeds or falls below a specified setting, the alert writes an event to the application log, sends a network message to a computer, starts a performance log, or runs a program that you specify.

To create an alert, follow these steps:

1. Select Start | Programs | Administrative Tools | Performance.
2. Double-click Performance Logs and Alerts, and then click Alerts.
3. Right-click a blank area in the right pane and choose New Alert Settings.
4. In the New Alert Settings dialog box, type the name of the alert and click OK.
5. In the Comment box, type a comment that describes the alert and click Add.
6. In the Select Counters dialog box choose the computer for which you want to create an alert.
7. In the Performance Object list, select an object to monitor.
8. Select the counters you want to monitor and click Add. Then, click Close.
9. In the Alert When The Value Is list, specify Under or Over, and in the Limit box, choose the value that triggers the alert.
10. In the Sample Data Every section, choose the amount and measurement characteristic for the update interval.
11. In the Action tab of the alert's dialog box, select the action that occurs when the alert is triggered.
12. In the Schedule tab of the alert's dialog box, configure the schedule used for the alert. Then, click OK.

Using Compiler Optimizations

Visual Basic .NET includes "automatic" optimization options. These options are available with the new Visual Basic.NET compiler. You use the Property Pages to enable these optimizations within the application.

To access the settings, follow these steps:

1. Right-click your project in the Solution Explorer.
2. Choose Properties from the context menu.
3. Choose the Optimizations link in the Configuration Properties folder.

The following optimizations are included on this page:

- **Remove integer overflow checks** This option turns on or off overflow error checking for integer operations. Checking this option prevents the compiler from checking integer calculations for errors such as overflow or division by zero. Choosing this option can make integer calculations faster. However, without error checking, if data type capacities are exceeded, incorrect results may be stored without raising an error.

- **Enable optimizations** Enabling compiler optimizations makes the output file smaller, faster, and more efficient. However, because optimizations cause code rearrangement in the output file, choosing this option can make debugging difficult.
- **Enable incremental build** This option optimizes the build process by building only those parts of the project that changed since the last compilation. If there are so many changes that the system cannot determine where changes have occurred, a full build occurs.
- **Base address** This option allows a default base address to be specified when creating a DLL.

Configuring Security in an Application

Implementing security mechanisms within applications is critical. Security means protecting code from "hackers" and other computer criminals who want to steal, damage, or modify an application or the data within it, for example an underlying database.

Permissions

The primary objects of security in Visual Basic .NET applications are permissions. These code objects represent users, identities, or code resources. Permissions implement the IPermission interface. The methods of this interface are critical to the functionality of security in an application. Table 17-8 describes the methods of the IPermission interface.

All security permissions must implement the IPermission interface; in fact, they use the Demand method to actually enforce security. As described in Table 17-8, the Demand method requires that callers have been granted appropriate permission to access the secured code. If a caller has not been granted the correct permission, a SecurityException is thrown.

Table 17-8 Methods of the IPermission Interface

Method	Description
Copy	Creates and returns an identical copy of the current permission
Demand	Forces a SecurityException at runtime if all callers higher in the call stack have not been granted the permission specified by the current instance
Intersect	Creates and returns a permission that is the intersection of the current permission and the specified permission
IsSubsetOf	Determines whether the current permission is a subset of the specified permission
Union	Creates a permission that is the union of the current permission and the specified permission

Role-Based Authorization

Developers frequently use role-based security in applications. This type of security authorization grants or denies access to an application based on the identity (roles) of the end user. For example, a Director might be allowed to access all aspects of a financial accounting application, while lower-level staff might be restricted to certain portions of the application. The security system built into the Windows operating system will assist you with role-based authorization.

The underlying .NET Framework enables authenticated users to be represented in code using the **Principal** object. You use this object with the **PrincipalPermission** object to implement role-based authorization and protect sensitive resources in an application.

Another important security object, the **WindowsPrincipal** object, represents the current Windows user. You can associate this object with an application by setting the principal policy of the application, as shown in the following code.

```
AppDomain.CurrentDomain.SetPrincipalPolicy _
      (PrincipalPolicy.WindowsPrincipal)
```

WindowsPrincipal contains a reference to the **WindowsIdentity** object. **WindowsIdentity** represents the current user. With these objects, obtaining information regarding the current user of an application is as simple as accessing **WindowsIdentity**. Specifically, **WindowsPrincipal** returns the Identity property as an IIdentity interface so you must convert it to a **WindowsIdentity** object as shown in the following code.

NOTE This example assumes that the principal policy of the application has been set to **WindowsPrincipal**.

```
Dim myPrincipal As WindowsPrincipal
myPrincipal = CType(Threading.Thread.CurrentPrincipal, _
      WindowsPrincipal)
Dim myIdentity As WindowsIdentity
myIdentity = CType(myPrincipal.Identity, WindowsIdentity)
```

These security objects allow you to use *imperative security checks*. To create such a check, you use the **PrincipalPermission** object to specify a user, and then demand that the current user match this value, as shown in the following example.

```
Dim myPermission As New PrincipalPermission("ASmith", _
      "Director")
myPermission.Demand()
```

TIP You can specify Nothing for either the name or the role in the **PrincipalPermission** object. This provides flexibility when checking security by allowing you to match only a name or a role for a user.

PART V

You can also authenticate membership of users of the built-in Windows roles (groups). Perhaps to ensure that a user is a member of the built-in Power Users group, for example. To do so, specify BUILTIN\ in front of the group name. The code in the following example allows you to check for users of the Administrators group.

```
Dim myPermission As New PrincipalPermission(Nothing, _
      "BUILTIN\Administrators")
```

You can also take a *declarative security* approach in an application. Using this method, you attach permission attributes to the members these permissions protect in order to specify the level of access. The following example demonstrates how to implement declarative, role-based security for a method called myMethod.

```
<PrincipalPermission(SecurityAction.Demand, _
      Name:="JaneS", Role:="Acct_Clerk")> _
      Public Sub myMethod()
            ' Method code omitted
      End Sub
```

Code Access Security

Protecting code from computer criminals and other unauthorized users is extremely important. Fortunately, it is relatively easy in Visual Basic .NET. Like role-based security, code access security is based on permissions; however, in this type of security, permissions represent system resources. Table 17-9 describes some of the most common permissions used to implement code access security.

Name	Description
DirectoryServicesPermission	Controls access to Active Directory
EnvironmentPermission	Controls the ability to read and set environment variables
EventLogPermission	Controls the ability to read and write to event logs
FileDialogPermission	Controls the ability to access files or folders via a dialog box
FileIOPermission	Controls the ability to read and write to the file system
OleDbPermission	Controls the ability to access an OleDb database
PrintingPermission	Controls access to a printer
ReflectionPermission	Controls the ability to use the **System.Reflection** classes to discover type information at runtime
RegistryPermission	Controls the ability to read and write to the registry
SecurityPermission	Controls several rights including the ability to execute code
SQLClientPermission	Controls the ability to access a Microsoft SQL Server database
UIPermission	Controls the ability to access the user interface

Table 17-9 Security Permissions Used for Code Access Security

You can easily create permissions that provide unrestricted access to resources or that deny access to resources. You use the PermissionState.Unrestricted flag to permit unrestricted access; you use the PermissionState.None flag to deny access. The following code provides an example of denying access.

```
Dim myPermission As New _
      OleDbPermission(PermissionState.None)
```

Summary

It is easy to make applications more user-friendly by providing intelligent, context-sensitive Help. You use the **Help** class and the HelpProvider component to easily implement these types of help.

Print capabilities are typically required in an application, and Visual Basic .NET includes easily used classes and components dedicated to the print process. The core component for almost all these mechanisms is the **PrintDocument** object.

You can assist users that have visual or auditory impairments by incorporating Accessibility aids using the Accessibility properties in Visual Basic .NET. These properties include AccessibleDescription, AccessibleName, AccessibleRole, AccessibilityObject, and AccessibleDefaultActionDescription. It is a good idea to develop the habit of using them all.

Visual Basic .NET applications provide the ability to configure properties once the application is deployed using an external configuration file. You can also optimize an application using application properties.

Visual Basic .NET also provides mechanisms for securing applications. Securing applications includes protecting code, as well as "hiding" particular areas of the application from specific users.

Test Questions

1. Which method is used to display help in an application?
   A. ShowHelp
   B. ShowHelpDialog
   C. Help
   D. DisplayHelp
2. Which of the following parameters do you use to display a particular help location?
   A. Navigator
   B. Help
   C. HelpPlace
   D. HelpNavigator

3. You want your users to receive very specific help regarding a control if they press F1 while the control has focus. Which of the following components should you use in your application?
   A. Help
   B. HelpF1
   C. HelpProvider
   D. HelpControl
4. Thanks to the properties, methods, and events of the __________, this class features all the logic necessary to print pages within an application.
   A. Printer
   B. PrintDocument
   C. PrintObject
   D. PrintClass
5. Which of the following controls allows you to quickly and easily create a dialog-based preview utility in an application?
   A. PrintPreviewDialog
   B. PrintPreview
   C. PrintDocument
   D. Printer
6. Which Accessibility property contains an enum value that helps determine how an accessibility aid treats a control?
   A. AccessibleName
   B. AccessibleRole
   C. AccessibleDescription
   D. AccessibilityTreatment
7. Which area of the Properties window do you use to create properties in an application that can be controlled after the application is deployed?
   A. DynamicProperties
   B. Post-mortem
   C. PostProperties
   D. ConfigFileProperties

8. Which of the following methods forces a SecurityException at runtime if all callers higher in the call stack have not been granted the permission specified by the current instance?
   A. Intersect
   B. Demand
   C. Copy
   D. IsSubsetOf
9. Which of the following permissions is used to control the ability to read and write to the file system?
   A. ReflectionPermission
   B. RegistryPermission
   C. FileDialogPermission
   D. FileIOPermission
10. Which of the following flags do you use to permit unrestricted access to a resource?
   A. State.Unrestricted
   B. State.None
   C. PermissionState.Unrestricted
   D. PermissionState.None

Test Answers

1. A.
2. D.
3. C.
4. B.
5. A.
6. B.
7. A.
8. B.
9. D.
10. C.

CHAPTER 18

Data Binding in Windows Forms Applications

In this chapter, you will

- Study data providers and data consumers
- Implement simple bound controls
- Understand how to implement data binding at design time and runtime
- Learn how to implement complex bound controls
- Find out how to navigate data bound controls
- See how to filter and sort data
- Learn about the **DataViewManager** class

Earlier in this book you learned how easy it is to access data in a Visual Basic .NET application using ADO.NET. In this chapter you explore binding data to a Windows application using form controls. Doing so allows data to be easily viewed and manipulated. You also learn how to create filtered and sorted views of data for more powerful viewing.

Data Binding

The terms *data provider* and *data consumer* are commonly used in discussions of data binding. A data provider refers to the source of data for an application; a data consumer refers to a control in an application that displays or uses the data. For example, the records from a column of data may appear in a TextBox on a form. In this very common example, the column of data is the data provider, and the TextBox control is the data consumer.

In the .NET Framework, any object that implements the IList interface can serve the role of data provider. This includes **DataSets**, **DataTables**, **DataColumns**, arrays, collections, or even **DataViews**. Each of these objects includes the **CurrencyManager** object, which tracks the current record; **CurrencyManager** objects are managed through a form's **BindingContext** object.

In addition, the .NET Framework enables any runtime-accessible property of any control to be bound to a data source. This provides many options for the use of data binding in an application. Database records can literally control the behavior of controls in a form, or you can view/update database records using intuitive controls such as Back and Forward style buttons.

There are two forms of data binding: simple and complex. Simple binding means that one record at a time is bound to a control. For example, a Label control may display data one record at a time. Complex binding permits multiple records to be bound to a single control. For example, a ListBox control can be bound to an entire column of data. Some controls, such as a DataGrid, allow even more complex binding. The DataGrid can be bound to all the columns and rows of a **DataTable**, **DataView**, or **DataSet**.

Simple Binding

You use the DataBindings property of the **ControlBindingsCollection** class to create simple bound controls. During design time, you use the DataBindings node of the Properties window to configure simple bindings. This node expands and automatically displays the most commonly bound properties for the control. To bind one of the displayed properties, simply click in the appropriate field to view a drop-down menu of options. These options are the data providers. Expand the **DataSet** object and the **DataTable** or **DataView** to select the particular column for binding.

Remember, you can bind any property of a control. If the property does not automatically appear in the DataBindings node, click the Ellipses button next to the (Advanced) field to bind the property using the Advanced Data Binding dialog box.

Exercise 18-1: Implementing Simple Binding In this exercise you practice implementing simple data binding in a Windows form.

1. Launch Microsoft Visual Studio .NET.
2. Select New Project on the Get Started pane of the Start page.
3. Create a new Windows Application entitled **Chapter18**.
4. Access the Server Explorer window in the IDE. This window is typically docked to the left-hand side of the design environment. If it is not, select View | Server Explorer.
5. In the Server Explorer window, right-click the Data Connections node and choose Add Connection from the context menu. The Data Link Properties window appears with the Connection tab selected.

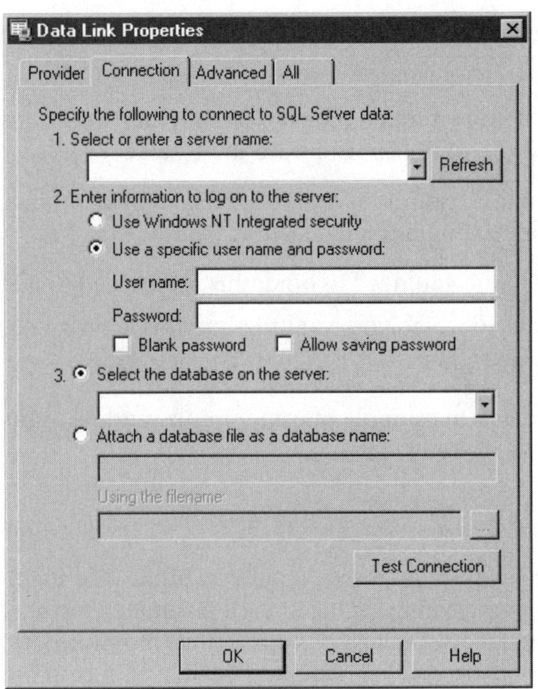

NOTE This exercise uses a sample Microsoft Access database named FPNWIND.MDB. You may choose any database for this exercise, but understand that steps may differ slightly.

6. Select the Provider tab. Choose Microsoft Jet 4.0 OLE DB Provider and click Next. The Connection tab appears.
7. Use the Ellipses button to browse to the location of your database.
8. Click Test Connection to test the database connection.
9. Click OK in the Data Link Properties window.
10. In the Server Explorer, expand the node for the database connection and view the contents of the Tables node.
11. To create a sample **DataAdapter** object in the application, drag a sample table to the Windows Form Designer.
12. Create a new **DataSet** as you learned in Chapter 12 and as shown in the following example.

```
Dim myDataSet As New DataSet()
OleDbDataAdapter1.Fill(myDataSet)
```

13. Add a **TextBox** object to the Windows Form in the designer using the Toolbox.
14. Access the Properties window and expand the DataBindings node.
15. Access the drop-down menu for the Text property and choose the column you would like bound to the control from the **DataSet** object.

It is possible to bind a control to a particular data provider during runtime. This is accomplished using the DataBindings.Add method. This Add method uses three parameters:

- The property name you need to bind; this is provided as a String.
- The data source to which you want to bind; this is provided as an object.
- The data member of the data source to which you want to bind.

The following code is an example of using simple binding to bind a TextBox control during runtime.

```
myTextBox.Databindings.Add("Text", _
     myDataSet.Employees, "EmployeeID")
```

You might not always use all three parameters of the Add method. When this is the case, you supply an empty string for the unused parameter. A classic case of this is when you bind a control to an object that does not possess multiple data members, for example, an array. The following code is an example of binding an array to the property of a control.

```
Dim mySampleStrings(4) As String
mySampleStrings(0) = "Sample"
mySampleStrings(1) = "String"
mySampleStrings(2) = "Array"
mySampleStrings(3) = "For"
mySampleStrings(4) = "Binding"
mySampleTextBox.DataBindings.Add _
      ("Text", mySampleStrings, "")
```

You can also remove a data binding in code during runtime. To do so, call the DataBindings.Remove method and use the **Binding** object as the parameter for the method, as shown in the following example.

```
txtMyTextBox.DataBindings.Remove _
     txtMyTextBox.DataBindings("Text"))
```

To quickly and efficiently remove all the data bindings from a control, use the DataBindings.Clear method, as shown in the following example.

```
txtMyTextBox.DataBindings.Clear()
```

Maintaining Data Currency

The **CurrencyManager** object allows developers to navigate through records and update data-bound properties. If multiple data sources in an application are bound to multiple controls, each maintains its own **CurrencyManager**. In fact, each Windows Forms uses a central object called the **BindingContext** to manage multiple **CurrencyManager** objects.

You use the BindingContext property of each form to manage record positions in the data. In the following example, you use the **BindingContext** object of the current form to access the **CurrencyManager** of a data source. The data source is a table named Employees from a **DataSet** object named mySampleDataSet.

```
Me.BindingContext(mySampleDataSet.Employees)
```

The **BindingContext** object simplifies navigation through records thanks to the Position property of these objects. For example, the following code sets the current record to the first record of the data source.

```
Me.BindingContext(mySampleDataSet.Employees). _
      Position = 0
```

The following sample code advances the current record by one.

```
Me.BindingContext(mySampleDataSet.Employees). _
      Position += 1
```

The following sample code moves the current record back by one.

```
Me.BindingContext(mySampleDataSet.Employees). _
      Position -= 1
```

The following sample code advances to the last record in the set.

```
Me.BindingContext(mySampleDataSet.Employees). _
      Position = mySampleDataSet.Tables("Employees"). _
      Rows.Count - 1
```

Developers often provide users with a user interface change if they reach the beginning or end of a set of data. For example, a common approach disables Next or Back buttons in the event the user reaches the beginning or end. To code this, use the PositionChanged event of the **CurrencyManager**, as shown in the following example.

```
Public Sub OnPositionChanged(ByVal Sender As Object, _
      ByVal e As System.EventArgs)
      If Me.BindingContext(myDataSet, "Employees"). _
            Position = 0 Then
            btnBackButton.Enabled = False
      Else
            btnBackButton.Enabled = True
      End If
      If Me.BindingContext(myDataSet.Employees). _
            Position = myDataSet.Tables("Employees"). _
            Rows.Count -1 Then
            btnForwardButton.Enabled = False
      Else
            btnForwardButton.Enabled = True
      End If
End Sub
```

Note that you must also tie this event to the method that is to handle it. Use the following code in the form's constructor.

```
AddHandler Me.BindingContext(myDataSet.Employees). _
     PositionChanged, AddressOf Me.OnPositionChanged
```

Complex Binding

As discussed earlier, binding more than one record at a time to a control property is referred to as complex binding. Developers often use this technique to allow an end user to choose an option from several database-driven choices.

To create complex bound controls, you set the DataSource property of a control that supports complex binding. Use the Properties window to set the property during design time. During runtime, it is easy to use code, as shown in the following example.

```
myDataGrid.DataSource = mySampleDataSet.Employees
```

Certain controls that permit complex binding only allow binding to a single column of the data set. Examples of these controls include ListBox, CheckedListBox, and ComboBox. You must set the DisplayMember property for these controls. This property takes a string value that represents the name of the bound column, as shown in the following example.

```
myListBox.DataSource = myDataSet.Employees
myListBox.DisplayMember = "Emp_LName"
```

Filtering, Sorting, and Editing Bound Data

The **DataView** object is the key object that allows developers to filter, sort, and edit data bound to Windows controls. It is a filter that presents a subset of the data in an underlying **DataTable** object.

Creating DataViews

To create a **DataView** object during design time, use the DataView button of the Data tab in the Toolbox to drag a **DataView** object to the Windows Form Designer. Next, with the **DataView** object selected, set the Table property using the Properties window. Then, bind controls to the **DataView** using the DataBindings property of the Properties window.

Creating a **DataView** in code is also very simple. Just be sure to specify the **DataTable** object that the **DataView** object will filter, as shown in the following code.

```
Dim myDataView As New DataView(myDataTable)
```

It is also possible to create a **DataView** that is not associated with a **DataTable**. This is fine, as long as you dynamically set the Table property of the view later in the code. The following sample code creates the **DataView** without specifying a **DataTable** object.

```
Dim myDataView As New DataView()
```

The following code associates the appropriate DataTable later in the code.

```
myDataView.Table = myDataTable
```

Sorting Data

The **DataView** object includes a Sort property to enable developers to easily sort data in an application. Simply assign a String value to the Sort property. Visual Basic parses this String value and converts it to an expression.

To sort the data based on a particular column, simply provide the column name as the String value, as shown in the following example.

```
myDataView.Sort = "Emp_LName"
```

To sort data by more than one column, specify the column names as Strings, separating each with a comma, as shown in the following example.

```
myDataView.Sort = "Emp_LName, Emp_FName"
```

Data is sorted in ascending order by default. To sort data in descending order, add the keyword DESC to the column name. The code in the following example sorts both the employee last name and employee first name columns in descending order.

```
myDataView.Sort = "Emp_LName DESC, Emp_FName DESC"
```

Filtering Data

The RowFilter property of the **DataView** object allows developers to easily filter data. As with the Sort property, use a String to specify the criteria for filtering. Just as with Sort, this String value is parsed to an expression. The code in the following example presents only employees whose last name is Smith.

```
myDataView.RowFilter = "Emp_LName = 'Smith'"
```

To ensure that RowFilter expressions do not produce syntax errors, use SQL syntax in the strings. For example, you must enclose String literals in single quotes while dates must be enclosed in pound symbols. You can also use logical operators such as And, Or, and Not, as shown in the following example.

```
myDataView.RowFilter = "Emp_LName = 'Smith" _
      OR Emp_FName = 'John'"
```

Arithmetic, concatenation, and relational operators add even more flexibility to filtering, as shown in the following example.

```
myDataView.RowFilter = "Price * 1.15 <= 10"
```

Or perhaps you would like to use In and Like operators to search for specific string values, as shown in the following example.

```
myDataView.RowFilter = "Emp_FName IN ('John', 'Bill', 'Bob')"
myDataView.RowFilter = "Emp_FName LIKE 'S%'"
```

NOTE In SQL syntax, * is a wildcard that stands for any single character, while % is a wildcard that stands for any number of characters.

The RowState property of the **DataView** object enables developers to also filter data based upon the state of rows. Table 18-1 summarizes the values that can be used with this property.

EXAM TIP It is a little known fact that you can set this property to multiple values at once. For example, you can set RowState to *Added, Deleted* in order to view newly added or deleted rows.

Editing Data

A **DataView** object is also the key to editing data. Developers use three properties to determine whether the underlying data can be edited. Table 18-2 describes these properties.

Using the DataViewManager Class

Developers use the **DataViewManager** object to create and manage **DataView** objects for **DataSet** tables on demand. Creating a new **DataViewManager** is simple, as shown in the following code.

```
Dim myDataViewManager As New DataViewManager(myDataSet)
```

You can also create the **DataViewManager** using the following method.

```
Dim myDataViewManager As New DataViewManager
myDataViewManager.DataSet = myOtherDataSet
```

Once the **DataViewManager** is associated with the appropriate **DataSet**, you manage RowFilter, Sort, and other relevant properties using the **DataViewSettings** collection. This collection exposes the DataView properties—there is one property for each table in

Name	Description
Unchanged	Displays rows that have not been changed
Added	Displays added rows
Deleted	Displays rows that have been deleted
OriginalRows	Displays all original rows including unchanged and deleted rows
CurrentRows	Displays all of the current rows including added, modified, and unchanged rows
ModifiedCurrent	Displays the current version
ModifiedOriginal	Displays the original version although it has been modified

Table 18-1 Values for the RowState Property

Table 18-2 DataView Properties Permitting Data Modifications

Name	Description
AllowDelete	Allows the deletion of rows
AllowEdit	Allows the editing of rows
AllowNew	Allows the addition of rows

the **DataSet**. You set the values for these properties by specifying which table to set DataView properties for and then specifying the property itself, as shown in the following example.

```
myDataViewManager.DataViewSettings("Employees"). _
      RowFilter = "Emp_FName = 'John'"
```

You can also retrieve DataViews from the **DataViewManager** using the CreateDataView method. This requires a reference to a **DataTable**, as shown in the following example.

```
Dim myDataView As DataView
myDataView = myDataViewManager.CreateDataView _
      (myDataSet.Tables(0))
```

Summary

To view and manipulate data in applications, developers use a process called data binding. Data binding uses data providers and data consumers. The data providers are the sources of data, while the data consumers are the Windows controls that use the data in the application.

Simple binding means that one record at a time is bound to a control. Complex binding permits multiple records to be bound to a single control.

To navigate through records in a data provider, you use the BindingContext property of each form. The Position property permits you to do this easily.

DataView objects allow you to increase the flexibility with which you display data. These objects permit the easy sorting, filtering, or editing of data. You can even create these powerful objects dynamically in code using **DataViewManager** objects.

Test Questions

1. Which of the following objects can serve the role of data provider in a Windows Forms application? Choose all that are correct.

   A. DataSets

   B. DataViews

   C. Collections

   D. DataColumns

2. What type of binding allows you to bind multiple records to a single control, such as a DataGrid or ListBox?

   A. Simple

   B. Complex

   C. Inferior

   D. Sophisticated

3. Which of the following properties of the **ControlBindingsCollection** class do you use to create simple bound controls?

   A. DataBindings

   B. Bindings

   C. SimpleBindings

   D. Fill

4. Which of the following code samples sets the current record to the first record of the data source?

   A. Me.BindingContext.Position = 0

   B. Me.BindingContext(mySampleDataSet).Position = 0

   C. Me.BindingContext(mySampleDataSet.Employees).Position = 0

   D. Me.BindingContext(mySampleDataSet.Employees).Position.Start = 0

5. Which of the following properties of a control that supports complex binding do you set to create complex bound controls?

   A. Binding

   B. BindingContext

   C. Context

   D. DataSource

6. Which of the following lines of code creates a new **DataView** object?

   A. Dim myDataView

   B. Dim myDataView As New View(Data)

   C. Dim myDataView As New DataView(myDataTable)

   D. New DataView(myDataTable)

7. The Sort property of a **DataView** object accepts what type of value?

   A. Numeric

   B. String

   C. Integer

   D. Boolean

8. The **DataView** object includes which of the following properties to allow for the filtering of bound data?
   A. Filter
   B. Sort
   C. Reorganize
   D. RowFilter
9. Which character allows you to specify any number of characters?
   A. *
   B. &
   C. #
   D. %
10. Which of the following lines of code creates a new **DataViewManager**?
   A. Dim myDataViewManager As New DataViewManager(myDataSet)
   B. Dim myDataViewManager
   C. New myDataViewManager
   D. New Data

Test Answers

1. A, B, C, D.
2. B.
3. A.
4. C.
5. D.
6. C.
7. B.
8. D.
9. D.
10. A.

CHAPTER 19

Testing and Deploying a Windows Forms Application

In this chapter, you will

- Find out about the debugging tools of Visual Basic .NET
- Learn how to use the **Debug** and **Trace** classes
- Understand how to create a unit test plan
- Learn how to handle and throw exceptions
- Study options for deploying an application

Once you have constructed a Windows Forms application, you are not finished by any means. You still must determine whether the application contains any bugs, and you also must formulate a plan of deployment. Once the deployment plan is formulated, you must actually implement the deployment to ensure its success. This chapter ensures that you are ready for the tasks involved in these processes. It can save hours of frustration not only for you, but also for your end users.

Using the Debugging Tools

Bugs in an application are inevitable. It is up to you to eliminate as many as possible prior to the application's deployment. Three types of errors are commonly introduced into applications:

- Syntax errors
- Runtime errors
- Logic errors

Syntax errors are perhaps the easiest to deal with. These simple errors indicate that the Visual Basic .NET compiler does not understand the code. A typical example is a typo within a command or the omission of a required character such as a period.

Visual Basic .NET is unique in that it can help debug syntax errors in code as they are entered. These errors are underlined in red as they occur and are added to the Task List window.

Double-clicking the error in this window displays and highlights the error where it exists in the code. Because the item is already highlighted, you simply press F1 to obtain additional information about the error.

As their name implies, runtime errors occur when the application is executed and typically include operations that are impossible to carry out such as division-by-zero errors or attempted security breaches. When these errors occur, they raise a special class called an exception. Later in this chapter, you learn to write code to handle exceptions as they occur so that the application does not halt its execution.

Logical errors can be the toughest to track down and eliminate. These errors occur when an application works fine but produces incorrect results. For example, an application is to return calculations, but the calculations are not accurate when they are produced. Logical errors typically require intensive testing to track down. They are one of the main error types that is addressed using the tools explored in this section.

Using Break Mode

Break mode is a powerful way to test an application. When you build and run an application in Break mode, you can halt execution at a specific point and execute code line by line. While you execute the application in this manner, you can observe variable values and property values. Visual Basic can enter Break mode in any of the following circumstances:

- You force Break mode by choosing an option from the Debug main menu or the Toolbar.
- Execution reaches a line of code that you have flagged with a breakpoint.
- Execution reaches a Stop statement.
- An unhandled exception is raised in the application.

Once you are in Break mode, you can take advantage of a number of options to debug code. These options are located on the Debug menu. They are described in Table 19-1.

Table 19-1 Debug Menu Options

Option	Description
Windows	Allows you to access the many debugging menu windows in Visual Basic .NET
Start/Continue	Runs the application in Debug mode; or if the application is in Break mode, this option continues execution
Break All	Halts execution and causes entry into Break mode
Stop Debugging	Stops the debugging process and returns to design mode
Detach All	Detaches the debugger from all processes and does not halt program execution
Restart	Terminates and restarts the program's execution

Table 19-1 Debug Menu Options *(continued)*

Option	Description
Apply Code Changes	Used only for C/C++ programming
Processes	Displays the Processes window
Exceptions	Displays the Exceptions window
Step Into	Runs the next executable line of code; if this line calls a method, execution halts at the beginning of the method
Step Over	Runs the next executable line of code; if this line calls a method, the method executes and execution halts at the next line within the current method
Step Out	Executes the remainder of the current method and halts at the next line of code in the calling method
QuickWatch	Displays the QuickWatch window
New Breakpoint	Displays the New Breakpoint window
Clear All Breakpoints	Removes all breakpoints from the application
Disable All Breakpoints	Disables all breakpoints but does not delete them

Although the Debug menu presents many options for debugging an application, there are other options. Some debugging functions are accessed by right-clicking an element in the code window, and then accessing the function from the context menu. Table 19-2 lists these functions.

Setting Breakpoints

A powerful method for debugging an application involves halting execution at specific locations within the code by setting breakpoints. Breakpoints are lines of code or particular conditions that trigger Break mode in the application. Developers use three basic breakpoint types when debugging an application. Table 19-3 summarizes these breakpoints.

Table 19-2 Debugging Functions Available from the Context Menu

Function	Description
Insert Breakpoint	Inserts a breakpoint at the selected line
New Breakpoint	Displays the New Breakpoint window
Add Watch	Adds the selected expression to the Watch window
QuickWatch	Displays the QuickWatch window
Show Next Statement	Highlights the next statement to be executed
Run To Cursor	Runs program execution to the selected line
Set Next Statement	Designates the selected line as the next line of code to execute

Table 19-3 Breakpoint Types in Visual Basic .NET

Breakpoint	Description
Function	Halts execution at a specified location within a function
File	Halts execution when a specified location in a file is reached
Address	Halts execution when a specified memory address is reached

Function breakpoints are used most often. There are several ways to set these breakpoints. You can click in the gray bar to the left of code in the code window. You can right-click the line of code and choose Insert Breakpoint from the pop-up window. Finally, you can choose the New Breakpoint option from the Debug menu.

If you set breakpoints using the Debug menu, you are led to the new Breakpoints window as shown in Figure 19-1. The Breakpoints window allows you to manage all the breakpoints in an application; see Figure 19-2. It also allows you to specify conditions or hit counts that must be met in order to trigger the breakpoint. Finally, the Breakpoints window makes it very easy to disable or delete breakpoints from an application.

EXAM TIP A common condition to set on breakpoints is to pause the execution of an application only if the value of a specified variable changes.

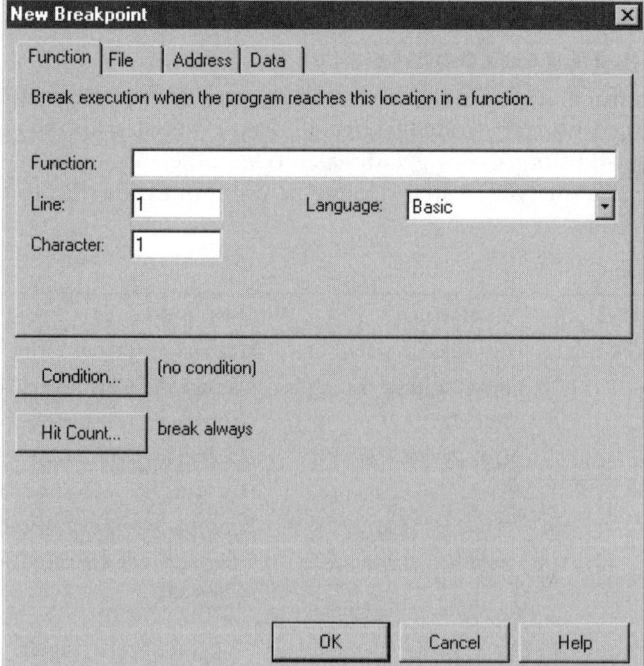

Figure 19-1 The New Breakpoint window

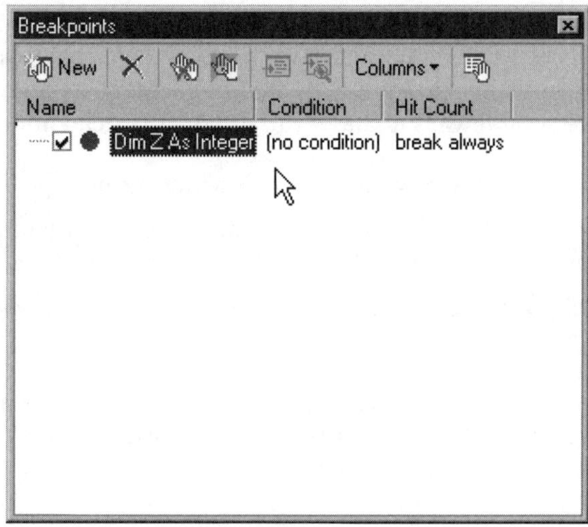

Figure 19-2 The Breakpoints window

Using the Debugging Windows

In addition to the Breakpoints window, Visual Basic .NET includes other windows for debugging. Most of these windows are displayed by selecting the appropriate option from the View menu.

One of these windows is the Output window, which provides details regarding the compilation and execution of an application. This information can include notifications about the loading of assemblies, and more importantly it can include output from any Debug or Trace statements in the application. We discuss the **Debug** and **Trace** classes later in this chapter.

Other useful debugging windows are the Locals, Autos, and Watch windows. Developers use these integrated development environment (IDE) elements to monitor and edit the value of variables during execution of the application. To access these windows while debugging, choose Debug, then Windows, and then the appropriate window.

Developers use the Locals window to monitor the value of all the variables in the current procedure during execution in debug mode. If complex variable types are used, they appear in the Locals window as an expandable node that permits the viewing of member settings. To modify the value of a variable using this window, simply type over the value as displayed by the Value column. Notice that when you modify a value in this manner, it appears in red within the Locals window.

The Autos window is a "shorthand" version of the Locals window. This window displays the same data in the same presentation as the Locals window, but it only displays the variable on the current line and the variables on the three lines above and below the current line.

NOTE For testing purposes, you can change variable values in the Autos window just as you would in the Locals window.

Visual Basic .NET also provides four Watch windows. These windows allow you to add variables whose values you want to track. Use the Watch windows instead of the Locals or Autos window when you want to track variables even if they are no longer within scope.

There are several ways to add a variable to a Watch window:

- Select an empty row in the Watch window and type the variable name.
- Find the variable in the appropriate Code Editor window and right-click it; then, choose Add Watch from the context menu.
- Highlight and drag a variable from the Code Editor window to the Watch window.

If you need to quickly evaluate a variable's value, and do not expect to view the information for an extended time period, you can use the QuickWatch window. This window displays variable information for a single variable only.

TIP The QuickWatch window enables you to add a variable to the full-featured Watch window using the Add Watch button.

To add a variable to the QuickWatch window, simply right-click the appropriate variable in the Code Editor and choose QuickWatch from the context menu.

- Developers use the Command window to either issue commands or to debug and evaluate expressions. This window has two different operating modes: Command mode and Immediate mode.

Command mode allows developers to execute commands or aliases directly in the Visual Basic .NET IDE without accessing the menu system. Obviously, this mode of the Command window is also useful for executing commands that have no menu item equivalent.

TIP Command mode is the default mode for the Command window. Command mode is indicated by the appearance of the words "Command Window" in the title bar and the greater than (>) sign, which appears in the window as a prompt.

When the Command window is running in Command mode, use a question mark character (?) to preface an expression you would like to evaluate, as shown in the following example.

```
? mySampleVariable
```

Use the *immed* Command to enter Immediate mode.

CEDevelopers typically use the Immediate mode of the Command window strictly for debugging. This might include evaluating expressions, executing statements, or printing variable values.

NOTE To issue a command while in Immediate mode, you must preface the command with a greater than (>) sign.

The Break mode of the Command window is very useful for debugging. It allows developers to preempt an expression or property value with a question mark in the Command window and have the value returned, as shown in the following example.

```
? txtMyTextBox.Text
```

Table 13-4 summarizes additional windows that are useful for debugging tasks.

EXAM TIP The Me window is very useful for viewing all the properties and their values of the currently executing object.

Using the Debug and Trace Classes

When debugging simple applications, the tools previously described in this chapter are typically sufficient. But complex applications might require more sophisticated troubleshooting methodologies. The **Trace** and **Debug** classes are designed for more complex troubleshooting environments.

The **Debug** class allows developers to create and log informative messages about program conditions while the application is executing. The **Trace** class allows developers to create sophisticated diagnostic information and deliver these messages even after the application is compiled and released.

Figure 19-4 Miscellaneous Debugging Windows in Visual Basic .NET

Window	Description
Running Documents	Displays a list of documents currently loaded into the process you are running
Me	Displays the data members of the object associated with the current method
Call Stack	Displays the names of functions on the call stack, parameter types, and parameter values
Threads	Displays threads running in the program you are debugging
Modules	Displays the modules used by the application
Memory	Displays the raw values stored in memory
Disassembly	Displays assembly code corresponding to the instructions created by the compiler
Registers	Displays register contents

Both the **Debug** and **Trace** classes contain methods that permit you to test conditions during runtime and log the results. These results can be written to the Output window for viewing and/or they can be sent to the Listeners collection. The Listeners collection includes Listeners that write to files, write to event logs, and more.

As mentioned, you write output to the Listeners collection using methods of the **Trace** and **Debug** classes. Table 13-5 describes the six methods for writing this debugging output.

EXAM TIP Although the **Debug** and **Trace** classes may seem identical, the **Debug** class is used typically for debugging during the design phase of development. The **Trace** class is used for testing and optimizing an application after it has been compiled.

The following code is a simple example of the use of the WriteIf method with the **Debug** class.

```
Debug.WriteIf(X<=Y, "X is less than or equal to Y")
```

EXAM TIP To ensure that you can view the output of Debug statements, select the Debug build configuration. Breakpoints and methods of the **Debug** class are ignored when the solution configuration is set to Release.

To create a hierarchical display of error messages, use the Indent and Unindent methods or you can set the IndentSize and IndentLevel properties.

Figure 19-5 Methods of the Debug and Trace Classes

Method	Description
Write	Used to write text to the Listeners collection unconditionally
WriteLine	Used to write text to the Listeners collection and includes a carriage return
WriteIf	Used to write text to the Listeners collection only if the specified Boolean expression is True
WriteLineIf	Used to write text to the Listeners collection (including a carriage return) only if the specified Boolean expression is True
Assert	Used to write an assertion message to the Listeners collection if the specified Boolean expression is False; it also causes a message box to appear containing the assertion message
Fail	Used to create an assertion that automatically fails without a test condition; Fail writes an assertion message to the Listeners collection and displays a message box to the user

The following example increments and decrements the indent level and emits tracing messages.

```
Trace.WriteLine("List of errors:")
Trace.Indent()
Trace.WriteLine("Error 1: File not found")
Trace.WriteLine("Error 2: Directory not found")
Trace.Unindent()
Trace.WriteLine("End of list of errors")
Trace.WriteLine("List of errors:");
 Trace.Indent();
 Trace.WriteLine("Error 1: File not found");
 Trace.WriteLine("Error 2: Directory not found");
 Trace.Unindent();
 Trace.WriteLine("End of list of errors");
```

This example produces the following output.

```
List of errors:
     Error 1: File not found
     Error 2: Directory not found
 End of list of errors
```

By default, the Listeners collection contains a member named DefaultTraceListener. This member is created automatically and receives Trace and Debug output even if no other Listeners have been employed. The Trace and debug output appears in the Output window of Visual Studio.

To log Trace messages in a more sophisticated fashion, you must create at least one more Listener. The .NET Framework provides the TextWriterTraceListener and the EventLogTraceListener members for this purpose.

As its name implies, you use the TextWriterTraceListener to write Trace output to a text file. First, you must create or open the text file to be used for this purpose. Next, you create an instance of the TextWriterTraceListener that specifies the file as a target. Finally, you add the TextWriterTraceListener to the Listeners collection.

Here is an example.

```
Dim mySampleLog As New System.IO.FileStream _
      ("C:\mySampleLog.txt", IO.FileMode. _
      OpenOrCreate)
Dim mySampleListener As New TextWriterTraceListener _
       (mySampleLog)
Trace.Listeners.Add(mySampleListener)
```

Although the preceding code sample looks complete, it is not. In order for all of the output from the **Debug** and **Trace** classes to be written to the file, you must flush the Trace buffer using the Flush method, as shown in the following example.

```
Trace.Flush()
```

You can also set the AutoFlush property of the **Trace** class to True, as shown in the following example. This causes the buffer to be automatically flushed after every write.

```
Trace.AutoFlush = True
```

You use the EventLogTraceListener to log **Trace** output to an **EventLog** object. First, you must create or open an event log. Next you create an EventLogTraceListener, and, finally, you add it to the Listeners collection.

The following code shows an example of logging **Trace** output to an event log.

```
Dim mySampleLog As New EventLog("Debug Log")
mySampleLog.Source = "Trace Output"
Dim mySampleListener As New EventLogTraceListener _
      (mySampleLog)
```

NOTE Remember to call Trace.Flush after each write, or set the AutoFlush property to True.

For added flexibility, you can use Trace switches in an application. These configurable switches are used to determine whether Trace statements are displayed. Typically, you configure these switches after the application is distributed using the application configuration file.

There are two basic types of Trace switches: BooleanSwitch and TraceSwitch.

The following code is an example of the creation of a new TraceSwitch. The creation requires you to provide two parameters: DisplayName and Description. DisplayName determines the name of the switch in the user interface; Description contains a short description of the switch.

```
Dim mySampleTraceSwitch As New TraceSwitch _
      ("SampleSwitch", "This is a sample descrip.")
```

The **BooleanSwitch** class returns a Boolean value; the **TraceSwitch** class allows you to set the level represented by the switch to one of five settings depending on the output you desire. These settings are exposed by the TraceSwitch.Level property. Table 19-6 describes the settings.

The **TraceSwitch** class also exposes four read-only Boolean properties representing the different trace levels. These properties are TraceSwitch.TraceError, TraceSwitch.TraceWarning, TraceSwitch.TraceInfo, and TraceSwitch.TraceVerbose.

Figure 19-6 TraceSwitch Settings

Setting	Description
TraceLevel.Off	A TraceSwitch not currently active; integer value = 0
TraceLevel.Error	A very brief error message; integer value = 1
TraceLevel.Warning	Error messages and warnings; integer value = 2
TraceLevel.Info	Error messages, warnings, and short informative messages; integer value = 3
TraceLevel.Verbose	Error messages, warnings, and detailed descriptions of program execution; integer value = 4

These read-only properties correspond to the levels of the same name; when the TraceSwitch.Level property is set, these Boolean properties are automatically set to the appropriate level.

Remember, Trace switches are used to test whether to write Trace output, as shown in the following example.

```
Trace.WriteLineIf(mySampleTraceSwitch.TraceInfo _
        = True, "Sample Error Text")
```

When configuring an application's configuration file, use the DisplayName property you configured for the Trace switch for identification purposes in the .config file. When you make the change to the .config file, remember that you must also specify the value to which the switch is set. The value must be an integer in this file.

When configuring the .config file, follow these rules:

- For **BooleanSwitch** objects, 0 represents Off, and any non-zero value represents On.
- For **TraceSwitch** objects, the values 0 through 4 correspond to the appropriate values, while any integer greater than 4 is treated as TraceLevel.Verbose.

The following code is an example of a .config file configuration.

```
<?xml version="1.0" encoding="Windows-1252"?>
<configuration>
<system.diagnostics>
      <switches>
            <add name="mySampleBooleanSwitch" _
                  value="0" />
            <add name="mySampleTraceSwitch" _
                  value="3" />
      </switches>
</system.diagnostics>
</configuration>
```

EXAM TIP Setting the Trace switch level to 4 provides the greatest level of detail in Trace messages.

Creating a Unit Test Plan

Typically, during the testing phase of application development, developers test the code method by method, testing each individual method with a variety of inputs and execution parameters. This approach is referred to as unit testing. This name is appropriate because the application is tested using the individual units that make it up.

When testing units in an application, developers typically provide representative sample inputs. These sample inputs are commonly called test cases. It is critical to design test cases carefully, because this process is fundamental to the overall success of the testing. One important decision is the number of test cases to implement. Using too few may cause errors to exist in the application, while using too many may waste time and other resources.

It is up to you to ensure that your application can handle different kinds of data. If data is provided outside normal bounds, the application should still behave gracefully and not crash. Consider including the following types of data when creating test cases:

- **Normal data** Do not forget the obvious. Be sure to test application units against data that would be normal and typical. Normal data spans the normal range of operation and should include normal minimum values and normal maximum values. Although you usually cannot test every possible occurrence of data, test enough to help guarantee a working application.
- **Boundary conditions** Also consider testing data that is "off by one" from the normal minimum and maximum parameters. For example, to test a maximum value, you should test not only the maximum value, but also the maximum value minus one, and the maximum value plus one.
- **Bad data** Do not forget to test the application against bad data. This includes data that is well outside the scope of acceptable values. Again, you should ensure that the application does not crash and responds to the bad data gracefully. What is sometimes worse than crashing is an application that accepts bad data and then produces erroneous results. Be sure to test for this condition as well.
- **Data combinations** Test cases should include a variety of the data forms included in this list. Perhaps your application works fine if certain combinations of normal and bad data are used.

Handling and Throwing Exceptions

To enable applications to gracefully respond to errors and continue functioning, Visual Basic .NET provides structured exception handling.

When an application encounters a runtime error, it raises an exception. An exception is an instance of a class called **System.Exception**. Exceptions contain features that allow you to respond to the error condition. For example, you might use the Message property of the exception to provide a readable description of the error.

TIP Besides system-defined exceptions, you can create your own exceptions using the **System.ApplicationException** class, which is covered later in this chapter.

When a runtime error occurs and an exception is created in an application, an exception handler is searched for in the method where the error occurred. If no exception handling structure is discovered there, the next method higher up in the application is checked for an exception handling structure. If exception handling code is not found anywhere in the stack, a default system message box appears and the application terminates. In addition, the end user is not given the opportunity to save work or recover from the error in any way. For this reason, it is very important to provide appropriate exception handlers in an application.

Creating Exception Handlers

You create exception handlers on a per method basis. You should definitely create exception handlers for methods that are likely to encounter errors, such as methods dealing with file access. Exception handlers in Visual Basic .NET use a Try . . .Catch . . . Finally syntax.

To use this syntax, follow these steps:

1. Wrap the code the handler is associated with in a Try block.
2. Add one or more Catch blocks to handle the possible exceptions.
3. Add any code that always must be executed to a Finally block.

The following example demonstrates how this approach is structured in code.

```
Public Sub
      Try
            ' The code placed here is monitored for exceptions
      Catch e As System.ArgumentNullException
            ' Code is placed in this block that should execute
            ' if there is a System.ArgumentNullException thrown
      Catch e As System.Exception
            ' Code is placed here to execute if any other
            ' Exceptions might occur
      Finally
            ' Code is placed here that executes no matter what
      End Try
End Sub
```

Notice that if an error is encountered within a Try block, execution transfers immediately to the Catch blocks. Once the code in the appropriate Catch block executes, the code in the Finally block executes.

EXAM TIP Only one Catch block executes per exception. For this reason, be sure to compose Catch blocks from the most specific to the least specific.

Throwing Exceptions

There are times in application programming when you want to throw exceptions in code. For example, perhaps the exception handling code cannot fully handle all possible problems. So you have the code throw a problem it cannot handle farther up the stack. This is simple to do using the Throw keyword, as shown in the following example.

```
Try
      ' Here is the code that is being
      ' checked for exceptions
Catch e As Sytem.NullReferenceException
      ' This code attempts to handle the exception
      ' If it cannot - notice the next line
      ' Throws the exception, sending it
      ' Further up the stack
      Throw e
End Try
```

PART V

If you want to throw the exception and provide additional information to the next application level, you can wrap the exception in a new exception. The following example creates a new exception by wrapping the original exception. Notice that an informative message is included using a string.

```
Try
      ' Here is the code that is being
      ' checked for exceptions
Catch e As Sytem.NullReferenceException
      Throw New NullReferenceException _
           ("This is a sample string", e)
```

Creating Custom Exceptions

When developing your own components in an application, it is often necessary to create and throw custom exceptions. You accomplish this by inheriting from the **System.ApplicationException** class. This class encapsulates all the functionality that you need, including Message, StackTrace, and InnerException properties that serve as a base for the custom functionality. The following example demonstrates custom exception creation.

```
Public Class mySampleComponentException
Inherits System.ApplicationException
      Private mySampleComponent As SampleComponent
      Public ReadOnly Property ErrorSampleComponent() _
            As SampleComponent
            Get
                 Return mySampleComponent
            End Get
      End Property

Public Sub New(ByVal As SampleComponent, _
      ByVal Message As String)
      MyBase.New(Message)
      mySampleComponent = M
End Sub
End Class
```

Once you have created an exception class, you can throw a new instance of it when conditions become unacceptable, as shown in the following example.

```
Dim mySample As New SampleComponent()
Throw New mySampleComponentException _
      (mySample, "mySample is corrupt!")
```

NOTE In the preceding example, the code that actually corrupts the component is missing.

Deploying an Application

Once you have designed, constructed, tested, and debugged an application, you must still deploy it. Whether your plan is to deploy the application via a Web site, a network server, or a removable medium such as a CD or floppy disk, Visual Basic .NET makes the process simple.

Planning Deployment

There are many ways to deploy a Visual Basic .NET application. These methods range from the simple to the complex. The first thing you must do is plan your deployment, selecting a deployment method that is appropriate for the situation. This section walks you through the various options for deployment.

Deploying with XCOPY

The most basic form of deployment is an XCOPY deployment. This method derives its name from the very simple DOS XCOPY command. The XCOPY utility simply copies the application directory on the development machine to the target directory on the client system.

You utilize the XCOPY deployment process from the command prompt. Use a /S switch to indicate that you are copying subdirectories as well as the parent directory. The following example copies the SampleApplication directory including all its subdirectories from the D: drive to the C: drive.

```
XCOPY D:\SampleApplication C:\SampleApplication /s
```

As shown, you supply the source and then the destination in XCOPY syntax. Table 19-7 describes the switches that are available with this utility for copying applications to a target.

Figure 19-7 Switches for the XCOPY Utility

Switch	Description
/A	Copies only files that have the Archive attribute set; does not change the attribute
/M	Copies only files that have the Archive attribute set; turns off the attribute
/D:m-d-y	Copies only files changed on or after the date specified
/EXCLUDE:file1[+file2]	Specifies a list of files to exclude from the copy
/P	Prompts you before creating each destination file
/S	Copies subdirectories
/E	Copies subdirectories, including those that are empty
/V	Verifies each new file created
/W	Prompts for a key press before the copy operation
/C	Continues the copy operation even if errors occur
/I	If the destination does not exist and more than one file is being copied, assumes the destination is a directory
/Q	Does not display file names while copying
/F	Displays full source and destination file names while copying
/L	Displays files that are to be copied

Figure 19-7 Switches for the XCOPY Utility *(continued)*

Switch	Description
/G	Allows the copying of encrypted files
/H	Copies hidden and system files
/R	Overwrites read-only files
/T	Creates the directory structure, but does not copy files
/U	Copies only the files that already exist in the destination
/K	Copies file attributes
/N	Copies using the generated short names
/O	Copies file ownership and ACL information
/X	Copies file audit settings
/Y	Suppresses prompting to confirm that you want to overwrite an existing file
/-Y	Causes prompting for file overwrites
/Z	Copies networked files in restartable mode

There are several important factors to consider if you use XCOPY for deployments. First, all the files required by your application must exist in the directory structure you are copying. This includes any compiled .EXE files and .DLL files that the application requires. Second, the .NET Framework must be installed on the target machine. Finally, additional resources that the application requires (such as a database) must also reside on the target machine.

Creating Setup Projects

Because XCOPY is inadequate for many application deployments, you must use Visual Studio .NET to create a Windows Installer setup project. Setup projects provide a complete, robust set of installation options that cover almost all your deployment needs. They are easily added to a solution, enabling their seamless deployment once the application is finished.

For Windows Forms applications, there are two types of setup projects: merge module projects and setup projects. Merge module projects deploy controls or components that do not exist as standalone applications and cannot be deployed to a target system directly. Setup projects deploy executable applications.

EXAM TIP Merge modules are setup applications that can only be called from other setup applications.

The Setup Project Wizard in Visual Studio .NET enables developers to easily create a base setup project, which can then be customized in the Visual Studio IDE.

Exercise 19-1: Using the Setup Project Wizard In this exercise you will use the Setup Project Wizard to create a standard setup for a Windows application.

1. Open an existing project in Visual Studio .NET.

2. Choose File | Add Project | New Project to display the Add New Project dialog box.
3. Select the Setup and Deployment Projects folder in the Project Types pane.
4. Choose the Setup Wizard in the Templates area.
5. Name your project **MySampleSetupProject** in the Name field.

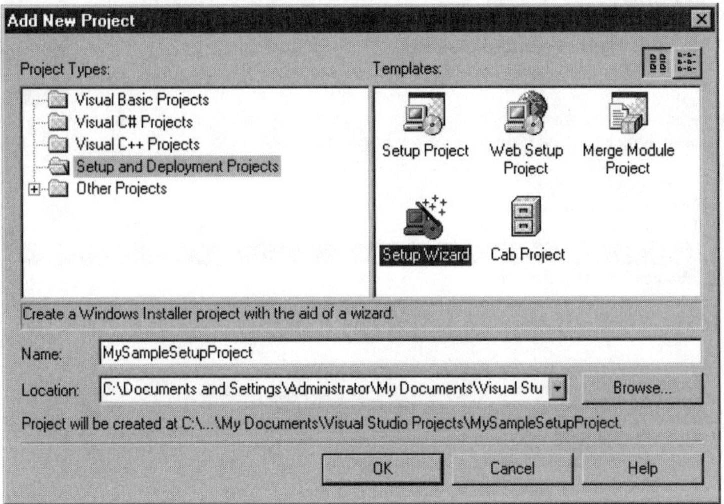

6. Click OK, and then click Next in the Welcome dialog box that appears.
7. The Choose A Project Type page appears. Notice how easy it is to designate that you would like to create a merge module for your Windows application. In this exercise, accept the default and create a standard setup for your Windows application. Click Next.

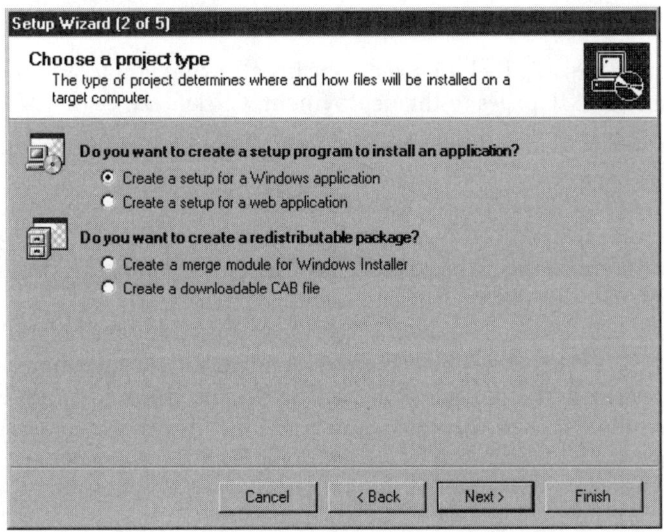

8. The Choose Project Outputs To Include page allows you to specify the files from your solution that you want to include in the deployment. To view a description of each category, click the category and view the Description field. Choose the Primary Output, Localized Resources, and Content Files categories. Then, click Next.

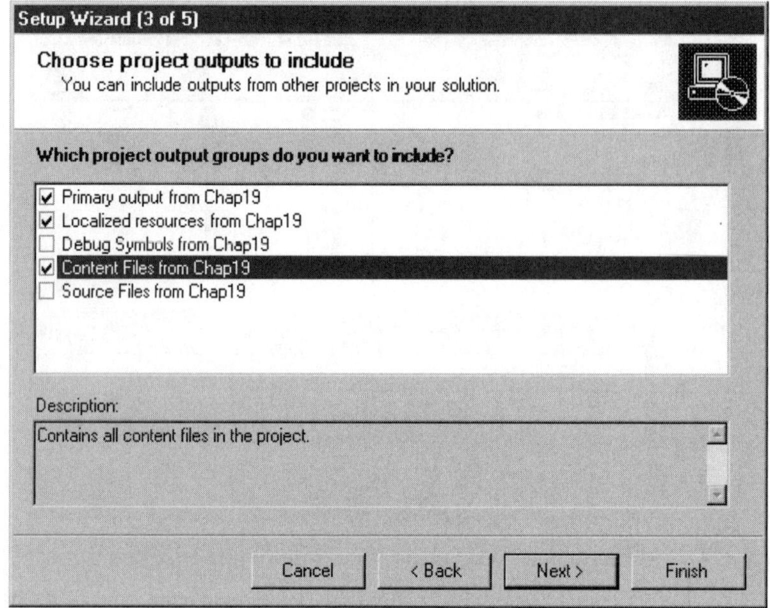

NOTE Although source files and debugging symbols are useful in test deployments, they are usually not needed for deployments.

9. The Choose Files To Include page appears, allowing you to add files such as ReadMe or HTML pages to the deployment. Click Next.
10. Use the Summary area to review the selected options, and then click Finish to create the project.

Once you create the setup project, it is added to the Solution Explorer of the IDE. Adding other content to the project is as simple as right-clicking the project and choosing the appropriate option from the Add menu.

Notice that in addition to the files you specified while using the Setup Project Wizard, Visual Studio .NET automatically detects any dependencies and adds them to the Detected Dependencies folder of the project. However, by default, the automatically detected dependency is excluded from the deployment. To add the file to the deployment, right-click the file and choose Exclude to clear the check mark from the context menu.

TIP By default, the Setup Project Wizard includes the .NET Framework redistribution files as a detected dependency. If you include these files in an application, the deployment will be considerably larger. You only need to do this if the target machine does not have the .NET Framework installed.

Once you have properly created the setup project, you configure its output by setting the Build properties. Typically, this involves creating a Windows Installer file (.MSI) that contains all the information needed to install the application on a target system.

TIP You can also configure additional files to install your application on systems that do not possess the Windows Installer technology for using .MSI files.

To access the Build properties of a project, right-click the setup project in the Solution Explorer and choose Properties. See Figure 19-3.

Use the Output File Name field to control the name and location of the Windows Installer file. Note that the default for this field is

```
configuration\projectname.extension
```

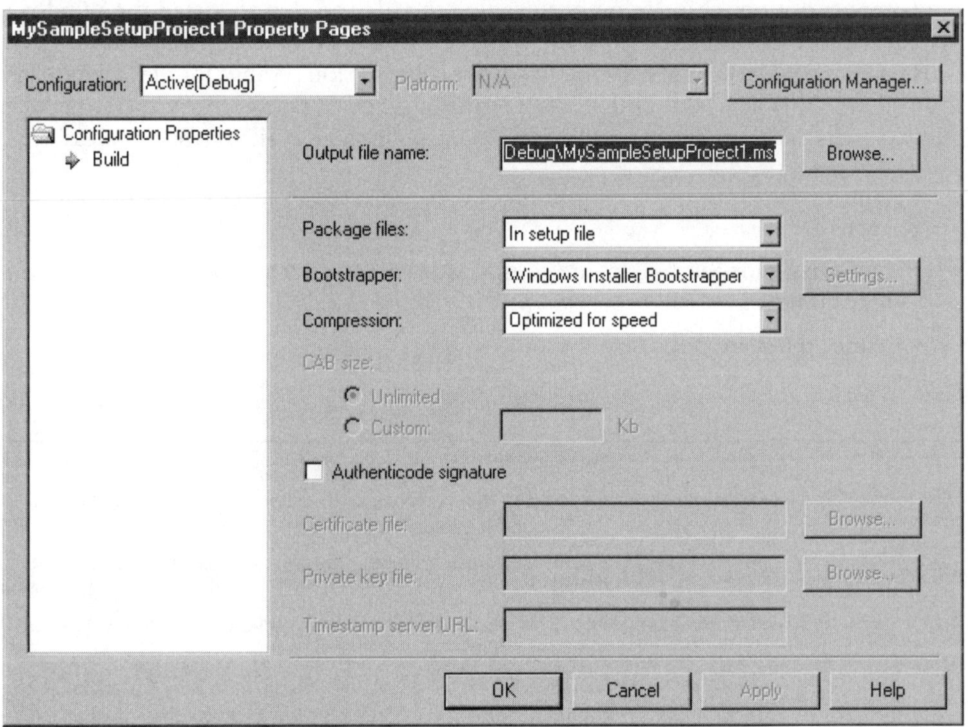

Figure 19-3 The Property Pages of the setup project

PART V

Use the Browse button to assist you in selecting a new location for the file, should you need to.

The Package Files drop-down menu allows you to control how the solution output files are packaged into the setup project. The default selection causes output files to be compressed and packaged into the setup file itself. The CAB option allows you to package output files in CAB files. The last option allows you to deploy the files as loose uncompressed files.

NOTE If you choose to deploy files in CABs, you can then specify the CAB file size. Setting the maximum size is critical if you plan to distribute the application on removable media such as floppy disks.

The Bootstrapper option lets you install the Windows Installer application on the target machine prior to the installation of the application. Specifically, using the Bootstrapper option allows installation of Windows Installer 1.5 on systems that require it—essentially, systems not running Windows XP. If you must include the Windows Installer Bootstrapper in a deployment, four additional files are included in the Build directory. Table 19-8 describes these files.

If your application is going to be downloaded from the Web, choose the Web Bootstrapper option. This option ensures that the files needed to install the Windows Installer 1.5 are downloaded from the Web and installed on the target machine.

The Compression field allows you to specify compression settings for files included in the installer. Obviously, this option is not available when As Loose Uncompressed Files is selected as the Package Files option. The following options are available for compression:

- **Optimized for Speed** Output files are compressed to install more quickly, but are larger in size.
- **Optimized for Size** Files are compressed to a smaller size, but the installation may be slower.
- **None** Files are not compressed.

Table 19-8 Files Used for the Windows Installer Bootstrapper

File	Description
setup.exe	Checks for the existence of Windows Installer 1.5 or higher; if not found it initiates the installation process
instmsia.exe	Installs Windows Installer 1.5 on a Microsoft Windows 95 or 98 system
instmsiw.exe	Installs Windows Installer 1.5 on a Microsoft Windows NT or Windows 2000 system
setup.ini	Contains the name of the .MSI file to be run by setup.exe after the installation of the Windows Installer has been verified

The remaining options of the Property Pages for the setup project allow you to control the following security settings for the application deployment:

- **Authenticode Signature** Determines whether the outputs of the deployment project are signed using Authenticode signing
- **Certificate File** Specifies an Authenticode certificate file (.SPC) used to sign the files. Use the Browse button to select a certificate file
- **Private Key File** Specifies a private key file (.PVK) that contains the digital encryption key for the signed files. Use the Browse button to select a private key file
- **Timestamp Server URL** Specifies the Web location for a timestamp server used to sign the files. This location must be a valid URL. If left blank, this setting is ignored

Deploying with the Setup Project

Once you have configured the appropriate properties for the setup project, you can build it and use it to deploy your application.

To build the setup project, follow these steps:

1. Select the setup project in the Solution Explorer.
2. From the Build menu, choose Build *<projectname>*.

Once you build the setup project, the files needed for the deployment are conveniently located in the folder specified in the setup project's Property Pages.

Further Tailoring a Deployment

You can use additional properties to control the setup project. To access these properties, select the setup project in the Solution Explorer and access the Properties window of the IDE. Table 19-9 describes these properties.

Table 19-9 Setup Project Properties

Property	Description
AddRemoveProgramsIcon	Specifies an icon to be displayed in the Add/Remove Programs dialog box on the target computer
Author	Specifies the name of the author of an application or component
Description	Specifies a free-form description for an installer
Keywords	Specifies keywords used to search for an installer
Localization	Specifies the locale for string resources and the runtime user interface
Manufacturer	Specifies the name of the manufacturer of an application or component

Table 19-9 Setup Project Properties *(continued)*

Property	Description
ManufacturerUrl	Specifies a URL for a Web site containing information about the manufacturer of an application or component
ProductName	Specifies a public name that describes an application or component
Subject	Specifies additional information describing an application or component
SupportPhone	Specifies a phone number for support information for an application or component
SupportUrl	Specifies a URL for a Web site containing support information for an application or component
Title	Specifies the title of an installer

Finally, to add even more flexibility to application deployment, Visual Basic .NET includes various installation editors. Table 19-10 describes these editors.

EXAM TIP The File System Editor is very popular because you can use it to create folders on target systems and add files to those folders.

Summary

For an application to be successful, you must carefully debug it and develop the setup project for its deployment. Debugging includes properly using the debugging tools of Visual Basic .NET and exploiting the powers of the **Debug** and **Trace** classes. You should also consider carefully creating a unit test plan, and creating and throwing exceptions where appropriate.

When it comes to deploying an application, you must properly configure deployment options. The options you set should ensure proper deployment whether the actual method of deployment is Web-based, on removable media, or on a network server.

Table 19-10 Installation Editors

Installation Editor	Description
File System Editor	Allows you to configure an application's installation to the target file system
Registry Editor	Allows you to write entries to the registry
File Types Editor	Allows you to set associations
User Interface Editor	Allows you to edit the user interface seen during installation
Custom Actions Editor	Allows you to define custom actions to be performed during installation
Launch Conditions Editor	Allows you to set conditions for launching the installation

Test Questions

1. Which of the following errors is a simple error indicating that the Visual Basic .NET compiler does not understand your code?
   A. Syntax
   B. Logic
   C. Runtime
   D. Compiler
2. This Debug menu option runs the next executable line of code; if this line calls a method, the method executes and execution halts at the next line within the current method. To which Debug menu option does this statement refer?
   A. Step Into
   B. Step Over
   C. Break
   D. Break All
3. Which of the following windows is a "shorthand" version of the Locals window?
   A. Command
   B. Watch
   C. Registry
   D. Autos
4. Which of the following TraceSwitch settings allows you to provide a very brief error message?
   A. TraceLevel.Error
   B. TraceLevel.Message
   C. TraceLevel.Warning
   D. TraceLevel.ErrorMessage
5. Which type of data causes you to test data based upon the normal minimum and maximum values as well as data that is "off by one" from these parameters?
   A. Bad data
   B. Clean data
   C. Boundary conditions
   D. Dirty data
6. When an application encounters a runtime error, it raises an exception. Of which class is this exception an instance?
   A. Exception
   B. System.Exception

   C. SystemNull.Exception
   D. Error.Exception

7. To throw an exception, which of the following keywords do you use?
   A. Throw
   B. Raise
   C. Exception
   D. Launch
8. To create a complex project for deploying an application, what should you use?
   A. XCOPY
   B. Setup Project Wizard
   C. Wizard
   D. New Project Wizard
9. Which of the following editors allows you to set file associations on a target system?
   A. File System Editor
   B. File Types Editor
   C. User Interface Editor
   D. Registry Editor
10. You need to make custom modifications to the interface for deploying your application. Which editor should you use to do this?
   A. User Interface Editor
   B. Registry Editor
   C. File Types Editor
   D. File System Editor

Test Answers

1. A.
2. B.
3. D.
4. A.
5. C.
6. B.
7. A.
8. B.
9. B.
10. A.

PART VI

Web Forms Applications

CHAPTER 20

Web Forms and Server Controls

In this chapter, you will

- Create a Web application
- Create ASP.NET pages
- Add Web server controls and HTML server controls to ASP.NET pages
- Set the properties on Web controls
- Instantiate and invoke an ActiveX control
- Validate user input
- Create custom and user controls
- Host a user control
- Incorporate existing and new code into ASP.NET pages
- Use and edit intrinsic objects
- Implement error handling in the user interface

ASP.NET is the technology of the Microsoft .NET Framework in which you build Web applications. You use Web forms to build the Internet user interface within a Web application. This development environment is very different from the previous ASP development environment, and you need to understand this new framework. You cannot rely on your previous ASP development knowledge as many aspects of the process are new and/or different.

Web forms follow the object model as described in Chapter 6. When you compile a Web form, a new class is dynamically generated. This class is derived from the ASP.NET Page class and extended by the controls and logic you add to the Web form. Your Web form contains both the visual interface for your user and the custom logic you write for handling this interface. You use server controls, HTML controls, and static HTML to create the visual user interface. You use code-behind pages to write the custom logic.

Creating a Web Application in ASP.NET

The Visual Studio .NET IDE (VS.NET IDE) gives you a quick start creating a Web application. It adds the virtual directory to IIS and creates several files used by ASP.NET. You start a new Web application by selecting the ASP.NET Web Application template for a Visual Basic project type as shown in Figure 20-1. Be sure that you change the Location to reflect the name of the application. It is much easier to do it when you are creating the Web application than to have to do it later.

NOTE This chapter assumes that you have IIS 5.0 or greater installed on your local computer. If you have IIS installed on another computer, you need to change *localhost* to the *computername* for that computer.

Click OK to create a new Web application. The VS.NET IDE then creates the virtual directory you specified in the Location text box and creates the following files in the root of that virtual directory:

- **webappname.vbproj** VS.NET IDE project support file
- **webapname.vbproj.webinfo** VS.NET IDE web support file
- **webappname.vsdisco** Web application discover document
- **AssemblyInfo.vb** Web application assembly information
- **Global.asax** Application-level globals
- **Global.asax.resx** Application-level resource file
- **Global.asax.vb** Application-level event code
- **Styles.css** Cascading style sheet
- **Web.config** Configuration file for the Web application
- **WebForm1.aspx** Web ASP.NET page
- **WebForm1.aspx.resx** Web page resource file
- **WebForm1.aspx.vb** Web page code-behind file

CAUTION When creating a new Web application, you may get an error message that the VS.NET IDE cannot find your local IIS. The usual problem is that your Internet connection is set up to use a proxy server and the option is not set to bypass the proxy server for local addresses. To change this in IE 6, go to Tools | Internet Options | Connections | Lan Settings, and check the box for "Bypass the proxy server for local addresses."

In addition, the VS.NET IDE creates a subdirectory in the Visual Studio project directory. This subdirectory has the same name as the Web application name you specified in the Location text box in Figure 20-1. The webappname.sln and webappname.suo files are added to this directory.

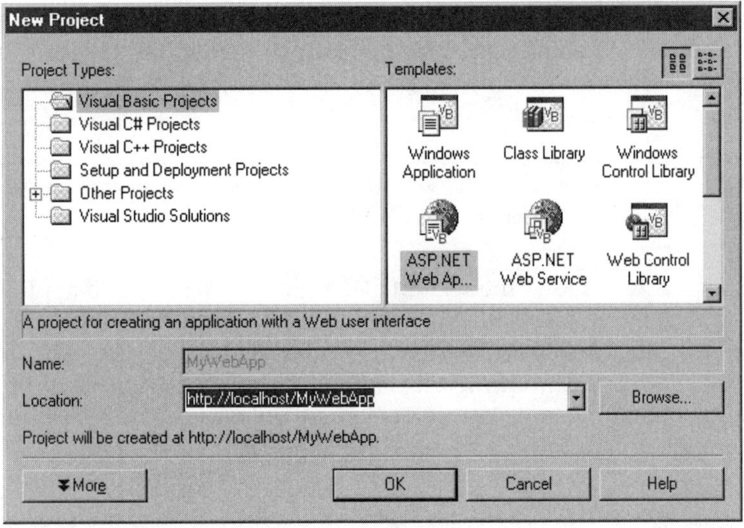

Figure 20-1 Creating a new Web application

NOTE You can change the default location of your Visual Studio project directory at Tools | Options | Environment | Projects and Solutions.

In Exercise 20-1, you will create a new Web application. After it is created you will be ready to start working with Web forms.

Exercise 20-1: Creating a New Web Application

1. Select Start | All Programs | Microsoft Visual Studio .NET | Microsoft Visual Studio .NET.
2. Select New Project.
3. Under Project Types, select Visual Basic Projects.
4. Under Templates, select ASP.NET Web Application
5. Change the Location text box to read http://localhost/MyWebApp.
6. Click OK.

Creating a Web Form in a Web Application

A Web form provides the primary user interface for ASP.NET applications. When you created the application in Exercise 20-1, the VS.NET IDE created a default Web form for you. The Web form consists of three files, WebForm1.aspx, WebForm1.aspx.vb, and

WebForm1.aspx.res. WebForm1.aspx is the main Web form file and is distributed with the completed application. The WebForm1.aspx.vb file contains the server-side code for the form and is compiled for distribution. The WebForm1.aspx.res file is the resource file for the Web form.

EXAM TIP Files with the extensions aspx and aspx.vb contain the aspx page and the server-side code, respectively.

Figure 20-2 shows the VS.NET IDE right after a new Web application has been created. The figure shows the Web application with the Web form displayed in the center window, the Toolbox window, the Properties window, and the Solution Explorer window.

Before you start working with a Web form, you should change the name of the form to a meaningful name. You can rename WebForm1.aspx, but this does not change the name everyplace. It is best to delete this Web form and add a new Web form to the project.

NOTE The terms *Web form* and *ASP.NET page* are used interchangeably.

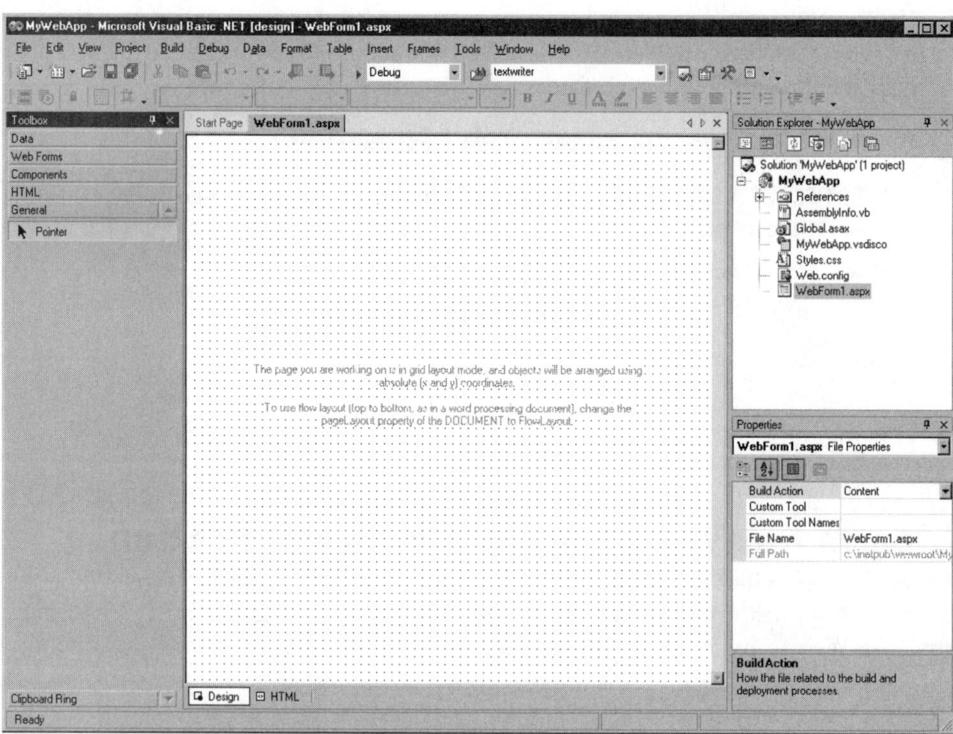

Figure 20-2 VS.NET Web form window with Solution Explorer and Properties windows displayed

In Exercise 20-2, you will rename the default Web form, delete the default Web form from the Web application, and add a new Web form with a different name.

Exercise 20-2: Renaming the Default Web Form

1. Open the Solution Explorer window in the VS.NET IDE.
2. Select Show All Files in the Solution Explorer window.
3. Expand the WebForm1.aspx node by clicking the + sign in front of the node.
4. Right-click the WebForm1.aspx node and rename the Web form to MyWebForm .aspx. The VS.NET IDE renames the WebForm1.aspx.vb node.
5. Select the HTML view in the lower left side of the MyWebForm.aspx window. There are still references to WebForm1 in the HTML, as shown here:

```
<%@ Page Language="vb" AutoEventWireup="false"
Codebehind="MyWebForm.aspx.vb" Inherits="MyWebApp.WebForm1"%>
```

6. Right-click the MyWebForm.aspx node in the Solution Explorer window and select Delete.
7. Click OK to permanently delete the Web form.
8. Select the MyWebApp project in the Solution Explorer window.
9. Right-click in the Solution Explorer window and select Add | Add Web Form.
10. Change the Name text box to MyWebForm.aspx as shown in Figure 20-3.
11. Click Open.

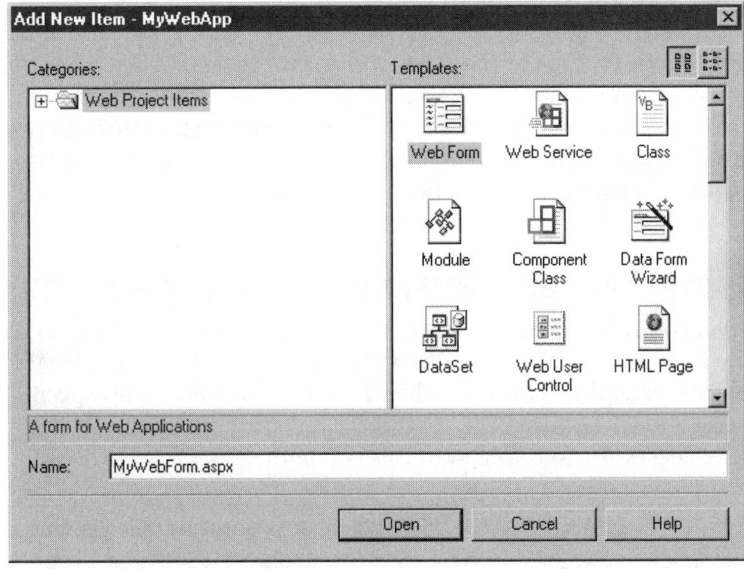

Figure 20-3 Adding a new Web form to a Web application

Placing a Control on a Web Form

An ASP.NET page can be designed using either a grid layout or a flow layout. The page layout used affects how controls and text are added to the page and how they are positioned on the page. The default for a Web form is the grid layout. This is a WYSIWYG (what you see is what you get) design. The controls are placed on the page at the absolute location you place them. The flow layout is more like building a standard HTML page. The text and controls flow together except for the specific spacing that you add.

NOTE Grid layout gives you a close approximation of the actual layout. As with most Web pages, their look can vary depending on the browser.

Adding Controls to a Web Form in Flow Layout

When you add controls in flow layout, most of the time you add them to the end of a document. You place the cursor over the control you want to add, then press and hold the left mouse button. While holding the button down, you move the cursor over the form and release the mouse (this is called *drag and drop*). If you release the mouse while over an existing control or text, the control is inserted into the HTML at that position and all other controls are moved accordingly. If you release the mouse while over an area past the end of the last text or control, the control is added to the end of the existing HTML. You can resize the control after you have dropped it onto the form.

Adding Controls to a Web Form in Grid Layout

You can also add controls in grid layout using the drag and drop technique. However, when you drop them on existing controls or text, they are placed on top of those controls, not inserted as with flow layout.

You can also add controls in grid layout by clicking the control, then moving the cursor from the toolbox to the form, where the cursor will change from a pointer to a plus sign. Move the cursor to the location on the form where you want to place the control. Then press and hold the left mouse button, moving the cursor to size the control on the form. The control is placed on the form when you release the mouse. You can also resize the form after you have dropped it on the form.

Using Server Controls on a Web Form

Server controls are used to implement the user interface of a Web form. In ASP you are able to write code that executes on the server and generates HTML. In ASP.NET, server controls extend this functionality. A server control defines specific behavior using an object model with events, methods, and properties. It automatically generates the HTML necessary to implement this behavior.

EXAM TIP The .NET Framework automatically generates browser-specific code for ASP.NET server controls.

The events, methods, and properties of a server control are available on the server. ASP.NET implements two types of server controls: HTML server controls and Web controls.

Adding HTML Server Controls to a Web Form

HTML server controls are standard HTML elements that support server-side code. You can make many HTML elements into server controls by specifying the runat attribute as "server" to the element, as shown here:

```
<input type="text" runat="server" id="FirstName"/>
```

EXAM TIP Know that you add runat="server" to change an HTML element into a server control.

You use the id attribute to assign a name to the control. This name is used in code that is executed on the server. You reference the server-side properties and methods with this name, as well.

EXAM TIP The namespace for HTML server controls is System.Web.UI.HtmlControls.

You add an HTML server control to a Web form using the VS.NET IDE. Figure 20-4 shows the HTML toolbox menu on the left side of the window and an HTML text field that has been added to the form.

NOTE It is best not to have the toolbox set to auto-hide when adding controls to a form. It tends to get in the way of placing a control on the form as it expands over the form. You can allow the control to float or dock it without auto-hide set. Right-click in the toolbox title bar to change this setting.

An HTML control is placed on the form as a normal HTML control. You need to explicitly make it a server control. To do this, right-click the control and select Run As Server Control. This adds a small icon at the top left of the control to indicate this is a server control.

In Exercise 20-3, you will add an HTML control to the Web form you created earlier and change it to a server control. Also, you will view the resulting HTML that was generated by the VS.NET IDE.

PART VI

Exercise 20-3: Adding an HTML Control to a Web Form

1. Open MyWebApp solution using the VS.NET IDE.
2. Make sure that MyWebForm.aspx is visible in the main window. You may need to open the Solution Explorer window, select MyWebForm.aspx, and click the Designer icon in the Solution Explorer toolbar (just below the Solution Explorer title bar).

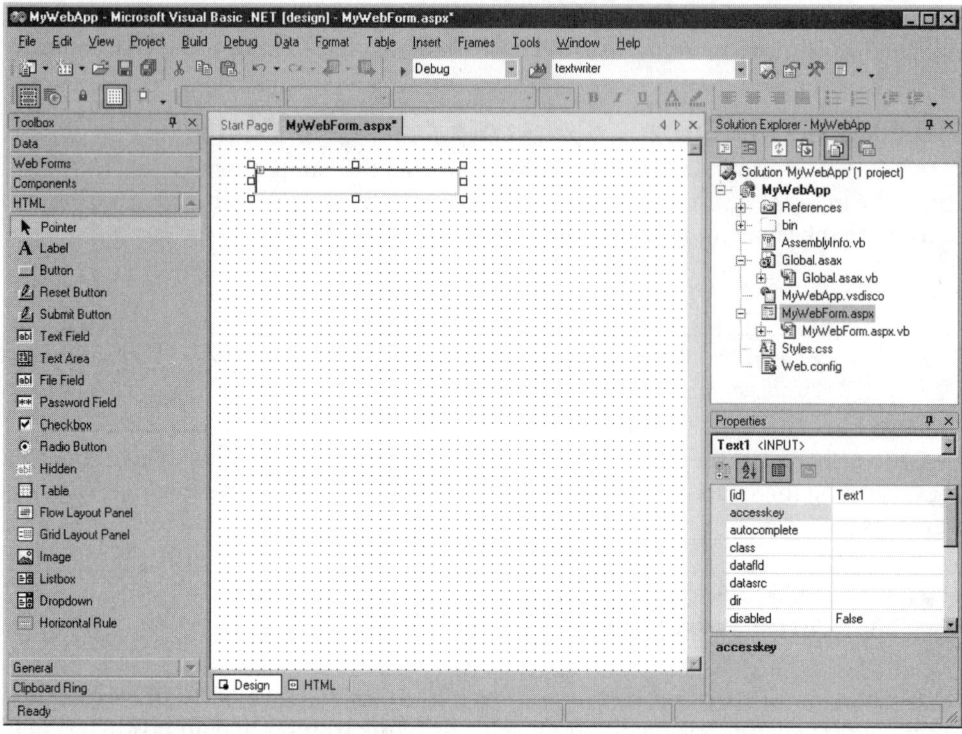

Figure 20-4 Adding an HTML server control to a Web form

3. Open the Toolbox window if it is not already open.
4. There are several options (buttons) to select on the toolbox. Select the HTML option. This shows a list of available HTML controls.
5. Review the list of HTML controls. There are several different types of input, button, and text controls.
6. Click the Text Field HTML control and move the cursor over the Web form. The cursor changes from an arrow to a plus sign.
7. Position the cursor at the location you want to place the HTML control on the Web form. Press the left mouse button and hold it down while you size the HTML control.
8. Release the left mouse button. The text field is now placed on the form.
9. Right-click within the control on the Web form. Select Run As Server Control on the pop-up menu. A small icon is placed in the upper left corner of the control.

10. Click the HTML selection at the bottom of the Web form and examine the HTML:

```
<INPUT style="Z-INDEX: 101; LEFT: 18px; WIDTH: 192px;
 POSITION: absolute; TOP: 17px; HEIGHT: 26px"
 type="text" size="26" id="Text1" name="Text1" runat="server">
```

EXAM TIP An HTML control is not a server control when placed on the form. You need to change it. This change cannot be made in the properties window. It needs to be changed by right-clicking the control or editing the HTML.

11. Click the Design selection at the bottom of the Web form to return to the Design view.
12. Add several more controls on the form and examine the HTML for each.
13. Delete the controls from the form. (To delete a control, click the control and press the DELETE key.)

Adding Web Controls to a Web Form

The second type of server control is the Web control. Web controls include many of the standard Windows form controls, enhanced controls, and validation controls. Label, TextBox, and CheckBox are some of the standard Window form controls. DataGrid and Calendar are two of the enhanced controls. RequiredFieldValidator and RangeValidator are two validation controls.

NOTE A standard Windows form control is a control available for .NET Windows applications as covered in Chapter 16. An enhanced control is a custom control that provides functionality beyond that available with the standard windows form controls.

Web controls belong to the System.Web.UI.WebControls namespace. When you add a Web control to a Web form you need to include the tag for this namespace. The Web form (ASP.NET page) automatically includes the asp tag for the namespace.

```
<asp:TextBox id="FrstName" runat="server"></asp:TextBox>
```

You add a Web control to a Web form the same way you add an HTML control. The only difference is that all Web controls are server controls and you do not need to set the Run As Server Control property. In fact, the VS.NET IDE does not let you change this property. If you edit the HMTL and remove the runat="Server" attribute, the control does not work.

Figure 20-5 shows a Web form with the Web Forms toolbox option open and listing the available Web controls. The Properties window shows the namespace for the currently selected control.

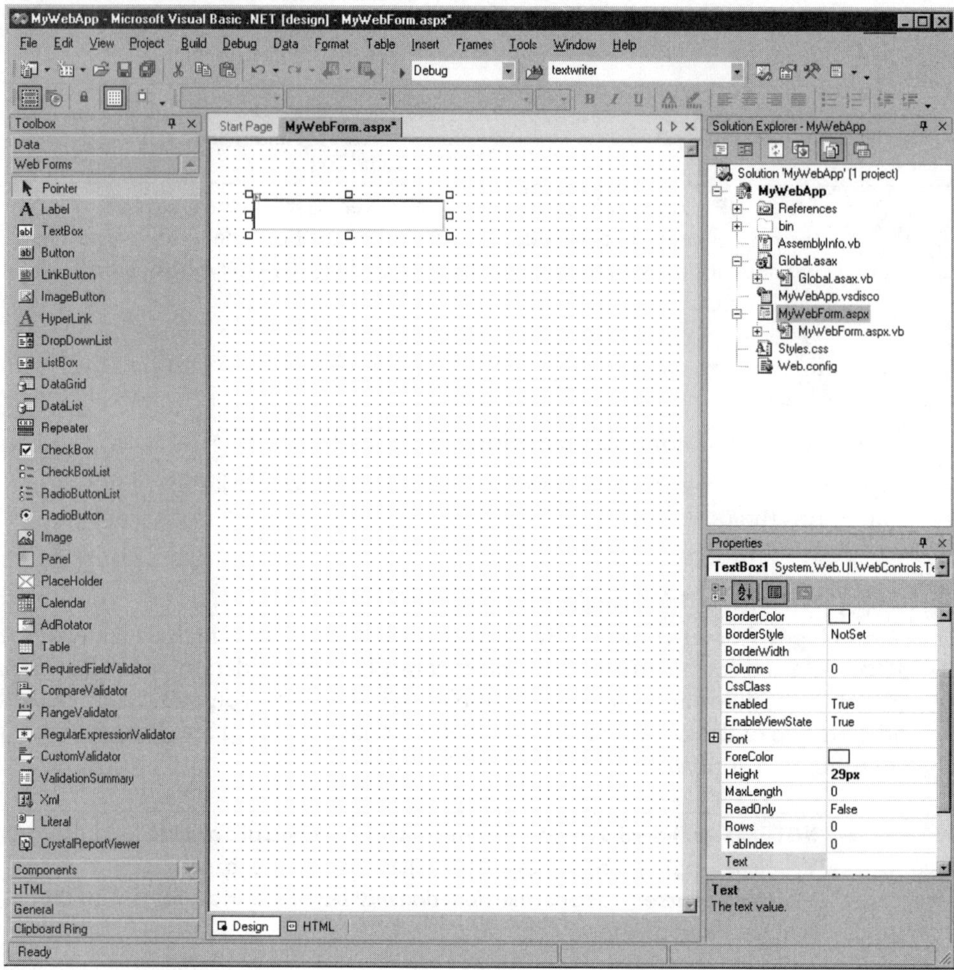

Figure 20-5 Adding a Web Forms control to a Web form

In Exercise 20-4, you will add a Web server control to the MyWebForm form and review the HTML for the Web server control.

Exercise 20-4: Adding a Web Control to a Web Form

1. Open MyWebApp solution using the VS.NET IDE.
2. Make sure that MyWebForm.aspx is visible in the main window.

3. Open the Toolbox window if it is not already open.
4. Select the Web Forms option. This shows a list of available Web Forms controls.
5. Review the list of the available Web Forms controls.
6. Click the TextBox control and place it on the form. The server icon is already shown in the upper left corner of the control.
7. Click the HTML selection at the bottom of the Web form and examine the HTML for control. There is an <asp> tag for the text box and a closing </asp:TextBox> tag to make the HTML well formed.

```
<asp:TextBox id="TextBox1" runat="server"></asp:TextBox>
```

8. Switch back to Design view and add several more Web form controls and review the HTML for each.
9. Delete the controls from the Web form.

Using Validation Controls to Validate User Input

Users do not always enter correct information on a Web form. If they did, a developer's life would be much easier. Unfortunately, developers spend much of their development effort handling errors made during user input. The .NET Framework has input validation controls to help.

Input validation may run at the client if supported by the client's browser. This gives quick feedback to the user when incorrect information is entered. A round trip to the server is saved when validation can be done on the client's machine. In addition, the validation is always performed at the server when information is posted to the server. You can make your applications friendlier, faster, and more secure using validation controls.

Validation is performed by comparing the user input against input formats. If the input does not match the input formats, an error is generated. There are several types of input formats available. These formats can be as simple as character and numeric checks or as complicated as mathematical formulas. Checking Social Security numbers, telephone numbers, percent ranges, and age limits are examples of validations you are able to perform.

Validation

You define the validation you want to do once and it is performed at both the client and the server. If the client's browser supports the validation, it is performed on the client's machine. This allows all the input to be validated prior to being sent to the server, saving round trips between the client's machine and the server just to report errors. Even though the client's input may be checked at the client's machine, it is always checked at the server when submitted by the client.

Validation Performed at the Client

Client-side validation is performed using JavaScript and dynamic HTML scripts. For those client browsers that support the client-side script, that script is sent to the client. For most browsers that support client-side validation, the validation is performed when the Submit button is clicked. The user input is not sent to the server until all input is valid.

If the client's machine is using Internet Explorer 5 or later, the validation is performed when the user moves off a control. This gives immediate feedback to the user when there is an error in the input.

Validation Performed at the Server

Validation is always performed at the server even if it has already been performed on the client's machine. In addition to the defined validation for a control, you can write server-side validation code in any Microsoft .NET based language.

EXAM TIP Validation is always done on the server, even if it is also done on the client.

Always performing validation at the server provides better security and safer applications. It protects the application from spoofing and malicious code. Spoofing is when the user modifies your page to circumvent error checking and sending invalid data to the server. Malicious code can cause buffer overruns, inappropriate database commands, and incorrect authentication.

Validation Controls

There are six validation controls defined in ASP.NET. These controls are divided into five controls that perform the validation and one control that provides validation feedback to the user. The five controls that perform (and define) the validation are:

- **CompareValidator** You can perform comparisons against specific values or another control.
- **CustomValidator** You can write custom code for validation requirements you have that are not available with the other validation controls. Validation against a database is a common use for this control.
- **RangeValidator** You can compare using a specified range.
- **RegularExpressionValidator** You can write a regular expression to perform the validation.
- **RequiredFieldValidator** Input is required from the user.
- Each of these five validation controls provides the display error information to the user. The sixth control, ValidationSummary, displays validation feedback to the user for all controls on the Web form.

Adding Validation Controls to a Web Form

You add and set properties of a validation control to a Web form just as you add any other control. Normally, you place the validation control next to the control you are validating. Once you drag and drop the control onto the Web form, you set the properties for the control.

There are several common properties for the validation control. The main common properties that require setting are:

- **ControlToValidate** A validation control must be associated with the appropriate control that is being validated. The VS.NET IDE provides a drop-down list of controls that can be validated.
- **Display** An error message can be displayed within the validation control. If you choose to display the error message within the control it is important that you size the control to fit the error message. You can choose not to display the error message by setting this property to None. You can specify that the display area for the error message is Static or Dynamic. Static requires that the control is sized appropriately for the error message. Dynamic causes the page layout to change based on the length of the error message.
- **Text** This text is displayed in the validation control when there is an error. If you do not set this property, the ErrorMessage property is used for the error text.
- **ErrorMessage** This is the error message that is displayed in the ValidationSummary control. This message is also displayed in the validation control if the Text property is empty.
- **EnableClientScript** For browsers that support client-side script, you can inhibit client-side script generation by setting this property to False. The default value is True.

Each of the validation controls has custom properties that are discussed in following sections.

You can have more than one validation control for the same input control. In fact, this is a common practice. All validations must be passed for a control to pass multiple validation controls. If you require multiple patterns, you must use a single control for all of the patterns.

Using the CompareValidator Validation Control

The CompareValidator control compares the input value to a specific value or to a second input value. The comparison is made using the standard comparison operators of equal, not equal, greater than, greater than or equal, less than, and less than or equal. Also, it allows for a data type comparison. An empty input passes the validation test. The data type comparison is useful in the .NET Framework where the variant type is not allowed.

The custom properties for the CompareValidator control are:

- **ValueToCompare** This is a constant value. You can separate multiple values with the pipe character (|), for example, 1|2|3|4.
- **ControlToCompare** This is the name of the control to compare to. A common example is when you are asking for a password and a confirmation of the password word. You would set the validation control for the confirmation password control to validate against the password control.
- **Type** You set the data type when you are using the data type operator. The valid data types are string, integer, double, date, and currency.
- **Operator** The valid operators are Equal, NotEqual, GreaterThan, GreaterThanEqual, LessThan, LessThanEqual, and DataTypeCheck.

Using the RangeValidator Validation Control

The RangeValidator control is very similar to the CompareValidator control except that it compares for a range of values. An empty input passes the validation test. That is, if the user does not enter any information, the validation does not fail. The custom properties for the RangeValidator are:

- **MinimumValue** The minimum numeric value for numeric data types or the minimum length for character strings.
- **MaximumValue** The maximum numeric value for numeric data types or the maximum length for character strings.
- **Type** You set the data type when you are using the data type operator. The valid data types are string, integer, double, date, and currency.

Using the RequiredFieldValidator Validation Control

The RequiredFieldValidator control makes input for the control being validated a required entry. Any value can be entered except an empty input (no characters) or all spaces. The other four validation controls allow empty input. The custom property for the RequiredFieldValidator control is:

- **InitialValue** The naming and some of the documentation for this control may be misleading. If the InitialValue property is set to a value, the input control fails if the input is equal to the InitialValue property. The comparison is made after all extra spaces are removed. The RequiredFieldValidator control is really a validation that the input control cannot be equal to the value in the InitialValue property. By default this property is empty and requires input.

NOTE The process of requiring a user to change a password is an example of using the control to validate against a value. You put the old password in the InitialValue. This requires that the user change the value to something other that the original password.

Using the CustomValidator Validation Control

The CustomValidator control allows you to write both client-side functions and server-side functions that are used to validate the input. The IsValid property is set by these functions. The custom properties for the CustomValidator control are:

- **ClientValidationFunction** This is the name of the JScript or VBScript client-side function that you include in the aspx file for client-side validation.
- **OnServerValidate** This is the name of the server-side function you write to handle the ServerValidate event.

Using the RegularExpressionValidator Validation Control

The RegularExpressionValidator control is used to check the input against one or more patterns. The pattern matching is performed using regular expressions. Regular expressions are a cryptic set of notations that perform powerful pattern matching. The custom property for the RegularExpressionValidator is:

- **ValidationExpression** This is the regular expression used to validate the input.

The VS.NET IDE provides a dialog box to allow you to choose from several predefined regular expressions. These are very useful. In addition to speeding the process of setting the regular expressions for common patterns, the examples help you learn how regular expressions work. You can use these examples as templates for your own regular expressions. The following is an example of the regular expression for an e-mail address:

```
\w+([-+.]\w+)*@\w+([-.]\w+)*\.\w+([-.]\w+)*
```

You can study the .NET Framework documentation for a complete description of regular expressions.

Using the ValidationSummary Validation Control

The ValidationSummary control enables you to display all the errors on a page in a single location. Typically, you display the error messages in the ValidationSummary control near the Submit button on the form. The custom properties for the ValidationSummary control are:

- **ShowSummary** Set this property to True to display the validation summary on the Web form.
- **ShowMessageBox** Set this property to True to display the validation summary in a message box. The EnableClientScript property must also be set to True for the message box to be displayed.
- **DisplayMode** This property controls how the validation summary messages are formatted. The possible values for the property are List, BulletList, and SingleParagraph.

Each validation control has a Text property and an ErrorMessage property. When the validation summary is displayed, the ErrorMessage property is used in the ValidationSummary control or the message box. The Text property is displayed in the validation control itself. A common practice is to have descriptive text for the ErrorMessage property and a red asterisk for the Text property. This results in the display of detailed error messages near the Submit button with red asterisks identifying the individual fields.

Creating and Using User Controls

Several HTML server controls and Web controls are included with the .NET Framework. After you have worked with these for a while, you may notice that you are using one or more of the controls in the same way. You continually repeat the same implementation of these controls. The .NET Framework allows you to encapsulate this repetitive functionality into your own user controls. This can be as simple as formatting a Social Security number or more complex entry of complete name and address information. Within the name and address user control, you may use another user control that you created for the city, state, and zip code.

A user control is an ASP.NET page that you can use as a server control on other ASP.NET pages. User control pages have a file extension of ascx instead of the standard aspx extension for an ASP.NET page. A user control allows you to group and reuse common UI interfaces. Also, a user control is compiled the first time it is requested and stored in memory. This provides for faster response time when next requested.

Creating a User Control

Creating a user control is very similar to creating an ASP.NET page. In fact, a user control *is* an ASP.NET page with some minor differences. You can create a user control using your favorite text editor or the VS.NET IDE. Or you can convert an existing Web form into a user control.

In Exercise 20-5, you will create a user control with two text boxes for entering an area code and phone number. In subsequent exercises, you will add validation to the user control and use the control on a Web form.

Exercise 20-5: Creating a User Control

1. Open the MyWebApp solution you created using the VS.NET IDE.
2. Open the Solution Explorer.
3. Right-click the MyWebApp solution and select Add.
4. Select Add Web User Control.
5. Change the name to ucPhoneNumber.ascx.

6. Type **Area Code:** followed by two spaces into the user control. The user control is in flow layout. No matter where you place the cursor and click within the user control, the cursor moves to the beginning of the control. You cannot change the page layout for a user control.
7. Drag and drop a Web form TextBox control in the user control. You can drop the TextBox anyplace (except on the text entered previously) on the user control and it automatically positions itself after the text you typed into the control.
8. Change the ID property of the text box to cAreaCode.
9. Resize the text box to allow for approximately three characters.
10. Type two spaces and **Phone Number:** followed by two more spaces after the cAreaCode text box.
11. Drag and drop another Web form TextBox onto the user control after the text you entered. Rename the text box cPhoneNumber and size it for a typical phone number.
12. Select the HTML selection at the bottom left of the ucPhoneNumber.ascx window.
13. Examine the HTML that has been created automatically by the VS.NET IDE. The user control has a Control directive instead of a Page directive. The spaces you entered were entered as non-breaking spaces.

```
<%@ Control Language="vb" AutoEventWireup="false"
Codebehind="ucPhoneNumber.ascx.vb" Inherits="MyWebApp.ucPhoneNumber"
TargetSchema="http://schemas.microsoft.com/intellisense/ie5" %>
Area Code: 
<asp:TextBox id="cAreaCode" runat="server" Width="42px"></asp:TextBox> 
Phone Number: 
<asp:TextBox id="cPhoneNumber" runat="server" Width="76px"></asp:TextBox>
```

14. Select the Design view at the bottom left of the ucPhoneNumber.ascx window.

NOTE It is important that you change the name to the name you want for the control when you create it. When you rename a control name, all of the references to that original name are not changed by the VS.NET IDE. This may not affect the operation of the control, but it can be confusing for those who modify your implementation.

PART VI

Your user control should look similar to Figure 20-6 when you have completed Exercise 20-5.

Differences Between a Web Form and a User Control

Just like a Web form, user controls contain HTML and code. However, user controls are used on a Web form; therefore, you do not include <HEAD>, <BODY>, or <FORM> HTML tags in the user control. These tags already exist for the Web form.

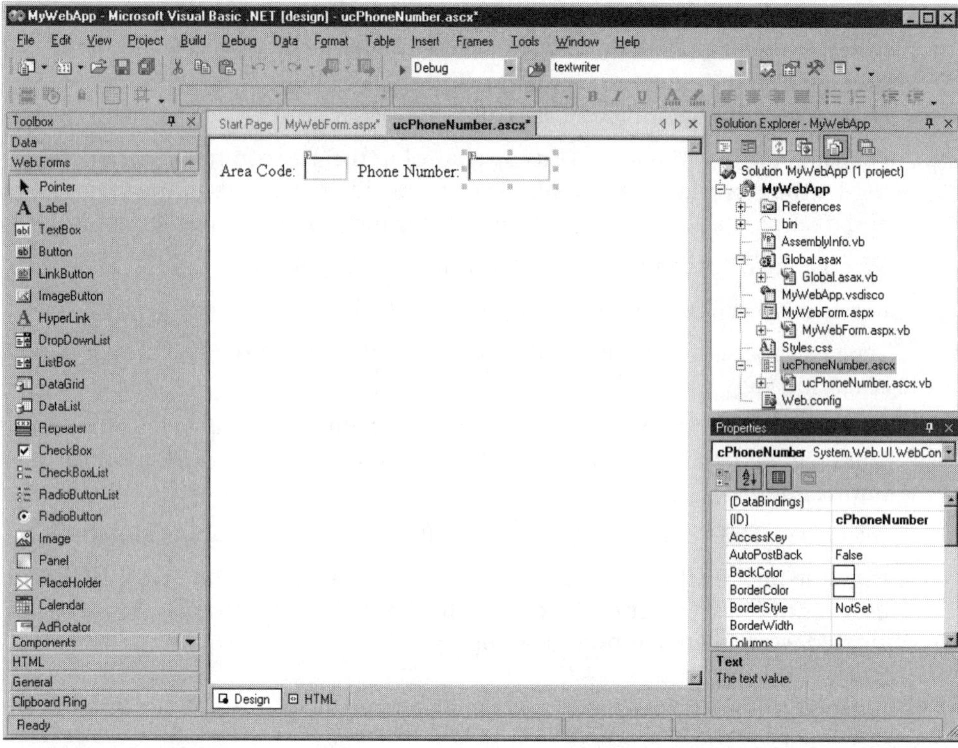

Figure 20-6 Creating a user control

You use the Page directive on a Web form to specify the code-behind page on a Web form. The user control can also contain a code-behind page. You use the Control directive to set the code-behind page for a user control. Most of the attributes of the Control directive are the same as the attributes for the Page directive.

NOTE You cannot set the trace attribute in the Control directive. It needs to be set in the Page directive for the Web form. The trace attribute applies to an entire page and all of its controls.

Enhancing the User Control

The user control you created in Exercise 20-5 sets standard wording and sizing for phone numbers. In Exercise 20-6, you will extend the functionality of the control by adding validation controls.

Exercise 20-6: Adding Validation Controls

1. Start with the ucPhoneNumber.ascx window displayed within the VS.NET IDE.
2. Drag and drop a RangeValidator control after the cAreaCode text box.
3. Change the ID property to vAreaCode.
4. Change the Type property to Integer.
5. Set the MinimumValue property to 201.
6. Set the MaximumValue property to 980.
7. Set the ControlToValidate property to cAreaCode
8. Change the Text property to an asterisk.
9. Set the ErrorMessage property to Invalid Area Code.
10. Drag and drop a RegularExpressionValidator control after the cPhoneNumber text box.
11. Change the ID Property to vPhoneNumber.
12. Set the ControlToValidate property to cPhoneNumber.
13. Change the Text property to an asterisk.
14. Set the ErrorMessage property to Invalid phone number format (*nnn-nnnn*).
15. Enter \d{3}-\d{4} for the ValidationExpresson property.

Your user control should look similar to Figure 20-7 when you have completed Exercise 20-6.

Adding a User Control to a Web Form

You are ready to place a user control on a Web form after you have created it within an application. There are some rules that you should keep in mind, however:

- User controls can be used only in the Web application in which they are created.
- You cannot share user controls between Web applications.
- You must copy the user control to the Web application in which you want to use the user control.

The Web form on which you place the user control is called the host for the user control. You must register the user control on all Web forms using the Register directive to include a user control on a Web form. A example is:

```
<%@ Register TabPrefix="uc1" TagName="ucPhoneNumber",
Scr="ucPhoneNumber.ascx" %>
```

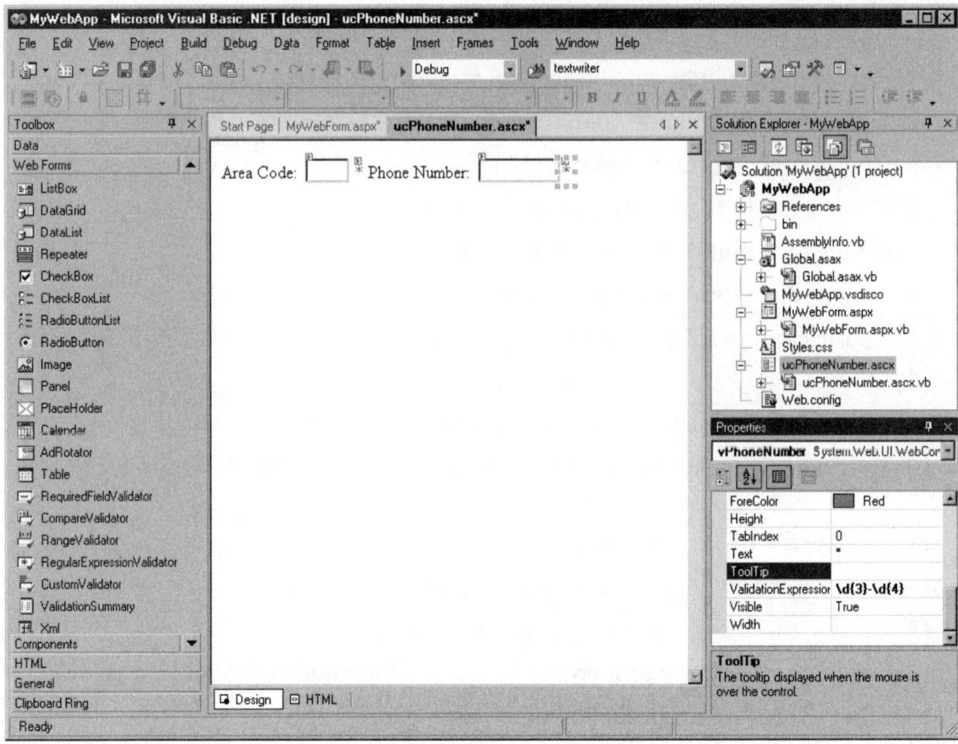

Figure 20-7 Using validation controls

The Register directive has three attributes for registering user controls. They are:

- **TagPrefix** A unique namespace for the user control. As with namespaces in general, the tag prefix distinguishes this user control from other user controls that may have the same name.
- **TagName** A unique name for the control within the namespace.
- **Scr** The location and file name, including the extension, for the source file for the control. The location can be relative or absolute.

After the user control is registered, you simply place the user control on the form. You reference the user control using both the TagPrefix and the TagName. You also include the runat="server" attribute:

```
<uc1:ucPhoneNumber id="cContactPhone" runat="server" />
```

You can drag and drop the user control from the Solution Explorer window using the VS.NET IDE. It automatically adds the Register directive with default TagPrefix and

TagName. The user controls are placed on the Web form in flow layout even if the page is in grid layout.

NOTE Even if you add positioning information to the user control, it is not used during the rendering of the page.

In Exercise 20-7, you will add a user control to a Web form.

Exercise 2-7: Adding a User Control to a Web Form

1. Start with the MyWebForm.aspx window displayed in the VS.NET IDE in Design view. Make sure you have deleted all controls from the form.
2. Drag and drop the ucPhoneNumber.ascx file from the Solution Explorer window onto the Web form.
3. Examine the HTML of MyWebForm.aspx. The Register directive has been added to the form. A default TagPrefix of uc1 has been generated and the control added to the form.

```
<%@ Register TagPrefix="uc1" TagName="ucPhoneNumber"
Src="ucPhoneNumber.ascx" %>
. . .
<uc1:ucPhoneNumber id="UcPhoneNumber1" runat="server"></uc1:ucPhoneNumber>
```

4. Return to Design view and try to move the control (you should still be working in grid layout for the page). The VS.NET IDE does not allow you to specifically position the control.

NOTE Even if you manually add a style to position the control, the control is not positioned when rendered.

5. Change the page layout to flow layout using the custom properties dialog box (right-click the page and select Properties) or selecting Document in the normal properties window and changing the page layout.
6. Place the cursor in front of the user control on the Web form and press ENTER. This moves the user control down one line.
7. Move the cursor up one line and enter **Contact Name:** followed by a space.
8. Add a text box after the space above and set the ID property for the text box to cContactName. Set the Text property to <Enter Contact Name>.
9. Add a space after the cContactName text box and drag and drop a RequiredFieldValidator control after the space. Set the ID property of the control to vContactName. Set the ErrorMessage property to "Please enter a contact name". Set the Text property to an asterisk. Set the InitialValue property to <Enter Contact Name>.

10. Add a button below the custom control. Set the ID property to cSubmit and the Text property to Submit. To place the control on the line following the custom control, you must place the cursor after the custom control and press ENTER. You can then drag and drop the control onto the form.
11. Drag and drop a ValidationSummary control after the cSubmit control.
12. Set MyWebForm.aspx as the start page for this Web application. Right-click the MyWebForm.aspx file in the Solution Explorer window and select Set As Start Page.
13. Press F5 to compile and run the Web application.
14. Click Yes to save the changes.
15. Click Submit without changing or entering any information. A red asterisk appears next to the contact name control and the ValidationSummary window is displayed by the Submit button.
16. Delete the text in the contact name control and click the Submit button. You do not receive an error. An empty entry is valid since it does not match the IntitialValue property of the validation control.
17. Enter various combinations of phone number and click Submit. Since you are probably using Internet Explorer 5, the red asterisk appears whenever you enter an incorrect area code or phone number. The validation summary always appears when there is an error and the Submit button is clicked.

The completed Web form should look like Figure 20-8.

Adding ActiveX Controls to a Web Form

ActiveX controls can still be included on Web forms. The VS.NET IDE does not reference ActiveX controls by default. However, you can add ActiveX controls to the Toolbox, and then drag and drop them to your Web form.

Use the following steps to add ActiveX controls to the Toolbox:

1. Make sure the Toolbox window is open and accessible.
2. Right-click on an open area of the Toolbox and select Add Tab.
3. Name the tab ActiveX Controls.
4. Right-click on an open area of the ActiveX Controls tab and select Customize Toolbox. The Customize Toolbox dialog box opens.
5. Select the COM components tab and check the ActiveX controls you want to add to the Toolbox window.

Now that you have access to the ActiveX control within the VS.NET IDE, you can add them to your Web forms.

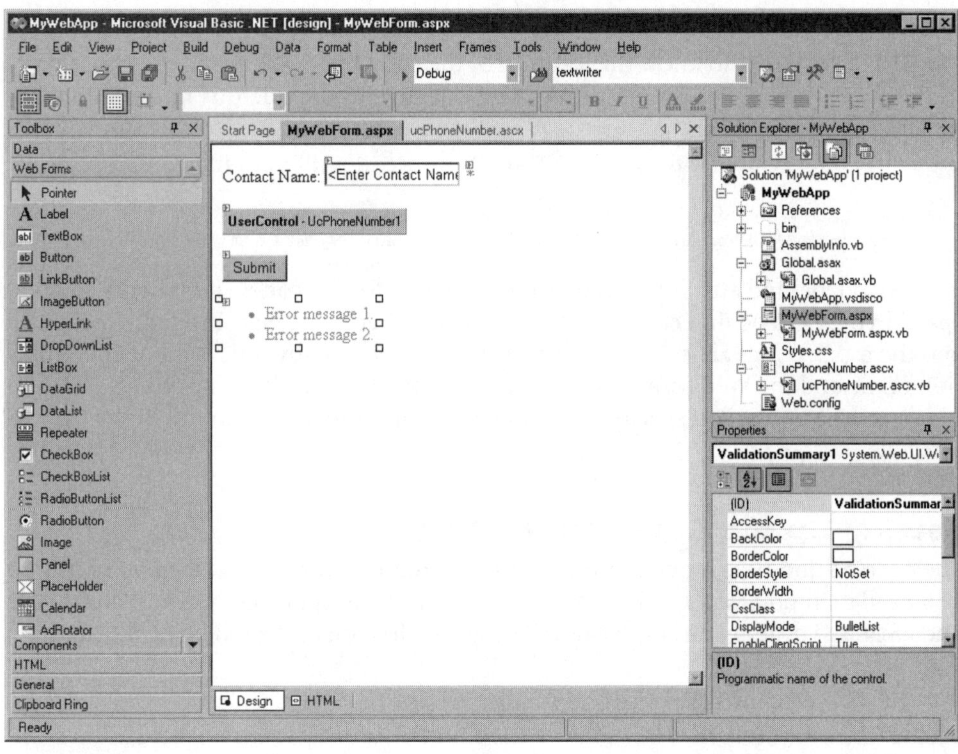

Figure 20-8 Adding a user control to a Web form

Adding Server-Side Code to a Web Form

HTML server controls, Web form server controls, and user controls provide many features for developing your Web forms. However, you eventually need to implement more complex processing. You do this with code-behind pages within the .Net Framework. Although you do not need to use the code-behind pages to write VB or C# code, it is the best practice. It separates the code from the user interface. This separation allows for easier maintenance and reduces errors when writing the code.

The syntax of the VB.NET code is the same whether you are coding for ASP.NET or for Windows forms. In addition, you have access to the ASP.NET intrinsic objects of Response, Request, Session, and Application. These objects allow you to maintain properties between ASP.NET pages and perform ASP.NET operations.

Defining the Code-Behind File and Class

The Web form needs to know the location of the code-behind files and the class related to this form. You use attributes of the Page directive to provide this information. The VS.NET IDE automatically creates the Page directive, including its attributes for you. The following is an example of an Page directive:

```
<%@ Page Language="vb" AutoEventWireup="false"
Codebehind="MyWebForm.aspx.vb" Inherits="MyWebApp.MyWebForm"%>
```

The Codebehind attribute specifies the file name for the code. The Inherits attribute specifies the Codebehind class that the Web form inherits. When compiled, the aspx file and the aspx.vb files are combined into a single class. Usually, this is the Web application name and the Web form name as shown in the Inherits attribute above.

For user controls, you specify the Codebehind and Inherits attributes in the Control directive.

Setting Up the Code-Behind Page

The code-behind page requires a minimum amount of information when you set it up. You need to import System and System.Web. The class must inherit System.Web.UI.Page. The VS.NET IDE automatically creates these entries for you as the following illustrates:

```
Imports System
Imports System.Web
Public Class MyWebForm
Inherits System.Web.UI.Page
. . .
End Class
```

EXAM TIP The ASP.NET code-behind pages must inherit from System.Web.UI.Page.

Using the Code-Behind Page

The Web form and the code-behind page are compiled into a single class that runs on the server. You have access to the controls on the page from within the code-behind page and you can respond to events generated from the Web form.

In order to access the controls and respond to events from the controls, you must declare each control in the code-behind page. Again, the VS.NET IDE takes care of most of this for you.

```
Protected WithEvents cContactName As System.Web.UI.WebControls.TextBox
Protected WithEvents cValidationSummary As
System.Web.UI.WebControls.ValidationSummary
Protected WithEvents cSubmit As System.Web.UI.WebControls.Button
Protected WithEvents vContactName As
System.Web.UI.WebControls.RequiredFieldValidator
```

However, it does not provide the declaration for user controls that you use. You need to provide these declarations yourself.

```
Protected cPhoneNumber as MyWebApp.ucPhoneNumber
```

The class for the user control declaration is the Web application and the user control name.

Using Code-Behind Pages to Add Properties to a User Control

One use of code-behind pages is to expose controls that are on a user control. You may have noticed that the phone number user control created in previous exercises does not provide the host form access to the area code and the phone number. You need to explicitly provide access to information entered by the user. You provide access to this information by adding properties to the user control in the code-behind page for the user control.

In Exercise 20-8, you will expose the area code and phone number as properties of the ucPhoneNumber user control.

Exercise 20-8: Adding Properties to a User Control

1. Start with the ucPhoneNumber.aspx window displayed in the VS.NET IDE in Design view.
2. Double-click the ucPhoneNumber.aspx window. The ucPhoneNumber.aspx.vb window is displayed.
3. Review the control declarations that have automatically been created by the VS.NET IDE:

```
Protected WithEvents cPhoneNumber As System.Web.UI.WebControls.TextBox
Protected WithEvents vAreaCode As
System.Web.UI.WebControls.RangeValidator
Protected WithEvents cAreaCode As System.Web.UI.WebControls.TextBox
Protected WithEvents vPhoneNumber As
System.Web.UI.WebControls.RegularExpressionValidator
```

4. Review the Inherits statement for the user control. Since this is a user control and not a page, the code-behind page must inherit from the UserControl instead of Page.

```
Inherits System.Web.UI.UserControl
```

5. Add the following code to expose the area code and the phone number:

```
Public Property AreaCode as String
    Get
        Return cAreaCode.Text
    End Get
    Set
        cAreaCode.Text = Value.ToString
    End Set
 End Property
```

PART VI

```
Public Property PhoneNumber as String
    Get
        Return cPhoneNumber.Text
    End Get
    Set
        cPhoneNumber.Text = Value.ToString
    End Set
End Property
```

You have now exposed the two text boxes in the user control. This allows the host of the control to have access to this information.

Accessing User Control Properties

After you have exposed the properties of a user control to the host Web form, the host form needs to be able to access these properties. You create a code-behind page for the host form and add a declaration of the user control to the page. You can then access the properties of the user control.

In Exercise 20-9, you will access the area code from the user control and store it in a session variable for later use.

Exercise 20-9: Accessing User Control Properties

1. Start with the MyWebForm.aspx window displayed in the VS.NET IDE in Design view.
2. Double-click in the MyWebForm.aspx window to open the MyWebForm.aspx .vb window. Alternatively, you can access this window by selecting MyWebForm .aspx in the Solution Explorer window, or you can double-click MyWebForm.aspx .vb in the Solution Explorer window.
3. Review the Inherit statement and the declarations that the VS.NET IDE automatically built for you.
4. Add a declaration for the user control ucPhoneNumber:

   ```
   Protected cPhoneNumber as MyWebApp.ucPhoneNumber
   ```

5. In the left drop-down list located at the top of the MyWebForm.aspx.vb window, select the cSubmit control. This selects the cSubmit control and populates the right drop-down list with the events available for that control.
6. In the list on the right, select the Click event. The following code is added to the MyWebForm.aspx.vb window:

   ```
   Private Sub cSubmit_Click(ByVal sender As Object, ByVal e As
   System.EventArgs) Handles cSubmit.Click)
   End Sub
   ```

7. Add the following line of code within the event handler for the cSubmit_Click event:

   ```
   Session.add("ContactAreaCode", cPhoneNumber.AreaCode.ToString)
   ```

8. Press F5 to run the application. The application runs the same. However, the area code is saved in a session variable when the Submit button is clicked.

Using the Intrinsic Objects

When you are writing VB.NET code, you have access to the ASP.NET intrinsic objects. Intrinsic objects that you commonly use are the Response, Request, Application, and Session. The Response and Request objects are part of the ASP.NET request/response model.

- **Request** Contains the request for the resource
- **Response** Contains the response to the client

The Application and Session objects allow you to save information for the entire Web application or between pages for a specific user.

- **Application** Shares information for all uses of the Web application
- **Session** Shares information for all pages in a client's session

The properties and methods of these objects are available within your VB.NET code. You can find the details of all of the available properties and methods in their corresponding sections of the .NET documentation. The following examples demonstrate some of the most common uses of these objects.

When the client browser or another Web form makes a request, the request often contains a query string to provide parameters. The following code accesses the query string using the Request object:

```
Dim QueryString as String = Request.querystring
```

The Response object is used in creating a response to the client. The write method is commonly used to provide information to be sent in the response.

```
Response.write("Customer Name:" & custName)
```

The Application object is used to store information that is available to all sessions and users of the entire Web application. The follow code shows how to save information in the Application object:

```
Application("VisistorCount") += 1
```

You can later display this information on a Web form using the following code:

```
Response.write("Number of visits: " & Application("VisitorCount"))
```

This code demonstrates using both the Response object and the Application object.

The Session object is used to store information between pages for a single session. A session is identified on a per client basis. It is normally the time from when the client accesses the site to when the client leaves the site. While the client is at your site, you can make information available between pages using the Session object. This information is not available to other users. The following code is an example of assigning a session variable:

```
Session("UserName") = FirstName & " " & LastName
```

Once you have set the information in the Session object, you use it on other Web forms for this user.

```
Response.write("Current User: " & Session("UserName"))
```

Implementing User Interface Error Handling

Validation controls handle many of the user interface errors that you can anticipate. You know the possible formats for a phone number and you can check for them. Other errors are not as easily detected. ASP.NET provides for several methods of trapping and responding to errors when they occur:

- Page_Error event
- Page.ErrorPage property
- Application_Error event
- Application configuration file

Using the Page_Error Event

The Page_Error event is used to trap errors that happen at the page level. You can place code in this event to display an error message, log an error, and/or redirect the user to a different page. There are four methods that are useful in working with page and application errors. They are:

- **Server.GetLastError** Gets the last unhandled error
- **Server.ClearError** Clears the error to avoid passing it to the next level
- **EventLog.WriteEntry** Writes an entry to the event log
- **Response.Redirect** Redirects to another page

Using the Page.errorPage Property

Each page has an errorPage property. When an error is encountered and not handled on the page, the user is redirected to the page specified in the errorPage property for the page. You can set this in code:

```
Me.errorPage = "ErrorPage.aspx"
```

Or you can use the Page directive:

```
<%@ Page @ErrorPage="ErrorPage.aspx" %>
```

Using the Application_Error Event

You can create an event handler for an application error in global.asax. If you do not handle an exception on a page, the application error event in global.asax handles the error. The following code segment is provided in global.asax:

```
Sub Application_Error(ByVal sender As Object, ByVal e As EventArgs)
    ' Fires when an error occurs
End Sub
```

Specifying web.config Settings to Handle Errors

You can specify a default error page handler in the web.config file to handle errors that are not handled by the page or application. You specify the default page in the customErrors section of the web.config file, as shown here:

```
<customErrors
defaultRedirect="http://MyWebServer/MyWebApp/DefaultError.aspx" mode="on">
      <error StatusCode="404" redirect="FileNotFound.aspx">
      <error StatusCode="500" redirect="ServerError.aspx">
</customErrors>
```

Summary

The .NET Framework has simplified creating a Web application. It also creates a new development environment. Developing using ASP.NET and the VS.NET IDE is significantly different than developing in the previous version of ASP.

The VS.NET IDE creates the Web application's virtual directory and manages the application development, user interfaces, and logical code. You create the Web forms for the Web application and add HTML, Web, and user server controls to provide the user interface.

In addition, you use the validation controls to provide reliable and efficient user input validation that runs on both the client's machine and on the server. You can add custom code written in any .NET supported language and provide for the automatic generation of client HTML, DHTML, and JScript.

Errors and exceptions not handled at the control level can be handled at the page and application levels. You have server options of trapping the error with a page event, an application event, or by default error pages.

Test Questions

1. You have created a new Web application called MyWebApp. Which of the following files is not created by the VS.NET IDE?
   A. MyWebApp.vbproj
   B. Global.asax
   C. WebForm1.aspx
   D. WebForm1.ascx
   E. Web.config
2. What is the default page layout for a Web form?
   A. Grid layout
   B. Flow layout

C. You must specify when you create the Web form
D. None of the above

3. What must be added to an HTML element to make it a server control?
A. type="server"
B. runat="server"
C. runat="iis"
D. server=true

4. What attribute of the server control is used to define the reference in server code?
A. name
B. type
C. runas
D. id

5. When you place either an HTML control or a Web form control on an Web form, they are automatically created as server controls.
A. True
B. False

6. What is the namespace for an HTML server control?
A. Application.Web.Html
B. System.HtmlControl
C. System.UI.HtmlControl
D. Application.UI.HtmlControl
E. System.Web.UI.HtmlControl

7. All controls on a Web form must be in either grid layout or flow layout.
A. True
B. False

8. You can create a user control by modifying a Web form.
A. True
B. False

9. What is the extension of the user control file?
A. aspx
B. actl

C. uc

D. ascx

E. None of the above

10. You have added a user control that you created to an existing Web form. Now your control covers up some of the host form. What is the most likely cause?

A. Your user control was designed in grid layout.

B. Your host form is in grid layout and you have not allowed enough room for your user control.

C. Your host form is in flow layout and your control is in grid layout.

D. Your browser is not compatible with flow layout.

11. You should only place validation controls after all other controls on the page.

A. True

B. False

12. Which of the following validation controls does not validate user input?

A. RequiredFieldValidator

B. RangeValidator

C. ValidationSummary

D. CompareValidator

13. The RequiredFieldValidator will never accept empty input.

A. True

B. False

14. If a control is validated on the client with a validation control, it is validated again on the server.

A. True

B. False

15. In what file can you define a default error page?

A. global.asax

B. global.ini

C. web.config

D. AssemblyInfo.config

Test Answers

1. D.
2. A.
3. B.
4. D.
5. B.
6. E.
7. B.
8. A.
9. D.
10. B.
11. B.
12. C.
13. B.
14. A.
15. C.

CHAPTER 21

Web Forms Applications Options

In this chapter, you will

- Implement navigation for the UI
- Apply cascading style sheets
- Configure a Web application
- Configure security for a Web application
- Configure authorization
- Configure and implement session state

Creating Web forms to provide the user interface is just one part of developing a complete Web application. A Web application is made up of several Web forms. You need to be able to navigate between forms, maintain information from one form to another, and authenticate and authorize users of the forms. In addition, there are several configuration settings you can make for your Web application that determine how it will function.

Implementing Navigation of Web Forms

When a user moves between forms, you usually want to maintain some information about the user and information the user has entered on other Web forms visited. As in previous versions of ASP, you can use the Session object to maintain this information. The Session object is covered later in this chapter and in Chapter 20. Two features have been added in addition to the Session object, the ViewState control and the Page.IsPostBack property.

The ViewState control is an automated method of storing information within the form that you send to the user. When the form is posted back to the server, the ViewState control value is returned with the form.

With the addition of server controls, the form can be posted back to the server several times prior to the user leaving the form. The Page.IsPostBack page property allows you to distinguish between the initial page load event and the page load events caused by a server control.

Using ViewState

In ASP, you could add hidden elements to a form to store information that you wanted returned to you when the user posted the form back to the server. In ASP.NET, this has been automated for you. An ASP.NET Web form makes several trips between the server and the user because server controls may require processing on the server. Each time the form is posted back to the server, the Web form gets rebuilt. During this rebuild process, you want the form to retain the look it had when sent by the user. ASP.NET uses a ViewState control to store information between round trips between the client and the server. Like a control you may have used in ASP for this purpose, the ViewState control is a hidden control named __VIEWSTATE.

By default, ViewState is enabled for ASP.NET forms. When enabled, ASP.NET automatically adds the hidden __VIEWSTATE control to the HTML that is sent to the user. The control stores a list of name value pairs. These pairs are the control's name and the control's value. When the form is sent to the user, these values are updated with the current values of the control. When the request is posted to the server, these values are updated with any user input and sent to the server.

The following shows HTML code for the ViewState control that is generated by ASP.NET when ViewState is enabled:

```
<form name="Form1" method="post" action="MyWebForm2.aspx" id="Form1">
<input type="hidden" name="__VIEWSTATE"
value="dDwtNTMwNzcxMzI0Ozs+md/MHNkRWpkzSS8twVIXHDPSN7E=" />
. . .
</form>
```

NOTE The value of the ViewState control is converted to a string of characters to optimize storage and transmission of the information (serialized). As you can see in the example, the information is not human-readable. Some controls contain data that cannot be serialized and you should disable ViewState for these controls.

There are times when you do not want ViewState to be enabled. An example is when you populate a data grid that cannot be changed by the user and that you repopulate every time you send the form to the user. The data grid can create a large amount of data that is sent to the user. By repeating this data in the ViewState control, the bandwidth used to send and receive the data is significantly increased. This reduces response time for the user and increases the load on the server.

EXAM TIP To increase performance on a Web form that contains large amounts of data, you can disable ViewState for a Web form.

You can disable ViewState for an entire Web form and then enable it for specific controls on the Web form. You use the EnableViewState attribute of the Page directive to control the ViewState for a Web form. This is shown in the following code sample:

```
<%@ Page EnableViewState="False" %>
```

You then enable ViewState for specific controls using the EnableViewState attribute of the control. This is shown in the following code sample:

```
<asp:ListBox id="ListBox1" EnableViewState="true" runat="server">
```

NOTE ViewState only applies to those controls between <form> and </form> tags and to Web form server controls (ASP.NET server controls).

You can also set the EnableViewState attribute of the Web form and controls using the VS.NET IDE. This attribute is listed in the Properties window for each Web form server control. Select DOCUMENT in the Properties window to set the ViewState for the Web form.

Using the Page.IsPostBack Property

In ASP.NET, a Web form makes several round trips between the server and client during a single presentation of the form to the user. These round trips are necessary whenever server-side code needs to be executed in support of the form. This may happen as a result of server-side events fired by a control on the form or by validation required on the server. Each time the form is returned by the user to the server, the page load event is executed on the server. When you write code in the page load event, you need to be able to distinguish between the initial page load event and the page load caused by control events on the form. The Page.IsPostBack property is used to make this distinction.

When a Web form is first loaded, you may want to set certain default values for controls or access a database to populate a listbox. Later, when the page load happens as a result of a control server-side event, you do not want to set these default values, because the user might have changed them. Also, you do not need to make another access to the database because the listbox data is already populated.

The Page.IsPostBack property is set by the .NET Framework. It sets it to False during the initial page load. It sets it to True during a page load caused by a server-side event on the Web form. You can then check the Page.IsPostBack value to determine if this is an initial page load or a page load caused by a server-side event on the Web form. The following sample code is an example of using the Page.IsPostBack property:

```
   Private Sub Page_Load(ByVal sender As System.Object, ByVal e As
System.EventArgs) Handles MyBase.Load
       If Not Page.IsPostBack Then
          cCountry.Text = "USA"
          ... (database access code to populate a state list)
       End If
   End Sub
```

This code checks the Page.IsPostBack property to determine if this is the initial page load. If it is the initial page load, the cCountry control is set to USA and a state list control is populated from a database.

EXAM TIP The Page.IsPostBack property is used to distinguish between the initial page load event and page load events as a result of a control's server-side event processing.

PART VI

Configuring Your Web Application

ASP.NET provides flexible configuration for your Web applications. This configuration exists in the web.config files. A web.config file can exist in the root of a virtual directory and any of the subdirectories. If configuration information does not exist in web.config files, the configuration defaults to the machine.config file configuration settings if they exist. The machine.config file is located in the %system%\Microsoft.NET\Framework\v1.0.3705\CONFIG\ directory. v1.0.3705 is the current release of .NET.

You can modify the configuration files while ASP.NET is processing. The changed file is detected and the new configuration is loaded. This dynamic updating of the configuration information eliminates the need to restart Web applications just to change a configuration setting.

EXAM TIP It is not necessary to restart a Web application for changes in a web.config file to be available to the applications. When the web.config file changes, the .NET Framework automatically reads the new file.

How Configuration Settings Are Applied

Understanding how the same configuration settings in multiple configuration files are applied is necessary when configuring your Web applications. Settings that are in the machine.config file apply until a setting in a web.config file changes them. The path that is followed from the virtual root of the Web site is the URL path, not the file system path.

NOTE The URL path is the virtual directory structure of your Web site. This may not be the same as the Windows operating system's logical directory structure, the file system path.

The easiest way to illustrate the application of configuration settings is with an example. First, assume the following virtual directory structure:

```
MyWebApp
  -BusinessPages
    -OrderPages
  -CompanyPages
```

Now, assume a configuration setting of LoggingLevel with the following values:

```
machine.confg - LoggingLevel=1
MyWebApp web.config - no entry in web.config for LoggingLevel
  -BusinessPages web.config - LoggingLevel=2
    -OrderPages web.config - web.config file does not exist
  -CompanyPages web.config - LoggingLevel=0
```

Any Web forms that exist in the MyWebApp virtual directory inherit the LoggingLevel=1 from the machine.config file. Although the web.config file exists in the MyWebApp directory, it does not contain an entry for LoggingLevel, thus it inherits the value from its parent's configuration file, machine.config.

Any Web forms that exist in the MyWebApp/BusinessPages virtual directory have LoggingLevel=2 because it is explicitly set in the web.config file that exists in the MyWebApp/BusinessPages virtual directory.

Any Web forms that exist in the MyWebApp/BusinessPages/OrderPages virtual directory have LoggingLevel=2 because it does not have a web.config file, thus it inherits the value from its parent's web.config file, in the MyWebApp/BusinessPages virtual directory.

Any Web forms that exist in the MyWebApp/CompanyPages virtual directory have LoggingLevel=0 because it is explicitly set in the web.config file that exists in the MyWebApp/CompanyPages virtual directory.

Setting Values in the Configuration Files

The VS.NET IDE automatically creates a web.config file when you create a Web application. It also provides quick access to the file for editing from the Solution Explorer. In addition, you can use an XML editor or a text editor to modify the web.config file.

NOTE The web.config file that is created by the VS.NET IDE contains documentation and several predefined sections. In practice, it is best to remove the documentation, except what applies to your application, and any sections that are not used by your application. This improves maintenance and readability of the file.

The web.config file is a well-formed XML file. See Chapter 13 for more details on the structure of XML files. The root node of the file is <configuration> and all configuration information is located between the <configuration> and </configuration> XML tags. Each section of the web.config file has special attributes and elements dependent on the settings required. The following is a sample web.config file with an appSettings section:

```
<?xml version="1.0" encoding="utf-8"?>
<configuration>
  <appSettings>
    <add key="DefaultCountry" value="USA"/>
  </appSettings>
</configuration>
```

The appSettings section in the web.config file is the section that you use for the settings you define. Most of the other sections are for configuring ASP.NET or the .NET Framework settings. Once you have assigned a value to an appSetting as shown in the previous sample file, you can access it from application code as shown here:

```
cCountry.Text =
System.Configuration.ConfigurationSettings.AppSettings("DefaultCountry").tostring
```

You use the System.Configuration.ConfigurationSettings.AppSettings method to access values that are set in the web.config file.

PART VI

NOTE You cannot change the values set in the web.config file in code. If you have application variables that you need to change in code, you need to use the Application intrinsic object. This is discussed in Chapter 20 and also later in this chapter in the "Using Application State" section.

Applying Cascading Style Sheets

The VS.NET IDE creates a default cascading style sheet, Styles.css, when you create a new Web application. You can modify this style sheet or you can create your own custom style sheet. This section describes how to apply, modify, and create these style sheets in your Web forms.

Most Web applications are composed of several Web forms. If you want all of the Web forms to have the same look, you can define a single cascading style sheet and have it apply to all the Web forms. Many times, you have groups of Web forms with Web forms in each group having the same look but with each group having a slightly different look. A simple example is that you may want one group to have all text that appears between the <H1> and </H1> tags to be black and in another group you want the text to be blue. In this case, you define two cascading style sheets, one for each group.

Figure 21-1 shows the VS.NET IDE with the Styles.css file selected in the Solution Explorer window (right side), the file contents in the main window, and the file outline displayed in the window on the left. You can modify the cascading style sheet within the VS.NET IDE.

Apply a Cascading Style Sheet to a Web Form

Although Styles.css is included in a Web application when you create it using the VS.NET IDE, the style sheet is not applied to any of the Web forms. There are several methods you can use to apply a cascading style sheet to a Web form. The easiest is to simply drag the file from the Solution Explorer and drop it onto the Web form while the Web form is in Design view. The LINK tag is added to the HTML of the Web form as shown in the following HTML code:

```
<HTML>
  <HEAD>
    . . .
        <LINK href="Styles.css" type="text/css" rel="stylesheet">
  </HEAD>
  . . .
</HTML>
```

Another method is to simply edit the HTML code and add the LINK tag as shown in the previous code.

A third option is to use the Document Styles window to add the LINK tag. This is a more complicated method and you need to be sure to have the correct files and views

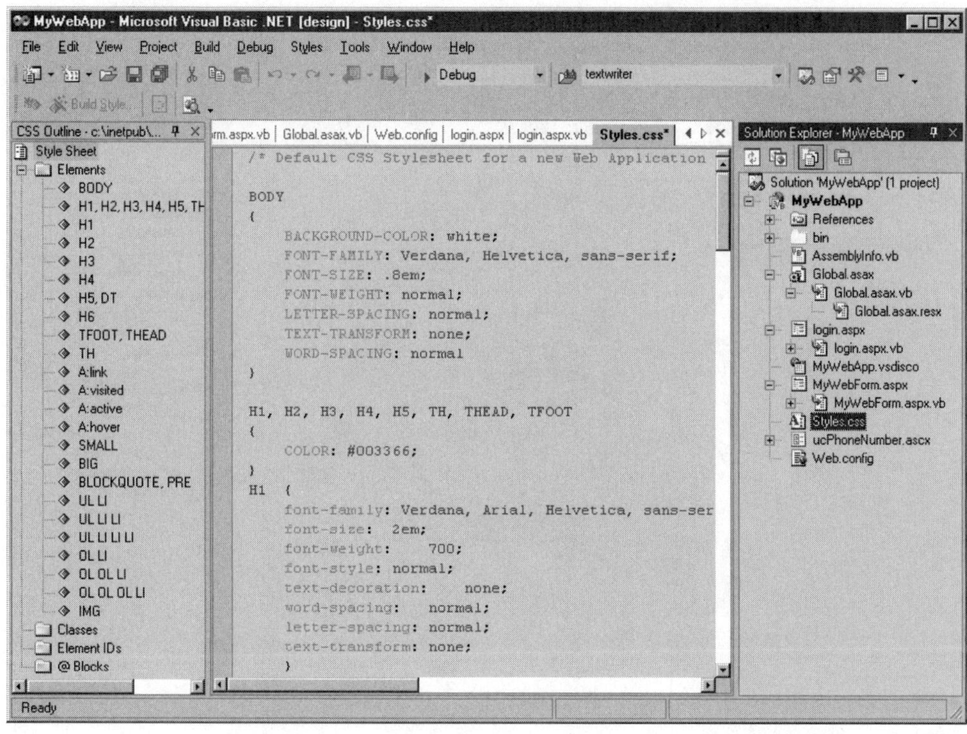

Figure 21-1 VS.NET IDE showing the default cascading style sheet

selected. Use the following steps to add the cascading style sheet file to the Web form by using the Document Styles window:

1. Select the Web form in the Solution Explorer window.
2. Be sure that the Web form is displayed in the main window.
3. Be sure that you are in Design view for the Web form.
4. Click an area of the Web form that does not contain any controls or be sure that DOCUMENT is selected in the Properties window.
5. Click Format on the VS.NET IDE menu.
6. Click Document Styles (the last entry in the pop-up menu). Figure 21-2 shows the VS.NET IDE ready for you to select Document Styles, with the Solution Explorer window and the Properties window properly selected.

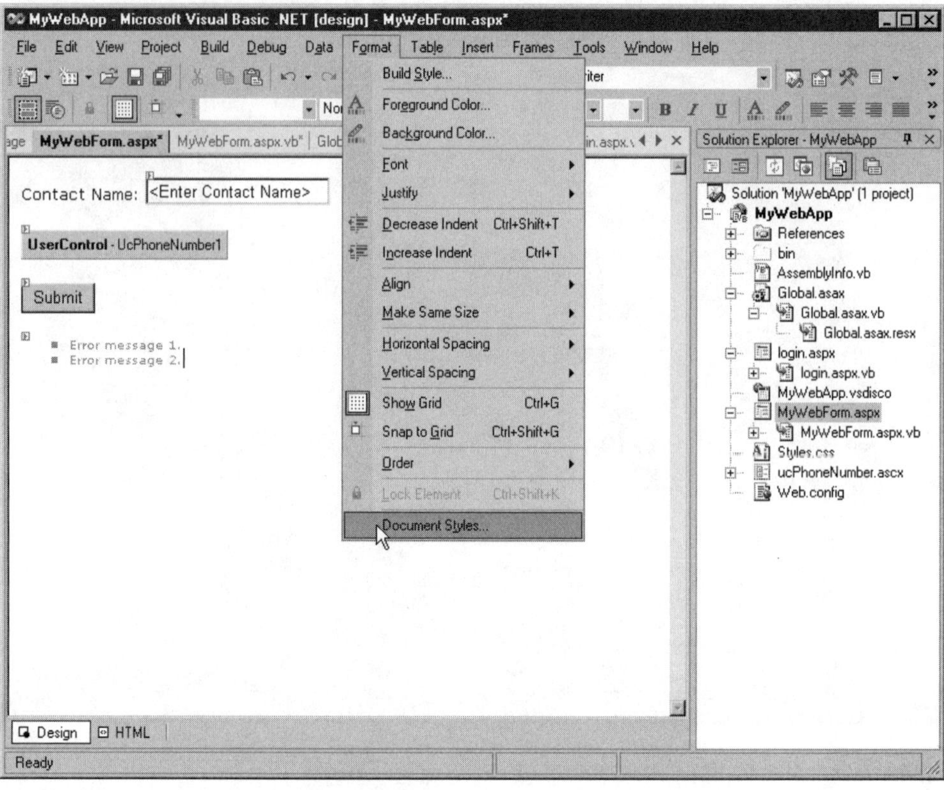

Figure 21-2 VS.NET IDE with the Document Styles ready to be selected

7. Click the Add Style Link icon in the Document Styles toolbar. This is the third icon from the left. Figure 21-3 shows the Document Styles window and the Select Style Sheet window.
8. Select Styles.css in the left window, Contents of "MyWebApp."
9. Click OK and close the Document Styles window.

Adding a Class to a Cascading Style Sheet

The default Styles.css cascading style sheet file contains styles for the common elements in HTML. It does not contain any style *classes*. You need to add these classes to the file in order to apply them to both Web form server controls and HTML controls.

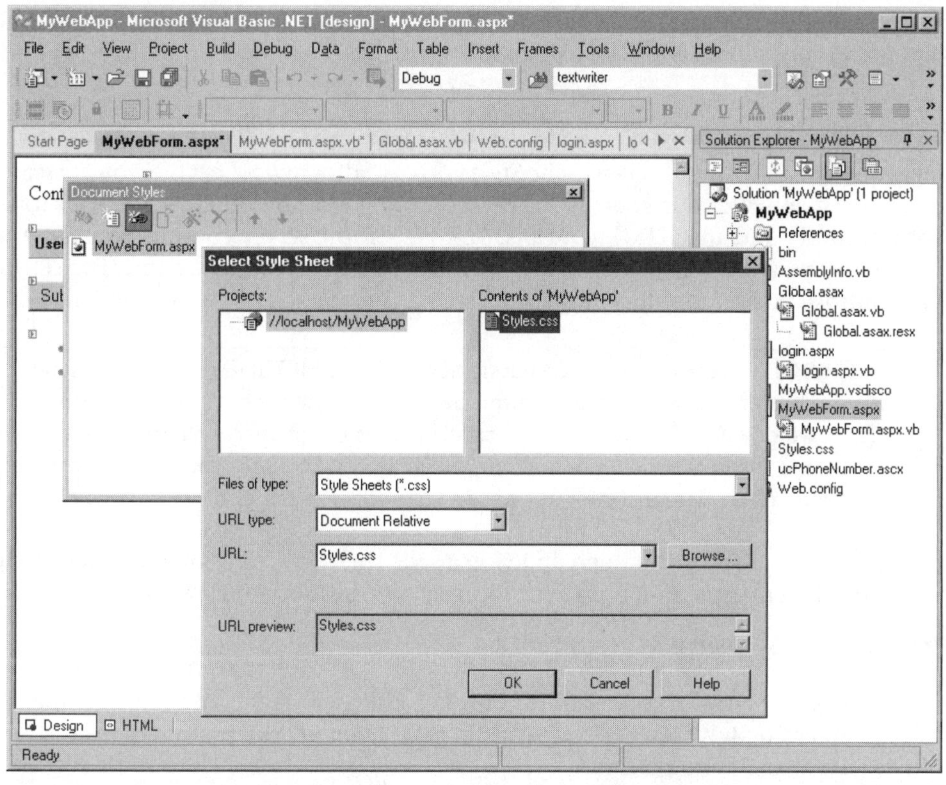

Figure 21-3 Document Styles and the Select Style Sheet windows open and ready to select a cascading style sheet for the current Web form

Adding a Style Class Directly to the Styles.css File

It is not difficult to add a simple style class (one with a few lines of code) directly to the Styles.css file in the VS.NET IDE. You prefix the name of the class with a period (.) and define the attributes of the style as shown in the following sample code:

```
.MyStyle
{
    font-weight: bold;
    color: red;
    font-family: Arial;
}
```

Using the VS.NET IDE Dialog Boxes to Build Style Classes

The VS.NET IDE provides dialog boxes to help you build style classes. This is convenient for learning the different attributes of styles and for building complex styles. The VS.NET IDE refers to the style classes as *style rules*. There are two steps in adding a new style rule.

First you add the rule and then you build the rule. Exercise 21-1 takes you through the steps of creating a new style class using the VS.NET IDE.

Using the Cascading Style Sheet on Web Form Controls

After you have added a style class to the Styles.css cascading style sheet file, you are ready to use the style with your controls. The procedure is slightly different for Web form server controls and for HTML controls. For Web form server controls, you set the CssClass property in the VS.NET IDE Properties window to the class name. For HTML Web controls, you set the class property to the class name.

NOTE Terminology is confusing here. The VS.NET IDE refers to the style class as a style rule in adding the class to the style sheet. The Properties window for Web form server controls uses the property named CssClass and the Properties window for the HTML controls uses the property named class. As Exercise 21-1 demonstrates, they are all basically the same.

Exercise 21-1 takes you through applying a style sheet to a Web form, adding a style class, and using that class on both Web form server controls and HTML controls.

Exercise 21-1: Using Style Sheets

1. Start with MyWebApplication as completed in Chapter 20. You can copy the Chapter 20 MyWebApp directory from the CD into C:\Inetpub\wwwroot\MyWebApp if you need to.
2. Open MyWebForm.aspx in the main edit window in Design view (double-click MyWebForm.aspx in the Solution Explorer window and click Design at the bottom of the main window showing MyWebForm.aspx).
3. Select Styles.css in the Solution Explorer window and drag and drop it on the MyWebForm.aspx main window. This adds the style sheet to the Web form.
4. Select the HTML view for MyWebForm.aspx display and find the following line of code to verify that Styles.css has been added to the Web form:

```
LINK href="Styles.css" type="text/css" rel="stylesheet">
```

5. Select the Design view for MyWebForm.aspx display.
6. Open Styles.css in the main window (double-click Styles.css in the Solution Explorer window).
7. Select the Styles menu item in the VS.NET IDE.
8. Select Add Style Rule from the drop-down menu. This opens the Add Style Rule dialog box as shown in Figure 21-4.
9. Select the Class Name radio button option.
10. Enter MyStyle for the class name.

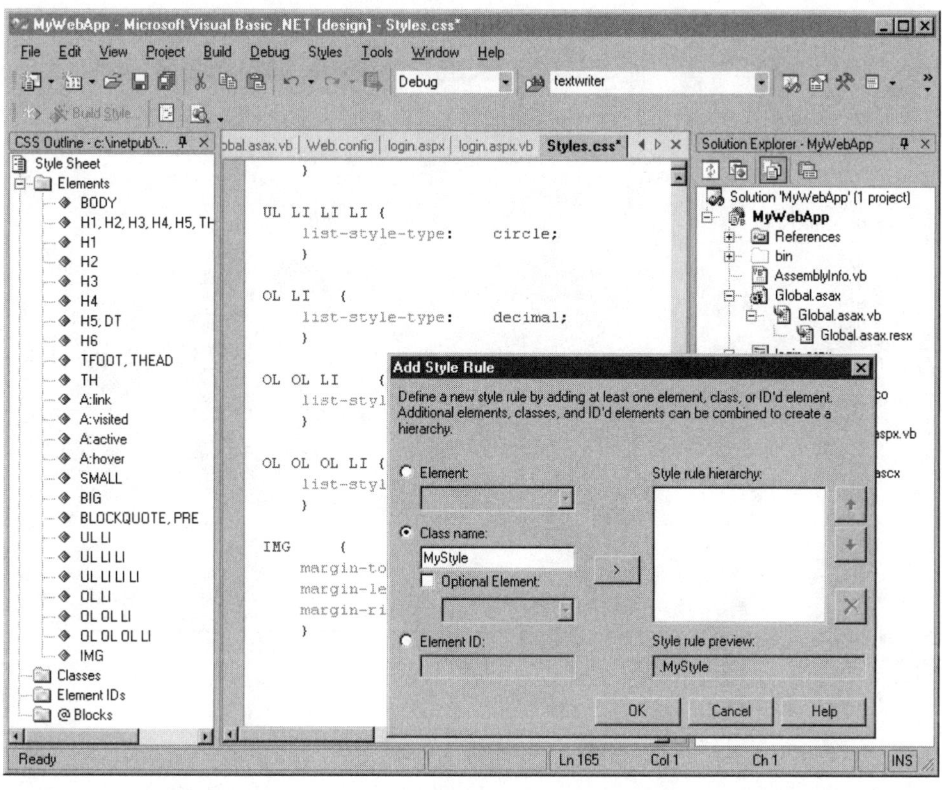

Figure 21-4 Adding a new style rule using the Add Style Rule dialog box

11. Click OK. This adds the style class to the Styles.css file. You can see the results in the main window.
12. Be sure that the cursor is positioned somewhere within the definition of the new style in the Styles.css file.
13. Select the Styles menu item.
14. Select the Build Styles option from the drop-down menu. If the Build Styles option is not available, you do not have the cursor properly positioned as specified in Step 12. This opens the Style Builder dialog box as shown in Figure 21-5.
15. Make the following Font selections in the Style Builder dialog box:
    - Family: Arial
    - Color: Red
    - Bold: Absolute

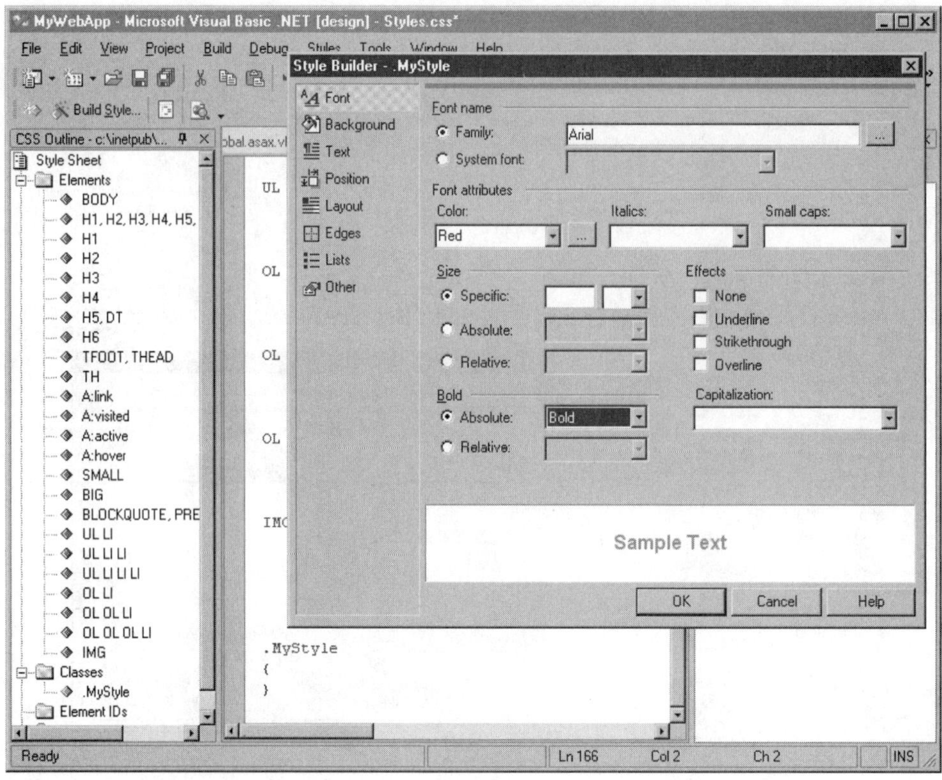

Figure 21-5 Creating a new style using the Style Builder dialog box

16. Click OK. This adds the attributes to the style class.
17. Open MyWebApp.aspx in the main window in Design view.
18. Place the cursor within the Contact Name label in MyWebApp.aspx.
19. In the Properties window, set the class property to MyStyle.
20. Click the cContactName TextBox control.
21. In the Properties window, set the CssClass property to MyStyle.
22. Press F5 to run the Web application.

User Authentication

Your Web application may allow all users access to all forms and data within the Web application. In this case, you do not have to worry about authenticating that the user is who he says he is or authorizing the user to access Web forms within the application. Many Web applications allow this universal access to some of the Web forms but not all.

Most commerce sites follow this model. You can access the site's general Web forms, browse the product catalog, and even create an order. However, when it comes to buying the items, you are asked for account information or asked to create a new account. Once you have a valid account, you can access the check-out Web forms of the Web site and proceed with your purchase.

The processing of logging in to an account is the authentication process. Authentication confirms that you are who you say you are. Once you are authenticated, the login information is used to authorize your access to specific Web forms and related data within the Web application.

EXAM TIP Authentication allows a user access to your site. Authorization allows user access to specific Web forms.

Authentication Methods in ASP.NET

Authentication is divided into two steps. First, you get the authentication information from the user. This information makes up the user's *credentials*. Then the user's credentials are validated against some authentication process or authority. The first release of ASP.NET supports three authentication providers to aid you with these two steps of authentication. These authentication providers are:

- **Windows** Uses a combination of Windows and IIS authentication
- **Microsoft Passport** Uses the Microsoft Passport authentication service
- **Forms-based** Uses ASP.NET form and custom code for authentication

Windows Authentication

Windows authentication uses the Windows operating system's IIS authentication to authenticate the user. When a user requests a Web form that requires authorization, the user must be authenticated by IIS prior to determining if the user is authorized for the Web form. If the user is not already authenticated, IIS sends a login Web form requiring a user login and password. IIS has four methods of authentication:

- **Anonymous** No user login or password is required. IIS does not request this information.
- **Basic** User login and password are sent as clear text. The user login and password can be encrypted using SSL. The user login and password are provided to the Web application for authorization.
- **Digest** User login and password are sent as encoded hash. This requires IE 5 or later and Active Directory. The user must have an Active Directory service domain account.
- **Integrated Windows** Either Windows NT LAN Manager or Kerberos is used for encrypting and authenticating the user. The user must be a valid Windows domain user.

Since Windows-based authentication uses the Windows operating system to provide the authentication, it requires the minimum amount of ASP.NET coding. However, it is recommended only for intranets where all users already have Windows user accounts. Establishing Windows user accounts for a public Internet Web application is not a realistic approach to authentication. For public Internet Web applications, forms-based authentication is the more appropriate option.

Microsoft Passport Authentication

Microsoft Passport authentication uses the Microsoft Passport service to provide user authentication. This service allows a single user login and password to have access to all sites for which the user is registered with the Microsoft Passport service. This reduces the number of logins and passwords that the user has to remember. Some users may like this centralization and some may not. Organizations may not want Microsoft to store their user information, and users may not want Microsoft to store their login information.

To use Microsoft Passport authentication, you set up IIS to validate users as anonymous users. When a user sends a request for a Web form that requires authorization, the request is sent to ASP.NET as an anonymous user. ASP.NET checks to see if the user has been authenticated. If not, the client is redirected to the Passport.com Web site for authentication. After, and if, the user enters the appropriate credential, the Passport.com Web site returns an authentication ticket to your Web site. Your Web site then authenticates the user authentication ticket and returns the Web form to the user.

NOTE When a Web form requires *authorization*, the user must be *authenticated*. It is important to understand this difference. A registered user of a Web site and an employee for the owner of the Web site may both be authenticated to access a Web site, but the employee may be authorized to access different Web forms.

Microsoft Passport authentication is a fee-based service. This and the fact that users and Web site owners are reluctant to have their user information stored at Microsoft has hindered the acceptance and use of the Microsoft Passport service. Also, this provides a single point of failure for your Web site that is not within your control.

Forms-Based Authentication

The most common authentication method implemented is forms-based authentication. When you developed a forms-based authentication in ASP, you had to do all of the implementation yourself. ASP.NET has simplified the process and made the implementation of forms-based authentication more secure.

Forms-based authentication is processed as part of ASP.NET. It does not rely on the Windows operating system, IIS, or Passport for authentication providers. You provide the authentication process and ASP.NET manages the requesting, saving, and checking of credentials. The following section describes the implementation of forms-based authentication in more detail.

Implementing Forms-Based Authentication

Forms-based authentication is the most popular means of user authentication because it gives you control over the authentication process and does not rely on other processes.

Of course, you have to provide the mechanism to determine if the user is who he says he is. Most often, the user is authenticated by verifying his login credentials against a database.

All requests for ASP.NET Web forms must go through IIS. In order to let these requests through to ASP.NET, you must configure IIS authentication to Anonymous access. Once the request for a Web form requiring authorization reaches ASP.NET and you have configured forms-based authentication, ASP.NET and your custom processes proceed with authentication.

EXAM TIP IIS must be configured for Anonymous access when using forms-based authentication.

ASP.NET checks to see if the user has already been authenticated. If a valid authentication cookie is attached to the request, the user has already been authenticated. Since the user is already authenticated, the user is checked to see if he is authorized to access the requested Web form. Details of Web form authorization are discussed in the next section. If the user is authorized, access to the Web form is allowed. If the user is not authorized and access fails, the user is returned an Access Denied message.

If the request has not been authenticated—that is, the request does not have a valid authentication cookie—the user is redirected to a login Web form. The login Web form requests the login information required and authenticates the information. Once the user has been authenticated, the authorization to the Web form is checked. If the user is authorized, access to the Web form is allowed. If the user is not authorized and access fails, the user is returned an Access Denied message.

Configuring ASP.NET for Forms-Based Authentication

You must configure ASP.NET when you want it to perform forms-based authentication. To do this, you set the authentication method in the <authentication> subsection of the <system.web> section in the web.config file as the following shows:

```
<system.web>
   <authentication mode="Forms"/>
</system.web>
```

The mode attribute specifies the type of authorization. In the above case, you set the mode to Forms. The other possible values are Windows, Passport, and None. When a request for a secure Web form is received, the request is redirected to the login.aspx Web form. This is the default login Web form, and you need to create this login.aspx Web form or specify a different login Web form by adding the form element to the authentication section as shown here:

```
<system.web>
   <authentication mode="Forms">
        <forms name=".MyAppAuth" loginUrl="MyAppLogin.aspx"/>
   </authentication>
</system.web>
```

In this element you identify the suffix used for the cookies in the name attribute and your custom login Web form in the loginUrl attribute.

Creating a Login Web Form

The login Web form accepts the user credential, authenticates the credentials, and redirects the user back to the original Web form requested, or a different Web form if desired. It is an ASP.NET Web form that requests the user credential and submits the information. The Submit button for the HTML form has a Click event. The Click event validates the user credential and calls the FormAuthentication.RedirectFromLoginPage method if valid. If the credentials are not valid, the user is notified on the login Web form that the credentials are not valid. In Exercise 21-3, after the "Web Form Authorization" section, you will create a login Web form.

Web Form Authorization

After a user is authenticated, he must be authorized to access secured Web forms. Just like in the Windows security model and the SQL Server security model, authentication is different than authorization. A user can be authenticated for access to a Web site, but he may not be authorized to access all of the Web forms within the Web site. A user can log in to a Windows domain but may not be allowed to access all of the resources within that domain. Or a user may be able to log in to SQL Server but not be able to access all of the databases managed by SQL Server.

The previous section described the process of authentication. Now you will learn about authorization.

Web forms that require authorization are called *secured* Web forms, and you allow users or roles access to those secured Web forms. This access is specified for the Web application, for directories, and/or for specific aspx files.

Authorization is configured within the <authorization> subsection of the <system.web> section in the Web.config files. The <system.web> section can be a subsection of the <configuration> section or of a <location> section.

```
<configuration>
  <system.web>
     <authorization>
       <allow users="*" />
     </authorization>
  </system.web>
  <location path="MyWebForm.aspx">
    <system.web>
      <authorization>
        <deny verb="POST" roles="customer, buyer"/>
      </authorization>
    </system.web>
  </location>
</configuration>
```

The <system.web> section exists twice in the previous authorization example. It first appears as a subsection of the <configuration> section. This tells ASP.NET that this authorization applies to the folder in which the web.config file exists.

The second <system.web> section is a subsection of a <location> section. You can modify the authorization that you specified for the entire folder and its subfolders in this section. The <location> section contains a path attribute to identify the specific subfolder and/or file to which the subsequent configuration information applies.

You define two elements within the <authorization> section: allow and deny. The allow and deny elements contain attributes for users, roles, and specific HTTP verbs as shown in the previous example. The HTTP verbs are POST, GET, and HEAD.

More than one allow or deny element can exist in each <authorization> section. They are applied in the sequence in which they are encountered. For example, you allow access to specific users or roles and then deny access to all users. If you denied access to all users and then allowed access to specific users or roles, no one would be allowed access to your site.

Also, you can specify multiple <location> sections. When you specify a folder in the path attribute, the authorization applies to that folder and all of its subfolders. Of course, you can override this authorization in a web.config file in a subfolder.

EXAM TIP Remember that the authorization in a subfolder's web.config file overrides authorization in the parent's web.config file. Read the question carefully to determine where the authorization is specified.

There are two special characters you may use when specifying a user. They are the asterisk (*) and the question mark (?). The asterisk specifies all users. The question mark identifies anonymous users. The following code denies access to all anonymous users:

```
<deny users="?" />
```

The default setting in machine.config is:

```
<configuration>
  <system.web>
    <authorization>
      <allow users="*" />
    </authorization>
  </system.web>
</configuration>
```

The default setting in the machine.config file allows access to all users.

In the following exercise, you change the web.config setting for authentication and authorization, create a login Web form and test the login process.

Exercise 21-2: Configuring Authentication and Authorization

1. In the Solution Explorer window of the VS.NET IDE, double-click the web.config file. This should open the web.config file in the main edit window of the VS.NET IDE.
2. Find the following line:

   ```
   <authentication mode="Windows" />
   ```

   Change it to:

   ```
   <authentication mode="Forms" />
   ```

3. Find the following line:

   ```
   <allow users="*" /> <!-- Allow all users -->
   ```

PART VI

Change it to:

```
<deny users="?" />
```

4. Run the MyWebApp application by pressing the F5 key. You should get an HTTP error "404 The resource cannot be found." The Requested URL is MyWebApp/login.asp. Because you changed the authentication mode to Forms in Step 2, and then denied access to anonymous users in Step 3, when you tried to access the MyWebForm form, ASP.NET tried to redirect you to the login.aspx form. Since you have not created a login.aspx form, the request failed.
5. Find the following line:

```
<deny users="?" />
```

Change it to:

```
<deny users="*" />
```

6. Add the following line before the line you modified in Step 5.

```
<allow users="MyWebUser1, MyWebUser2" />
```

Figure 21-6 shows the results of Exercise 21-2 with the changes made to the default web.config files authentication and authorization sections. Since the login.aspx form does not exist, you are not able to access this application. You create this Web form in Exercise 21-3.

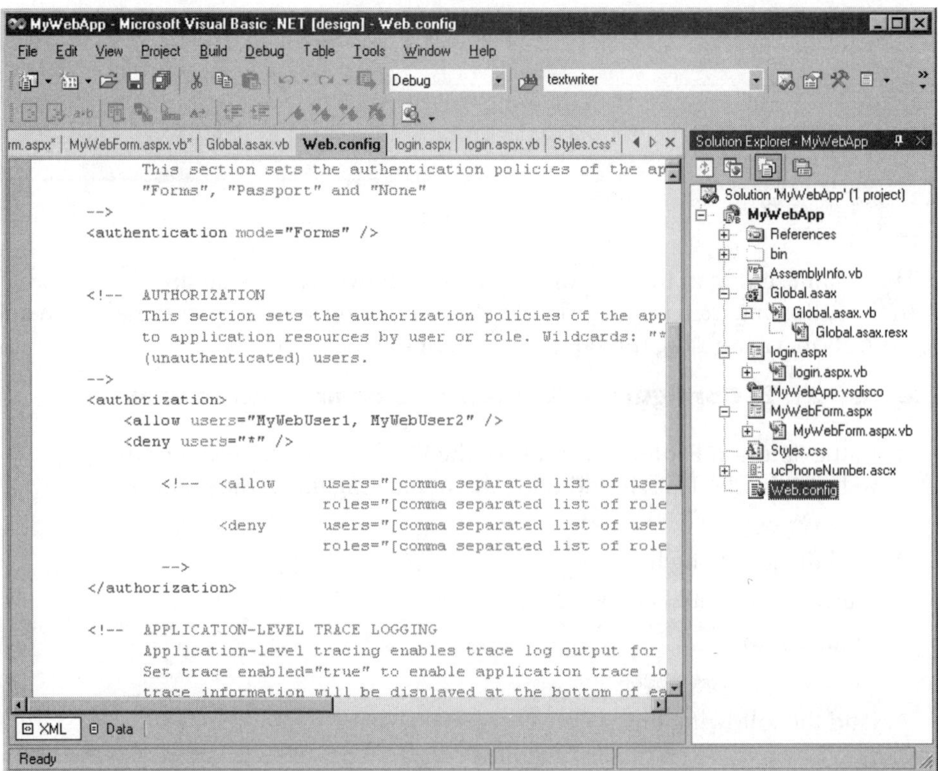

Figure 21-6 The web.config file with changes made to the authentication and authorization sections

Exercise 21-3: Creating the Default Login Web Form

1. From the menu bar of the VS.NET IDE, click Project and then click Add Web Form.
2. The Add New Item - MyWebApp dialog box appears. Change the name to login.aspx.
3. Click Open.
4. Add a Web forms Label control to the form.
5. Change the label's text property to User Name.
6. Add a Web forms TextBox control to the form after the label you added above.
7. Rename the TextBox control to cUserName.
8. Add a Web forms Button control to the form.
9. Rename the Button control to cSubmit.
10. Change the cSubmit control Text property to Submit. Figure 21-7 shows the login.aspx Web form after you have completed this step.
11. Double-click the cSubmit button. This should open the code-behind page for the login.aspx Web form.

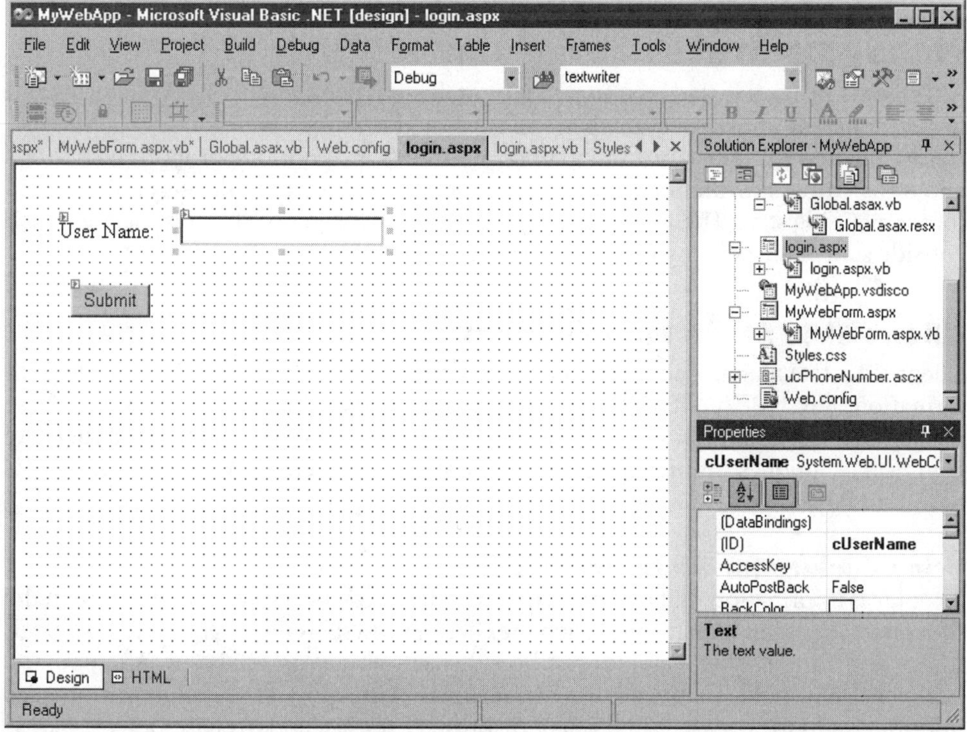

Figure 21-7 The login form with the cUserName and cSubmit controls

12. Add the following code to the cSubmit_Click event:

```
Dim UserName as String = cUserName.Text.ToString
If UserName <> "" Then
System.Web.Security.FormsAuthentication.RedirectFromLoginPage(UserName,False)
End If
```

Exercise 21-3 implements a very simple authentication and authorization process. You usually provide more detailed user authorization by calling your own business rules in the cSubmit_Click event. Exercise 21-4 tests the authentication and authorization that you defined in the previous two exercises.

Exercise 21-4: Testing the Login and Authorization Configuration

1. Start the MyWebApp by pressing F5. Although the application has MyWebForm.aspx set as the start page for the application, security redirects you to the login.aspx Web form.
2. Enter Test in the User Name text box.
3. Click the Submit button. The login page is redisplayed because Test is not *authorized* to access MyWebForm.aspx.
4. Enter MyWebUser1 in the User Name text box.
5. Click the Submit button. The MyWebForm.aspx Web form is displayed because MyWebUser1 is *authorized* to access MyWebForm.aspx.

Managing State

A Web form by itself is stateless. That is, it is totally independent of other Web forms and has no inherent knowledge of what has happened on other Web forms. Maintaining state is providing a mechanism to manage information about one or more Web forms and transferring information between Web forms. ASP.NET provides several processes for maintaining state. These can be categorized into two types of state management: client-side state management and server-side state management.

Client-Side State Management

Client-side state management uses the client's system or the Web form itself to store information. ASP.NET provides three methods to manage client-side server state. These are cookies, query strings, and the ViewState property. Cookies and query strings are common techniques for managing client-side state; however, the ViewState property is new to ASP.NET.

Using Cookies for State Information

A cookie is information that is stored on the client's machine, either in memory or in the file system, between Web forms. When the client's browser sends a request to the server, it also sends the cookie. Cookies can be either temporary or persistent. A temporary, non-persistent cookie is information that is stored in the browser's session memory. The information in the cookie is lost when the browser session ends. A temporary cookie is also known as a session cookie. A persistent cookie is stored in the client's file system.

The client must provide permission for the cookie to be saved on their system. How long a persistent cookie is stored on the client's system is dependent on the client's operating system and browser settings. You cannot depend on the cookie being available.

The amount of information that can be stored in a cookie is limited. The client's computer may only allow cookies up to a certain size and each cookie can contain no more than four kilobytes of information. Since the cookie is stored on the client's computer, it can be modified by the client. This is a potential security risk because these changes may cause your application to perform unexpectedly.

Using Query Strings for State Information

A query string is information that is appended to the URL to provide parameters to the requested Web form. It is limited in size and is fully visible. The query string information is appended to the URL with a question mark (?) followed by value pairs, a value name and a value. The following is an example of a query string:

```
http://www.myWebSite.com/myWebForm.aspx?name=Smith&ZipCode=80111
```

The query string contains two value pairs, one for the name of Smith and one for the zip code of 80111.

Query strings are limited in size and are a potential security risk. Most browsers limit the length of a URL to 255 characters. This query string is transmitted with the URL and is visible to the user. This is a security risk because not only can the user see the parameters your page is receiving, the user can change these parameters and submit requests your application is not expecting.

Using the ViewState Property for State Information

As you learned earlier in the chapter, Web forms in ASP.NET have a ViewState property that is a built-in structure for maintaining state. This property is maintained in a hidden control in the Web form, __VIEWSTATE. The hidden __VIEWSTATE control is added to a form and returned to the server with the next request. ASP.NET automates the process of populating and using the ViewState property to maintain state information.

Server-Side State Management

Server-side state management uses server resources to store state information. ASP.NET provides two intrinsic objects to maintain state. They are the Application object to maintain application state and the Session object to maintain session state. ASP.NET also provides application cache to optimize application state information. The application cache is covered in Chapter 23.

Using Application State

Application state saves information that is available to all Web forms and users within the Web application. This application information is saved in the Application intrinsic object, which we explored in Chapter 20. You simply place a value in the Application object as shown in the following sample code:

```
Application("DefaultCountry") = "USA"
```

This code sets the DefaultCountry to USA. All Web forms can now access this value as shown in the following sample code:

```
cCountry.Text = Application("DefaultCountry")
```

You normally initialize application variables in the Application_Start event in the global.asax file. The global.asax file contains code for responding to Web application events. Just like you have the code-behind page for a form, you can think of the global .asax file as the code-behind page for a Web application. It is also called the ASP.NET application file. The following sample code shows DefaultCountry being set within the *Application_Start* event of the global.asax file:

```
Sub Application_Start(ByVal sender As Object, ByVal e As EventArgs)
    Application("DefaultCountry") = "USA"
End Sub
```

You can access the global.asax file directly from the VS.NET IDE when you are developing a Web application.

NOTE The VS.NET IDE creates a global.asax.vb file for the code you create. The global.asax and global.asax.vb files are located in the root virtual directory of the application.

Application information can also be maintained in cache. This is an optimization feature of ASP.NET and is covered in detail in Chapter 23.

Using Session State

A user is assigned a SessionID when they first access a Web application. This SessionID is used to track that user while he is within the Web application. You can maintain information for the user during this session. This is referred to as *session state*. As you learned in Chapter 20, you may store session variables is the Session intrinsic object. Setting and retrieving information for the Session object is identical to the process of using an Application object as shown in the following sample code:

```
Session("UserName") = cFirstName.Text & " " & cLastName.Text
```

Once you have set the information in the Session object, you use it on other Web forms for this user, as shown here:

```
cName.Text = Session("UserName")
```

You use the Session object to maintain information between Web forms. As in the preceding sample code, the user may enter his first name and last name on one Web form. You store this information in the Session object and then access it on other Web forms the user visits.

You can initialize session information in the Session_Start event in the global.asax file. This is similar to initializing information for the Application object in the Application_Start event in the global.asax file described in the previous section. The following sample code shows initialization of the EmailRequired variable to True:

```
Sub Session_Start(ByVal sender As Object, ByVal e As EventArgs)
    Session("EmailRequired") = True
End Sub
```

Implementing Online User Assistance and Accessibility Features

The .NET Framework provides features for both online user assistance and accessibility features for Windows forms. See Chapter 17 for details on these features. These features are not available in ASP.NET because they are dependent on the Windows operating system and the .NET Framework. Access to an ASP.NET application is through a browser that may not be operating within the Windows operating system and the .NET Framework.

You use the same techniques in ASP.NET as you did in ASP to implement online user assistance. You specify tool tips for controls and you provide links to specific Web forms to display help information.

The same applies for accessibility features. You use the same techniques in ASP.NET as you did in ASP. For example, you can provide alternate text displays for images and design your forms to work with large fonts.

Summary

Creating a Web form is just the start of developing a complete Web application. You need to transfer information between forms, authenticate users for access to your Web application, and authorize users for different parts of your Web application. Also, you can control the look of your Web application using cascading style sheets and modify the operation of your Web application by simply changing settings in the web.config files.

You maintain information that is required between forms using either client-side state or server-side state. Client-side state includes cookies (persistent and non-persistent), query strings, and the ViewState property. Server-side state includes the Application and Session intrinsic objects.

You control access to your Web application using different authentication processes and you control access to specific Web forms using authorization. The .NET Framework provides for Windows, Passport, and forms-based authentication processes.

The .NET Framework allows for dynamic configuration of your Web application using the web.config files. Each virtual directory within your Web application can have different web.config files. When you change and save these files, the new values are immediately available to your Web application. You do not have to stop and restart your Web application.

Test Questions

1. Which of the following is not a method to maintain client-side state?
   A. Cookies
   B. ViewState
   C. QueryStrings
   D. Session
   E. None of the above

2. Your Web form contains several server-side controls that require processing on the server. What do you need to do to keep from reloading default values that you set in the page_load event?
   A. Do nothing. The page_load event is only fired the first time a page is accessed.
   B. Set the ViewState values to the current values returned by the user.
   C. Populate the controls from the ViewState values.
   D. If the Page.IsPostBack value is True, do not set the default values.
3. Is it easy for the user to view the ViewState information that is sent to the client?
   A. Yes
   B. No
4. Where is the most likely place you would find the machine.config file?
   A. The root directory of the Web application.
   B. Every directory of the Web application contains a machine.config file.
   C. WinNT\Microsoft.NET\Framework\v1.0.3705\CONFIG\
   D. Program Files\Microsoft.NET\CONFIG\
5. If all web.config files and the machine.config file set the same configuration value, which setting applies for a specific Web form?
   A. The web.config file in the root directory for the Web application
   B. The value in the machine.config file
   C. The web.config file in the same directory as the Web form
   D. None of the above
6. What is the name of the section in the web.config file that you can use to define your own settings?
   A. userSettings
   B. userConfig
   C. appConfig
   D. appSettings
   E. appVariables
7. If you make a change to a setting in a web.config file and save that change, what must you do for your Web application to access the changed information?
   A. Stop and start IIS
   B. Stop and start the Web application
   C. Read the web.config file from the Web application to reset all the values
   D. Nothing, the new configuration values will automatically be available

8. When you create a new application using the VS.NET IDE, it automatically creates the Styles.css cascading style sheet and applies it to all Web forms you create.
   A. True
   B. False
9. Which of the following is not a type of IIS authentication?
   A. Anonymous
   B. Forms
   C. Basic
   D. Digest
10. Which of the following is not true for forms authentication?
    A. IIS must be configured for Anonymous authentication.
    B. The VS.NET IDE automatically creates a login.aspx Web form for you.
    C. The default login page is login.aspx.
    D. It does not rely on the Windows operating system.
11. If you want to set up specific authorization for a specific page, where do you define this authorization?
    A. Windows registry
    B. The <location> section of the web.config file
    C. The <pageSettings> section of the web.config file
    D. The <allow> element for the specific page section of the web.config file
12. Where do you place code that you want to be executed every time an application starts?
    A. You repeat code in each page_load event of each Web form.
    B. The application_load event of each Web form.
    C. The session_load event in the global.asax (global.asax.vb) file.
    D. The application_load event in the global.asax (global.asax.vb) file.
13. You can change the value of a configuration application setting from code in a Web application.
    A. True
    B. False
14. What intrinsic object do you use for values that you want available to all users and Web forms?
    A. Session
    B. Page
    C. AllUsers

D. Application

E. System

15. What is the name of the default form to request user credentials when using forms authentication?

A. UserCredentials.aspx

B. Logon.aspx

C. Login.aspx

D. User.aspx

Test Answers

1. D.
2. D.
3. B.
4. C.
5. C.
6. D.
7. D.
8. B.
9. B.
10. B.
11. B.
12. D.
13. B.
14. D.
15. C.

CHAPTER 22

Data Binding in ASP.NET Applications

In this chapter, you will

- Use controls to display data
- Bind data to the user interface
- Transform and filter data
- Use templates
- Dynamically add controls

In Chapter 12, we explored using ADO.NET for accessing and updating data sources. Because ADO.NET is designed to work with disconnected data, it is ideal for use in Web applications, as well. This chapter covers how to use ADO.NET in an ASP.NET Web application.

Preparing to Use Data in ASP.NET

One of the key features of the .NET Framework is the use of ADO.NET's DataReader class, DataSet class, and DataView class as common interfaces for data access. Chapters 12, 13, and 14 cover how to use the DataReader, DataSet, and DataView objects. Once you have a DataReader object, a DataSet object, or a DataView object, you can use them in either a Windows forms application or a Web application.

You use the DataReader class to provide one-time access to the data. A DataReader object is primarily used to populate controls of a Web form from VB code in the code-behind page. The DataSet class provides you with access to data that you want to bind to controls on the form and that you may want to update. If you want to transform, filter, or sort information in a DataSet object, you create a DataView object from the DataSet object. Then you use the DataView object to bind to controls on the Web form.

NOTE The examples in this chapter and many of the examples provided by Microsoft create a direct connection to a SQL Server database to create a DataSet object. This simplifies the examples. In a real application you should use business classes that return DataSets. This isolates the user interface from the data source, which provides better security, more scalability, and easier future enhancements.

Populating a Control Using the DataReader

When the user first accesses a page, you may wish to populate controls with information from a database. For example, you may want to populate a Web server control with information from the Regions table in the Northwind database. The following listing shows the necessary code in the Page_Load event of the Web form:

```
Private Sub Page_Load(ByVal sender As System.Object, ByVal e As
System.EventArgs) Handles MyBase.Load
    If Not Page.IsPostBack Then
        Dim cnNWind as New SqlConnection
        cnNWind.ConnectionString = _
            "Data Source=(local);Initial Catalog=Northwind;" & _
            "Integrated Security=SSPI"
        cnNWind.Open()
        Dim cmdRegions as New SqlCommand("Select * FROM Region", cnNWind)
        Dim drRegions as SqlDataReader = Cmdregions.ExecuteReader()
        Do While drRegions.Read()
            cRegions.Items.Add(drRegions.Item("RegionDescription").toString)
        Loop
        drRegions.Close
        cnNWind.Close
    End If
End Sub
```

In this code, you want to load the region information into the control the first time the Web form is loaded. You check the Page.IsPostBack property to determine if you need to populate the control. If it is not a page postback—that is, if this is the first time the page is being loaded—you connect to the database, create a command to execute against the database, and execute the command to create the DataReader. You then use the DataReader, drRegions, to add each RegionDescription to the DropDown control, cRegions. After you have completed populating the control, you need to be sure to close both the DataReader object, drRegions, and the SQLConnection object, cnNWind, to free up the SQL Server resources.

EXAM TIP Connections need to be explicitly closed to release database resources.

In Exercise 22-1, you will create a new Web application and populate a Web form control with regions from the Regions table in the Northwind database.

Exercise 22-1: Populating a Web Server Control Using the DataReader

1. Open the VS.NET IDE and create a new Web application called MyWebADOApp. Refer to Chapter 20 if you need instructions on creating a new Web application.
2. In the Solution Explorer window, right-click the WebForm1.aspx and click Delete.
3. Click OK to delete the Web form.
4. Right-click MyWebADOApp in the Solution Explorer window, select Add, and select Add Web Form.

5. Change the Name property to Regions.aspx and click OK.
6. From the Toolbox window, select Web Forms to provide access to the Web forms controls.
7. Add a Web forms Label control to the Regions.aspx Web form.
8. Change the Text property of the Label control to **Select region to display**.
9. Add a Web forms DropDownList control to the Regions.aspx Web form.
10. Change the ID property of the DropDownList control to cRegions. Your Web application should look similar to Figure 22-1.
11. Double-click on the Region.aspx form in the main window in an area that does not contain a control. This opens the Regions.aspx.vb file in the main window.
12. Place the following code in the Page_Load event of the Regions.aspx.vb file:

```
Private Sub Page_Load(ByVal sender As System.Object, ByVal e As
System.EventArgs) Handles MyBase.Load

    If Not Page.IsPostBack Then
        ' Loading Region data into a control
        Dim cnNWind as New SqlConnection
        cnNWind.ConnectionString = _
            "Data Source=(local);Initial Catalog=Northwind;" & _
            "Integrated Security=SSPI"
        cnNWind.Open()
        Dim cmdRegions as New SqlCommand("Select * FROM Region", cnNWind)
        Dim drRegions as SqlDataReader = Cmdregions.ExecuteReader()
        Dim liRegion as ListItem
        cRegions.Items.Add("") ' Blank item for no selection
        Do While drRegions.Read()
            liRegion = New ListItem
            liRegion.Value = drRegions.Item("RegionID").toString
            liRegion.Text = drRegions.Item("RegionDescription").toString
            cRegions.Items.Add(liRegion)
        Loop
        drRegions.Close
        cnNWind.Close
    End If
End Sub
```

This code shows the use of the ListItem object to populate the DropDownList, cRegions. The previous example simply added the RegionDescription to the cRegions control. This Web form is going to be used in Exercise 22-3 and that exercise needs access to the RegionID. Therefore, a ListItem is created to contain both the RegionID and the RegionDescription. Also, this code adds a blank item to the cRegions control, cRegions.Items.Add(""). This allows the user to select no region when a region is not required.

8. In the Solution Explorer window, right-click the Regions.aspx file and select Select As Start Page.
9. Press F5 to compile and run the application.
10. Select the DropDownList control down arrow to open the DropDownList. The results should look similar to Figure 22-2.

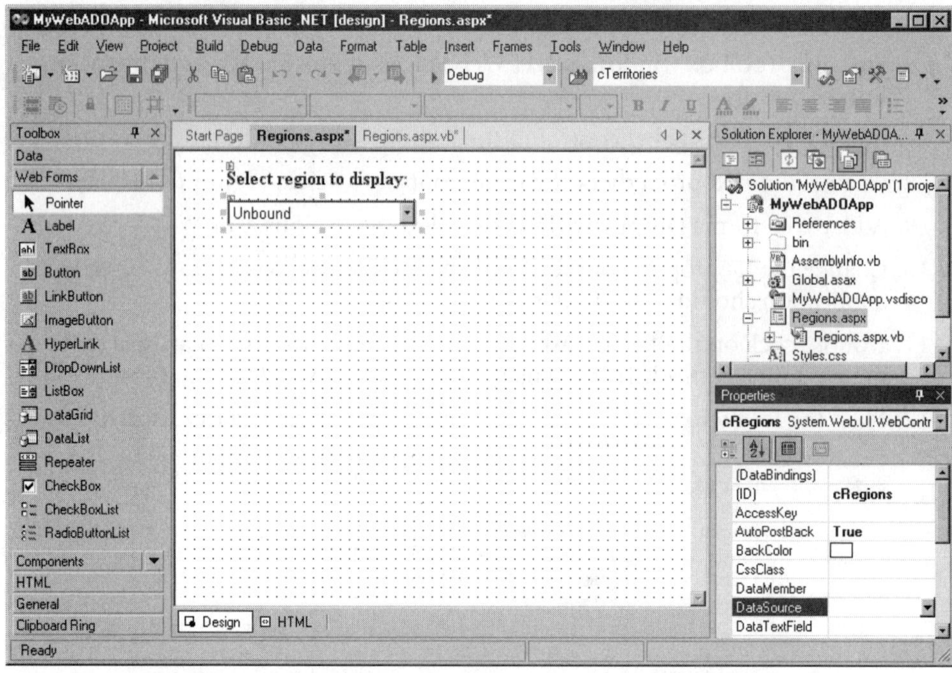

Figure 22-1 Regions.aspx form with controls added

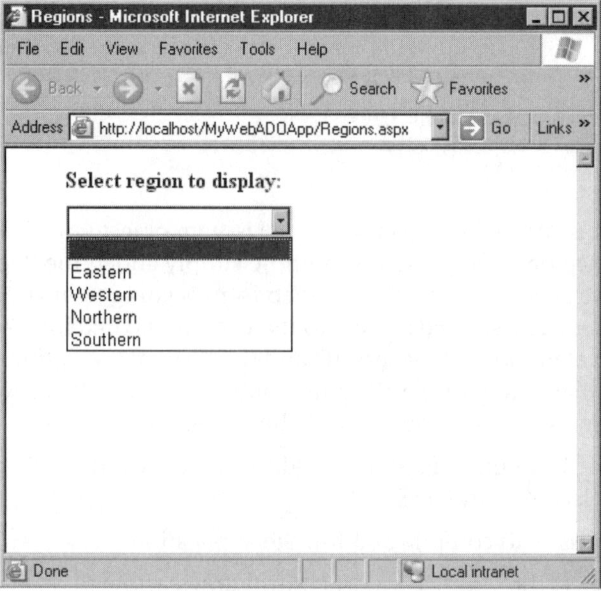

Figure 22-2 Completed Exercise 22-1 with DropDownList control open

Dynamically Adding Controls

When you are designing a form, you may not always know the number or type of controls you want on the form. In many cases, the controls you want on the form may be driven by data. Take regions, for example. Instead of providing a drop-down list for the user to select a region, you may want to provide radio buttons for the user to click. At design time, you do not know how many regions are going to be defined. You want to make the number of radio buttons and their description dynamic based on the data in your database.

ASP.NET allows you to load controls dynamically. First, you need to add a "place keeper" control to your Web form. The Panel Web form server control is a good choice for this place keeper control. The Panel Web form server control is simply a set of HTML <div></div> tags used to separate sections of your HTML. It is used as a container to place the control you are going to dynamically add to the Web form.

The following listing shows the necessary code to dynamically add a radio button for each region in the Regions table of the Northwind database:

```
If Not Page.IsPostBack Then
    Dim cnNWind as New SqlConnection
    cnNWind.ConnectionString = _
        "Data Source=(local);Initial Catalog=Northwind;" & _
        "Integrated Security=SSPI"
    cnNWind.Open()
    Dim cmdRegions as New SqlCommand("Select * FROM Region", cnNWind)
    Dim drRegions as SqlDataReader = Cmdregions.ExecuteReader()
    Dim rButton as RadioButton
    Dim lcLine as LiteralControl
    Do While drRegions.Read()
        rButton = New RadioButton()
        rButton.Text = drRegions.Item("RegionDescription").ToString
        rButton.GroupName = "Regions"
        cRegionButtons.Controls.Add (rButton)
        lcLine = New LiteralControl("<br>")
        cRegionButtons.Controls.Add(lcLine)
    Loop
    drRegions.Close
    cnNWind.Close
End If
```

The data access portion of this code is identical to the code in the previous section. The difference is in the Do While loop and the objects used in it. The code creates a RadioButton object, **rButton**, that is used to add new buttons to the Panel control, cRegionButtons, that has been added to the Web form. Also, a Literal Control object, **lcLine**, is created as a separator for the radio buttons. In this case, the separator is a new line (<br>). The Do While loop adds a new radio button and a line separator for each record in the Regions table.

EXAM TIP You dynamically add controls to the Controls collection of a control container object using the Add method. The Page object has a Controls collection, thus you can add controls directly to the page without a separate control such as the Panel control.

PART VI

In Exercise 22-2, you will add a radio button to a Web form for each region in the Regions table in the Northwind database.

Exercise 22-2: Dynamically Adding Controls to a Web Form

1. Add a new Web form named DynamicControls.aspx to the MyWebADOApp. See Exercise 22-1 for more details on adding a Web form.
2. Add a Web forms Label control to the DynamicControls.aspx Web form.
3. Change the Text property of the Label control to **Select region to display**.
4. Add a Web forms Panel control to the DynamicControls.aspx Web form.
5. Change the ID property of the Panel control to cRegionButtons. Your Web application should look similar to Figure 22-3.
6. Double-click on the DynamicControls.aspx form in the main window in an area that does not contain a control. This opens the DynamicControls.aspx.vb file in the main window.

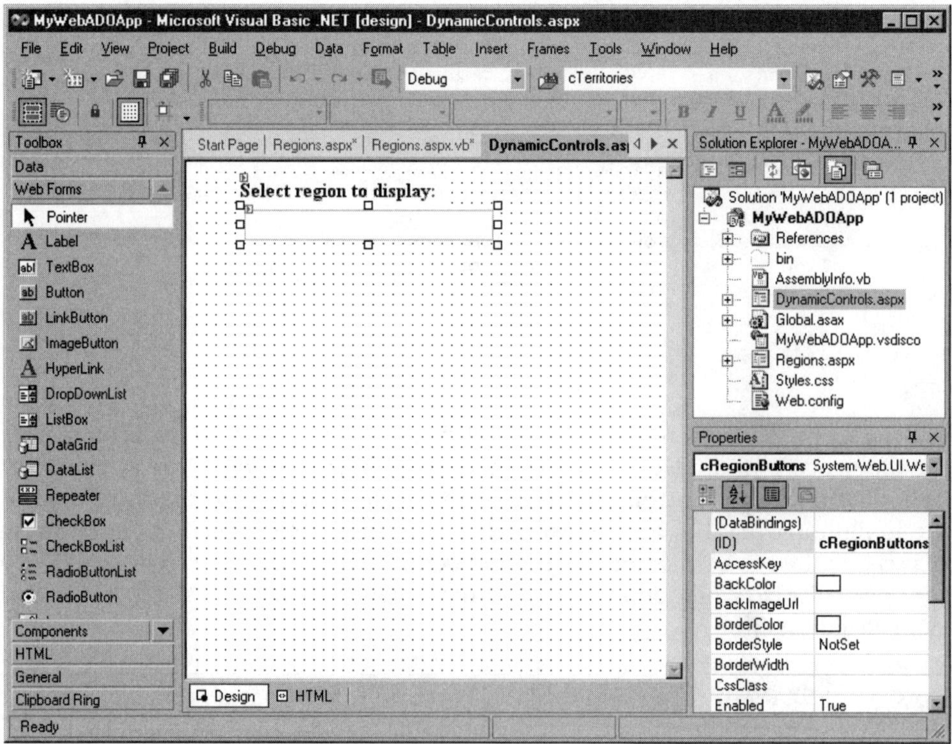

Figure 22-3 DynamicControls.aspx form with controls added

7. Place the following code in the Page_Load event of the DynamicControls.aspx.vb file:

```
Private Sub Page_Load(ByVal sender As System.Object, ByVal e As
System.EventArgs) Handles MyBase.Load
    If Not Page.IsPostBack Then
        ' Adding a new radio button for each control
        Dim cnNWind as New SqlConnection
        cnNWind.ConnectionString = _
            "Data Source=(local);Initial Catalog=Northwind;" & _
            "Integrated Security=SSPI"
        cnNWind.Open()
        Dim cmdRegions as New SqlCommand("Select * FROM Region", cnNWind)
        Dim drRegions as SqlDataReader = Cmdregions.ExecuteReader()
        Dim rButton as RadioButton
        Dim lcLine as LiteralControl
        Do While drRegions.Read()
            rButton = New RadioButton()
            rButton.ID = "cRegion_" & drRegions.Item("RegionID").ToString
            rButton.Text = drRegions.Item("RegionDescription").ToString
            rButton.GroupName = "Regions"
            cRegionButtons.Controls.Add (rButton)
            lcLine = New LiteralControl("<br>")
            cRegionButtons.Controls.Add(lcLine)
        Loop
        drRegions.Close
        cnNWind.Close
    End If
End Sub
```

8. In the Solution Explorer window, right-click the DynamicControls.aspx file and select Select As Start Page.

9. Press F5 to compile and run the application. The results should look similar to Figure 22-4.

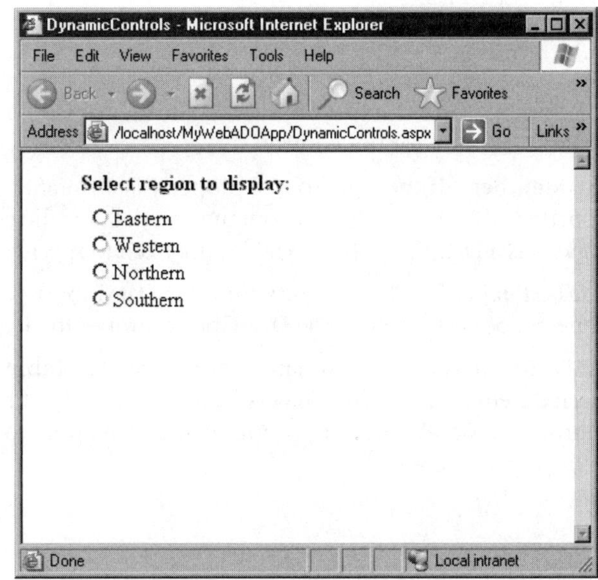

Figure 22-4 Completed Exercise 22-2 with dynamic radio buttons added for each region

Using ASP.NET List-Bound Controls

ASP.NET includes several list-bound controls that you bind to DataSets. A list-bound control is connected to either a DataSet object or a DataView object and works with one or more rows of data. References in this chapter to a data source refer to either a DataSet object or a DataView object. ASP.NET automatically populates the list-bound control with data from the data source. The list-bound controls included in ASP.NET are:

- **CheckBoxList** Dynamically creates multiple check boxes based on the number of rows in the data source
- **DataGrid** Lists multiple rows from the data source displaying each field in a column
- **DataList** Lists multiple rows from the data source. The placement and formatting of the data is controlled by a template. Templates are discussed later in this chapter.
- **DropDownList** Provides a drop-down list from which the user can make a single selection
- **ListBox** Displays multiple rows from which the user can select one or more rows
- **RadioButtonList** Dynamically creates multiple radio buttons based on the number of rows in the data source
- **Repeater** Has no visual user interface. The display of information is controlled by a template. You have control over how the columns from the rows are displayed.

Special Properties of List-Bound Controls

Special properties apply to the list-bound controls. These properties define the data source for the control and information about the data source. The special properties for list-bound controls are:

- **DataSource** The DataSet object, DataReader object, or DataView object that contains the data for the control
- **DataMember** If the DataSource property is a DataSet object, the DataMember property is the DataTable that contains the data for the control. If the DataSource property is a DataView object, you do not need to specify a DataMember property.
- **DataTextField** The field name within the DataTable to display. The DataTextField property does not apply to the DataGrid control or the Repeater control.
- **DataValueField** The field name within the DataTable that is the value of a selected item in a list. This may be different than the text displayed within the control. The DataValueField property does not apply to the DataGrid control or the Repeater control.

Binding a List-Bound Control to a Data Source

Once you have a data source available, it is easy to bind the data source to the list-bound control. You just set the special list-bound properties. The following example shows the code necessary to bind a DataSet to a DataGrid control:

```
Private Sub PopulateTerritories(RegionID as String)
    Dim SQL as String
    If RegionID = "" then
        cTerritories.Visible = False
    else
        cTerritories.Visible = True
    End If
    SQL = "SELECT * FROM Territories WHERE RegionID='" & RegionID & "'"
    Dim cnNWind as New SqlConnection
    cnNWind.ConnectionString = _
        "Data Source=(local);Initial Catalog=Northwind;" & _
        "Integrated Security=SSPI"
    cnNWind.Open()
    Dim daTerritories as New SqlDataAdapter(SQL, cnNWind)
    Dim dsTerritories as New DataSet
    daTerritories.Fill(dsTerritories)
    cTerritories.DataSource = dsTerritories
    cTerritories.DataBind()
End Sub
```

The DataGrid control, cTerritories, is the control on the Web form that is being bound to a DataSet. The DataSet object, dsTerritories, is created using the SqlDataAdapter object, daTerritories. daTerritories provides access to the Northwind database using the SQL statement, SQL, to retrieve all territories in a specific region. Chapter 12 describes the data adapters in detail. After the SqlDataAdapter fills the DataSet object, the DataGrid's DataSource property is set to the DataSet, dsTerritories. The final and most important step is to bind the DataSet to the DataGrid control. The DataBind method is used to perform this binding.

EXAM TIP It is not sufficient to set the DataSource property of a control to populate the control with data. The control must explicitly be bound by the DataBind method of the control.

In Exercise 22-3, you will modify the form you created in Exercise 22-1 to display all of the territories within a selected region. In addition to demonstrating the binding of a DataSet to the DataGrid control, the exercise demonstrates the changes necessary to force a post back to the server when a region is selected.

Exercise 22-3: Binding a Dataset to the DataGrid Control

1. In the Solution Explorer window, double-click the Regions.aspx Web form. This opens the Regions.aspx Web form in the main window.
2. From the Toolbox window, drag and drop the Web forms DataGrid control onto the Regions.aspx Web form.

3. Change the ID property of the DataGrid control to cTerritories.
4. Click the cRegions DropDownList control.
5. Change the AutoPostBack property of the cRegions control to True. The Regions.aspx Web form should look similar to Figure 22-5.
6. Double-click on the cRegions control on the Regions.aspx form. This opens the Regions.aspx.vb file in the main window and adds code for the cRegions_SelectedIndexChanged event.
7. Place the following code in the cRegions_SelectedIndexChanged event of the Regions.aspx.vb file:

```
PopulateTerritories(cRegions.SelectedItem.Value.ToString)
```

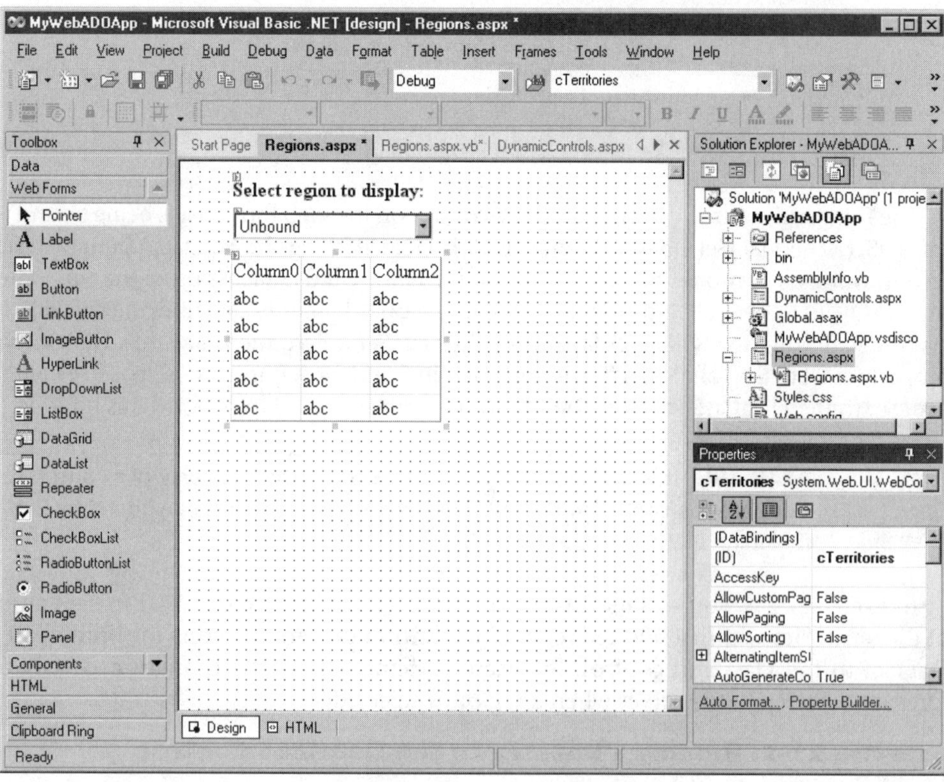

Figure 22-5 The Regions.aspx Web form with the DataGrid control added

8. Add the following PopulateTerritories subroutine to the Regions.aspx.vb file:

```
Private Sub PopulateTerritoryList(RegionID as String)
    Dim SQL as String
    If RegionID = "" then
        cTerritories.Visible = False
    else
        cTerritories.Visible = True
    End If
    SQL = "SELECT * FROM Territories WHERE RegionID='" & RegionID & "'"
    Dim cnNWind as New SqlConnection
    cnNWind.ConnectionString = _
        "Data Source=(local);Initial Catalog=Northwind;" & _
        "Integrated Security=SSPI"
    cnNWind.Open()
    Dim daTerritories as New SqlDataAdapter(SQL, cnNWind)
    Dim dsTerritories as New DataSet
    daTerritories.Fill(dsTerritories)
    cTerritories.DataSource = dsTerritories
    cTerritories.DataBind()
    cnNWind.Close
End Sub
```

9. In the Solution Explorer window, right-click the Regions.aspx file and select Select As Start Page.
10. Press F5 to compile and run the Web application.
11. Select a region to display the territories for that region. The results should look similar to Figure 22-6.

The DataGrid control in Exercise 22-3 was automatically built and formatted by ASP.NET based on the data in the DataSet. In Exercise 22-4, you will change this formatting using the VS.NET IDE.

Exercise 22-4: Changing the Formatting of the DataGrid Control

1. In the Solution Explorer window, double-click the Regions.aspx Web form. This opens the Regions.aspx Web form in the main window.
2. Click the DataGrid control, cTerritories.
3. Change the AutoGenerateColumns property of the cTerritories control to False.
4. Right-click the cTerritories control and select Property Builder. The cTerritories Properties dialog window is displayed.
5. In the cTerritories Properties dialog window, select Columns in the list on the left side of the window.
6. In the Available Columns window, select Bound Column.
7. Click the > symbol to move the Bound Column to the Selected Columns window.
8. Under the BoundColumn Properties section, set the Header Text to Id.

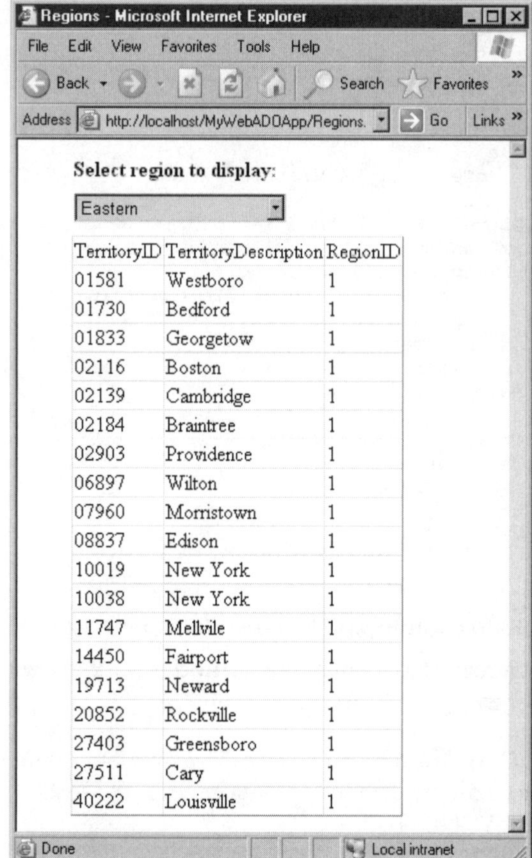

Figure 22-6 Completed Exercise 22-3 displaying territories in a DataGrid control for a selected region

9. Set the Data Field to TerritoryID.
10. Repeat Steps 6 through 9 setting the Header Text to Description and the Data Field to TerritoryDescription. Figure 22-7 shows the completed cTerritories Properties dialog box.
11. Click the OK button.
12. Press F5 to compile and run the Web application.
13. Select a region to display the territories for that region. The results should look similar to Figure 22-8.

Using Templates with List-Bound Controls

The DataGrid, DataList, and Repeater list-bound controls allow you to create templates for the user interface for the controls. Templates are required for the DataList and the Repeater controls, and you have the option of using templates for columns of the DataGrid control. ASP.NET provides you with the flexibility to define your own display within the HTML code. The following listing is sample template code for a DataList control.

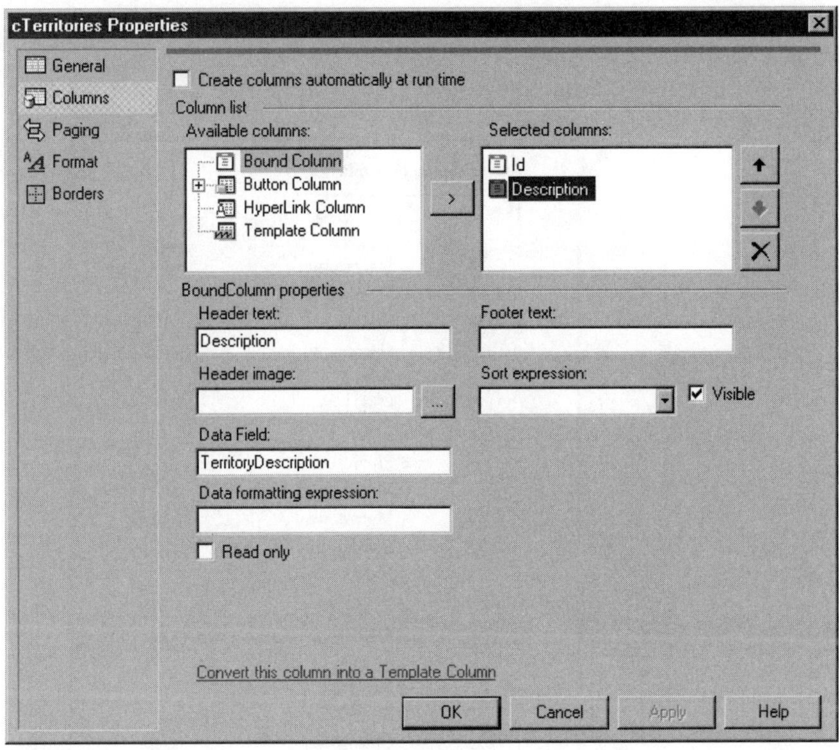

Figure 22-7 The complete Property Builder dialog box for the cTerritories DataGrid control

EXAM TIP The DataList and Repeater control require templates.


```
<asp:DataList id="cTerritoryList" style="Z-INDEX: 104; LEFT: 362px;
POSITION: absolute; TOP: 88px" runat="server" Height="132" Width="284">
    <HeaderTemplate>
        <B>Territories</B>
    </HeaderTemplate>
    <ItemTemplate>
        <%# Container.DataItem("TerritoryDescription")%>
    </ItemTemplate>
</asp:DataList>
```

NOTE This is HTML code that you add to the aspx file. It is not VB code in the code-behind aspx.vb file. When the form is displayed in the main window of the VS.NET IDE, you select the HTML option instead of the Design option at the bottom of the window.

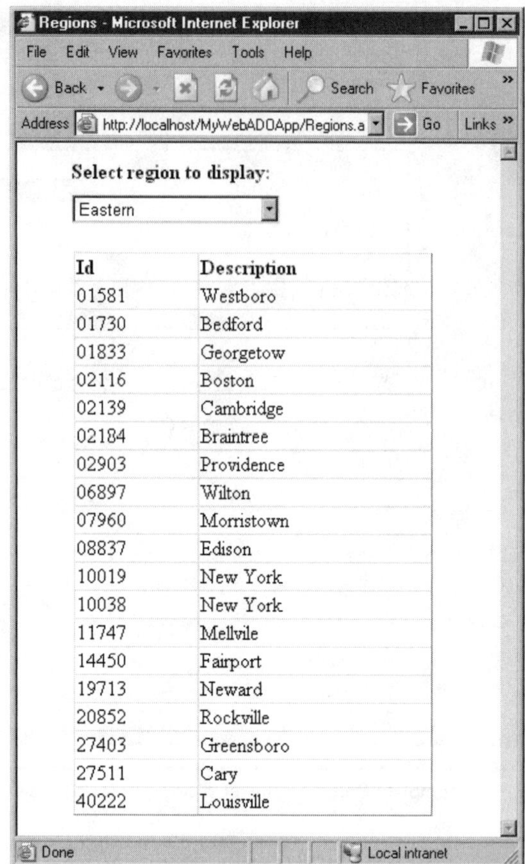

Id	Description
01581	Westboro
01730	Bedford
01833	Georgetow
02116	Boston
02139	Cambridge
02184	Braintree
02903	Providence
06897	Wilton
07960	Morristown
08837	Edison
10019	New York
10038	New York
11747	Mellvile
14450	Fairport
19713	Neward
20852	Rockville
27403	Greensboro
27511	Cary
40222	Louisville

Figure 22-8 Regions.aspx Web form with a formatted DataGrid

The template sections are enclosed by the list-bound controls tags, <asp:DataList …> and </asp:DataList>. There are two template sections shown in the code, the HeaderTemplate and the ItemTemplate. The HTML code for displaying the data is included within each of these sections. The key to accessing the bound data is the <%# …%> section. The <% … %> syntax identifies the enclosed code as inline server-side code, and the # indicates that this code is a data binding process. You use the Container.DataItem collection to access specific fields from a data row.

While only two are shown in the example above, there are actually seven types of templates for the list-bound controls. Not all of the templates are available for all controls. The following list identifies each type of template and the control to which they apply:

- **HeaderTemplate (DataGrid, DataList, Repeater)** Contains the display code that is listed prior to any of the data
- **FooterTemplate (DataGrid, DataList, Repeater)** Contains the display code that appears after all of the data is displayed
- **ItemTemplate (DataGrid, DataList, Repeater)** Contains the display code that is displayed for each row (column for the DataGrid control)

- **AlternatingItemTemplate (DataList, Repeater)** Contains the display code for every other row
- **SeparatorTemplate (DataList, Repeater)** Contains the display code to separate each row of data
- **SelectedItemTemplate (DataList)** Contains the display code for those rows that have been selected by the user
- **EditItemTemplate (DataList, DataGrid)** Contains the display code for the current row that is being edited by the user

In Exercise 22-5, you add a DataList control to the existing Regions.aspx Web form and create a template for displaying rows from a DataSet.

Exercise 22-5: Applying Templates to the DataList Control

1. In the Solution Explorer window, double-click the Regions.aspx Web form. This opens the Regions.aspx Web form in the main window.
2. From the ToolBox window, drag and drop a Web forms DataList control onto the Regions.aspx Web form to the right of the cTerritories DataGrid control.
3. Change the Text property in the Properties window of the DataList control to cTerritoryList.
4. Change to the HTML view of the Regions.aspx page by clicking the HTML option at the bottom of the main window.
5. Add the following code to the cTerritoryList DataList control:

```
<asp:datalist id="cTerritoryList" style="Z-INDEX: 104; LEFT: 362px;
POSITION: absolute; TOP: 88px" runat="server" Width="284" Height="132">
   <HeaderTemplate>
       <B>Territories</B>
   </HeaderTemplate>
   <ItemTemplate>
       <%# Container.DataItem("TerritoryDescription")%>
        (<%# Container.DataItem("TerritoryID")%>)
   </ItemTemplate>
</asp:datalist>
```

6. Switch back to Design view for the Regions.aspx page.
7. Double-click the cRegion DropDownList control to open the Regions.aspx.vb page in the main window.
8. Modify the cRegions_SelectedIndexChanged event of the Regions.aspx.vb file as shown in the following code:

```
Private Sub cRegions_SelectedIndexChanged(ByVal sender As System.Object,
ByVal e As System.EventArgs) Handles cRegions.SelectedIndexChanged
   PopulateTerritories(cRegions.SelectedItem.Value.ToString)
   PopulateTerritoryList(cRegions.SelectedItem.Value.ToString)
End Sub
```

9. Add the following code for the PopulateTerritoryList subroutine to the Regions.aspx.vb file:

```
Private Sub PopulateTerritoryList(RegionID as String)
    Dim SQL as String
    If RegionID = "" then
        cTerritories.Visible = False
    else
        cTerritories.Visible = True
    End If
    SQL = "SELECT * FROM Territories WHERE RegionID='" & RegionID & "'"
    Dim cnNWind as New SqlConnection
    cnNWind.ConnectionString = _
        "Data Source=(local);Initial Catalog=Northwind;" & _
        "Integrated Security=SSPI"
    cnNWind.Open()
    Dim daTerritories as New SqlDataAdapter(SQL, cnNWind)
    Dim dsTerritories as New DataSet
    daTerritories.Fill(dsTerritories)
    cTerritories.DataSource = dsTerritories
    cTerritories.DataBind()
    cnNWind.Close
End Sub
```

10. Open the Regions.aspx Web form in the main window in Design view. It should look similar to Figure 22-9.

11. Press F5 to compile and run the Web application.

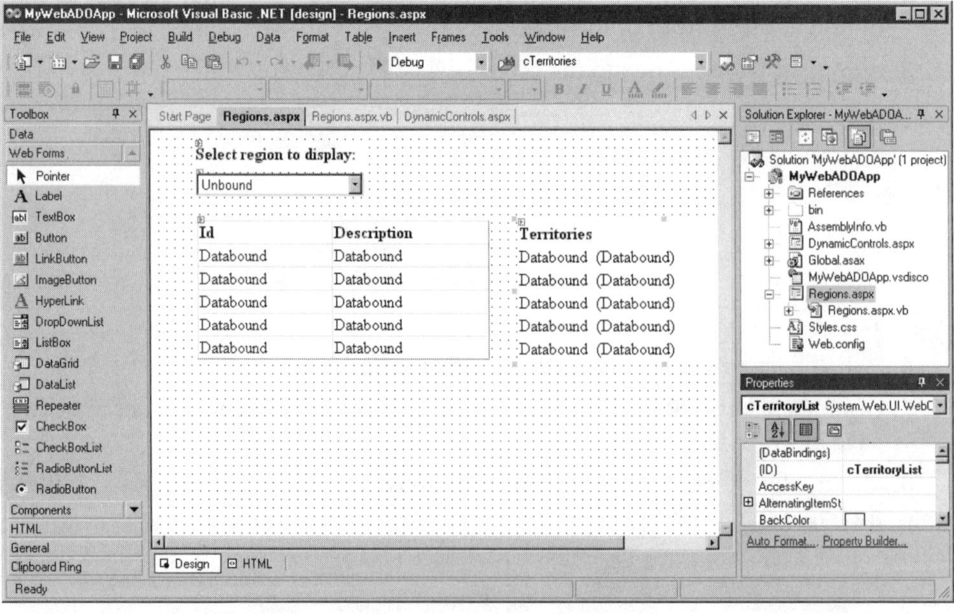

Figure 22-9 Regions.aspx form in Design view with the cTerritoryList DataList control and its template defined

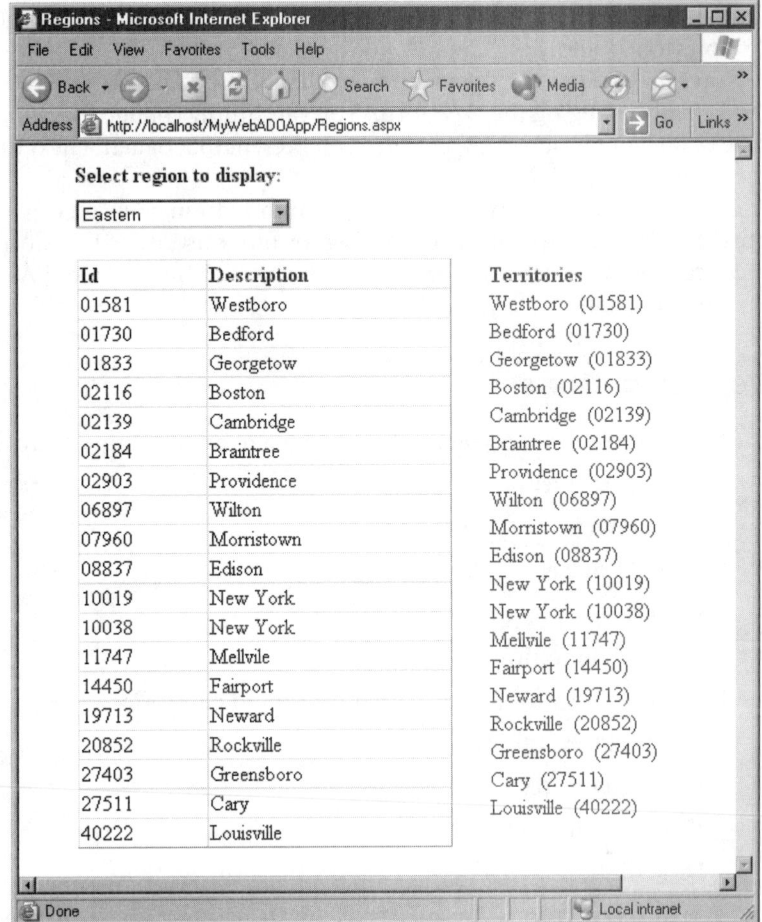

Figure 22-10 Regions.aspx with both the cTerritories DataGrid control and the cTerritoryList DataList control displays territories for a selected region

12. Select a region from the DropDownList control. This will show two lists of territories for that region. One list is in the cTerritories DataGrid control and the other is in the cTerritoryList DataList control. Figure 22-10 shows the resulting Web form.

Summary

Over the past several years, using dynamic information on the Internet has increased as it is employed to provide content that can change or is user specific. The .NET Framework provides several new features to incorporate information from databases and other sources into your Internet or intranet application. You can use DataReader, DataSet, and DataView objects to bind data to Web form controls. You can also use this information to dynamically add HTML elements and controls to Web forms. ASP.NET also allows you to create templates to control the presentation of the information to the user.

Overall, ASP.NET has made the dynamic creation of Web forms easier and faster than ASP previously allowed.

You can use dynamic information to change the look of your Web forms daily without actually changing the Web form. You can simply change the information in a database or an xml file and the Web form will present that data the next time a user accesses the page.

Also, if you have captured user-specific information, you can use this information to provide order status, shipment tracking, or other user-specific information. Although these capabilities existed for ASP pages, the .NET Framework and ASPX pages simplify the implementation.

Test Questions

1. Which objects can you use to bind data to a Web from control? (Choose two.)
   A. DataAdapter
   B. DataView
   C. SQLDataSet
   D. DataSet
   E. SQLConnection
2. Which of the following is not a list-bound control?
   A. CheckBoxList
   B. DropDownList
   C. DataGrid
   D. RadioButton
3. Which objects can you specify as the DataSource for a list-bound control? (Choose two.)
   A. DataReader
   B. DataView
   C. DataSet
   D. SQLConnection
4. Which of the following list-bound controls uses templates? (Choose two.)
   A. CheckBoxList
   B. DataList
   C. DropDownList
   D. Repeater

5. Which list-bound control can you use with a SelectedItemTemplate template?
   A. DropDownList
   B. ListBox
   C. DataList
   D. DataGrid
6. You have added a list-bound control to your form and have properly filled its DataSet and set the DataSource property. The control is not displaying on your Web form. What is the most likely cause?
   A. The control's Enabled property is set to False.
   B. There is no data in the DataSet.
   C. You have not issued the BindData method.
   D. The SQL Server database is not available.
7. Where do you specify the template information for list controls?
   A. In the code-behind page for the Web form
   B. In the HTML code for the aspx file
   C. In the web.config file
   D. In the machine.config file
8. If cRegionButtons is the name of a Web forms Panel control, what is the command to dynamically add the cButton control to cRegionButtons?
   A. cRegionButtons.AddControl(cButton)
   B. cButton.AddTo(cRegionButtons)
   C. cRegionButtons.Controls.Add(cButton)
   D. AddControl(cRegionButtons, cButton)
9. Which of the following is not a template for the Repeater control?
   A. HeaderTemplate
   B. FooterTemplate
   C. EditItemTemplate
   D. SeparatorTemplate
10. The DataGrid control allows you to define templates for which of the following? (Choose all that apply.)
    A. Data rows
    B. Data columns
    C. Paging
    D. DataGrid label

Test Answers

1. A, D.
2. D.
3. A, C.
4. B, D.
5. C.
6. C.
7. B.
8. C.
9. A.
10. B.

CHAPTER 23

Testing and Deploying a Web Forms Application

In this chapter, you will

- Create a unit test plan
- Implement tracing
- Debug, rework, and resolve defects in code
- Create a setup program for installing a Web application
- Deploy a Web application
- Optimize the performance of a Web application
- Diagnose and resolve errors and issues
- Configure and implement caching
- Configure session state
- Install and configure Web services

You have now created a Web application, designed and developed all of the Web Forms, and they compile. So you must be done, right? Wrong. You've just completed the easy part. Now comes the hard part. In the best-practice situation, you should have been doing unit testing for each Web Form as you designed and developed it. This is a very important part of the development cycle and .NET Framework provides many tools to aid in testing your application.

During the testing cycle, you may find that you need to optimize the application to increase performance and provide better scalability. This chapter covers several optimization and scalability techniques, including caching, using the session state server, and using SQL Server to manage state.

After you have determined the logical and physical layout of your production environment, you need to develop a deployment strategy. This chapter covers different techniques for deploying your Web application, as well as installation of the IIS server and the FrontPage Server extensions necessary in your production environment.

Creating a Unit Test Plan

Unit testing is a very important part of the .Net Framework development cycle. Also, it is one of the most often skipped tasks. Being able to identify and fix problems in a unit saves time, money, and frustration as opposed to waiting until the entire application is complete or even waiting until a set of Web pages is complete.

The first question that needs to be answered is, what is a unit in ASP.NET? A unit is a small, isolatable, and testable piece of the application. In ASP.NET, this is usually a Web Form or a user control.

Once you have decided what a unit is, you need to decide how to isolate and test that unit. First, unit testing should not be done within the Web application you are developing. Part of unit testing is isolating the unit you are testing from other units. This isolation is required to verify that the unit is independent of other parts of the application—in other words, it does not require information that you do not expect it to need and does not alter information that you do not expect it to alter. Also, after you have completed testing the unit, you need to be able to come back and test it later when changes are made to the unit. For Web applications, this means setting up a different Web application just for unit testing.

Creating the unit test for a user control in the unit-testing Web application is fairly easy. You simply create one or more Web Forms that exercise all of the features of the user control.

Creating the unit test for a Web Form can be more complicated. You need to set any application and session variables that are required by the Web Form. You need to set any query strings that the form might be expecting. In addition, in an Internet application, you do not have control over how the user requested your form. The request may have come from one of your Web Forms, the user may have clicked the browser's back or forward buttons, or the user may have selected the Web Form from the browser's history list. You need to be able to handle all these conditions in your unit-testing Web application, just like you need to handle them in the production Web application.

Many developers consider it too time consuming and difficult to extract a single Web Form from a sequence of Web Forms and develop the necessary environment to test that one form. It *is* time consuming and difficult, but these costs are recovered over the life of the Web application. Also, once the unit-testing Web application is developed, it is easier to add new forms to the environment.

NOTE Remember that you need to be able to test a Web Form in an isolated environment while you are developing the Web Form. This exercise will lead to better implementation of the Web Form. If you do not take this into consideration during the development of the Web Form, incorporating it into the test environment can be very difficult.

Testing Your Web Application

The VS.NET IDE provides many testing and debugging features to help you develop solid Web applications. In fact, there are so many different tools available, a developer usually uses just a subset of the tools that work for how he likes to test and debug programs. However, it is important to be familiar with all of the tools so that when you encounter a problem that may require a tool you do not normally use, you know that it is available.

Setting Up the VS.NET IDE for Debugging

The VS.NET IDE provides compile time configurations for a debug version of your Web application and a release version of your Web application. You can then request that the VS.NET IDE generate either a debug version or release version of your Web application. The debug version of your Web application contains symbolic debug information and is not optimized. The release version of your Web application is optimized and contains no debug information.

During the testing and debugging of your Web application, you have the VS.NET IDE create the debug version of your Web application. You can select the version for the VS.NET IDE to generate from the VS.NET IDE standard toolbar Solution Configuration list. The following illustration shows the VS.NET IDE with the Solution Configuration list open and ready to choose the version. The Solution Configuration list in the figure contains the Debug, Release, and Configuration Manager. It does not show a title for the list.

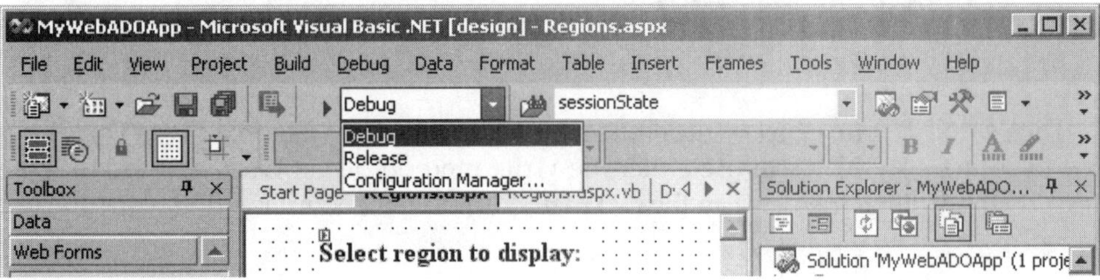

You can change the debug and release configuration settings from the Property Pages window for the project. Figure 23-1 shows the project Property Pages window with the debugging configuration options displayed.

The specific configuration values for the debug and release versions are automatically set for you when you create a new Web application using the VS.NET IDE.

Using ASP.NET Tracing

The Trace object and the Debug object, along with trace listeners, were covered in Chapter 19. These objects are used to write messages to the VS.NET IDE output window, files, and the event log. This functionality is still available within ASP.NET. If you have not read Chapter 19, you may wish to review this information. ASP.NET provides a special version of tracing that is designed specifically for Web applications. The object name is also Trace, so this can be confusing. The Trace object covered in Chapter 19 is part of the System.Diagnostics namespace. The Trace object that is part of ASP.NET and covered here is part of the System.Web namespace. For the rest of this chapter, when we refer to the Trace object, we are referring to the ASP.NET Trace object.

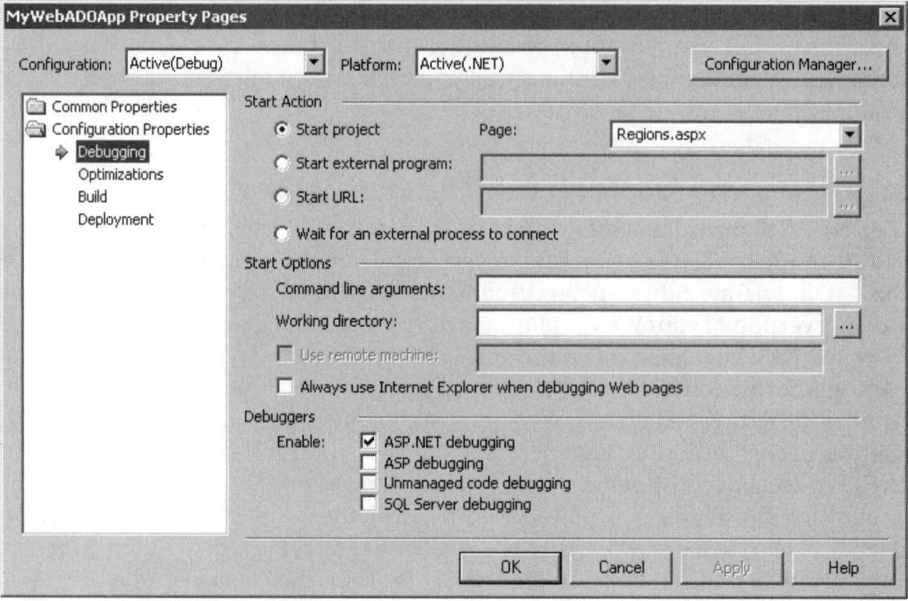

Figure 23-1 The project Property Pages window showing the debugging configuration options

The ASP.NET Trace object writes information either to the Response (Web Form) object or to memory. You can use either the Write method or the Warn method to write text. The only difference between the two methods is that the Warn method writes the text in red.

EXAM TIP The Trace object that is in the System.Web namespace is different than the Trace object in the System.Diagnostics namespace.

You need to enable tracing before the Trace object will write information. You can still include code to use the Trace object, but no output is generated until you enable tracing. You can enable tracing for an individual page or for the entire Web application. You enable tracing for a page by setting the Trace attribute of the Page directive as shown in the following code:

```
<%@ Page Language="VB" Trace="true" %>
```

EXAM TIP You enable tracing for a Web Form in the Page directive setting the Trace attribute to "true."

When you enable tracing using the Page directive, you not only receive the output resulting from Trace object's Write method and Warn method, you also receive more detailed results information on the Web page. This information includes:

- **Request Details** General information about the request, including Session ID, time of request, and type of request
- **Trace Information** Information generated by the event executed by the page and trace messages that you generated
- **Control Tree** Information about the control on your Web Form
- **Cookies Collection** Information about the cookies for the Web Form
- **Headers Collection** Information from the HTTP header
- **Forms Collection** Controls and the control values of the form that is posted
- **Server Variable** List of the server variables and their values

Figure 23-2 shows a partial trace output when you turn on tracing for a page. This trace result information is appended to the bottom of your Web Form if you have designed your form using FlowLayout. If you are using GridLayout, the trace result starts at the top of the page and overlays your controls. This not only makes your controls readable, it also renders the result information unreadable. To overcome this problem, you can configure tracing in the web.config file.

You add a trace element to the web.config file as shown in the following code:

```
<configuration>
    <system.web>
        <trace enabled="true" pageOutput="false"/>
    </system.web>
</configuration>
```

By enabling tracing in the web.config file and setting the pageOutput attribute of the trace element to false, you force the trace information to be maintained in memory. To view this trace information, open an instance of Internet Explorer and browse to http://server/project/trace.axd. You can view the application Web page in one browser window while your application is running and monitor the trace information in a different browser window. Turning off the pageOutput and viewing the trace information with trace.axd is the preferred method of monitoring your trace information.

PART VI

EXAM TIP To view trace information for a Web Form that uses GridLayout, you set the pageOutput attribute of the trace element in the web.config file to false and view the trace information using trace.axd.

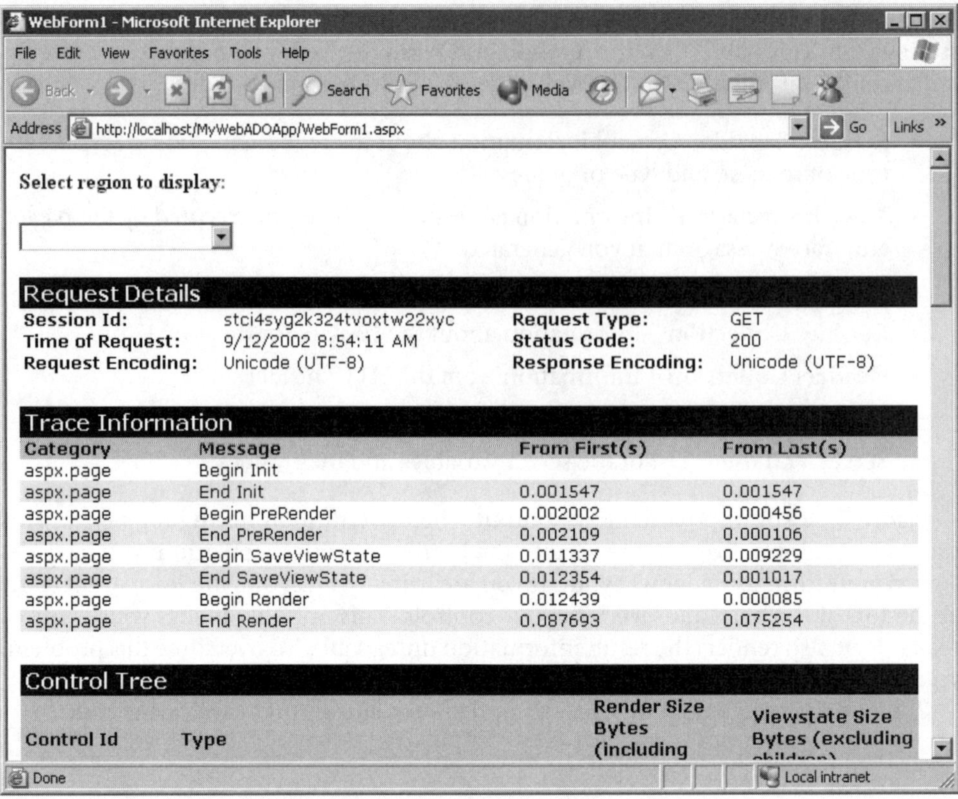

Figure 23-2 Trace information appended to the bottom of a Web Form

You use the Trace object's Write and Warn methods to write information to the Response object or to memory. The Write method and the Warn method have three parameters:

- **Category** You can assign a category to the message for grouping and sorting.
- **Message** This is the message you want written.
- **Exception object** If you are processing an exception, you can pass the exception object to get more details about the error in the trace information.

The following is sample code using the Trace object's Write and Warn methods:

```
Try
    Trace.Write("DataAccess", "Reading territories")
    . . . (data access code)
```

```
Catch x as Exception
    Trace.Warn("SQLError", "Error reading territories", x)
End Try
```

In Exercise 23-1, you will configure tracing for ASP.NET and add tracing to the Regions.aspx Web Form from Chapter 22.

Exercise 23-1: Configuring and Using Tracing in ASP.NET

1. Start with the MyWebADOApp as completed in Chapter 22. You can copy the Chapter 21 MyWebADOApp directory from the CD into C:\Inetpub\wwwroot\MyWebADOApp if you need to.
2. Open the MyWebADOApp using the VS.NET IDE.
3. Open the Regions.aspx file in HTML view in the main window.
4. Add Trace="true" to the Page directive. Figure 23-3 shows the HTML code with the Trace attribute set to "true".

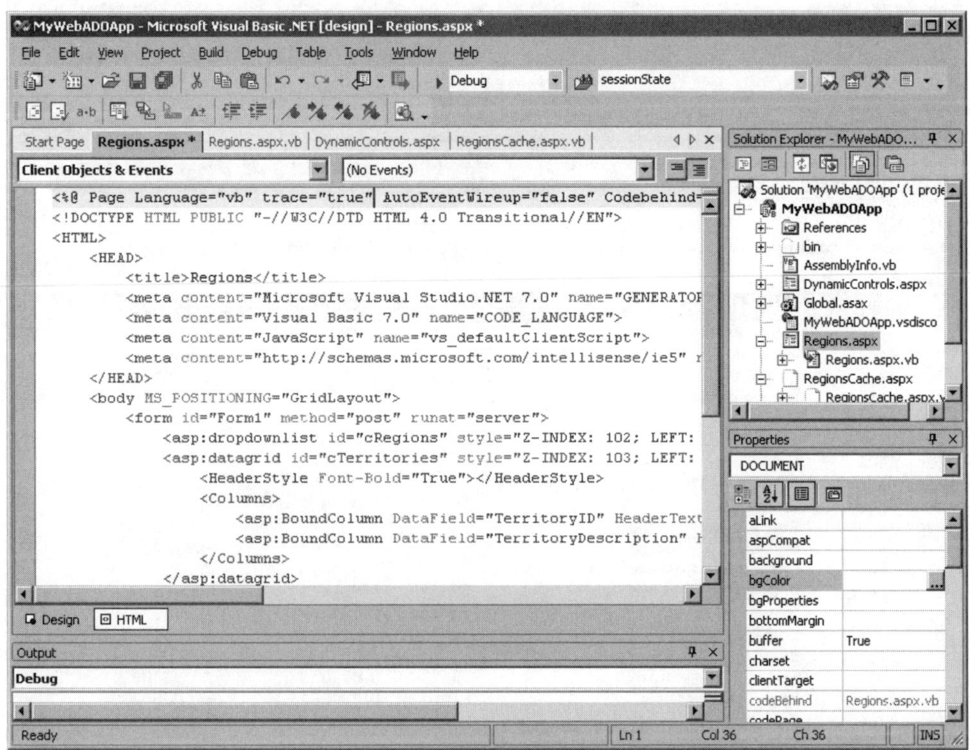

Figure 23-3 Regions.aspx form in HTML view with the Trace attribute added to the Page directive

5. Press F5 to run the Web application. You will see the trace results overlapping the Web controls.
6. Select a region to display the territory information. Figure 23-4 shows the resulting Web Form with the trace results overlapping the Web Form controls. This is because the Regions.aspx Web Form is designed with a page layout of GridLayout.
7. Close Internet Explorer to end the Web application.
8. Remove Trace="true" from the Page directive.
9. Open the web.config file in the main window.
10. Locate the trace element in the web.config file.
11. Set the enable attribute of the trace element to true, enabled="true". Figure 23-5 shows the web.config file with tracing enabled.
12. Open the Regions.aspx.vb file in the main window.

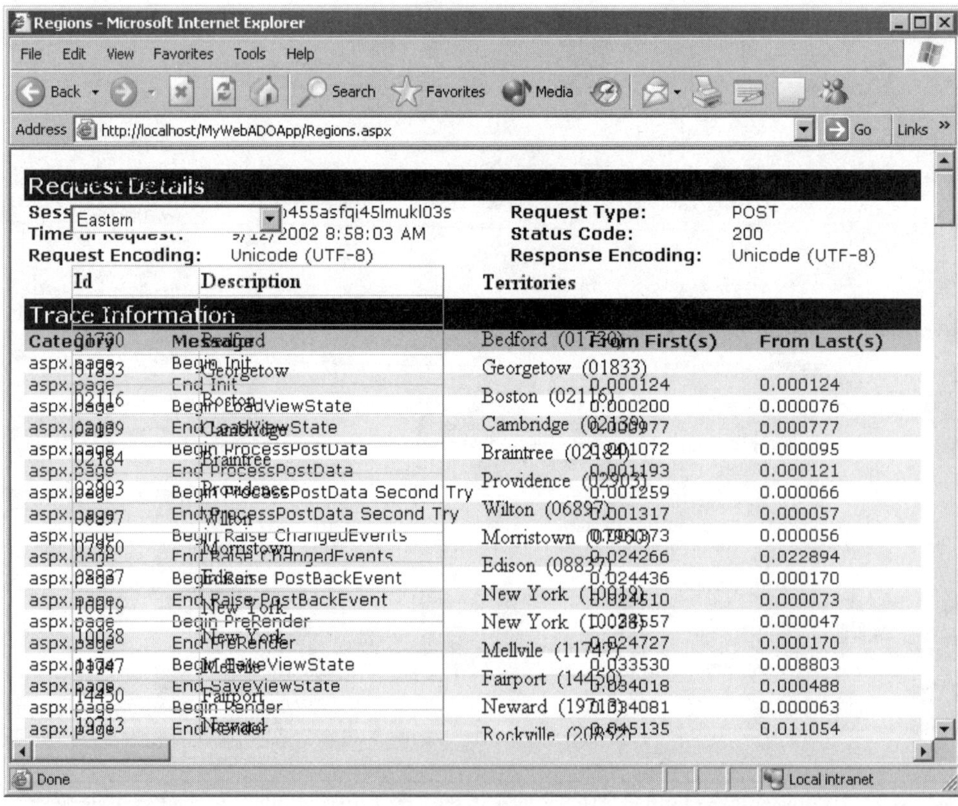

Figure 23-4 Regions.aspx Web Form trace results overlapping the Web Forms controls

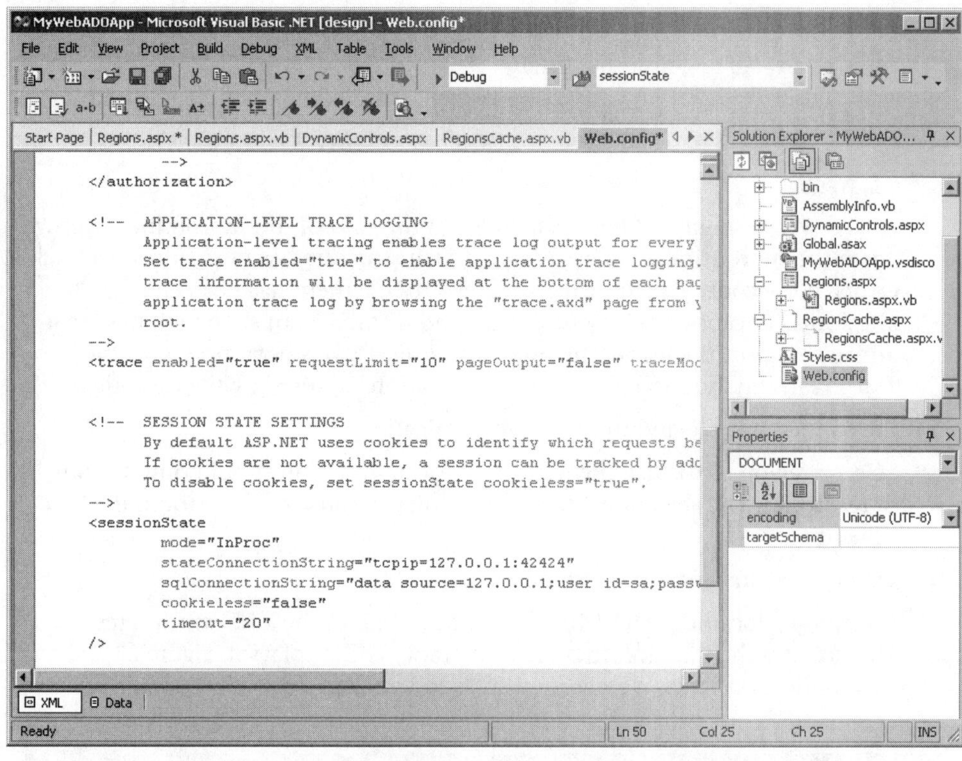

Figure 23-5 The web.config file with tracing enabled

13. Change the PopulateTerritoryList subroutine the match the following code. Changes are identified in bold.

```
Private Sub PopulateTerritoryList(RegionID as String)
    Dim SQL as String
    Trace.Write("ADOApp", "Populating Territories")
    If RegionID = "" then
        cTerritoryList.Visible = False
    else
        cTerritoryList.Visible = True
    End If
    Try
        SQL = "SELECT * FROM Territories WHERE xRegionID='" & RegionID & "'"
        Dim cnNWind as New SqlConnection
        cnNWind.ConnectionString = _
            "Data Source=(local);Initial Catalog=Northwind;" & _
            "Integrated Security=SSPI"
        cnNWind.Open()
        Dim daTerritories as New SqlDataAdapter(SQL, cnNWind)
        Dim dsTerritories as New DataSet

        daTerritories.Fill(dsTerritories)
```

```
            cTerritoryList.DataSource = dsTerritories

            cTerritoryList.DataBind()
            cnNWind.Close
        Catch x as Exception
            Trace.Warn("SQLError", "Error accessing territories", x)
        End Try
    End Sub
```

A Trace.Write statement has been added at the start of the subroutine to record when the subroutine is called. A Try…Catch structure has been added to catch errors in the code. The RegionID in the SQL statement has been changed to xRegionID to cause a SQL Server error, and a Trace.Warn statement has been added to report the error. The exception object x has been passed to the Trace.Warn method to report error information captured by the exception.

14. Press F5 to compile and run the Web application.
15. Select a region to display the territory information. You should only see one list of territories. The second list does not display because of the error in the SQL statement.
16. Open a new instance of Internet Explorer.
17. Enter http://localhost/MyWebADOApp/trace.axd for the address and press ENTER. This accesses the trace information in memory and displays it. Figure 23-6 shows the Application Trace Web Form displayed by trace.axd.

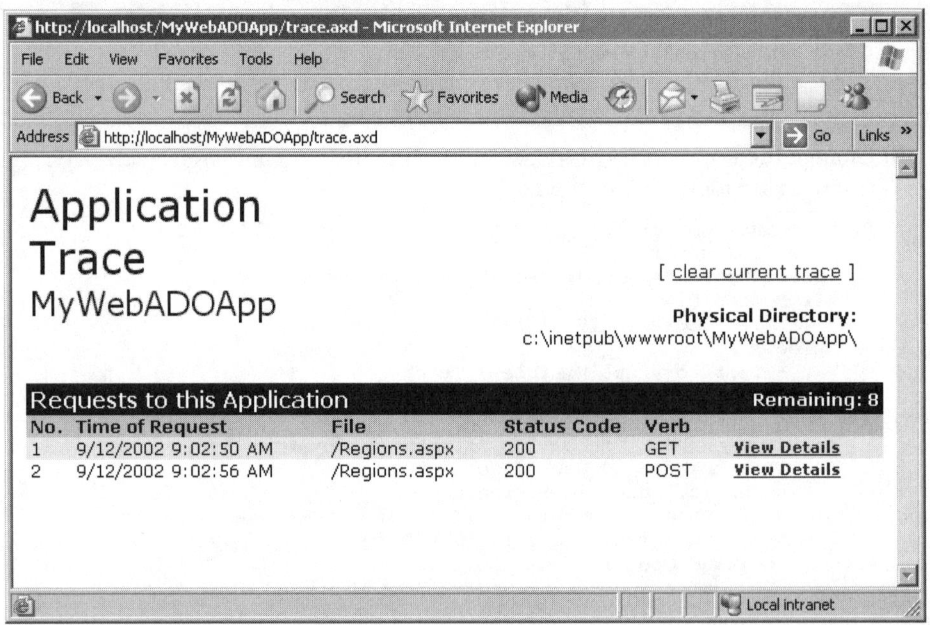

Figure 23-6 Displaying trace information using trace.axd

18. Select the ViewDetail for the second line in the trace information. This shows the Request Detail and both the Populating Territories trace message and the Error Accessing Territories trace message. The error detail is also displayed reporting "Invalid column name 'xRegionID'". Figure 23-7 shows the Request Detail including the SQL error message.
19. Close both Internet Explorer windows.
20. Change the xRegionID in the SQL statement to RegionID to avoid future errors.

Debugging in ASP.NET

Debugging a Web application written with VB.NET using the VS.NET IDE is similar to debugging any VB.NET application. The main difference is that instead of a Windows Form or the console to present the user interface, Internet Explorer is used for the user interface.

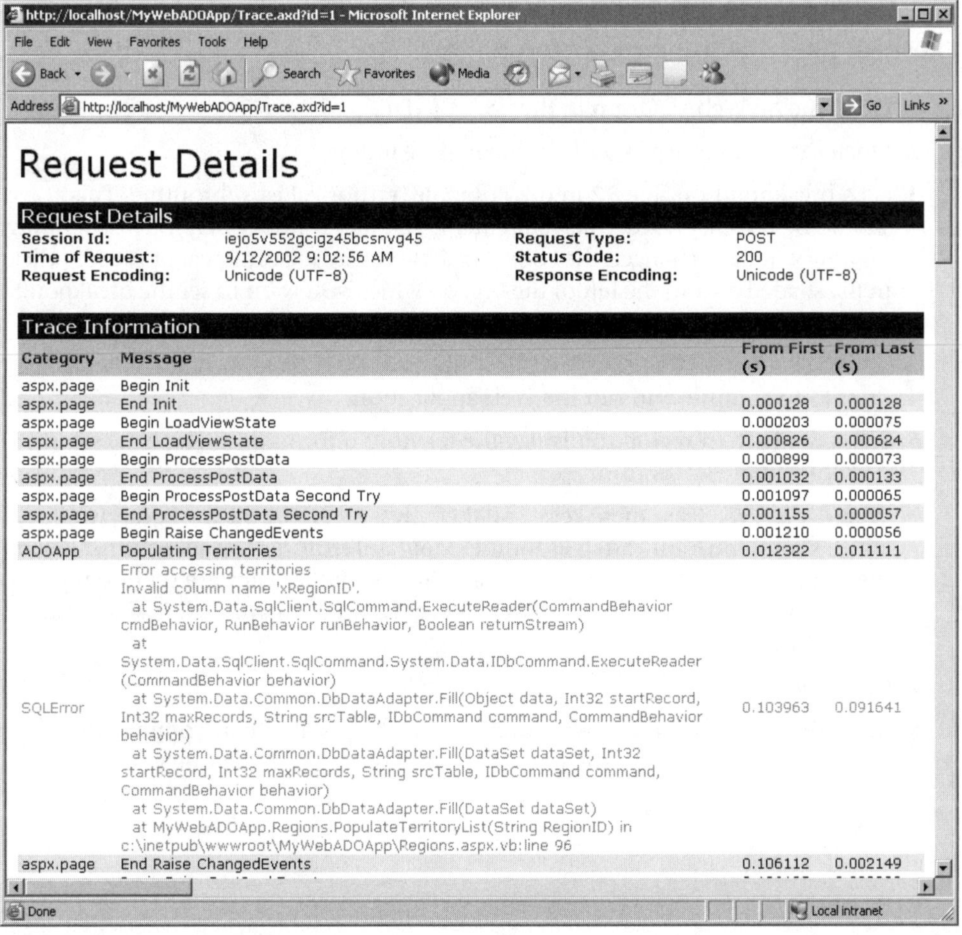

Figure 23-7 Trace.axd Request Detail showing the SQL error message

You can still set breakpoints, view and set variables, and add debug statements that are not compiled into the final release of the Web application. Chapter 2 covers the debugging tools available in the VS.NET IDE in detail. In this section, we provide an example of using these tools in an ASP.NET Web application.

You need to enable debugging in the web.config file for the Web application. When you create a Web application using the VS.NET IDE, it automatically enables debugging. Prior to releasing the Web application, you need to disable debugging. You enable/disable debugging in the compilation element in the web.config file as shown in the following code:

```
<configuration>
    <system.web>
        <compilation language="vb" debug="true" />
    </system.web>
</configuration>
```

Exercise 23-2 takes you through a debugging session for the Regions.aspx form. In this exercise, you will set breakpoints, view variables, and change variable values.

Exercise 23-2: Debugging a Web Form

1. Open the MyWebADOApp in the VS.NET IDE.
2. Open the Regions.aspx.vb file in the main window.
3. Set a breakpoint on line 92 in the PopulateTerritoriesList subroutine. This should be the cnNWind.Open statement. The line number may vary depending on how you have changed the code. The easiest way to set a breakpoint is to click in the shaded area to the left of the line on which you want to set the breakpoint. Alternatively, you can click on the line and then press F9. This toggles the breakpoint on or off.
4. Press F5 to compile and run the Web application.
5. Select the Eastern region to display the territory information. The code stops executing at the breakpoint.
6. Press CTL-ALT-V, release these keys, and then press L. This opens the Locals window, which shows the local variables for the PopulateTerritoriesList subroutine. Review the values for the RegionID variable and SQL variable. They are set to retrieve information for region "1" from SQL Server. The Locals window is shown in Figure 23-8.
7. Close the Locals window.
8. Move the point of execution up to the SQL = "…" statement. To move the execution point, click on the yellow arrow and drag it to the line you want

it to start on. Figure 23-9 shows the VS.NET IDE with the breakpoint set and the execution point moved to the SQL statement line.

9. Press CTL-ALT-I to open the Immediate window.
10. Enter RegionID="3" into the Immediate window and press ENTER. This changes the value of the RegionID.
11. Press F5. The execution stops on the breakpoint.

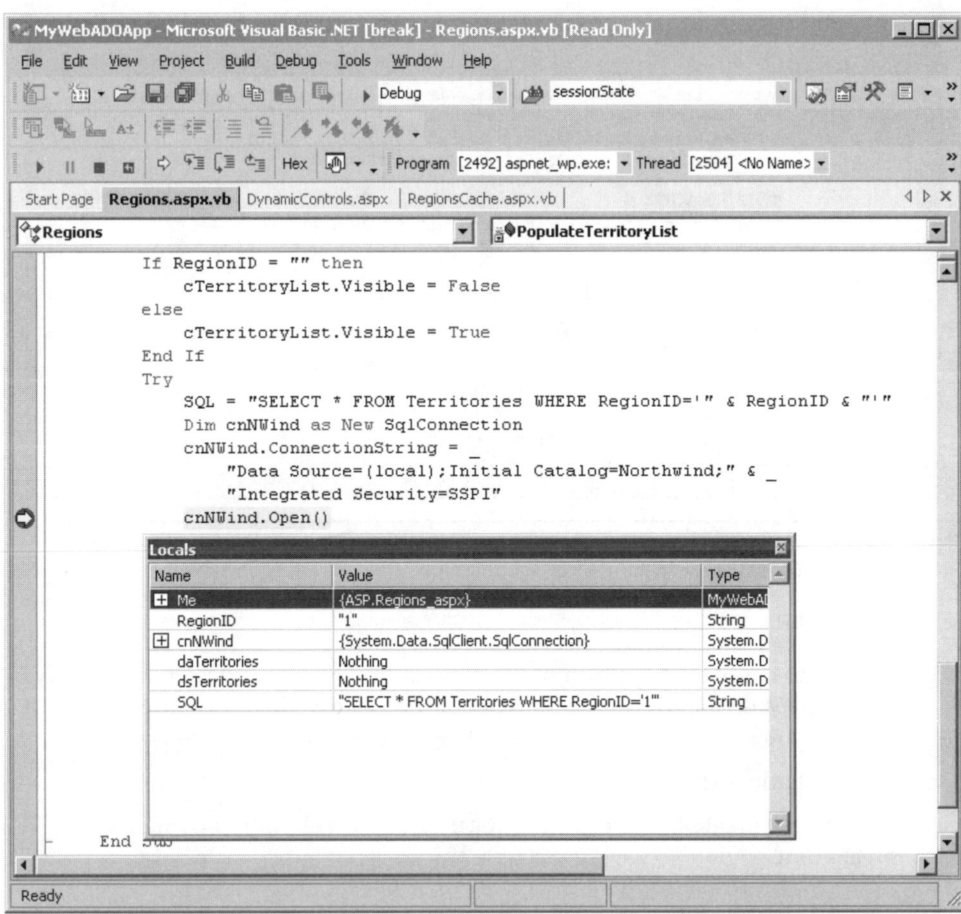

Figure 23-8 The debug Locals window for the PopulateTerritoryList subroutine

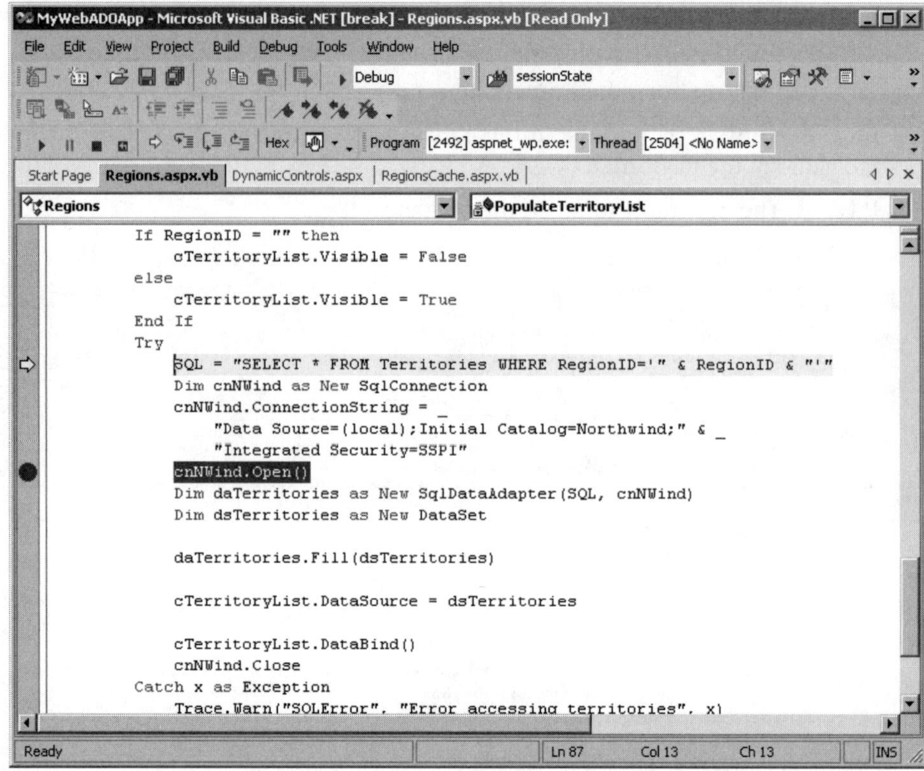

Figure 23-9 Regions.aspx VB.NET code with a breakpoint set and the execution point moved to the SQL statement line

12. Press F5 to continue execution of the application. Now you have two territory lists displayed. The list on the right is not the same as the list on the left because you changed the value of the RegionID while debugging the code.
13. Close Internet Explorer.
14. Remove the breakpoint. See Step 3 for information about removing the breakpoint.

Using the Try...Catch Structure to Resolve Code Errors

You should be using the Try…Catch structure within your application to avoid propagating meaningless error messages to the user and to gracefully allow the user to correct input errors. You can also use the Try…Catch structure to isolate problems in your code. By surrounding sections of code with the Try…Catch structure, you can use the exception information provided by the Exception object to identify the source of the error. Chapter 3 covers the details of .NET Framework's structured exception handling.

Review Exercise 23-1, which uses the Try...Catch structure to capture and report errors in the code. When the RegionID was incorrectly spelled in the SQL statement, the error was caught and reported in the Trace.Warn message.

Optimizing and Increasing Performance of Your Web Application

You can optimize your Web application by implementing caching. There are two types of caching that affect performance. You can use the cache object within your application and you can use ASP.NET output caching for caching pages.

You can also increase performance by using a Web farm. In order to implement a Web farm you need to change how you maintain session state. In addition, the cache objects and cache output are not available across Web farms.

Using the Cache Object

You can use the Cache object to cache application data. For certain types of data, it is better to use the Cache object than to use the Application intrinsic object. The Cache object is meant to store data that consumes a large amount of server memory, such as a list of valid state codes and their descriptions for an application. This list consumes memory, but you do not want to have to rebuild the list every time it is needed. If you put the list in the Application object, it consumes memory and that memory is not available if needed. If you put the state list in the Cache object and memory resources become low, the .NET Framework will remove it from memory.

The Cache object is created when the Web application starts and removed when the Web application terminates. It is also private to each Web application running on the server.

EXAM TIP An instance of the Cache object is created when a Web application starts and is removed when the Web application terminates. It is available to all Web Forms in the application.

Data is maintained in the Cache object as name-value pairs. The following code adds a value to the Cache object using a simple assignment statement:

```
Cache("Regions")=dsRegions
```

You can also use the Add method or the Insert method to add a value to the Cache object. The Add and Insert methods are identical except that the Add method returns an object representing the object that is being added. The Add and Insert methods provide for additional parameters that take advantage of features of the Cache object. The parameters of the Add method and Insert method are:

- **Key** The name of the object being added. It is used to later retrieve the object.
- **Value** The object that is being saved to the Cache object

PART VI

- **Dependencies** Identifies files or key values that this object depends upon. If any one of the files or keys changes, this object is removed from cache. Use Nothing for this parameter if there are no dependencies.
- **AbsoluteExpiration** The date and time that this object expires and will be removed from cache. Use Cache.NoAbsoluteExpiration for this parameter if you are going to specify a SlidingExpiration.
- **SlidingExpiration** The length of time after the last time the object was accessed that the object expires. You cannot specify both an AbsoluteExpiration and a SlidingExpiration. Cannot be less than zero or more than one year. Use Cache.NoSlidingExpiration for this parameter if you specified an AbsoluteExpiration.
- **Priority** Allows you to set different priority levels for the automatic removal of objects from the Cache object when the .NET Framework needs to remove items from the Cache object. The priorities are defined in the CacheItemPriority enumeration.
- **OnRemoveCallback** Specifies a delegate that is called when this object is removed from the Cache object. Use Nothing for this parameter if there is no delegate.

The following code shows a value being added using the Add method:

```
cTerritories.DataSource = Cache.Add("Territories", dsTerritories, Nothing,
Cache.NoAbsoluteExpiration, TimeSpan.FromHours(3),
Caching.CacheItemPriority.Default, Nothing)
```

The following code shows the same functionality using the Insert method:

```
Cache.Insert("Territories", dsTerritories, Nothing,
Cache.NoAbsoluteExpiration, TimeSpan.FromHours(3),
Caching.CacheItemPriority.Default, Nothing)
cTerritories.DataSource = dsTerritories
```

EXAM TIP Use Nothing when you are not going to provide a Dependencies object or a OnRemoveCallback object. Much of the .NET Framework documentation states to use null, which does not work.

In Exercise 23-3, you will create a new Web Form, RegionsCache.aspx, that implements caching of a DataSet for the Regions table in the Northwind database.

Exercise 23-3: Implementing Caching for a DataSet

1. Open the MyWebADOApp Web application in the VS.NET IDE.
2. Add a new Web Form called RegionsCache.aspx.
3. Add a Button Web Form control with ID property of cPopulateRegions and Text property of Populate Regions.

4. Add a Button Web Form control with ID property of cRemoveCache and Text property of Remove From Cache.
5. Add a DataGrid Web Form control with ID property of cRegionsGrid. Figure 23-10 shows the completed form.
6. Double-click on the form or any of its controls to open the code-behind page, RegionsCache.aspx.vb, for the form.
7. Add the Imports System.Data.SQLClient statement at the top of the listing.
8. Enter the following code for the cPopulateRegions_Click subroutine:

```
Private Sub cPopulateRegions_Click(ByVal sender As System.Object, ByVal e As
System.EventArgs) Handles cPopulateRegions.Click
    Dim dsRegions As DataSet
    dsRegions = Cache("RegionsDataSet")
    If dsRegions Is Nothing Then
        Dim SQL As String
        SQL = "SELECT * FROM Region"
        Dim cnNWind As New SqlConnection()
        cnNWind.ConnectionString = _
            "Data Source=(local);Initial Catalog=Northwind;" & _
            "Integrated Security=SSPI"
        cnNWind.Open()
        Dim daRegions As New SqlDataAdapter(SQL, cnNWind)
        dsRegions = New DataSet()
        daRegions.Fill(dsRegions)
        Cache("RegionsDataSet") = dsRegions
        cnNWind.Close()
    End If
    cRegionsGrid.DataSource = dsRegions
    cRegionsGrid.DataBind()
End Sub
```

9. Enter the following code for the cRemoveCache_Click subroutine:

```
Private Sub cRemoveCache_Click(ByVal sender As System.Object, ByVal e As
System.EventArgs) Handles cRemoveCache.Click
 Cache.Remove("RegionsDataSet")
End Sub
```

10. Set a breakpoint on the SQL = "SELECT * FROM Region" statement.
11. Press F5 to compile and run the Web application.
12. Click the Populate Regions button. Execution should stop on the breakpoint.
13. Press F5 to continue execution. The cRegionsGrid should display.
14. Click the Populate Regions button. Execution should *not* stop on the breakpoint. You have saved a round trip to SQL Server to access the region information. It is now in cache.
15. Click the Remove From Cache button.
16. Click the Populate Regions button. Execution should stop on the breakpoint.
17. Press F5 to continue execution.
18. Close Internet Explorer to stop the Web application.
19. Remove the breakpoint.

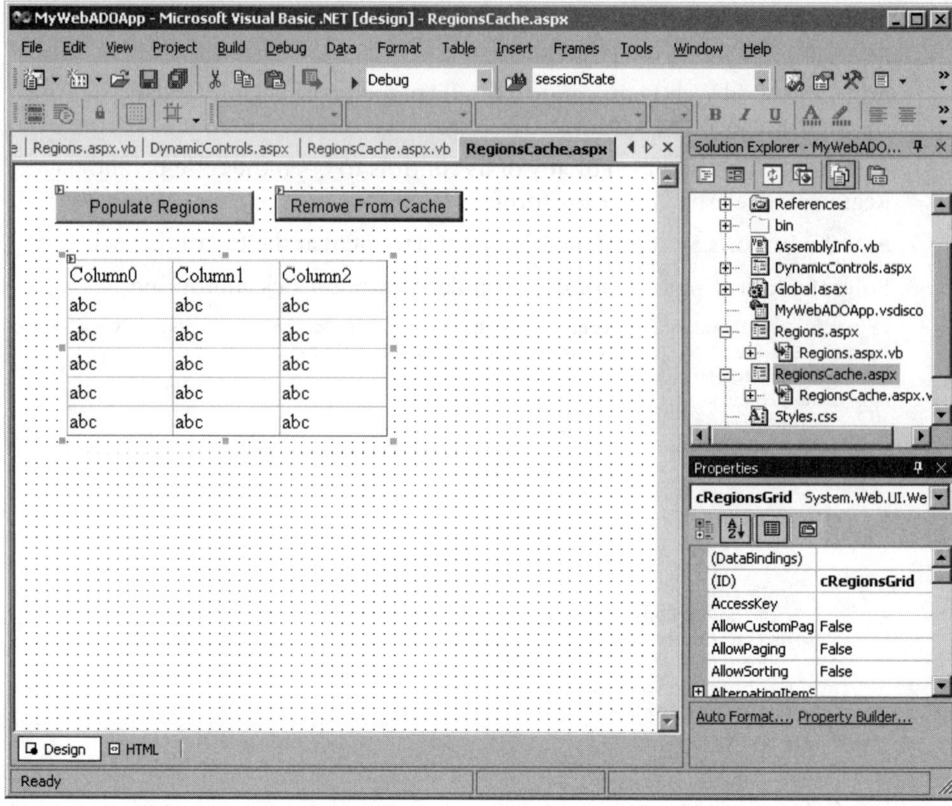

Figure 23-10 RegionsCache.aspx Web Form in Design view

Using the Cache Output

The .NET Framework can cache either complete page output or page fragments. When a Web page (form) is first requested, it is compiled and the code is executed creating an output page. You can direct the .NET Framework to cache this page so that the next request for the page is not compiled and the code is not executed. The page is returned to the user from the cache (a copy of the form that has been saved in memory).

You can also cache page fragments by making the page fragments into user controls and directing the .NET Framework to cache the user control. Caching user controls is useful for page headers, footers, and sidebars. Caching pages provides a significant performance increase for a server with high activity against common pages.

NOTE Caching output increases performance for the server on which the application is running. The cached pages are not available to other servers in a Web farm.

To direct the .NET Framework to cache a page or user control, you simply add the OutputCache directive to the page as shown in the following code:

```
<%@ OutputCache Duration="600" VaryByParam="none" %>
```

The Duration attribute and the VaryByParam attribute are required attributes. You receive a parsing error if you do not include both attributes.

The Duration attribute specifies how long the page stays in cache before it is removed. You specify the duration in seconds.

NOTE If the source page changes prior to the duration time elapsing, the .NET Framework reloads the page the next time it is requested.

The VaryByParam attribute allows you to cache multiple versions of the same page. Your Web Form may receive parameters in the query string or as part of a Post request. You can specify one or more of these parameters as the value of the VaryByParam attribute. The .NET Framework will then cache a separate page for each parameter. In the following code, a separate page is cached for each different value of RegionID. The values are case sensitive so that if one request for the page has RegionID in all upper case and another request has RegionID in mixed case, two copies of the page will exist in cache.

EXAM TIP The value of the VaryByParam is case sensitive. A separate page is cached if the value is the same except for its case.

```
<%@ OutputCache Duration="600" VaryByParam="RegionID" %>
```

Since the VaryByParam is a required attribute, you specify "none" if you do not need to use this feature.

EXAM TIP Both the Duration attribute and VaryByParam attribute are required for the OutputCache directive. If you are not caching a page based on parameters, you set the VaryByParam attribute to "none."

You need to be careful of the pages that you cache. Pages that change based on data that is not a page parameter may not get refreshed to reflect the changes. In Exercise 23-4, you will add the OutputCache directive to the Regions.aspx Web Form. Since this Web Form changes based on the region selection, it will not behave properly—the territory lists are not refreshed when the region changes. The exercise demonstrates how caching works and also demonstrates that you need to be careful when applying it to pages.

Exercise 23-4: Implementing Page Caching

1. Open the MyWebADOApp Web application in the VS.NET IDE.
2. Open the Regions.aspx Web Form in HTML view in the main window.
3. Enter the OutputCache directive after the Page directive at the top of the HTML code as shown in the following code:
   ```
   <%@ OutputCache Duration="600" VaryByParam="none" %>
   ```
4. Set the Regions.aspx page as the start page.
5. Press F5 to compile and run the Web application.
6. Select the Eastern region to display territory information.
7. Select the Western region. The territory information for the Western region is not displayed because the page is cached. This demonstrates both the caching of a page and the fact that not all pages should be cached, specifically those pages that can change based on user input from the page itself.
8. Close Internet Explorer to stop the Web application.
9. Remove the OutputCache page directive from the HTML code.

Configuring Session State

One method of increasing performance is to implement a Web farm. Although we are not covering Web farm implementation specifically, you can change how the Session intrinsic object is handled to take advantage of a Web farm.

By default the Session object is maintained as an in-process object. That is, it is saved in memory allocated to the Web application. This means that the session information is only available to the Web application that is running on the Web server that created it. The .NET Framework allows you to configure a Web application to maintain the session state information out of process, allowing access to session information from other Web servers in a Web farm.

The .NET Framework provides for out-of-process session information to be maintained on a state server or in a SQL Server database. Providing the session information in an out-of-process session has the following advantages:

- The session information is available to your Web applications running on other servers in a Web farm.
- If your Web application crashes, it can be recovered without losing session information because the session information is in another process.
- Performance is enhanced because the session information is being processed by separate worker processes.
- SQL Server state allows the additional benefit of recovery even if the server running SQL Server crashes, because the session information is persisted in the database. The state server keeps the session information in memory. If it crashes, the session information is lost.

EXAM TIP SQL Server is the only method provided by the .NET Framework that does not keep session state in memory. It persists it to a database.

There are two steps in setting up SQL Server to maintain state. First, you need to run the InstallSQLState.sql script on the server that is running SQL Server. This sets up the database in SQL Server for the session state information. The InstallSQLState.sql script is located in the %System%\Microsoft.NET\v.1.0.3705 directory.

Second, you need to configure the sessionState element in the web.config file to enable SQL Server as your session state mode and to set the connection string to the server. The following listing shows the web.config settings:

```
<configuration>
    <system.web>
        <sessionState
            mode="SQLServer"
            sqlConnectionString="data source=SQLComputerName;
                Integrated security=true"
            timeout="20"
            cookieless="false"
        />
    </system.web>
</configuration>
```

In the preceding listing, SQLComputerName is the name of your SQL Server computer.

Configuring the state server is also a two-step process. You need to be sure that the apsnet_estate.exe service is running on the server computer that is acting as the state server. The program is in the %System%\Microsoft.NET\v.1.0.3705 directory. It is installed as part of ASP.NET. However, when it is installed, it is not started. To start the service you need to locate it in the Services plug-in for the Computer Management MMC as shown in Figure 23-11.

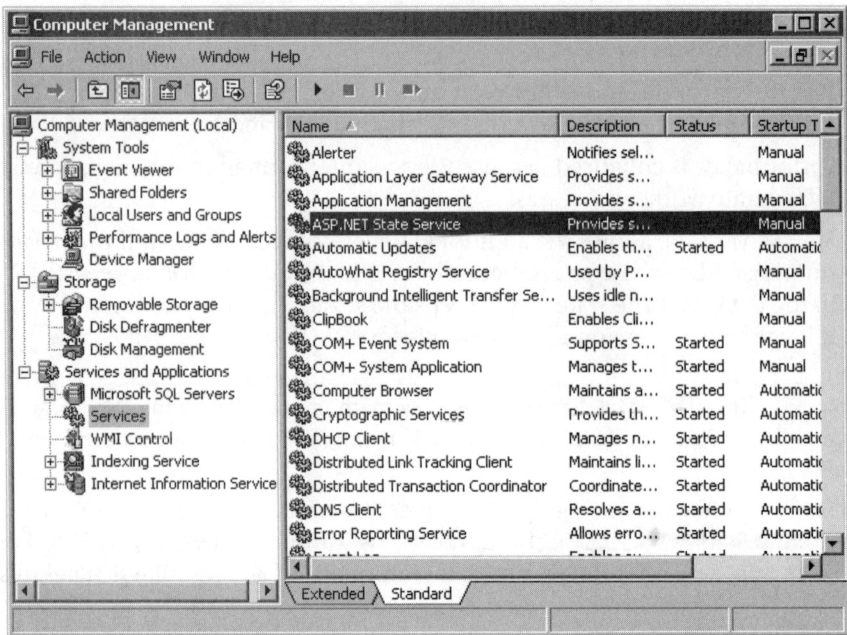

Figure 23-11 The ASP.NET State Service in the Services plug-in for the Computer Management MMC

You then need to set it to start automatically as shown in Figure 23-12. To access the ASP.NET State Services Properties dialog box, double-click the service shown in Figure 23-12. If you are not going to restart the state server computer, you also need to start the service. To start the service, click the Start button in the ASP.NET State Service Properties dialog box.

Second, you need to configure the sessionState element in the web.config file to enable the state server computer as your session state mode and to set the connection string to the server. The following listing shows the web.config settings:

```
<configuration>
    <system.web>
        <sessionState
            mode="StateServer"
            stateConnectionString="tcip=ServerComputerName:42424"
            timeout="20"
            cookieless="false"
        />
    </system.web>
</configuration>
```

In the preceding listing, ServerComputerName is the name of the state server computer or its TCP/IP address.

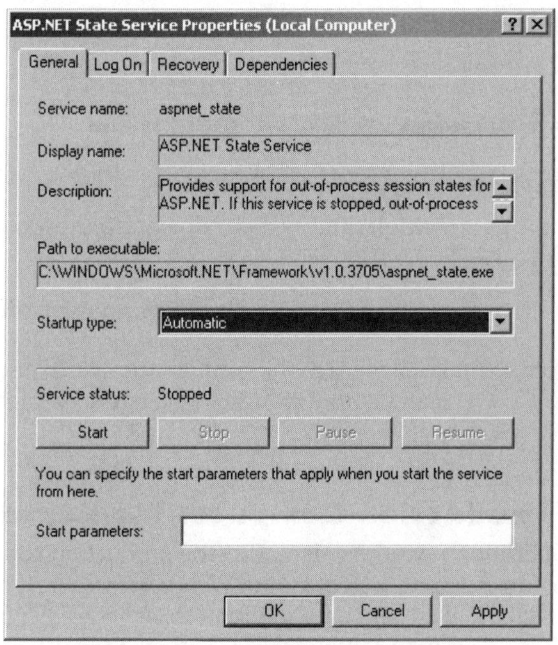

Figure 23-12 Setting the ASP.NET State Service to start automatically

Deploying Your Web Application

The .NET Framework has made deploying your application very easy. You simply follow these steps:

1. Prepare the Web application for deployment.
2. Prepare the production computer for deployment.
3. Copy the Web application into the production machine's virtual directory.
4. Modify the production machine's machine.config file if necessary.
5. Copy any common assemblies into the Global Assembly Cache.

Preparing Your Web Application for Deployment

To prepare your Web application for deployment, you must first compile the Web application as a release version. This removes all debug information from the compiled version and optimizes the compiled version. You then need to make a copy of the Web application files and directories, removing all unnecessary files.

The following is the list of all unnecessary files:

- Project or solution files (.sln, .vbproj, etc.)

- Code-behind files (.vb, .cs)
- Resource files (.resx)

The following is a list of all necessary directories and files:

- The \bin directory and all dll files within it
- All Web Forms, user controls, and Web services (.aspx, .ascx, .asmx)
- All configuration files required
- Any support directories and files, such as xsd files and xml files

You may also need to make changes to the configuration and other support files that are server dependent (SQL Server connection strings, state server machine names, and so on).

Prepare the Production Computer for Deployment

Once your Web application is ready to deploy to the production computer, you need to prepare the production machine to receive the Web application. If the production machine does not have IIS installed, you need to install IIS. If you didn't install the FrontPage Server Extension when you installed IIS, you need to add the FrontPage Server Extension.

To install IIS and/or add the FrontPage Server Extension, open the Control Panel and click on Add Or Remove Programs. You then select Add Or Remove Windows Components in the left sidebar. In the Windows Components dialog box, check Internet Information Services (IIS) and then click Details. In the Internet Information Services (IIS) dialog box, check the subcomponents you want, being sure to check the FrontPage 2000 Server Extension. Figure 23-13 shows the Internet Information Services (IIS) dialog box with subcomponents selected. Click OK and complete the wizard to install IIS and the FrontPage Server Extensions.

Once IIS and the FrontPage Server Extension are installed, you can use the IIS Man agement Console to create the virtual directory (or directories) required for the application. You need to also configure the IIS authentication for the virtual directory. If you are using Form Authentication, the IIS authentication is automatically set and you do not need to change the configuration.

Copying the Web Application to the Production Computer

After the virtual directory for your Web application is created, you simply copy the files that you created in Step 1 to the appropriate directories. If you do not have access to the production computer from the development computer via the network or through FTP, you can copy the files to removable media and then install them locally on the production computer.

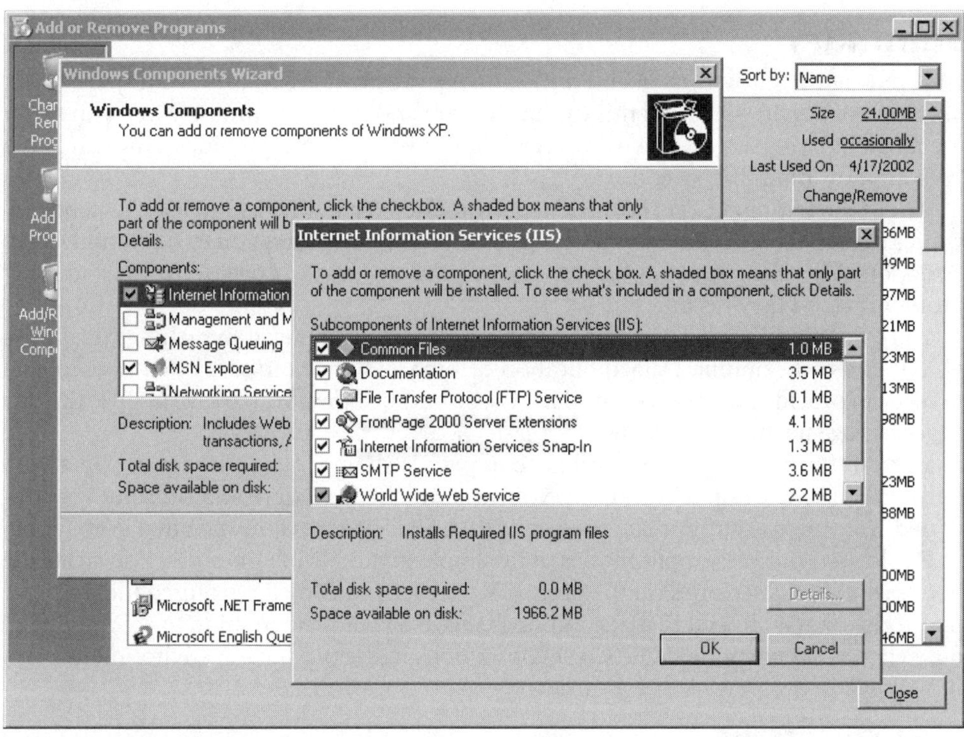

Figure 23-13 Internet Information Services (IIS) dialog box with subcomponents selected

Modify the machine.config File

You should not copy the machine.config file from the development computer to the production computer. If you have made changes to the machine.config file on the development machines that are required by your application, you need to manually make these changes to the machine.config file on the production machine.

Copying Global Assembly Cache Assemblies

If you have common assemblies that are used in more than one Web application or are used in other applications that need to be installed on the production machine, you need to add them to the Global Assembly Cache. See Chapter 10 for more details about adding assemblies to the Global Assembly Cache.

Summary

Unit testing the individual Web Forms and user controls is an important part of the development cycle. Although this can be difficult and time consuming when you are in the midst of trying to get everything together, it saves time and provides a more reliable Web application in the long run.

Part of the testing process is to add tracing to the Web Forms and to use the debug facilities of the VS.NET IDE. The VS.NET IDE environment allows you to find and resolve errors quickly. Also, you can use tracing in your production release to help identify problems when they occur.

You can optimize your Web application by using data application caching (the Cache object) and cache output. Data application caching allows you to save often-needed data in cache to provide fast access to the data. Cache output allows you to save frequently used pages or page fragments in memory for faster access.

You can further increase performance of your Web application by setting up a Web farm. When you set up a Web farm, you need to change where session state is maintained. You can use either a state server or SQL Server for session state in a Web farm.

Deploying your Web application is quite simple in the .NET Framework. You create the necessary virtual directories on the production server and copy the required files to those directories. You may need to make minor changes to your configuration to accommodate different server names and SQL Server connections in the production environment.

Test Questions

1. Which two methods are part of the System.Web Trace class? (Choose two.)
   A. Write
   B. Assert
   C. Warn
   D. Writeline
2. Where do you enable tracing for an individual Web Form?
   A. In VB.NET code by setting Trace.On = True
   B. In the @Tracing directive in the HTML code
   C. In the @Page directive in the HTML code
   D. In the web.config file trace element
3. You have set tracing so that it displays on the Web Form, and your Web Form is designed using a page layout of GridLayout. What problem will you encounter?
   A. The trace messages will be interspersed in your Web Form.
   B. No problems will be encountered. Trace is designed to work in the environment.

C. The trace result information will overlay the Web Form display.

D. The trace result information will not be displayed because it would overlay the Web Form display.

4. What configuration attribute do you set in the trace element to avoid displaying trace results on the Web Form?

A. pageOutput

B. resultsLocation

C. enabled

D. outputPage

5. Where is Web Form trace information stored when it is not being displayed on the Web Form?

A. A SQL Server database

B. On the session state server

C. In memory

D. In a log file

6. How do you display trace information that has not been displayed on the Web page?

A. You run the trace.exe program.

B. You display it using Internet Explorer and the //localhost/WebAppName/trace.axd URL.

C. You view the trace.log file using notepad.exe.

D. You run the viewtrace.exe program.

7. If you set a breakpoint in your Web application and run the Web application, but execution does not stop at the breakpoint even though you are sure that the line was executed, what is the most likely problem?

A. The line could not have executed, otherwise the execution would have stopped at the breakpoint.

B. You have the compile option set to compile a release version of the application.

C. You have programmatically turned debugging off in the VB.NET code.

D. You are running the beta version of VS.NET.

8. If you want to view all the variables available within the subroutine you have stopped executing in, what debug window do you use?

A. Output window

B. Watch window

C. Locals window

D. Immediate window

9. If you want to change the value of a variable while debugging, what debug window can you use? (Choose two.)

   A. Output window

   B. Watch window

   C. Locals window

   D. Immediate window

10. Which of the following is a valid Cache.Insert statement?

   A. Cache.Insert("Regions", dsRegions, null, Cache.NoAbsoluteExpiration, Cache.NoSlidingExpiration, Caching.CacheItemPriority.Default, null)

   B. Cache.Insert("Regions", dsRegions, Nothing, Cache.NoAbsoluteExpiration, Cache.NoSlidingExpiration, Caching.CacheItemPriority.Default, Nothing)

   C. Cache.Insert("Regions", dsRegions, null, Cache.NoAbsoluteExpiration, TimeSpan.FromHours(1), Caching.CacheItemPriority.Default, null)

   D. Cache.Insert("Regions", dsRegions, Nothing, Cache.NoAbsoluteExpiration, TimeSpan.FromHours(1), Caching.CacheItemPriority.Default, Nothing)

11. If you want to use cache output for part of a page, what must you do?

   A. Isolate the code into a subroutine.

   B. You cannot cache a part of a page.

   C. Create a user control that contains the part of the page that you want to cache.

   D. Enclose the HTML code for the part of the page you want to cache in <cache></cache> tags.

12. What are the two required attributes of the OutputCache directive? (Choose two.)

   A. Timeout

   B. Duration

   C. Location

   D. VaryByParam

13. Which of the following Web application files should not be included on a production server? (Choose two.)

   A. .aspx files

   B. .resx files

   C. web.config

   D. .vb files

14. What are the units for the Duration attribute for the @OutputCache directive?
    A. Millisecond
    B. Seconds
    C. Minutes
    D. Hours
15. What is the maximum time duration that can be specified for the SlidingExpiration parameter of the Trace object?
    A. One minute
    B. One hour
    C. One day
    D. One year

Test Answers

1. A, C.
2. C.
3. C.
4. D.
5. C.
6. B.
7. B.
8. C.
9. B, D.
10. D.
11. C.
12. B, D.
13. B, D.
14. B.
15. D.

PART VII

Remoting, Windows Services, and Using Web Services

CHAPTER 24

Windows Services

In this chapter, you will

- Write code that is executed when a Windows service is started and stopped
- Access unmanaged code from a Windows service
- Configure client computers and servers to use a Windows service

As a developer, you probably develop applications that have some interaction with the end user. A user will provide input, and the application provides output in response. Users start an application when they want to begin using the application's functionality, then exit the application when they're finished. This type of application is very client heavy—that is, an application of this type is usually installed on multiple workstations, making it more expensive to manage. The functionality that is provided by the application is duplicated from one machine to the next. This focus on functionality to an end user brought on the era of client/server programming, where most of the application ran on the server, with a small portion running on the client. Usually only enough of the application is implemented on the client to render the information provided by the server.

These types of applications don't provide functionality directly to the end user, but instead manage resources that other applications or users can share. These applications were sometimes implemented as extensions to an OS because they executed from system boot to shutdown or were responsible for interacting with a specialized device such as a fax card. Such applications or services had some common characteristics, such as:

- **A service usually does not implement a user interface.** Interaction directly with the end user is generally not a requirement of these types of applications. In fact, service applications run in a different Windows station altogether than other applications. Because of this, dialog boxes raised from within a service application will not be seen and may cause your program to stop responding. Similarly, error messages should be logged in the Windows Event Log rather than raised in the UI. If the application requires configuration, this can be done through settable configuration parameters in the registry that are read upon startup of the service.
- **A service doesn't depend on a user logging on to the system.** The application can be developed to run under the context of the system account or specific credentials can provide the necessary permissions to access resources required by the service.
- **A service starts and shuts down when the system starts and shuts down.** If you are familiar with Unix, you will recognize the similarities to a Unix daemon.

In Windows 2000 and Windows NT, developing a service proved to be challenging. Environmental issues such as resource access depend on the account the service is running under. For instance, if the local system account is used, you have to be aware that this account is only known locally to your machine. The local system account cannot be used to access network resources such as file shares, named pipes, the registry, and access to a remote computer's event logs. This is because NTLM authentication (the mechanism used for authenticating access to network resources) tries to access network resources based on NULL credentials. When a network resource is accessed in this way, it is referred to as a NULL session. Access is only allowed if the remote machine allows NULL session access. By default, this is not allowed in Windows NT, which necessitated reconfiguring the operating system or the application not being able to use network resources. This and other difficulties such as debugging proved to be onerous tasks for the Windows NT services developer.

With the introduction of Microsoft .NET, the development of services has become much easier. This chapter will delve into the Microsoft .NET approach to Windows services development. We will finish the chapter with a discussion on how to debug a service developed using Visual Basic .NET.

Windows Services Architecture

Service applications are processes that run in conjunction with various components that make up the services architecture in Windows operating systems (OS), and extensions to the OS provided by the common language runtime (CLR) of Microsoft .NET. Each Windows NT/2000 system consists of a Service Control Manager (SCM) that is implemented within services.exe, an executable in %systemroot%\system32. The SCM acts as a central broker for services on your system. This component is responsible for service communication within your system and provides services such as starting and stopping services, pausing them, continuing them, and so on.

Before a service can be started and stopped by the SCM, of course, it must be installed. Visual Studio .NET ships installation components that can be used to install resources associated with your service applications. Installation components register an individual service in the SCM database on the system to which it is being installed and let the Services Control Manager know that the service exists. The SCM database is implemented via the registry under HKEY_LOCAL_MACHINE\SYSTEM\CurrentControlSet\Services. The installation components register the service by defining a services registry key which contains the parameters for the service. These parameters include the service type, the location of the service image file, an optional description of the service, and whether the service starts automatically when the system boots.

The service itself is developed using a component called ServiceController. This component is used to start, stop, and communicate directly with the service. (Actually, the ServiceController makes calls to the Service Control Manager which in turn does work on its behalf.) This component allows the service to communicate status information back to the SCM and to receive commands from the SCM that control the execution of the service. Once the SCM initiates the service by loading it as a background process, the service runs indefinitely until it is either stopped, paused, or the computer shuts down. Loading a service is often done at bootup, before any user logs in, and is independent of any specific user. Once loaded, the service is started by the SCM and control is passed to the OnStart method which begins processing any code you have defined in the method.

Many services are launched automatically by the system at boot time. They can also be manually launched by a user at the console, via the NT Control Panel's Services applet, as shown in Figure 24-1.

This applet is used to communicate with the Service Control Manager and is known as the Service Control Program (SCP). An SCP allows you to command the SCM to start a stopped service, stop a started service, pause a started service, or continue a paused service. Each of these actions calls an associated procedure within the service (OnStop, OnPause, or OnContinue), in which you can define additional processing to be performed based on the change in state as defined through the SCP. If you are manually starting a service, you can pass command-line arguments to the service by filling in the Startup Parameters edit box.

Although Windows NT/2000 comes with its own SCP within the Control Panel, it is possible to develop your own SCP that will interact with the SCM. Many services define their own SCP to allow for the configuration of the service by the end user. You can see this with the Services applet itself, as it provides a very rudimentary facility that will allow you to enter parameters that are then passed to the service upon startup. Each SCP is implemented with special Win32 function calls that let it talk to the SCM.

EXAM TIP Make sure you have an understanding of how Windows services work in the context of the Windows operating system. This will help you to understand how Windows services are developed.

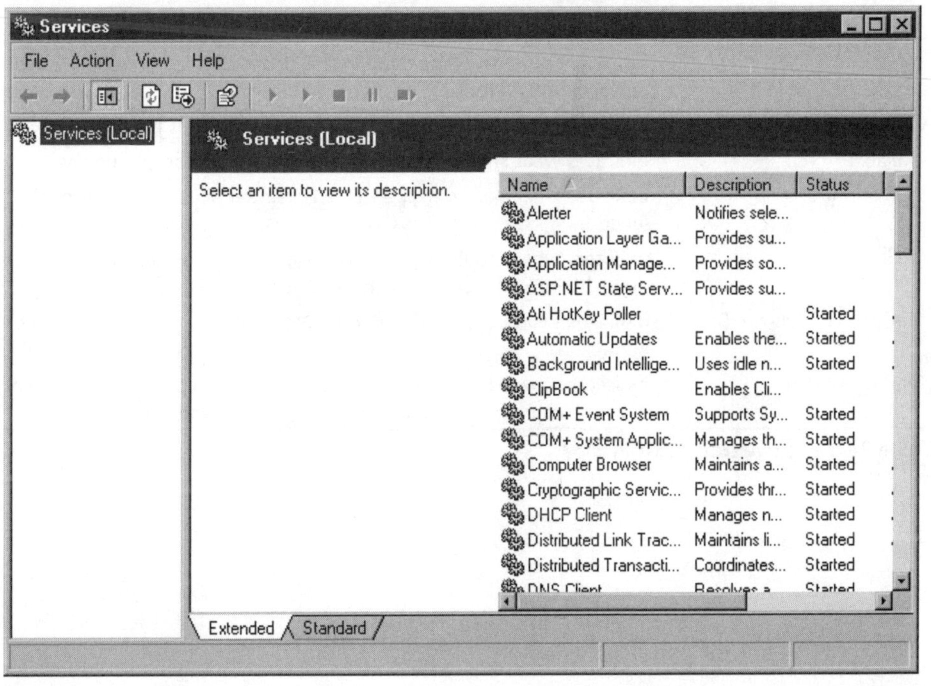

Figure 24-1 Services applet

Developing Windows Services

Microsoft made great strides with .NET to ease the development effort that is required when developing a Windows service. Defining a service with Visual Basic .NET requires you to use the System.ServiceProcess namespace and the four classes within it. These classes include the ServiceBase class, ServiceInstaller class, ServiceProcessInstaller class, and the ServiceController class. These classes provide most of the functionality you need to create a service. The ServiceInstaller and ServiceProcessInstaller classes are used to install the service and will be discussed later. The ServiceController class is used to manipulate the service itself. This class is not involved in the creation of a service, but can be used to start and stop the service, pass commands to it, and return a series of enumerations. The ServiceBase class provides the core methods that you can implement within your derived class to define the functionality of your service and how your service will behave.

The ServiceBase class is the primary class from which you will derive your own class for defining a service application. The other classes will be discussed later. Table 24-1 provides an overview of the methods that are exposed by the ServiceBase class.

When the state of your service changes via an event generated by the Services Control Manager, one of the methods in Table 24-1 is invoked based on the associated state change. For instance, when a user stops a particular service through the Services applet in Control Panel, the Services applet communicates with the Service Control Manager,

Method	Description
OnStart	Indicates what actions should be taken when your service starts running. You must write code in this procedure for your service to perform useful work.
OnStop	Indicates what should happen when your service is paused.
OnPause	Indicates what should happen when your service stops running.
OnContinue	Indicates what should happen when your service resumes normal functioning after being paused.
OnShutdown	Indicates what should happen just prior to your system shutting down, if your service is running at that time.
OnCustomCommand	Indicates what should happen when your service receives a custom command.
OnPowerEvent	Indicates how the service should respond when a power management event is received, such as a low battery or suspended operation.

Table 24-1 ServiceBase Class Methods

which in turn invokes one of the methods in the ServiceBase class. If the service is stopped, the OnStop method is invoked to perform processing that will occur when the service is stopped. Similarly, any of the other methods defined by the ServiceBase class can be called based on actions carried out by the SCM as you interact with the service. None of these methods is required, but you can use them to provide specific behavior in reaction to requests from the SCM's user interface or from other services.

As a developer, you have some control in your code as to which of these methods can and cannot be called by your service. Control of which of these methods can be called on your service by the SCM is handled through properties set on the ServiceBase class itself. These properties specify which of the methods in your service can be called. For example, if the CanStop property is set to true, the OnStop method on your service can be called. When the CanPauseandContinue property is set to true, the OnPause and OnContinue methods can be called. When you set one of these properties to true, you should then override and define processing for the associated methods.

There is one last method that you need to be concerned about in the ServiceBase class. This is the run method. The run method allows your service to begin execution by defining an entry point into your executable. The run method provides the routine that will load the remainder of the service code into memory. At this point the service is ready to be controlled through the SCM. When the service is started it is done through one of the controlling functions such as OnStart. If you would like your executable to support multiple services, you will need to define a run method for each service. This can be done by creating an array of ServiceBase objects with each element corresponding to one of your defined services.

Let's put this into practice by developing a Windows services application in Visual Studio .NET. To ease the development effort for services, Microsoft has included a project template that provides much of the configuration for you by adding the necessary classes, namespaces, and setting up the inheritance from the ServiceBase class. This is an improvement over previous releases of Visual Studio, where much of the work to set up a service needed to be done manually. In Exercise 24-1, you will create a service that will set the ServiceName property, and override and specify code for the OnStart and OnStop methods. We will look at how to set up the installers for your service application in depth later in this chapter.

Exercise 24-1: Developing a Windows Service

1. In this application, you will define a service which will send a mail message to a predefined address every three seconds. Start by invoking Microsoft Visual Studio .NET.

2. Create a new Windows service application by selecting New under the File menu. From the New submenu, select Project. This will bring up the New Project dialog box as shown here.

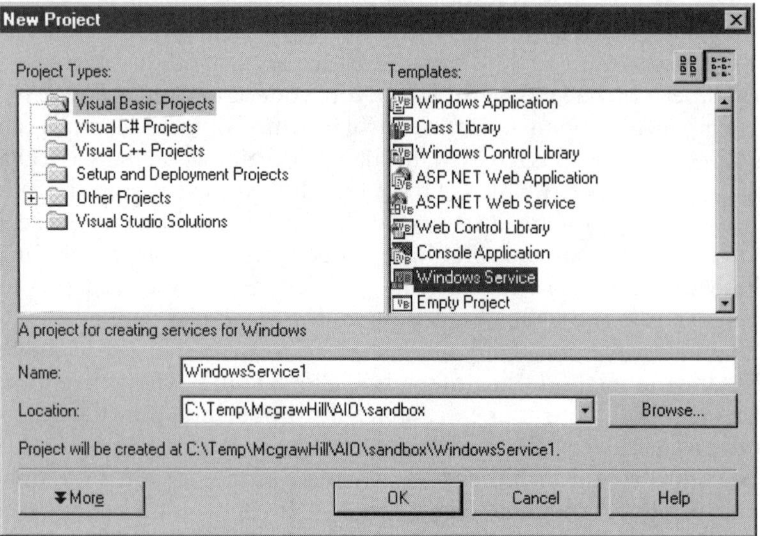

3. Select Windows Service from the Templates pane.
4. Specify the name of your application and the path to where it will be located and click OK. Once you have done this, Visual Studio .NET will use the project template to add a component class called service1 that inherits from System.ServiceProcess.ServiceBase.
5. Click Design view. Then, in the Properties window, set the ServiceName property for Service1 to MailService, as shown in Figure 24-2.
6. Set the Name property to MailService.
7. Set the AutoLog property to true. This specifies that the service should automatically log to the event log common events such as Install and Start.
8. In the code editor, edit the Main method to create an instance of MailService. When you renamed the service in Step 5, the class name was not modified in the main method. To access the main method in Visual Basic, expand the Component Designer generated code region and make modifications to match the following:

```
Shared Sub Main()
   Dim ServicesToRun() As System.ServiceProcess.ServiceBase

   ServicesToRun = New System.ServiceProcess.ServiceBase() {New MailService()}
   System.ServiceProcess.ServiceBase.Run(ServicesToRun)
End Sub
```

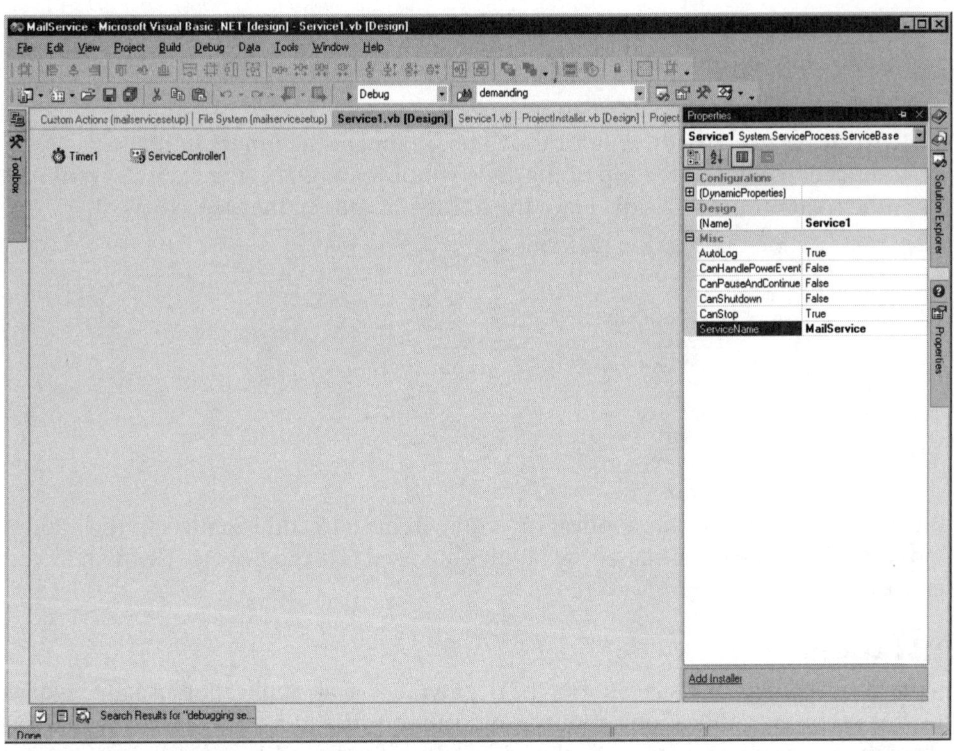

Figure 24-2 Setting the ServiceName property

9. Click Design view, open the Toolbox, and click on the Components tab. Drag a timer control from the Toolbox onto the MailService component. This will add a timer control to the design surface with the name timer1.
10. In the Properties window for timer1, change the Interval property to a value of 3000. This sets the timer's value to 3000 milliseconds, which causes the timer to fire every three seconds.
11. In Solution Explorer, select Service1.vb, right-click, and select View Code. In the code window, enter the following code into the OnStart event:

```
Timer1.Enabled = True
```

12. Before setting up the timer event for the application, you need to add in the code to send e-mail. To do this, you need to add a reference to the System.Web assembly. Right-click on References in Solution Explorer and select Add Reference. Select the System.Web.dll component, then click Select and OK.

13. Now that a reference has been added to the proper assembly, you can add the following code just after the Imports System.ServiceProcess:

```
Imports System.Web.Mail
```

14. To create an elapsed event for the timer, highlight the timer1 in the left drop-down box at the top of the code window and select the elapsed event in the right drop-down box. Place the following code in the elapsed event:

```
Dim Mailmsg As New MailMessage()

With Mailmsg
     .From = you@yourcompany.com
     .To = administrator@yourcompany.com
     .Subject = "Message from MailService"
End With

'Use the local SMTP Service to send the message
SmtpMail.SmtpServer = "127.0.0.1"
SmtpMail.Send(Mailmsg)
```

Before you can build this application, you will need to add installers to the application. Let's take a look at installers, what they are used for, and how to use them in your services application.

Installers

In previous versions of Visual Studio, the deployment of an application usually involved copying all of the application's runtime and support files to a location on the machine where the application was to be deployed. In Visual Studio .NET, an application consists not only of the traditional program files but also of associated resources, such as message queues, event logs, performance counters, databases, and configuration files, that must be created on the target computer as well. You can configure your application to create these resources when your application is installed and to remove them if your application is uninstalled, using what are called installation components.

Installers are particularly important to Windows services. Whereas Windows applications can be run directly from within Visual Studio .NET, Windows service applications cannot. This is due to the fact that the service being created in the development environment must be installed before it can be run. The installer for Windows service applications is responsible for doing the work required to register the service with the SCM.

The ServiceInstaller and ServiceProcessInstaller classes do work specific to the service with which they are associated. These classes are used by the installation utility to write registry values associated with the service to the SCM database in the registry. Typical values written to the database include the service name, services type, the location of the service image file, an optional description of the service, and whether the service starts automatically when the system boots.

There are a couple of things you need to consider when adding installers to your service application. The first is the security context in which the service will run. By default, services run in the context of the LocalSystem account, which gives the service different access privileges to system resources than a user account typically provides. If there is a requirement to change the account that the service runs under, the developer chooses one of four account types:

- **LocalService** Provides the service with extensive local privileges and presents the computer's credentials to any remote server the service may communicate with.
- **LocalSystem** Runs the service with an account that is non-privileged on the local computer. If the service is required to communicate with a remote server, anonymous credentials will be provided to the remote system when the LocalSystem account is used.
- **NetworkService** Runs the service with an account that acts as a non-privileged user on the local system. If the service is required to communicate with a remote computer, the computer's credentials will be provided to the remote server.
- **User** Runs the service in the context of the user account specified. When the service is installed, the system will prompt for a valid username and password for the account specified.

The second consideration for your service application when adding an installer is to consider any methods you may need to override within the installer. By default, every installation component contains the methods outlined in Table 24-2.

Each of these methods contains code that will carry out the required work without modification. If you require custom processing, however, it is possible to override the processing in each method to add your own functionality. For example, you can modify the commit method so that the installation process starts the service after it has been successfully installed. You could also modify the uninstall method so that each service is stopped before it is uninstalled.

In Exercise 24-2, you will add an installer to your MailService application.

Method	Description
Install	Any installation functions that must be performed during installation are carried out with this method. The ProjectInstaller class calls the install method on each of the installation components it contains, and then calls either commit if the installations were all successful or rollback if any errors occurred.
Commit	Commit is called after the install method has been successfully run on all of the installation components the installer class contains.
Rollback	The rollback method is used to undo all previous installation work if an error occurs anywhere in the installation process. If any of the installation components contained by the installer class raises an error, all of the installations carried out so far are undone.
Uninstall	Uninstall is used to remove installation component resources from the system. Unlike installation, uninstall is not transactional. If one uninstall process fails, the system still attempts to uninstall all of the other resources.

Table 24-2 Installer Methods

Exercise 24-2: Adding an Installer to an Application

1. Open the MailService application you developed previously in Exercise 24-1.
2. In Solution Explorer, right-click on Service1.vb and select View Designer. Click anywhere within the Design window.
3. In the description area of the Properties window, click the Add Installer link. A new class, ProjectInstaller, and two installation components, ServiceProcessInstaller and ServiceInstaller, are added to your project and the property values for the service are copied to the components. Be aware that property values for your service are copied from the service class to the installer class. If you update the property values subsequently on the service class, they will not be automatically updated in the installer after the initial copy.
4. To set the startup value for your service, click the ServiceInstaller component and set the StartType property to the appropriate value. This can be manual, automatic, or disabled. Manual causes the service to be started in a stopped state, and requires the service to be manually started after installation. Automatic and disabled are self-explanatory.
5. To determine the security context in which your service will run, click the ServiceProcessInstaller component and set the appropriate value on the Properties tab.
6. In Solution Explorer, right-click your project and select Properties. The project's Property Pages dialog box appears.
7. In the left pane, select the General tab in the Common Properties folder.
8. From the Startup object list, choose Service1 and click OK.
9. Select Build Solution from the Build menu.

After you have added the installer, Visual Studio .NET takes care of adding the majority of code for the ServiceProcessInstaller and ServiceInstaller objects. You are now ready to install your service application. To do so, you will use the command-line utility InstallUtil.exe that comes with Visual Studio .NET. To use the InstallUtil.exe utility, you pass the path to the services executable file. The easiest way to do this is to use Windows Explorer to find InstallUtil.exe on your drive and then copy it to the directory where your service executable is located. Then bring up a command prompt window, run installutil, and pass it the name of your executable. An example of the output is shown here:

```
C:\Temp\MailService\bin>installutil mailservice.exe
Microsoft (R) .NET Framework Installation utility Version 1.0.3705.0
Copyright (C) Microsoft Corporation 1998-2001. All rights reserved.

Running a transacted installation.
Beginning the Install phase of the installation.
See the contents of the log file for the
c:\temp\mailservice\bin\mailservice.exe assembly's progress.
The file is located at c:\temp\mailservice\bin\mailservice.InstallLog.
Installing assembly 'c:\temp\mailservice\bin\mailservice.exe'.
```

```
Affected parameters are:
   assemblypath = c:\temp\mailservice\bin\mailservice.exe
   logfile = c:\temp\mailservice\bin\mailservice.InstallLog
Installing service MailService...
Service MailService has been successfully installed.
Creating EventLog source MailService in log Application...
The Install phase completed successfully, and the Commit phase is beginning.
See the contents of the log file for the
c:\temp\mailservice\bin\mailservice.exe assembly's progress.
The file is located at c:\temp\mailservice\bin\mailservice.InstallLog.
Committing assembly 'c:\temp\mailservice\bin\mailservice.exe'.
Affected parameters are:
   assemblypath = c:\temp\ mailservice\bin\mailservice.exe
   logfile = c:\temp\mailservice\bin\mailservice.InstallLog
The Commit phase completed successfully.
The transacted install has completed.
```

To uninstall the service, you must first close the Service Management Console. If the console is open, it must be closed and reopened to allow the uninstall process to complete. Use the syntax installutil /u mailservice.exe to perform this operation.

EXAM TIP Have a good understanding of installers and how they are used in the development of Windows services. Pay particular attention to the security context within which services run.

Deploying the Service

One of the features of Microsoft .NET applications that attract developers is the ability to use XCOPY to deploy an application. While this works well for client applications, it doesn't work so well for service applications. As you've seen, a service application cannot simply be copied to the target computer. The SCM would have no knowledge of the service since it has not been properly installed. Microsoft addresses this issue through the use of a setup project. A setup project allows you to create installers to distribute your service application. The resulting Windows Installer (.msi) file contains the application, any dependent files, information about the application such as registry entries, and instructions for installation. When the .msi file is distributed to the target computer, it is distributed as a self-contained application that includes all the necessary functionality to ensure that the service application is installed properly on the target machine. If for any reason the installation fails, the installation will be rolled back and the computer returned to its preinstallation state.

When creating a setup package for a service application, not only must you create the package itself, you must also include a custom action that will be run from the package. Custom actions can help in determining which components are part of the install, which you should roll back in case of error, and which you should remove when the service is uninstalled. In this case, your custom action will invoke the ServiceProcessInstaller and ServiceInstaller components associated with the project and install your service from the setup package.

In Exercise 24-3, you will create a setup project for your service application that will contain a custom action to install the MailService application you have been creating throughout this chapter.

Exercise 24-3: Creating a Setup Project

1. Open the MailService application.
2. From the File menu, select Add Project, then select New Project. This will bring up the Add New Project dialog box as shown here.

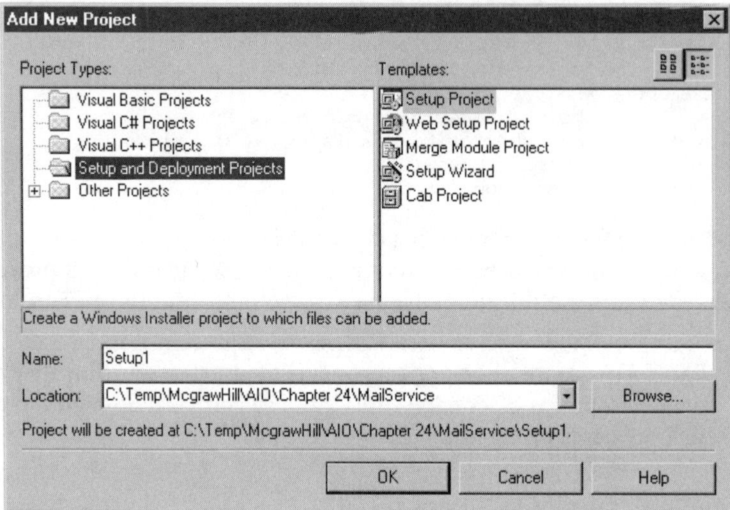

3. Select Setup And Deployment Projects in the Project Types pane.
4. In the Templates pane, select Setup Project.
5. Specify the project name and location and click OK.

   This creates the setup project for you. To complete the deployment package, you will need to specify what needs to be included in the installer and where to install it on the target computer. To do this you will add the project output for your service application to the setup project.
6. Open the File System editor (one of six editors used to configure installers created with a deployment project) by first selecting the deployment project in Solution Explorer.
7. From the View menu, select Editor and the File System editor, as shown in the illustration.

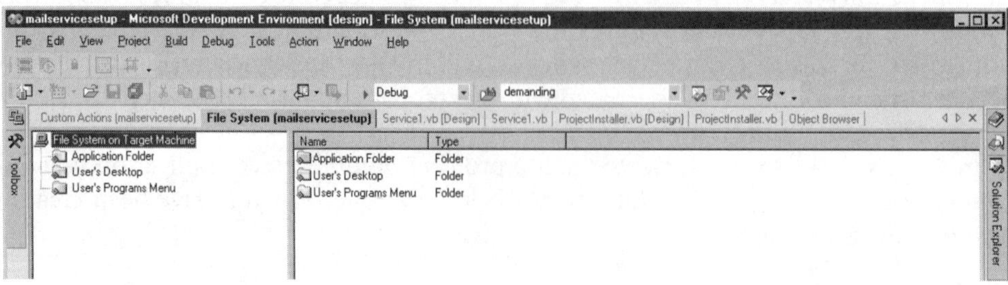

8. Select a folder on the target computer where the item will be installed.
9. From the Action menu, select Add, and then click Project Output. This will bring up a dialog box in which you can select the items you want to add, as shown in the following illustration. Click on Primary Output and click OK.

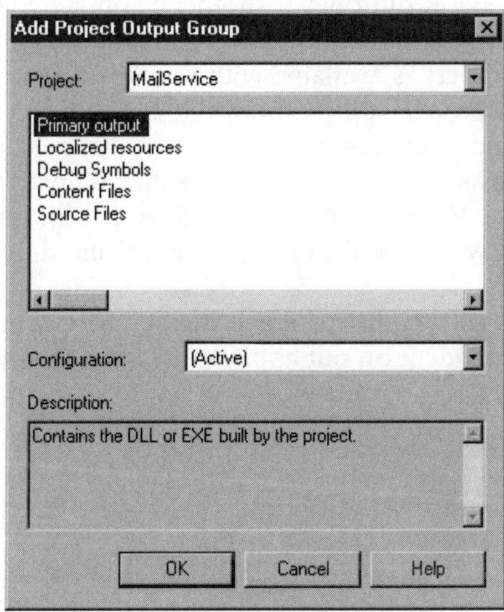

10. To add a custom action for your application, right-click on the MailServiceSetup node in Solution Explorer, then select View. From the View menu, select Custom Actions. This will set up the designer for custom actions.
11. In the Design View, right-click on the Custom Actions node and select Add Custom Action.
12. Double-click on the Application Folder node and select the primary output added previously and click OK. This adds an item to each of the four custom actions.
13. Build the application and associated setup package by selecting Build Solution from the Build menu.

Once the package is built, you can install your service application by running the setup application. To remove the service from the system, use the Add/Remove Programs option in Control Panel.

PART VII

Controlling Your Service

Once you have developed your service application and installed it, you can start the service from the Services Control Manager, from Server Explorer, or from within code. This section will discuss controlling your application through code.

To manipulate your service within code, you will use the ServiceController class. This class allows you to do things like start and stop the service, pass commands to it, and determine its status. Once you have created an instance of the ServiceController class, you set its properties so it interacts with a specific Windows service. This is done by specifying the computer name where the service is running and the name of the service you want to control. By default the computer name takes on the value of the local computer that your code is running on. If this is what you intended, this will not need to be changed unless you want to point the ServiceController at another computer. Some of the other properties that are available with the ServiceController class are outlined in Table 24-3.

In addition to the properties available with the ServiceController class, there are a number of methods that are available to the developer. Table 24-4 provides an overview of common methods and their uses.

Using these methods and properties, you have the ability to manipulate any service in your system. The ServiceController class provides the facilities for manipulating your services programmatically from within an application and developing your own management services.

In Exercise 24-4, you will modify your existing MailService application to pause any services that may be dependent on our application service every time your application service has paused itself.

Exercise 24-4: Pausing Dependent Services

1. Open the MailService application.
2. Select the Design View for your service application.
3. From the Toolbox, select the Components tab. Drag a copy of the ServiceController component to the designer.
4. Right-click the ServiceController component and select Properties.
5. Specify MailService for the ServiceName property. Leave the default MachineName property.
6. In the code window for your application, add the following code:

```
Protected Overrides Sub OnPause()
    Dim services() As ServiceController
    Dim intCounter As Integer

    services = Me.ServiceController1.DependentServices()
    For intCounter = 0 To UBound(services)
        If services(intCounter).CanPauseAndContinue Then
            services(intCounter).Pause
        End If
    Next
End Sub
```

7. From the Build menu, select Build Solution to create your application.

Debugging Windows Services

Debugging an application in Visual Studio .NET is typically done by selecting Start or Step Into from the Debug menu. This usually begins the debug process and as the developer you can start to trace through your code, examine variables, set breakpoints, and so on. However, with a service application it is a little more complex.

Property	Description
CanPauseandContinue	Specifies whether the service can be paused and resumed
CanShutDown	Specifies whether the service should be notified when the system is shutting down
CanStop	Specifies whether the service can be stopped after it has started
DependentServices	Specifies the set of services that depend on the service associated with this instance of the ServiceController class
DisplayName	Specifies the name for the service
MachineName	Specifies the computer on which this service resides
ServiceName	Specifies the name of the service that this instance references
ServicesDependOn	Specifies the set of services that this service depends on
Status	Specifies the status of the service that is referenced by this instance of the ServiceController class

Table 24-3 ServiceController Properties

The first thing to consider is the security context that the service application will run in. Depending on the account your service is running under, it may not have access to resources that normal applications have access to. For instance, opening a named pipe server with no security attributes in a normal application will have client access to the named pipe. If a service application is used to open and access the same named pipe, it will fail, unless your service is set to run logged in as the same user the client is logged in as. As such, keeping the security context in mind when developing and debugging service applications will go a long way in helping to improve your overall productivity.

Another consideration that you need to take into account when developing and debugging service applications is the interaction your service may have with the desktop. The Win32 subsystem associates every Win32 process with a window station. A window station contains the desktop interface, and only one window station can be visible on a console and receive user mouse and keyboard input. Win32 names the visible window

Method	Description
Close	Disconnects this ServiceController instance from the service and frees all the resources that the instance allocated
Continue	Continues a service after it has been paused
GetDevices	Retrieves the device driver services on a computer
GetServices	Retrieves the non-device driver services on a computer, and those that are not drivers
Pause	Suspends a service's operation
Refresh	Refreshes all the property values, setting them to the current values
Stop	Stops this service and any services that are dependent on this service
Start	Overloaded—starts the service
WaitForStatus	Waits for the service to reach the specified status

Table 24-4 ServiceController Methods

station WinSta0, and all interactive processes access WinSta0. Unless the system directs otherwise, the SCM associates services with a different window station than WinSta0 because they are not interactive. By default, services are associated with an invisible window station that all non-interactive services share, which is different than the window station associated with an interactive user. Services running with the default service window station therefore can't receive input from a user or display windows on the console. In fact, if a service were to present a dialog box on the window station, the service would appear to hang because a user wouldn't be able to see the dialog box or enter keyboard or mouse input to dismiss the box and let the service continue executing. This happens even if the service is set to run logged in as the same user who interactively uses the system.

Suffice it to say, debugging a service application is not as simple as selecting Start or Step Into from the Debug menu in Visual Studio .NET. To debug a service, you must start the service and then attach a debugger to the process in which it is running. You can then debug your application by using all the standard debugging functionality of the Visual Studio IDE.

Before debugging a service application, you should understand the consequences of attaching to and possibly killing the service. Attaching the debugger to a running service that is required by the operating system to provide services can be detrimental to the stability of your machine. Attaching a debugger interrupts the functioning of your service instead of stopping or pausing the service's processing. While the service is still running as you are debugging it, the processing is suspended. For instance, if you attach a debugger to the Workstation process and it stops processing, the system will halt, as it cannot function without it. You need to understand the impact of your service application on the system.

In Exercise 24-5, you will debug your MailService application.

Exercise 24-5: Debugging a Service Application

1. If you have not already done so, install your MailService application as outlined earlier.
2. Start your service, either from Services Control Manager, Server Explorer, or from code.
3. In Visual Studio .NET, select Processes from the Debug menu. This will bring up the Processes dialog box as shown in the illustration on the following page.

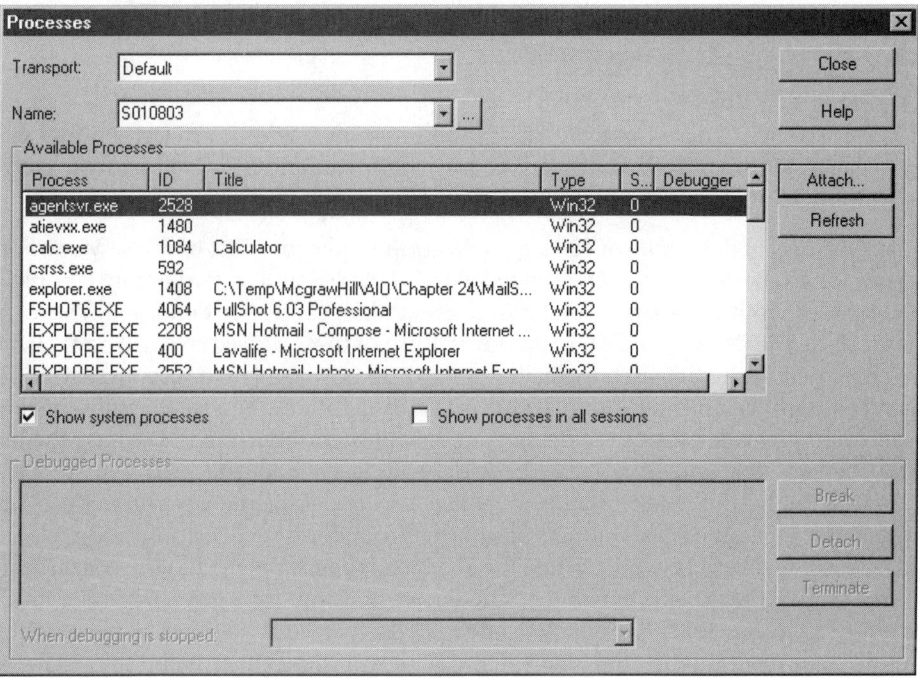

4. Select Show System Processes.
5. Under Available Processes, click the process for your service, and then click Attach. The Attach To Process dialog box appears as shown here.

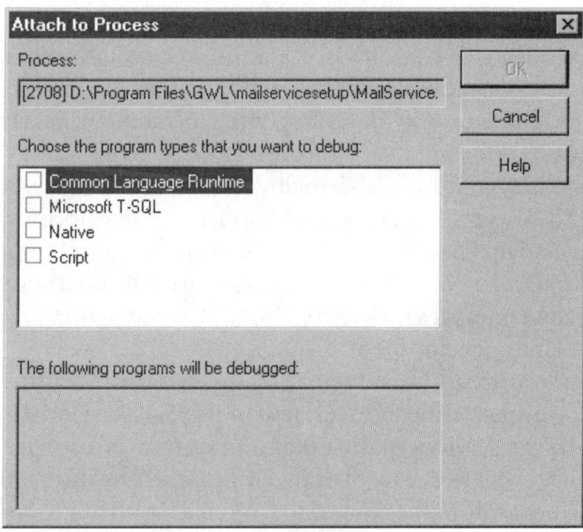

6. Choose any appropriate options, and then click OK to close the dialog box. You will now be in debug mode.
7. Set any breakpoints you want to use in your code.
8. Access the Services Control Manager and manipulate your service, sending stop, pause, and continue commands to hit your breakpoints and debug your service application.

This process of debugging a service application works for most of the service's code, but not for all. Because your service needed to be loaded and started before it could be debugged, the routines used to load it in the first place cannot be debugged. These routines include the OnStart and Main methods. Both of these procedures will have already been executed by the time debugging has started. So how can you debug these routines? The recommended approach to this issue is to create a second service in your service application for the sole purpose of debugging. Install both services and then use the temporary service that you have created for debugging to load and start your intended service. By doing this you can take advantage of the debugging environment to trace through the OnStart and Main methods of the production service application.

There is one caveat, however. When the SCM loads and starts the service, it is under the control of the SCM. The SCM will load the service and wait for a given period of time to see if the service has loaded properly. By default, this period is 30 seconds. If the method does not return within this time interval, the SCM will show an error and the service will not be started. When debugging the OnStart method for your service, you must be aware of this 30-second interval. If you place a breakpoint in the code in the OnStart method and do not step through it within 30 seconds, the SCM will not start the service.

Summary

This chapter introduced you to developing Windows service applications. With the introduction of Visual Studio .NET, Microsoft has introduced another chapter in the evolution of Windows service development, making it much easier than in previous versions of Visual Studio. Not only have they introduced the necessary templates in the design environment to alleviate much of the background work of developing a Windows service application, they have also included within the core of the CLR the necessary namespaces and classes to make service application development less of an effort. This is especially true with Visual Basic .NET. Support for service application development in previous versions of Visual Basic .NET was very painful, especially when it came to debugging. With all languages now using the CLR as the platform to run in, they have a consistent approach to development.

This chapter began with an introduction to the Windows services architecture and how services function, including an overview of the Service Control Manager (SCM), the central broker for all services in the operating system. No service is allowed to execute unless it is done under the control of the SCM. To allow interaction between yourself and the SCM, Microsoft makes use of the Service Control Program. An example of such a program is the Services applet in the Control Panel. This program acts as the user interface to the SCM and provides the facilities to start, stop, pause, and manage your service. While the Services applet will likely act as the interface to the SCM for the majority of your service applications, Microsoft provides the necessary facilities for you to develop your SCP if the functionality of the Services applet does not provide it.

Various classes allow you to create services, interact with services, and install services. You deploy your Windows service application using a setup project. Deploying a Windows service application for the most part does not differ from deploying a regular Windows application with the exception of how the service is installed. Because the service requires installation into the operating system as part of the deployment, it is necessary to make special accommodations to arrange this through your setup package. The way with which to handle this is to make use of custom actions.

ServiceController class methods and properties provide you with the capability to control and manage the services that have been installed on your machine through the SCM. This chapter provided an example that showed how to manipulate a list of dependent services for your sample MailService application, and concluded with a discussion of debugging.

Test Questions

1. Which of the following accounts will present the computer's credentials to a remote server when a service application interacts with a remote system?
   A. LocalService
   B. LocalSystem
   C. NetworkService
   D. User account
2. Where is the Service Control Manager database located?
   A. In SCM.MDB located in %SYSTEMROOT%\SYSTEM32
   B. In the registry
   C. In SAM located in %SYSTEMROOT%\SYSTEM32\CONFIG
   D. In SERVICES.INI located in %SYSTEMROOT%\SYSTEM32
3. Which of the following service installation component methods will undo all previous installation work if an error occurs anywhere in the installation process?
   A. Uninstall
   B. Commit
   C. Rollback
   D. Install

Test Answers

1. A, C.
2. B.
3. C.

CHAPTER 25

COM Interoperability

In this chapter, you will

- Instantiate and invoke a COM or COM+ component
- Implement a serviced component
- Create a strong-named assembly
- Create interfaces that are visible to COM
- Manage the component by using the component services tool

When introducing a new product or technology, the commercial success of it will, to a large extent, be based on how well it supports or interoperates with legacy products and technologies. This is particularly relevant when the new technology runs the majority of computer systems in the world. For Microsoft to introduce a new runtime environment in which future applications will run, it is necessary that they support legacy applications. While corporations may introduce a new technology within their company, they will not wholeheartedly swap out all applications because there is no support in the new runtime environment. For instance, Windows 3.0 not only allowed existing DOS applications to run, but also multitasked them better than any other product up to that time and provided a platform for writing Windows applications that were better than any DOS application.

As such, Microsoft has taken great steps in ensuring that the Microsoft .NET runtime is interoperable with previous versions of COM components. This was necessary since the majority of Windows is based on COM and essentially all code for the Windows environment is neck-deep in COM. This chapter will look closely at the support Microsoft has embedded in Microsoft .NET for interoperability between the COM world and the .NET common language runtime (CLR).

The Anatomy of COM

The fundamental goal of COM was to enable the developer to create applications that could be assembled from prebuilt parts—that is, components. Providing this type of programming environment did much to promote productivity for the developer. There are a number of challenges in developing component-based applications, however. These include:

- A standard way to locate components and create objects using those components. These must be easy to use and not introduce unnecessary overhead.
- Unique identifiers to prevent scenarios in which an application developer asks for one type of object and gets a completely different type.

- A standard way of interacting with objects. This standard mechanism for object interaction would not care where an object was located.
- Compatibility with any programming language or tool used to create the components.
- The ability to create new versions of applications and components and ensure they will work with existing applications.

The binary standard for object interaction helps COM meet all of these requirements. This standard defines a way of laying out virtual function tables (vtables) in memory, and a way for developers to call functions through these vtables. The implementation of this standard provides system services that do the actual work of locating components and loading them into memory, as well as providing the facilities to support interprocess and remote communications.

As a developer, you create objects in your application and then use these objects to manipulate information for you. When an application accesses a COM object, it does so through something called an interface pointer. An interface pointer is actually a pointer from the variable in your application to a pointer in your COM object, which in turn is a table of more pointers to the actual binary code for the method in the interface. This is shown in the illustration.

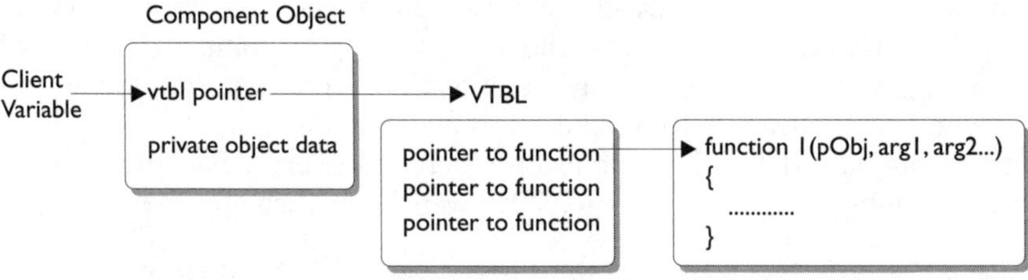

Each COM object contains an interface pointer for each interface it supports. Each interface that is supported is represented by a vtable which itself is a collection of pointers to logically related operations that define a particular behavior for the object. It is possible to have multiple interfaces for your object, each providing its own particular behavior. To identify the interface you want to work with, each interface is represented by a unique interface identifier. Indeed, the COM object itself is represented by a unique identifier. These are known as globally unique identifiers (GUIDs).

The COM object is the actual object that is created when your application instantiates a copy of the class. The class is just a template or logical representation of the COM component. For your application to instantiate it, it actually calls the COM component and then loads the physical implementation of it, which could be a Windows service, a dll, or an executable. Each physical component can contain one or more classes which represent the implementation or actual code for your interfaces.

Each class in your component is represented by a class identifier (CLSID) so that when you create an instance of your component using your application, your application knows how to locate the particular class it wants to work with. However, you don't want to use a CLSID, which is a long string of hexadecimal digits that are useful and understandable to the system, but not to the developer. Instead, you want to use a ProgID, which is a text representation of the CLSID. Think of the CLSID as the numeric IP address and the ProgID as the host name address. As with IP addresses, you usually refer to the host name, not the IP address itself. The translation occurs through the domain name server (DNS). With COM, this translation occurs in the registry where ProgIDs are mapped to CLSIDs.

COM Programming Model

As a Visual Basic developer, you are accustomed to using automation. Automation was originally developed as a way for applications, such as Word and Excel, to expose their functionality to other applications. The intention was to provide a simple way to access properties and call methods and allow calls to be made without needing type information about the object being accessed. It was not easy for developers to determine the type information or the vtable offset for a method. All this is especially tricky with a text-based interpreted language such as Visual Basic.

Automation defines a standard COM interface called IDispatch. Implementing IDispatch in your components can expose any number of functions to clients. Clients access all functionality through a single well-known function called IDispatch Invoke. As a Visual Basic developer, you would use automation to call objects without any prior knowledge of methods exposed by the objects. Within the application you would create an instance of the object and request the IDispatch interface. To determine the functionality that is available for the object, the client calls the IDispatch GetIDsOfNames method with the text name of the function it intends to call. When the function returns, a dispatch ID (DISPID) identifying the object's function is returned. The client will then build a package of parameters to the function in a standard data structure and call IDispatch Invoke. The underlying COM services will then instantiate the object and call Invoke. COM services uses the DISPID that was passed to Invoke to determine which internal function to call. The information passed in the data structure is then used to build a method call to the internal function. Implementing automation in this fashion is known as late binding and your application pays a penalty in terms of performance by using this process.

To alleviate the performance issue of late binding, you can bind the DISPIDs for methods in your application. This will avoid the call to GetIDsOfNames and the overhead associated with it. This form of automation involves binding the components into the application at build time. To do this, Visual Basic uses type libraries to determine DISPIDs during the development process. Type libraries are binary files that contain interface definitions. Using Visual Basic, you read the type library to determine the syntax of the interfaces. Once you have read the type library, you then have the capability to use the methods associated with the component in your application at design time. When the application is compiled, it already has the DISPID and the application will incur no additional overhead in determining it.

COM Interoperability Support

To provide support for COM components in .NET applications, you use a tool that is shipped by Microsoft in the .NET SDK. This tool is known as the type library importer or TLBIMP.EXE. This tool converts classes and interfaces contained in a COM type library to metadata. The metadata is stored in an assembly called the interop assembly. An example of the TLBIMP.EXE command is provided here:

```
tlbimp.exe COMServer.tlb
```

Executing this command generates a .NET assembly in the form of a dll called COMServer.dll. Once you have created your dll, the metadata will be available to your application so that it can create COM object instances and call its methods, just as if it were a .NET instance.

COM+

COM was a technology that was really only applicable to the local workstation. Trying to instantiate a COM object on another machine and make use of its methods and properties, Microsoft has sold a lot of desktop operating systems, in addition to servers. It would be nice to harness the power of these desktops or servers and distribute your application on these systems. Doing so would provide your application with additional scalability and transactional capability, among other advantages. This has led Microsoft to build its own set of services to support this distributed approach to component development.

COM+ can be thought of as the runtime environment for COM components. COM+ provides a way for you to declare services or interest in services that you want to use. Microsoft provides the infrastructure that makes COM+ services work. This infrastructure is based on Microsoft Transaction Server (MTS), which is a Distributed Transaction Coordinator (DTC) environment that lets you compose components into larger units of functionality and makes sure that resources that need to be updated as a group are updated either all at once or not at all. COM+ allows middle-tier objects running on Windows-based platforms to run and control distributed transactions from the middle tier. However, COM+ is much more than a transaction monitor. It provides additional infrastructure support that was not included in COM at the middle-tier level. In particular, it added new support for the following:

- **Integrated security** MTS security is based on the notion of roles. A role is an abstraction that represents a security profile for one or more users in an MTS application. At design time, a developer can set up security checks using roles in either a declarative or a programmatic fashion. At deployment time, an administrator maps a set of roles to user accounts and group accounts inside a Windows NT domain.
- **Thread pooling** Is a scheme to manage concurrency of threads. COM+ introduced an abstraction called an activity, which represents a logical thread of execution in a COM+ application. Multitier applications that use a thread-pooling scheme scale better than those that use a single-threaded model or a thread-per-client model. A single-threaded model removes any chance of concurrency because it can't execute methods for two or more clients at the same time. A thread-per-client model results in unacceptable resource usage in larger applications because of the ongoing need to create and tear down physical threads.

- **Improved configuration and administration** COM+ administration tools make it much easier to configure and manage the server computers that run middle-tier objects. Unlike COM, COM+ makes it possible to manage many server computers from a single desktop. COM+ also provides the tools to generate client-side and server-side setup programs, making it easier to deploy the client functionality required to invoke COM+ components on the back end.

COM+ doesn't stop at providing a transaction monitor. Other services are available from COM+, including Queued Components. Queued Components is a service provided by COM+ that provides the same functionality as Microsoft Message Queue Services without having to explicitly program against the MSMQ API. You author Queued Components in almost exactly the same way that you do standard COM+ components. Queued Components provides an infrastructure that allows you to tie applications together that are not necessarily implemented on the same system. It allows you to send messages in a standard environment between applications and guarantee their delivery. The primary design goal of Queued Components is to provide the convenience of COM method calls together with the benefits of asynchronous, connectionless communication. In essence, Queued Components uses MSMQ as an underlying transport protocol instead of remote procedure calls (RPC). Queued Components can thus get around many of the limitations of connection-oriented, synchronous protocols such as RPC.

Other services included with COM+ include Internet Information Server and Active Server Pages (ASP). Components encapsulate much of the work that you will do in these ASP pages, and you will use script commands to trigger actions on the components. Using ASP you have the ability to provide the user interface for your application and invoke components that will process the data passed from the back end. Components implemented in this fashion act as the middle tier to your application.

The purpose of this section has been to provide a brief overview of COM+ in preparation for further discussion of how .NET handles COM+ components in the new world of Microsoft .NET. We have only touched on some of the features that are available in the COM+ infrastructure. Some of the additional services that are provided as part of COM+ are outlined in Table 25-1.

Discussing COM+ could be a chapter unto itself. We recommend that you refer to Microsoft's MSDN site and specifically the Microsoft .NET SDK documentation for further information regarding COM+. The COM+ infrastructure provides the plumbing needed to tie COM to a distributed world. Using these services, it is possible to develop distributed applications that will be geographically dispersed.

EXAM TIP Ensure you have a good understanding of the different COM+ services that are available within the Microsoft .NET environment.

Service	Description
Automatic Transaction Processing	Applies declarative transaction-processing features
BYOT (bring your own transaction)	Allows a form of transaction inheritance
COM Transaction Integrator (COMTI)	Encapsulates CICS and IMS applications in Automation objects
Compensating Resource Manager (CRM)	Applies atomicity and durability properties to non-transactional resources
Just-in-time activation	Activates an object on a method call and deactivates when the call returns
Loosely coupled events	Manages object-based events
Object construction	Passes a persistent string value to a class instance on construction of the instance
Object pooling	Provides a pool of ready-made objects
Private Components	Protect components from out-of-process calls
Queued Components	Provides asynchronous message queuing
Role-based security	Applies security permission based on role
SOAP services	Publish components as XML Web services
Synchronization	Manages thread concurrency
XA interoperability	Supports the X/Open transaction-processing model, an industry standard for processing transactions

Table 25-1 COM+ Services

The .NET Approach to Components

COM provided developers with a binary standard for integrating components into their applications without referring to or altering their source code. With the introduction of COM, programmers were able to integrate binary components into their applications, similar to the way you plug and play hardware components into your desktop PC.

While COM permits you to integrate binary components developed using any language, you must obey the COM identity, lifetime, and binary layout rules. You must also write the underlying plumbing code for your component that is required to register your component. These are implemented using well-defined entry points, including DllGetClassObject, DllCanUnloadNow, DllRegisterServer, and DllUnRegisterServer. As a developer of a COM component, you must provide the capability for a COM component to be located and for a COM object to be instantiated.

Another benefit of .NET component development is the removal of the registry as a central source of information for your component. You are no longer required to register your component in the registry; this removes the need for the plumbing code used to create a registry entry for your COM component. This results in a significant improvement in productivity for application developers, as they now do not have to deal with the underlying complexity of how to register a COM component.

With .NET, this has all changed. Microsoft has taken the rules of COM development out of the developers' hands so as to make their life easier. In the .NET world, all classes are ready to be reused at the binary level. You don't have to write extra plumbing code to support the registering of components or the instantiation of a COM object. To create a component in .NET, you simply write a .NET class, which then becomes a part of an assembly, at which point applications can use its plug and play functionality. In the next section, we will explore the assembly manifest's metadata support for interoperability. For further discussion on assemblies, refer to Chapter 9.

Managed and Unmanaged Code

One of the major components of the .NET Framework is the common language runtime (CLR). The CLR provides an environment with a richer set of services than the standard Win32 operating system. This environment includes facilities for the developer for exception handling, security, debugging, and versioning.

When a compiler compiles for the CLR, the code that is generated is said to be managed code. This code is native to the CLR and takes advantage of the services offered by the CLR. This differs from legacy code that is run from the CLR, which is known as unmanaged code.

For the runtime to work with managed or unmanaged code, the assembly manifest that supports the code contains the appropriate metadata to support its execution. This metadata is created during the compilation process by compilers targeting the CLR and is stored with the compiled code. Metadata contains information about the types, members, and references in the code. Among other things, the CLR uses this metadata to locate classes, load classes, generate native code, and provide security.

It is this metadata that provides the facilities to support interoperability with COM. Because it offers a common format for specifying types, metadata allows different components, tools, and runtimes to support interoperability.

Locating Assemblies

You have learned how COM locates components for use in applications, but how are .NET assemblies located since the registry is no longer used? When an application calls a referenced assembly, the reference contains the following information:

- The name of the assembly
- The version of the assembly required
- Culture information
- The public key and digital signature for strong-named assemblies

Based on this information the CLR will then use one of the following methods to locate the assembly:

- **Using codebases** Codebases are values that are specified in a configuration file associated with the assembly. The configuration file is used to specify reference information that can change. This lets the application developer configure a particular version of an assembly for your application, allowing you to force an application to bind to a particular version of your component, which ensures that the application does not suffer from "dll hell." When the runtime loads the file pointed to by the codebase, it checks the version information to make sure it matches what is in the application's reference. By default, if the assembly pointed to by the codebase is the same version or higher, the binding will occur.
- **Using probing** If there is no codebase, the runtime begins a probing process. The runtime will first look in the global assembly cache (GAC). The GAC provides a global cache for assemblies to be used by multiple applications on the same machine. Even if the assembly is found through probing or codebases, the runtime will look for updated versions of the component in the GAC. If the assembly is private, the search is performed only in the application's root directory, referred to as the AppBase. If the assembly is not found in the AppBase directory, the runtime searches based on the path setup in the configuration file. This path is specified with the <AppDomain> tag. If this does not locate the assembly, the CLR uses probing heuristics to further try and locate the assembly. For further information on the types of heuristics used, refer to the Microsoft .NET SDK documentation.

.NET Interoperability Support

So how can you provide support for .NET assemblies in legacy applications? Microsoft ships two tools with the .NET SDK that support interoperability of .NET assemblies in a COM environment.

The first tool is the assembly registration tool (REGASM.EXE). This tool registers a .NET assembly into the registry so that COM clients can use it. Under the HKEY_CLASSES_ROOT /CLSID registry key, REGASM.EXE creates a new entry for the CLSID of the .NET class. Regardless of the number of times you use REGASM.EXE on a specific class, the class always has the same CLSID in COM.

Under the HKEY_CLASSES_ROOT\CLSID\{0000…0000} key, the default value is set to the ProgID of the class, and two new named values, Class and Assembly, are added. The runtime reads the Assembly value from the registry and passes it on to the runtime assembly resolver. The assembly resolver attempts to locate the assembly, based on assembly information such as the name and version number. Before the assembly resolver can locate the assembly, however, the assembly must be signed and installed in the global assembly cache or it must be found along the application path.

The second tool that ships with the Microsoft .NET SDK to support interoperability of .NET assemblies in a COM environment is the type library exporter tool (TLBEXP.EXE). This tool generates a type library file (.tlb) based on the .NET assembly that is passed to it. Clients cannot access type information from an assembly directly. Assembly, module, type, parameter, and field representations must first be exported from the assembly to a type library. Once you have generated a type library from a given .NET assembly, you can import the type library into your Visual Basic application and use the .NET assembly in exactly the same way as if you were using a COM component. For example, you would generate a type library for the .NET assembly called hello.exe as follows:

```
TLBEXP.EXE hello.exe
```

Creating .NET Classes

To begin our exploration of interoperability, let's begin by creating a .NET class in VB.NET. VB.NET refers to one or more classes compiled into a file as a *class library*, rather than a COM component. Class libraries are compiled into an assembly, which often has a .dll extension. To use the classes in the library, you instantiate an object in your application based on the class. In Exercise 25-1, you will create a .NET class.

Exercise 25-1: Creating .NET Classes

1. Start Visual Studio .NET and from the Start Page, click Create New Project. This will open the New Project dialog box.
2. Create a new Windows service application by selecting New under the File menu. From the New submenu, select Project. This will open the New Project dialog box.
3. Choose Visual Basic Projects in the Project Types list box and then choose Class Library in the Templates list box.
4. Name the project DentalRecords and click the OK button.
5. Before we define our Patient class, we will define a Dentist class that will be used within our Patient class definition. Do so by adding the following code.

```
Public Class Dentist
   Dim miDentistID as Integer
   Public Property DentistID() as Integer
      Get
         Return miDentistID
      End Get
      Set
         miDentistId = Value
      End Set
   End Property
End Class
```

6. In the code window for your class library, change the class definition from Class 1 to the following:

```
Public Class Patient
End Class
```

7. This will provide the template for your Patient class. Because you have created a class library project, the initial class template is fairly bare-bones. You will add a component definition in the next step that provides more of the necessary code

PART VII

required for creating classes, but first you need to make sure your filenames match your class names. In Solution Explorer, rename class1.vb to dentalRecords.vb.

8. To add an additional class to your class library project, add a component to your project through Solution Explorer as shown in Figure 25-1.
9. This will open the Add New Item dialog box with the Component class preselected, as shown in Figure 25-2.
10. Double-click on the design view to open the code window for your new class. Note that Visual Studio .NET has added the template code for your class along with code for constructors. Constructors are special methods that allow control over initialization of your class. These are always called when you instantiate an object. You will also notice that Visual Studio .NET has added the following line:

```
Inherits System.ComponentModel.Component
```

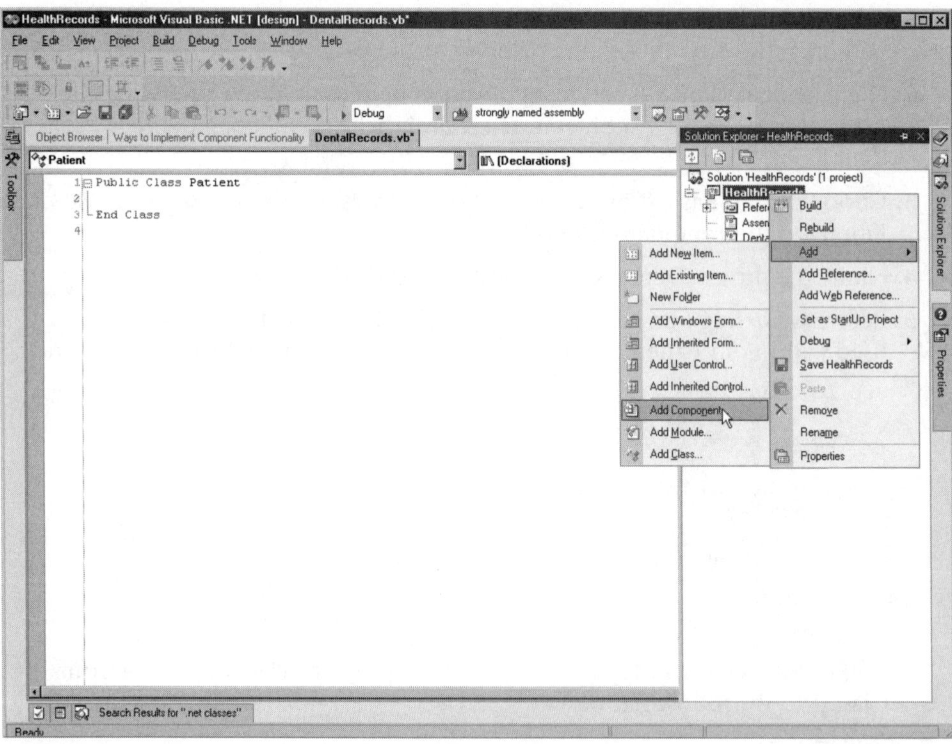

Figure 25-1 Add Component

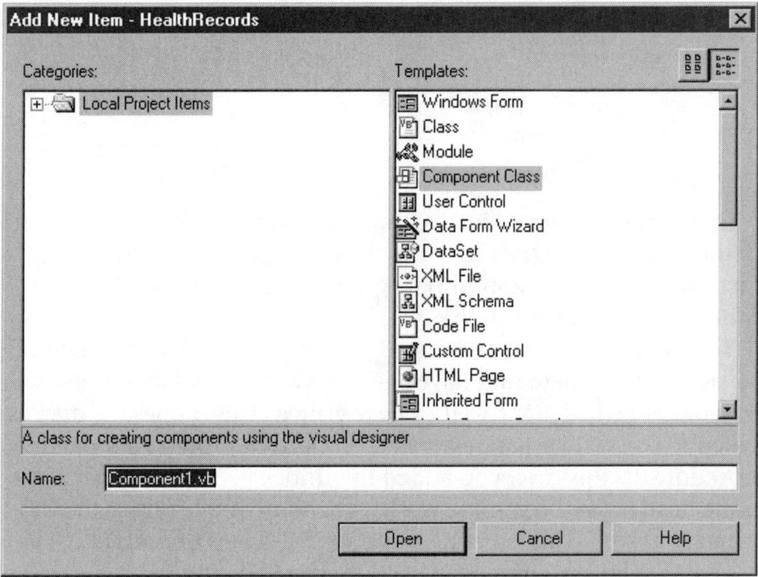

Figure 25-2 Add New Item dialog box

11. This line makes the class inherit from the base Component class. You will now add properties, methods, and events to your Patient class. Click on the code window for your Patient class and add the following code:

```
Dim DentistsList As New Collection()
Dim miPatientID As Integer
Dim msFirstName As String

Public Property FirstName as String
   Get
      Return msFirstName
   End Get
   Set(ByVal Value as String)
      msFirstName = value
   End Set
End Property

Public ReadOnly Property Dentists(ByVal iIndex As Integer) As Dentist
   Get
      Return CType(DentistsList(iIndex), Dentist)
   End Get
End Property

Public Function Admit() As Boolean
   Return True
End Function

Event LabResult(ByVal LabType As String)

Public Property PatientID() As Integer
```

PART VII

```
        Get
            Return miPatientID
        End Get
        Set
            miPatientID = Value
            RaiseEvent LabResult("CBC")
        End Set
    End Property
```

In this example, you added a number of variable declarations that will be used by the methods and properties in your Patient class. You then created a property named FirstName and added appropriate get and set sections to allow you to store and retrieve information from your property.

You then added a parameterized property called Dentists that holds a collection. It is possible that a patient may have been to other dentists in the past, and you would like to keep track of which dentists they have visited. This property is then associated with your patients. To create a parameterized property, simply add a parameter to the property procedure. In this case, you added the iIndex property, which allows you to select the particular dentist you want to work with. Notice that you use the CType function in your property as well. This is because the DentistsList is defined as a base collection and the value you want to return is a collection of type dentist, which is different. Because of the Option Strict statement that is automatically added to all .NET applications, you will need to explicitly convert the object you want to return to the proper type. This is done through the CType function.

You then followed the properties up with a simple method that returns true if a patient was admitted, and an event that notifies you when there is a pending lab result for a patient. To add the event to your code, you declare it with the Event statement and the code for the actual event itself. This event can then be used in your client application with the RaiseEvent statement.

Now that you have created your .NET class, you need to test it. In Exercise 25-2, you will add a test client to your existing application.

Exercise 25-2: Creating a Test Client

1. From the File menu in Visual Studio .NET, choose New | Project. This will open the New Project dialog box.
2. Select Visual Basic Projects from the Project Type list and Windows Application from the Templates list. Name your Windows application DentalRecordsClient and save it to the same location that your class library is saved.
3. Before clicking the OK button, make sure you select the Add To Solution radio button as shown in Figure 25-3.
4. After you click OK, your test client application is added to your solution. Since you added the test client application after developing your class library, the startup project will be configured to be that of the class library. To set your test client application as the startup application, right-click on the DentalRecordsClient project in Solution Explorer and choose Set As Startup Project from the pop-up menu.

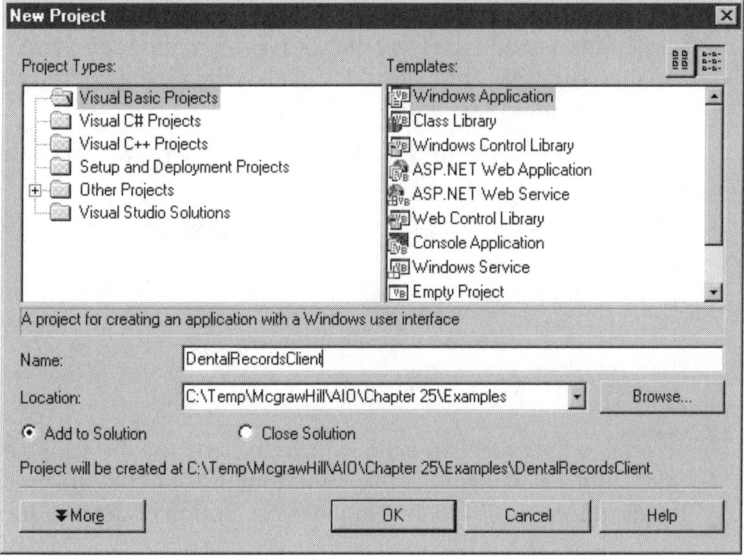

Figure 25-3 Add test client to your solution

5. You now need to add a reference to the classes you have defined in our DentalRecords project. To do this, right-click on the References node for the DentalRecordsClient in Solution Explorer and choose Add Reference. This will open the Add Reference dialog box as shown in Figure 25-4.

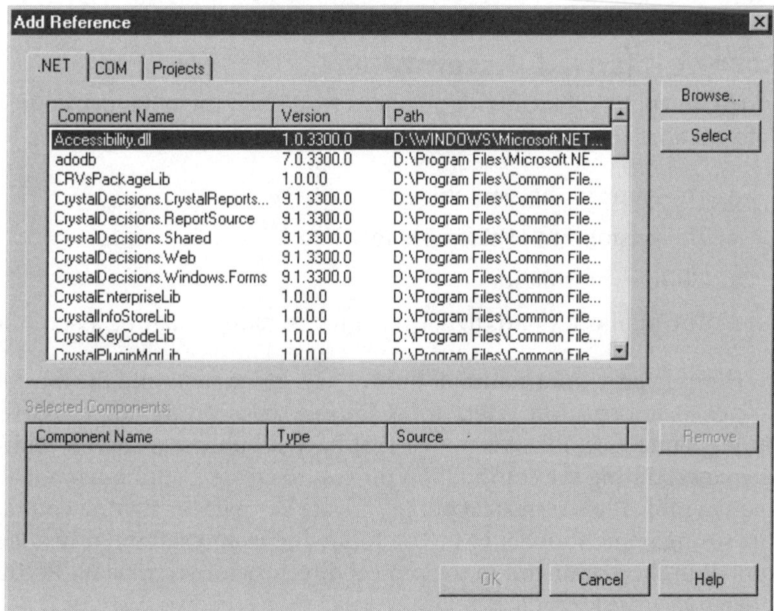

Figure 25-4 Add Reference dialog box

6. Click on the Projects tab and you should see the DentalRecords project. Click the Select button to add the DentalRecords project into the Selected Components box and then click OK. This will add your class library to your test client application so you can use the classes you have defined.
7. In design view for your test application, add a button from the Toolbox to the form.
8. Select the code window for your form by double-clicking on the form and enter the following code:

```
Protected Sub button1_Click(ByVal sender As Object, _
                          ByVal e As System.EventArgs) Handles button1.click
   Dim Patient as New DentalRecords.Patient()
   Patient.Firstname = "Bob"
   msgbox(Patient.FirstName)
End Sub
```

9. To process the event you defined in your client, use the AddHandler statement. The AddHandler statement ties the event from the object to the procedure you create to handle the event. To do this, modify your button click procedure as follows:

```
AddHandler Patient.LabResult, AddressOf Me.LabHandler
```

10. Define the event handler procedure by adding the following code to the code window for your form:

```
Private Sub LabHandler(ByVal LabType As String)
   msgbox("Your Lab results are ready")
End Sub
```

Once you have completed coding your test application, you can build it by selecting Build Solution from the Build menu.

Strong-Named Assemblies

When an application calls a referenced assembly, the reference contains the following information:

- The name of the assembly
- The version of the assembly required
- Culture information
- The public key and digital signature for strong-named assemblies

This reference information is known as a *strong name* and the assembly to which this reference information refers to is known as a strong-name assembly. To build a strong-name assembly, you must first have a public/private key pair. This key pair is then used during the compilation process to create a strong-named assembly and sign the assembly file. To create a public/private key pair for signing your assembly, you use the strong-name tool SN.EXE. The following is an example of using the strong-name tool. Run this command in the project directory for your DentalRecords component:

```
sn -k DentalRecords.snk
```

During the compilation process, the portable executable (PE) file containing the manifest is built, and the file's entire content is hashed. The resulting hash value is then signed with the private key that was created with the strong-name tool, which results in a digital signature being created. This digital signature is then stored in a reserved section in the PE file. The CLR header of the PE file is updated to reflect the location where the digital signature is embedded in the file. The publisher's public key is stored in the manifest's metadata as well. The combination of the filename and the public key gives the assembly a strong name. This strong name is then guaranteed to be unique among all assemblies in the system.

Suppose you want to write a strong-named assembly that lives in the global assembly cache. Let's use your DentalRecords component as an example of how to configure it with a strong name. To do this, you will use the AssemblyKeyFileAttribute attribute in the source code to specify the file that contains the key pair. Once the file is known, add the following code fragment to the top of the DentalRecords code view window:

```
Imports System.Reflection
<Assembly:AssemblyKeyFileAttribute("..\\..\\ DentalRecords.snk")>
```

You are now ready to build the solution.

Signing a file with a private key ensures the identity of the file and provides the ability to verify the security of the executable. When the assembly is installed in the GAC, the system hashes the PE file's contents and compares the hash value with the digital signature value embedded in the PE file (after unsigning it with the public key). If the values are identical, the file's contents have not been tampered with, and you know that you have the public key that corresponds with the publisher's private key. Note that the system only detects if the file containing the manifest has been altered at install time. Detecting whether one of the assembly's other files was tampered with is performed when the file is loaded at runtime.

EXAM TIP Be sure to have an understanding of what makes up a Strong-Named assembly.

Serviced Components

With the introduction of the .NET Framework, Microsoft did not attempt to replace the COM+ infrastructure. The COM+ services that were introduced as part of Windows 2000 to build enterprise class distributed applications are still available. Microsoft .NET has just introduced a new environment and constructs for interacting with the COM+ infrastructure. Specifically, Microsoft .NET introduced the concept of a serviced component, which is Microsoft's name for a .NET component that uses COM+ services.

A serviced component is a class that you develop in Visual Basic .NET by inheriting directly or indirectly from the System.EnterpriseServices.ServicedComponent class. To be a serviced component, the component must be strong-named and should be placed in the global assembly cache (GAC) for manual registration. To indicate which of the COM+ services you want to use from your serviced component, you add attributes to your class that specify which COM+ services your class will use. You then add attributes to your assembly which will configure the COM+ application your class will be used with.

Serviced components, just like COM+ components, have client and server parts to them. When you create an instance of your serviced component on the client, the CLR creates a COM+ application for your class and configures it according to the attributes you have specified in your assembly. The CLR then configures each class in your assembly using the class-level attributes you have specified. Let's look at an example. You want to specify that your DentalRecords component and, more specifically, your Patient class be hosted as a COM+ application. In Exercise 25-3, you will modify your existing DentalRecords application.

Exercise 25-3: Modifying the DentalRecords Application

1. You need to add a reference to the System.EnterpriseServices namespace to provide access to the necessary classes so you can set up a serviced component. To do this, click on Add Reference from the Project menu. This will open the Add Reference dialog box. Select System.EnterpriseServices from the .NET tab, as shown in Figure 25-5.
2. Once you have highlighted the reference, click the Select button and then click OK. This will add the EnterpriseServices namespace to your application. Add the following Import statement to the DentalRecords class module just before the Imports System.Reflection statement:

```
Imports System.EnterpriseServices
```

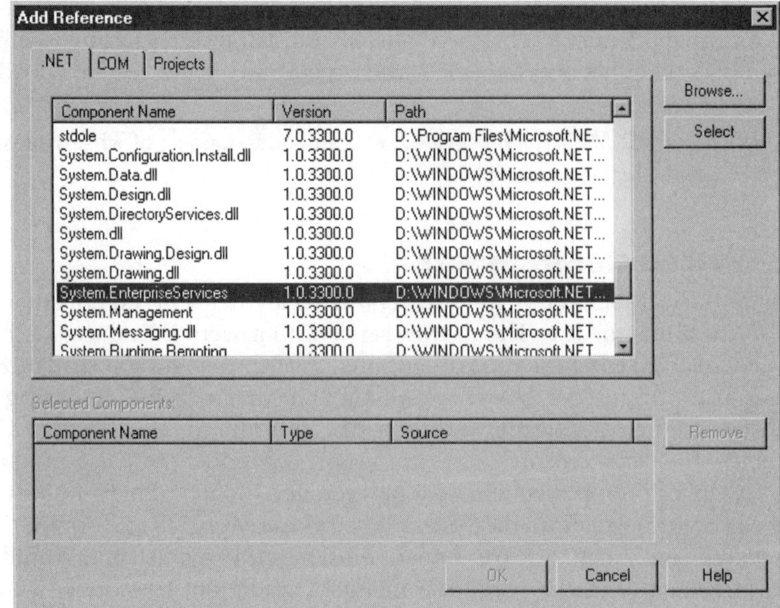

Figure 25-5 Add System.Enterprise Services reference

3. You now need to specify that your class will inherit from the ServicedComponent class. To do this, add the following line after your Patient class definition statement:

```
Public Class Patient
   Inherits ServicedComponent
```

Now that you have inherited the proper class, you will need to specify the COM+ attributes you want to use in your serviced component. In this example, you will use the ObjectPooling and Transaction attributes. Object pooling is a service provided by COM+ that enables you to configure a component so that instances of it are kept active in a pool, ready to be used by any client that requests the component. This saves significant overhead associated with instantiating a component every time it is used and increases scalability significantly. In this example, you will configure the ObjectPooling attribute to specify the minimum and maximum pool size and a creation timeout. To add this to your code, modify your DentalRecords module to add the following line before the Patient class definition statement:

```
<ObjectPooling(MinPoolSize := 2, MaxPoolSize := 5, CreationTimeout := 20000)>
Public Class Patient
```

Finally, you want to take advantage of the Transaction attribute. In your example component, you will specify that the component is required to be transactional by modifying the code as follows:

```
<ObjectPooling(MinPoolSize := 2, MaxPoolSize := 5, CreationTimeout := 20000)>
<Transaction(TransactionOption.Required)>
Public Class Patient
```

Starting and committing or aborting a distributed transaction with serviced components works the same way it does in previous versions of Visual Studio. If a component is marked with the Transaction required attribute, when you instantiate an object of your class a call will be made to a resource manager. COM+ will then start the Distributed Transaction Coordinator (DTC) transaction on behalf of the component, at which point the resource manager will take over. When the component completes its work, it calls SetComplete on its object context if it is satisfied that the transaction completed satisfactorily, or it calls SetAbort to roll back the transaction if it is not satisfied.

To use the SetAbort or SetComplete methods you need to access the object's context by using the ContextUtil class. In Exercise 25-4, you will modify your test client application to explicitly commit the transaction.

Exercise 25-4: Explicitly Committing a Transaction

1. Just as you needed to add a reference to the System.EnterpriseServices namespace in your DentalRecords component, you need to add the same namespace to your client application. Select Add Reference from the Project menu. This will open the Add Reference dialog box. Select System.EnterpriseServices from the .NET tab and click OK.

2. Add the following Import statement to the DentalRecords class module just before the Imports System.Reflection statement:

```
Imports System.EnterpriseServices
```

3. Modify the Button1_Click procedure as follows:

```
Protected Sub button1_Click(ByVal sender As Object, _
              ByVal e As System.EventArgs) Handles Button1.Click
    Dim Patient As New DentalRecords.Patient()
    AddHandler Patient.LabResult, AddressOf Me.LabHandler

    Patient.FirstName = "Bob"
    MsgBox(Patient.FirstName)
    If Patient.FirstName = "BOB" Then
       ContextUtil.SetAbort()
    Else
       ContextUtil.SetComplete()
    End If
End Sub
```

You have modified your button1_click procedure to automatically commit the transaction if the value of FirstName is anything other than BOB. If the value of FirstName is BOB, your transaction will be aborted. While this example is not very useful, it does serve to illustrate the concepts of transactions and serviced components in your application.

The final consideration you need to make is how you will deploy your serviced component. There are two options available to the developer. The simplest method is with dynamic registration, which consists of copying an assembly containing one or more serviced components to the COM+ application's directory. Assemblies that are dynamically registered are not placed in the global assembly cache.

Dynamic registration enables your client application to call your serviced components that are unregistered. The first time that your client application tries to create an instance of a serviced component, the CLR registers the assembly, the type library, and configures the COM catalog automatically. However, for dynamic registration to take place, you must configure your component properly to ensure that COM+ knows how to register it. To do this, use a set of application-level attributes that are available with the System.EnterpriseServices namespace. Make the following modifications to your DentalRecords component to include these registration attributes:

```
Imports System.EnterpriseServices
Imports System.Reflection
<Assembly: ApplicationName("DentalRecords")>
<Assembly: ApplicationActivation(ActivationOption.Server)>
<Assembly: Description("Testing of .NET Serviced Components)>
<Assembly: AssemblyKeyFileAttribute("..\\..\\DentalRecords.snk")>
```

Here you have specified that your COM+ component will be called DentalRecords and that it will be server activated by the client. Since the assembly is making use of Library activation, you will need to deploy the assembly into the same directory as the client application or in the configurable private path for the client application, which can be configured using the client application's configuration file.

To remove the overhead of allowing the system to dynamically register your component, you can use the Services Installation utility REGSVCS.EXE, which is part of the Microsoft .NET SDK. The Services Installation utility allows you to load and register the serviced component assembly, and generates, registers and installs the necessary type library information into your COM+ application. For example, to register the DentalCare component with your DentalCareTestClient application, you would use the following code:

```
regsvcs /appname:DentalCareTestClient DentalCare.dll
```

Managing Components Using the Component Services Tool

Since the introduction of Windows 2000, Microsoft has provided a tool called component services. Using this tool, you deploy and administer COM+ applications. This section will take a look at the component services tool and how it can be used to manage, configure, and administer COM components and COM+ applications.

When administering component services, there are a number of things to consider as part of deploying a COM+ application. These include configuring your system for component services and installing and configuring COM+ applications. We will begin with configuring Component Services for your organization. Before you can start using COM+ applications in your environment, you must perform a number of steps, including configuring your system to enable administrator control for the system application, making computers visible to component services, and configuring COM to communicate with machines across the network.

To configure component services for your organization, begin by configuring the system application. The system application is used to manage configuration and deployment in component services. To guard access to this important application, you must define who can administer the environment. This step is necessary for making any changes to your component services configuration, including installing an application or adding a computer. The system application uses role-based security to administer permissions in your COM+ application.

Computers in a distributed application require administration. You need to make any computer that is part of your distributed application visible to the component services administration tool. Unless a computer is visible to the component services administrative tool, you cannot set security or install applications for it.

The final step is to configure COM to allow communication between COM components running on different computers. This is known as distributed COM (DCOM). You must configure each computer that communicates across the network. Although disabling DCOM has no effect on communication between components on the same computer, all communication is disabled between components on separate computers.You have now configured component services in your environment. In Exercise 25-5, you will install and configure a COM+ application.

Exercise 25-5: Installing and Configuring a COM+ Application

1. Start by making settings for your application that govern how the COM+ application behaves on the network. To do this, install the application on a staging server that will allow you to simulate scenarios that are likely to occur after applications are deployed on the production computers in your network. Staging computers can be used to manage versioning and to update components. Rather than changing configurations or updating individual components on a production computer, you can modify the application, test it on a staging computer, and then export it as a unit to be installed on the production computer.
2. To ensure that the application performs correctly in your network environment and within the associated security context, you will need to add users to the application's roles and set the application's security identity.
3. Finally, when your COM+ application has been configured on the staging server, it is time to deploy it to clients and servers in your distributed environment.

While this is only an introduction to component services, it does provide some insight into what needs to be done to deploy a distributed application in your environment. For specific steps, refer to the documentation for the component services application.

Using COM Objects from .NET

Given the abundance of COM components, accessing a COM component from .NET is to be expected eventually. To do this, you use a runtime callable wrapper (RCW). The RCW wraps the COM object and mediates between it and the CLR environment, making the COM object appear to .NET clients just as if it were a native .NET object, and making the .NET client appear to the COM object just as if it were a standard COM client. As a developer, you can add a COM component to your application quite easily. For example, say you want to create a component that handles the conversion of cholesterol levels. This component will be called cholesterol.dll and will contain a single class called conversion. The class stores an internal variable representing a cholesterol level and handles conversion between millimoles per litre as used in Canada to milligrams per deciliter used in the United States. Table 25-2 shows the members of the conversion interface.

In Exercise 25-6, you will create this COM component in Visual Basic 6.0.

Member	Type	Explanation
Millimoles	Property	Current cholesterol level in millimoles per litre
Milligrams	Property	Current cholesterol level in milligrams per deciliter
GetMillimoles	Method	Returns the current cholesterol level in millimoles per litre
GetMilligrams	Method	Returns the current cholesterol level in milligrams per deciliter
AboveNormal	Event	Fires when a cholesterol level is dangerously high
Optimal	Event	Fires when a cholesterol level is optimal

Table 25-2 Interface for Conversion Class in cholesterol.dll

Exercise 25-6: Creating the COM Component

1. Launch Visual Basic 6.0 and create a new ActiveX dll project.
2. Click on the Class1 module in the Project Explorer window, and use the Properties window to change the name of the class to Conversion.
3. Click on the Project1 project in the Project Explorer window, and use the Properties window to change the name of the project to Cholesterol.
4. Add the following code to the Conversion class:

```
Option Explicit

Private mdblMillimoles As Double
Private mdblMilligrams As Double

Public Event AboveNormal()
Public Event Optimal()

Public Property Get Millimoles() as Double
   Millimoles = mdblMillimoles
End Property

Public Property Let Millimoles(NewCholesterolLevel As Double)
   mdblMillimoles = NewCholesterolLevel
   mdblMilligrams = NewCholesterolLevel * 38.598
   if mdblMillimoles > 6.19 then
      RaiseEvent AboveNormal
   end if
   if mdblMillimoles < 2.59 then
      RaiseEvent Optimal
   End if
End Property

Public Property Get Milligrams() As Double
   Milligrams = mdblMilligrams
End Property

Public Property Let Milligrams(NewCholesterolLevel As Double)
   mdblMilligrams = NewCholesterolLevel
   mdblMillimoles = NewCholesterolLevel/38.598
   If mdblMilligrams > 240 then
      RaiseEvent AboveNormal
   End if
   If mdblMilligrams < 100 Then

      RaiseEvent Optimal
   End if
End Property

Public Function GetMillimoles() As Double
   GetMillimoles = mdblMillimoles
End Function

Public Function GetMilligrams() As Double
   GetMilligrams = mdblMilligrams
End Function
```

```
Private Sub Class_Initialize()
   mdblMillimoles = 0
   mdblMilligrams = 10
End Sub
```

5. Click Project, and from the Visual Basic menu, click Cholesterol Properties. In the Project Properties dialog box, change the Project Description to Cholesterol Conversion Server. Click OK.
6. Save the project.
7. Click File, and to create the COM component, name it cholesterol.dll.

   To install this COM component on your Visual Studio .NET computer, complete the following:
8. Create a new folder named Legacy on your hard drive.
9. Copy cholesterol.dll to the Legacy folder.
10. Open a command prompt window and type:

```
regsvr32 c:\legacy\cholesterol.dll
```

   As the developer of a .NET client application, you generate the RCW to use in your code as follows:
11. From the Project menu, select Add Reference. This will open the Add Reference dialog box.
12. Select the COM tab to display a list of COM components registered on your system.
13. Highlight the cholesterol.dll component you have just registered, and click Select. Once finished selecting this component, click OK.

   By referencing the COM component in Visual Studio .NET in this way, you are allowing Visual Studio .NET do the work in the background to generate the necessary RCW. To use this component in your test application, modify the button1_click procedure as follows:

```
Protected Sub button1_Click(ByVal sender As Object, _
                            ByVal e As System.EventArgs) Handles Button1.Click
    Dim Patient As New DentalRecords.Patient()
    Dim RCWCholesterol As New cholesterol.conversion()
    Dim mdblMilliMoles As double
    AddHandler Patient.LabResult, AddressOf Me.LabHandler

    Patient.FirstName = "Bob"
    MsgBox(Patient.FirstName)
    RCWCholesterol.Milligrams = 5
    mdblMilliMoles = RCWCholesterol.GetMillimoles()
    MsgBox("The MilliMoles per Litre for 5 Milligrams per deciliter is" &
           CStr(mdbMilliMoles))
End Sub
```

As outlined in the preceding code, you create the RCW object simply by using the new operator, as you would for any other .NET object. When it's created, the RCW internally calls the native COM function CoCreateInstance, thereby creating the COM object that it wraps. Your .NET client program then calls methods that are wrapped with a RCW as if it were a native .NET object. The RCW automatically converts each call to the COM calling convention. The RCW converts the results returned from the COM object into native .NET types before returning them to the client.

Using .NET Classes from COM

So what if you want to create a .NET object from a COM-aware client? This scenario is less common but not impossible. There is a legacy of applications out there that will not disappear just because a new technology is being introduced into the organization. It is important that the technology being introduced be backward compatible. If an application requires new functionality to be added to it, a new technology that provides backward support needs to be considered. This is necessary because it introduces the organization to the new technology and provides it with experience, while at the same time meeting the requirements for legacy applications.

So how does Microsoft .NET provide backward support for legacy COM-based clients? Through the use of COM callable wrappers (CCW). The CCW wraps .NET objects and mediates between them and the CLR environment, making the .NET object appear to COM clients just as if it were a native .NET object.

To operate with a CCW, a .NET component assembly must meet some basic requirements. These include:

- A .NET component assembly must be signed with a strong name; otherwise, the CLR will not be able to uniquely identify it.
- The .NET component must reside in the global assembly cache or in the client's search path.
- The .NET component must provide a default constructor that requires no parameters. COM object creation functions don't know how to pass parameters to the objects they create, so you need to make sure the class you are designing does not require this. Your class can have as many parameterized constructors as you want for the use of .NET clients, as long as you have one constructor that requires none for use with COM clients.

For a COM client to find the .NET object, it is necessary to configure the environment with the .NET class. This means making the registry entries that COM requires, using the REGASM.EXE utility outlined earlier in this chapter. There is no need to do anything special in your COM client's code as the COM client will see your .NET class as a native COM object. Once you have done this, you are in a position to take advantage of the .NET assembly in your COM client.

When a client accesses a .NET object as if it were a native COM object, the client calls CoCreateInstance to create the object. COM searches the registry for the registered server associated with the .NET assembly. What it finds is a copy of mscoree.dll. This dll represents the CLR and allows unmanaged programs such as a COM client to run in "managed" mode long enough to execute the .NET assembly. This dll inspects the requested

CLSID, reads the registry to find the .NET class to create, and then creates the necessary CCW needed to run the .NET assembly. The CCW converts native COM types such as BSTRs to the .NET equivalent, in this case a string. Once it has converted types, the CCW packages the request and calls the .NET assembly. Upon return mscoree.dll converts the results that are generated by the .NET assembly back into a type that is suitable for consumption by the COM client, including any errors.

Perhaps you want to use your .NET class to provide support not only for COM, but also for .NET applications. Yet you do not want your COM clients to be able to have access to the methods, interfaces, or classes that are used to support your .NET applications. This is a reasonable request, as it is helpful to package up new functionality while supporting existing functionality. This has been taking place with dlls and COM since the inception of COM and it continues with .NET. To hide this new functionality from COM clients, the developer can use the metadata attribute called System.Runtime.InteropServices.ComVisible. You can use this attribute on an assembly, class, interface, or individual method. Items marked with this attribute set to false will not be visible to COM. The default CLR setting is true, so the absence of this attribute causes the item to be visible to COM. However, Visual Studio .NET's default behavior for assemblies is to set this attribute to false. Settings made lower in the hierarchy override those made higher up. Let's look at an example. Assume that in your DentalRecords class you do not want to make the patientID property available to COM clients. To explicitly configure the property to not be available, you modify your .NET class and your patientID property as follows:

```
<System.Runtime.InteropServices.ComVisible(false)> Public Property _
 PatientID() As Integer
   Get
      Return miPatientID
   End Get
   Set(ByVal Value As Integer)
       miPatientID = Value
       RaiseEvent LabResult("CBC")
   End Set
End Property
```

Summary

This chapter has introduced us to COM interoperability, the ability for .NET classes to interoperate with COM clients and for COM components to interact with .NET applications. The introduction of a new product or technology will only be commercially successful if it can ensure that it interoperates with legacy products and technologies. This is particularly relevant when the new technology runs the majority of computer systems in the world. For Microsoft to introduce a new runtime environment in which future applications will run, it is necessary that they support legacy applications. While corporations may introduce a new technology within their company they will not wholeheartedly swap out all applications because there is no support within the new runtime environment.

As such, Microsoft has taken great steps in ensuring that they are interoperable with previous versions. This was necessary since the majority of Windows is based on COM and essentially all code for the Windows environment is neck deep in COM. This chapter will look closely at the support Microsoft has embedded within Microsoft .NET for interoperability between the COM world and the .NET Common Language Runtime (CLR).

This chapter has provided insight into interoperability. The chapter started with an introduction to COM and COM+, exploring the fundamentals of how the two technologies work. This was necessary to provide a basis for the remainder of the chapter. The chapter introduced how a COM component worked, how COM services locates a COM component on your system, and how a COM component is deployed within your environment. COM+ is the next evolution of COM that supports distributed applications. The chapter provided a brief introduction to the different services that make up COM+ including the distribute transaction coordinator, queued components, etc.

We then moved on to discuss the .NET approach to component development. We explored how configuration information that used to be stored within the registry is now stored within an assembly. Now that the registry is no longer used for locating or holding configuration information for assemblies, we explored how they are located. We then moved on to discuss managed and unmanaged code—how assembly information can be exported for later use in configuring the .NET assembly for use in COM applications. The chapter then moved on to discuss the creation of.NET Classes. An example was presented that was then subsequently used as the basis for further examples throughout the chapter. The chapter then provided a discussion of serviced components. Serviced components replace COM+ components in the .NET world. We looked at how Serviced Components are created and how they interacted with COM+ services on the back end. Finally, we finished up the section with a brief introduction to the Component Services Administration tool. We provided a brief overview of what needed to be done to configure COM+ services within your environment and then finished off with a discussion of how a COM+ application can be installed.

The chapter finished off with the main topic: a discussion of interoperability between COM components and .NET applications and the use of .NET Classes within COM applications. We looked at wrappers both on the .NET side (runtime callable wrappers) and COM components (COM callable wrappers).

Test Questions

1. Which of the following COM+ services encapsulates CICS and IMS applications in Automation objects?

   A. COMTI service

   B. XA interoperability service

   C. Compensating Resource Manager service

   D. Just-in-time activation service

2. Which of the following is not part of a strong-named assembly?

   A. The name of the assembly

   B. The version of the assembly required

C. The location of the assembly

D. The public key and digital signature

3. For a COM client application to work with a .NET component via a COM callable wrapper (CCW), what must the assembly contain?

A. The assembly must be signed with a strong name.

B. The .NET component must reside in the global assembly cache or in the client's search path.

C. The CCW information must be explicitly configured within the assembly prior to it being used in a COM application.

D. The .NET component must provide a default constructor that requires no parameters.

Test Answers

1. A. The COMTI or COM Transaction Integrator service encapsulates CICS and IMS applications in Automation objects.
2. C. The location of the assembly is not required as a part of a strong-named assembly.
3. C. The CCW information does not need to be explicitly configured within the assembly for it to be used by a COM application. The CCW information is determined as part of the implementation of the .NET component on computer.

CHAPTER 26

.NET Remoting

In this chapter, you will

- Implement server-activated components
- Implement client-activated components
- Select a channel protocol and a formatter
- Create client configuration files and server configuration files
- Implement an asynchronous method
- Create the listener service
- Instantiate and invoke a .NET remoting object
- Access unmanaged code from a .NET remoting object
- Configure client computers and servers to use a .NET remoting object

Towards the .NET Remoting Architecture

Over the years, application design has evolved along with the introduction of new technologies. In the early days of computing, all applications were run on a single mainframe computer with the mainframe being shared among all the running applications. This was generally due to the fact that a mainframe computer was, and still is, quite expensive. Maximizing the use of the computer's resources amortized the cost across many applications.

With the introduction of personal computing technologies, the paradigm changed. Computing resources became plentiful and were relatively cheap compared with mainframe resources. Instead of sharing a single computer among many people, a computer was provided to each person. Even though computers were now distributed everywhere, there was still a need to centralize computing resources. Issues such as data backup, availability of applications, and application sharing among many people justified this centralization of resources. The question is how much centralization should take place and what this means for application design.

The introduction of computers to the desktop brought with it new issues in terms of management and software design. The model of dedicating an application to each computer became redundant and expensive. Instead, it made sense to centralize the application and have desktops use the application over a network. This introduced the client/server model of application development. The client would be provided with a relatively large application that contained the business logic and presentation services for the end user, while the data (and to some extent, application) logic was maintained centrally. This made management of the data much easier.

There were a number of problems with the client/server model. Distributing the client portion of the application to each desktop proved to be fraught with its own man agement issues, and having a single centralized back end did not bode well for scalability. Changes to any aspect of the application or its underlying database would necessitate the deployment of new logic to all clients. As the client base increased, especially with the introduction of the potential client base of the Internet, the scalability issues also increased by orders of magnitude.

As the introduction of the Internet started to reveal the weaknesses of the traditional client/server model, the development community responded with the introduction of a multi-tier application environment. In moving from a two-tier (client/server) model to a multi-tier design, two things occurred:

- A new class of server machine was introduced, commonly referred to as an application server.
- There was a more deliberate and precise partitioning of application logic. Now logic could be componentized and run on the application server. Rather than establishing a connection to the back-end database server for each user, one connection could be established and requests for data multiplexed over that one connection, thereby increasing performance.

The deployment of business services on application servers has the following advantages:

- Consistent use of business logic and rules across all clients that use the server
- Improved security in accessing different pieces of application logic
- Reduced reliance on proprietary Database Management System (DBMS) technologies for implementing business logic, enabling the use of tools and technologies offering optimal performance for the server platform
- More flexibility to exploit new server technologies as they become available
- Increased performance, availability, and throughput with transaction monitors and object request brokers

Microsoft responded to the multi-tier application development methodology by enhancing its Component Object Model (COM) technology to support this distributed approach to application development. COM has become the foundation of all of Microsoft's technologies. The fundamental goal of COM is to enable you to create applications that are assembled from prebuilt parts or components. For example, an order entry application might use a data entry grid component to make entering the ordered items easier. Another component could compute sales tax on the order. Each component isolates the responsibility for a piece of business logic to itself.

Running these "business components" in the middle tier on an application server benefited the user and optimized the use of network and computer resources. It became possible to remove the logic from the client, making the application easier to manage from a deployment perspective, while at the same time increasing the overall scalability of the application, because now the application logic could be shared by many clients. Designing the application with distribution in mind can accommodate different clients with different capabilities by running components on the client side when possible and on the server side when necessary.

The challenge with the original implementation of COM was that it did not really accommodate the distributed model of application development. Having two components interact across the network was not possible with the original implementation of COM. Applications could delegate the invocation of these components to an application server that would then run the component on behalf of the client, but there was no way for the client itself to invoke the component. This lead to the introduction of Distributed COM (DCOM).

DCOM extended the COM model to support communication among objects on different computers over a LAN, a WAN, or even over the Internet. DCOM allowed your application to be distributed at locations that make the most sense to your application. DCOM allowed you to preserve your existing investment in COM-based applications, while allowing you to move into the world of distributed computing. As you do so, DCOM handles the low-level details of network protocols, allowing you to focus on the business logic.

COM defines how components and their clients interact. A COM client instantiates an instance of the component and the client calls methods in the component without any overhead (see the illustration).

Invoking a COM application in this manner works well when the component and the client belong to the same process. Computers can run many processes, however, each in its own security context. The operating systems that run these computers shield the process from other processes without clear rules for how interprocess communication can occur. This is to ensure that a process does not violate another process due to bugs. To ensure that clients can still call components residing in another process, the client needs to communicate with the component using some form of interprocess communication provided by the operating system. COM provides this interprocess communication in a completely transparent fashion. It intercepts calls from the client and forwards them to the component in another process. The following illustration provides an overview of the facilities that enable this interaction.

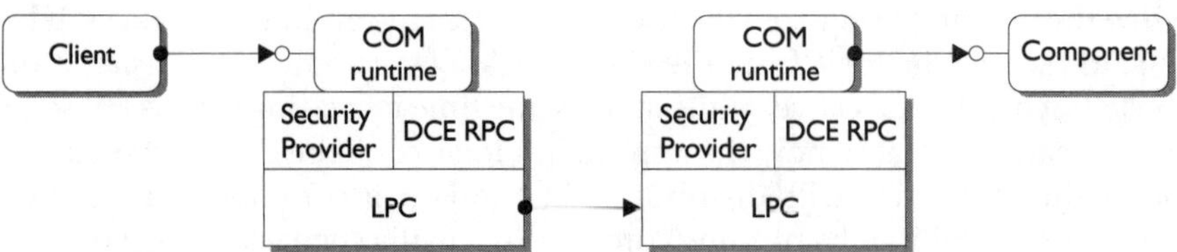

What happens if the component resides on a different computer? DCOM gets involved and simply replaces the local interprocess communication with a network protocol. Neither the client nor the component is aware that the wire that connects them has just become a little longer. The illustration provides an overview of this process.

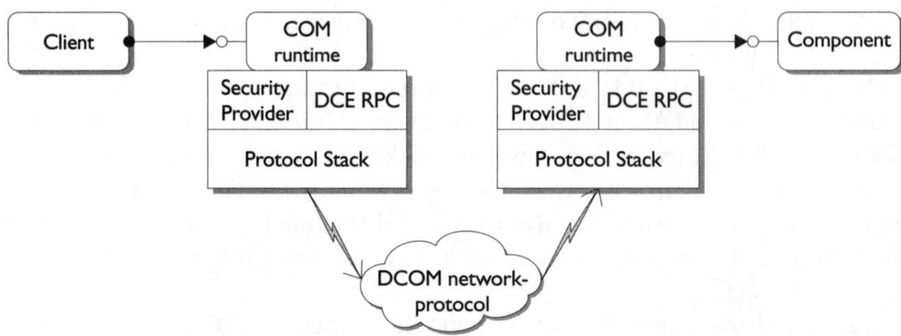

With the introduction of Microsoft .NET, DCOM has been replaced with remoting. The remoting infrastructure enables different applications to communicate with one another and provides a number of services to help facilitate this interaction. .NET remoting provides the facilities to

- Publish or consume services in any type of application domain, whether that domain is a console application, a Windows form, Internet Information Services (IIS) based, an XML Web service, or a Windows service
- Preserve full managed-code type-system fidelity in binary formatted communications
- Pass objects by reference and return to a particular object in a particular application domain
- Control activation characteristics and object lifetimes directly
- Implement and use third-party channels or protocols to extend communication to meet your specific needs
- Participate directly in the communication process to create the functionality you need

This chapter will introduce you to the remoting framework provide by Microsoft .NET and introduce you to the details needed to have an understanding of how to implement remoting in your application.

Overview of the .NET Remoting Architecture

The remoting infrastructure is an abstract approach to interprocess communication. Code running in one application cannot directly access code or resources from another application. The common language runtime enforces this isolation by preventing direct calls between objects in different processes or application domains.

Application Domains

Operating systems and runtime environments typically provide some form of isolation between applications. This isolation is necessary to ensure that code running in one application cannot adversely affect other applications. Each application is loaded into a separate process, which isolates the application from other applications running on the same computer. The applications are isolated because memory addresses are process-relative. A memory pointer passed from one process to another cannot be used in any meaningful way in the target process, as the target process or computer has its own memory space. Using the memory pointer in another process would not result in the same reference.

Application domains are objects that act like a process within a process. Every process has at least one application domain (the default), but can have additional ones as you create them. Everything running in an application domain is isolated from any other application domains within the same process, so if one application domain crashes it will not affect the other application domains. Individual application domains within a process can be independently started and stopped.

Most applications that you write probably only need the default application domain. You can choose to create additional application domains if you want to isolate code from other code in your application. For example, you might have an application that supports third-party plug-ins. You might develop your application to load each plug-in into a separate application domain to isolate them from the main program and from each other.

Code running in one application cannot directly access code or resources from another application. The common language runtime (CLR) enforces this isolation by preventing direct calls between objects in different application domains. Objects that pass between domains are either copied to the local application domain and run locally or accessed by proxy. If the object is accessed through a proxy, the call to the object is remote. In this case, the caller and the object being referenced are in different application domains. Cross-domain calls use the same remote call infrastructure as calls between two processes or between two machines. This is where .NET remoting comes into play.

Remoting Architecture

As mentioned in the previous section, when an application makes a call to a component that resides in a different application domain, it does so using the remoting framework available with Microsoft .NET. An example of what happens during one of these calls is illustrated in Figure 26-1.

When instantiating an instance of a particular class, you use the New keyword and define the class you want to create an instance of. If the class you instantiate is local to your application domain, you receive a local reference to the object. However, if your class is remote to your application domain, you receive a reference to a proxy, which allows you to use the methods and properties as though the object were local to your application domain or process. Because this remote object runs inside a process that is different from the client process (usually on a different system) the client does not call the object directly, but instead calls the object via the proxy which packages the call and creates a message to be sent to the remote server object. These messages are serialized using a formatter class, which takes the parameters and information to be passed to the object and converts the information into a form that can be transported. The message is then sent into the client channel.

Channels are objects that transport messages between application domains, processes, or computers. A channel can listen on an endpoint for inbound messages, send outbound messages to another endpoint, or both. The channel then takes the stream of data passed to it and creates a package according to a particular network protocol, and sends the package to another computer, even if the common language runtime is not at the other end of the channel. Some channels can only receive information, others can only send information, and still others, such as the default TcpChannel and HttpChannel classes, can be used in either direction.

Once the client channel communicates with the server part of the channel to transfer the message across the network, the server channel uses a formatter to deserialize the message, so that the methods can be invoked on the remote object. The remote object finishes processing the request and then packages its current state, represented by the value of its member variables, using a formatter class again, and passes it back to the client.

There are three types of objects that can be configured to serve as .NET remote objects.

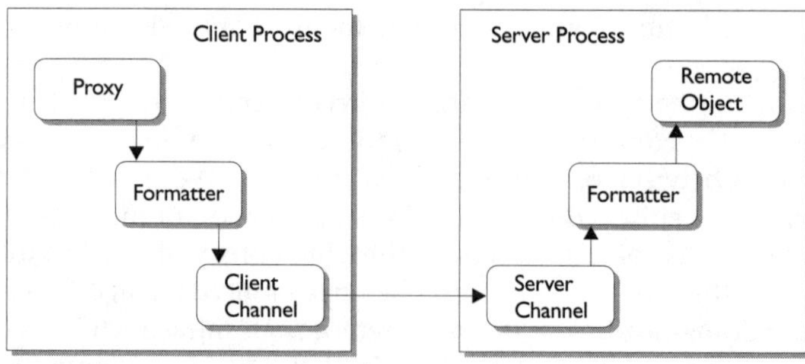

Figure 26-1 The remoting architecture

Each of these objects has its own set of functionality. Choosing which one to use depends on the requirements of your application. The types of objects that can be configured as remote objects include

- **Single call objects** Can process one and only one request coming in. These objects are useful in scenarios where the objects are required to do a finite amount of work and are not required to store state information. When an object is declared a single call object, the system creates a new object for each client method invocation.
- **Singleton objects** Objects that service multiple clients and share data by storing state information between client calls. They are useful in situations in which data needs to be shared explicitly between clients and also in situations in which the overhead of creating and maintaining objects is substantial. There will always be only one instance of a singleton object, regardless of how many clients there are for that object.
- **Client-activated objects** Server-side objects that are activated upon a request from the client. When the client submits a request for a server object using the new keyword, an activation request message is sent to the remote application. The server then creates an instance of the requested class and returns an ObjRef pointer back to the client application. A proxy is then created on the client side using the ObjRef. The client's method calls can then be executed on the proxy which in turn makes the calls on the remote object.

Server-activated objects can be either singleton objects or single call objects. Client-activated objects are activated similarly to the way objects are activated in the classic client/server activation model. When a client creates an object, it gets a dedicated object. A singleton server-activated object is shared by all clients, whereas a single call object is newly activated with each client and disposed of at the end of the call. The client decides whether it needs a client- or server-activated object, and the server decides whether it will activate a singleton object or a single call object.

Each of these objects has associated with it a lease lifetime that determines how long the object should be activated by the server, and at what time the client no longer needs the remote object. A single call object can be garbage collected immediately after it is used because it doesn't hold any state. A singleton object or a client-activated object generally has a longer lease lifetime and therefore needs to be managed over that lifetime to determine if the leases have expired and the resources consumed by the object can be recovered. When the lease manager determines that the lease has expired, it notifies one or more sponsors (the client applications that invoked the object through the lease manager), and asks if they would like to renew the lease on the object. If the lease is not renewed by any of the sponsors, the lease manager removes the lease, deletes the object, and the resources consumed by the object are recovered by the garbage collection process.

Now that you know the different objects that can be created and their particular types, let's look at the activation of marshal-by-reference objects. When a client application makes use of a marshal-by-reference object, it can activate the object using server activation or client activation.

Server activation creates objects whose lifetimes are directly controlled by the server, and the server's application domain creates these objects in one of two ways. The first method the server can use is to create the object directly when a client invokes the first method on a proxy object. The server will then create the object with a proxy being created in the client application. This occurs at the first method invocation, not when the object is instantiated using the New keyword. The second method is to declare an object as a singleton or single call object. In .NET remoting, however, a singleton-mode object is subject to the lifetime lease that is specified for it, so the object can be recycled by the garbage collector even if clients currently hold references to it. It is possible to create singleton objects that are not recycled by the garbage collector if there are still references to the object. To do so means overriding the initialization of the lifetime service object.

Client-activated objects are objects whose lifetimes are controlled by the calling application instead of the server. With client activation, when a client application creates an instance of a server object, the remoting infrastructure creates a proxy object using an object reference class that is returned by the remoting infrastructure on the server when the remote object is created. If a client application creates two instances of the remote object on the server, each of the client references will refer to the same remote object on the server. When dealing with lease life on client-activated objects, client applications specify the length of time that an object it creates should exist. If the lease life for the remote object expires, the client application is notified by the lease manager to determine if the client application wants to renew the lease for the application and for how long. If the client does not respond, the server can be configured to wait a specified amount of time for the client application to respond while continuing to try and contact the client app.

Developing an Application Using .NET Remoting

In Exercise 26-1, you will create a remote object class that will then be instantiated on a server by a client Windows application.

Exercise 26-1: Creating a Remote Object Class

1. Create a new Visual Basic .NET project using the Class library template.
2. In Solution Explorer, rename Class1.vb to RemoteHelloWorld.vb.
3. In the RemoteHelloWorld.vb code window, modify your class template code as follows:

```
Imports System
Imports System.Runtime.Remoting

Public Class RemoteHello
    Inherits MarshalByRefObject
```

```
        Public Function RemoteHelloWorld() As String
            Return ("Hello World! ")
        End Function

    End Class
```

4. Click Build Solution from the Build menu to build your remote object.

To use this remote object, you will need to specify the configuration information for the remoting infrastructure and then load the configuration information into the remoting infrastructure to activate the channel. The remoting infrastructure will take over and create the remote object and facilitate the communication between the remote object and the client. In Exercise 26-2, to implement the server side of your remote object, you will create a console application that will load configuration information for your remote object and activate the channel that will listen for client requests.

Exercise 26-2: Creating a Console Application

1. Add a new project to your existing solution by selecting Add Project from the File menu, and then selecting New Project as shown in Figure 26-2.

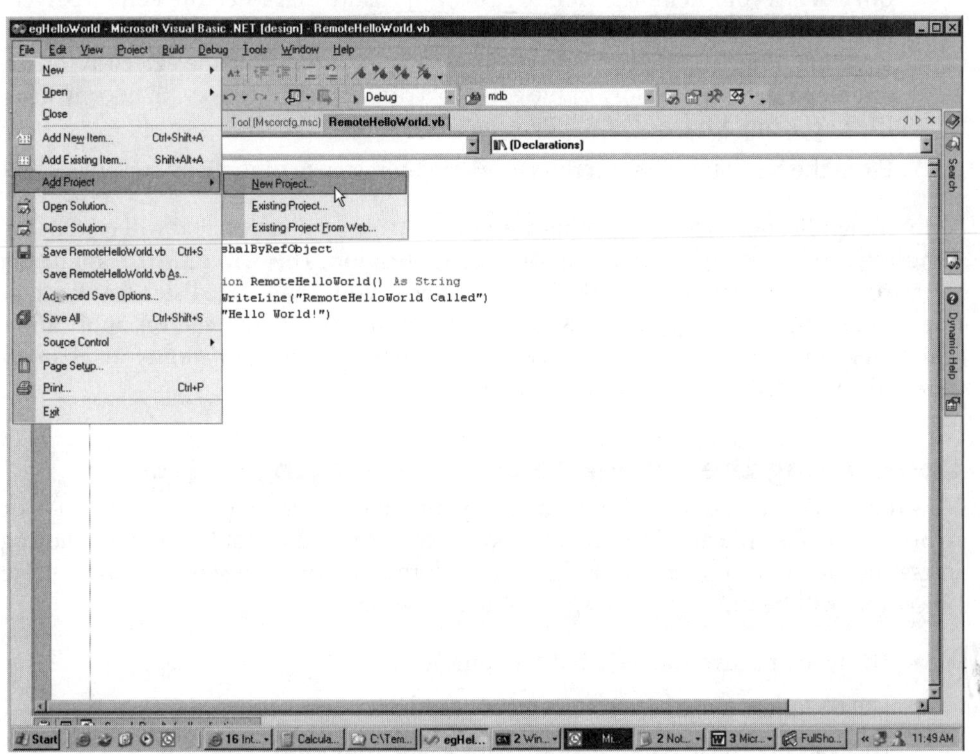

Figure 26-2 Adding a new project to your solution

2. The Add New Project dialog box opens. Create a new Visual Basic .NET project using the Console Application template. Name the application RemoteServer.
3. In Solution Explorer, rename Module1.vb to RemoteServer.vb.
4. In the RemoteServer.vb code window, modify your code to look as follows:

```
Imports System
Imports System.Runtime.Remoting

Module Module1

    Sub Main()
        RemotingConfiguration.Configure("RemoteServer.exe.config")
        Console.WriteLine("Press enter to finish")
        Console.ReadLine()
    End Sub

End Module
```

5. Click Build Solution from the Build menu.
6. To make your remote object available to your RemoteServer application, you must copy the egHelloWorld.dll created in the previous example to the same directory as your RemoteServer.exe. This will ensure that when the RemoteServer application is run, it can locate the egHelloWorld.dll you want to instantiate as a remote object. To do this, use Windows Explorer to locate the egHelloWorld .dll file in the bin directory of the egHelloWorld project directory, then copy this file to the bin directory of the RemoteServer project.
7. From the RemoteServer bin directory, run an instance of the RemoteServer.Exe.

In this application, you are creating a simple console application that will read in the remoting configuration information for your application. This will cause the remoting infrastructure to load your remote object and activate your channel to listen for client requests and return to your RemoteServer application. Your RemoteServer application will then go into a wait state until the ENTER key is pressed. This will allow your channel to remain activated, listening for client requests.

Configuring the Server to Use a Remoting Object

Now that you have an understanding of how your remote object will get loaded via your remote server console application, let's look at the file used to configure the remoting infrastructure on the server. To configure the information on your server for the remote object that will be run, you must specify the following:

- The type of activation required for your object
- The complete metadata describing your object
- The channel registered to handle requests for your object
- The URL that uniquely identifies your object

You can do this programmatically or you can set up a server configuration file for your application. A configuration file for remoting clients and servers has the advantage that the channel and remote object can be configured without changing a single line of code in your application. Specifying options for your remoting clients and servers programmatically has the advantage that you can get to the information during runtime.

When specifying configuration information for your remote objects, you have a number of options. As a developer, you can create remoting configuration information in your application's configuration file, a web.config file on your Internet Information Services (IIS) server, or in a machine.config file also on your IIS server. In this particular example, you will create an application configuration file. An application configuration file contains settings specific to an application that is read by the common language runtime prior to execution to configure the environment for the application. Here is an example of the configuration file you will use:

```
<configuration>
   <system.runtime.remoting>
      <application name="RemoteServer">
         <service>
            <wellknown mode="SingleCall"
                       type="egHelloWorld, egHelloWorld"
                       objectUri="egHelloWorld"/>
         </service>
         <channels>
            <channel ref="tcp server" port="7000"/>
         </channels>
      </application>
   </system.runtime.remoting>
</configuration>
```

In this configuration file, you have specified all configuration elements as children of the <system.runtime.remoting> element. Within this element, you specify the <application> element that indicates the name of your server application with the name attribute. This application offers a service and as such you need to specify the service with the <service> element and the channel that the service will listen on with the <channels> element. The <service> element is where you specify the information associated with the remote object you created earlier.

In this particular example, you have created a well-known object. The alternative would be to create a client-activated object. Well-known objects are server-activated objects where the client must know the endpoint of the object. The endpoint is used to identify the remote object. This differs from client-activated objects, which are activated based on the type of the class. As mentioned, client-activated objects' lifetimes are controlled by the calling application domain, whereas well-known objects are server-activated objects whose lifetimes are directly controlled by the server.

In this example, you have created a well-known single call object and specified the full type name of the object and the assembly name where the type implementation is located. You specify the objectURI attribute as the endpoint name of the remote object that will be used to connect from the client.

Finally, in the <channels> element you define the channel your server application will listen on. The <channels> element contains channel templates that the application uses to communicate with remote objects. Instead of explicitly defining your channel information, you will make reference to an existing predefined channel defined in your machine.config file, using the ref attribute of the <channel> element. Reference the predefined server channel using the TCP protocol "tcp server" and assign the port of this channel to the port attribute. In this example, you are using port 7000. Once you have configured the configuration file for your server application, save it as RemoteServer.Exe.Config in the same directory as your RemoteServer.exe application.

This example is almost complete. What remains is to create your client application and its associated configuration file. Let's develop the client application first. In this application, you will read the configuration file for the application to define the remoting configuration the client application. The application will then instantiate your remote object, calling your RemoteHelloWorld method defined on your remote object. In Exercise 26-3, you will define your RemoteClient application.

Exercise 26-3: Defining the RemoteClient Application

1. Add a new project to your existing solution by selecting Add Project from the File menu, and then selecting New Project.
2. The Add New Project dialog box opens. Create a new Visual Basic .NET project using the Console Application template. Name the application RemoteClient.
3. In Solution Explorer, rename Module1.vb to RemoteClient.vb.
4. Right-click on References in Solution Explorer and select Add Reference. In the Add Reference dialog box that appears, click on the Projects tab and select the egHelloWorld project. Click the Select button.
5. In the RemoteClient.vb code window, modify your code to look as follows:

```
Imports System
Imports System.Runtime.Remoting

Module Module1

    Sub Main()
        Dim objRemHello As New egHelloWorld.RemoteHello()

        RemotingConfiguration.Configure("RemoteClient.exe.config")
        Console.WriteLine(objRemHello.RemoteHelloWorld())
    End Sub
End Module
```

6. Click Build Solution from the Build menu.

Configuring the Client to Use a Remoting Object

Now that you have created your client application, all that remains is to create your client configuration file. The following outlines the contents of this file:

```
<configuration>
   <system.runtime.remoting>
      <application name="RemoteClient">
         <client url="tcp://localhost:7000/RemoteServer">
            <wellknown type="egHelloWorld, egHelloWorld"
                       url="tcp://localhost:7000/RemoteServer/egHelloWorld"/>
         </client>
         <channels>
            <channel ref="tcp client"/>
         </channels>
      </application>
   </system.runtime.remoting>
</configuration>
```

In this configuration file, you specify the name of the application you are working with using the name attribute of the <application> element. The <client> element specifies the URL of the server being used. In this example, you use TCP as the protocol to connect with and specify that the server runs on the localhost with port number 7000. The <wellknown> element specifies the remote object you want to access. The type attribute defines the type of the remote object and its associated assembly. The URL attribute defines the path to the remote object. Finally, the <channel> element specifies the channel that is configured with the client. In this case, you use the tcp client channel instead of the tcp server channel as used in the server configuration file.

Using Client-Activated Objects

In the last example, you used a well-known object, which is a server-activated object whose lifetime is directly controlled by the server. You used a single call object, which is instantiated with every method call. You could just as easily use a singleton object, which creates one object that can be shared between multiple clients. This allows you to maintain state information between clients and to facilitate sharing of that information.

A client-activated object is one in which the lifetime of the object is controlled directly by the calling application domain. When specifying the remote object configuration information for the client-activated object, the configuration file does not really change from the configuration file used to specify a well-known object. The client and server configuration files that follow are specified using the <activated> element instead of the <wellknown> element. You specify the client configuration file first:

```
<configuration>
   <system.runtime.remoting>
      <application name="RemoteClient">
         <client url="tcp://localhost:7000/RemoteServer">
            <activated type="egHelloWorld, egHelloWorld"/>
         </client>
         <channels>
            <channel ref="tcp client"/>
         </channels>
      </application>
   </system.runtime.remoting>
</configuration>
```

The server configuration file has a similar change:

```
<configuration>
   <system.runtime.remoting>
      <application name="RemoteServer">
         <service>
            <activated type="egHelloWorld, egHelloWorld"/>
         </service>
         <channels>
            <channel ref="tcp server" port="7000"/>
         </channels>
      </application>
   </system.runtime.remoting>
</configuration>
```

As you can see, configuring a remote object to be client activated is much simpler than configuring server-activated objects. With a client-activated object, you don't have to specify the endpoint or URL information for the object as you did for a well-known object. The remote object will be instantiated by its type information. The .NET runtime automatically creates a unique URL to the remote object instance for client-activated objects.

Using Client-Activated Objects

A configuration file for remoting clients and servers has the advantage that the channel and remote object can be configured without changing a single line of code in your application. There is an alternative way of configuring your clients and servers, however, and that is through code. Specifying options for your remoting clients and servers programmatically has the advantage that you can get to the information during runtime. Instead of using a configuration file to configure the channel startup, you can do this through code. The following provides a modification of your RemoteServer application code that includes remoting configuration code. To create this code, be sure you add a reference to the egHelloWorld component and the .NET System.Runtime.Remoting component in your application.

```
Imports System
Imports System.Runtime.Remoting
Imports System.Runtime.Remoting.Channels
Imports System.Runtime.Remoting.Channels.Tcp
Imports egHelloWorld

Module Module1

    Sub Main()
        Dim objChannel As New TcpServerChannel(7000)
        Dim objSrvcTypeEntry As New
WellKnownServiceTypeEntry(GetType(egHelloWorld.RemoteHello), _
                                  "RemoteServer/egHelloWorld", _
                                  WellKnownObjectMode.SingleCall)

        ChannelServices.RegisterChannel(objChannel)
        RemotingConfiguration.RegisterWellKnownServiceType(objSrvcTypeEntry)
```

```
        Console.WriteLine("Press enter to finish")
        Console.ReadLine()
    End Sub

End Module
```

In this example, you have replaced the code for reading configuration from a configuration file with code that defines a TCP server channel and registers it at port 7000. The code then registers this channel with the .NET remoting infrastructure using the ChannelServices.RegisterChannel method.

To configure your remote object with the .NET remoting infrastructure, you use the RemotingConfiguration class to register your well-known object on the server. To specify the information to be registered, you use the WellKnownServiceTypeEntry to specify the values that are required for your well-known object. Once an object is created with the information needed to register the object, it is passed to the RegisterWellKnownServiceType method, which registers the object with the .NET remoting infrastructure.

The last piece that we need to configure the example programmatically instead of through configuration files, is to change the client application to use code to configure the .NET remoting infrastructure. The following outlines the code that would be used within the client application to make this happen. As with the RemoteServer application, you will need to add a reference to the egHelloWorld component and the .NET System.Runtime.Remoting component to the application to ensure it compiles properly.

```
Imports System
Imports System.Runtime.Remoting
Imports System.Runtime.Remoting.Channels
Imports System.Runtime.Remoting.Channels.Tcp
Imports egHelloWorld

Module Module1

    Sub Main()
        Dim objRemHello As New egHelloWorld.RemoteHello()
        Dim objChannel As New TcpClientChannel()
        Dim objSrvcTypeEntry As New _
                     WellKnownClientTypeEntry(GetType(RemoteHello), _
                     "tcp://localhost:7000/RemoteServer/RemoteHello")

        ChannelServices.RegisterChannel(objChannel)
        RemotingConfiguration.RegisterWellKnownClientType(objSrvcTypeEntry)
        Console.WriteLine(objRemHello.RemoteHelloWorld())
    End Sub

End Module
```

In this code example, you have defined a TcpClientChannel and registered it with the .NET remoting infrastructure. As with the server application, you use the WellKnownClientTypeEntry to define the remote object and to specify the complete path to the remote object. You then use the RemotingConfiguration class to register the remote object with the .NET remoting infrastructure.

Client Proxy Objects

When a client instantiates a remote object, the .NET remoting infrastructure creates a proxy object on the client's behalf. When the client invokes methods or sets/retrieves property values, the client makes use of the proxy object, which packages the request and ensures that all calls made on the proxy are forwarded to the correct remote object instance.

When the .NET remoting infrastructure creates a proxy, it is in fact creating two proxies. The first proxy is known as a TransparentProxy and is the one used directly by the client application. The TransparentProxy looks like the remote object, with the same public methods and properties. When a TransparentProxy object is created, all method calls on the proxy are intercepted and a determination is made whether the remote object resides in the same application domain as the proxy. If the remote object does reside in the same application domain, the method call is routed to the actual object itself. If the object is in a different application domain, the call parameters are packaged as a message and forwarded to a second proxy object, known as a RealProxy. The RealProxy object is then responsible for forwarding messages to the remote object. Both the TransparentProxy and RealProxy classes are created under the covers when a remote object is activated, but only the TransparentProxy is returned to the client.

To have a better understanding of these proxy objects, it is necessary to understand something called an ObjRef. An ObjRef (object reference) is an object that stores all relevant information required to generate a proxy that will facilitate communication with a remote object. ObjRefs contain metadata describing the type of the object being marshaled, a unique uniform resource identifier (URI) for the object, and information indicating how to reach the application domain where the object lives. The process of passing these object references from the client application domain to the remote object application domain is known as marshaling. Unmarshaling is the process of creating an object from the marshaled data. The .NET remoting infrastructure can marshal data in one of two ways:

- It can make a complete copy of the object and pass it to the calling application domain. Once the copy is in the caller's application domain, calls to it are direct to that copy. This process is known as *marshal-by-value*. Marshal-by-value objects are used when it makes sense to move the entire object to the application domain because of performance and processing concerns. In some instances where there are many calls to the object, calling the object locally rather than over the network can make sense. This reduces the chatter over the network and can result in improved performance. Marshal-by-value objects are also used directly from within the object's original application domain just as any normal object would be used. This results in no copy or marshaling of the object being made.
- Depending on the type of object instantiated (single call, singleton, or client-activated), it can create an instance of the object in its own application domain, and then create a proxy object in the caller's application domain that acts as a stub for the remote object. The client application then makes calls to the proxy object. This process is known as *marshal-by-reference*. Marshal-by-reference should

be used when the object should reside centrally and be called from another application domain, generally over the network. This is desirable when passing an entire copy of the object around the network might not be the most feasible choice for your application. For instance, if your network connection happens to be over a dial-up line, passing an object that is very large can be time consuming to the point where the application becomes unusable.

When a client calls a method on a proxy, the proxy object creates a message containing all the information necessary to specify the remote object (the URI of the object) and all call information, and dispatches a message over the registered transport channel to the server application domain. With marshal-by-value, the object is serialized into the channel, and a copy of the object is created in the remote object's application domain. If any of the arguments in the method call are marshal-by-reference objects themselves, or if the return of the call is a marshal-by-reference object, an ObjRef is created and sent along with the message to become a proxy in the application domain that needs to use the reference. Let's look at this closely.

When a remote object is registered on the server, the remote object is marshaled to produce an ObjRef. The ObjRef contains all the information necessary to locate and access the remote object from anywhere on the network. When a client activates a remote object by calling new, the activation process on the client is used to make a call to the remote activator using the URL and object URI as the endpoint. The remote activator activates the object, and an ObjRef is streamed to the client where it is unmarshaled to produce a TransparentProxy that is then returned to the client. During the unmarshaling process, the ObjRef is parsed to extract the method information of the remote object and both the TransparentProxy and RealProxy objects are created. The content of the ObjRef is added to the internal tables of the TransparentProxy before it is registered with the CLR.

Let's look at an example of how to extend a Proxy object. We will use previous examples to provide the basis for the proxy example. To begin, modify the code for your object as follows:

```
Imports System
Imports System.Runtime.Remoting
Imports System.Reflection
Imports System.Runtime.Remoting.Proxies
Imports System.Runtime.Remoting.Messaging

Public Class RemoteHello
    Inherits MarshalByRefObject

    Public Function RemoteHelloWorld() As String
        Return ("Hello World!")
    End Function
End Class

Public Class MyProxy
    Inherits RealProxy
    Private Target As Object
```

```
    Public Sub New(ByVal typ As Type, ByVal obj As Object)
        MyBase.New(typ)
        Target = obj
    End Sub

    Public Overrides Function Invoke(ByVal mesg As IMessage) As IMessage
        Dim methMesg As IMethodMessage
        Dim Method As MethodInfo
        Dim myProps As IDictionary
        Dim myObject As MarshalByRefObject
        Dim retValue, key As Object

        myProps = mesg.Properties
        methMesg = mesg
        Console.WriteLine("Message Properties")
        For Each key In myProps.Keys
            Console.WriteLine(" Key: {0}\n Value: {1}", _
                              key.ToString(), MyProps(key))
        Next

        Method = Target.GetType().GetMethod(methMesg.MethodName, _
                    methMesg.MethodSignature)
        retValue = Method.Invoke(Target, methMesg.Args)
        Console.WriteLine("MyProxy.Invoke - Finish")
        Return New ReturnMessage(retValue, Nothing, 0, _
                  methMesg.LogicalCallContext, ethMesg)

    End Function
End Class
```

In this example, you have extended your class library with an additional class called myProxy that extends your RealProxy class. In this class, you define a new method which takes a type and an object. You also define a method called Invoke which overrides the RealProxy.Invoke method and is used to add the custom functionality to your extended RealProxy class. In the invoke method, you write the values of the message object passed in to the console. You then convert the message to a methodMessage whose MethodName, MethodSignature, and Args properties return the name of the method, an array of type representing the signature of the method, and an array of object containing the values of the parameters passed to the method. You use this information to obtain a reference to the corresponding method defined in the target remote object. You then forward the invocation to the target object using the invoke method. Finally, you wrap the object returned by the original method in a ReturnMessage instance and pass it back to the calling method of TransparentProxy.

To test this implementation, modify your remote client application as follows:

```
Imports System
Imports System.Runtime.Remoting
Imports System.Runtime.Remoting.Channels
Imports System.Runtime.Remoting.Channels.Tcp
Imports egHelloWorld

Module Module1

    Sub Main()
```

```
        Dim myProxy As egHelloWorld.MyProxy
        Dim myType As Type
        Dim objRemHello As egHelloWorld.RemoteHello
        Dim objChannel As New TcpClientChannel()
        Dim objSrvcTypeEntry As New _
                  WellKnownClientTypeEntry(GetType(RemoteHello), _
                            tcp://localhost:7000/RemoteServer/RemoteHello)

        ChannelServices.RegisterChannel(objChannel)
        RemotingConfiguration.RegisterWellKnownClientType(objSrvcTypeEntry)

        myProxy = New MyProxy(GetType(RemoteHello), _
                              New egHelloWorld.RemoteHello())
        objRemHello = myProxy.GetTransparentProxy
        Console.WriteLine(objRemHello.RemoteHelloWorld())
    End Sub
End Module
```

Here you instantiate a new instance of your custom proxy class and pass it the type of your method and a new instance of your remote object. You then retrieve the resulting TransparentProxy that is provided by the .NET remoting infrastructure and assign it to your local object where it is used to call the RemoteHelloWorld method.

Channels

In the previous examples, you have defined channels for both the client and the server in your applications and registered them with the .NET remoting infrastructure. We have not really gone into great depth as to what channels are or how to use them other than providing the basic functionality to make the example applications work. This section will introduce channels and some of the specifics behind them.

A channel is used to physically transport messages to and from remote objects in client applications. When a client calls a method on a remote object, the parameters as well as other details related to the call are packaged according to a particular protocol and then routed through the channel to the remote object. Any results from the call are returned back to the client in the same way.

A channel object listens for incoming messages and sends outbound messages. In both cases, the messages it handles can be made of packets written for a variety of protocols. For the developer, a channel is a .NET class that implements the IChannel interface. The channel object is required to implement IChannelReceiver and IChannelSender if it is expected to act as a receiver and/or a sender.

A client can select any of the channels registered on the server to communicate with the remote object. For a list of predefined channels, refer to the machine.config file located in the directory %SystemRoot%\Microsoft.NET\Framework\,vx.x.x>\CONFIG. In this file you will find six predefined channels as can be seen in the following XML segment:

```
<channels>

   <channel
      id="http"
      type="System.Runtime.Remoting.Channels.Http.HttpChannel,
            System.Runtime.Remoting,
```

PART VII

```
      Version=1.0.3300.0,
      Culture=neutral, PublicKeyToken=b77a5c561934e089"/>
   <channel id="http client"
           type="System.Runtime.Remoting.Channels.Http.HttpClientChannel,
                 System.Runtime.Remoting,
           Version=1.0.3300.0,
           Culture=neutral, PublicKeyToken=b77a5c561934e089"/>
    <channel id="http server"
            type="System.Runtime.Remoting.Channels.Http.HttpServerChannel,
                  System.Runtime.Remoting,
            Version=1.0.3300.0,
            Culture=neutral, PublicKeyToken=b77a5c561934e089"/>
    <channel id="tcp"
            type="System.Runtime.Remoting.Channels.Tcp.TcpChannel,
                  System.Runtime.Remoting,
            Version=1.0.3300.0,
            Culture=neutral, PublicKeyToken=b77a5c561934e089"/>
    <channel id="tcp client"
                type="System.Runtime.Remoting.Channels.Tcp.TcpClientChannel,
                      System.Runtime.Remoting,
                      Version=1.0.3300.0,
                      Culture=neutral, PublicKeyToken=b77a5c561934e089"/>
    <channel id="tcp server"
                type="System.Runtime.Remoting.Channels.Tcp.TcpServerChannel,
                      System.Runtime.Remoting,
                      Version=1.0.3300.0,
                      Culture=neutral, PublicKeyToken=b77a5c561934e089"/>
</channels>
```

There are two primary types of channels, HttpChannel and TcpChannel. Each define both server and client functionality. TcpChannel uses a binary formatter to serialize data to a binary stream and transport it to the target object using the TCP protocol. HttpChannel transports messages to and from remote objects using the SOAP protocol.

By defining different protocols over which clients can communicate with remote objects on the server, the developer has the freedom to select the channel that best suits his needs. For instance, if you have a client application that resides on the Internet and needs to communicate with a server located behind a corporate firewall, you will likely want to use HTTP as the communication protocol. This is preferred as HTTP on most firewalls is opened for Web traffic, allowing other applications to establish a tunnel using the protocol to enable communication between the client and the server. On the other hand, for clients in the corporate intranet that need to communicate with servers, the use of TCP as the transport protocol is preferable for performance reasons. When choosing a channel, consider the following points:

- At least one channel must be registered with the .NET remoting infrastructure before a remote object can be called. Channels must be registered before objects are registered.
- Channels are registered for each application domain. There can be multiple application domains in a single process. When a process is terminated, all channels that are registered for that domain are automatically destroyed.

- If you are not sure if a port is available, use 0 (zero) when configuring your channel's port and the .NET remoting infrastructure will choose an available port for you.
- It is illegal to register the same channel that listens on the same port more than once. Even though channels are registered per application domain, different application domains on the same machine cannot register the same channel listening on the same port. You can register the same channel listening on two different ports.
- Channel names must be unique in an application domain. For example, because the default channels have names, to register two HttpChannel objects in one application domain, you must change the names of the channels before registering them. This can be done by registering the name and port properties of the channel prior to registering it.
- Clients can communicate with a remote object using any registered channel. The .NET remoting infrastructure ensures that the remote object is connected to the right channel when a client attempts to connect to it. This is done through the RegisterChannel method on the ChannelService class before attempting to communicate with a remote object.

When a client makes a call to a remote object, it passes the call through a proxy which uses the channel to communicate with the remote object on the server. How does the remote object listen for the client communication if it has not been instantiated yet? The answer lies in the way a server application hosts a remote object. Server applications that host remote objects have to register the channels they require as well as the objects they want to expose with the .NET remoting infrastructure. When the channel is registered, an ObjRef is created for the object that resides in memory and stored in a table. When the remoting infrastructure receives a call on the registered channel, the message associated with the call is examined and the object being invoked is determined from the table, or is instantiated if not already present in memory, and the call is then forwarded to the object. In the case of synchronous calls, the connection from the client is maintained for the duration of the message call.

Asynchronous Remoting

When a client invokes a method on a remote object through its TransparentProxy, the TransparentProxy creates an IMessage object or message that encapsulates all information describing the nature of the call. Messages are containers that carry a set of named properties, including action identifiers, envoy information, and parameters. There are several types of messages that are supported by .NET. These message types include construction call messages and responses as well as method call messages and responses. Internally, the only difference between a "plain" IMessage implementation and another type of method call message is that the method call message uses a set of predefined dictionary entries. There are two types of delivery modes for messages:

- **Synchronous messages** Represent messages that are delivered and a response is expected immediately. By default, unless explicitly defined, all calls to remote objects are called in a synchronous fashion.
- **Asynchronous messages** Represent messages that are delivered, but the response is expected to be delayed or not delivered at all.

Let's look at the latter type of delivery mode. When calling methods across the network, it can take some time before the method returns. During this time that the method call is running on the server, your application can be doing other things on the client. To do this, .NET remoting lets you call your remote objects methods asynchronously. You "spin" off another thread in your process to make the remote call while the current thread answers user requests or does something else. To facilitate this process, the .NET remoting infrastructure uses delegates. Delegates provide the ability to call a synchronous method in an asynchronous manner.

To extend the example that we have been using throughout this chapter with asynchronous capabilities, you will extend your class library. The new class defines a procedure that takes as parameters two numbers and a third value specifying the time to go to sleep. When the procedure wakes up, it will calculate the value of the two numbers added together, and then write the results to the console. The class code is as follows:

```
Imports System.Threading
Public Class AsyncRemote
    Public Sub LongDisplay()

        Thread.Sleep(500)
        Console.WriteLine("Finished sleeping...Yawnnnnnnnn ")
    End Sub
End Class
```

To use this class remotely, you need to use a delegate from your client application. The following is the code for your client application:

```
Imports System
Imports System.Runtime.Remoting
Imports System.Runtime.Remoting.Channels
Imports System.Runtime.Remoting.Channels.Tcp
Imports System.Threading
Imports egHelloWorld

Module Module1

    Delegate Sub RemoteAsyncDelegate()

    Sub Main()

        Dim objRemHello As egHelloWorld.RemoteHello
        Dim objLngDsply As New egHelloWorld.AsyncRemote()
        Dim objLngDsplyDelegate As New _
            RemoteAsyncDelegate(AddressOf objLngDsply.LongDisplay)
```

```
        Dim objAsyncResult As IAsyncResult
        Dim objChannel As New TcpClientChannel()
        Dim intCounter As Integer
        Dim objSrvcTypeEntry As _
                New WellKnownClientTypeEntry(GetType(RemoteHello), _
                "tcp://localhost:7000/RemoteServer/RemoteHello")

        ChannelServices.RegisterChannel(objChannel)
        RemotingConfiguration.RegisterWellKnownClientType(objSrvcTypeEntry)

        objAsyncResult = objLngDsplyDelegate.BeginInvoke(Nothing, Nothing)
        objRemHello = New egHelloWorld.RemoteHello()
        Console.WriteLine(objRemHello.RemoteHelloWorld())

        intCounter = 0
        While Not objAsyncResult.IsCompleted
            intCounter = intCounter + 1
            Thread.Sleep(New TimeSpan(TimeSpan.TicksPerMillisecond))
        End While
        Console.WriteLine(vbCrLf & "Completed. " & _
                          "intCounter finished at, " & intCounter)
    End Sub
End Module
```

In this example, you have configured your channel and your remote object by defining it as a well-known object. You have defined the RemoteAsyncDelegate procedure as a delegate and then defined your remote object, created an instance of the delegate, and defined your asynchronous result object using IAsyncResult. The code snippet for this is as follows:

```
Dim objLngDsply As New egHelloWorld.AsyncRemote()
Dim objLngDsplyDelegate As New _
    RemoteAsyncDelegate(AddressOf objLngDsply.LongDisplay)
Dim objAsyncResult As IAsyncResult
```

You then invoke your remote method asynchronously with the BeginInvoke method call of objLngDsplyDelegate. The BeginInvoke method returns immediately and the remainder of the procedure finishes executing. If you do not wait for the results of the delegate call to complete, you will end the execution of the application and not see the results of your delegate call. Use the AsyncResult IsComplete property to determine whether the remote object that was started asynchronously has completed. If not, go into a loop and wait for it to finish. Once the remote object has completed, you then print out the results of how long it took to wait for the remote object to finish.

This is one example of how to make asynchronous calls. There is much more that we have not even begun to cover. For more information, refer to the documentation available on Microsoft's MSDN site.

Serialization Formatters

Formatters are used to encode and decode messages before they are sent along a channel. As you will recall, a message is composed of a dictionary of key/value pairs. The formatter's job is to convert these dictionaries into data streams and back again. Formatters are dynamically used by channels prior to sending the data over the wire. Based on how you have configured your channel to transport messages, the remoting infrastructure will invoke the appropriate formatter to translate the dictionary into the appropriate wire format before transferring the data. Out of the box, the .NET remoting infrastructure comes with a binary formatter and a SOAP formatter. The binary formatter is extremely fast and encodes method calls in a proprietary binary format. The SOAP formatter is slower, but it provides developers with a mechanism to encode messages in a standards-based SOAP format before transporting the message.

Formatters are implemented through a sink, which is a sort of message bucket. We will cover sinks in the next section. Essentially, a formatter takes a message and puts it through a process known as serialization. Serialization is the process of taking objects and converting their state information into a form that can be transported over the wire. An object writes its current state, usually indicated by the value of its member variables, to the network stream. During this process, the public and private fields of the object and the name of the class, including the assembly containing the class, are converted to the network stream as bytes, which are then transported over the wire to the destination machine and re-created by reading, or deserializing, the object's state from the stream. When the object is deserialized, an exact clone of the original object is created. What makes this process interesting is that you may also take the serialized representation, transport it to another context such as a different machine, rebuild your original object, and use it on the remote machine. It also provides the capability to write the current state of an application to disk, making it useful for preserving the state of an application during scheduled or unscheduled (using error handling) shutdowns of the computer or application. The .NET Framework features two serializing technologies:

- Binary serialization preserves type fidelity or type safety, which is useful for preserving the state of an object between different calls to an application. Remoting uses serialization to pass objects "by value" from one computer or application domain to another. It is usually not suitable to use binary serialization through a firewall.
- XML serialization or serialization using SOAP serializes only public properties and fields and does not preserve type fidelity. This is useful when you want to provide or consume data without restricting the application that uses the data. Because XML is an open standard, it is an attractive choice for sharing data across the Web and is suitable for passing data through a firewall without having to reconfigure the existing firewall to open up unnecessary ports. SOAP is an open standard, which makes it an attractive choice for organizations that want to maintain vender neutrality in their environment.

There are two aspects to serialization. There is the process of serializing objects at runtime, and then there is the process of marking objects for serialization at design time before they are serialized in code.

Let's examine serialization at design time first. The simplest way to make your classes eligible for serialization is to use the Serializable attribute during the design of your classes. By default, objects are not serializable, as .NET has no way of knowing whether a serial dump of the object state to a stream makes sense. Maybe the object members have some transient value (such as an open connection), or they may have information that has been calculated and can be recalculated on the remote client. Serializing transient values such as an open connection will likely produce errors during deserialization. Deserializing calculated data, while possible, probably does not make sense, since the data used to create the calculated value has likely been passed to the remote client. To save on network bandwidth, it makes sense to recalculate the values at the remote end of the connection based on the information provided instead of sending the calculated values across the stream. To inhibit the serialization of members, you can attach a NonSerialized attribute to those members.

You should consider serialization when designing new classes since a class cannot be made serializable after it has been compiled. Some questions to ask are:

- Do I have to send this class across application domains?
- Will this class ever be used with remoting?
- What will my users do with this class? Perhaps they can derive a new class from mine that needs to be serialized?

When in doubt, mark the class as serializable. It is probably better to mark all classes as serializable unless:

- They will never cross an application domain.
- The class stores special pointers that are only applicable to the current instance of the class. If a class contains unmanaged memory or file handles, for example, ensure these files are marked as NonSerialized or you will have to reacquire the same file resources on the remote end.
- Some of the data members contain sensitive information. In this case, it will probably be advisable to mark the class itself as serializable but mark the individual variables containing the sensitive information as NonSerialized. Another alternative is to implement ISerializable and serialize only the required fields.

To make instances (objects) of your class serializable, add the [Serializable] attribute to your class definition:

```
[Serializable]
public class MyClass
   public num1 As Integer
   public num2 As Integer
End Class
```

In most cases, this is all a developer has to do. If you have a member variable in the class that you would like to preclude from serialization, use the [NonSerialized] field attribute:

```
<Serializable()> public class MyClass
   public num1 As Integer

   <NonSerialized()> public num2 As Integer
End Class
```

The code to handle serialization in .NET is actually quite simple. In the following code, you will create a new console application:

```
Imports System
Imports System.Runtime.Serialization
Imports System.Runtime.Serialization.Formatter
Imports System.Runtime.Serialization.Formatters.Binary
Imports System.Runtime.Serialization.Formatters.Soap
Imports System.IO

<Serializable()> Public Class TestSimpleObject
    Public member1 As Integer
    Public member2 As String
    Public member3 As String
    Public member4 As Double

    <NonSerialized()> Public member5 As String

    Public Sub New()
        member1 = 11
        member2 = "hello"
        member3 = "hello"
        member4 = 3.14159265
        member5 = "hello world!"
    End Sub

    Public Sub Print()
        Console.WriteLine("member1 = '{0}'", member1)
        Console.WriteLine("member2 = '{0}'", member2)
        Console.WriteLine("member3 = '{0}'", member3)
        Console.WriteLine("member4 = '{0}'", member4)
        Console.WriteLine("member5 = '{0}'", member5)
    End Sub
End Class

Module Module1

    Sub Main()

        Dim objSimpleObject As TestSimpleObject
        Dim objBinStream As Stream
        Dim objSOAPStream As Stream
        Dim objBinFormatter As IFormatter
        Dim objSOAPFormatter As IFormatter
        Dim intCounter As Integer

        Console.WriteLine("Before serialization the object contains: ")
```

```
        objSimpleObject = New TestSimpleObject()
        objSimpleObject.Print()

        objBinStream = New FileStream("output.bin", FileMode.Create, _
                        FileAccess.Write, FileShare.None)
        objSOAPStream = New FileStream("output.xml", FileMode.Create, _
                        FileAccess.Write, FileShare.None)
        objBinFormatter = New BinaryFormatter()
        objSOAPFormatter = New SoapFormatter()

        objBinFormatter.Serialize(objBinStream, objSimpleObject)
        objSOAPFormatter.Serialize(objSOAPStream, objSimpleObject)
        objBinStream.Close()
        objSOAPStream.Close()
        objSimpleObject = Nothing

        objSOAPStream = File.Open("output.xml", FileMode.Open)
        objSimpleObject = CType(objSOAPFormatter.Deserialize(objSOAPStream), _
                            TestSimpleObject)
        objSOAPStream.Close()

        Console.WriteLine("")
        Console.WriteLine("After deserialization the object contains: ")
        objSimpleObject.Print()
    End Sub
End Module
```

In this example, you create a simple class called TestSimpleObject and define various public properties and the methods new and print. The new method is used to assign values to your properties, while the print method is used to write them to the console. In the main procedure of your application, you define an object of type TestSimpleObject. This is followed by the creation of two files and two formatters. The first formatter is used to serialize the object to a file in binary format, while the second formatter is used to serialize the object to a file as XML. The application then closes the files, deletes the object you serialized to disk, and then opens the XML file and deserializes the contents of the XML file into an the object, thereby instantiating the object on the client. The print method on the newly created object is then called again, to show how the methods and properties along with their state were preserved after the object was originally deleted.

Message Sinks

When a TransparentProxy object is created, all method calls on the proxy are intercepted and a determination is made whether the remote object resides in the same application domain as the proxy. If it does, the method call is routed to the actual object itself. If the object is in a different application domain, the call parameters are packaged as a message and forwarded to a second proxy object known as a RealProxy.

When the TransparentProxy calls the invoke method on the RealProxy, it passes the message object as a parameter. The invoke method on the RealProxy then takes the message and begins the process of passing the message through a chain of channel sink objects prior to sending or after receiving a message. It starts by passing the message to the first IMessageSink in the client-side message sink chain. This sink chain contains sinks required for basic channel functionality, such as formatter, transport, or stack builder sinks, but you can customize the channel sink chain to perform special tasks that suit your own purposes.

The client-side message sink chain processes the message before finally transporting the message to and from the channel for transport over the wire. The server-side message sink chain transports the message from the channel through a series of message sinks before passing it to the stack builder sink, which is the last sink in the chain. This sink builds a call stack and then makes the call on the remote object. In other words, a remote method call can be thought of as a message that goes from the client to the server, and possibly back again, passing through a chain of message sinks on each side of the transport channel. Each sink in each chain receives the message, performs a specific operation, and passes it on to the next sink in the chain.

Message sinks are the main location of customization in the remoting framework. Out of the box, there are two types of sinks in the remoting infrastructure, message sinks and channel sinks. Each occurs in a different location along the remoting chain and serves a different purpose. Message sinks allow you to intercept the method call message before the method call and its parameters are serialized into the stream. With a channel sink, once the method call message is serialized into a stream, you can intercept the stream before it's put on the wire for transport to the remote machine.

The IMessageSink interface is implemented by channels and the remoting infrastructure to accept messages. Any type that implements the IMessageSink interface can participate in the .NET remoting infrastructure as a message sink. Within the IMessageSink interface there is a NextSink property, which allows the building of chains of message sinks. When you implement your own message sink, you must ensure you honor this invocation sequence by passing any message which you do not want to handle yourself onward to the next sink.

To submit messages into a channel, you obtain a reference to the channel's message sink from the IChannelSender interface using the method CreateMessageSink(). To use channels, client code drops messages into the remoting infrastructure using the SyncDispatchMessage() or AsyncDispatchMethod() method on the ChannelServices class. To see how this all works in practice, look at the following code, which defines a class that implements the necessary IMessageSink and associated helper classes:

```
Imports System
Imports System.Runtime.Remoting
Imports System.Reflection
Imports System.Runtime.Remoting.Proxies
Imports System.Runtime.Remoting.Messaging
Imports System.Threading
Imports Microsoft.VisualBasic

Public Class AsyncReplyHelperSink
    Implements IMessageSink

    Public Delegate Function _
        AsyncReplyHelperSinkDelegate(ByVal msg As IMessage) As IMessage
    Public _NextSink As IMessageSink
    Public _Delegate As AsyncReplyHelperSinkDelegate
```

```
    ReadOnly Property NextSink() As IMessageSink _
                  Implements IMessageSink.NextSink
        Get
            NextSink = _NextSink
        End Get
    End Property

    Public Sub AsyncReplyHelperSink(ByVal nxt As IMessageSink, _
                      ByVal del As AsyncReplyHelperSinkDelegate)

        _NextSink = nxt
        _Delegate = del

    End Sub

    Public Function SyncProcessMessage(ByVal msg As IMessage) As _
                IMessage Implements IMessageSink.SyncProcessMessage
        Dim msg2 As IMessage
        Dim retmsg As ReturnMessage

        If Not IsDBNull(_Delegate) Then
            msg2 = _Delegate(msg)
            Return _NextSink.SyncProcessMessage(msg2)
        Else
            retmsg = New ReturnMessage(New _
            System.Exception("AsyncProcesssMessage _delegate is null"), msg)
        End If
    End Function

    Public Function AsyncProcessMessage(ByVal msg As IMessage, _
            ByVal replysink As IMessageSink) _
            As IMessageCtrl Implements IMessageSink.AsyncProcessMessage
        Return Nothing
    End Function
End Class
Public Class CustomMsgSink
    Implements IMessageSink

    Public _NextSink As IMessageSink

    ReadOnly Property NextSink() As IMessageSink _
                  Implements IMessageSink.NextSink
        Get
            NextSink = _NextSink
        End Get

    End Property

    Public Sub CustomMsgSink(ByVal nxt As IMessageSink)

        _NextSink = nxt

    End Sub

    Public Function SyncProcessMessage(ByVal msg As IMessage) _
                As IMessage Implements IMessageSink.SyncProcessMessage

        Return _NextSink.SyncProcessMessage(msg)
```

PART VII

```
    End Function

    Public Function AsyncProcessReplyMessage(ByVal msg As IMessage) As _
                IMessage
        Return msg
    End Function

    Public Function AsyncProcessMessage(ByVal msg As IMessage, _
            ByVal replysink As IMessageSink) As _
            IMessageCtrl Implements IMessageSink.AsyncProcessMessage

        Dim rsdelegate As AsyncReplyHelperSink.AsyncReplyHelperSinkDelegate

        rsdelegate = New _
         AsyncReplyHelperSink.AsyncReplyHelperSinkDelegate(AddressOf _
                    AsyncProcessReplyMessage)
        replysink = New AsyncReplyHelperSink()
        Return _NextSink.AsyncProcessMessage(msg, replysink)

    End Function
End Class
```

In this example, you have created two classes. The main class is CustomMsgSink, which defines your custom message sink. The AsynReplyHelperSink class serves as a delegate to a callback method that is invoked upon receiving an IMessage in IMessageSink .SyncProcessMessage. The CustomMsgSink implements very basic functionality in this example and simply passes the IMessage to the next sink in the chain. However, it does serve the purpose of showing how an IMessageSink is implemented.

The IMessage.SyncProcessMessage function in the CustomMsgSink class processes the message as it is passed to the message sink. This function simply passes the message on to the next sink in the chain in a synchronous fashion. Synchronous processing completes only after the .NET remoting infrastructure receives and returns the response message from the method call on the remote object.

The AsyncProcessMessage function processes message requests only, unlike the SyncProcessMessage method, which processes both the request and response messages. When the asynchronous operation completes, the .NET remoting infrastructure passes the response message to the IMessageSink.SyncProcessMessage method of the sink referenced. In this example, the second parameter to the AsyncProcessMessage method, replySink, is used to process the message.

Summary

This chapter gave you a brief introduction to the complex topic of remoting. With the introduction of Microsoft .NET, Microsoft has essentially replaced DCOM with the remoting infrastructure. This infrastructure provides an abstract approach to interprocess communication. Code running in one application cannot directly access code or resources from another application. The common language runtime enforces this isolation by preventing direct calls between objects in different processes or application domains. Using the facilities of remoting allows you to make calls across application domains.

Invoking a remote object allows you to distribute your application across machines, thereby improving the overall scalability of the application. The chapter introduced what needed to be done from the client and the server, to configure each to allow communication. Configuring applications to make use of remoteable objects can be done through the use of configuration files or through the use of code within the application. The chapter introduced both methods of accomplishing this. Each method configured the necessary channels and registered the remote object with the .NET remoting infrastructure for use in applications. We looked at the different types of objects that could be used remotely, including a single call object, which is instantiated and then destroyed once it is finished with, a singleton object that is instantiated and maintains state across calls, and a client activated object that is instantiated by the server upon a request by the client. The beauty of using remoteable objects is it provides you with the ability to let your client applications call objects asynchronously. This allows your client application to perform other processing while the remote object does its work. When the remote object is finished, it lets the client application know where it can retrieve the return values and continue processing.

Calling remote objects is done through proxy objects. This mechanism not only provides you with a method for calling remote objects asynchronously or synchronously, but also allows you to extend and customize the various components that make up the execution path in the .NET remoting infrastructure. To extend this infrastructure you need to be aware of how to marshal data across application domains and we looked at both Marshaling by Reference and Marshaling by Value. Once you have decided on how you want to pass data back and forth between your application and the remote object, you need to have an understanding of the channels that can be used to facilitate communication between application domains, or clients and servers when applications interact with remote objects. The .NET remoting infrastructure allows you to make use of HTTP as the primary protocol for transmitting information. Within the HTTP protocol you can encapsulate information using HTTP methods such as HTTP-GET and HTTP-POST, or you can make use of the SOAP protocol to encapsulate information. SOAP provides more functionality to the developer than HTTP-GET and HTTP-POST.

The .NET remoting infrastructure not only allows you to configure how the objects should be called, and the type of communication channel the call should occur over but also provides the facilities to translate objects, data, parameters, and calls from the client to the server and back again. This is done through a mechanism known as a formatter and the process of translating information is known as serialization. We looked at two types of formatters to allow this, the binary formatter and the SOAP formatter, and looked at the differences between the two and how they translate data prior to it being sent over the network. This was followed up by a discussion on serialization and how we could use the facilities of formatters within our code and the different phases within which the serialization process takes place.

Test Questions

1. Which of the following object types is not a valid remote object? (Choose all that apply.)
   A. Single call
   B. Single process
   C. Singleton
   D. Client-activated
2. When is it appropriate to mark a class as serializable?
   A. Public properties refer to calculated values.
   B. Public properties make reference to sensitive information.
   C. Public properties make reference to files.
   D. Public properties refer to data retrieved from a database.
3. Which of the following does not require configuration on your server for a remote object to run?
   A. The type of activation for your object
   B. The complete metadata describing your object
   C. The channel registered to handle requests for your object
   D. The IP address of the server where your remote object will be located

Test Answers

1. A, C, D.
2. D.
3. D.

CHAPTER 27

Creating and Using Web Services

In this chapter, you will

- Create and consume a Web service
- Control characteristics of Web methods by using attributes
- See how to create asynchronous Web methods
- Learn how to control the Network Encapsulation protocol for an XML Web service
- Learn how to instantiate and invoke an XML Web service
- Find out how to publish an XML Web service
- See how to enable static discovery
- Explore how to publish XML Web service definitions in the UDDI

Web services allow the Web to be used not only for presenting information, but also for creating applications that use Web-based applications and services. Using Web services is similar to using prebuilt components on your local PC to compose applications. For example, if you are designing an inventory application you can design an interface that connects via the Web to a manufacturer's inventory application and dynamically synchronizes inventory between the manufacturer and its customer.

To develop programs of this type, developers must be able to quickly and easily write code that communicates with other programs over the Internet, regardless of platform. Web services help to eliminate proprietary programmatic access by using standards-based development technologies that facilitate interaction among heterogeneous applications.

This chapter introduces you to Web services. It explains how to develop Web services as well as how to use them from your applications.

Web Service Architecture

Web services are distributed software components that are accessible through standard Web protocols. Unlike proprietary components such as COM and DCOM, Web services enable software to interoperate with a broad range of clients. They can be consumed by any application that understands how to parse an XML-formatted stream transmitted through Hypertext Transfer Protocol (HTTP) channels.

The diversity of devices on the Internet poses a challenge for developers who want to develop over the Internet. Randomly changing heterogeneous nodes must communicate with fixed servers and with each other. Their internal programming works in a variety of incompatible languages and if communication between different components breaks down, applications cannot function properly, if at all. Developers use the universally accepted HTTP to enable multiple, heterogeneous entities on the Internet to exchange data. Developers use the universally accepted Extensible Markup Language (XML)for encoding the data sent from one Web service entity to another. XML is the key technology used in Web services. It is used in the following components of the Visual Basic .NET Web services architecture:

- **Web service Network Encapsulation Protocols** Specifies how to perform data exchanges between the service provider and consumer, and defines the format of the data for the request and response. Three protocols are supported for interaction with Web services: HTTP Post, HTTP Get, and SOAP. This chapter concentrates on SOAP as it provides the richest functionality for applications.
- **Web service description** Describes how to use the Web service. Think of this as the instructions on the washing machine at the Laundromat telling you where to put quarters, what buttons to push, and so on. For clients to understand how to interact with a particular Web service, the service must include a description that defines the interactions it supports. The Web Services Description Language (WSDL) is used to provide the description of services in the form of a document.
- **Web service discovery** Refers to the process of advertising or publishing software as a service and enabling its discovery. Web service discovery defines a process of identifying a set of one or more related documents that describe a particular Web service. The Microsoft Discovery Protocol (DISCO) defines an algorithm for locating Web service descriptions.
- **Web service directory** Provides a central location to locate Web services provided by other organizations. Web services directories such as a Universal Description, Discovery, and Integration (UDDI) registry fulfill this role.

A Web service seamlessly enables objects on a server to accept incoming requests from clients using HTTP/XML. To create a Web service, you write a Visual Basic .NET object as if it were being accessed directly by local clients and mark it with an attribute indicating that it should be available to Web clients; ASP.NET does the rest. An example of this process is shown in Figure 27-1.

ASP.NET automatically associates the .NET Web services infrastructure that accepts incoming requests through HTTP and maps them to calls on the object. This saves developers the task of writing the infrastructure that handles Web communications.

On the client side, the .NET Web services infrastructure provides proxy classes that allow access to the Web services provided by a server that accepts HTTP requests. A developer tool reads the description of the Web service and generates a proxy class containing methods in whatever language you use to develop the client. When the client calls one

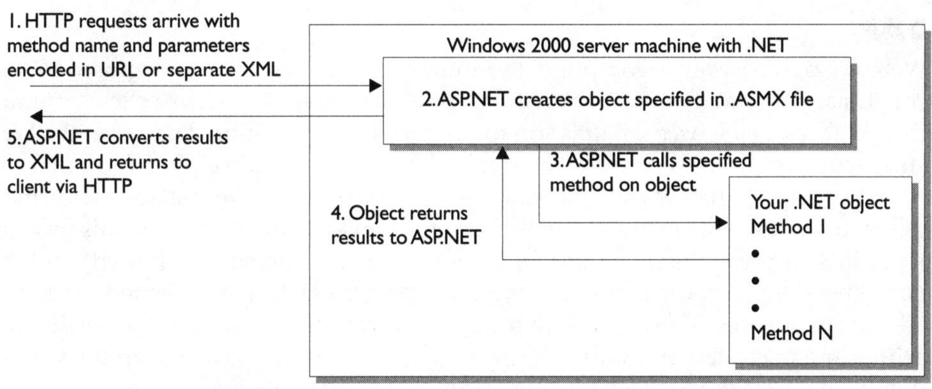

Figure 27-1 Server-side view of a Web service

of these methods, the proxy class creates an HTTP request and sends it to the server. When the response comes back from the server, the proxy class parses the results and returns them from the method. This process allows the client to seamlessly interact with any Web server and associated Web service that uses HTTP and XML. Figure 27-2 provides an example of the client-side proxy.

The protocols used within the .NET Web services infrastructure provide a discovery mechanism for locating Web services, a service description for defining how to use Web services, and standard network encapsulation protocols with which to communicate with Web services. These protocols are discussed in the following sections.

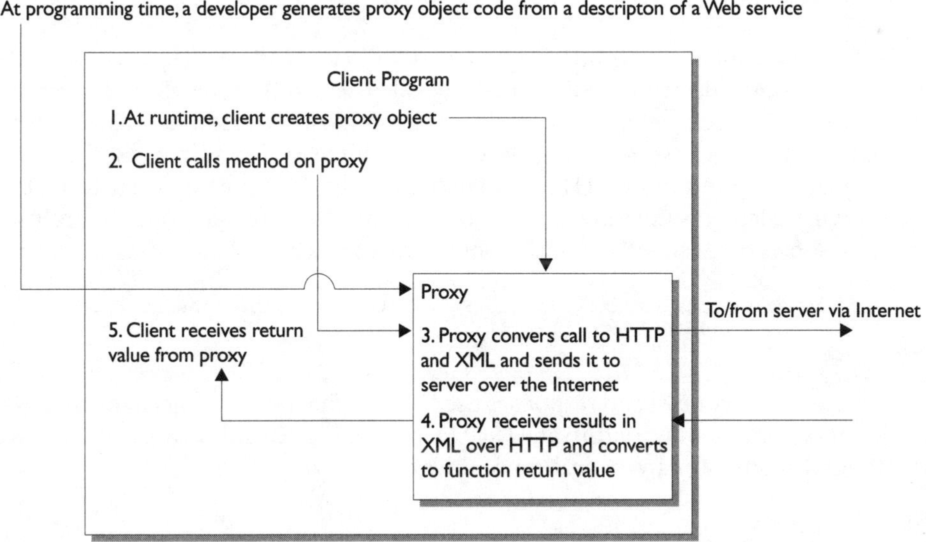

Figure 27-2 Client-side view of a Web service

PART VII

SOAP

A Web service is basically a component running on a Web server that is exposed for use through standard Internet protocols. As discussed in Chapter 26, when a client communicates with a server it uses serialization to package the information it passes to the Web component. Serialization converts the state information of objects into a form that can be transported over the network. Basically, an object writes its current state, usually indicated by the value of its member variables, to the network stream. During this process, the public and private fields of an object (if the object is being transported) and the name of the class, including the assembly containing the class, are converted to the network stream as bytes. These bytes are transported over the network to the destination machine and re-created by reading, or deserializing, the object's state from the stream. When the object is deserialized, an exact clone of the original object is created.

You can also transport the serialized representation to another context such as a different machine, rebuild the original object, and use it on the remote machine. The format that the information takes as it is passed in the form of requests and responses between the client and the Web service located on the server is based on XML. The Simple Object Access Protocol (SOAP) describes the format of these XML requests and responses.

SOAP is an encoding scheme for request and response parameters that uses HTTP as its transport mechanism. It defines a lightweight XML-based protocol for exchanging information in a decentralized, distributed environment and consists of three components:

- An envelope that defines a framework for describing what is in a message, who needs to handle it, and how to process it
- A set of encoding rules for expressing instances of application-defined data types and defining the mechanism for serializing the information
- A convention for representing remote procedure calls (RPC) and responses

SOAP is a complex specification. This chapter discusses the envelope construct and the framework for describing SOAP messages. For encoding rules, RPC conventions, and other information, refer to the MSDN Web site at http://msdn.microsoft.com/.

To illustrate the concepts underlying SOAP we will use the example of a simple Web service that communicates via HTTP and uses SOAP to define the message format. The Web service calculates the sales tax on the total price of a transaction. The following example shows the Visual Basic .NET code for this service.

```
Public Function GetSalesTax(ByVal dblSalesTotal As Double) As Double
    GetSalesTax = dblSalesTotal * 0.07
End Function
```

Because SOAP requests and responses use HTTP as the transport mechanism, a SOAP request message is defined within an HTTP POST request. The following code shows the HTTP POST request for an invocation of the example Web service.

```
POST /soap HTTP/1.1
Host: www.salestax.com
Content-Type: text/xml;
```

```
charset="utf-8"
Content-Length: 162
SOAPMethodName:"http://www.salestax.com/soap:TaxCalc#GetSalesTax"

<SOAP:Envelope xmlns:SOAP="urn:schemas-xmlsoap-org:soap.v1">
    <SOAP:Header></SOAP:Header>
    <SOAP:Body>
        <m:GetSalesTax xmlns:m="http://www.salestax.com/soap:TaxCalc">
            <SalesTotal>100</SalesTotal>
        </m:GetSalesTax>
    </SOAP:Body>
</SOAP:Envelope>
```

In this example, we define a simple SOAP request that complies with the SOAP encoding rules. Specifically we define a SOAP endpoint as an HTTP-based URL that identifies a target application method for invocation. As with remote objects, we must decide how to map the object endpoint identifier onto a server-side object. In this example, we specify an HTTP POST request that defines the text/xml content type. This type defines the content being carried within the message; a request URI that specifies the target object of the request (/soap); and the application method being invoked (http://www.salestax.com/soap:TaxCalc#GetSalesTax). The SOAPMethodName header indicates that the method name is GetSalesTax and that the scoping URI is "http://www.salestax.com/soap:TaxCalc", which specifies that we are calling the GetSalesTax method on the **TaxCalc** object at the URL http://www.salestax.com/soap.

The HTTP content of a SOAP request is a SOAP request document. This document consists of a SOAP <envelope> element, which in turn is made up of a SOAP <header> and a SOAP <body>. The <body> element encloses the <GetSalesTax> method call element, which contains the namespace URI of the SOAPMethodName HTTP header.

The SOAP response is similar to the SOAP request. The following code shows the response that the client receives after the requested method is called on the Web service.

```
200 OK
Content-Type: text/xml;
Content-Length: 162

<SOAP:Envelope xmlns:SOAP="urn:schemas-xmlsoap-org:soap.v1">
    <SOAP:Header></SOAP:Header>
    <SOAP:Body>
        <m:GetSalesTaxResponse xmlns:m="http://www.salestax.com/soap:TaxCalc">
             <SalesTax>4</SalesTax>
        </m:GetSalesTaxResponse>
    </SOAP:Body>
</SOAP:Envelope>
```

The response content contains the return call parameter of the method encoded as a child element of the <GetSalesTaxResponse> element. This element's name is the same as the request call element except that it is concatenated with the response suffix. Notice that the HTTP header is absent. This header is only required in the request message, not in the response.

WSDL

For a client application to understand how to interact with a Web service, there must be a description of the method calls and properties that are available from the service. This description specifies what the client application must "say" to the service to get it to perform as intended. It is defined as a document and is specified by the Web Services Description Language (WSDL). A WSDL document is like a type library that uses Interface Definition Language (IDL) to describe a COM component. Both IDL and WSDL files describe an interface's method calls and the parameters for a particular method call. The main difference between the two description languages is that all descriptions in the WSDL file are in XML. A WSDL document describes three fundamental components of a Web service:

- **Functionality** Operations (methods) that the service provides
- **Access methods** Details of the data formats and protocols used to access the service
- **Location** Details of the protocol-specific network address (URL)

The WSDL document defines these components by specifying the following XML elements:

- **<types>** Defines a container for data type definitions
- **<operation>** Describes an action supported by the service; each operation specifies the input and output messages defined as <message> elements
- **<services>** Defines a collection of ports or endpoints to a particular binding for each port
- **<ports>** Specifies an address for a binding, thus defining a single communication endpoint
- **<bindings>** Points to a corresponding port type and describes the data format and protocol for each interface
- **<porttypes>** Describes the operations that the service can implement; each operation description defines the input and output messages that the service uses
- **<messages>** Provides information about particular messages passed to and from the Web service; there is one input and one output message for every operation

The following code is an example of a WSDL document file:

```
<?xml version="1.0"?>
<definitions name="InventoryList"
targetNamespace="http://example.com/inventorylist.wsdl"
         xmlns:tns="http://example.com/ inventorylist.wsdl"
         xmlns:xsd1="http://example.com/ inventorylist.xsd"
         xmlns:soap="http://schemas.xmlsoap.org/wsdl/soap/"
         xmlns="http://schemas.xmlsoap.org/wsdl/">
```

```
    <types>
       <schema targetNamespace="http://example.com/ inventorylist.xsd"
              xmlns="http://www.w3.org/2000/10/XMLSchema">

          <element name="InventoryRequest">
             <complexType>
                <all>
                   <element name="PartNumber" type="string"/>
                </all>
             </complexType>
          </element>
          <element name="InventoryItem">
             <complexType>
                <all>
                   <element name="price" type="float"/>
                </all>
             </complexType>
          </element>
       </schema>
    </types>

    <message name="GetInventoryInput">
        <part name="body" element="xsd1:InventoryRequest"/>
    </message>

    <message name="GetInventoryListOutput">
        <part name="body" element="xsd1:InventoryItem"/>
    </message>

    <portType name="InventoryListPortType">
        <operation name="GetInventoryList">
           <input message="tns:GetInventoryListInput"/>
           <output message="tns:GetInventoryListOutput"/>
        </operation>
    </portType>

    <binding name="InventoryListSoapBinding" type="tns:InventoryListPortType">
        <soap:binding style="document"
                      Transport="http://schemas.xmlsoap.org/soap/http"/>
        <operation name="GetInventoryList">
           <soap:operation soapAction="http://example.com/GetInventoryList"/>
           <input>
               <soap:body use="literal"/>
           </input>
           <output>
               <soap:body use="literal"/>
           </output>
        </operation>
    </binding>

    <service name="InventoryListService">
        <documentation>My first service</documentation>
        <port name="InventoryListPort" binding="tns:InventoryListSoapBinding">
           <soap:address location="http://example.com/inventorylist"/>
        </port>
    </service>
</definitions>
```

Within the preceding document we specify a number of <type> elements that contain a physical type description in XML schema definition (XSD) format. These types are referred to from the <message> elements.

For each Web method in the Web service, two messages are defined for a particular port: an input message and an output message. In this example we use only the SOAP protocol; therefore, only two <message> elements are defined for the port: the <GetInventoryListInput> message and the <GetInventoryListOutput> message. The <portType> element specifies the operations for the protocol in use. Each operation is specified as an <operation> element. Although the port types are abstract operations for each port, the bindings provide concrete information on what protocol is used, how the data is transported, and where the service is located. Again, there is a <binding> element for each protocol supported by the Web service. In this example we specify a SOAP binding using the <soap:binding> element to indicate that the transport protocol for the SOAP messages is HTTP. The <soap:operation> element defines the HTTP header soapAction, which points to the Web method. Both the input and output of the SOAP call are SOAP messages.

Finally, we use the <service> element to specify the port for the Web service. For each supported protocol, there is one <port> element. Because we use only one protocol (SOAP) in this example, there is only one port definition. Within the port definition we specify the binding to the Web method defined earlier.

DISCO

To use a WSDL document, a client must obtain it. If the client knows where the WSDL document resides, it can simply request it via HTTP. However, if the client doesn't know the location of the document, it must use a discovery mechanism, which is enabled in Visual Basic .NET using the Microsoft discovery protocol called DISCO.

To advertise Web services publicly, developers post discovery files on the Internet. DISCO defines the document format and interrogation algorithm for retrieving the discovery document, making it possible to discover the Web services exposed by a given server at a specified URL. Web service clients can then browse the discovery files for WSDL document information about how to use the Web service. The process of looking up a service and reviewing the service description is called Web service discovery.

There are two basic ways of advertising a service: statically or dynamically. Static discovery is explicit. To advertise a Web service statically, you must explicitly create a .disco discovery file and point it to the WSDL document. To illustrate static discovery, we use the following .disco file, which is a continuation of the earlier WSDL example.

```
<?xml version="1.0">
<disco:discovery
   xmlns:disco="http://schemas.xmlsoap.org/disco/"
   xmlns:scl="http://schemas.xmlsoap.org/disco/scl/">
   <!-- reference to other DISCO document -->
   <disco:discoveryRef
      ref="related-services/default.disco"/>
   <!-- reference to WSDL and documentation -->
   <scl:contractRef ref="inventorylist.asmx?wsdl" docRef="inventorylist.asmx"/>
</disco:discovery>
```

To publish the DISCO file with our Web services application, we simply create a .disco file and place it in the vroot along with the other service-related configuration files for our Web service, as shown in the following code.

```
\inetpub
  \wwwroot
    \inventorylist  (vroot)
       inventorylist.asmx
       web.config
       inventorylist.disco
      \bin
         simpleInventory.dll
         complexInventory.dll
```

All .disco files begin with a <discovery> element, which is defined in the **http://schemas.xmlsoap.org/disco** namespace. This element is referred to as disco in this example. One or more <contactref> or <discoveryref> elements can be inside the <discovery> element. Both elements are described in the **http://schemas.xmlsoap.org/disco/scl** namespace. Developers use the <contractref> element to refer to the Web service URL that will return the WSDL document describing the Web service. Developers use the <discoveryref> element to refer to another discovery document. In this example we specify that the WSDL document be returned for the InventoryList Web service in the <contractref> element; we use the <discoveryref> element to refer to another discovery document located at "related-services/default.disco."

With dynamic discovery, you do not specify the URL for Web services directly. Instead, you specify all Web services underneath a specific URL on the Web site. Under your own Web site, for example, you might want to group related Web services under different directories and then provide a single dynamic discovery file in each directory. To use dynamic discovery you must change the XML within the .disco file. The following example outlines a .disco file that uses dynamic discovery.

```
<?xml version="1.0">
<dynamicDiscovery xmlns="urn://schemas-dynamic:disco.2000-03-17">
   <exclude path="_vti_cnf"/>
   <exclude path="_vti_pvt"/>
   <exclude path="_vti_log"/>
   <exclude path="_vti_script"/>
   <exclude path="_vti_text"/>
</dynamicDiscovery>
```

In this example, we specify not only that we want to use dynamic discovery, but also that we want to exclude paths so that the dynamic discovery algorithm does not traverse all subdirectories underneath the dynamic discovery file. Note that dynamic discovery files are not saved in the same way that static discovery files are saved. With static discovery files you save the XML to a .disco file; with dynamic discovery, you save the XML to a .vdisco file.

The preceding examples required the client to specify the exact address of the .disco file on the server. In most situations prospective clients won't know the exact address of the .disco file; for this reason, DISCO enables developers to provide hints in the vroot's default page.

If the vroot's default page is an HTML document, you can use the Link tag to redirect the client to the .disco file, as shown in the following example.

```
<HTML>
  <HEAD>
    <link type="text/xml" rel="alternate" href="inventorylist.disco"/>
  </HEAD>
</HTML>
```

If the vroot's default page is an XML document, you can use the XML Stylesheet processing instruction to accomplish the same thing, as shown in the following code.

```
<?xml-stylesheet type="text/xml" alternate="yes" _
                 href="inventorylist.disco"?>
```

With these redirects in place, clients can simply point the discovery tools to the vroot and they will be automatically redirected to the specified .disco file.

UDDI

The Universal Description, Discovery, and Integration (UDDI) specification is a public registry, much like a phone company's yellow pages, of publicly available Web services. UDDI provides a database of businesses that is searchable based on business criteria such as North American Industry Classification System (NAICS) codes and Standard Industrial Classification (SIC) codes. It also enables clients to search by business name or geographical location. Suppose that a company wants to purchase computer equipment electronically. To do this, it needs a directory of all businesses that expose Web services and sell computer equipment. If the company searches the UDDI for NAICS code 3341, which corresponds to computer manufacturers, the search would return a list of such companies that are registered with UDDI. The client application could then use the information to begin an application-to-application dialogue.

Using UDDI, developers can publish Web services by first modeling the UDDI entry and then registering it with the UDDI directory.

To model the entry, follow these steps:

1. Determine the WSDL files or tModels that your Web service will use to describe its behavior, which is referred to as a service type. Each tModel has a name, description, and Universally Unique Identifier (UUID) that represents its service type called a tModelKey.
2. Provide a brief description of your company as well as the central contacts for the company's Web services in case you need to contact them for support.
3. Identify the categories and identification codes appropriate to your company. Currently supported categories include North American Industry Classification System (NAICS), Universal Standard Products and Services Codes (UNSPSC), ISO 3166, Standard Industry Classification (SIC), and GeoWeb Geographic Classification.
4. Identify the Web services that your company provides through UDDI.

Once you have modeled the UDDI entry you are ready to register the Web services. To test services prior to registering them publicly, you can use the UDDI services that are available with the Windows .NET Server or you can install the UDDI on a local machine from the SDK.

To register services, you must register the WSDL file for each Web service as a tModel. Then you must register the access point for each Web service using a bindingTemplate. UDDI bindingTemplates are XML structures used to represent implementation details about a given Web service. You must add a binding for each service that you register. The following code provides an example of a UDDI bindingTemplate. Note that the serviceKey, bindingKey, and tModelKey are all generated by UDDI and are unique to the entities within the template. The keys generated by other UDDI registries will be different.

```
<bindingTemplate serviceKey="ef25102d-2171-454c-ade9-3dd7a4a914ee"
      bindingKey="f46fced9-2b8a-4817-b957-f8d8aca0a2f9">
   <accessPoint URLType="http">
      http://localhost/SalesReportUSA/SalesReport.asmx
   </accessPoint>
   <tModelInstanceDetails>
      <tModelInstanceInfo tModelKey=
            "uuid:b28fe40a-ea62-4657-88d5-752d8a6cdf77" />
   </tModelInstanceDetails>
</bindingTemplate>
```

Each binding must create a reference to the interfaces it supports. These references are known as specification signatures. A specification signature is the tModel that contains the WSDL interface. The accessPoint and bindingKey for the specified Web service provide information to the client application on how to connect to the server and the specified Web service.

To generate the proxy client, developers use the WSDL.EXE tool that is available with Visual Studio .NET. Based on the information that the UDDI publishes about the Web service, you can code the specification signature within the UDDI application. At design time, you would presumably discover the Web service in UDDI and retrieve its accessPoint and bindingKey, and then include the specification signature in an application configuration file. A configuration file is shown in the following example.

```
<?xml version="1.0" encoding="utf-8" ?>
<configuration>
   <appSettings>
      <add key="UDDI_URL" value="http://localhost/uddi/api/inquire.asmx" />
      <add key="bindingKey" value="f46fced9-2b8a-4817-b957-f8d8aca0a2f9" />
   </appSettings>
</configuration>
```

In this example, we point to a Microsoft UDDI server hosted on our local machine. The UDDI_URL or an internally hosted UDDI registry could also be one of the public UDDI nodes. We save the file using the naming convention for configuration files: app.config. When the application is compiled, the configuration file will be placed in the /bin directory and be named after the name of the .EXE file itself. We can now use this published service within our applications using the client proxy that was generated.

Building Web Services

As introduced in the preceding section, open standards-based protocols and the Web services infrastructure provided by the .NET Framework allow developers to create and use Web services. The following sections explore Web services creation and use in detail.

Creating and Using Web Services

In this section we describe how to develop a Web service, first from the server perspective, and then from the client perspective. Web service developers implement Web services and advertise them so that client applications can discover them and use the services they provide. Because Web services run on top of HTTP, there must be a Web server application on the machine that hosts the Web service. The .NET infrastructure currently supports only one Web server: Microsoft Internet Information Server (IIS).

In Exercise 27-1, you will create a Web service that converts temperatures between Fahrenheit and Celsius. The Web service has two methods: ToCelsius and ToFahrenheit.

Exercise 27-1: Creating a Simple Web Service

1. Create a new ASP.NET Web service application by selecting File | New. The New Project dialog box appears.
2. From the New Project dialog box select Visual Basic Projects from the Project Types pane, and then select ASP.NET Web Service from the Templates pane.
3. Within the Location field indicate the location of your new Web service as **http://localhost/TemperatureService** and click OK. The default designer window for the Web service opens.
4. Within Solution Explorer right-click on service1.asmx and rename it **TemperatureService.asmx**.
5. Double-click on the designer window to open up the code module for the Web service. Modify the code to match the following code.

```
Imports System
Imports System.Web.Services

<WebService(Namespace := "http://tempuri.org/")> _
Public Class TemperatureService
    Inherits System.Web.Services.WebService

    <WebMethod()> Public Function ToCelsius(ByVal TF As Double) As Double
        Return (5 / 9) * (TF - 32)
    End Function

    <WebMethod()> Public Function ToFahrenheit(ByVal TC As Double) As Double
        Return (9 / 5) * (TC + 32)
    End Function
End Class
```

6. Select Build Solution from the Build menu.

In the preceding exercise you define a public class named **TemperatureService** that inherits from the .NET **WebService** class. Next you declare two methods for the class: one to convert from Celsius to Fahrenheit and another to convert from Fahrenheit to Celsius. Each method is defined using Visual Basic functions and each is exposed by the Web service. The <WebMethod()> expression is used with every method that is defined in the class. It tells ASP.NET that a method is to be exposed to clients as a Web service. You might expect to obtain this functionality through the Public access modifier, and within Windows-based applications, this would be the case; functions declared with the Public access modifier can be accessed by all procedures in all classes of an application. However, the Public access modifier does not expose a function as a method of the Web service. To be exposed as a Web method, the function must be Public, and it must be flagged with the WebMethod attribute.

Setting Custom Attributes

Adding the WebMethod attribute to a method within a Web service created using ASP.NET allows remote Web clients to call the method. This attribute has the optional properties described in Table 27-1.

To provide a description for the ToCelsius method in Exercise 27-1, for example, you declare the method as shown in the following code.

```
<WebMethod(Description:="Converts Fahrenheit to Celsius")> _
   Public Function ToCelsius(ByVal TF As Double) As Double
   Return (5 / 9) * (TF - 32)
End Function
```

Property	Description
BufferResponse	Controls whether to buffer the method's response
CacheDuration	Specifies the length of time, in seconds, to keep the method response in cache. The default is to not hold the method response in cache.
Description	Provides additional information about a particular Web method
EnableSession	Enables or disables session state. If you don't intend to use session state for the Web method, you might want to generate and manage session IDs for each user accessing the Web method. This might improve performance. This flag is set to True by default.
MessageName	Distinguishes Web methods that have the same name
TransactionOption	Specifies whether a transaction is created. Can be one of five modes: disabled, notsupported, supported, required, and requiresnew. Even though there are five modes, Web methods can only participate as the root object in a transaction. This means both required and requiresnew result in a new transaction being created for the Web method. The disabled, notsupported, and supported settings result in no transaction being used for the Web method. Set to False by default.

Table 27-1 WebMethod Properties

In your example Web service, you use not only the WebMethod custom attribute, but also the WebService custom attribute. The WebService attribute allows you to specify properties for a Web service as a whole. To do this, you use the properties of the WebService **Attribute** class. Table 27-2 describes the properties of this class.

The Namespace property is particularly important. By default, the XML namespace in Exercise 27-1 is set to http://tempuri.org/. When developing Web services, you should modify the XML namespace to specify your own URL. The URL that you specify does not have to point to an actual Web page; it simply functions as a unique identifier so that Web services developed by your company can be distinguished from Web services developed by other companies.

Consuming a Web Service

As a client, you access a Web service from within an application by creating a Web service proxy class. This type of proxy class is a local representation of the properties and methods of a remote Web service class. After you create a proxy class, you can treat the class exactly like any other .NET Framework class. For example, imagine that the TemperatureService Web service is hosted at an Internet Service Provider located in central Africa. After you create a proxy class, you can invoke the methods of the remote Web service class within your application as though the class were located on your computer.

To generate a proxy class, you use the WSDL.EXE tool, which is provided with the Visual Studio .NET integrated development environment (IDE). This utility reads the description of the Web service from a WSDL document and generates a proxy for accessing its methods from the language you specify. Once the proxy has been generated, you can use any of the supported protocols, but the default is SOAP. To create a proxy class for the example Web service, you would run the following code to create a proxy class for the Web Service created in Exercise 27-1.

```
Wsdl /l:vb http://localhost/TemperatureService/TemperatureService.asmx?WSDL
```

Property	Description
Description	Provides a description for the Web service. This description appears in the Web service help page.
Name	Specifies a name for the Web service (by default, the class name is used)
Namespace	Specifies the XML namespace for the Web service (not to be confused with the .NET namespace)

Table 27-2 WebService Properties

The Visual Basic proxy class contains both synchronous and asynchronous versions of functions for retrieving temperature conversions from the Web service. The following code shows the output of the WSDL.EXE utility.

```
Imports System
Imports System.ComponentModel
Imports System.Diagnostics
Imports System.Web.Services
Imports System.Web.Services.Protocols
Imports System.Xml.Serialization

<System.Diagnostics.DebuggerStepThroughAttribute(),  _
 System.ComponentModel.DesignerCategoryAttribute("code"),  _
 System.Web.Services.WebServiceBindingAttribute(Name:= _
        "TemperatureServiceSoap", [Namespace]:="http://tempuri.org/")>  _
Public Class TemperatureService
    Inherits System.Web.Services.Protocols.SoapHttpClientProtocol

    Public Sub New()
        MyBase.New
        Me.Url = "http://localhost/temperature/TemperatureService.asmx"
    End Sub

<System.Web.Services.Protocols.SoapDocumentMethodAttribute( _
    "http://tempuri.org/ToCelsius", _
    RequestNamespace:="http://tempuri.org/", _
    ResponseNamespace:="http://tempuri.org/", _
    Use:=System.Web.Services.Description.SoapBindingUse.Literal, _
    ParameterStyle:=System.Web.Services.Protocols.SoapParameterStyle.Wrapped)> _
    Public Function ToCelsius(ByVal TF As Double) As Double
        Dim results() As Object = Me.Invoke("ToCelsius", New Object() {TF})
        Return CType(results(0),Double)
    End Function

    Public Function BeginToCelsius(ByVal TF As Double, _
                ByVal callback As System.AsyncCallback, _
                ByVal asyncState As Object) As System.IAsyncResult
        Return Me.BeginInvoke("ToCelsius", New Object() {TF}, callback, asyncState)
    End Function

    Public Function EndToCelsius(ByVal asyncResult As System.IAsyncResult) _
           As Double
        Dim results() As Object = Me.EndInvoke(asyncResult)
        Return CType(results(0),Double)
    End Function

<System.Web.Services.Protocols.SoapDocumentMethodAttribute( _
    "http://tempuri.org/ToFahrenheit", _
    RequestNamespace:="http://tempuri.org/", _
    ResponseNamespace:="http://tempuri.org/", _
    Use:=System.Web.Services.Description.SoapBindingUse.Literal, _
    ParameterStyle:=System.Web.Services.Protocols.SoapParameterStyle.Wrapped)> _
    Public Function ToFahrenheit(ByVal TC As Double) As Double
        Dim results() As Object = Me.Invoke("ToFahrenheit", New Object() {TC})
        Return CType(results(0),Double)
    End Function
```

```
    Public Function BeginToFahrenheit(ByVal TC As Double, _
                ByVal callback As System.AsyncCallback, _
                ByVal asyncState As Object) As System.IAsyncResult
        Return Me.BeginInvoke("ToFahrenheit", New Object() {TC}, _
                        callback, asyncState)
    End Function

    Public Function EndToFahrenheit(ByVal asyncResult As System.IAsyncResult) _
            As Double
        Dim results() As Object = Me.EndInvoke(asyncResult)
        Return CType(results(0),Double)
    End Function
End Class
```

In this example, the proxy class inherits from the base class **System.Web.Services.Protocols.SoapHttpClientProtocol**, which contains the actual code. Note that a URL property is defined as part of the New method. The proxy inherits this property from the base class. The property specifies the URL of the server to which the call is directed. It contains a default value, which it gets from the original WSDL file. The client calls the named method on the proxy by calling the Invoke method within the BeginToCelsius method or the BeginToFahrenheit method, depending on which method is called.

The BeginToCelsius method and the BeginToFahrenheit method are synchronous methods; when they are invoked by the client, the client waits until they are finished processing before continuing its work. Each of these methods creates a SOAP packet containing its method name and parameters and sends the SOAP packet via HTTP to the server. When the SOAP response packet comes back from the server, the base class parses out the return value and returns it to the proxy, which then returns it to the client.

Note the attributes that are attached to the function names; they contain information, such as method names, that tells the base class how to package the call. Visual Studio .NET uses these metadata attributes extensively to pass information to the prefabricated functionality of system code. In earlier days, this would probably have been done through member variables of the base class, where it would have been difficult to differentiate immutable runtime attributes from those that can change during program execution.

In this exercise you will create a console application that makes use of asynchronous calls from the example client application to invoke Web methods that convert temperature values for you.

Exercise 27-2: Making an Asynchronous Call

1. Create a new console application by selecting File | New. The New Project dialog box appears.
2. From the New Project dialog box select Visual Basic Projects from the Project Types pane, and then select Console Application from the Templates pane.
3. Within the Name and Location fields indicate the name of your application. For this example, call the application **SyncConsoleApp**.
4. Compile the proxy class that was generated from the WSDL.EXE utility using the following command.

```
vbc /t:library /r:System.dll,System.Web.Services.dll,System.Xml.dll
TemperatureService.vb
```

5. Make a reference to the proxy class by right-clicking the References node within Solution Explorer and clicking Add Reference. The Add Reference dialog box appears. Select the .NET tab and click Browse. Locate the proxy class DLL that was created in the preceding step and add it to your project.
6. Modify the code within the code window to match the following lines.

```
Imports System.Web.Services
Module Module1

    Sub Main()
        Dim SyncTempServiceProxy As TemperatureService
        Dim Result As Double

        SyncTempServiceProxy = New TemperatureService()
        SyncTempServiceProxy.Url = _
           "http://localhost/TemperatureService/TemperatureService.asmx"
        Result = SyncTempServiceProxy.ToCelsius(35)
        Console.WriteLine("The temperature in Celsius of 35 degrees " & _
                          "Fahrenheit is, " & Convert.ToString(Result))
        Result = SyncTempServiceProxy.ToFahrenheit(35)
        Console.WriteLine("The temperature in Fahrenheit of 35 degrees " & _
                          "Celsius is, " & Convert.ToString(Result))
    End Sub
End Module
```

7. Select Build Solution from the Build menu.

Invoking Asynchronous Web Methods

For most applications, calling the synchronous proxy method is not appropriate because the slow response time leaves the client with a "frozen" interface. Developers need a mechanism that allows a client to call a Web method from another thread that can go into a wait state while the Web method performs its processing. When the Web method is finished processing, it informs the thread that invoked the method and returns the results, which are passed to the application, all without interrupting the original application.

To enable applications to perform asynchronous calls against Web methods, Microsoft includes asynchronous proxy classes within the prefabricated code that is generated by WSDL.EXE. Instead of making a call and blocking until it completes, a program calls one method that transmits the request data to the server and returns immediately. Later, the application calls another method to retrieve the results that were returned by the server.

As shown in the preceding section, the code that is generated by WSDL.EXE contains asynchronous method calls. Here is the ToCelsius method asynchronous method for reference.

```
Public Function BeginToCelsius(ByVal TF As Double, _
                ByVal callback As System.AsyncCallback, _
                ByVal asyncState As Object) As System.IAsyncResult
```

```
        Return Me.BeginInvoke("ToCelsius", New Object() {TF}, callback, asyncState)
    End Function

    Public Function EndToCelsius(ByVal asyncResult As System.IAsyncResult) _
            As Double
        Dim results() As Object = Me.EndInvoke(asyncResult)
        Return CType(results(0),Double)
    End Function
```

In the preceding code, the proxy class contains a method with the name Begin*MethodName* for each temperature conversion method. (We identify only the BeginToCelsius method.) The parameter list for these function calls begins with the temperature being converted, as it does for the synchronous methods. Two more parameters are passed to the asynchronous call that are not passed to the synchronous call. The first of these parameters identifies a callback function that is invoked when the asynchronous call finally returns; the second of these parameters specifies the state of the call.

To use the example asynchronous code from a client application, we modify the Exercise 27-1 console application with the following code.

```
Imports System.Web.Services
Module Module1

    Sub Main()
        Dim ASyncTempServiceProxy As TemperatureService
        Dim AsyncResult As IAsyncResult
        Dim Result As Double
        Dim intCounter As Integer

        ASyncTempServiceProxy = New TemperatureService()
        ASyncTempServiceProxy.Url = _
            "http://localhost/TemperatureService/TemperatureService.asmx"
        AsyncResult = ASyncTempServiceProxy.BeginToCelsius(35, Nothing, Nothing)
        intCounter = 0
        Do While AsyncResult.IsCompleted <> True
            intCounter = intCounter + 1
        Loop
        Result = ASyncTempServiceProxy.EndToCelsius(AsyncResult)
        Console.WriteLine("The temperature in Celsius of 35 degrees " & _
                          "Fahrenheit is, " & Convert.ToString(Result))
        Console.WriteLine("We managed to count to " & _
                  Convert.ToString(intCounter) & " while our service ran")
        AsyncResult = ASyncTempServiceProxy.BeginToFahrenheit(35, Nothing, Nothing)
        intCounter = 0
        Do While AsyncResult.IsCompleted <> True
            intCounter = intCounter + 1
        Loop
        Result = ASyncTempServiceProxy.EndToFahrenheit(AsyncResult)
        Console.WriteLine("The temperature in Fahrenheit of 35 degrees " & _
                          "Celsius is, " & Convert.ToString(Result))
        Console.WriteLine("We managed to count to " & _
                  Convert.ToString(intCounter) & " while our service ran")
    End Sub
End Module
```

In this example we call both conversion methods asynchronously. In each case we pass the temperature we want to convert and Nothing for the remainder of the parameters. The call to BeginToCelsius starts the communication chain by sending out the request and then returns immediately. The return value is an **IAsyncResult** object, which we use to fetch the result later and to determine when the asynchronous Web method has completed its processing. While waiting for the processing to complete, the application remains in a loop continuously, incrementing a counter while waiting.

Once the asynchronous Web method has completed, we retrieve the results of the conversion by calling the EndToCelsius method and passing it the **IAsyncResult** object. Passing this object lets the infrastructure determine which result to return, as the client can have several outstanding requests at the same time (as is the case in our example, where we call both the ToCelsius and ToFahrenheit methods asynchronously).

Invoking a Web Service

HTTP Get is the standard HTTP protocol for transmitting requests for URLs or posting a form with METHOD="Get". You can also invoke the ToCelsius method of the TemperatureService Web service by adding the following hypertext link in an HTML document.

```
<a href="/Services/TemperatureService.asmx/ToCelsius?TF=32">Convert</a>
```

Alternatively, you can type the following URL directly into the address bar of your Web browser.

```
http://localhost/Services/TemperatureService.asmx/ToCelsius?TF=32
```

In either case, the ToCelsius Web method is invoked by passing the TF parameter with the value 32. The Web service returns the following XML document representing the results of converting the value 32 into degrees Celsius, which results in the value 0 being returned.

```
<?xml version="1.0" encoding="utf-8" ?>
   <double xmlns=http://tempuri.org/>0</double>
```

Instead of using an HTTP Get request, you can also invoke the Web service using an HTTP Post request. HTTP Post is the standard HTTP protocol for transmitting form data submitted with METHOD="Post". For example, you can invoke the ToCelsius method of TemperatureService by using the following HTML.

```
<form method="post" action="/Services/TemperaturesService.asmx/ToCelsius">
   <input name="TF" value="32">
   <input type="submit" value="Convert!">
</form>
```

Posting this form invokes the ToCelsius method of the TemperatureService Web service and returns the following XML document.

```
<?xml version="1.0" encoding="utf-8" ?>
   <double xmlns=http://tempuri.org/">0</double>
```

Finally, another method of invoking the Web service is to use the Simple Object Access Protocol (SOAP) to transmit more complex messages across the network. You can transmit data types with SOAP that you cannot transmit by using either HTTP Get or HTTP Post. For example, you can use SOAP to transmit DatasSets, custom classes, and binary files. The SOAP request that invokes the ToCelsius method of TemperatureService is shown in the following code.

```
<?xml version="1.0" encoding="utf-8"?>
<soap:Envelope xmlns:xsi="http://www.w3.org/2001/XMLSchema-instance"
               xmlns:xsd="http://www.w3.org/2001/XMLSchema"
               xmlns:soap="http://schemas.xmlsoap.org/soap/envelope/">
  <soap:Body>
    <ToCelsius xmlns="http://tempuri.org/">
      <TF>double</TF>
    </ToCelsius>
  </soap:Body>
</soap:Envelope>
```

This SOAP request contains the name of the function and its parameters, encoded in XML according to an agreed upon schema. When the SOAP packet reaches the server, ASP.NET recognizes it, parses the method name and its parameters out of the packet, creates the object, and makes the call. In this example, the SOAP request invokes the ToCelsius method by passing a TF parameter with the value 32. The Web service would return the following SOAP response.

```
<?xml version="1.0" encoding="utf-8"?>
<soap:Envelope xmlns:xsi="http://www.w3.org/2001/XMLSchema-instance"
               xmlns:xsd="http://www.w3.org/2001/XMLSchema"
               xmlns:soap="http://schemas.xmlsoap.org/soap/envelope/">
  <soap:Body>
    <ToCelsiusResponse xmlns="http://tempuri.org/">
      <ToCelsiusResult>0</ToCelsiusResult>
    </ToCelsiusResponse>
  </soap:Body>
</soap:Envelope>
```

Unlike HTTP Get and HTTP Post, the SOAP protocol is not tied to the HTTP protocol. Although you use SOAP over the HTTP protocol within this example, it is possible to use SOAP over other protocols such as Simple Message Transfer Protocol (SMTP).

SOAP Extensions and Serialization

During the serialization/deserialization process, the Web services infrastructure provides a mechanism known as SOAP extensions. SOAP extensions allow developers to intercept messages before or after they are transported by the Web services infrastructure and perform actions on them or modify their contents.

SOAP extensions can be used for many tasks, including the following:

- Tracing
- Compression

- Encryption and decryption
- Authentication and authorization
- Accessing and modifying SOAP headers
- Performance monitoring
- Other global operations

A SOAP extension consists of a pair of custom classes that derive from **System.Web.Services.Protocols.SoapExtension** and **SoapExtensionAttribute** and are associated with a Web method using declarative syntax.

When a Web service is called, the following sequence of events occurs:

1. The client application creates a new instance of the Web service proxy class.
2. The client application invokes a method on the proxy class.
3. The infrastructure on the client computer serializes the arguments of the Web service method into a SOAP message and sends it over the network to the Web service.
4. The infrastructure receives the SOAP message and deserializes the XML from the SOAP message. Then, it creates an instance of the class implementing the Web service and invokes the Web service method, passing in the deserialized XML as arguments.
5. The Web service method executes its code, eventually returning information to the client.
6. The infrastructure on the Web server serializes the return value and parameters into a SOAP message and sends it over the network to the client.
7. The Web services infrastructure on the client computer receives the SOAP message, deserializes the XML into the return value and parameters, and passes the value and parameters to the instance of the proxy class.
8. The client receives the return value and continues execution.

When the Web service infrastructure receives a SOAP message, the SOAP message is deserialized into objects (for example, **SoapHeader** objects or **SoapMessage** objects) and is eventually passed into the Web method. After the Web method has finished, the result, as well as any **SoapHeader** objects or **SoapException** objects, is serialized into a SOAP message and sent back out the execution chain to the client that originally invoked the Web service method. To provide hooks into this message stream, the SOAP extensions go through four stages:

- **BeforeDeserialize** This stage occurs before the SOAP message is deserialized into objects and sent to the requested Web service. Therefore, you still have access to the actual SOAP message.

- **AfterDeserialize** This stage occurs after the SOAP message is deserialized into objects and sent to the requested Web service, so you have access only to the objects that represent the SOAP message, such as the **SoapHeader** object and the **SoapMessage** object.
- **BeforeSerialize** This stage occurs after the Web service is finished processing and before the returned objects are serialized back into a SOAP message and sent to the client. Therefore, you still have access to all the objects that will ultimately be serialized into a SOAP message.
- **AfterSerialize** This stage occurs after the Web service is finished processing and after the returned objects are serialized back into a SOAP message and sent to the client, so you have access to the SOAP message being sent back to the client.

ASP.NET serializes and deserializes XML during phases on both the Web services computer and the Web services client computer. A SOAP extension can be injected into the infrastructure to inspect or modify the SOAP messages before and after each of these serialize and deserialize phases. Typically, when a SOAP extension modifies the contents of a SOAP message, the modifications must be performed on both the client and the server. For example, if a SOAP extension runs on the client and encrypts the SOAP message, a corresponding SOAP extension must decrypt the SOAP message on the server. If the SOAP message is not decrypted, then the ASP.NET infrastructure cannot deserialize the SOAP message into an object.

Of course, a SOAP extension that does not modify the SOAP message, such as a SOAP extension that simply logs the SOAP messages, does not have to run on both the client and server. In this case, the recipient receives the same SOAP message it would receive if a SOAP extension were not running, and the ASP.NET infrastructure can deserialize the SOAP message.

To explore how to use SOAP extensions, you will use the following exercises to write an example client application that takes as input a text string representing a name. This string is passed to your Web service, which then prepends the word "Hello" to it and returns it to the client. This example will implement two SOAP extensions: one on the client and one on the server. The SOAP extension on the server will reverse the text string that is accepted/returned, while the SOAP extension on the client will do the same thing. In essence, this is a very rudimentary encrypt/decrypt function.

In this exercise you will define your Web service.

Exercise 27-3: Defining a Web Service

1. In Visual Studio .NET create a new ASP.NET Web services application by selecting File | New. The New Project dialog box appears.
2. In the New Project dialog box select Visual Basic Projects from the Project Types pane, and then select ASP.NET Web Service from the Templates window.
3. In the Location field indicate the location of your new Web service as **http://localhost/ReverseHelloVB** and click OK. The default designer window for your Web service will open.

4. Within Solution Explorer right-click on Service1.asmx and rename it **ReverseHello.asmx**.
5. Double-click on the designer window to open the code module for the Web service.
6. Modify the code to match the following lines.

```
Imports System.Web.Services

<WebService(Namespace:="http://www.catinhat.com/")> _
Public Class Service1
    Inherits System.Web.Services.WebService

    <WebMethod(), MyOwnSoapExtensionAttribute()> _
    Public Function SayHello(ByVal strName As String) As String
        Return "Hello, " & strName
    End Function
End Class
```

In the preceding code, you specify a custom attribute for the Web method. This attribute is called MyOwnSoapExtensionAttribute. It specifies to ASP.NET that you want to use the SOAP extension. You will define this attribute in exercise 27-5, but first you will define the SOAP extension class that the custom attribute refers to.

In this exercise, you will define the SOAP extension class that the MyOwnSoapExtensionAttribute attribute refers to.

Exercise 27-4: Defining a SOAP Extension Class

1. Add a class module to your application by selecting File | Add New Item. The Add New Item dialog box appears.
2. In the Templates pane click Class and specify **MyOwnSoapExtension.vb** as the file name.
3. Modify the code within the class module as shown in the following lines.

```
Imports System
Imports System.Web.Services
Imports System.Web.Services.Protocols
Imports System.IO

Public Class MyOwnSoapExtension
    Inherits System.Web.Services.Protocols.SoapExtension

    Private m_oldStream As Stream
    Private m_newStream As Stream

    Public Overrides Sub Initialize(ByVal initializer As Object)
    End Sub

    Public Overrides Sub ProcessMessage(ByVal message As _
           System.Web.Services.Protocols.SoapMessage)

        Select Case message.Stage
            Case SoapMessageStage.BeforeDeserialize
                InReverse()
            Case SoapMessageStage.AfterDeserialize

            Case SoapMessageStage.BeforeSerialize
```

```
            Case SoapMessageStage.AfterSerialize
                OutReverse()
        End Select
    End Sub

    Public Overloads Overrides Function GetInitializer(ByVal serviceType As System.Type) _
                As Object
        Return serviceType
    End Function

    Public Overloads Overrides Function GetInitializer(ByVal methodInfo As _
          System.Web.Services.Protocols.LogicalMethodInfo, ByVal attribute As _
          System.Web.Services.Protocols.SoapExtensionAttribute) As Object
        Return Nothing
    End Function

    Public Sub InReverse()
        Dim length As Integer = m_oldStream.Length
        Dim buffer(length) As Byte
        Dim Newbuffer(length) As Byte
        Dim i As Integer

        m_oldStream.Read(buffer, 0, length)
        For i = 1 To length
            Newbuffer(length - (i - 1)) = buffer(i)
        Next
        m_newStream.Write(Newbuffer, 0, length)
        m_newStream.Position = 0
    End Sub

    Public Sub OutReverse()
        m_newStream.Position = 0
        Dim length As Integer = m_newStream.Length
        Dim buffer(length) As Byte
        Dim newbuffer(length) As Byte
        Dim i As Integer

        m_newStream.Read(buffer, 0, length)
        For i = 1 To length
            newbuffer(length - (i - 1)) = buffer(i)
        Next
        m_oldStream.Write(newbuffer, 0, length)
    End Sub

    Public Overrides Function ChainStream(ByVal stream As _
                              System.IO.Stream) As System.IO.Stream
        m_oldStream = stream
        m_newStream = New MemoryStream()
        Return m_newStream
    End Function
End Class
```

In the preceding code, the SOAP extension class begins by deriving from the system base class **System.Web.Services.Protocols.SoapExtension**, as all SOAP extension classes do. You must override the methods of this base class, as well as supply your own custom methods to perform custom processing as required. The primary method used to override is the ProcessMessage method, which ASP.NET calls when it is the SOAP extension's turn to look at the SOAP packet. The single parameter, here called "message", is of type System.Web.Services.Protocols.SoapMessage. If you look this up, you'll find it contains a member named Stage.

The SOAP extension is called at four separate locations in the Web service process, as described earlier. Instead of forcing you to write four separate handler functions,

ASP.NET calls the same method every time, differentiating them by means of the Stage property. On input, the function is called before and after the incoming SOAP packet is deserialized from the network. On output, it is called before and after the Web service method's return values are serialized into XML. In this case, you use the InReverse method in the BeforeDeserialize case to reverse the buffer that the client has passed over the network. The remaining method, OutReverse, is used in the AfterSerialize case to reverse the buffer just before the message is passed on the network to the client.

Exercise 27-5: Defining a Custom Attribute In this exercise you will define the custom attribute to be used with the SOAP extension you defined in Exercise 27-4.

1. Add a class module to your application by selecting File | Add New Item. The Add New Item dialog box appears.
2. In the Templates pane click Class and specify **MyOwnSoapExtensionAttribute.vb** as the file name.
3. Modify the code within the class module as shown in the following lines.

```
<AttributeUsage(AttributeTargets.Method)> Public Class _
    MyOwnSoapExtensionAttribute
    Inherits System.Web.Services.Protocols.SoapExtensionAttribute

    Public Overrides ReadOnly Property ExtensionType() As System.Type
        Get
            Return GetType(MyOwnSoapExtension)
        End Get
    End Property

    Public Overrides Property Priority() As Integer
        Get
            Return 0
        End Get
        Set(ByVal Value As Integer)
        End Set
    End Property
End Class
```

In the preceding code, the custom attribute is defined as a class module that inherits from the base class **System.Web.Services.Protocols.SoapExtensionAttribute**. You override the ExtensionType property, writing code that responds with the .NET type name of the SOAP extension. The Priority property specifies the order in which SOAP extensions should be invoked if more than one exists. This would be useful, for example, if you had defined compression code and wanted to ensure that your reverse algorithm ran after compression code, not before. In this exercise, you explicitly specify a value of 0.

In this exercise you will define the client application that will access Web services.

Exercise 27-6: Defining a Client Application

1. In Visual Studio .NET create a new project by selecting File | New Project. The New Project dialog box appears.
2. From the New Project dialog box select Visual Basic Projects from the Project Types pane, and then select Console Application from the Templates pane.

3. In the Name field enter the name of the client application. For this exercise, call the application **ReverseHelloClientVB**.
4. Add a Web reference to the Web service by right-clicking References within Solution Explorer and selecting Web Reference. The Add Web Reference dialog box appears.
5. In the Address field enter the address of the Web service. For this exercise, use the address **http://localhost/reversehellovb/service1.asmx**.
6. Modify the code within the code window to match the following lines.

```
Module Module1
    Sub Main()
        Dim strResult As String
        Dim objRemoteHello As New localhost.Service1()

        strResult = objRemoteHello.SayHello("Larry")
        Console.WriteLine(strResult)

    End Sub
End Module
```

7. Select Build Solution from the Build menu.

Just as you have to reverse input and output on the server, you also must reverse the input and output on the client. To do so, you must add the SOAP extension attribute class and SOAP extension class to your client project. The code for these modules is the same as listed in Exercise 27-4; therefore, we do not list it here.

Locating Web Services Using DISCO

As discussed earlier, clients use a discovery mechanism to locate ASP.NET Web services. This mechanism is usually in the form of an XML-based discovery file (DISCO). The DISCO file involves the use of one or more of the following extensions:

- **.disco** Refers to a physical .disco file that you can customize and place anywhere. Visual Studio .NET does not create this file automatically when you create an ASP.NET Web services project.
- **?disco** By appending ?disco to the .asmx Web address in a Web browser or in the Add Web Reference dialog box in Visual Studio .NET, you can view the XML that is generated automatically by the ASP.NET runtime. Note that this item does not generate a physical .disco file.
- **.vsdisco** Refers to a physical .vsdisco file. The *vs* in the file extension means that the file contains XML-based pre-processor directives that the ASP.NET runtime uses to search for and discover any additional .vsdisco or .disco files in the same directory or child directories. Visual Studio .NET creates a .vsdisco file every time you create a new ASP.NET Web services project. A default .vsdisco file also resides in the localhost server root.

Each of the preceding items generates XML that can be processed to more easily discover your Web Services. Note that although DISCO is a Microsoft technology designed to support ASP.NET Web services, .disco files are simply XML text files that can be hosted on any server and parsed by any XML parser. Only the dynamic search and discovery functionality of the .vsdisco file is unavailable outside of the ASP.NET runtime.

The DISCO standard defines five main XML element types and their related attributes, all of which serve to make it easier for clients to discover the location of Web services. To be well-formed, every XML document must contain a single root element, and the .disco file is no exception. The root element is <discovery>. It contains references to the various unique namespaces related to DISCO and its standards. These standards include the following elements:

- **<contractRef>** This element contains a mandatory Ref attribute that can only contain a pointer to the WSDL document. (Other file types are not allowed.) You can also use the optional docRef attribute to include a link to a Web service support page, such as the .asmx file that the ASP.NET runtime uses to generate a Web service information "home" page.
- **<discoveryRef>** Optional. This is the key element used to link to related Web services to facilitate their discovery by potential customers and search engines that are "Disco-aware". It references another discovery document.
- **<schemaRef>** Optional. This element is used to specify additional XML schema definition (XSD) files that are needed to describe the data types used by the Web service. It is used for more advanced Web services in which the WSDL document is not sufficient to fully describe the Web service's return types.
- **<soap>** This element restates a portion of the information that is already contained in the WSDL document concerning SOAP binding. It enables clients to more easily discover the most relevant binding information.

In this exercise you will create a DISCO file for the ReverseHelloVB Web service that you created in the last section. This file will enable discovery of your Web service.

Exercise 27-7: Creating a DISCO File

1. Open the ReverseHelloVB Web service created in the last section by starting Visual Studio .NET and selecting File | Open | Project from Web. The Open Project from the Web dialog box appears.
2. Enter **http://localhost/ReverseHelloVB/ReverseHelloVB.vbproj** in the text box.
3. In the Solution Explorer right-click ReverseHelloVB, point to Add, and then click Add New Item.
4. In the Categories window expand Web Project Items and select the Utility category.
5. In the Templates pane click Static Discovery File. In the Name field type **ReverseHelloVB.disco**, and then click Open. Visual Studio .NET creates the file with an empty <discovery> root element.

6. Modify the contents of the file to match the following code.

```
<?xml version="1.0" encoding="utf-8" ?>

<discovery xmlns:xsd="http://www.w3.org/2001/XMLSchema"
           xmlns:xsi="http://www.w3.org/2001/XMLSchema-instance"
           xmlns="http://schemas.xmlsoap.org/disco/">

  <contractRef ref="http://localhost/reversehellovb/service1.asmx?wsdl"
               docRef="http://localhost/reversehellovb/service1.asmx"
               xmlns="http://schemas.xmlsoap.org/disco/scl/" />

  <soap address="http://localhost/reversehellovb/service1.asmx"
        xmlns:q1="http://tempuri.org/" binding="q1:Service1Soap"
        xmlns="http://schemas.xmlsoap.org/disco/soap/" />
</discovery>
```

7. You now have a physical .disco file that is equivalent to the dynamically generated DISCO contents. Note that any changes made to the Web service will not be automatically reflected in this file. Deploy the discovery document to a Web server by copying it to a virtual directory on the Web server.
8. Optionally, if you would like to allow prospective consumers to navigate to a URL by specifying an IIS application instead of a document, you can add a link to the default page for the IIS application. This allows consumers to access the discovery document without having to know its name. Users can then supply URLs during the discovery process, as shown in the following example.

   ```
   http://Localhost/ReverseHelloVB
   ```

   You add the link to the discovery document in the <head> tag of the default Web page for the Web server. For example, if you name your discovery document ReverseHelloVB.disco and place it in the same directory as the default page, place the following tag in the default Web page.

   ```
   <HEAD>
   <link type="text/xml" rel="alternate" href="ReverseHelloVB.disco"/>
   </HEAD>
   ```

Using UDDI

An alternative to using static discovery to locate a Web service is to use a Universal Description, Discovery, and Integration (UDDI) directory. As discussed earlier, UDDI can act as a central repository for Web service registration either on the Internet or internally within a company. Through a native implementation of a UDDI directory on a Windows .NET server or through a UDDI directory that is installed on a local server, developers can publish Web services internally much like publishing address records in a Domain Name Service (DNS) directory. If a Web service is commercially available to clients it can be published to the public UDDI server.

Figure 27-3 identifies the UDDI components that Visual Basic developers can use to interact with the UDDI registry and add Web service registration features to applications.

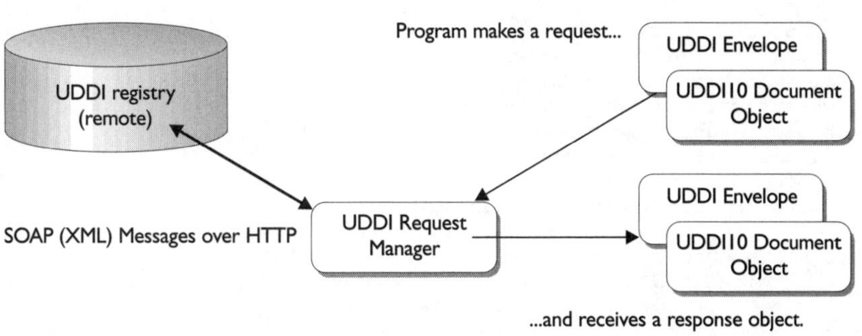

Figure 27-3 UDDI development environment

As shown in Figure 27-3, three components allow you to register with a UDDI directory. The request manager provides the bulk of the functionality and masks the details of XML SOAP authentication and error management. By default, the request manager connects to the Production instance of the UDDI registry at http://uddi.Microsoft.com. However, you can set the Mode property of the request manager to switch between Production and Test when developing your applications. Using Test mode while you work out kinks in an application is always a good practice during software development. The Mode property can be set to Production, Test, or Custom. When the property is set to Test or Production, the addresses that the request manager communicates are set automatically to predefined values. To communicate with an internal UDDI directory, you must set the mode to Custom and configure the following properties:

- **UDDI_Address** This property specifies where inquiry messages are sent.
- **UDDI_SecureAddress** This property specifies where publishing messages are sent and is used when you want to communicate securely with the UDDI server. The address is usually an SSL connection.

In the following code example, we use the UDDI SDK to register the ReverseHelloVB Web service that you defined earlier. In this example we specify the code to register a business named WebServicesRUs. The business contains a single service description named ReverseHelloVB that exposes a single binding for the ReverseHelloVB service. The binding exposes the URL where we can send messages to the ReverseHelloVB service using the specifications in the unique specification signature referenced in the tModelKey value.

```
Dim objBusEntity As New save_business
Dim objBusDetail As New businessDetail
Dim env As New UDDIEnv.Envelope
Dim ret As UDDIEnv.Envelope
Dim objreqManager as new UDDIEnv.requestManager

objreqManager.authenticate "MyUserID", "MyPassword"
```

```
Set env.Plugin = objBusEntity
With objBusEntity.AddbusinessEntity
    .Name = "WebServicesRUs Inc."
    .Adddescription = "We reverse the word Hello, for you"
    With .businessServices.AddbusinessService
        .Name = "Buy components"
        .Adddescription = "Bindings for our ReverseHelloVB service"
        With .bindingTemplates.AddbindingTemplate
             .accessPoint = "http://www.WebServicesRUs.com/RevereseHello.asp"
            .addescription = "ReverseHello example"
            With .tModelInstanceDetails.AddtModelInstanceInfo
                .tModelKey = GUID_REVERSEHELLO
            End With
        End With
    End With
End With
Set ret = objreqManager.UDDIRequest(env)
If objreqManager.UDDIErrno = 0 Then
    Set ret.Plugin = objBusDetail
    Debug.print objBusDetail.businessEntity.businessKey
End If
```

The UDDI registry communicates with software programs using XML messages. Developers can use approximately 20 different types of messages to interact with a UDDI registry. Each message is represented in an XML text stream. Because the XML interface to UDDI is based on the SOAP format, each message is comprised of an envelope section and a body section. The envelope objects manage SOAP details and transmission, and the request/response processing that occurs between the application and the directory.

To interact with a UDDI directory, the application uses a **requestManager** object, which is referenced by the **objreqManager** variable. This object manages all HTTP and SOAP interactions, sets up each request, waits for the response, and then detects any errors that have been flagged by the remote UDDI directory. For requests that require authentication, the **requestManager** object manages the housekeeping associated with authentication. In the previous code we begin by authenticating to the UDDI directory. This authentication step uses a Microsoft Passport user ID and password pair to authenticate against the directory. All the messages involved in publishing information to the UDDI registry require that a person first become authorized to publish.

In the previous code listing, a new registration is made because businessKey values are not provided in the data being saved. The response to the save_business request as outlined by the code

```
Set ret = objreqManager.UDDIRequest(env)
```

returns a businessDetail message, provided that the call is successful. A businessDetail message contains the new keys assigned to the businessEntity data, the businessServiceData, and the bindingTemplate data. A last thing to note regarding the example application is the tModel reference made in the bindingTemplate structure. This data represents the unique technical signature that is used to identify the Web service.

Summary

Web services are distributed software components that are accessible through standard Web protocols. Web services enable software to interoperate with a broad range of clients. Web services can be consumed by any application that understands how to parse an XML-formatted stream transmitted through HTTP channels.

XML plays a significant role in the Web services infrastructure. It uses the Simple Object Access Protocol (SOAP) to define all communications between the client and the server. SOAP is the underlying XML-based transport format used for exchanging messages between a Web service and a client application or other Web-based application.

The Web service description process and the Web Services Description Language (WSDL) are used to specify how applications communicate and interact with the Web service. Once a description is in place, an application must be able to locate a Web service. Discovery services are provided through the Microsoft discovery specification (DISCO) or a Universal Description, Discovery, and Integration (UDDI) directory server, which provides a central repository for Web service descriptions similar to a DNS server.

When developing a Web service you use the WebMethod attribute to expose a method as a Web service. You use the WebService attribute to specify properties about your Web service. You can invoke a Web service using an HTTP Get request, an HTTP Post request, or a SOAP request. The SOAP method provides the most functionality for interaction between a client application and a Web service. You can use the WSDL.EXE utility to develop a proxy class that enables a client to interact with a Web service both synchronously and asynchronously. SOAP extensions give you a mechanism for hooking into the execution code path of a client application/Web service dialogue, allowing you to modify or work with the information being passed back and forth. Extensions have many uses including adding functionality such as encryption or compression, or enabling you to log and trace information before it is passed over the network.

You can use static discovery to enable the discovery of a Web service. Static discovery uses a DISCO file to provide information about a Web service. You can also use UDDI for registering Web services and locating services that have been registered.

Test Questions

1. Which of the following statements is false?
   - A. SOAP consists of an envelope that defines a framework for describing what is in a message, who must handle it, and how to process it.
   - B. SOAP is a set of encoding rules for expressing instances of application-defined data types and the mechanism for serializing the information.
   - C. SOAP is a convention for representing remote procedure calls (RPC) and responses.
   - D. SOAP consists of methods for invoking Web services.

2. Which property should you set when you want to communicate securely with your own UDDI directory server?
   A. UDDI_Address
   B. UDDI_Directory
   C. UDDI_SecureRegistry
   D. UDDI_SecureAddress
3. Which element is not part of the DISCO specification?
   A. <contractRef>
   B. <discoveryRef>
   C. <schemaRef>
   D. <directoryRef>

Test Answers

1. **D.** The SOAP specification does not provide a set of methods for invoking Web services.
2. **D.** To communicate securely with your own UDDI server, you must set the address of the directory server in the UDDI_SecureAddress property.
3. **D.** The <directoryRef> element is not a valid element of the DISCO specification.

CHAPTER 28

Testing, Deploying, and Securing Web Services

In this chapter, you will

- Learn how to create a unit test plan
- See how to implement tracing and display trace output
- Debug a Web service
- Understand how to control debugging in the web.config file
- Use SOAP extensions for debugging
- Deploy an XML Web service
- Understand how to create a setup program that installs a Web service
- Learn how to configure and implement security for a Web service

Software bugs are a fact of life; even the best developers cannot write error-free code all the time. On average, even well-written programs have one to three bugs for every 100 statements. It is estimated that testing to find these bugs consumes half the labor involved in producing a working application. This chapter shows you how to use debugging tools and SOAP extensions to identify and correct problems with Web services. It also explains how to use trace and monitor facilities to watch the execution of Web services and to log information to help you understand what is happening when a service is running. Finally, the chapter discusses how to deploy a Web service and provide security.

Unit Testing

Developers conduct unit testing to ensure proper functionality and code coverage after the coding of an application component has been completed. The primary goal of unit testing is to take the smallest piece of self-contained software in an application, isolate it from the remainder of the code, and determine whether it behaves as expected. Unit test case design usually begins after a technical reviewer approves the high-level design. The unit test cases are derived from the functional specification, and then the components of the application are tested to ensure that the design has been coded correctly. Each unit is tested separately before integrating units into modules to test the interfaces between modules.

There are three main approaches to unit testing. The first approach uses a technique called black-box testing, which is also called functional testing or responsibility-based testing. In this approach software is exercised over a full range of inputs, and the outputs are observed for appropriate behavior. How the outputs are achieved, or what is inside the box, doesn't matter. The second approach to unit testing uses a technique called white-box testing. Other terms for this technique are structural testing and implementation testing. White-box testing strategies include executing every line of source code at least once or requiring every function to be individually tested.

Of the two approaches, black-box testing is the more common because it ensures that the intended functionality of the application is actually delivered. The third approach to unit testing uses a technique called use-case analysis. A use case is a sequence of actions, performed by a system, that produces a result for the user. Because use cases describe the "process flows" through a system based on likely scenarios, they are useful in uncovering defects that might occur in the process flows during actual system use.

White-Box Testing

White-box testing is used to test both the modules and the procedures that support the modules. The white-box testing technique ignores the function of the program being tested and focuses only on the program's code and the structure of that code. White-box testing uses a statement and condition technique. Test case designers generate cases that not only cause each condition to take on each possible value at least once, but also cause each condition to be executed at least once. In other words:

- Each decision statement in the program takes a True value and a False value at least once during testing.
- Each condition takes on each possible outcome at least once during testing.

Generally, very few white-box tests can be performed without modifying the program—changing values to force different execution paths or to generate a full range of inputs to test a particular function. This modification is usually done by using interactive debuggers or changing the source code. Although this technique may be adequate for small programs, it does not scale well to larger applications.

White-box testing is based on knowing the internal code of the class. Having this information allows the tester to write tests that exercise boundary conditions, conditional branches, and state transitions. In white-box testing, the tester should attempt to test the following elements:

- All branches of the method
- All boundary conditions in the method
- All possible combinations of state transitions

Although it is necessary for ensuring code coverage, white-box testing is limited. It can reveal defects in how the code handles branches, unusual input, boundary conditions, and so on. It can verify that the code works as built, but it cannot verify that the code does what it is supposed to do.

To illustrate white-box testing, we will create a MeanValue function that calculates the mean value of a list of scores read from a file. The following code listing will provides the basis for the example.

```
    Function dblfindmean(ByVal objFileScoreData As filesystemobject) As Double
01      Dim dblSumofScores As Double
01      Dim intNumberofScores As Integer
01      Dim dblScore As Double
01      Dim txtScore As String
01
01      txtScore = objFileScoreData.Readline
02      Do While Not objFileScoreData.AtEndofStream
02          dblScore = CDbl(txtScore)
03          If dblScore > 0.0 Then
04              dblSumofScores = dblSumofScores + dblScore
04              intNumberofScores = intNumberofScores + 1
05            End If
06            txtScore = objFileScoreData.Readline
        Loop
07      If intNumberofScores > 0 Then
08          dblfindmean = dblSumofScores / intNumberofScores
08          wscript.echo "The mean score is, " && Cstr(dblfindmean)
        Else
09          dblfindmean = 0
09          wscript.echo("No scores were found in the file")
        End If
    End Function
```

One approach used in white-box testing is to check that all possible paths through the program have been exercised during software testing. To do this, the tester must prepare a flowgraph representing the action's structure. Note that generating a test case for this function cannot occur until the source code is available. Therefore this type of testing is more suitable for finding errors after the code is complete instead of during the development phase. Testing after code is complete, however, can result in longer development schedules because of the sequential nature of development and testing.

A flowgraph has three constituents, representing sequence, selection, and iteration. These components are shown in Figure 28-1.

The first flowgraph in Figure 28-1 represents a sequence of actions in which the flow of control enters at point A and leaves at point B. The second flowgraph represents a selective structure in which flow of control moves from point C to point D via the left- or right-hand path. This structure can be used to represent an If structure or a case structure.

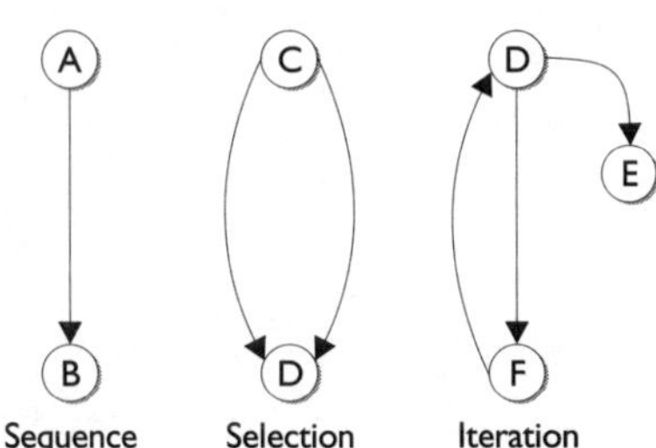

Figure 28-1 Constituent flowgraphs

If required, the number of paths can be increased. The third flowgraph represents an iterative structure in which flow of control can enter at point D and leave immediately at point E without ever executing the body of the loop. Otherwise, flow of control enters at point D and follows the path to point F, representing the body of the loop, and then returns to point D for the loop condition to be re-evaluated.

For the MeanValue example we will create a flowgraph based on the routine's logic. The code in the example is numbered with the entry points in the flowgraph. For example, the lines labeled 01 are initialization code and are represented by a sequence; the line labeled 02 provides the condition of the While loop and is represented by the iterative structure within the flowgraph. Figure 28-2 shows the final MeanValue flowgraph.

Once the flowgraph is created, it can be used to generate test cases that exercise all parts of the code.

Black-Box Testing

Black-box tests are generally constructed using the functional specification document. Testers examine each specification to identify appropriate test cases, generate tests based on what is required for input to the application, and then examine the results to ensure that they are accurate. Black-box test cases are the largest component of the functional test plan.

Black-box tests assume that the tester is not familiar with the underlying code. They are typically designed to simulate the user experience and to anticipate as many potential operating mistakes as possible. They are also used to test, and ideally exceed, the boundary conditions built in to the software.

Figure 28-2 MeanValue flowgraph

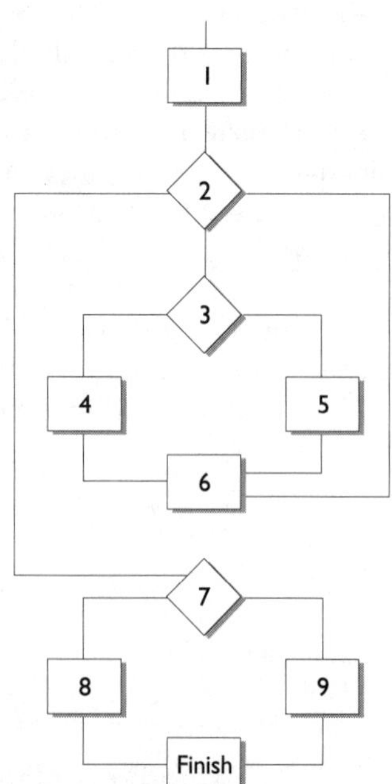

By themselves, however, black-box tests are not sufficient. First, real-life systems have many different kinds of inputs, resulting in virtually unlimited combinations of test cases. It is fine to run a set of representative test cases on a 100-line check-balancing program, but a commercial 747 pilot simulator/trainer has too many inputs and outputs to be able to test sufficiently using only black-box techniques. Second, the correct operation of the program may not produce a measurable output. The output of a check-balancing program is the current account balance, which is simple to verify. A 747 pilot simulator, however, has some outputs that are not so obvious—the height of the bounce on a too-aggressive approach, for example. Third, it is impossible to determine whether all portions of the code have been executed during black-box testing. Code that has not been executed during testing has not been tested, and untested code is a sleeping bomb in any software package. Finally, although typical black-box tests analyze the functional specifications, software paths, and boundary values of a system, they cannot describe the process flows through a system based on the system's actual use.

Use-Case Analysis

As mentioned earlier, a use case is a sequence of actions, performed with an application, that produces a result for the end user. Because use cases are based on likely scenarios, they are useful in uncovering defects that might occur in process flows during actual system use. Use cases serve the following purposes:

- Identify the business process and all activities, from start to finish.
- Document the context and environmental issues for all business and user requirements.
- Facilitate common understanding of the application.
- Trace a path between business needs and user requirements.
- Describe needs and requirements in the context of usage.
- Organize the functional specification.

Use cases are most useful in exposing defects that might occur in process flows during real-world use of the system. They also help uncover integration bugs caused by the interaction and interference of multiple features, which individual feature testing cannot detect.

Debugging

Debugging an application usually involves the use of a debugger. A debugger allows you to observe your application in action at runtime so that you can identify logic errors or unexpected behavior. Besides using a debugger, you might use debugging features that are built in to the programming language and its associated libraries. Many developers are first exposed to debugging when they attempt to isolate a problem by adding calls to output functions such as MsgBox, which allows you to see the results of an execution. This is a legitimate debugging technique, but once you have located and fixed the problem, you must go back through the code to remove all the extra calls, which may introduce new bugs. This section examines debugging and the facilities that are available within Visual Studio .NET and the .NET Framework to assist you with this process.

Debugging a Web Service

The .NET Framework includes a visual debugger that enables you to step line-by-line through the statements of a Web service. You can use the debugger to create breakpoints and watches, which allow you to view the values of variables at any point during service execution. Although the debugger included with the .NET Framework is very similar to the debugger included with Visual Studio .NET, it does not support remote debugging and some other features that the Visual Studio .NET debugger supports.

Exercise 28-1: Setting Up a Web Service In this exercise you will create a very basic Web service that takes as input from the client the user's name, and then returns as output the user's name prepended with the word Hello. You will use this Web service in later exercises to explore the process of debugging a Web service using the .NET Framework debugger.

1. Create a new ASP.NET Web service application by selecting File | New. The New Project dialog box appears.
2. From the New Project dialog box select Visual Basic Projects from the Project Types pane, and then select ASP.NET Web Service from the Templates pane.
3. In the Location field indicate the location of the new Web service as **http://localhost/DebugHelloVB** and click OK. The default designer window for the Web service opens.
4. Within Solution Explorer right-click Service1.asmx and rename it **DebugHello.asmx**.
5. Double-click the designer window to open the code module for the Web service. Then, modify the code to match the following lines.

```
Imports System.Web.Services

<WebService(Namespace:="http://www.catinhat.com/")> _
Public Class Service1
    Inherits System.Web.Services.WebService

    <WebMethod()> Public Function SayHello(ByVal strName As String) As String
        Return "Hello, " & strName
    End Function
End Class
```

6. To debug the application, you can use the various options listed in the Debug menu.

The project template that you use to create the Web service sets the default project settings for debugging automatically. When you choose Start from the Debug menu, these settings cause Visual Studio to launch the browser selected in the project's Property Pages and to dynamically generate a test page. On the test page you can enter commands and observe the data that is returned by the Web service. Using Visual Studio .NET to debug Web services is very convenient; a lot of the tasks necessary to set up the Web service for debugging are done for you. However, you may not always have access to a rich development environment such as Visual Studio .NET. For this reason, you should understand how to debug applications without using the facilities of Visual Studio .NET.

The Microsoft .NET Framework provides the capability to develop ASP.NET Web services without the use of Visual Studio .NET. To create a Web service manually, you must create a virtual directory that contains the files that make up the Web service.

Exercise 28-2: Creating a Virtual Directory In this exercise you will create a virtual directory that contains the files that comprise your Web service. This directory will be used in your debugging application. This exercise assumes that Microsoft Internet Information Server (IIS) and the .NET Framework are installed on your computer.

1. Launch Internet Services Manager by selecting Start | Administrative Tools | Internet Services Manager.
2. Right-click your default Web site and select New | Virtual Directory.
3. Provide the virtual directory with an alias. For this exercise, name the alias **ManualDebugHelloVB**.
4. Choose a physical directory for the virtual directory. It can be located anywhere on the hard drive. For this exercise, name the directory **C:\Temp\ManualDebugHelloVB**.
5. Choose the access permissions for the virtual directory. You must enable both Read and Run scripts to execute ASP.NET pages.

   Once you have created the virtual directory, you can access pages in the application by using URLs that look like the following URL.

   ```
   http://localhost/ManualDebugHelloVB/DebugHelloVB.asmx
   ```

   Every Web service contains a /bin directory that must be located in the root directory of the application. The /bin directory contains custom components and controls that are used by the Web service. Any component or control added to the /bin directory is automatically visible to all pages executing within the application.
6. Create the \bin directory as a subdirectory of C:\Temp\ManualDebugHelloVB.

A configuration file is an important component of a Web services application. Besides providing configuration files for Windows or console-based applications, Visual Basic .NET enables you to define a configuration file for Web-based applications. This file is called web.config. It specifies configuration information for the entire application and is similar to a .config file that is used to configure a Windows application or a console application created with Visual Studio .NET. The web.config file is a standard XML file that you can open and modify using any text editor. You use it to specify the settings for a Web service application. The web.config file contains a variety of settings, and many are irrelevant to this chapter. The two relevant settings are Debug and Trace. (We will look at the Trace setting later.)

Exercise 28-3: Associating an Application with a Debugging Process In this exercise you will prepare the Web service for debugging by associating a web.config file with the Web service.

1. Create a web.config file. This file will be associated with your Web service in the directory that you defined in Exercise 28-1. The XML for the web.config file is provided in the following code.

```
<?xml version="1.0" encoding="utf-8" ?>
<configuration>
   <system.web>
      <compilation debug="true"/>
   </system.web>
</configuration>
```

2. Create a ManualDebugHelloVB.asmx file within the application directory where the web.config file resides and associate the file with the following code.

```
<%@ webservice Language="VB" Class="Service1"%>
Imports System
Imports System.Web.Services

Public Class Service1
    Inherits System.Web.Services.WebService

    <WebMethod()> Public Function SayHello(ByVal strName As String) As String
        Return "Hello, " & strName
    End Function
End Class
```

3. Launch the DbgClr.exe debugger. It is located in the GuiDebug subdirectory of the Microsoft .NET Framework SDK install directory.
4. To open the Web service page that you want to debug (ManualDebugHelloVB.asmx), click Open File.
5. To open the Processes dialog box, select Debug | Processes.
6. Select Show System Processes, and then select aspnet_wp.exe. To attach the debugger to the ASP runtime process, Select Debug | Processes. Then, close the Processes dialog box.

To debug a Web service, you must define a breakpoint within the application. The breakpoint allows you to view the values of variables and perform other debugging operations. To set a breakpoint within the debugger, click the margin to the left of the statement where you want the breakpoint to occur. Doing so highlights the line of code you want to break at and defines a dot within the margin. To test this, define a breakpoint for your Web service application, and then start Internet Explorer. Within the Address field type the following text:

```
http://localhost/ManualDebugHelloVB/ManualDebugHelloVB.asmx
```

The page shown in Figure 28-3 appears.

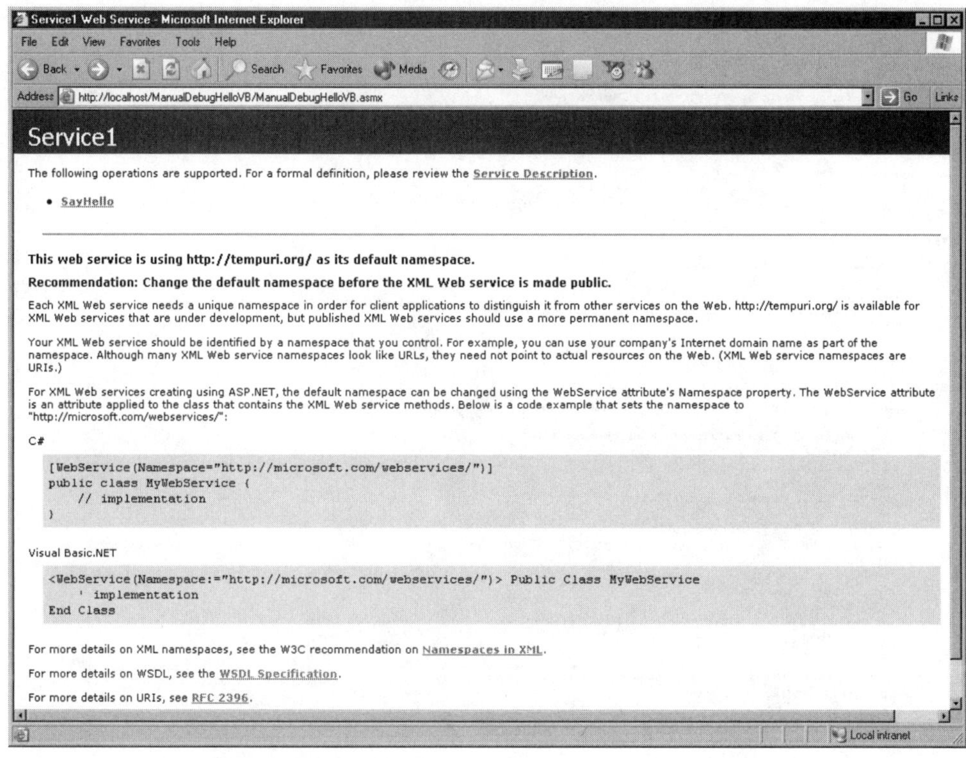

Figure 28-3 Web service page

The page lists the operations that are supported by your Web service. In this case, there is just the one SayHello operation. Click this link to bring up the page shown in Figure 28-4.

This page allows you to test the operations defined in your service. It provides a field for specifying the values of parameters that are to be passed to the operation, and it returns the output of the operation after you click Invoke. In this field you enter a string for the operation or Web method. When you click Invoke, you should be taken into the debugger at the point where you defined a breakpoint. You can now perform operations within the debugger environment such as examining variables, stepping through code, and applying watch expressions.

Using Tracing

Some applications contain thousands of lines of code. Stepping through this type of application can be very time consuming. Fortunately, you do not have to step through an application line-by-line to determine what is happening. The **Systems.Diagnostics** namespace includes **Trace** and **Debug** classes (which are essentially identical) that include a number of static methods that cause code to gather information about code-execution

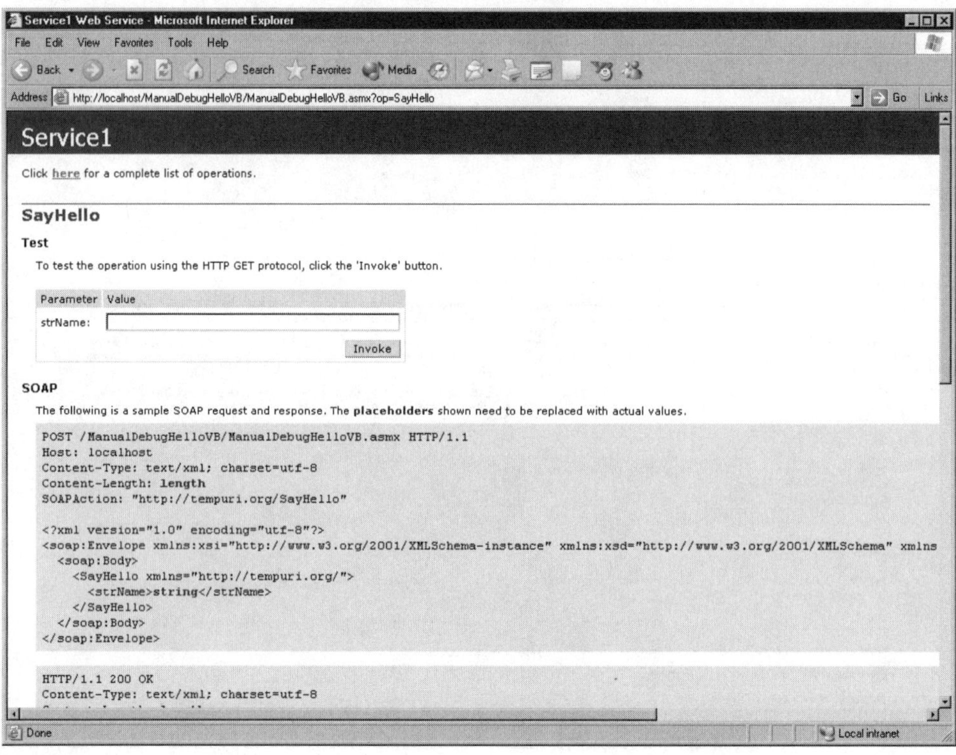

Figure 28-4 Web service operation page

paths, code coverage, and performance profiling. This section explains how to trace the execution of Web applications and monitor their performance using instrumentation. It also introduces you to methods for reading and adding information to the server event log and custom event logs to monitor the health of an application. By taking advantage of tracing, you can more easily debug applications.

To trace the execution of a Web application you must enable application-level tracing within the application's web.config file. The following example shows a web.config file that enables application-level tracing.

```
<configuration>
   <system.web>
      <trace enabled="true" requestLimit="50"
            pageOutput="false" localOnly="false"/>
   </system.web>
</configuration>
```

This web.config file enables application-level tracing for the local application. The trace configuration contains the following elements:

- **Enabled** Boolean value that indicates whether tracing is enabled for the application.
- **Requestlimit** Number of requests to list in the trace.axd page. The trace.axd page collects trace information from all the pages in an application.
- **pageOutput** Boolean value that indicates whether trace information is displayed at the bottom of every page.
- **localOnly** Boolean value that indicates whether trace messages should be displayed only on the local computer, not remote computers.

To enable application-level tracing for your example Web service, modify the web.config file for the ManualDebugHelloVB Web service to include the <trace> element, as shown in the preceding code example.

Application-level tracing is also referred to as "post-mortem" trace debugging. When you configure the system to capture trace events globally, ASP.NET writes the output details to an application-wide trace viewer application called trace.axd. Trace.axd is an HTTP handler that you can use to view application trace details for the most recent requests. (You configure how many requests to save by setting the requestLimit attribute in the web.config file, as shown in the preceding code example.) To view the most recent requests to your application using trace.axd, issue a request to trace.axd in the same application directory as your Web service (for example, http://webserver/applicationname/trace.axd).

Exercise 28-4: Creating a Test Client Application for Application-Level Tracing In this exercise you will create a test client application. You use this client during application-level testing to call the ManualDebugHelloVB Web service.

1. Create a new console application by selecting File | Add Project | New Project. The New Project dialog box appears.
2. From the New Project dialog box select Visual Basic Projects from the Project Types pane, and then select Console Application from the Templates pane.
3. In the Name field enter a name for the console application. For this exercise, call the application **DebugHelloClientVB**. Then, click OK. The application's code window opens.
4. Add a reference to the Web service by right-clicking References within Solution Explorer and selecting Add Web Reference. The Add Web Reference dialog box appears. Type in the URL to the Web service. For this example, it is http://localhost/ManualDebugHelloVB/ManualDebugHelloVB.asmx.
5. Within the code window for the console application modify the code to match the following code.

```
Module Module1

    Sub Main()
        Dim ws As New localhost.Service1()
        Dim cnsleString As String
```

```
            cnsleString = Console.ReadLine()
            Console.WriteLine(ws.SayHello(cnsleString))
        End Sub
    End Module
```

Once you have created the client application, execute it and enter a name. When you press ENTER, the application returns with the name you entered prepended with the word Hello. Because you modified the web.config file to enable application tracing, you can now look at the trace.axd page for the debug application by specifying http://localhost/ManualDebugHelloVB/trace.axd within a browser window. This will bring up the Web page shown in Figure 28-5.

As shown in the figure, each request for the Web service is reflected within the application-level trace. To view the details of an individual request, you can click the View Details link to bring up a Web page, as shown in Figure 28-6.

An application-level trace consolidates traces for all pages within an application, allowing you to observe the execution trail of previously executed pages. This is very helpful during the quality assurance phase of a project. For example, a QA team member can

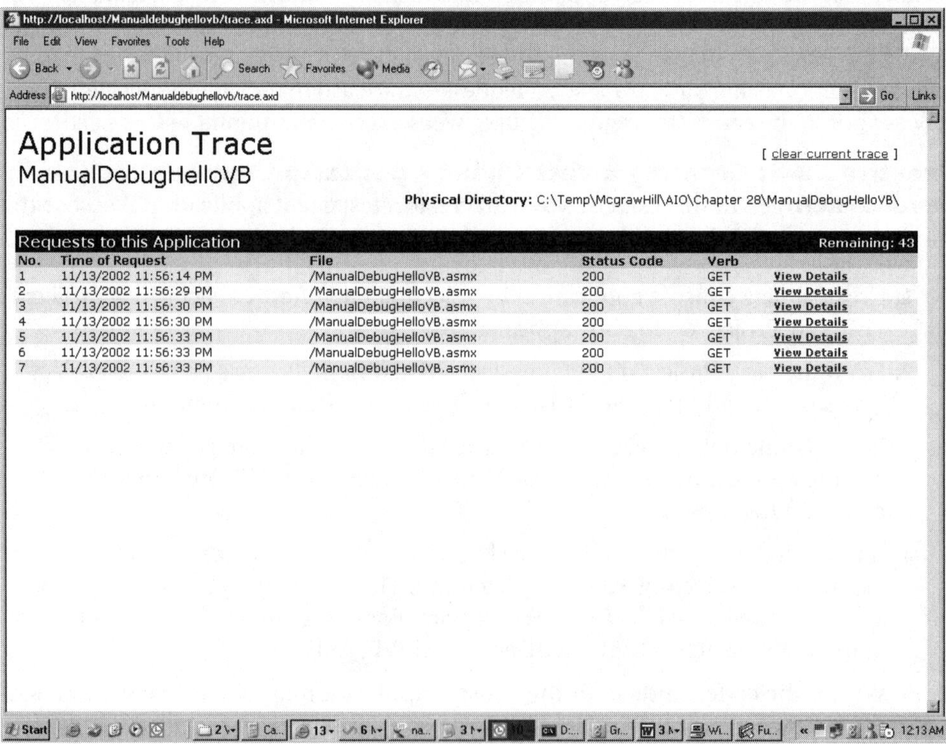

Figure 28-5 Application-level trace

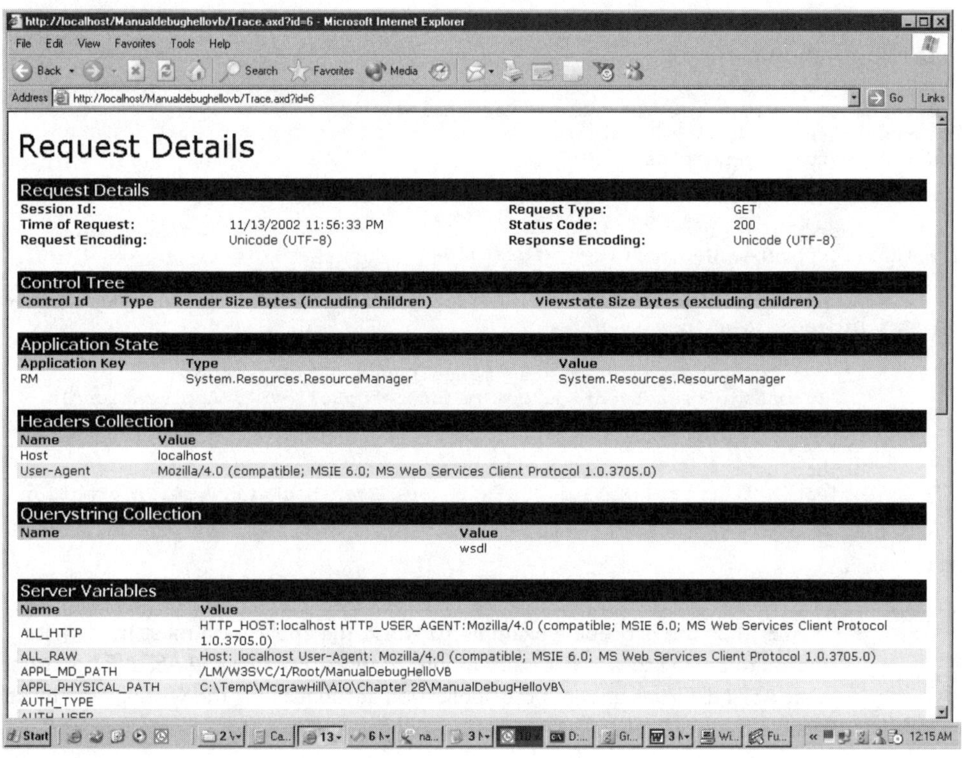

Figure 28-6 Application-level trace details

notify a development team member of a page that returned an error. You (or the QA team member) can pull up the page request using the trace.axd page and review the detailed trace information. The trace feature can also be useful during production. However, it adds significant overhead to your Web application, so do not enable it unless you are in development or debugging a specific problem.

Logging Events

The Windows 2000 operating system includes a centralized set of system event logs. You can use these logs to record events from your Web service to a standard location. The logs help trace what is happening with the Web service and provide valuable information to the people who must administer the service.

To add entries or retrieve existing entries from the server's event logs, you use the **EventLog** class. In the following example, we modify the ManualDebugHelloVB Web service code not only to return a string to the console application, but also to write it out to the application event log.

```
<%@ webservice Language="VB" Class="Service1"%>
Imports System
Imports System.Diagnostics
Imports System.Web.Services

Public Class Service1
    Inherits System.Web.Services.WebService

    <WebMethod()> Public Function SayHello(ByVal strName As String) As String
        Dim objLog as new EventLog

        If Not EventLog.SourceExists("manualDebugHelloVB") then
           EventLog.CreateEventSource("manualDebugHelloVB","Application")
        End if

        objLog.Source = "manualDebugHelloVB"
        objLog.WriteEntry("Hello, " & strName, EventLogEntryType.Information)
        Return "Hello, " & strName
    End Function
End Class
```

NOTE For the preceding example to work, the application must have write access to the log to which it is attempting to write. Because the ASP.NET account that ASP.NET runs under is the application account doing the writing, you must enable this account to write to the appropriate event log.

In the preceding code, we add a new event to the application event log. We do this by first creating a new event source named manualDebugHelloVB, which is associated with the Application event log. Next we instantiate an instance of the **EventLog** class and set the Source property with the event source. Finally, we call the WriteEntry method to add the event to the event log. The first parameter passed to the WriteEntry method represents the message to add to the event log. You can write any message you want as long as it is no larger than 16KB. The second parameter represents the type of message and has the following possible values:

- Error
- FailureAudit
- Information
- SuccessAudit
- Warning

Using Performance Counters

Performance counters provide a valuable tool for monitoring the performance of an application and the system it is running on. ASP.NET supports two groups of performance counters:

- ASP.NET System performance counter group
- ASP.NET Application performance counter group

You can access the ASP.NET System group through the Performance Monitor Application (PerfMon.exe) under the ASP.NET System performance counter object. This group contains information about every executing ASP.NET application. Table 28-1 describes some of the System performance counters included with ASP.NET.

The Application performance counter group is accessible via the ASP.NET Application performance counter object. ASP.NET also supports the creation of custom performance counters. These performance counters contain information about a particular ASP.NET application. Table 28-2 describes some of the Application performance counters included with ASP.NET.

Using performance monitor counters within an application allows you to determine the health of the execution environment. It also helps you determine whether the Web service should behave in a certain manner depending on the values of specific performance monitor counters. For example, you may provide a Web service that is very memory intensive. If memory is becoming critically short, and the application cannot function properly without sufficient memory (i.e., requests to the Web service will queue up), you can write a message to the event log indicating that there is insufficient memory and the service cannot function properly. Then, you can decide whether the application needs to somehow free memory resources, gracefully shut itself down, or continue to run letting requests queue up.

Table 28-1 System Performance Counters

Counter	Description
Application Restarts	The total number of ASP.NET application restarts since Internet Information Server was last started. Specifically, this counter counts each Application_End event
Application Running	The total number of executing ASP.NET applications
Requests Disconnected	The total number of requests that were disconnected due to a communication failure
Requests Queued	The total number of requests waiting in the queue
Request Wait Time	The amount of time, in milliseconds, that the last request waited for processing in the queue
Worker Process Restarts	The total number of times that the ASP.NET process has been restarted
Worker Process Running	The total number of executing ASP.NET processes

Counter	Description
Authentication Anonymous Requests	The total number of anonymous requests
Authentication Anonymous Requests/Sec	The number of anonymous requests made per second
Debugging Requests	The number of requests that occurred while debugging was enabled
Errors During Compilation	The number of errors that occurred during compilation
Errors During Execution	The total number of errors that occurred during the execution of an HTTP request
Errors During Preprocessing	The number of errors that occurred during parsing
Errors Unhandled During Execution	The total number of unhandled errors that occurred during the execution of HTTP requests
Errors Unhandled During Execution/Sec	The number of unhandled exceptions per second that occurred during the execution of HTTP requests
Total Errors	The total number of errors that occurred during the execution of HTTP requests, including parsing, compilation, or runtime errors
Total Errors/Sec	The number of errors per second that occurred during the execution of HTTP requests, including parsing, compilation, or runtime errors
Request Bytes In Total	The total size of all requests in bytes
Request Bytes Out Total	The total size of responses sent to a client in bytes (not including standard HTTP response headers)
Requests Executing	The number of requests currently executing
Requests Failed Total	The total number of failed requests, including requests that timed out, requests that were not authorized (status code 401), or requests that were not found (404 or 414)
Requests Not Found	The number of requests that failed because resources were not found (status code 404,414)
Requests Not Authorized	The number of requests that failed due to lack of authorization (status code 401)
Requests Succeeded	The number of requests that executed successfully and returned with status code 200
Requests Timed Out	The number of requests that timed out
Requests Total	The total number of requests since the service was started
Requests/Sec	The number of requests executed per second
Sessions Active	The number of currently active sessions
Sessions Abandoned	The number of sessions that have been explicitly abandoned
Sessions Timed Out	The number of sessions that have timed out
Sessions Total	The total number of sessions

Table 28-2 Application Performance Counters

To retrieve an object that represents a particular performance counter, you must supply the performance counter category name, the performance counter name, and the performance counter instance name.

In the following example we modify the ManualDebugHelloVB Web service code to specify which message will be displayed based on the value of a performance monitor counter.

```
<%@ webservice Language="VB" Class="Service1"%>
Imports System
Imports System.Diagnostics
Imports System.Web.Services

Public Class Service1
   Inherits System.Web.Services.WebService

   <WebMethod()> Public Function SayHello(ByVal strName As String) As String
       Dim objCounter as new PerformanceCounter("ASP.NET Applications", _
                               "Requests Total", "__Total__")

       if objCounter.NextValue < 5 then
          Return "Hello, " & strName & _
                 "sigh...you have called me less than 5 times"
       else
          Return "Hello, " & strName & " you just never seem to go away." & _
                 "You have called " & _
                 Convert.ToString( objCounter.NextValue) & " times"
       end if
   End Function
End Class
```

In this example, we declare a performance monitor counter using the PerformanceCounter method of the **System.Diagnostics** namespace. The first parameter that we pass to this method is the performance monitor category we would like to work with. In this case, we specify the ASP.NET Application counters. The second parameter represents a particular performance monitor counter. In this case, we specify the Requests Total performance counter. The last parameter, __Total__, represents the performance counter instance name. Within this code we use the NextValue property on the **PerformanceCounter** object to specify the message to display. This property returns the calculated value of the counter. The Performance-Counter class also includes the following methods:

- **RawValue** Returns the raw value of the performance counter at the time the counter is read.
- **NextSample** Returns a sample of the counter value that you can use when calculating statistics for the counter with the Calculate method of the **CounterSample** class.

Using SOAP Extensions for Debugging

As discussed in Chapter 27, SOAP extensions enable you to capture and manipulate SOAP messages as they are exchanged between the Web service and the client. This capability provides a valuable mechanism for debugging information at the network level. SOAP extensions can be invoked before/after a SOAP request message is deserialized into an object and before/after the response object is turned back into a SOAP message. Each invocation generates an event that allows you to examine the content of messages before they proceed in the call chain.

One difficulty when working with SOAP is viewing the actual SOAP messages being sent and received between the Web service and the client application. To address this problem, you can develop a custom SOAP tracing extension to view the messages' contents and write the SOAP messages to a text file so that their contents can be examined.

In the following exercises you will extend the DebugHelloVB Web service application to take advantage of SOAP trace extensions.

Exercise 28-5: Creating SOAP Extensions In this exercise you will define a class library that implements the SOAP extensions and SOAP attribute. This will allow you to tie the SOAP extensions to Web methods within the Web service.

1. In Visual Studio .NET, create a new class library application by selecting File | New. The New Project dialog box appears.
2. From the New Project dialog box select Visual Basic Projects from the Project Types pane, and then select Class Library from the Templates pane.
3. In the Name field enter **SOAPExtensions** and click OK. The code window for the class opens.
4. Add a reference to the System.Web.Services component by right-clicking References within Solution Explorer. The Add Reference dialog box appears. Select the component and add it to your application.
5. Within the code window, modify your code to match the following lines.

```
Imports System.IO
Imports System.Web.Services.Protocols

<AttributeUsage(AttributeTargets.Method)> _
Public Class TraceExtensionAttribute
    Inherits SoapExtensionAttribute

    Public Overrides ReadOnly Property ExtensionType() As Type
        Get
            Return GetType(TraceExtension)
        End Get
    End Property

    Private _priority As Int32
    Public Overrides Property Priority() As Integer
        Get
            Return _priority
        End Get
```

```
        Set(ByVal Value As Integer)
            _priority = Value
        End Set
    End Property

    Private _traceFilePath As String
    Public Property TraceFilePath() As String
        Get
            Return _traceFilePath
        End Get
        Set(ByVal Value As String)
            _traceFilePath = Value
        End Set
    End Property
End Class

Public Class TraceExtension
    Inherits SoapExtension

    Private _originalStream As Stream
    Private _processStream As Stream
    Private _traceFilePath As String

    Public Overloads Overrides Function GetInitializer(ByVal serviceType _
           As System.Type) As Object
        Return serviceType
    End Function

    Public Overloads Overrides Function GetInitializer(ByVal methodInfo _
           As  LogicalMethodInfo, _
           ByVal attribute As SoapExtensionAttribute) As Object
        Return attribute
    End Function

    Public Overrides Sub Initialize(ByVal initializer As Object)
        _traceFilePath = CType(initializer, TraceExtensionAttribute).TraceFilePath
    End Sub

    Public Overrides Function ChainStream(ByVal stream As Stream) As Stream
        _originalStream = stream
        _processStream = New MemoryStream()
        Return _processStream
    End Function

    Public Overrides Sub ProcessMessage(ByVal message As SoapMessage)
        Select Case message.Stage
            Case SoapMessageStage.BeforeDeserialize
                CopyStream(_originalStream, _processStream)
                WriteStream("Sent to Web service at " & _
                   Now.ToString & vbCrLf)

            Case SoapMessageStage.AfterDeserialize
            Case SoapMessageStage.BeforeSerialize
            Case SoapMessageStage.AfterSerialize

                WriteStream("Returned from Web service at " & _
                    Now.ToString & vbCrLf)

                CopyStream(_processStream, _originalStream)
```

```
        End Select
    End Sub

    Private Sub CopyStream(ByVal _from As Stream, ByVal _to As Stream)
        Dim textR As TextReader = New StreamReader(_from)
        Dim textW As TextWriter = New StreamWriter(_to)
        textW.WriteLine(textR.ReadToEnd())
        textW.Flush()
    End Sub

    Private Sub WriteStream(ByVal _title As String)
        _processStream.Position = 0

        Dim sr As New StreamReader(_processStream)
        Dim sw As New StreamWriter(_traceFilePath, True)
        sw.WriteLine(_title)
        sw.WriteLine(sr.ReadToEnd)
        sw.Close()

        _processStream.Position = 0
    End Sub
End Class
```

In Exercise 28-5, you define two classes: one to define the SOAP extension attribute, and the other to define the SOAP extension. You define the SOAP extension attribute so that you can attach it to a Web method. Within the class definition you define and override several properties. The first property is the ExtensionType property, which returns the SOAP extension class that will actually do the work. This property forms the connection between the custom extension attribute and the custom extension class. The second property that you override is the Priority property. You must override it to properly implement a custom extension attribute. The Priority property determines the order in which multiple SOAP extensions are applied to the same Web service method. Finally, you define a property that lets you send a TraceFilePath argument to the extension attribute when it attaches to a Web method.

The second class that you define is the SOAP extension itself. In the **SOAPExtensions** class you define a number of methods to add custom processing to the class; you also override a number of methods so that you can implement the SOAP extension. Note that the GetInitializer method is overridden twice. The first override applies only if you attach the extension to a Web service using a configuration file (which is not the case here). The second GetInitializer method is passed to the **TraceExtensionAttribute** object that contains the file name that you want to work with. Within this method you simply return the attribute class. The Web services infrastructure will then cache the object and pass it to the Initialize method each time the Web method is called.

As mentioned, the attribute that was returned by GetInitializer is passed into the Initialize method. This method extracts the file name from the object so that it can be used in the ProcessMessage method. You use the ChainStream method to intercept the incoming stream from the Web services infrastructure so that the stream can be manipulated within the SOAP extension.

Finally, the ProcessMessage method is the heart of the SOAP extension. It is the main method that is called as messages are passed to and from the Web service. This method is called four times on a Web server during the process of invoking a Web method. (A proxy version on the client also is called four times, but in reverse order.) Within the Web service, the SOAP request is received and processed as shown here:

- **BeforeDeserialize** Called before any work is done. The SOAP request is passed in as a stream of unprocessed bytes from the client. It is at this stage that the application copies the contents of the original stream into a temporary worker stream for processing and writes the contents of the SOAP stream to a file.
- **AfterDeserialize** Called when the SOAP request has been parsed. At this point the method, arguments, and header are known and available programmatically to the client application. (The example SOAP extension does not do any processing at this point.)
- **BeforeSerialize** Called after the Web method has been executed. At this point any necessary post-processing can be performed. (The example SOAP extension does not do any post-processing on the results of the Web method.)
- **AfterSerialize** Called when the SOAP response has been serialized as a stream and is ready to be sent to the client. (At this point in the example, the contents of the SOAP stream are written to the file, and the processed stream is copied back into the original stream, where the SOAP response message is then sent back to the client.)

Exercise 28-6: Associating SOAP Extensions with a Web Service In this exercise you will associate the SOAP extensions with the Web method that you defined within the **SOAPExtensions** class.

1. Create a new ASP.NET Web service application by selecting File | Add Project | New Project. The New Project dialog box appears.
2. From the New Project dialog box select Visual Basic Projects from the Project Types pane, and then select ASP.NET Web Service from the Templates pane.
3. In the Location field indicate the location of the new Web service as **http://localhost/SOAPExtHelloVB** and click OK. The default designer window for the Web service opens.
4. Within Solution Explorer right-click Service1.asmx and rename it **SoapExtHelloVB.asmx**.
5. Add a reference to the class by right-clicking References within Solution Explorer and selecting Add Reference. The Add Reference dialog box appears. Select the Projects tab and choose the **SOAPExtensions** project. Click OK.
6. Double-click the designer window to open the code module for the Web service. Modify the code to match the following lines.

```
Imports System.Web.Services

<WebService(Namespace:="http://www.catinhat.com/")> _
Public Class Service1
    Inherits System.Web.Services.WebService

    <WebMethod(), _
```

PART VII

```
SOAPExtensions.TraceExtension(TraceFilePath:="c:\SOAPExt\ServerTrace.txt")> _
 Public Function SayHello(ByVal strName As String) As String
   Return "Hello, " & strName
 End Function
End Class
```

Exercise 28-7: Enabling a Client to Interact with the Extension-Enabled Web Service In this exercise you will create a client application that can interact with the Web service that has SOAP extensions attached to it.

1. Create a new console application by selecting File | Add Project | New Project. The New Project dialog box appears.
2. From the New Project Dialog box select Visual Basic Projects from the Project Types pane, and then select Console Application from the Templates pane.
3. In the Name field provide a name for the console application. For this exercise, name the application **SOAPClient**. Click OK. The code window for the console application appears.
4. Add a reference to the Web service by right-clicking References within Solution Explorer and selecting Add Web Reference. The Add Web Reference dialog box appears. Type in the URL to the Web service. In this exercise the URL is **http://localhost/SoapExtHelloVB/SoapExtHelloVB.asmx**.
5. Within the code window for the console application modify the code to match the following lines.

```
Module Module1

    Sub Main()
        Dim ws As New localhost.Service1()
        Dim cnsleString As String

        cnsleString = Console.ReadLine()
        Console.WriteLine(ws.SayHello(cnsleString))
    End Sub
End Module
```

Before building the client application, you must complete two security-related administrative tasks using the Windows NT File System (NTFS). The trace files do not have to exist at runtime, but the path to them does. Therefore you must ensure that the C:\SoapExt path exists and has the proper permissions applied to it. Because the Web server will have to write to the SOAPExt folder, you must add the ASP.NET user account to the folder's access control list (ACL), and then grant Write permissions to the ASP.NET user.

Exercise 28-8: Enabling an ASP.NET User Account to Write to a SOAP Extension Folder In this exercise you will define the necessary file permissions that will allow the Web service to write to a SOAP Extension folder.

1. Open Windows Explorer and create a **SOAPExt** folder in the C root.
2. Right-click the SOAPExt folder and select Properties. Then, select the Security tab.
3. In the Properties dialog box click Add.

4. In the Select Users or Groups dialog box click Advanced.
5. In the dialog box that appears click Find Now. From the list of users, select ASP.NET and click OK. In the first Select Users dialog box click OK.
6. In the Select Users or Groups dialog box click OK.
7. In the Properties dialog box click ASP.NET in the list of users.
8. From the Permissions list check Write, and then click OK.

The ASP.NET user account can now create and write to a text file in the SOAPExt folder.

Deploying a Web Service

To deploy a Web service you must create the directories and files listed in Table 28-3.

Manually creating the required files and directories for a Web service and configuring IIS to support the application is labor-intensive. In addition, it is easy to introduce errors when typing directory names and other information. Fortunately, Visual Studio .NET enables you to deploy Web services automatically using a Web Setup project.

Exercise 28-9: Adding a Web Setup Project In this exercise you will add a Web Setup project to your Web service project.

1. Within Visual Studio .NET select File | Add Project | New Project. The New Project dialog box appears.
2. Within the New Project dialog box select Setup and Deployment Projects from the Project Type pane, and then select Web Setup Project from the Templates pane.
3. In the Name field enter the name of the setup project. For this exercise, name the project **HelloSetup**.
4. Within Solution Explorer right-click the deployment project, click Add, and then click Project Output.
5. In the Add Project Output Group dialog box, select the following:
    - **Primary output** Consists of the project .DLL and its dependencies.

Table 28-3 Required Components for Web Deployment

Item	Description
Web application directory	The <vroot> for a Web service; lists all files that make up a Web service, with the exception of binary components.
WebService.asmx file	Provides the main reference point for a Web service. The file name is used as the endpoint for the URL that is used to reference the service.
WebService.disco file	Optional; allows the Web service to be discovered.
web.config file	Optional; specifies configuration options for the Web service.
\bin directory	Contains binary components for the Web service.

- **Debug symbols** Consist of the project PDB file used for symbol information by the debugger.
- **Content files** Consist of the remaining files for the Web service, such as .asmx, .config, and .disco files.

6. Within Solution Explorer right-click the deployment project and click Build to build the deployment project.

Securing a Web Service

Web services run as a Web application under ASP.NET and therefore participate in the same security model as any ASP.NET application. When a request is made to a Web server, the ASP.NET subsystem performs security services such as authentication and authorization on behalf of the system. Authentication ensures that users are who they say they are. To authenticate a user, the security infrastructure collects the user's credentials, usually in the form of a user ID and password, and then checks the credentials against a credential store, such as Active Directory. If the credentials provided by the user are valid, the user is considered to be an authenticated user.

Once the system authenticates a user and determines that the user's credentials are valid, it checks the user's authorization. Authorization ensures that the authenticated user has sufficient rights to access the requested resource. If a user has sufficient rights, the operation proceeds; otherwise, it fails.

For Web services created using ASP.NET, you can use the authentication and authorization options offered by ASP.NET or develop a custom SOAP-based security infrastructure. This section explores both options.

Authentication

ASP.NET provides several mechanisms for authenticating clients. Each mechanism has validity in different environments and different scenarios. For example, using a Windows-based authentication mechanism for a Web service that is accessible from the Internet is probably not feasible as it would require a Windows account and associated license for every user accessing the service from the Internet. Using Windows-based authentication for a Web service that is used within the corporate intranet, however, is a preferred mechanism for authenticating access. When choosing a mechanism for authentication it is important to understand the requirements of the situation. The following authentication options are available when developing Web services:

- **Integrated Windows authentication** This mechanism enables clients to securely pass a user's credentials over the network. It uses either Windows NT LAN Manager (NTLM) or Kerberos authentication. For users to have one of these protocols, they must be Windows clients. This is the best scheme for intranet environments using Windows, but it is not suitable for Internet use because it works only with Windows clients.

- **Basic authentication** This mechanism does not require users to be Windows clients. Instead of computing a hash of the user's credentials, as in integrated Windows authentication, credential information is encoded using base64 encoding and then transmitted to the server. Most browsers, proxy servers, and Web servers support this method. However, anyone who knows how to decode a base64 string can decode the user's credentials, making this mechanism unsuitable for many security requirements.
- **Basic authentication with SSL** Basic authentication usually is insufficient for most security requirements. However, when combined with Hypertext Transfer Protocol over Secure Sockets Layer (HTTPS), which encrypts all communication between the client and server, basic authentication can be useful. The advantage of this option is that you can easily use it on the Internet without facing any problem from proxy servers.
- **Digest authentication** This new type of authentication is available in Windows 2000 domains, and is only supported in Internet Explorer 5.0 or later. Instead of user credentials being sent over the network in the form of text, they are encrypted using a hashing mechanism called Message Digest (5). This option is good for Internet-based Web services, but the server and client requirements limit its adoptability.
- **Certificate-based authentication** This type of authentication uses digital certificates. Server certificates ensure that the identity of the server is valid. Similarly client certificates ensure that the identity of the client is valid. When invoking a Web service using this method, a client must present a valid client certificate to the Web server. The Web server uses the client certificate to authenticate the client's identity.

Regardless of which Windows authentication option you use, setting up the Web service and Web service client are similar. You do not have to add code to the Web service to use Windows authentication, as the authentication options are set in a configuration file and in IIS.

Configuring IIS Security

Before you can use Windows authentication, you must configure Internet Information Server (IIS). When a user requests a page that requires authorization, the user must be authenticated through IIS. IIS 5.0, included with Windows 2000, supports the following authentication methods:

- **Basic authentication** Compatible with all browsers, firewalls, and proxy servers. However, user names and passwords are transmitted across the network in plain text.
- **Integrated Windows authentication** Compatible with Internet Explorer. User names and passwords are not transmitted across the network in plain text. This form of authentication is not compatible with all firewalls and proxy servers.

- **Digest authentication** Compatible with Internet Explorer. User names and passwords are not transmitted across the network in plain text. This form of authentication is compatible with all firewalls and proxy servers. However, it requires you to save Windows user names and passwords in a plain text file on the domain server.

Typically, you enable either basic authentication or integrated Windows authentication. If your application must be compatible with Netscape browsers, you have no choice but to use basic authentication. If you can mandate that all users use Internet Explorer and you are not using a firewall or proxy server, you can use Windows authentication.

To enable basic or integrated Windows authentication for a directory or file, complete the following steps:

1. Start Internet Services Manager from the Administrative Tools menu.
2. Open the property sheet for a directory or file.
3. Choose the Directory Security or File Security tab.
4. In the section labeled Anonymous Access and Authentication, click Edit.
5. Enable one or more authentication mechanisms.

After you enable an authentication mechanism, you can use either of two methods to force users to log on to your Web site through IIS. You can disable anonymous access to the Web server, or you can disallow anonymous access by modifying the NTFS permissions on a file or directory. To disable anonymous access on the Web server, complete the preceding steps but remove the check mark from the Anonymous Access option.

By default, files in the wwwroot directory can be accessed by members of three groups: the System group, the Administrators group, and the Everyone group. The IUSER_machinename account that is created as part of IIS installation is a member of the Everyone group. Because the IUSER_machinename account represents every anonymous user who accesses your Web site through IIS, all anonymous users can access files in the wwwroot directory by default.

If you remove the Everyone group from any directory in the Web site, anonymous users can no longer access the files in the directory.

To remove the Everyone group from a directory, complete the following steps:

1. In Internet Explorer right-click the directory you want to modify.
2. Choose the Security tab.
3. Select Everyone.
4. Click Remove.

Once you prevent anonymous users from accessing files in a directory, if a request for a file in the directory comes in, a dialog box appears forcing the user to log on with an account that has access to the directory, such as the Administrator user account. To enable an authorized user or group to access a directory or file in the Web site, simply add the user or group by using the Security tab associated with the file or directory.

Configuring a Client

To pass the client credentials to the Web service, you must add code to the Web service client.

Exercise 28-10: Configuring a Web Service To Use Windows Authentication In this exercise you will configure the ManualDebugHelloVB Web service to use Windows authentication.

1. Modify the web.config file for the ManualDebugHelloVB Web service to include an authentication element, as shown in the following code.

```
<?xml version="1.0" encoding="utf-8" ?>
<configuration>
  <system.web>
    <compilation debug="true" />
    <trace enabled="true" requestLimit="50" pageOutput="true"
           localOnly="false"/>
    <authentication mode="Windows" />
  </system.web>
</configuration>
```

2. In Visual Studio .NET open the client code for the Web service and modify the code as shown in the following lines.

```
Imports System
Imports System.Net
Imports System.Diagnostics
Module Module1

    Sub Main()
        Dim ws As New localhost.Service1()
        Dim objCredentialCache As CredentialCache
        Dim objCredentials As NetworkCredential
        Dim cnsleString As String

        objCredentialCache = New CredentialCache()
        objCredentials = New NetworkCredential("username", "password", "domain")
        objCredentialCache.Add(New Uri(ws.Url), "Basic", objCredentials)
        ws.Credentials = objCredentialCache
        cnsleString = Console.ReadLine()
        Console.WriteLine(ws.SayHello(cnsleString))
    End Sub
End Module
```

In this example you use the **NetworkCredential** class to set the user name and password that will be used to authenticate to the Web service. The resulting **NetworkCredential** object is cached using the **CredentialCache** class, and the object is assigned to the Credentials property of the Web service proxy object. These credentials are passed to the Web service upon each call.

Role-Based Authentication

If you have ever managed a large-scale e-mail system and imposed limits on the size of mailboxes, you may have had users that exceeded their mailbox limits. Depending on the role of the user, this may or may not have been allowed. If the user was the president of the company, his or her role may have provided the privilege of exceeding the limits.

A role can be thought of as a group that contains users or principals that all have the same privileges. For example, a teller or manager role could include multiple people or principals. Applications use role membership to determine whether a user is authorized to perform a requested action. Within Visual Basic .NET the **Principal** and **Identity** objects provide the basis for role-based authentication.

Principals and Identities

To represent a user, the system uses the **Principal** object and the **Identity** object. A **Principal** object is constructed from an associated **Identity** object. It represents the identity and role of a user, as well as the security context under which code runs. Developers can use this object to enable authorization decisions based on the principal's identity or role membership, or both. The .NET Framework includes the following types of **Principal** objects:

- Generic principals represent users and roles that exist outside of Windows NT and Windows 2000. Use this principal when you have your own user/role database. To populate the **GenericPrincipal** object, use the OnAuthenticate event.
- Windows principals represent Windows users, their roles, or their Windows NT and Windows 2000 groups. A Windows principal can impersonate another user, which means that the principal can access a resource on another user's behalf while presenting the identity that belongs to that user. This object is automatically created when you use integrated Windows authentication in IIS. It allows you to check the Windows group membership of a Windows user account and restrict access accordingly.
- Custom principals can be defined in any way that is needed for a particular application.

Using **Principal** objects, you can discover the identity or the role of users as well as the security context in which they are allowed to use the system.

The **Identity** object for an individual contains information about the user being validated. At the most basic level, **Identity** objects contain a name and an authentication type (NTLM, Kerberos, Passport, and so on). The .NET Framework defines the following identities. These match up closely and are used in conjunction with the **Principal** objects.

- Generic identities represent users that exist outside of Windows NT and Windows 2000.
- Windows identities encapsulate information about Windows accounts. Use the **WindowsIdentity** object to make authorization decisions based on a user's Windows account.
- Custom identities are defined by specifying your own **Identity** class, which encapsulates custom user information that a generic identity does not provide. The custom identity can then be used in any way that is needed for the particular application.

Code developed using Visual Basic .NET can discover the identity or the role of a principal through the **Principal** object, which contains a reference to the **Identity** object. You can think of these two objects much like you would think of user and group accounts. In most network environments, user accounts represent people or programs, while group accounts represent specific combinations of users and the rights they possess. In the .NET world, **Identity** objects represent users, while roles represent memberships and the security context of the user. Applications developed using Visual Basic .NET grant rights to the principal based on the identity of users or, more commonly, their roles.

The PrincipalPermission Object

Once you have defined **Identity** and **Principal** objects, your application can perform security checks against them to determine whether a particular **Principal** object is a member of a role or has a known identity. To enable this check, you must create a security demand for a **PrincipalPermission** object.

The **PrincipalPermission** object is used by the application to demand that the identity and roles of the active user or principal match the identity and roles defined within the **PrincipalPermission** object. During a security check, the common language runtime examines the caller's **Principal** object to determine whether its identity and role match those represented by the **PrincipalPermission** object being demanded. If the Principal object does not match, a SecurityException is thrown indicating that the user does not have permission to make the request. In addition, the code can perform basic operations against the current permissions using the Union and Intersect methods of the **PrincipalPermission** object.

In the following example we create two different administrative users: Sylvain and Annie. We combine the two using the Union method of the **PrincipalPermission** object. Then, we demand that the user or principal have the permissions specified by the **PrincipalPermission** object. In this particular case, the demand will succeed only if the current user is either Sylvain in the role of Supervisor, or Annie in the role of Manager.

```
Dim strUser1 As String = "Sylvain"
Dim strRole1 As String = "Supervisor"
Dim PrincipalPerm1 As New PrincipalPermission(strUser1, strRole1)

Dim strUser2 As String = "Annie"
Dim strRole2 As String = "Manager"
Dim PrincipalPerm2 As New PrincipalPermission(strUser2, strRole2)

PrincipalPerm1 = PrincipalPerm1.Union(PrincipalPerm2)
PrincipalPerm1.Demand()
```

The following example provides an overview of the **Principal**, **Identity**, and **PrincipalPermission** objects. In the example we prompt the user for a user name and password. If the user name and password are matched, the application creates the Principal and Identity objects needed to access the Privatedata method, and the message "You have accessed this procedure" is displayed in the console. If the proper credentials are not supplied, an exception is thrown when the Privatedata method is called.

```
Imports System
Imports System.Security.Permissions
Imports System.Security.Principal
Imports System.Threading
Imports Microsoft.VisualBasic

Module Module1
    Public Sub Main()
        Dim objIdentity As New GenericIdentity("User")
        Dim arrUserRoles As String() = {"Administrator", "User"}
        Dim objPrincipal As New GenericPrincipal(objIdentity, arrUserRoles)
        Dim strUsername As String
        Dim strPassword As String

        Console.Write("Username:")
        strUsername = Console.ReadLine()
        Console.Write(ControlChars.CrLf & "Password:")
        strPassword = Console.ReadLine()

        If strPassword.Equals("password") And strUsername.Equals("username") Then
            Thread.CurrentPrincipal = objPrincipal
        End If
        Privatedata()

    End Sub

    'The protected method.
    Public Sub Privatedata()
        Dim MyPermission As New PrincipalPermission("User", "Administrator")

        MyPermission.Demand()
        Console.WriteLine(ControlChars.CrLf & "You have accessed this procedure")
    End Sub
End Module
```

IsInRole

Creating a **PrincipalPermission** object can incur additional overhead because you have to allocate it. Instead of using the **PrincipalPermission** object, you may want to consider using the IsInRole method of the **Principal** object. Using the IsInRole method you can determine whether the current principal belongs to a particular user group. Using the IsInRole method with a **WindowsPrincipal** object has the added advantage of allowing you to check for membership in Windows Groups in addition to checking role membership.

In the following example we create a Visual Basic .NET console application and modify the code. We create a **WindowsPrincipal** object and then use it to determine whether the user running the application is a member of the Administrators group. If so, a message is written to the console to indicate that the user is a member. If not, a message indicates this fact.

```
Imports System
Imports System.Threading
Imports System.Security.Principal
Imports Microsoft.VisualBasic

Module Module1
```

```
    Public Sub Main()
        Dim objIdentity As WindowsIdentity = WindowsIdentity.GetCurrent()
        Dim objPrincipal As New WindowsPrincipal(objIdentity)

        If objPrincipal.IsInRole("Administrators") Then
            Console.WriteLine("The user is a member of the Administrators Group")
        Else
            Console.WriteLine("The user is not a member of the Administrators _
                               Group")
        End If
    End Sub

End Module
```

Passport Authentication

Microsoft Passport is a centralized authentication service that offers single logon (single signon) capabilities and core profile services for member sites. Users who log on to a Web site that has enabled Passport authentication are automatically redirected to the Passport Web site where they are authenticated and then returned to the original site.

Passport authentication has advantages over Windows authentication. First and most important, users can use the same user name and password that they currently use at other Web sites. Therefore, they are less likely to forget passwords. This also centralizes information, allowing registration to be more easily updated. Second, when using Passport authentication, you don't have to set up and maintain a database to store identity information. Microsoft does all the work in the background.

Passport authentication provides options to customize the appearance of the Registration and Sign In pages using templates.

Enabling Passport Authentication

To use Microsoft Passport, you must pay an initial subscription fee and download and install the Microsoft Passport Software Development Kit (SDK) from www.passport.com/business. The Passport SDK contains the Passport Manager, the Passport Manager Administrator utility, and a sample site that implements Passport authentication.

After you download and install the SDK, you can create a site in test mode. Certain features of Passport do not work in test mode, however. For example, you cannot read all the information from a user's profile, nor can you customize the appearance of the Sign In or Registration pages. The sign out process doesn't work either. To use these features you must enter production mode. To enter production mode, you must register to become a Passport participant site. After you register and sign the necessary agreements, you are issued a Site ID and an encryption key.

After you download and install Microsoft Passport, you enable Passport authentication for an application by creating a web.config file in the root directory. The following web.config file contains the necessary authentication section to enable Passport authentication.

```
<configuration>
   <system.web>
      <authentication mode="Passport">
      <passport redirectUrl="login.aspx" />
   </system.web>
</configuration>
```

This file sets the application's authentication mode to use Passport authentication. It also sets the value of the redirectUrl attribute. If a user is not authenticated and requests a page in a directory that requires authentication, the user is redirected to the page specified by the RedirectUrl attribute.

Allowing Users To Sign In and Sign Out

To use Passport authentication within an application, you must use the Logo2Tag method of the **PassportIdentity** object. This method automatically displays a Sign In button and a Sign Out button on the Web page. In the following example we use the LogoTag2 method to display a Sign In button at the top of the page.

```
<Script Runat="Server">
Sub Page_Load
   Dim objPassportID as PassportIdentity

   objPassportID = user.identity
   if objPassportID.GetFromNetworkServer then
      response.redirect(request.path)
   End if
   plhPassport.controls.add(New LiteralControl(objPassportID.LogoTag2()))
End sub
</script>

<html>
<head><title>Default.aspx</title></head>
<body>

<asp:PlaceHolder
   ID="plhPassport"
   runat="server" />
<hr>
<h2>Welcome to our Web site</h2>
</body>
</html>
```

In this example, we use the Page_load routine to create the **PassportIdentity** object. This object is then used to call the LogoTag2 method to retrieve the HTML tag for a Sign In button, which is displayed at the top-left corner of the page. After the user signs in, the LogoTag2 method displays a Sign Out button instead of the Sign In button.

Custom Authorization

If you are building an application that includes calls to a Web service, you must be sure that you have appropriate credentials before making the call, or the call will fail. At runtime, you can pass credentials to the Web service by setting the Credentials property of the client-side object representing the Web service. Because other ASP.NET security options might not be sufficiently flexible, Web services can implement a custom authentication solution in which credential information is passed in SOAP headers. In this solution, credentials are passed in an optional part of the message exchanged between client and server. You can then write a custom HttpModule (implementing the IHttpModule interface) that listens for the information in the header and calls your authentication code.

Another common way of doing this is to use the SoapHeader attribute to pass the user-defined **DW** authentication object.

Summary

To ensure that Web services function properly once deployed, developers perform unit testing during the quality control process. Unit testing includes black-box testing, white-box testing, and use-case analysis.

Debugging is another important task. The .NET Framework provides easy-to-use facilities for debugging applications. You can attach a debugger to a Web service and invoke it to debug Web services interactively. You can also configure debugging for a Web service manually, using the web.config file.

Special debugging tools allow you to monitor or measure a Web service's performance and diagnose errors. Tools include tracing, event logging, and performance monitoring. You use tracing to review information that is generated by the system. You use event logging to generate messages from the application to an event log. You use performance counters to monitor the performance of the application and to make decisions based on the values returned by the counters. SOAP extensions enable you to trace what is happening within the messages that are being passed back and forth between a client and the server.

To deploy a Web service, you can deploy the service manually or you can build a custom setup application that installs the Web service for you. To ensure that only users with valid identification and appropriate permissions access a Web service, you must implement security in the application. The .NET Framework provides a number of mechanisms for authenticating Web service clients and allows you to easily configure security and authentication.

Test Questions

1. Which of the following mechanisms is not a valid authentication mechanism for Web services?

   A. Integrated Windows authentication

   B. Basic authentication

   C. SQL Server native authentication

   D. Certificate authentication

2. Which of the following files/directories are optional when deploying a Web service?
   A. Web.config
   B. .disco file
   C. vroot directory
   D. \bin directory
3. You want to encrypt a SOAP message so that it is secure as it travels over the network. Which phase would you do this in?
   A. AfterSerialize
   B. BeforeSerialize
   C. AfterDeserialize
   D. BeforeDeserialize

Test Answers

1. C.
2. A, B.
3. A.

PART VIII

Advanced .NET Programming

CHAPTER 29

File and Data Streams

In this chapter, you will

- Learn how to manage directories and files including creating, deleting, and accessing their property information
- Understand how to read and write files as streams of data both synchronously and asynchronously
- Learn how to access file data at the binary level
- See how to monitor the file system and respond to basic system events

It is very important that an application be able to manipulate files on the local file system. However, enabling this capability often presents problems for new Visual Basic developers. The good news is that the Visual Basic .NET Framework provides tools and techniques to make this task easier and more straightforward than ever before.

This chapter covers the basics of file and data streams, including both asynchronous and synchronous reads and writes. It also covers the access of file data at the binary level.

Manipulating Files and Directories

Because all the Visual Basic .NET applications that you compose contain information that is stored in files in some manner, all your applications must interact with the file system at some level. In fact, many of the applications you compose require you to read, write, or manipulate files and directories. The .NET Framework **System.IO** namespace provides a rich set of tools to write effective file I/O code as efficiently as possible.

The System.IO Namespace

The **System.IO** namespace encapsulates functionality related to both synchronous and asynchronous reads and writes to files and streams. Table 29-1 describes the key classes contained in the namespace. You typically use these classes when implementing features based on directories, files, and streams.

As shown in Table 29-1, to access directories and files using the .NET Framework Class Library, you use two primary classes: **DirectoryInfo** and **FileInfo**. These classes provide most of the file system functionality and information that an application needs.

Table 29-1 Key Classes for File and Data Streams

Class	Description
Directory	Creates, moves, and enumerates directories and subdirectories; uses static methods and requires a security check for each call
DirectoryInfo	References a specific directory; a security check is performed only when the instance is created
Path	Processes directory strings across platforms
File	Creates, copies, deletes, moves, and opens files; its methods are static and therefore perform a security check on every call
FileInfo	References a specific file; a security check is performed only when the instance is created
FileStream	Creates a stream instance based on a file
StreamReader	Implements a **TextReader** object that reads characters from a byte stream in a particular encoding
StreamWriter	Implements a **TextWriter** object for writing characters to a stream in a particular encoding
StringReader	Implements a **TextReader** object that reads from a string
StringWriter	Implements a **TextWriter** object that writes information to a string; the information is stored in an underlying **StringBuilder** class (from the **System.Text** namespace)
BinaryReader	Accesses file data at the binary level
BinaryWriter	Writes binary data to files
FileSystemWatcher	Listens to the file system change notifications and intercept events when a directory or file changes

Using the Classes of the System.IO Namespace

The **DirectoryInfo** and **Directory** classes create, move, and enumerate through directories and subdirectories. The **Directory** class contains the associated static methods, whereas **DirectoryInfo** contains the instance methods.

An instance of the **DirectoryInfo** class represents one physical directory. With it, you call the GetDirectories method to return a list of the directory's subdirectories. You can also return a list of files in the directory with the GetFiles method. Of course, there are a number of important properties and methods within the **DirectoryInfo** class. Tables 29-2 and 29-3 describe these properties and methods.

Property	Description
Attributes	Gets or sets the FileAttributes of the current **FileSystemInfo** object
CreationTime	Gets or sets the creation time of the current **FileSystemInfo** object
Exists	Overridden; gets a value indicating whether the directory exists
Extension	Gets the string representing the file extension
FullName	Gets the full path of the directory or file
LastAccessTime	Gets or sets the time the current file or directory was last accessed
LastWriteTime	Gets or sets the time the current file or directory was last written to
Name	Overridden; gets the name of the DirectoryInfo instance
Parent	Gets the parent directory of a specified subdirectory
Root	Gets the root portion of a path

Table 29-2 Properties of the DirectoryInfo Class

Method	Description
Create	Creates a directory
CreateObjRef	Creates an object that contains all the information required to generate a proxy used to communicate with a remote object
CreateSubdirectory	Creates a subdirectory or subdirectories on the specified path
Delete	Overloaded and overridden; deletes the **DirectoryInfo** class and its contents from a path
Equals	Overloaded; determines whether two object instances are equal
GetDirectories	Overloaded; returns the subdirectories of the current directory.
GetFiles	Overloaded; returns a file list from the current directory
GetFileSystemInfo	Overloaded; retrieves an array of strongly typed **FileSystemInfo** objects
GetHashCode	Serves as a hash function for a particular type; suitable for use in hashing algorithms and data structures like a hash table
GetLifetimeService	Retrieves the current lifetime service object that controls the lifetime policy for the instance
GetType	Gets the type of the current instance
InitializeLifetimeService	Obtains a lifetime service object to control the lifetime policy for the instance
MoveTo	Moves a **DirectoryInfo** instance and its contents to a new path
Refresh	Refreshes the state of the object
ToString	Overridden; returns the original path that was passed by the user

Table 29-3 Methods of the DirectoryInfo Class

As shown in the preceding tables, the **DirectoryInfo** class provides many useful properties and methods. In the following example, the GetDirectories method is used to print a listing of directories from the underlying file system.

```
Imports System
Imports System.IO


Public Class myGetDirectoriesTest

    Public Shared Sub Main()
        Dim mySampleDirectoryInfo As _
            New DirectoryInfo("c:\")
        Dim mySampleDInfoArray As _
            DirectoryInfo() = di.GetDirectories()
        Dim myDirectoryInfo As DirectoryInfo
        For Each myDirectoryInfo In mySampleDInfoArray
            Console.WriteLine(myDirectoryInfo.Name)
        Next myDirectoryInfo
    End Sub 'Main
End Class myGetDirectoriesTest
```

The **FileInfo** and **File** classes create, copy, delete, move, and open files. The **File** class contains the associated static methods, whereas **FileInfo** contains the instance methods. Using an instance of the **FileInfo** class, you return specific attributes of a given file. For example, you can read the file's name, size, and parent directory. The content of a file is accessed using the **FileStream** object. The **FileStream** class allows both synchronous and asynchronous read and writes to a file. Tables 29-4 and 29-5 describe properties and methods of the **FileInfo** class.

Table 29-4 Properties of the FileInfo Class

Property	Description
Attributes	Gets or sets the file attributes of the current **FileSystemInfo** object
CreationTime	Gets or sets the creation time of the current **FileSystemInfo** object
Directory	Gets an instance of the parent directory
DirectoryName	Gets a string representing the directory's full path
Exists	Overridden; gets a value indicating whether a file exists
Extension	Gets the string representing the file extension
FullName	Gets the full path of the directory or file
LastAccessTime	Gets or sets the time the current file or directory was last accessed
LastWriteTime	Gets or sets the time the current file or directory was last written to
Length	Gets the size of the current file or directory
Name	Overridden; gets the name of the file

Table 29-5 Methods of the FileInfo Class

Method	Description
AppendText	Creates a **StreamWriter** that appends text to the file represented by the instance of the **FileInfo** object
CopyTo	Overloaded; copies an existing file to a new file
Create	Creates a file
CreateObjRef	Creates an object that contains all the information required to generate a proxy used to communicate with a remote object
CreateText	Creates a **StreamWriter** that writes a new text file
Delete	Overridden; permanently deletes a file
Equals	Overloaded; determines whether two object instances are equal
GetHashCode	Serves as a hash function for a particular type; suitable for use in hashing algorithms and data structures like a hash table
GetLifetimeService	Retrieves the current lifetime service object that controls the lifetime policy for the instance
GetType	Gets the type of the current instance
InitializeLifetimeService	Obtains a lifetime service object to control the lifetime policy for the instance
MoveTo	Moves a specified file to a new location, providing the option to specify a new file name
Open	Overloaded; opens a file with various read/write and sharing privileges
OpenRead	Creates a read-only FileStream
OpenText	Creates a **StreamReader** with UTF8 encoding that reads from an existing text file
OpenWrite	Creates a write-only FileStream
Refresh	Refreshes the state of the object
ToString	Overridden; returns the fully qualified path as a string

The addition of the **FileInfo** class to the .NET Framework enables developers to easily create files and write to files. In addition, the properties of the **FileInfo** object make it very simple to obtain information regarding files, as shown in the following example.

```
Dim myFileInfo As New FileInfo("myFile")
Dim s As StreamWriter = fileInfo.CreateText()
s.WriteLine("Sample output to the file")
s.Close()
myFileInfo.Refresh()
Console.WriteLine("File '{0}' now has size {1} bytes", _
      myFileInfo.Name, myFileInfo.Length)
```

The **System.IO** namespace contains classes that allow you to access data streams and files both synchronously and asynchronously. Understand that file and data streams are essentially the same thing. Each is a type of stream with the main difference being their backing store. The backing store is the storage medium, such as a disk, tape, memory, or network. Every backing store implements its own stream type as a version of the **Stream** class. This allows each stream type to read and write bytes to and from its own backing store. These streams that connect directly to backing stores are called base streams in Visual Basic .NET. An example of a base stream is the **FileStream** class, which lets you access files stored on disk inside of directories.

The **FileInfo** class makes extensive use of the **FileStream**, **StreamWriter**, and **StreamReader** classes, which expose the necessary functionality to read and write to files in Visual Basic .NET. These objects are designed to work with persisted text files. They are based on the **TextWriter** and **TextReader** classes.

You create the **FileStream** class explicitly. The code examples that follow demonstrate the different types of FileStream constructors you can use to create **FileStream** objects for different purposes.

You use the following constructor when you have a valid file pointer and need to specify the read/write permissions. In this sample, handle is a valid handle to a file, and access is a member of the FileAccess enumeration (Read, ReadWrite, and Write).

```
New FileStream (ByVal handle as _
      IntPtr, ByVal access as FileAccess)
```

You use the following constructor when you know the file's path and want to specify how the file is opened. In this sample, path is a valid path to the file that the **FileStream** object represents, and mode is a member of the FileMode enumeration (Append, Create, CreateNew, Open, OpenOrCreate, or Truncate) that specifies how the file should be opened.

```
New FileStream (ByVal path as String, _
      ByVal mode as FileMode)
```

You use the following constructor when you have a valid file pointer, need to specify the read/write permissions, and want to own (or disown) the file's handle. If the **FileStream** object owns the file's handle, a call to the Close method also closes the file's handle and thus decrements its handle count by one. In this sample code, ownsHandle indicates whether the file's handle is owned by the given instance of the **FileStream** object.

```
New FileStream (ByVal handle as IntPtr, _
      ByVal access as FileAccess,  _
      ByVal ownsHandle as Boolean)
```

You use the following constructor when you know the file's path, want to specify how the file is opened, and need to specify the read/write permissions on the file. In this sample code, access is a member of the FileAccess enumeration (Read, ReadWrite, or Write).

```
New FileStream (ByVal path as String, _
      ByVal mode as FileMode, _
      ByVal access as FileAccess)
```

You use the following constructor when you have a valid file pointer, need to specify the read/write permissions, want to own the file's handle, and need to set the stream's buffer size. In this sample code, bufferSize indicates the size of the buffer in bytes.

```
New FileStream (ByVal handle as IntPtr, _
      ByVal access as FileAccess, _
      ByVal ownsHandle as Boolean, _
      ByVal bufferSize as Integer)
```

You use the following constructor when you know the file's path, want to specify how the file is opened, and need to specify the read/write permissions on the file. In this sample code, share is a member of the FileShare enumeration that indicates how the file is shared. FileShare controls how other **FileStream** objects access the same file. Values include Inheritable, None, Read, ReadWrite, and Write.

```
New FileStream (ByVal path as String, _
      ByVal mode as FileMode, _
      ByVal access as FileAccess, _
      ByVal share as FileShare)
```

You use the following constructor when you have a valid file pointer, need to specify the read/write permissions, want to own the file's handle, need to set the buffer size, and want to indicate that the file should be opened asynchronously. In this sample code, isAsync indicates whether the file should be opened asynchronously.

```
New FileStream (ByVal handle as IntPtr, _
      ByVal access as FileAccess, _
      ByVal ownsHandle as Boolean, _
      ByVal bufferSize as Integer, _
      ByVal isAsync as Boolean)
```

You use the following constructor when you know the file's path, want to specify how the file is opened, need to specify the read/write permissions on the file, and need to set the stream's buffer size.

```
New FileStream (ByVal path as String, _
      ByVal mode as FileMode, _
      ByVal access as FileAccess, _
      ByVal share as FileShare, _
      ByVal bufferSize as Integer)
```

Finally, you use the following constructor when you know the file's path, want to specify how the file is opened, need to specify the read/write permissions on the file, need to set the stream's buffer size, and need to indicate whether the file is being opened for asynchronous read/write.

```
New FileStream (ByVal path as String, _
      ByVal mode as FileMode, _
      ByVal access as FileAccess, _
      ByVal share as FileShare, _
      ByVal bufferSize as Integer, _
      ByVal useAsynch as Boolean)
```

Reading and Writing Asynchronously

As stated earlier, streaming with the Visual Basic .NET Framework classes can be accomplished both synchronously and asynchronously. Synchronous reading and writing prevent methods from continuing until the operation is complete.

For more efficient use of resources, you typically read data asynchronously. This way, once you execute the BeginRead method, you can continue executing other program logic.

With asynchronous file I/O, the main thread of the application continues to execute code while the I/O process finishes. In fact, multiple asynchronous IO requests can process simultaneously. Generally, an asynchronous design offers an application better performance, yet there is a downside. Coding this way requires greater effort on your part.

To master reading and writing asynchronously, you must be comfortable with the properties and methods of the **FileStream** class. Tables 29-6 and 29-7 describe these properties and methods.

Notice that the **FileStream** class provides the BeginRead method for asynchronous file input and the BeginWrite method for asynchronous file output. Simply pass the name of the method you want to have called when the operation is complete (userCallback as AsynchCallback), as shown in the following example.

```
New AsyncCallback(AddressOf myCallbackMethod)
```

Note that myCallbackMethod is the name of the method that intercepts and processes the completed operation notification. From within this callback method, you call EndRead or EndWrite, as needed. These methods end their respective operation. EndRead returns the number of bytes that were read during the operation. Both methods take a reference to the pending asynchronous I/O operation (AsynchResult as IAsynchResult). This object returns your custom callback method as a parameter.

Table 29-6 Properties of the FileStream Class

Property	Description
CanRead	Overridden; gets a value indicating whether the current stream supports reading
CanSeek	Overridden; gets a value indicating whether the current stream supports seeking
CanWrite	Overridden; gets a value indicating whether the current stream supports writing
Handle	Gets the operating system file handle for the file that the current **FileStream** object encapsulates
IsAsync	Gets a value indicating whether the FileStream was opened asynchronously or synchronously
Length	Overridden; gets the length in bytes of the stream
Name	Gets the name of the FileStream that was passed to the constructor
Position	Overridden; gets or sets the current position of the stream

Table 29-7 Methods of the FileStream Class

Method	Description
BeginRead	Overridden; begins an asynchronous read
BeginWrite	Overridden; begins an asynchronous write
Close	Overridden; closes the file and releases any resources associated with the current file stream
CreateObjRef	Creates an object that contains all the information required to generate a proxy used to communicate with a remote object
EndRead	Overridden; waits for the pending asynchronous read to complete
EndWrite	Overridden; ends an asynchronous write, blocking until the I/O operation has completed
Equals	Overloaded; determines whether two object instances are equal
Flush	Overridden; clears all buffers for the stream and causes any buffered data to be written to the underlying device
GetHashCode	Serves as a hash function for a particular type; suitable for use in hashing algorithms and data structures like a hash table
GetLifetimeService	Retrieves the current lifetime service object that controls the lifetime policy for the instance
GetType	Gets the type of the current instance
InitializeLifetimeService	Obtains a lifetime service object to control the lifetime policy for the instance
Lock	Prevents access by other processes to all or part of a file.
Read	Overridden; reads a block of bytes from the stream and writes the data in a given buffer
ReadByte	Overridden; reads a byte from the file and advances the read position one byte
Seek	Overridden; sets the current position of the stream to the given value
SetLength	Overridden; sets the length of the stream to the given value
ToString	Returns a string that represents the current object
Unlock	Allows access by other processes to all or part of a file that was previously locked
Write	Overridden; writes a block of bytes to the stream using data from a buffer
WriteByte	Overridden; writes a byte to the current position in the file stream

Binary Reading and Writing

Although you usually have to write and read from text files, you occasionally might have to code using files of a proprietary type. To read and write to proprietary files, you access them at the binary level. Suppose, for example, that you need to accept an Excel file streaming across the network. Chances are you will want to persist it to disk using a binary reader and writer. Or suppose you want to read image files and store them in your database. Again, a binary reader will make this operation go smoothly.

You have a number of options for file I/O at the binary level. Typically, you use the **BinaryReader**, **BinaryWriter**, and **FileStream** classes. **BinaryReader** and **BinaryWriter** are similar to **StreamReader** and **StreamWriter**. Like these classes, **BinaryReader** and **BinaryWriter** take an instance of a valid **Stream** object as a parameter of their constructor. The **Stream** object represents the backing store that is being read from or written to.

The **BinaryReader** class provides a number of read methods that allow developers to access primitive data types from file streams. Table 29-8 describes the methods of the **BinaryReader** class.

Each of the Read methods in Table 29-8 returns the given data from the stream and advances the current position in the stream ahead of the returned data. Typically, developers use the ReadByte method most often. This method returns one byte of data from the stream and advances the current stream position to the next byte. When the end of the stream is reached, the exception, EndOfStreamException, is thrown by the method.

Method	Description
Close	Closes the current reader and the underlying stream
Equals	Overloaded; determines whether two object instances are equal
GetHashCode	Serves as a hash function for a particular type; suitable for use in hashing algorithms and data structures like a hash table
GetType	Gets the type of the current instance
PeekChar	Returns the next available character and does not advance the byte or character position
Read	Overloaded; reads characters from the underlying stream and advances the current position of the stream
ReadBoolean	Reads a Boolean from the current stream and advances the current position of the stream by one byte
ReadByte	Reads the next byte from the current stream and advances the current position of the stream by one byte
ReadBytes	Reads count bytes from the current stream into a byte array and advances the current position by the number of count bytes
ReadChar	Reads the next character from the current stream and advances the current position of the stream in accordance with the encoding used and the specific character being read from the stream
ReadChars	Reads count characters from the current stream, returns the data in a character array, and advances the current position in accordance with the encoding used and the specific character being read from the stream

Table 29-8 Methods of the BinaryReader Class

Method	Description
ReadDecimal	Reads a decimal value from the current stream and advances the current position of the stream by sixteen bytes
ReadDouble	Reads an eight-byte floating-point value from the current stream and advances the current position of the stream by eight bytes
ReadInt16	Reads a two-byte signed integer from the current stream and advances the current position of the stream by two bytes
ReadInt32	Reads a four-byte signed integer from the current stream and advances the current position of the stream by four bytes
ReadInt64	Reads an eight-byte signed integer from the current stream and advances the current position of the stream by four bytes
ReadSByte	Reads a signed byte from the stream and advances the current position of the stream by one byte
ReadSingle	Reads a four-byte floating point value from the current stream and advances the current position of the stream by four bytes
ReadString	Reads a string from the current stream; the string is prefixed with the length, encoded as an integer seven bits at a time
ReadUInt16	Reads a two-byte unsigned integer from the current stream using little endian encoding and advances the position of the stream by two bytes
ReadUInt32	Reads a four-byte unsigned integer from the current stream and advances the position of the stream by four bytes
ReadUInt64	Reads an eight-byte unsigned integer from the current stream and advances the position of the stream by eight bytes
ToString	Returns a string that represents the current object

Table 29-8 Methods of the BinaryReader Class *(continued)*

Once you master the **BinaryReader** class, **BinaryWriter** is simple. This class provides a number of write methods for writing primitive data to a stream. Unlike **BinaryReader**, **BinaryWriter** exposes only one method, WriteByte, for executing binary writes. This method presents overloads, allowing you to specify whether you are writing byte, string, decimal, and so on. Calls to WriteByte write out the given data to the stream and advance its current position by the length of the data.

The **FileStream** class also exposes the basic binary methods, ReadByte and WriteByte. ReadByte and WriteByte behave in the same manner as BinaryReader.ReadByte and BinaryWriter.WriteByte.

TIP Consider using the **FileStream** class for all basic implementations.

Monitoring the File System

In addition to creating files and directories, and reporting information regarding these objects, the Visual Basic .NET Framework makes it very simple to monitor the file system. The **FileSystemWatcher** class is a key element for monitoring the file system. Developers use this class to easily monitor events within directories. Before the inclusion of this class within the .NET Framework, early Visual Basic developers often had to implement a message queue application, monitor Simple Message Transfer Protocol (SMTP), or write a service which, at different intervals, queried a directory to check for changes.

Developers typically use **FileSystemWatcher** to monitor changes made to files and subdirectories of a specified parent directory. **FileSystemWatcher** works with the local file system, a directory on the local network, or a remote machine.

NOTE The **FileSystemWatcher** class does not permit you to monitor a remote Windows NT 4.0 computer from another Windows NT 4.0 computer, nor does it work with CDs or DVDs because files on these devices are fixed and cannot change.

The power of the **FileSystemWatcher** class emanates from its properties and methods, which are described in Tables 29-9 and 29-10.

Once you have determined which objects you want to monitor on the file system, you must determine what you want to monitor. The **FileSystemWatcher** can monitor changes in the directory's or file's properties, size, last write time, last access time, and security settings.

To specify which changes to watch for in files and directories, developers use the NotifyFilters enumeration of the **FileSystemWatcher** class. Using this enumeration, an event is raised when any change is made to a monitored object. Table 29-11 describes the members of the NotifyFilters enumeration.

Property	Description
Container	Gets the IContainer that contains the component
EnableRaisingEvents	Gets or sets a value indicating whether the component is enabled
Filter	Gets or sets the filter string; used to determine which files are monitored in a directory
IncludeSubdirectories	Gets or sets a value indicating whether subdirectories within the specified path should be monitored
InternalBufferSize	Gets or sets the size of the internal buffer
NotifyFilter	Gets or sets the type of changes to watch for
Path	Gets or sets the path of the directory to watch
SynchronizingObject	Gets or sets the object used to marshal the event handler calls issued as a result of a directory change

Table 29-9 Properties of the FileSystemWatcher Class

Method	Description
BeginInit	Begins the initialization of a **FileSystemWatcher** used on a form or used by another component; the initialization occurs at runtime
CreateObjRef	Creates an object that contains all the information required to generate a proxy used to communicate with a remote object.
Dispose	Overloaded; releases the resources used by the component
EndInit	Ends the initialization of a **FileSystemWatcher** used on a form or used by another component; the initialization occurs at runtime
Equals	Overloaded; determines whether two object instances are equal
GetHashCode	Serves as a hash function for a particular type; suitable for use in hashing algorithms and data structures like a hash table
GetLifetimeService	Retrieves the current lifetime service object that controls the lifetime policy for the instance
GetType	Gets the type of the current instance
InitializeLifetimeService	Obtains a lifetime service object to control the lifetime policy for the instance
ToString	Returns a string that represents the current object
WaitForChanged	Overloaded; a synchronous method that returns a structure that contains specific information on the change that occurred

Table 29-10 Methods of the FileSystemWatcher Class

The following sample code creates a **FileSystemWatcher** object to watch the directory specified at runtime. The component is set to watch for changes in LastWrite and LastAccess, as well as the creation, deletion, or renaming of text files in the directory. If a file

Member	Description
Attributes	Watches for changes made to the attributes of a file or directory
CreationTime	Watches for changes made to the time the file or directory was created
DirectoryName	Watches for changes made to the name of the file or directory
FileName	Watches for changes made to the name of a file
LastAccess	Watches for changes made to the date the file or directory was last opened
LastWrite	Watches for changes made to the date the file or directory had data written to it
Security	Watches for changes made to the security settings of the file or directory
Size	Watches for changes made to the size of the file or directory

Table 29-11 Members of the NotifyFilters Enumeration

is changed, created, or deleted, the path to the file prints to the console. If a file is renamed, the old and new paths print to the console.

```
Public Class myWatcher
        Public Shared Sub Main()
        Dim args() As String = _
            System.Environment.GetCommandLineArgs()
        If args.Length <> 2 Then
            Console.WriteLine("Usage: Watcher.exe (directory)")
            Return
        End If
        Dim myWatcher As New FileSystemWatcher()
        myWatcher.Path = args(1)
        myWatcher.NotifyFilter = (NotifyFilters.LastAccess _
            Or NotifyFilters.LastWrite _
            Or NotifyFilters.FileName _
            Or NotifyFilters.DirectoryName)
        myWatcher.Filter = "*.txt"
        AddHandler myWatcher.Changed, AddressOf OnChanged
        AddHandler myWatcher.Created, AddressOf OnChanged
        AddHandler myWatcher.Deleted, AddressOf OnChanged
        AddHandler myWatcher.Renamed, AddressOf OnRenamed


        myWatcher.EnableRaisingEvents = True


        Console.WriteLine("Press 'q' to quit the sample.")
        While Chr(Console.Read()) <> "q"c
        End While
    End Sub


    Public Shared Sub OnChanged _
      (source As Object, e As FileSystemEventArgs)
        Console.WriteLine_
         "File: " & e.FullPath & " " & e.ChangeType)
    End Sub


    Public Shared Sub OnRenamed_
      source As Object, e As RenamedEventArgs)


        Console.WriteLine _
      "File: {0} renamed to {1}", e.OldFullPath, e.FullPath)
    End Sub
End Class
```

Summary

The Visual Basic .NET Framework provides a variety of classes to simplify the manipulation of files and directories on file systems. The **System.IO** namespace contains almost all the classes you require for these tasks. These classes allow you not only to read information regarding directories and files, but also to create and manipulate these files and directories.

You can write or read data in streams with the .NET Framework classes. This can be accomplished both synchronously and asynchronously. Synchronous reading and writing prevent methods from continuing until the operation is complete, whereas asynchronous reading permits additional code to execute with no delay.

If you need to read from or write to files of a proprietary type, there are classes that permit you to read and write at the binary level. The **BinaryReader** and **BinaryWriter** classes permit a wide degree of flexibility in this regard.

In addition to creating files and directories, and reporting information regarding these objects, the .NET Framework makes it very simple to monitor the file system. Perhaps you need to know when a particular file or directory is modified, for example. The **FileSystemWatcher** class is a key element for monitoring the file system.

Test Questions

1. Which namespace of the .NET Framework provides a rich set of tools to write effective file I/O code efficiently?

   A. System.Directories

   B. System.Files

   C. System.Drawing

   D. System.IO

2. Which of the following classes allows you to reference a specific directory and only causes a security check when the instance is created?

   A. Directory

   B. DirectoryInfo

   C. DirRead

   D. DirectoryRef

3. Which of the following classes allows you to reference a specific file and only causes a security check when the instance is created?

   A. File

   B. FileInfo

   C. FileRead

   D. FileRef

4. Which of the following methods of the **DirectoryInfo** class would you use if you wanted to print a listing of all directories on a particular file system?

   A. Directories

   B. PrintDirectories

   C. GetDirectories

   D. SetDirectories

5. For more efficient use of resources, how should you typically read data?
   A. Asynchronously
   B. Synchronously
   C. Binarily
   D. Serially
6. Which property of the **FileStream** class retrieves a value indicating whether the **FileStream** was opened asynchronously or synchronously?
   A. Handle
   B. CanRead
   C. CanWrite
   D. IsAsync
7. Which method of the **BinaryReader** class reads the next byte from the current stream and advances the current position of the stream by one byte.
   A. ReadByte
   B. ReadBytes
   C. RByte
   D. RBytes
8. Which of the following classes is a key element for monitoring the file system?
   A. Watcher
   B. FileWatcher
   C. FileSystemWatcher
   D. SystemWatcher
9. Which of the following file systems is the **FileSystemWatcher** unable to monitor?
   A. Local file system
   B. Remote file system
   C. CD-ROM file system
   D. Local network file system
10. To specify which changes to watch for in files and directories, which enumeration of the **FileSystemWatcher** class should you use?
    A. NotifyFilters
    B. FileSystem
    C. Filters
    D. SystemFilters

Test Answers

1. D.
2. B.
3. B.
4. C.
5. A.
6. D.
7. A.
8. C.
9. A.
10. A.

CHAPTER 30

Network I/O

In this chapter, you will

- Learn how to utilize the **System.Net.Sockets** namespace for network I/O
- Understand how to use the **NetworkStream** class
- Learn how to create TCP/IP networking services

Besides building code that allows applications to communicate with local file systems, you should be prepared to write code that permits communication with remote file systems. The popularity of the Internet and intranets requires you to write code for communicating with systems located virtually anywhere in the world. This chapter explores the components that enable network I/O.

The System.Net.Sockets Namespace

A key to successfully coding network I/O is to master the classes in the **System.Net.Sockets** namespace. This namespace provides a managed implementation of the Windows Sockets (Winsock) interface for developers. Tables 30-1 and 30-2 detail the classes and enumerations that are available in this namespace.

Class	Description
LingerOption	Contains information about a socket's linger time, which is the amount of time the socket is available after closing if data remains to be sent
MulticastOption	Contains IP address values for IP multicast packets
NetworkStream	Provides the underlying stream of data for network access
Socket	Implements the Berkeley sockets interface
SocketException	The exception that is thrown when a socket error occurs
TCPClient	Provides client connections for Transmission Control Protocol (TCP) network services
TCPListener	Listens for connections from TCP network clients
UDPClient	Provides User Datagram Protocol (UDP) network services

Table 30-1 Classes of the System.Net.Sockets Namespace

Enumeration	Description
AddressFamily	Specifies the addressing scheme that an instance of the **Socket** class can use
ProtocolFamily	Specifies the type of protocol that an instance of the **Socket** class can use
ProtocolType	Specifies the protocols that the **Socket** class supports
SelectMode	Defines the polling modes for the Socket.Poll method
SocketFlags	Provides constant values for socket messages
SocketOptionLevel	Defines socket option levels for the Socket.SetSocketOption and Socket.GetSocketOption methods
SocketOptionName	Defines socket option names for the **Socket** class
SocketShutdown	Defines constants used by the Socket.Shutdown method
SocketType	Specifies the type of socket an instance of the **Socket** class represents

Table 30-2 Enumerations of the System.Net.Sockets Namespace

Using the NetworkStream Class

As discussed in Chapter 29, streams provide a way to write and read bytes to and from a backing store that can be one of several storage mediums. The **NetworkStream** class assists with the manipulation of network backing store locations by implementing the standard .NET Framework stream mechanism to send and receive data through network sockets. This very useful class supports both synchronous and asynchronous access to the network data stream.

Representing network resources as streams has advantages. By treating resources in this generic manner, the .NET Framework offers a common mechanism for sending and receiving Internet data regardless of the format of the data files. These files can be HTML, TXT, or XML. Using the **NetworkStream** class, an application can use Stream.Write and Stream.Read to send and receive data.

Using streams also ensures compatibility with other streams across the .NET Framework. For example, an application that reads XML data from a FileStream can be modified to read data from a NetworkStream by changing only the few lines of code that initialize the stream. The main difference between the **NetworkStream** class and other streams is that **NetworkStream** is not "seekable". This means that the CanSeek property always returns False, and the Seek and Position methods throw a NotSupportedException.

Using the stream approach also permits an application to process data as it arrives instead of waiting for an entire data set to download from a remote location before it resumes processing.

Tables 30-3 and 30-4 describe the properties and methods of the **NetworkStream** class.

Using the WebRequest and WebResponse Classes

The **WebRequest** class is a request/response model for accessing data from the Internet. Using this class developers can request data from the Internet in a protocol-agnostic manner, in which the application works with instances of the **WebRequest** class while protocol-specific descendant classes carry out the details of the request.

Property	Description
CanRead	Overridden; gets a value indicating whether the current stream supports reading
CanSeek	Overridden; gets a value indicating whether the stream supports seeking; this value always returns False
CanWrite	Overridden; gets a value that indicates whether the current stream supports writing
DataAvailable	Gets a value indicating whether data is available on the stream to be read
Length	Overridden; gets or sets the length of the data available on the stream; this property always throws a NotSupportedException
Position	Overridden; gets or sets the current position in the stream; this property always throws a NotSupportedException

Table 30-3 Properties of the NetworkStream Class

Method	Description
BeginRead	Overridden; begins an asynchronous read from a stream
BeginWrite	Overridden; begins an asynchronous write to a stream
Close	Overridden; closes the stream and optionally closes the underlying socket
CreateObjRef	Creates an object that contains all the relevant information required to generate a proxy used to communicate with a remote object
EndRead	Overridden; handles the end of an asynchronous read
EndWrite	Overridden; handles the end of an asynchronous write
Equals	Overloaded; determines whether two object instances are equal
Flush	Overridden; flushes data from the stream
GetHashCode	Serves as a hash function for a particular type; suitable for use in hashing algorithms and data structures like a hash table
GetLifetimeService	Retrieves the current lifetime service object that controls the lifetime policy for the instance
GetType	Gets the type of the current instance
InitializeLifetimeService	Obtains a lifetime service object to control the lifetime policy for the instance
Read	Overridden; reads data from the stream
ReadByte	Reads a byte from the stream and advances the position within the stream by one byte, or returns -1 if at the end of the stream
Seek	Overridden; sets the current position of the stream to the given value; this method always throws a NotSupportedException
SetLength	Overridden; sets the length of the stream; this method always throws a NotSupportedException
ToString	Returns a string that represents the current object
Write	Overridden; writes data to the stream
WriteByte	Writes a byte to the current position in the stream and advances the position within the stream by one byte

Table 30-4 Methods of the NetworkStream Class

Requests are sent from an application to a particular uniform resource identifier (URI), such as a Web page on a server. The URI determines the proper descendant class to create from a list of **WebRequest** descendants registered for the application. Although **WebRequest** descendants are typically registered to handle a request to a specific protocol, such as HTTP or FTP, they can be registered to handle a request to a specific server or path on a server.

Table 30-5 describes the methods of the **WebRequest** class.

To send data to the network using the returned stream, simply call the GetRequestStream method of the WebRequest instance. The WebRequest sends request headers to the server; then you can send data to the Internet resource by calling the BeginWrite, EndWrite, or Write method on the returned stream.

TIP With some protocols, such as HTTP, you may need to set protocol-specific properties before sending data.

Method	Description
Abort	Cancels an asynchronous request to an Internet resource
BeginGetRequestStream	When overridden in a descendant class, provides an asynchronous version of the GetRequestStream method
BeginGetResponse	When overridden in a descendant class, begins an asynchronous request for an Internet resource
Create	Overloaded; initializes a new WebRequest
CreateDefault	Initializes a new WebRequest instance for the specified URI scheme
CreateObjRef	Creates an object that contains all the relevant information required to generate a proxy used to communicate with a remote object
EndGetRequestStream	When overridden in a descendant class, returns a stream for writing data to the Internet resource
EndGetResponse	When overridden in a descendant class, returns a WebResponse
Equals	Overloaded; determines whether two object instances are equal
GetHashCode	Serves as a hash function for a particular type; suitable for use in hashing algorithms and data structures like a hash table
GetLifetimeService	Retrieves the current lifetime service object that controls the lifetime policy for the instance
GetRequestStream	When overridden in a descendant class, returns a stream for writing data to the Internet resource
GetResponse	When overridden in a descendant class, returns a response to an Internet request
GetType	Gets the type of the current instance
InitializeLifetimeService	Obtains a lifetime service object to control the lifetime policy for the instance
RegisterPrefix	Registers a WebRequest descendant for the specified URI
ToString	Returns a string that represents the current object

Table 30-5 Methods of the WebRequest Class

The **WebResponse** class is similar to the **WebRequest** class. To receive data from the network, you call the GetResponseStream method of the WebResponse instance. You can then read data from the Internet resource by calling the BeginRead, EndRead, or Read method on the returned stream.

When using streams to manipulate network resources, remember the following points:

- When you use WebRequest and WebResponse, stream instances created by calling GetResponseStream are read-only, and stream instances created by calling GetRequestStream are write-only.
- Use the StreamReader class to simplify encoding.
- The call to GetResponse may be blocked if network resources are not available. Consider using an asynchronous request with the BeginGetResponse and EndGetResponse methods.
- The call to GetRequestStream may be blocked while the connection to the server is created. Consider using an asynchronous request for the stream when using the BeginGetRequestStream and EndGetRequestStream methods.

Creating TCP/IP Networking Services

As shown in Table 30-1, the **System.Net.Sockets** namespace provides classes that facilitate the creation of TCP/IP networking services. Specifically, the **TCPClient**, **TCPListener**, and **UDPClient** classes encapsulate the details of creating Transmission Control Protocol (TCP) and User Datagram Protocol (UDP) connections to specific TCP/IP locations on the Internet or an intranet.

The TCPClient Class

The **TCPClient** class enables developers to easily code client connections for TCP network services. The key properties and methods of this class are listed in Tables 30-6 and 30-7, respectively.

The members listed in Tables 30-6 and 30-7 enable developers to use the **TCPClient** class as a simple mechanism for connecting, sending, and receiving data over an IP net-

Property	Description
LingerState	Gets or sets information about the socket's linger time
NoDelay	Gets or sets a value that enables a delay when send or receive buffers are not full
ReceiveBufferSize	Gets or sets the size of the receive buffer
ReceiveTimeout	Gets or sets the amount of time a TCPClient will wait to receive data once data transmission is initiated
SendBufferSize	Gets or sets the size of the send buffer
SendTimeout	Gets or sets the amount of time a TCPClient will wait to receive confirmation after a data transmission is initiated

Table 30-6 Properties of the TCPClient Class

Method	Description
Close	Closes the TCP connection
Connect	Overloaded; connects the client to a remote TCP host using the specified host name and port number
Equals	Overloaded; determines whether two object instances are equal
GetHashCode	Serves as a hash function for a particular type; suitable for use in hashing algorithms and data structures like a hash table
GetStream	Returns the stream used to send and receive data
GetType	Gets the type of the current instance
ToString	Returns a string that represents the current object

Table 30-7 Methods of the TCPClient Class

work. To use this class to connect with a remote host on the IP network, you have two choices:

- Create an instance of the **TCPClient** class using a local IPEndPoint or, alternatively, no parameters, and then call one of the three available **TCPClient** Connect methods.
- Create an instance of the **TCPClient** class using the host name and port number of the device to which you intend to connect. This constructor automatically establishes the connection.

To send and receive data, use the GetStream method to obtain a NetworkStream that sends and receives data on the underlying connected socket. After utilizing the Write and Read methods available through the **NetworkStream** class, use the Close method to release all resources associated with the TCPClient.

TIP The **TCPClient** class provides a set of convenient properties that you can use to adjust common socket settings. To set socket options that these properties do *not* address, use the Client property to retrieve the underlying socket.

The following sample code creates a TCPClient connection using the host name www.abc-company.com on port 10500. We then use the underlying NetworkStream instance to send and receive simple string statements.

```
Dim myTCPClient As New TCPClient()
Try
      myTCPClient.Connect("www.abc-company.com", 10500)
      Dim myNetworkStream As _
            NetworkStream = myTCPClient.GetStream()
      If myNetworkStream.CanWrite _
            And myNetworkStream.CanRead Then
            Dim mySendBytes As [Byte]() = _
```

```
                Encoding.ASCII.GetBytes("Sample Send String")
          myNetworkStream.Write _
                (sendBytes, 0, sendBytes.Length)
          Dim MyBytes(myTCPClient.ReceiveBufferSize) _
                As Byte
          myNetworkStream.Read _
                (myBytes, 0, CInt _
                (myTCPClient.ReceiveBufferSize))
          Dim myReturnData As String = _
                Encoding.ASCII.GetString(myBytes)
          Console.WriteLine _
                (("This is what the host returned _
                to you: " + myReturnData))
    Else
          If Not myNetworkStream.CanRead Then
                Console.WriteLine _
                      ("You cannot write data to this stream")
                TCPClient.Close()
    Else
          If Not myNetworkStream.CanWrite Then
          Console.WriteLine("You cannot read _
                data from this stream")
          TCPClient.Close()
          End If
    End If
End If
Catch e As Exception
   Console.WriteLine(e.ToString())
End Try
```

The TCPListener Class

The **TCPListener** class allows developers to code an application so that it listens for connections from TCP/IP clients in the internetwork. This class consists of only one public property:

- **LocalEndpoint** This property gets the underlying endpoint of the current TCPListener.

Table 30-8 describes the methods of the **TCPListener** class.

Method	Description
AcceptSocket	Accepts a pending connection request
AcceptTCPClient	Accepts a pending connection request
Equals	Overloaded; determines whether two object instances are equal
GetHashCode	Serves as a hash function for a particular type; suitable for use in hashing algorithms and data structures like a hash table
GetType	Gets the type of the current instance
Pending	Determines whether there are pending connection requests
Start	Starts listening to network requests
Stop	Closes the listener
ToString	Returns a string that represents the current object

Table 30-8 Methods of the TCPListener Class

You create an instance of the **TCPListener** class by providing one of the following constructor argument lists:

- An IPEndPoint containing your local IP address and port number
- Your IP address and port number
- Only your port number; in this case, the default network interface will be used

To begin listening for incoming connection requests, use the Start property. You can also use the Pending method to determine whether connections are pending.

As indicated in Table 30-8, use AcceptSocket to retrieve a socket, or AcceptTCPClient to retrieve a TCPClient used for facilitating communication with the remote machine. Also, use Stop to close the underlying listening socket.

NOTE Using Stop only closes the socket used to listen for incoming connections. You must close any instances returned from AcceptSocket or AcceptTCPClient as well.

The following code example demonstrates the creation of a TCPListener on port 10600.

```
Const myPortNumber As Integer = 10600
Dim myTCPListener As New TCPListener(myPortNumber)
myTCPListener.Start()
Console.WriteLine("Waiting for connection...")
Try
      Dim myTCPClient As TCPClient _
            = myTCPListener.AcceptTCPClient()
      Console.WriteLine("Connection accepted.")
      Dim myNetworkStream As NetworkStream _
            = myTCPClient.GetStream()
      Dim myResponseString As String _
            = "You have successfully connected."
      Dim mySendBytes As [Byte]() = _
            Encoding.ASCII.GetBytes(myResponseString)
      myNetworkStream.Write _
            (mySendBytes, 0, mySendBytes.Length)
      Console.WriteLine(("Message Sent /> : " + myResponseString))
      myTCPClient.Close()
      myTCPListener.Stop()
Catch e As Exception
      Console.WriteLine(e.ToString())
End Try
```

The UDPClient Class

User Datagram Protocol (UDP) is a connectionless protocol that runs on top of IP networks. UDP is an alternative to TCP for communicating across IP networks. Unlike TCP/IP, UDP/IP provides very few error-recovery services. Instead, this protocol offers a direct way to send and receive datagrams over an IP network. Because of its low overhead (compared to TCP), UDP is used primarily for broadcasting messages over a network.

The **UDPClient** class provides UDP network services. Table 30-9 describes the methods of this class of the **System.Net.Sockets** namespace.

Method	Description
Close	Closes the UDP connection
Connect	Overloaded; establishes a connection to a remote host
DropMulticastGroup	Leaves a multicast group
Equals	Overloaded; determines whether two object instances are equal
GetHashCode	Serves as a hash function for a particular type; suitable for use in hashing algorithms and data structures like a hash table
GetType	Gets the type of the current instance
JoinMulticastGroup	Overloaded; adds a UDP client to a multicast group
Receive	Returns a UDP datagram that was sent by a remote host
Send	Overloaded; sends a UDP datagram to a remote host
ToString	Returns a string that represents the current object

Table 30-9 Methods of the UDPClient Class

Because UDP is a connectionless transport protocol, you are not required to establish a remote host connection prior to sending and receiving data. However, you have the option of establishing a default remote host using one of the following methods:

- Create an instance of the **UDPClient** class using the remote host name and port number as parameters.
- Create an instance of the **UDPClient** class and then call the Connect method.

You use any of the Send methods provided in the **UDPClient** class to send data to a remote device. You use the Receive method to receive data from remote devices.

NOTE If you have already specified a default remote host, do not use the Send method using a host name or IP endpoint. Coding in this manner causes UDPClient to throw an exception.

As indicated in Table 30-9, the UDPClient methods also allow you to receive multicasted datagrams. Use JoinMulticastGroup and DropMulticastGroup to associate and disassociate a UDP client with a multicast group.

The following code sample creates a UDP client connection using the host name www.abc-company.com on port 10500. In this code, a sample string message is sent to two separate remote host machines. The Receive method blocks execution until a message is received.

```
Dim myUDPClient As New UDPClient()
Try
      myUDPClient.Connect("www.abc-company.com", 10500)
      Dim mySendBytes As [Byte]() _
            = Encoding.ASCII.GetBytes("Sample message")
      myUDPClient.Send(mySendBytes, mySendBytes.Length)
      Dim myUDPClient2 As New UDPClient()
```

PART VIII

```
        MyUDPClient2.Send(mySendBytes, mySendBytes.Length, _
              "Another Sample String", 10500)

        Dim myRemoteIPEndPoint As New IPEndPoint _
              (IPAddress.Any, 0)
        Dim myReceiveBytes As [Byte]() = _
              myUDPClient.Receive(RemoteIPEndPoint)
        Dim myReturnData As String = _
              Encoding.ASCII.GetString(myReceiveBytes)

        Console.WriteLine(("This is the message you received " _
              + myReturnData.ToString()))
        Console.WriteLine(("This message was sent from " _
              + myRemoteIPEndPoint.Address.ToString() + _
              " on their port number " + _
              myRemoteIPEndPoint.Port.ToString()))
        myUDPClient.Close()
        myUDPClient2.Close()
   Catch e As Exception
        Console.WriteLine(e.ToString())
  End Try
  End Sub
```

Summary

The popularity of TCP/IP based internetworks has fueled the need for sophisticated and dependable network I/O in today's applications. The good news for Visual Basic .NET developers is that the .NET Framework provides a variety of classes to facilitate simple and effective network I/O in your applications. Key classes include **NetworkStream**, **TCPClient**, and **TCPListener**. The **NetworkStream** class provides the underlying stream of data for network access, while the **TCPClient** class provides client connections for TCP network services.

The **NetworkStream** class provides a mechanism for writing and reading bytes to and from network locations. This includes both synchronous and asynchronous access to network information. This class also offers a common way to send and receive Internet data regardless of the format of the data files.

As for the creation of TCP/IP based networking services, the **TCPClient**, **TCPListener**, and **UDPClient** classes encapsulate the details of creating TCP and UDP connections to specific TCP/IP locations on the Internet. While the **TCPClient** and **TCPListener** classes handle Transmission Control Protocol (TCP) communications, the **UDPClient** class provides User Datagram Protocol (UDP) network services.

Test Questions

1. Which of the following classes allows an application to listen for connections from TCP network clients?

   A. TCPClient

   B. TCPScan

   C. TCPListener

   D. UDPClient

2. Which System.Net.Sockets enumeration specifies the type of protocol that an instance of the **Socket** class can use?
   A. ProtocolFamily
   B. ProtocolSocket
   C. Protocol
   D. ProtocolInclude
3. Which of the following is the main difference between the **NetworkStream** class and other streams?
   A. The **NetworkStream** class is only useful for the creation of asynchronous reads.
   B. The **NetworkStream** class is used only to read data, not to write data.
   C. The **NetworkStream** class cannot be used to interact with a traditional backing store.
   D. The **NetworkStream** class is not "seekable."
4. Which of the following properties of the **NetworkStream** class always throws an exception?
   A. CanWrite
   B. CanSeek
   C. CanRead
   D. Length
5. To send data to the network using the returned stream, which of the following methods of the WebRequest instance should you call?
   A. GetRequestStream
   B. GetResponse
   C. RegisterPrefix
   D. BeginGetRequestStream
6. What is the single public property of the **TCPListener** class?
   A. GetType
   B. Duration
   C. Length
   D. LocalEndpoint
7. Which protocol does not use acknolwedgement mechanisms and is, therefore, considered unreliable?
   A. IP
   B. UDP

C. ICMP

D. ARP

8. Which of the following methods allows a UDPClient to be associated with a multicast group?

A. MulticastGroup

B. MulticastGroupJoin

C. JoinMulticastGroup

D. Multicast

9. To receive data from the network, which of the following methods of the WebResponse instance should you call?

A. GetResponseStream

B. ResponseStream

C. Response

D. Stream

10. Which of the following classes can make encoding easier when you are using streams to manipulate network resources?

A. NetworkStreams

B. Streams

C. StreamReader

D. GetRequestStream

Test Answers

1. C.
2. A.
3. D.
4. D.
5. A.
6. D.
7. B.
8. C.
9. A.
10. C.

CHAPTER 31

Serialization

In this chapter, you will

- Learn about the classes of the **System.Runtime.Serialization** namespace
- Find out how to utilize basic serialization techniques
- Understand how to implement binary and SOAP serialization
- Learn about object graphs
- Learn how to implement custom serialization
- Study the StreamingContext structure
- Understand how to implement XML Serialization

Serialization is the process of saving an object onto a storage medium and later deserializing it from the storage medium to re-create an object instance that can be considered identical to the original object. The runtime uses this key feature of the .NET Framework frequently. For example, besides saving information to files in this manner, the runtime uses serialization to marshal objects by value to another application.

As an advanced Visual Basic developer, you might use serialization in any of the following situations:

- Sending an object to another application
- Saving an object on a storage medium, such as a disk or a buffer in memory
- Saving an object in a database field
- Saving an object in an ASP.NET session object
- Using an exception object in another application

TIP You might hear serialization and persistence used as synonyms. According to Microsoft, however, persistence refers to data stored in a durable medium, such as a file. Serialization works with durable and nondurable media, such as memory buffers.

This chapter strives to cover the most important aspects of serialization. This includes the use of the key classes for serialization. It also provides coverage of XML serialization.

Class	Description
Formatter	Provides base functionality for the common language runtime (CLR) serialization formatters
FormatterConverter	Represents a base implementation of the IFormatterConverter interface that uses the **Convert** class and the IConvertible interface
FormatterServices	Provides static methods to assist in the implementation of a Formatter for serialization
ObjectIDGenerator	Generates IDs for objects
ObjectManager	Keeps track of objects as they are deserialized
SerializationBinder	Allows users to control class loading and mandate what class to load
SerializationException	The exception thrown when an error occurs during serialization or deserialization
SerializationInfo	Holds all the data needed to serialize or deserialize an object
SerializationInfoEnumerator	Provides a formatter-friendly mechanism for parsing the data in **SerializationInfo**
SurrogateSelector	Assists formatters in selecting the serialization surrogate to delegate the serialization or deserialization process to

Table 31-1 Classes of the System.Runtime.Serialization Namespace

The System.Runtime.Serialization Namespace

Developers use the classes of the **System.Runtime.Serialization** namespace for serializing and deserializing objects. Tables 31-1, 31-2, 31-3, and 31-4 describe the key members of this namespace.

Interface	Description
IDeserializationCallback	Indicates that a class is to be notified when deserialization of the entire object graph has been completed
IFormatter	Provides functionality for formatting serialized objects
IFormatterConverter	Provides the connection between an instance of **SerializationInfo** and the formatter-provided class best suited to parse the data inside the **SerializationInfo**
IObjectReference	Indicates that the current interface implementer is a reference to another object
ISerializable	Allows an object to control its own serialization and deserialization
ISerializationSurrogate	Implements a serialization surrogate selector that allows one object to perform serialization and deserialization of another
ISurrogateSelector	Indicates a serialization surrogate selector class

Table 31-2 Interfaces of the System.Runtime.Serialization Namespace

Structure	Description
SerializationEntry	Holds the value, type, and name of a serialized object
StreamingContext	Describes the source and destination of a given serialized stream, as well as a means for serialization to retain that context and an additional caller-defined context

Table 31-3 Structures of the System.Runtime.Serialization Namespace

Implementing Basic Serialization

To serialize or deserialize basic objects, such as numbers, strings, or arrays of these objects, you simply utilize the proper formatter object. As indicated in Table 31-2, a formatter is any object that implements the IFormatter interface. Although you can create a formatter by creating a class that implements IFormatter, you typically rely on one of the following formatter objects provided by Visual Basic .NET:

- **BinaryFormatter** This Visual Basic .NET object serializes and deserializes an object, or an entire graph of connected objects, in binary format. Because the actual bits in memory are persisted, the serialization and deserialization processes tend to be quite fast.
- **SoapFormatter** This Visual Basic .NET object serializes and deserializes an object, or an entire graph of connected objects, in Simple Object Access Protocol (SOAP) format. Doing so persists the data in a human readable format (XML). As a result, the serialization and deserialization processes tend to be slower.

Implementing Binary Serialization

The key methods that all formatter objects provide for serialization and deserialization are Serialize and Deserialize. In the following code sample the Serialize method accepts a **Stream** object as its first argument and then accepts the object to be serialized in the second argument.

Enumeration	Description
StreamingContextStates	Defines a set of flags that specifies the source or destination context for the stream during serialization

Table 31-4 Enumeration of the System.Runtime.Serialization Namespace

```
Imports System.IO
Imports System.Runtime.Serialization
Imports System.Runtime.Serialization.Formatters.Binary

Sub SampleSerialization()
      Dim mySampleArray() As Integer = {1, 10, 20, 40, 60}

      Dim mySampleFileStream As FileStream = _
            New FileStream("c:\sample.dat", FileMode.Create)

      Dim mySampleBinaryFormatter As New BinaryFormatter()
      mySampleBinaryFormatter.Serialize(mySampleFileStream, _
            mySampleArray)
      mySampleFileStream.Close()
End Sub
```

The Deserialize method is used to read back the data. Specifically, notice in the following sample code that we simply indicate the **Stream** object and cast the returned object value to the appropriate typed variable.

```
Imports System.IO
Imports System.Runtime.Serialization
Imports System.Runtime.Serialization.Formatters.Binary

Sub mySampleDeserialization()
      Dim mySampleFileStream As FileStream = _
            New FileStream("c:\sample.dat", FileMode.Open)

      Dim myBinaryFormatter As New BinaryFormatter()

      Dim mySampleArray() As Integer
      mySampleArray = CType(myBinaryFormatter.Deserialization _
            (mySampleFileStream), Integer())
End Sub
```

Implementing SOAP Serialization

The **SoapFormatter** object of the **System.Runtime.Serialization.Formatters.Soap** namespace enables developers to easily serialize objects using the SOAP format. Unfortunately, this namespace is not available in the default installation of Visual Studio .NET.

To add the namespace, follow these steps:

1. Open your Visual Basic project.
2. Select Add Reference from the Project menu.
3. Select the .NET tab in the Add Reference window.
4. In the list box select System.Runtime.Serialization.Formatters.Soap, and then click Select.
5. Click OK in the Add Reference window.

The following sample code saves an object to a file using the SOAP format. Notice the use of the **StreamingContext** object to specify where the serialization data is stored. Also notice how similar this code is to the sample code that used binary serialization.

```
Imports System.IO
Imports System.Runtime.Serialization
Imports System.Runtime.Serialization.Formatters.SOAP

Sub mySampleSOAPSerialization(ByVal myPath As String, _
      ByVal myObject As Object)
      Dim mySampleFileStream As FileStream = _
            New FileStream(myPath, FileMode.Create)
      Dim mySoapFormatter As New SoapFormatter(Nothing, _
            New StreamingContext(StreamingContextStates.File))
      mySoapFormatter.Serialize(mySampleFileStream, myObject)
      mySampleFileStream.Close()
End Sub
```

The following code provides an example of deserializing the object using a SOAP format.

```
Imports System.IO
Imports System.Runtime.Serialization
Imports System.Runtime.Serialization.Formatters.SOAP

Function DeserialSoapData(ByVal myPath as String) _
      As Object
      Dim myFileStream As FileStream = New FileStream _
           (myPath, FileMode.Open)
      Dim mySoapFormatter As New SoapFormatter(Nothing, _
            New StreamingContext(StreamingContextStates. _
                  File))
      DeserialSoapData = mySoapFormatter.Deserialize _
            (myFileStream)
      myFileStream.Close()
End Function
```

Using the Serializable and NonSerialized Attributes

To make a class serializable, use the Serializable attribute, as shown in the following code. Notice how simple this is as the constructor takes no arguments.

```
<Serializable()> Public Class mySampleClass
```

Classes often contain fields that should not be serialized. To prevent member variables from being serialized, mark them with the NonSerialized attribute, as shown in the following example.

```
<NonSerialized()> Public mySample As String
```

Understanding Object Graphs

Serialization in the .NET Framework relies upon the **Formatter** class, the **ObjectIDGenerator** class, and the **ObjectManager** class.

The **Formatter** class is a key class in the serialization process. It converts atomic data to the output stream, interprets the bits in the stream, and converts the bits back to data during deserialization.

The **ObjectIDGenerator** class generates unique IDs for the objects being serialized. When you ask for the ID of an object, the **ObjectIDGenerator** knows whether to return the existing ID or generate and remember a new ID. The IDs are unique for the life of the

ObjectIDGenerator instance. Generally, an **ObjectIDGenerator** lives as long as the formatter that created it. Object IDs have meaning only within a given serialized stream; they are used for tracking which objects have references to others within the serialized object graph. Using a hash table, the **ObjectIDGenerator** tracks what ID is assigned to what object. The object references, which uniquely identify each object, are addresses in the runtime garbage-collection heap. Object reference values can change during serialization; the table is updated automatically so the information is correct.

The **ObjectManager** class is used to keep track of objects being deserialized. During deserialization, the formatter queries the **ObjectManager** to determine whether a reference to an object in the serialized stream refers to an object that has already been deserialized (a backward reference), or to an object that has not yet been deserialized (a forward reference). If the reference in the serialized stream is a forward reference, then the formatter can register a "fixup" with the **ObjectManager**. If the reference in the serialized stream is a backward reference, the formatter immediately completes the reference. *Fixup* refers to the process of finalizing object references that were not completed during the object deserialization process. After the required object has been deserialized, the **ObjectManager** completes the reference.

The **ObjectManager** follows a set of rules that dictate the fixup order. All objects that implement ISerializable or have an ISerializationSurrogate will have all the objects that they transmitted through SerializationInfo available when the object tree is deserialized. However, you cannot presume that a parent object will have all its child objects fully completed when it is fully deserialized. All child objects will be present, but not necessarily all the grandchild objects will be present. If an object must take actions that depend on executing code on its child objects, it can delay these actions, implement the IDeserializationCallback interface, and execute the code only when it is called back on this interface.

The **ObjectIDGenerator** and the **ObjectManager** classes are critical to serialization, and this becomes apparent when dealing with an object graph. An object graph is a set of multiple objects with references to each other. For example, suppose you have an ArrayList that contains references to individual objects. When you serialize the ArrayList, you indirectly serialize all the referenced objects inside it. If there are no circular references among the objects, no **ObjectIDGenerator** is required as the objects are serialized and deserialized. Typically, however, such references do exist and these classes are required.

Implementing Custom Serialization

Besides the capabilities provided by the Serializable attribute, Visual Basic .NET includes the ISerializable interface to allow developers to customize serialization capabilities to meet specific requirements.

The ISerializable Interface

To customize the serialization capability in your own classes, you can implement the ISerializable interface. This interface exposes a single method, GetObjectData, which utilizes the following syntax.

```
Sub GetObjectData(ByVal info As SerializationInfo, _
     ByVal context As StreamingContext)
End Sub
```

GetObjectData is invoked when the object passes to the Formatter.Serialize method. It fills the **SerializationInfo** object with all the information about the object being serialized. The code inside this method examines the StreamingContext structure and retrieves additional details about the serialization process.

The ISerializable interface creates a special constructor method that has the following syntax.

```
Private Sub New(ByVal info As SerializationInfo, _
     ByVal context As StreamingContext)
End Sub
```

The preceding constructor is called by the runtime when the object is deserialized.

NOTE It is a good idea to use a Private scope with the preceding constructor. Doing so prevents other clients from calling it.

If you omit this constructor, no error appears during compilation. However, an error appears during runtime when deserialization is attempted.

The **SerializationInfo** object of this constructor works like a dictionary object. You use the AddValue method in order to add one or more values, as shown in the following example.

```
Info.AddValue("Anthony", FirstName)
```

You retrieve values at a later time using the GetValue method. Simply specify the value name and type, as shown in the following example.

```
FirstName = CStr(info.GetValue("FirstValue", _
     GetType(String)))
```

The **SerializationInfo** object presents many methods. Table 31-5 describes these methods.

Method	Description
AddValue	Overloaded; adds a value into **SerializationInfo**
Equals	Overloaded; determines whether two object instances are equal
GetBoolean	Retrieves a Boolean value from **SerializationInfo**
GetByte	Retrieves an 8-bit unsigned integer value from **SerializationInfo**
GetChar	Retrieves a Unicode character value from **SerializationInfo**
GetDateTime	Retrieves a date/time value from **SerializationInfo**
GetDecimal	Retrieves a decimal value from **SerializationInfo**
GetDouble	Retrieves a double-precision, floating-point value from **SerializationInfo**
GetEnumerator	Returns a **SerializationInfo** enumerator used to iterate through the name-value pairs in **SerializationInfo**

Table 31-5 Methods of the SerializationInfo Object

Method	Description
GetHashCode	Serves as a hash function for a particular type; suitable for use in hashing algorithms and data structures like a hash table
GetInt16	Retrieves a 16-bit signed integer value from **SerializationInfo**
GetInt32	Retrieves a 32-bit signed integer value from **SerializationInfo**
GetInt64	Retrieves a 64-bit signed integer value from **SerializationInfo**
GetSByte	Retrieves an 8-bit signed integer value from **SerializationInfo**
GetSingle	Retrieves a single-precision, floating-point value from **SerializationInfo**
GetString	Retrieves a string value from **SerializationInfo**
GetType	Gets the type of the current instance
GetUInt16	Retrieves a 16-bit unsigned integer value from **SerializationInfo**
GetUInt32	Retrieves a 32-bit unsigned integer value from **SerializationInfo**
GetUInt64	Retrieves a 64-bit unsigned integer value from **SerializationInfo**
GetValue	Retrieves a value from **SerializationInfo**
SetType	Sets the type of the object to serialize
ToString	Returns a string that represents the current object

Table 31-5 Methods of the SerializationInfo Object *(continued)*

The StreamingContext Structure

As mentioned in the preceding section, the ISerialization interface utilizes a StreamingContext structure, which allows developers to learn additional details about the serialization and deserialization process.

Typically, you use the value returned by the State property to learn additional information regarding serialization/deserialization. The State property returns a bit-coded enumeration value. Table 31-6 describes these values.

Name	Value	Description
All	127	Specifies that the serialized data can be transmitted to or received from any of the other contexts
Clone	64	Specifies that the object graph is being cloned; you can assume that the cloned graph continues to exist within the same process and is safe to access handles or other references to unmanaged resources
CrossAppDomain	128	Specifies that the source or destination context is a different AppDomain
CrossMachine	2	Specifies that the source or destination context is a different computer
CrossProcess	1	Specifies that the source or destination context is a different process on the same computer

Table 31-6 Values of the State Property

Name	Value	Description
File	4	Specifies that the source or destination context is a file; you can assume that files last longer than the process that created them and therefore serialize objects in such a way that deserialization does not require accessing data from the current process
Other	32	Specifies that the serialization context is unknown
Persistence	8	Specifies that the source or destination context is a persisted store, which may include databases, files, or other backing stores
Remoting	16	Specifies that the data is remoted to a context in an unknown location

Table 31-6 Values of the State Property *(continued)*

The following code example demonstrates the use of the StreamingContext structure.

```
Imports System
Imports System.Runtime.Serialization

<Serializable()> Public Class mySampleClass
    Implements ISerializable

    Public Shared Sub Main()
    End Sub

    Public winhandle As Integer
    Public value As Double = 3.14159265

    Public Sub New _
(info As SerializationInfo, context As StreamingContext)
If context.State = StreamingContextStates.CrossProcess _
Then winhandle = CInt(info.GetValue("winhandle", _
GetType(Integer)))
        Else
            winhandle = - 1
      End If
      value = CDbl(info.GetValue("mySampleClass_value", _
      GetType(Double)))
    End Sub

    Public Sub GetObjectData(info As SerializationInfo, _
      context As StreamingContext) _
      Implements ISerializable.GetObjectData

      info.AddValue("MyClass_value", value)

      If context.State = StreamingContextStates.CrossProcess _
   Then
           info.AddValue("winhandle", winhandle)
        End If
    End Sub
End Class
```

The IDeserializationCallback Interface

There is a potential problem when engaging in serialization as described in this chapter. Sometimes the serialization infrastructure can call the object's constructor even though the object graph is not completely deserialized. The IDeserialization interface addresses this problem by indicating that a class is to be notified when deserialization of the entire object graph has been completed.

Use of the interface is very simple. It has only one public method, OnDeserialization, which runs when the entire object graph has been deserialized.

Implementing XML Serialization

The .NET Framework also enables developers to implement XML serialization.

NOTE Do not confuse XML serialization with SOAP serialization. As discussed in the following text, you do not have the same levels of control with SOAP serialization that you have with XML serialization.

XML serialization allows developers to persist an object's state in an XML stream while maintaining control over the XML elements used to persist the data. Using XML serialization, developers can easily perform the following tasks:

- Select an XML namespace for use with the application
- Control whether a property is serialized as an XML element or attribute
- Set the name of the element or attribute

Although XML serialization has its advantages, it also has the following shortcomings:

- It only works with public classes
- Only public fields and properties can be serialized
- Object graphs containing circular references cannot be serialized
- Data in classes can be serialized, but object identity is lost
- Information about the assembly is lost

XML serialization is often used to stream data to another application that is designed to understand the XML stream. It is also common to read XML streams from other applications for import into your own application.

Understanding the XmlSerializer Class

At the core of an application's capability to engage in XML serialization is the **XmlSerializer** class, which is a member of the **System.Xml.Serialization** namespace.

NOTE ASP.NET actually relies upon the **XmlSerializer** class to encode XML Web service messages.

As you know, you describe the data in objects using programming language constructs like classes, fields, and properties. Perhaps you even use embedded XML in the form of **XmlElement** or **XmlAttribute** objects. You can create your own classes or use the XML schema definition tool (XSD.EXE) to generate the classes based on an existing XML schema definition (XSD) document. Typically, if you have an XML schema, you run XSD.EXE to produce a set of classes that are strongly typed to the schema and annotated with attributes to adhere to the schema when serialized.

To transfer data between objects and XML, you must create a mapping from the programming language constructs to the XML schema and vice versa. The **XmlSerializer** class, and related tools like XSD.EXE, allow you to bridge between these technologies during design time and runtime.

During design time you can use XSD.EXE to produce an XML schema document (XSD) from your custom classes, or you can produce classes from a given schema. Regardless of which method you choose, the classes are annotated with custom attributes to instruct the **XmlSerializer** how to map between the XML schema system and the common language runtime.

During runtime, instances of the classes can be serialized into XML documents that follow the given schema. Likewise, these XML documents can be deserialized into runtime objects.

To control the generated XML, you apply special attributes to classes and members. For example, to specify a different XML element name, apply XmlElementAttribute to a public field or property, and set the ElementName property. Table 31-7 describes the attributes that you can use with the **XmlSerializer** class.

If you must generate XML code that conforms to section 5 of the World Wide Web Consortium document, *Simple Object Access Protocol (SOAP) 1.1*, you must construct the **XmlSerializer** with an XmlTypeMapping. You can further control the encoded SOAP XML serialization using the attributes listed in Table 31-8.

XmlSerializer enables you to work with strongly typed classes while maintaining the flexibility of XML. Using fields or properties of type XmlElement, XmlAttribute, or XmlNode in strongly typed classes, you can read parts of the XML document directly into XML objects.

If you work with extensible XML schemas, you can also use the XmlAnyElementAttribute and XmlAnyAttributeAttribute attributes to serialize and deserialize elements or attributes that are not found in the original schema. To use the objects, simply apply XmlAnyElementAttribute to a field that returns an array of **XmlElement** objects, or apply an XmlAnyAttributeAttribute to a field that returns an array of **XmlAttribute** objects.

Attribute	Description
XmlAnyAttributeAttribute	When deserializing, specifies that the array will be filled with **XmlAttribute** objects that represent all XML attributes unknown to the schema
XmlAnyElementAttribute	When deserializing, specifies that the array will be filled with **XmlElement** objects that represent all XML elements unknown to the schema
XmlArrayAttribute	Specifies that the members of the array will be generated as members of an XML array
XmlArrayItemAttribute	Specifies the derived types that can be inserted into an array; usually applied in conjunction with an XmlArrayAttribute
XmlAttributeAttribute	Specifies that the member will be serialized as an XML attribute
XmlChoiceIdentifierAttribute	Further distinguishes the member by using an enumeration
XmlElementAttribute	Specifies that the field or property will be serialized as an XML element
XmlEnumAttribute	Specifies the element name of an enumeration member
XmlIgnoreAttribute	Indicates that the property or field should be ignored when the containing class is serialized
XmlIncludeAttribute	Indicates that the class should be included when generating schemas (to be recognized when serialized)
XmlRootAttribute	Indicates that the class represents the root element of the XML document; use this attribute to further specify the namespace and element name
XmlTextAttribute	Indicates that the property or field should be serialized as XML text
XmlTypeAttribute	Indicates the name and namespace of the XML type

Table 31-7 Attributes for XML Serialization Control

Attribute	Description
SoapAttributeAttribute	Specifies that the class member will be serialized as an XML attribute
SoapElementAttribute	Specifies that the class will be serialized as an XML element
SoapEnumAttribute	Specifies the element name of an enumeration member
SoapIgnoreAttribute	Indicates that the property or field should be ignored when the containing class is serialized
SoapIncludeAttribute	Indicates that the type should be included when generating schemas (to be recognized when serialized)
SoapTypeAttribute	Indicates that the class should be serialized as an XML type

Table 31-8 Attributes for Controlling Encoded SOAP Serialization

You can also override the serialization of any set of objects and their properties by creating the appropriate attribute, and then adding it to an **XmlAttributes** class. Overriding serialization in this way has two purposes:

- To control and augment the serialization of objects found in a DLL; even if you do not have access to the source
- To create one set of serializable classes, but serialize the objects in multiple ways

Summary

Serialization is the process of saving an object onto a storage medium and later deserializing it from the storage medium to re-create an object instance that can be considered identical to the original object. You might use serialization if you plan to send an object to another application or you plan to save an object in a database field. You use the classes of the **System.Runtime.Serialization** namespace for serializing and deserializing objects.

To serialize or deserialize objects, you simply use the proper formatter object. You can utilize the binary formatter or the SOAP formatter depending on your needs. Binary serialization is simple using the Serialize and Deserialize methods. SOAP serialization is just as simple using the **SoapFormatter** object of the **System.Runtime.Serialization.Formatters.Soap** namespace.

You can use the Serializable attribute to make a class serializable. You can also prevent member variables from being serialized by marking them with the NonSerialized attribute.

The **ObjectIDGenerator** and the **ObjectManager** objects are critical for the serialization and deserialization of object graphs. An object graph is a set of multiple objects with references to each other.

If the serialization capabilities provided by the Serializable attribute do not meet your needs, you can implement custom serialization using the ISerializable interface. This simple interface exposes one method: GetObjectData. This method is invoked when the object passes the Formatter.Serialize method.

You use the StreamingContext structure to learn additional information regarding the serialization and deserialization process. This is accomplished through the State property that returns a bit-coded enumeration value.

A potential problem exists with serialization. Sometimes the serialization infrastructure can call the object's constructor even though the object graph has not been completely deserialized. The IDeserialization interface assists with this problem. It indicates that a class is to be notified when deserialization of the entire object graph has been completed.

XML serialization is also possible in the Visual Basic .NET Framework. XML serialization allows you to persist an object's state in an XML stream while maintaining control over the XML elements used to persist the data.

Test Questions

1. Which of the following is not a reason to implement serialization?
   A. You plan to send an object to another application.
   B. You plan to save an object in a database field.
   C. You are saving an object in an ASP.NET session object.
   D. You need to better secure an object in your application.
2. Which of the following namespaces do you use for serializing and deserializing objects?
   A. System.Objects.Serialize
   B. System.Runtime.Serialization
   C. System.Serialize
   D. System.Serialize.Deserialize
3. Which of the following objects is used to keep track of objects as they are deserialized?
   A. SerializationException
   B. FormatterConverter
   C. FormatterServices
   D. ObjectManager
4. If you are having problems with deserialization of complex objects, you should consider using which of the following interfaces?
   A. IDeserializationCallback
   B. IFormatter
   C. IObjectReference
   D. ISerializable
5. Which method do you use in order to implement basic serialization?
   A. Serialize
   B. BasicSerialize
   C. SerializationInterface
   D. BeginSerialize

6. Serialization using the SOAP format is simple using which object of the **System.Runtime.Serialization.Formatters.Soap** namespace?

   A. IFormatter

   B. Soap

   C. SoapFormatter

   D. SoapSuds

7. Often your classes contain fields that should not be serialized. You can prevent member variables from being serialized by marking them with which of the following attributes?

   A. NonSerialized

   B. Serialized

   C. Serializable

   D. NoSerialized

8. Which of the following classes is used to keep track of objects being deserialized?

   A. Formatter

   B. ObjectManager

   C. ObjectIDGenerator

   D. Multicast

9. Which of the following interfaces is used to implement custom serialization?

   A. ISerializable

   B. IObjectReference

   C. ISerializable

   D. ISerializationSurrogate

10. Which of the following classes does ASP.NET rely upon to encode XML Web service messages?

    A. XmlSerial

    B. Xml

    C. XmlSerializer

    D. XmlSerialization

Test Answers

1. D.
2. B.
3. D.
4. A.
5. A.
6. C.
7. A.
8. B.
9. C.
10. C.

CHAPTER 32

Reflection

In this chapter, you will

- Learn how to work with the **Assembly** class
- Learn how to work with the **Module** class
- Learn how to work with the **Type** class
- Discover how to invoke members and create objects

Reflection enables you to access and manipulate assemblies and modules as well as the types and metadata they contain. You can use reflection to dynamically create an instance of a type, bind the type to an existing object, or get the type from an existing object. Then you can invoke the type's methods or access its fields and properties.

In this chapter you learn to implement reflection thanks to powerful classes like Assembly, Module, and Type. You also discover how to invoke members and create objects.

What is Reflection?

Reflection is a critical feature of the Visual Basic .NET Framework. Here are some typical uses of reflection:

- Use the **Assembly** class to define and load assemblies, load modules that are listed in the assembly manifest, and locate a type from the assembly in order to create an instance.
- Use the **Module** class to discover information such as the assembly that contains a specific module and the classes in the module. You can also use the **Module** class to retrieve global methods or specific nonglobal methods.
- Use the **ConstructorInfo** class to discover information such as the name, parameters, access modifiers (such as public or private), and implementation details (such as abstract or virtual) of a constructor.
- Use the GetConstructors or GetConstructor methods of a **Type** object to invoke a specific constructor.
- Use the **MethodInfo** class to discover information such as the name, return type, parameters, access modifiers (such as public or private), and implementation details (such as abstract or virtual) of a method.

- Use the GetMethods or GetMethod method of a **Type** object to invoke a specific method.
- Use **FieldInfo** class to discover information such as the name, access modifiers (such as public or private), and implementation details (such as static) of a field, and to get or set field values.
- Use the **EventInfo** class to discover information such as the name, event-handler data type, custom attributes, declaring type, and reflected type of an event, and to add or remove event handlers.
- Use the **PropertyInfo** class to discover information such as the name, data type, declaring type, reflected type, and read-only or writable status of a property, and to get or set property values.
- Use the **ParameterInfo** class to discover information such as a parameter's name, data type, whether a parameter is an input or output parameter, and the position of the parameter in a method signature.
- Use the classes of the **System.Reflection.Emit** namespace to implement a specialized form of reflection that enables you to build types at runtime.
- Use reflection to create applications called type browsers, which enable users to select types and then view the information about those types.
- Compilers use reflection for languages such as JavaScript in order to construct symbol tables.
- Classes in the **System.Runtime.Serialization** namespace use reflection to access data and to determine which fields to persist.
- Classes in the **System.Runtime.Remoting** namespace use reflection indirectly through serialization.

Using the Assembly Class

Developers use the **Assembly** class to define an assembly, which is a reusable, versionable, and self-describing building block of a common language runtime application. Tables 32-1 and 32-2 describe the properties and methods of this class.

Be aware when using the **Assembly** class that the word *Assembly* is a reserved word for Visual Basic .NET. This means you must use the complete class name in code or use brackets in order to prevent a syntax error. The following example demonstrates three ways you can reference the class in code without causing an error.

```
Dim mySampleAssembly As System.Reflection.Assembly
Dim mySampleAssembly As Reflection.Assembly
Dim mySampleAssembly As [Assembly]
```

Properties	Description
CodeBase	Gets the location of the assembly as specified originally, for example, in an **AssemblyName** object
EntryPoint	Gets the entry point of the assembly
EscapedCodeBase	Gets the uniform resource identifier (URI), including escape characters, that represents the code base
Evidence	Gets the evidence for the assembly
FullName	Gets the display name of the assembly
GlobalAssemblyCache	Gets a value indicating whether the assembly was loaded from the global assembly cache
Location	Gets the location, in code base format, of the loaded file that contains the manifest if not shadow-copied

Table 32-1 Properties of the Assembly Class

Method	Description
CreateInstance	Overloaded; locates a type from this assembly and creates an instance of it using the system activator
CreateQualifiedName	Creates the name of a type qualified by the display name of its assembly
Equals	Overloaded; determines whether two object instances are equal
GetAssembly	Gets the assembly in which the specified class is defined
GetCallingAssembly	Returns the assembly of the method that invoked the currently executing method
GetCustomAttributes	Overloaded; gets the custom attributes for the assembly
GetEntryAssembly	Gets the process executable in the default application domain
GetExecutingAssembly	Gets the assembly that the current code is running from
GetExportedTypes	Gets the exported types defined in the assembly
GetFile	Gets a FileStream for the specified file in the file table of the manifest of the assembly
GetFiles	Overloaded; gets the files in the file table of an assembly manifest
GetHashCode	Serves as a hash function for a particular type; suitable for use in hashing algorithms and data structures like a hash table
GetLoadedModules	Overloaded; gets all the loaded modules that are part of the assembly
GetManifestResourceInfo	Returns information about how the given resource has been persisted
GetManifestResourceNames	Returns the names of all the resources in the assembly
GetManifestResourceStream	Overloaded; loads the specified manifest resource from the assembly
GetModule	Gets the specified module in the assembly

Table 32-2 Methods of the Assembly Class

Method	Description
GetModules	Overloaded; gets all the modules that are part of the assembly
GetName	Overloaded; gets an AssemblyName for the assembly
GetObjectData	Gets serialization information with all the data needed to reinstantiate the assembly
GetReferencedAssemblies	Gets the **AssemblyName** objects for all the assemblies referenced by this assembly
GetSatelliteAssembly	Overloaded; gets the satellite assembly
GetType	Overloaded; gets the **Type** object that represents the specified type
GetTypes	Gets the types defined in the assembly
IsDefined	Indicates whether a custom attribute identified by the specified type is defined
Load	Overloaded; loads an assembly
LoadFrom	Overloaded; loads an assembly
LoadModule	Overloaded; loads the module internal to the assembly
LoadWithPartialName	Overloaded; loads an assembly from the application directory or from the global assembly cache using a partial name
ToString	Overridden; returns the full name of the assembly; also known as the display name

Table 32-2 Methods of the Assembly Class *(continued)*

The **Assembly** class does not offer a constructor method. This is because you never actually create an assembly; you reference an existing assembly when you use the class. As shown in Table 32-2, several methods return a reference to an assembly.

The following example retrieves a reference to the assembly in which the code is running.

```
myAssembly = Reflection.Assembly. _
      GetExecutingAssembly()
```

The following example retrieves a reference to an assembly given its file name.

```
myAssembly = Reflection.Assembly. _
      LoadFrom("c:\sample\sample.dll")
```

The following example retrieves a reference to an assembly given its display name.

```
myAssembly = Reflection.Assembly.Load _
      ("sampleassem")
```

NOTE The argument provided in the preceding code can also be the full name of the assembly, which includes version, culture, and public key.

You can even retrieve a reference to an assembly when you do not have the assembly's full name, as shown in the following code.

```
myAssembly = Reflection.Assembly. _
      LoadWithPartialName("sample.xml")
```

Finally, you can retrieve a reference to an assembly that contains a given type, as shown in the following code. Notice that the argument you provide must be a System.Type value, so you must use the GetType method.

```
myAssembly = Reflection.Assembly. _
      GetAssembly(GetType(String))
```

Once you have obtained a valid reference to the assembly using one of the preceding methods, you can learn all types of information about it. For example, the following code uses the FullName property to obtain information about the version and public key token.

```
myAssembly = Reflection.Assembly.Load _
      ("mscorlib")
Console.Write(myAssembly.FullName)
```

NOTE You can try the preceding code as is, because mscorlib is one of the key .NET Framework assemblies.

Developers use the Location and CodeBase properties (these properties are read-only) to learn where assemblies of the global assembly cache (GAC) are stored. You can also use the GlobalAssemblyCache property to determine whether the assembly was loaded from the GAC. This property returns a Boolean value for the indication.

Most of the instance methods in Table 32-2 allow developers to enumerate the modules, files, and types of an assembly. For example, the GetModules method returns an array of references for all **Module** objects, while the GetFiles method returns an array of **FileStream** objects pointing to physical files. The following code uses the GetModules method to enumerate all of the modules in a particular assembly.

```
Dim myModule As [Module]
For Each myModule In myAssembly.GetModules
Console.WriteLine(myModule.FullyQualifiedName)
Next
```

Developers use the GetTypes method to view information regarding all the types defined in an assembly. This method returns an array with all the classes, interfaces, and other types defined, as shown in the following code.

```
Dim myTypes As Type
For Each myTypes In myAssembly.GetTypes
      Console.WriteLine(myTypes.FullName)
Next
```

Developers use the GetExportedTypes method to view information regarding only the public types that an assembly contains.

To return a specific **Type** object from the assembly, developers use the GetType method. The **Assembly** class overloads this method, which is inherited from **System.Object**. The following example assumes you are still referencing mscorlib.

```
Dim myType As Type = myAssembly.GetType _
      ("System.Int32")
```

The GetType method in the preceding example returns Nothing if the named type does not exist. You can use second and third arguments set to True if you want an exception to be raised on Nothing and if you want the search for the type to occur in a case-insensitive manner, as shown in the following code.

```
Dim myType As Type = myAssembly.GetType _
      ("system.int32", True, True)
```

The CreateInstance method allows developers to create an instance of the specified type. This type must be defined in the assembly where you invoke the method, as shown in the following code.

```
Dim myObject As Object = myAssembly.CreateInstance _
      ("System.Int32")
Console.Write(myObject.GetType.FullName)
```

Using the AssemblyName Class

The **AssemblyName** class creates the objects that the .NET Framework uses to describe the identities of shared assemblies. Specifically, the assembly cache manager uses **AssemblyName** objects for binding and retrieving information about assemblies.

Assembly identification information consists of the following components:

- Simple name
- Version number
- Cryptographic key pair
- Supported culture

Tables 32-3 and 32-4 describe the properties and methods of the **AssemblyName** class.

Although many methods and properties exist, developers most often use the GetName property of the **Assembly** object to get a reference to an existing **AssemblyName** object, as shown in the following example.

```
Dim myAssembly As [Assembly] = Reflection. _

      Assembly.Load("mscorlib")
Dim myAssemblyName As AssemblyName = myAssembly.GetName
```

Property	Description
CodeBase	Gets or sets the location of the assembly as a URL
CultureInfo	Gets or sets the culture supported by the assembly
EscapedCodeBase	Gets the URI, including escape characters, that represents the code base
Flags	Gets or sets the attributes of the assembly
FullName	Gets the full name of the assembly; also known as the display name
HashAlgorithm	Gets or sets the hash algorithm used by the assembly manifest
KeyPair	Gets or sets the public and private cryptographic key pair generated by the originator of the assembly
Name	Gets or sets the simple, unencrypted name of the assembly
Version	Gets or sets the major, minor, revision, and build numbers of the assembly
VersionCompatibility	Gets or sets information related to the assembly's compatibility with other assemblies

Table 32-3 Properties of the AssemblyName Class

Method	Description
Clone	Makes a copy of the **AssemblyName** object
Equals	Overloaded; determines whether two object instances are equal
GetAssemblyName	Gets the AssemblyName for a given file
GetHashCode	Serves as a hash function for a particular type; suitable for use in hashing algorithms and data structures like a hash table
GetObjectData	Gets serialization information with all of the data needed to reinstantiate the AssemblyName
GetPublicKey	Gets the public key identifying the originator of the assembly
GetPublicKeyToken	Gets a strong name consisting of a public key, a given name, and version parts
GetType	Gets the type of the current instance
OnDeserialization	Implements the ISerializable interface and is called back by the deserialization event when deserialization is complete
SetPublicKey	Sets the public key identifying the originator of the assembly
SetPublicKeyToken	Sets a strong name consisting of a public key, a given name, and version parts
ToString	Overridden; returns the full name of the assembly; also known as the display name

Table 32-4 Methods of the AssemblyName Class

You can also retrieve an array of **AssemblyName** objects using the GetReferencedAssemblies method, as shown in the following example.

```
Dim myArray() As AssemblyName
myArray = [Assembly].GetExecutingAssembly. _
      GetReferencedAssemblies()
```

Note that many properties of the **AssemblyName** class are identical to properties of the **Assembly** class.

Also be aware that several methods of the **AssemblyName** class return information about the assembly in the form of byte arrays. For example, the GetPublicKey and GetPublicKeyToken methods function in this manner. The following example demonstrates their usage.

```
Dim myByte As Byte
For Each myByte in myAssemblyName.GetPublicKeyToken()
      Console.WriteLine(myByte.ToString & ",")
Next
```

To modify the public key information stored in an assembly, developers use the SetPublicKey and SetPublicKeyToken methods.

To examine the culture supported by a particular assembly, developers use the CultureInfo property. If an assembly is culture neutral, this property returns a value of Nothing.

Developers use the VersionCompatibility property to get or set a value that reports the degree of compatibility of the assembly with other versions of the same assembly running in the same process, application domain, or machine. This value is actually a bit-coded AssemblyVersionCompatibility value belonging to the System.Configuration.Assemblies enumerated type. For this reason, using this value in code can be a bit tricky. The following example uses this value with the And operator.

```
Dim myAssemblyVerCompat As System.Configuration. _
      Assemblies.AssemblyVersionCompatibility
myAssemblyVerCompat = myAssemblyName.VersionCompatibility
If(myAssemblyVerCompat And Configuration. _
      Assemblies.AssemblyVersionCompatibility. _
      SameMachine) <> 0 Then
      Console.WriteLine("Compatibility check out OK!")
End If
```

Using the Module Class

Developers use the **Module** class to perform reflection on modules. Tables 32-5 and 32-6 describe the properties and methods of the **Module** class.

Property	Description
Assembly	Gets the appropriate assembly for the instance of Module
FullyQualifiedName	Gets a string representing the fully qualified name and path to the module
Name	Gets a string representing the name of the module with the path removed
ScopeName	Gets a string representing the name of the module

Table 32-5 Properties of the Module Class

Here is a simple example of code utilizing the **Module** class.

```
Dim myAssembly As [Assembly] = Reflection.Assembly. _
      Load("mscorlib")
Dim myModule As [Module]
For Each myModule in myAssembly.GetModules
      Console.WriteLine(myModule.Name & myModule. _
      ScopeName)
Next
```

Method	Description
Equals	Overloaded; determines whether two object instances are equal
FindTypes	Returns an array of classes accepted by the given filter and filter criteria
GetCustomAttributes	Overloaded; returns custom attributes
GetField	Overloaded; returns a specified field
GetFields	Returns an array of fields implemented by a class
GetHashCode	Serves as a hash function for a particular type; suitable for use in hashing algorithms and data structures like a hash table
GetMethod	Overloaded; returns a method having the specified criteria
GetMethods	Returns an array of all the global methods defined on the module
GetObjectData	Provides an ISerializable implementation for serialized objects
GetSignerCertificate	Returns an **X509Certificate** object corresponding to the certificate included in the Authenticode signature of the assembly that the module belongs to
GetType	Overloaded; returns the specified class
GetTypes	Returns all the classes defined within the module
IsDefined	Determines whether the specified attribute type is defined on the module
IsResource	Gets a value indicating whether the object is a resource
ToString	Overridden; returns the name of the module

Table 32-6 Methods of the Module Class

PART VIII

In this example the Name property of the **Module** class returns the name of the actual .DLL or .EXE. The ScopeName property returns a string used to represent the module. For example, the ScopeName for the Module mscorlib.dll is "CommonLanguageRuntimeLibrary".

Developers often opt for the use of the FullyQualifiedName property as it returns the module file name and the path to the module.

Using the Type Class

Perhaps one of the most important classes in reflection is the **Type** class. This class represents a managed type and includes class types, interface types, array types, value types, and enumeration types. Using this class you can enumerate a type's fields, properties, methods, and events. You can also set properties and fields and invoke methods dynamically. Tables 32-7 and 32-8 describe the properties and methods of the **Type** class.

Property	Description
Assembly	Gets the assembly that the type is declared in
AssemblyQualifiedName	Gets the fully qualified name of the type, including the name of the assembly from which the type was loaded
Attributes	Gets the attributes associated with the type
BaseType	Gets the type from which the current type directly inherits
DeclaringType	Overridden; gets the class that declares this member
DefaultBinder	Gets the default binder used by the system
FullName	Gets the fully qualified name of the type, including the namespace of the type
GUID	Gets the GUID (Globally Unique Identifier) associated with the type
HasElementType	Gets a value indicating whether the current type encompasses or refers to another type
IsAbstract	Gets a value indicating whether the type is abstract and must be overridden
IsAnsiClass	Gets a value indicating whether the string format attribute AnsiClass is selected for the type
IsArray	Gets a value indicating whether the type is an array
IsAutoClass	Gets a value indicating whether the string format attribute AutoClass is selected for the type
IsAutoLayout	Gets a value indicating whether the class layout attribute AutoLayout is selected for the type
IsByRef	Gets a value indicating whether the type is passed by reference
IsClass	Gets a value indicating whether the type is a class; that is, not a value type or interface
IsCOMObject	Gets a value indicating whether the type is a component object model (COM) object
IsContextful	Gets a value indicating whether the type can be hosted in a context

Table 32-7 Properties of the Type Class

Property	Description
IsEnum	Gets a value indicating whether the current type represents an enumeration
IsExplicitLayout	Gets a value indicating whether the class layout attribute ExplicitLayout is selected for the type
IsImport	Gets a value indicating whether the type was imported from another class
IsInterface	Gets a value indicating whether the type is an interface; that is, not a class or a value type
IsLayoutSequential	Gets a value indicating whether the class layout attribute SequentialLayout is selected for the type
IsMarshalByRef	Gets a value indicating whether the type is marshaled by reference
IsNestedAssembly	Gets a value indicating whether the type is nested and visible only within its own assembly
IsNestedFamANDAssem	Gets a value indicating whether the type is nested and visible only to classes that belong to both its own family and its own assembly
IsNestedFamily	Gets a value indicating whether the type is nested and visible only within its own family
IsNestedFamORAssem	Gets a value indicating whether the type is nested and visible only to classes that belong to either its own family or to its own assembly
IsNestedPrivate	Gets a value indicating whether the type is nested and declared private
IsNestedPublic	Gets a value indicating whether a class is nested and declared public
IsNotPublic	Gets a value indicating whether the top-level type is not declared public
IsPointer	Gets a value indicating whether the type is a pointer
IsPrimitive	Gets a value indicating whether the type is primitive
IsPublic	Gets a value indicating whether the top-level type is declared public
IsSealed	Gets a value indicating whether the type is declared sealed
IsSerializable	Gets a value indicating whether the type is serializable
IsSpecialName	Gets a value indicating whether the type has a name that requires special handling
IsUnicodeClass	Gets a value indicating whether the string format attribute UnicodeClass is selected for the type
IsValueType	Gets a value indicating whether the type is a value type
MemberType	Overridden; gets a bitmask indicating the member type
Module	Gets the module (the .DLL) in which the current type is defined
Name	Gets the name of the member
Namespace	Gets the namespace of the type
ReflectedType	Overridden; gets the class object that was used to obtain the member
TypeHandle	Gets the handle for the current type
TypeInitializer	Gets the initializer for the type
UnderlyingSystemType	Indicates the type provided by the common language runtime

Table 32-7 Properties of the Type Class *(continued)*

Method	Description
Equals	Overloaded; overridden; determines whether the underlying system type of the current type is the same as the underlying system type of the specified object or type
FindInterfaces	Returns an array of **Type** objects representing a filtered list of interfaces implemented or inherited by the current type
FindMembers	Returns a filtered array of **MemberInfo** objects of the specified member type
GetArrayRank	Gets the number of dimensions in an array
GetConstructor	Overloaded; gets a specific constructor of the current type
GetConstructors	Overloaded; gets the constructors of the current type
GetCustomAttributes	Overloaded; when overridden in a derived class, returns all attributes defined for the member
GetDefaultMembers	Searches for the members defined for the current type whose DefaultMemberAttribute is set
GetElementType	When overridden in a derived class, returns the type of the object encompassed or referred to by the current array, pointer, or reference type
GetEvent	Overloaded; gets a specific event declared or inherited by the current type
GetEvents	Overloaded; gets the events that are declared or inherited by the current type
GetField	Overloaded; gets a specific field of the current type
GetFields	Overloaded; gets the fields of the current type
GetHashCode	Overridden; returns the hash code for the instance
GetInterface	Overloaded; gets a specific interface implemented or inherited by the current type
GetInterfaceMap	Returns an interface mapping for the specified interface type
GetInterfaces	When overridden in a derived class, gets all the interfaces implemented or inherited by the current type
GetMember	Overloaded; gets the specified members of the current type
GetMembers	Overloaded; gets the members (properties, methods, fields, events, and so on) of the current type
GetMethod	Overloaded; gets a specific method of the current type
GetMethods	Overloaded; gets the methods of the current type
GetNestedType	Overloaded; gets a specific type nested within the current type
GetNestedTypes	Overloaded; gets the types nested within the current type
GetProperties	Overloaded; gets the properties of the current type
GetProperty	Overloaded; gets a specific property of the current type
GetType	Overloaded; gets the type with the specified name
GetTypeArray	Gets the types of the objects in the specified array

Table 32-8 Methods of the Type Class

Method	Description
GetTypeCode	Gets the underlying type code of the specified type
GetTypeFromCLSID	Overloaded; gets the type associated with the specified class identifier (CLSID)
GetTypeFromHandle	Gets the type referenced by the specified type handle
GetTypeFromProgID	Overloaded; gets the type associated with the specified program identifier (ProgID)
GetTypeHandle	Gets the handle for the type of a specified object
InvokeMember	Overloaded; invokes a specific member of the current type
IsAssignableFrom	Determines whether an instance of the current type can be assigned from an instance of the specified type
IsDefined	When overridden in a derived class, indicates whether one or more instance of attributeType is defined for the member
IsInstanceOfType	Determines whether the specified object is an instance of the current type
IsSubclassOf	Determines whether the current type derives from the specified type
ToString	Overridden; returns a string representing the name of the current type

Table 32-8 Methods of the Type Class *(continued)*

As shown in Table 32-8, the GetType shared method allows you to easily retrieve a **Type** object. This method accepts a class name in quotes as its parameter, enabling you to build the class name in code dynamically, as shown in the following example.

```
Dim myType As Type
myType = Type.GetType("System.Int64")
Console.WriteLine(myType.FullName)
```

The GetType method in the preceding code searches the current assembly for the **Type** object, and then it searches the system assembly, mscorlib.dll. The method returns Nothing if the specified type does not exist. As with the **Assembly** class GetType method, you can pass True for the second and third arguments if you want a TypeLoadException raised and if you want the search to proceed in a case-insensitive manner.

The **Type** class includes several methods that are useful only for retrieving the **Type** object that corresponds to a COM component. GetTypeFromCLSID works with a given CLSID, while GetTypeFromProgID relies upon a given ProgID.

Another popular (and generic) method of the **Type** class for reflection is GetMembers. This property returns an array of MemberInfo elements that contains all the fields, properties, methods, and events that the type exposes.

The GetMembers method also supports an optional BindingFlags enumerated argument. The bit-coded BindingFlags value allows you to narrow the enumeration. For example, suppose you want only the members declared in the current type as opposed to members inherited from the base class. The BindingFlags members you might find useful include

- Public
- NonPublic

- Instance
- Static
- DeclaredOnly
- FlattenHierarchy

If you have to perform more sophisticated searches, consider the FindMembers method. This method accepts the following four arguments to permit sophisticated searches:

- **memberType** A **MemberTypes** object indicating the type of member to search for
- **bindingAttr** A bitmask comprised of one or more BindingFlags that specify how the search is conducted
- **filter** The delegate that performs the comparisons, returning True if the member being inspected matches the filterCriteria and returning False otherwise
- **filterCriteria** The search criteria that determines whether a member is returned in the array of **MemberInfo** objects

Invoking Members and Creating Objects

It is also possible to execute a type's method that you discovered via reflection. For example, you can use the simple GetValue and SetValue methods to read or write to fields, as shown in the following code.

```
Sub SampleReadWriteFields
     Dim myCar As New Car("Ford", "Mustang")
     Dim myType As Type = myCar.GetType
     Dim myFieldInfo As FieldInfo = myType. _
           GetField("Make")
    myFieldInfo.SetValue(myCar, "GM")
End Sub
```

To execute a method, use the Invoke method or use the **Type** object's InvokeMember method. This method accepts the following data:

- The name of the member
- A flag that details whether the member is a field, property, or method
- The object for which the member should be invoked
- An array of objects for the arguments

Finally, you can dynamically create an object once you have obtained the class name by using the CreateInstance method of the **System.Activator** class or invoking one of the type's constructor methods.

Summary

Both you and Visual Basic .NET rely heavily on reflection capabilities in Visual Basic .NET programming. Using reflection you can access and manipulate assemblies and modules as well as the types and metadata they contain. You can use reflection to dynamically create an instance of a type, bind the type to an existing object, or get the type from an existing object. Then, you can invoke the type's methods or access its fields and properties.

You use the **Assembly** class to define an assembly, which is a reusable, versionable, and self-describing building block of a common language runtime application. Although you use the **AssemblyName** class to create the objects that the .NET Framework uses to describe the identities of shared assemblies, the assembly cache manager uses **AssemblyName** objects for binding and retrieving information about assemblies.

To perform reflection on modules, you use the **Module** class. The Name property of the **Module** class returns the name of the .DLL or .EXE, while the ScopeName property returns a string used to represent the module.

The **Type** class is one of the most important classes used in reflection. This class represents a managed type and includes class types, interface types, array types, value types, and enumeration types.

To invoke methods you can use the GetValue, SetValue, and InvokeMember methods. Objects can be dynamically created using the CreateInstance method of the **System.Activator** class.

Test Questions

1. Which property of the **Assembly** class gets the location of the assembly as specified originally, for example, in an **AssemblyName** object?

   A. Code

   B. FullName

   C. Location

   D. CodeBase

2. Which of the following code samples retrieves a reference to the assembly in which the code is running?

   A. myAssembly = Reflection.Assembly.GetExecutingAssembly()

   B. myAssembly = Reflection.Assembly.GetAssembly()

   C. myAssembly = Reflection.Get()

   D. myAssembly = Reflection.GetCurrentAssembly()

3. Which of the following properties can be used to retrieve a string representing the name of the module?

   A. Assembly

   B. FullyQualifiedName

C. Name

D. ScopeName

4. You would like to view the file name of a particular module and the location of this module on the file system. Which property of the **Module** class should you use?

A. FullyQualifiedName

B. ScopeName

C. Name

D. Assembly

5. Which Visual Basic function do you typically use to retrieve a **Type** object?

A. Type

B. RetrieveFunction

C. GetType

D. SetType

6. Which of the following shared methods allows you to easily retrieve a **Type** object and accepts a class name in quotes as its parameter?

A. GetTypeHandle

B. IsDefined

C. GetType

D. GetTypeFromProgID

7. Which of the following methods of the **Type** class returns an array of MemberInfo elements that contains all the fields, properties, methods, and events of the type?

A. GetMembers

B. GetType

C. Get

D. GetMemberInfo

8. You would like to narrow the enumeration returned with the GetMembers method. How should you do this?

A. Using the Limit argument.

B. Using the BindingFlags argument.

C. Using the DeclaredOnly argument.

D. This is not possible.

9. Which of the following methods should you use if you need to perform sophisticated searches for particular type objects?
   A. GetTypes
   B. FindMembers
   C. GetMembers
   D. RetrieveMembers
10. Which of the following methods of the **Type** class can you use to execute a method that you have discovered via reflection?
   A. InvokeMember
   B. IsAssignableFrom
   C. GetMethod
   D. FindInterfaces

Test Answers

1. D.
2. A.
3. D.
4. A.
5. C.
6. C.
7. A.
8. B.
9. B
10. A.

PART IX

Appendixes

- **Appendix A** About the CD
- **Appendix B** Exam Objective Mapping Document

APPENDIX

About the CD

The CD included with this book contains three practice exams—one for each of the following Microsoft certification exams:

- **Exam 70-305**—Developing and Implementing Web Applications with Microsoft Visual Basic .NET and Microsoft Visual Studio .NET
- **Exam 70-306**—Developing and Implementing Windows-Based Applications with Microsoft Visual Basic .NET and Microsoft Visual Studio .NET
- **Exam 70-310**—Developing XML Web Services and Server Components with Microsoft Visual Basic .NET and the Microsoft .NET Framework

The CD also includes MasterExam, MasterSim, an electronic version of this book, and Session #1 of two of LearnKey's online training. The software is easy to install on any Windows 98/NT/2000 computer. You must install it to access the MasterExam and MasterSim features. You can, however, browse the electronic book directly from the CD without installation. To register for LearnKey's online training and a second bonus MasterExam, click the Online Training link on the Main Page and follow the directions to the free online registration.

System Requirements

The CD software requires Windows 98 or higher, Internet Explorer 5.0 or higher, and 20MB of hard disk space for full installation. The electronic book requires Adobe Acrobat Reader. To access the online training from LearnKey, you must have RealPlayer Basic 8 or the Real1 plug-in, which is installed automatically when you launch the online training.

LearnKey Online Training

The LearnKey Online Training link allows you to access online training from Osborne.Onlineexpert.com. The first session of this course is provided free of charge. You can purchase additional sessions for this course and other courses directly from www.LearnKey.com or by calling (800) 865-0165.

Prior to running the online training, you must add the Real plug-in and the RealCBT plug-in to your system. This is facilitated automatically when you attempt to run the training the first time. You must also register the online product. Follow the instructions for a first-time user. Please be sure to use a valid e-mail address.

Installing and Running MasterExam and MasterSim

If your computer's CD-ROM drive is configured to auto-run, the CD will automatically start up when you insert it. From the opening screen, you can install MasterExam or MasterSim by clicking the MasterExam or MasterSim button. This begins the installation process and creates a program group named LearnKey. To run MasterExam or MasterSim, select Start | Programs | LearnKey. If the auto-run feature does not launch your CD, browse to the CD and double-click the RunInstall icon.

MasterExam

MasterExam simulates the actual exam. The number of questions, the type of questions, and the time allowed are intended to represent the exam environment. You have the option to take an open-book exam that includes hints, references, and answers; a closed-book exam; or the timed MasterExam simulation.

When you launch the MasterExam simulation, a digital clock appears in the top center of your screen. The clock counts down to zero unless you end the exam before the time expires.

MasterSim

MasterSim is a set of interactive labs that provide a wide variety of tasks that allow you to experience the software environment even if the software is not installed. Once you have installed MasterSim, you can access it through the CD launch page or Start | Programs | LearnKey.

Electronic Book

The CD includes the entire contents of the Exam Guidein PDF. The Adobe Acrobat Reader is included on the CD to allow you to read the file.

Help

A help file is provided and can be accessed by clicking the Help button on the main page in the lower-left corner. Individual help features are also available through MasterExam, MasterSim, and LearnKey's online training.

Removing Installation(s)

MasterExam and MasterSim are installed on your hard drive. For *best* results for removal of programs, use the Start | Programs | LearnKey | Uninstall options to remove MasterExam or MasterSim.

To remove RealPlayer, use the Add/Remove Programs icon in the Control Panel. You can also remove the LearnKey training program from this location.

Technical Support

For questions regarding the technical content of the electronic book or MasterExam, please visit www.osborne.com or e-mail customer.service@mcgraw-hill.com. For customers outside the United States, please e-mail international_cs@mcgraw-hill.com.

LearnKey Technical Support

For technical problems with the LearnKey software (installation, operation, and removing installations) and for questions regarding LearnKey online training and MasterSim content, please visit www.learnkey.com or e-mail techsupport@learnkey.com.

APPENDIX B

Exam Objective Mapping Document

MCSD Visual Basic .NET All-in-One Exam Guide
Exams 70-305, 306 and 310
Exam 70-305: Developing and Implementing Web Applications with Microsoft Visual Basic .NET and Microsoft Visual Studio .NET

Microsoft Exam Objective	Covered in Chapter #
Creating User Services	5, 7, 11, 20, 21, 22, 25, 26, 27
Create ASP.NET pages	20
Add and set directives on ASP.NET Pages	20
Separate user interface resources from business logic	20
Add Web server controls, HTML server controls, user controls, and HTML code to ASP.NET pages	20
Set properties on controls	20
Load controls dynamically	20
Apply templates	20
Set styles on ASP.NET pages by using cascading style sheets	20
Instantiate and invoke an ActiveX control	20
Implement naviation for the user interface	21
Manage the view state	21
Manage data during postback events	21
Use session state to manage data across pages	21
Validate user input	20
Validate non-Latin user input	20
Implement error handling in the user interface	20
Configure custom error pages	20
Implement global.asax, application, page-level, and page event error handling	20
Implement online user assistance	21
Incorporate existing code into ASP.NET pages	20
Display and update data	22
Transform and filter data	22
Bind data to the user interface	22
Use controls to display data	22
Instantiate and invoke Web Services or components	22
Instantiate and invoke a Web Service	27
Instantiate and invoke a COM or COM+ component	25
Instantiate and invoke a .NET component	7
Call native functions by using platform invoke	26
Implement globalization	11
Implement localizability for the user interface	11
Convert existing encodings	11
Implement right-to-left and left-to-right mirroring	11

Microsoft Exam Objective	Covered in Chapter #
Prepare culture-specific formatting	11
Handle Events	5
Creating User Services	5, 7, 11, 20, 21, 22, 25, 26, 27
Create event handlers	5
Raise events	5
Implement accessibility features	21
User and edit intrinsic objects. Intrinsic objects include response, request, session, server and application	20
Retrieve values from the properties of intrinsic objects	20
Set values on the properties of intrinsic objects	20
Use intrinsic objects to perform operations	20
Creating and Managing Components and .NET Assemblies	9, 11, 20
Create and modify a .NET assembly	9
Create and implement satellite assemblies	9
Create resource-only assemblies	11
Create custom controls and user controls	20
Consuming and Manipulating Data	12, 13
Access and manipulate data from a Microsoft SQL Server database by creating and using ad hoc queries and stored procedures	12
Access and manipulate data from a data store. Data stores include relational databases, XML documents, and flat files. Methods include XML techniques and ADO.NET	12, 13
Handle data errors	12
Testing and Debugging	23
Create a unit test plan	23
Implement tracing	23
Add trace listeners and trace switches to an application	23
Display trace output	23
Debug, rework, and resolve defects in code	23
Configure the debugging environment	23
Create and apply debugging code to components, pages, and applications	23
Provide multicultural test data to components, pages, and applications	23
Execute tests	23
Resolve errors and rework code	23
Deploying a Web Application	10, 21, 23
Plan the deployment of a Web application	23
Plan a deployment that uses removable media	23
Plan a Web-based deployment	23
Plan the deployment of an application to a Web garden, a Web farm, or cluster	23
Create a setup program that installs a Web application and allows for the application to be uninstalled	23
Deploy a Web application	23
Add assemblies to the global assembly cache	10
Maintaining and Supporting a Web Application	10
Optimize the performance of a Web application	23
Diagnose and resolve errors and issues	23
Configuring and Securing a Web Application	21, 23

Microsoft Exam Objective	Covered in Chapter #
Deploying a Web Application	10, 21, 23
Configure a Web application	21
Modify the Web.config File	10, 23
Modify the machine.config file	10, 23
Add and modify application settings	10, 23
Configure security for a Web application	21
Select and configure authentication type. Authentication types include Windows Authentication, None, forms-based, Microsoft Passport, Internet Information Services (IIS) authentication, and custom authentication	21
Configure authorization. Authorization methods include file-based methods and URL-based methods	21
Configure role-based authorization	21
Implement impersonation	21
Configure and implement caching. Caching types include output, fragment, and data	21
Use a cache object	21
Use cache directives	21
Configure and implement session state in various topologies such as a Web garden and a Web farm	21
Use session state within a process	21
Use session state with session state service	21
Use session state with Microsoft SQL Server	21
Install and configure server services	21
Install and configure a Web server	23
Install and configure Microsoft FrontPage Server Extensions	23

Exam 70-306: Developing and Implementing Windows-based Applications with Microsoft Visual Basic .NET and Microsoft Visual Studio .NET

Microsoft Objective	Covered in Chapter #
Creating User Services	3, 15, 16
Create a Windows Form by using the Windows Form Designer	15
Add and set properties on a Windows Form	15
Create a Windows Form by using visual inheritance	15
Build graphical interface elements by using the System.Drawing namespace	15
Add controls to a Windows Form	16
Set properties on controls	16
Load controls dynamically	16
Write code to handle control events and add the code to a control	16
Instantiate and invoke an ActiveX control	16
Configure control licensing	16
Create menus and menu items	16
Implement navigation for the user interface (UI)	16
Configure the order of tabs	16
Validate user input	15
Validate non-Latin user input	15
Implement error handling in the UI	15
Create and implement custom error messages	3, 15
Create and implement custom error handlers	3, 15

Microsoft Objective	Covered in Chapter #
Creating User Services	3, 7, 11, 15, 16, 17, 18, 25, 27
Raise and handle errors	3
Implement online user assistance	17
Incorporate existing code into a Microsoft Windows-based application	15
Display and update data	18
Transform and filter data	18
Bind data to the UI	18
Instantiate and invoke a Web service or component	27
Instantiate and invoke a Web service	27
Instantiate and invoke a COM or COM+ component	25
Instantiate and invoke a .NET component	7
Call native functions by using platform invoke	26
Implement globalization	11
Implement localizability for the UI	11
Convert existing encodings	11
Implement right-to-left- and left-to-right mirroring	11
Prepare culture-specific formatting	11
Create, implement, and handle events	5, 16
Implement print capability	17
Implement accessibility features	17
Creating and Managing Components and .NET Assemblies	9, 11, 16
Create and modify a .NET assembly	9
Create and implement satellite assemblies	9
Create resource-only assemblies	11
Create a Windows control	16
Create a Windows visual inheritance	16
Host a Windows control inside Microsoft Internet Explorer	16
Consuming and Manipulating Data	12, 13
Access and manipulate data from a Microsoft SQL Server database by creating and using ad hoc queries and stored procedures	12
Access and manipulate data from a data store. Data stores include relational databases, XML documents, and flat files. Methods include XML techniques and ADO.NET	12, 13
Handle data errors	12
Testing and Debugging	19
Create a unit test plan	19
Implement tracing	19
Add trace listeners and trace switches to an application	19
Display trace output	19
Debug, rework, and resolve defects in code	19
Configure the debugging environment	19
Create and apply debugging code to components and applications	19
Provide multicultural test data to components and applications	19
Execute tests	19
Resolve errors and rework code	19

Microsoft Objective	Covered in Chapter #
Deploying a Windows-based Application	10, 19
Plan the deployment of a Windows-based application	19
Plan a deployment that uses removable media	19
Plan a Web-based deployment	19
Plan a network-based deployment	19
Ensure that the application conforms to Windows Installer requirements and Windows Logo Program requirements	19
Create a setup program that installs an application and allows for the application to be uninstalled	19
Register components and assemblies	10
Perform an install-time compilation of a Windows-based application	19
Deploy a Windows-based application	19
Use Setup and Deployment Projects	19
Add assemblies to the Global Assembly Cache	10
Verify security policies for a deployed application	10
Launch a remote application (URL remoting)	10
Maintaining and Supporting a Windows-based Application	19
Optimize the performance of a Web-based application	19
Diagnose and resolve errors and issues	19
Configuring and Securing a Windows-based Application	17
Configure a Windows-based application	17
Configure security for a Windows-based application	17
Select and configure authentication type. Authentication types include Windows Authentication, None, forms-based, Microsoft Passport, and custom authentication	17
Specify the security level for an application	17
Use custom attributes to configure security	17
Configure authorization	17
Configure role-based authorization	17
Implement identity management	17

Exam 70-310: Developing XML Web Services and Server Components with Microsoft Visual Basic .NET and the Microsoft .NET Framework

Microsoft Objective	Covered in Chapter #
Creating and Managing Microsoft Windows® Services, Serviced Components, .NET Remoting Objects, and XML Web Services	10, 24, 25, 26, 27, 28
Create and manipulate a Windows service	24
Write code that is executed when a Windows service is started or stopped	24
Create and consume a serviced component	24
Implement a serviced component	25
Create interfaces that are visible to COM	25
Create a strongly named assembly	25

Microsoft Objective	Covered in Chapter #
Creating and Managing Microsoft Windows® Services, Serviced Components, .NET Remoting Objects, and XML Web Services	10, 24, 25, 26, 27, 28
Register the component in the global assembly cache	10
Manage the component by using the Component Services tool	25
Create and consume a .NET Remoting object	26
Implement server-activated components	26
Implement client-activated components	26
Select a channel protocol and a formatter. Channel protocols include TCP and HTTP./ Formatters include SOAP and binary	26
Create client configuration files and server configuration files	26
Implement an asynchronous method	26
Create the listener service	26
Instantiate and invoke a .NET Remoting object	26
Create and consume an XML Web service	27
Control characteristics of Web methods by using attributes	27
Create and use SOAP extensions	27
Create asynchronous Web methods	27
Control XML wire format for an XML Web service	27
Instantiate and invoke an XML Web service	27
Implement security for a Windows service, a serviced component, a .NET Remoting object, and an XML Web service	28
Access unmanaged code from a Windows service, a serviced component, a .NET Remoting object, and an XML Web service	24, 26, 27
Consuming and Manipulating Data	12, 14
Access and manipulate data from a Microsoft SQL Server™ database by creating and using ad hoc queries and stored procedures	12
Create and manipulate DataSets	12
Manipulate a DataSet schema	12
Manipulate DataSet relationships	12
Create a strongly typed DataSet	12
Access and manipulate XML data	14
Access an XML file by using the Document Object Model (DOM) and an XmlReader	14
Transform DataSet data into XML data	14
Use Xpath to query XML data	14
Generate and use and XSD schema	14
Write a SQL statement that retrieves XML data from a SQL Server database	14
Update a SQL Server database by using XML	14
Validate an XML document	14
Testing and Debugging	28
Create a unit test plan	28
Implement tracing	28
Configure and use trace listeners and trace switches	28
Display trace output	28
Instrument and debug a Windows service, a serviced component, a .NET Remoting object, and an XML Web service	28
Configure the debugging environment	28

Microsoft Objective	Covered in Chapter #
Testing and Debugging	28
Create and apply debugging code to components and applications	28
Provide multicultural test data to components and applications	28
Execute tests	28
Use interactive debugging	28
Log test results	28
Resolve errors and rework code	28
Control debugging in the Web.config file	28
Use SOAP extensions for debugging	28
Deploying Windows Services, Serviced Components, .NET Remoting Objects, and XML Web Services	10, 24, 26, 27, 28
Plan the deployment of and deploy a windows service, a serviced component, a .NET Remoting object, and an XML Web service	28
Create a setup program that installs a Windows service, a serviced component, a .NET Remoting object, and an XML Web service	28
Register components and assemblies	28
Publish an XML Web service	27
Enable static discovery	27
Publish XML Web service definitions in the UDDI	27
Configure client computers and servers to use a Windows service, a serviced component, a .NET Remoting object, and an XML Web service	24, 26, 27
Implement versioning	10
Plan, configure and deploy side-by-side deployments and applications	10
Configure security for a Windows service, a serviced component, a .NET Remoting object, and an XML Web service	28
Configure authentication type. Authentication types include Windows authentication, Microsoft .NET Passport, custom authentication and none.	28
Configure and control authorization. Authorization methods include file-based authorization and URL-based authorization.	28
Configure and implement identify management	28

INDEX

Symbols and Numbers

A

B

C

D

G

H

I

N

O

T

W

INTERNATIONAL CONTACT INFORMATION

AUSTRALIA
McGraw-Hill Book Company Australia Pty. Ltd.
TEL +61-2-9900-1800
FAX +61-2-9878-8881
http://www.mcgraw-hill.com.au
books-it_sydney@mcgraw-hill.com

CANADA
McGraw-Hill Ryerson Ltd.
TEL +905-430-5000
FAX +905-430-5020
http://www.mcgraw-hill.ca

GREECE, MIDDLE EAST, & AFRICA (Excluding South Africa)
McGraw-Hill Hellas
TEL +30-210-6560-990
TEL +30-210-6560-993
TEL +30-210-6560-994
FAX +30-210-6545-525

MEXICO (Also serving Latin America)
McGraw-Hill Interamericana Editores S.A. de C.V.
TEL +525-117-1583
FAX +525-117-1589
http://www.mcgraw-hill.com.mx
fernando_castellanos@mcgraw-hill.com

SINGAPORE (Serving Asia)
McGraw-Hill Book Company
TEL +65-863-1580
FAX +65-862-3354
http://www.mcgraw-hill.com.sg
mghasia@mcgraw-hill.com

SOUTH AFRICA
McGraw-Hill South Africa
TEL +27-11-622-7512
FAX +27-11-622-9045
robyn_swanepoel@mcgraw-hill.com

SPAIN
McGraw-Hill/Interamericana de España, S.A.U.
TEL +34-91-180-3000
FAX +34-91-372-8513
http://www.mcgraw-hill.es
professional@mcgraw-hill.es

UNITED KINGDOM, NORTHERN, EASTERN, & CENTRAL EUROPE
McGraw-Hill Education Europe
TEL +44-1-628-502500
FAX +44-1-628-770224
http://www.mcgraw-hill.co.uk
computing_neurope@mcgraw-hill.com

ALL OTHER INQUIRIES Contact:
Osborne/McGraw-Hill
TEL +1-510-549-6600
FAX +1-510-883-7600
http://www.osborne.com
omg_international@mcgraw-hill.com

LICENSE AGREEMENT

THIS PRODUCT (THE "PRODUCT") CONTAINS PROPRIETARY SOFTWARE, DATA AND INFORMATION (INCLUDING DOCUMENTATION) OWNED BY THE McGRAW-HILL COMPANIES, INC. ("McGRAW-HILL") AND ITS LICENSORS. YOUR RIGHT TO USE THE PRODUCT IS GOVERNED BY THE TERMS AND CONDITIONS OF THIS AGREEMENT.

LICENSE: Throughout this License Agreement, "you" shall mean either the individual or the entity whose agent opens this package. You are granted a non-exclusive and non-transferable license to use the Product subject to the following terms:

(i) If you have licensed a single user version of the Product, the Product may only be used on a single computer (i.e., a single CPU). If you licensed and paid the fee applicable to a local area network or wide area network version of the Product, you are subject to the terms of the following subparagraph (ii).

(ii) If you have licensed a local area network version, you may use the Product on unlimited workstations located in one single building selected by you that is served by such local area network. If you have licensed a wide area network version, you may use the Product on unlimited workstations located in multiple buildings on the same site selected by you that is served by such wide area network; provided, however, that any building will not be considered located in the same site if it is more than five (5) miles away from any building included in such site. In addition, you may only use a local area or wide area network version of the Product on one single server. If you wish to use the Product on more than one server, you must obtain written authorization from McGraw-Hill and pay additional fees.

(iii) You may make one copy of the Product for back-up purposes only and you must maintain an accurate record as to the location of the back-up at all times.

COPYRIGHT; RESTRICTIONS ON USE AND TRANSFER: All rights (including copyright) in and to the Product are owned by McGraw-Hill and its licensors. You are the owner of the enclosed disc on which the Product is recorded. You may not use, copy, decompile, disassemble, reverse engineer, modify, reproduce, create derivative works, transmit, distribute, sublicense, store in a database or retrieval system of any kind, rent or transfer the Product, or any portion thereof, in any form or by any means (including electronically or otherwise) except as expressly provided for in this License Agreement. You must reproduce the copyright notices, trademark notices, legends and logos of McGraw-Hill and its licensors that appear on the Product on the back-up copy of the Product which you are permitted to make hereunder. All rights in the Product not expressly granted herein are reserved by McGraw-Hill and its licensors.

TERM: This License Agreement is effective until terminated. It will terminate if you fail to comply with any term or condition of this License Agreement. Upon termination, you are obligated to return to McGraw-Hill the Product together with all copies thereof and to purge all copies of the Product included in any and all servers and computer facilities.

DISCLAIMER OF WARRANTY: THE PRODUCT AND THE BACK-UP COPY ARE LICENSED "AS IS." McGRAW-HILL, ITS LICENSORS AND THE AUTHORS MAKE NO WARRANTIES, EXPRESS OR IMPLIED, AS TO THE RESULTS TO BE OBTAINED BY ANY PERSON OR ENTITY FROM USE OF THE PRODUCT, ANY INFORMATION OR DATA INCLUDED THEREIN AND/OR ANY TECHNICAL SUPPORT SERVICES PROVIDED HEREUNDER, IF ANY ("TECHNICAL SUPPORT SERVICES"). McGRAW-HILL, ITS LICENSORS AND THE AUTHORS MAKE NO EXPRESS OR IMPLIED WARRANTIES OF MERCHANTABILITY OR FITNESS FOR A PARTICULAR PURPOSE OR USE WITH RESPECT TO THE PRODUCT. McGRAW-HILL, ITS LICENSORS, AND THE AUTHORS MAKE NO GUARANTEE THAT YOU WILL PASS ANY CERTIFICATION EXAM WHATSOEVER BY USING THIS PRODUCT. NEITHER McGRAW-HILL, ANY OF ITS LICENSORS NOR THE AUTHORS WARRANT THAT THE FUNCTIONS CONTAINED IN THE PRODUCT WILL MEET YOUR REQUIREMENTS OR THAT THE OPERATION OF THE PRODUCT WILL BE UNINTERRUPTED OR ERROR FREE. YOU ASSUME THE ENTIRE RISK WITH RESPECT TO THE QUALITY AND PERFORMANCE OF THE PRODUCT.

LIMITED WARRANTY FOR DISC: To the original licensee only, McGraw-Hill warrants that the enclosed disc on which the Product is recorded is free from defects in materials and workmanship under normal use and service for a period of ninety (90) days from the date of purchase. In the event of a defect in the disc covered by the foregoing warranty, McGraw-Hill will replace the disc.

LIMITATION OF LIABILITY: NEITHER McGRAW-HILL, ITS LICENSORS NOR THE AUTHORS SHALL BE LIABLE FOR ANY INDIRECT, SPECIAL OR CONSEQUENTIAL DAMAGES, SUCH AS BUT NOT LIMITED TO, LOSS OF ANTICIPATED PROFITS OR BENEFITS, RESULTING FROM THE USE OR INABILITY TO USE THE PRODUCT EVEN IF ANY OF THEM HAS BEEN ADVISED OF THE POSSIBILITY OF SUCH DAMAGES. THIS LIMITATION OF LIABILITY SHALL APPLY TO ANY CLAIM OR CAUSE WHATSOEVER WHETHER SUCH CLAIM OR CAUSE ARISES IN CONTRACT, TORT, OR OTHERWISE. Some states do not allow the exclusion or limitation of indirect, special or consequential damages, so the above limitation may not apply to you.

U.S. GOVERNMENT RESTRICTED RIGHTS: Any software included in the Product is provided with restricted rights subject to subparagraphs (c), (1) and (2) of the Commercial Computer Software-Restricted Rights clause at 48 C.F.R. 52.227-19. The terms of this Agreement applicable to the use of the data in the Product are those under which the data are generally made available to the general public by McGraw-Hill. Except as provided herein, no reproduction, use, or disclosure rights are granted with respect to the data included in the Product and no right to modify or create derivative works from any such data is hereby granted.

GENERAL: This License Agreement constitutes the entire agreement between the parties relating to the Product. The terms of any Purchase Order shall have no effect on the terms of this License Agreement. Failure of McGraw-Hill to insist at any time on strict compliance with this License Agreement shall not constitute a waiver of any rights under this License Agreement. This License Agreement shall be construed and governed in accordance with the laws of the State of New York. If any provision of this License Agreement is held to be contrary to law, that provision will be enforced to the maximum extent permissible and the remaining provisions will remain in full force and effect.